PRAISE FOR THE *NEW YORK TIMES* BESTSELLING
ECLIPSE BAY TRILOGY . . .

"An entertaining mix of . . . sex and mystery."   —*Publishers Weekly*

"Features a pair of classic Krentz protagonists and some exceptionally
well-drawn and appealing secondary characters."   —*Library Journal*

"Entertaining."   —*Booklist*

ALSO BY
JAYNE ANN KRENTZ . . .

SMOKE IN MIRRORS

"Quick and witty, and the romance sizzles . . . What else could you
want?"   —*The Columbia State*

"A suspenseful journey into unexpected danger and romance."
                                          —*Seattle Post-Intelligencer*

"A quintessential romantic hero . . . Written solidly, with a plot that
puts the two protagonists in convincing peril from a number of
directions . . . Entertaining."   —*The Seattle Times*

"[An] enticing blend of suspense and top-notch romance."
                                                     —*Booklist*

continued . . .

LOST & FOUND

"Delightful."
—*People*

"A compelling mystery laced with an equally compelling romance."
—*The Newark Star-Ledger*

"Romantic suspense at its most enjoyable, enhanced by Krentz's trademark humor and quirky characters. Fans will be very happy with this entertaining and delightful read."
—*Library Journal*

SOFT FOCUS

"Another well-polished tale."
—*Seattle Post-Intelligencer*

"All the flirtatious banter and steamy sex one would expect."
—*Kirkus Reviews*

"A healthy dose of suspense . . . Krentz has so much fun sending up the noir genre that you won't mind going along for the ride."
—*People*

Praise for the novels of *New York Times* bestselling author Jayne Ann Krentz . . .

"GOOD FUN."   *—Cosmopolitan*

"ENTERTAINING."   *—People*

"FAST-PACED . . . interesting characters . . . a good time is had by the reader."   *—Chicago Tribune*

"A lot of fun."   *—Minneapolis Star Tribune*

"Sexy, romantic."   *—Library Journal*

"A delight."   *—Publishers Weekly*

"Along with Nora Roberts, Krentz is one of the most reliably satisfying romance writers publishing."   *—Sunday Times* (CA)

"Pure pleasure."   *—The San Jose Mercury News*

"AN ABSOLUTELY, POSITIVELY FUN READ . . . Krentz's characters are always people you'd like to meet for yourself and know more about."   *—Southern Pines Pilot*

TOGETHER IN ECLIPSE BAY

JAYNE ANN KRENTZ

BERKLEY BOOKS, NEW YORK

A Berkley Book
Published by The Berkley Publishing Group
A division of Penguin Group (USA) Inc.
375 Hudson Street
New York, New York 10014

First edition: September 2003

Library of Congress Cataloging-in-Publication Data

Krentz, Jayne Ann.
    Together in Eclipse Bay / Jayne Ann Krentz.
        p.   cm.
    Contents: Eclipse Bay—Dawn in Eclipse Bay—Summer in Eclipse Bay.
    ISBN 0-425-19250-4
    1. Love stories, American.   2. Oregon—Fiction.   I. Title: Eclipse Bay.   II. Title: Dawn in
Eclipse Bay.   III. Title: Summer in Eclipse Bay.   IV. Title.

PS3561.R44T64   2003
813'.54—dc21

                                                                                2003051816

Printed in the United States of America

10   9   8   7   6   5   4   3   2   1

Contents

ECLIPSE BAY

Prologue

"IT'S going to be a long walk home."

The voice was low and rough around the edges, unmistakably masculine. The kind of voice that sent little shivers down a woman's spine. It came out of the bottomless shadows near the base of Eclipse Arch, the stone monolith that dominated this secluded stretch of rocky beach.

Hannah Harte jerked her gaze away from the sight of Perry Decatur's disappearing taillights and spun around. Her pulse, already beating briskly as a result of the unpleasant tussle in the front seat, shifted into high gear.

Maybe getting out of the car had not been one of her brighter ideas. This stretch of Bayview Drive was a very lonely place at this hour of the night. Nice going, Hannah, she thought. The old frying-pan-into-the-fire trick. And you're supposed to be so sensible and cautious. The one who never takes chances. The one who never gets into trouble.

"Who's there?" She edged back a step and prepared to run.

The man on the beach sauntered casually out of the dense darkness of the arched rock and stepped into the cold light of the late-summer moon. He was less than twenty feet away.

"You're a Harte," he said. Cold, ironic amusement filtered through the words. "Don't you recognize a no-good, low-down, untrustworthy Madison on sight?"

She took in the stark profile, the glint of silver light on midnight-dark hair, and the air of arrogant, prowling grace. She didn't need the additional clues of a leather jacket, a black crew-neck T-shirt, and jeans.

Rafe Madison. Her generation's most notorious member of the disreputable, thoroughly scandalous Madison clan. For three generations, ever since the legendary street fight between Mitchell Madison and Sullivan Harte in front of Fulton's Supermarket, the Hartes had dutifully warned their offspring not to get involved with the wild, unruly Madisons.

Rafe had apparently made it a point to live up to his family's scandalous heritage. The product of an affair between his sculptor father and a model, Rafe had been orphaned along with his brother at the tender age of nine. Both boys had been raised by their disreputable grandfather Mitchell, who was, according to Hannah's mother, in no way qualified to be a father.

Rafe had blossomed into the quintessential bad boy, but he had somehow managed, by the skin of his teeth, to stay out of jail. As far as most people in Eclipse Bay were concerned, it was only a matter of time before he wound up behind bars.

He was twenty-four, four years older than herself, Hannah thought. It was common knowledge that his grandfather was furious with him because he had dropped out of college in the middle of his sophomore year. Rafe had done a short stint in the military, and from all accounts, he had managed to prove all the recruitment posters wrong and emerge with no marketable skills. Word had it that this summer Mitchell was trying to coerce him into going to work for his older brother, Gabe, who was attempting, against all odds, to revive the family business. No one expected Gabe to succeed in that endeavor.

Although she and her family spent every summer and many weekends and vacations here in Eclipse Bay, Hannah had had no direct contact with Rafe while she was growing up. The four years' difference in their ages had, until tonight, served to keep their orbits safely separated, even in this small seaside community where both families had deep roots. Four years was a chasm when one was a kid.

But tonight was her twentieth birthday. In the fall she would start her junior year of college in Portland. For some reason the four years between herself and Rafe Madison no longer seemed an impenetrable barrier.

Her first reaction to the realization that he had witnessed the struggle in the front seat of Perry's car was overwhelming mortification. Hartes did not indulge in public scenes. Just her dumb luck to have a Madison hanging around when she broke that unwritten rule. Anger warred with acute embarrassment.

"Do you do this a lot?" she asked gruffly.

"Do what a lot?"

"Hide behind large rocks in order to spy on people who want to have private conversations?"

"You've got to admit that the entertainment options in this town are a little limited."

"I suppose that's especially true if you've got a severely *limited* concept of what constitutes entertainment." Everyone knew that Rafe's motorcycle was frequently spotted in the small parking lot behind Virgil's Adult Books and Video Arcade. "What do you do when you're not being a voyeur?"

"A voyeur?" He whistled softly. "That's a fancy word for a Peeping Tom, isn't it?"

She stiffened. "Yes, it is."

"Thought so. Wasn't absolutely sure, though. I dropped out of college before we got to some of the more upscale words."

He was mocking her. She knew it, but she was not certain how to deal with it.

"I wouldn't brag about leaving school if I were you." She clutched her purse more tightly in front of her body, as if it were a magic shield she could use to ward off any demonic vibes Rafe might be emitting. "My father says that it's too bad you blew off your future like that. He says you have potential."

Rafe's teeth flashed briefly in a sardonic grin. "Lots of people have said that over the years, starting with my first-grade teacher. But they've all concluded that I won't ever live up to whatever potential I've got."

"You're an adult now. It's your responsibility to make your life work properly. You can't blame your failure on others."

"I never do that," he assured her earnestly. "I'm proud to say that I am solely to blame for my own screwups."

She was out of her depth here. She tightened her grip on the purse and took another step back.

"You sort of implied that you and the guy who just took off came here to talk privately." His words pursued her in the darkness. "But I didn't get the feeling that the two of you were having what you'd call a meaningful conversation. Who was the jerk, anyway?"

For some oblique reason she felt compelled to defend Perry, who, unlike Rafe Madison, would amount to something someday. Or maybe it was her own self-image she wanted to protect. She did not like to think of herself as the kind of woman who dated jerks.

Not that Perry was a jerk. He was a budding academic.

"His name is Perry Decatur," she said coolly. "He's a grad student at Chamberlain. Not that it's any of your business."

"Guess he thought the evening was going to end a little differently."

"Perry's okay. He just got a little pushy tonight, that's all."

"Pushy, huh? Is that what you call it?" Rafe gave an easy shrug. "Well, it looked like you pushed back pretty good. For a minute there, I thought you might need a little help, but then I realized that you were handling him just fine on your own."

"Perry is hardly the violent type." Outrage flared. "He's a grad student, for crying out loud. He plans to teach political science."

"Is that right? Since when is politics a science?"

She was pretty sure that was a rhetorical question. "He expects to be offered a position on the faculty at Chamberlain as soon as he gets his Ph.D."

"Well, shoot. If I'd known that, I wouldn't have worried about you even half a minute while the two of you were staging that arm-wrestling contest. I mean, a guy who's going for his Ph.D. and plans to become a hotshot professor at Chamberlain wouldn't try to force himself on a woman. Don't know what I was thinking."

She was profoundly grateful for the simple fact that it was midnight. At least Rafe could not see the hot color she was almost sure was staining her face a vivid shade of pink. "There's no call to be sarcastic. Perry and I had a disagreement, that's all."

"So, do you date a lot of jerks?"

"Stop calling Perry a jerk."

"I was just curious. Can't blame me under the circumstances, can you?"

"Yes, I can and I do." She glared. "You're being deliberately obnoxious."

"But not quite as obnoxious as the jerk, huh? I haven't even touched you."

"Oh, shut up. I'm going home."

"I hate to mention it, but you are standing alone here on an isolated stretch of road in the middle of the night. Like I said, it's going to be a long walk back to your folks' place."

She seized the only weak point she could find in his logic. "I'm not alone."

In the pale moonlight, his smile gleamed dangerously. "We both know that as far as your family is concerned, the fact that I'm here with you makes your situation worse than being alone. I'm a Madison, remember?"

She raised her chin. "I don't give a darn about that stupid feud. Ancient history, as far as I'm concerned."

"Right. Ancient history. But you know what they say about history. Those who don't learn from it are condemned to relive it."

Startled, she stared at him. "You sound just like Aunt Isabel. She's always saying things like that."

"I know."

Hannah was floored. "You've talked to my aunt?"

"She talks to me." He raised one shoulder in another dismissive gesture. "I do some work around that big house of hers sometimes. She's a nice old lady. A little strange, but then, she is a Harte."

She wondered what her parents would say if they discovered that Aunt Isabel hired Rafe to do odd jobs around Dreamscape. "I guess that explains where you picked up the quote."

"You didn't think I'd actually read it in a book, did you?"

"Everyone knows you do most of your reading at Virgil Nash's porn shop." Lord, she sounded prissy. "I doubt that you'd find a quote like that in any of the books or magazines he stocks."

Rafe was silent for a beat, as if her comment had surprised him. But he recovered immediately. "Right. Mostly I just look at the pictures, anyhow."

"I believe it."

"I'll bet the jerk reads a lot."

Quite suddenly she'd had enough. It was time to level this playing field. Rafe Madison had four years and a lifetime of experience on her, but she was a Harte. She could hold her own against a Madison.

"If you didn't come here to play some voyeuristic games," she said coldly, "what are you doing at Eclipse Arch at this time of night?"

"Same thing you are," he said very smoothly. "My date and I had a little disagreement, and she kicked me out of her car."

Hannah was astonished. "Kaitlin Sadler threw you out of her car because you wouldn't have sex with her?"

"We didn't argue about having sex," he said with devastating honesty. "We argued about the fact that she's dating other guys."

"I see." It was no secret that Kaitlin had been seeing other men. "I hear she wants to marry someone who can take her away from Eclipse Bay."

"You heard right. Obviously I'm not in a position to do that, what with my failure to achieve my full potential and all."

"Obviously."

"Hell, I don't even have a steady job."

"I don't suppose Kaitlin would consider flipping veggie burgers at Snow's Café a position with a lot of guaranteed upward mobility," Hannah mused.

"No, she doesn't. She made that real clear."

Hannah was appalled to realize that she felt an insidious little tendril of sympathy for him. "You've got to admit that you certainly can't afford to keep her in the style to which she wants to become accustomed."

"I know. But I thought we had an understanding that while we were seeing each other, neither of us would fool around with anyone else."

"Kaitlin, I take it, didn't share that understanding?"

"Nope. She said she didn't want to be tied down to me. Made it clear that her first priority was finding a rich husband. Naturally, I was crushed to learn that I was nothing more than a plaything for her."

"Yeah. Crushed."

"Hey, Madisons have feelings too."

"Really?" she murmured. "I've never heard that."

"The family likes to keep it quiet."

"I'm not surprised. Sort of ruins the image."

"Yeah. You know, you'd be surprised how irritating it is to date a woman who is actively hunting elsewhere for a wealthy husband."

"Kaitlin's definitely active," Hannah said neutrally. "Everyone in town knows it."

Rafe smiled thinly. "As of tonight she can be active with someone else."

"I suppose she was upset when you told her you didn't want to continue in the role of, uh, plaything?"

"She was pissed as hell."

She tried to read his face in the shadows, but it was impossible to tell what he was thinking or feeling. Assuming that is, that he was thinking or feeling anything at all.

"I get the impression that you are not particularly devastated by the breakup in your relationship," she ventured cautiously.

"Sure, I'm devastated. I just told you, I'm a sensitive guy. But I'll get over it."

"What about Kaitlin?"

"Worrying about Kaitlin's feelings is not real high on my list of priorities at the moment."

Hannah gazed at him in amazement. "You mean you've actually *got* a list of priorities?"

"Okay, so it isn't a computer-generated five-year master plan like the one you've probably got tacked up on your bedroom wall. But some of us have to make it up as we go along."

She winced at the thought of the list of personal goals she had made for herself at the start of the summer. It was, indeed, hanging on the bulletin board over her dresser. It was an updated, more finely tuned version of the list she had made when she graduated from high school. Formulating objectives and then plotting a course to reach those objectives was second nature to her. Everyone in her family was trained to be organized and forward-looking. As her father, Hamilton, was fond of saying, an unplanned life was a messy life.

Madisons, on the other hand, were notorious for their propensity to be driven by quixotic obsessions, quirky desires, and the occasional wild hair. When a Madison was consumed by a passion, people said, nothing was allowed to get in the way. Rafe's casual attitude toward the breakup with Kaitlin Sadler tonight was convincing evidence that she did not rank as his passion.

"Okay, I'll bite," Hannah said, still uncertain about whether or not Rafe was teasing her. "What's on your list of priorities?"

For a moment she thought he was not going to respond. Then he shoved his hands deeper into the pockets of his leather motorcycle jacket and turned slightly to face the bay.

"I don't think my plans would be of much interest to you," he said laconically. "It's not like I'm going to get a Ph.D. or anything."

She watched him, unwillingly fascinated now. "Tell me."

He fell silent for a moment. She had the impression that he was engaged in some kind of internal debate.

"My grandfather says that when I'm not busy screwing around I have a head for business," he said eventually. "He wants me to go to work for Gabe."

"But you don't want to do that?"

"Madison Commercial is Gabe's baby. He's in charge, and that's the way it has to be. We get along okay, but I learned a few things about myself in the army. One of them was that I'm not cut out to take orders."

"No surprise there, I guess."

Rafe took one hand out of his pocket, scooped up a small stone, and sent it skipping out across the dark water of the bay. "I want to do my own thing."

"I can understand that."

He glanced over his shoulder. "You do?"

"I don't want to work in a corporation or a bureaucracy either," she said quietly. "I'm going to open my own business as soon as I graduate."

"Got it all planned, huh?"

"Not entirely. But by the time I get out of college I should have most of the details nailed down. What about you? What's your chief objective?"

"To stay out of jail."

"That's certainly an impressive career goal. I'll bet you need to study for years and years and probably do an internship and a residency as well in order to achieve that objective."

"Everyone I know seems to think that not ending up in prison will be a major accomplishment for me." He swung back around to look at her. "What about you? What kind of business are you planning to open, Ms. Most Likely to Achieve?"

She took a few steps across the pebbly beach and sank down on a rock. "I'm not sure yet. I'm still researching possibilities. I've been talking to my dad. He says that the secret is to carve out a small niche in the service sector. One that big companies can't fill because of their size."

"Something along the lines of outcall massage, or maybe one of those private escort services?"

"Very funny."

"I've seen the ads in the Yellow Pages. You know, the ones aimed at traveling businessmen and conventioneers. *Discreet personal services offered in the privacy of your hotel room.*"

"You know, your sense of humor is as limited as your idea of an evening's entertainment."

"Well, what do you expect from a guy who doesn't have his Ph.D.?"

"Too much, obviously." She drew up her knees and wrapped her arms around them.

He moved to stand next to her rock. "Sorry. I shouldn't have teased you like that."

"Forget it."

"I'm sure you'll find your niche or whatever. Good luck."

"Thanks."

"Is marriage on your list of personal objectives?"

She glanced up at him, startled. "Well, yes, of course."

"I guess you'll probably marry someone like the jerk, right?"

She sighed. "I was never serious about Perry. He was just someone to have fun with this summer." She wrinkled her nose. "Not that he turned out to be a lot of fun tonight."

"Definitely not Mr. Right."

"No."

"Bet you've got a long list of requirements that Mr. Right will have to meet before you agree to marry him, don't you?"

The dry question made her uncomfortable. "So, I know what I want in a husband. So what? Just because you don't make long-range plans doesn't mean everyone else has to play their life by ear."

"True." Without warning, he dropped down onto the rock beside her. The movement was easy, almost catlike. "Tell me, what kind of hoops will Mr. Right have to jump through before you'll agree to marry him?"

Stung, she held up one hand and ticked off the basics. "He'll be intelligent, well educated, a graduate of a good school, and successful in his field. He'll also be loyal, honorable, decent, and trustworthy."

"No criminal record?"

"Definitely no criminal record." She held up her other hand and continued down the list. "He'll be dependable, kind, sensitive, and capable of making a commitment. Someone I can talk to. Someone who shares my interests and goals. That's very important, you know."

"Uh-huh."

"He'll also get along well with my family, love animals, and be very supportive of my career."

Rafe lounged back on his elbows. "But other than that, just an ordinary guy?"

For some inexplicable reason his mockery hurt. "You think I'm asking too much?"

He smiled faintly. "Get real. The guy you're looking for doesn't exist. Or if he does, he'll have some fatal flaw that you didn't expect."

"Is that so?" She narrowed her eyes. "How about your Mrs. Right? Got any idea of what she'll be like?"

"No. Doubt if there is one. Not that it matters."

"Because you're not interested in a monogamous commitment?" she asked acidly.

"No, because the men in my family aren't much good when it comes to marriage. Figure the odds are against me getting lucky."

She could hardly argue that point. His grandfather's four spectacularly failed marriages were common knowledge. Rafe's father, Sinclair, had had two wives before he had engaged in the tumultuous affair with his model that had produced his sons. The assumption was that if he had not died in the motorcycle accident, Sinclair would have racked up a string of divorces and affairs that would have made Mitchell's record pale in comparison.

"Marriage should not be viewed as a lottery or a crapshoot," she said sternly. "It's a serious step, and it should be treated in a logical, rational manner."

"You think it's that easy?"

"I never said it's easy. I said it should be approached with intelligence and sound common sense."

"Where's the fun in that?"

She gritted her teeth. "You're teasing me again."

"Face it—we Madisons don't usually do things that involve common sense. We probably lack that gene."

"Don't give me that garbage. I'm serious about this, Rafe. I refuse to believe that you can't change what you see as your destiny."

He slanted her an appraising glance. "You really think I could be the one to break the mold?"

"If you want to break it badly enough, yes, I really think you can do it."

"Amazing. Who would have thought a Harte would be such a dreamer?"

"All right, what *are* you going to do with your life?"

"Well," he drawled, "I've noticed that the cult and guru businesses are profitable."

"Get serious. You've got your whole life ahead of you. Don't throw it away. Think about what you want. Make some concrete plans. Develop solid goals and then work toward them."

"You don't think my present career objective is a worthy goal?"

"Staying out of jail is okay as far as it goes. But it's not enough, Rafe. You know it isn't enough."

"Maybe not, but it's all I've got at the moment." He glanced at his watch. The dial glowed in the moonlight. "I think it's time that you went home."

Automatically she looked at her own watch. "Good grief, it's after one. It's going to take at least half an hour to walk home from here. I've got to get going."

He came up off the rock in a fluid movement. "I'll walk with you."

"That's not necessary."

"Yes it is. I'm a Madison and you're a Harte."

"So what?"

"So, if something were to happen to you between here and your place and your folks found out that I was the last guy to see you, I'd get the blame, for sure."

She smiled. "And maybe get tossed into jail by Chief Yates?"

"Yeah. And that would put a real crimp in the only viable career plan I've got at the moment."

The broad, semicircular sweep of the bay began in the distance behind Hannah, near the treacherous waters of Hidden Cove. It ended somewhere up ahead in the darkness, at a jutting piece of land known as Sundown Point. There were no streetlamps on the long, curving bluff road that rimmed the restless waters of Eclipse Bay. The sparse lights of the pier, the marina, and the town's tiny business district lay more than two miles to the rear, in the direction of Hidden Cove.

Up ahead, Hannah could make out only a vast pool of darkness. Sundown Point was invisible in the all-enveloping night. She knew that a handful of cottages and homes were scattered along the heavily wooded bluffs, but she saw no illuminated windows. Her family's summer place was nearly a mile from here, perched over a small, sheltered cove. Her aunt's big house, Dreamscape, was at least another half mile beyond that.

It was, indeed, going to be a long walk.

She glanced back over her shoulder. The faint glare of a well-lit parking lot could be seen on the hillside. It emanated from a clearing in the trees above the town. The parking facility belonged to the Eclipse Bay Policy Studies Institute, a recently established think tank that had been built close to Chamberlain College.

"My parents are up there at the institute tonight," she said at one point, just for something to say. "They're attending the reception for Trevor Thornley."

"The hotshot who's running for the state legislature?"

"Yes." She was surprised that he was aware of Thornley's campaign. He didn't seem like the type who paid attention to politics. But she refrained from making that observation aloud. "It looks like the event is running late. I may even get home ahead of Mom and Dad."

"Lucky for you, hmm? You won't have to go into a lot of awkward explanations about why you came home with me instead of the jerk tonight."

She glanced at him, surprised. "I'll tell them what happened in the morning."

He slapped his forehead with the heel of his palm. "That's right, I keep forgetting. I'm with Ms. Goody Two-shoes here. Of course you'll tell your parents that you spent the night on the beach with me."

Shock brought her to a sudden halt. "I did *not* spend the night on the beach with you, Rafe Madison. And if you dare tell your friends down at the Total Eclipse Bar and Grill that I did, I swear I will . . . I will *sue* you. Or something."

"Don't worry," he muttered. "I'm not planning to announce to the whole town that we did it under Eclipse Arch."

"You'd better not." She gripped her purse more tightly and started walking quicker. The sooner she got back to the house, the better.

Rafe fell into step beside her again. She was intensely aware of him. She had walked this road many times over the years, but never at this hour. Crime was minimal in Eclipse Bay, but not completely absent, especially during the summer when out-of-town visitors flocked to the beach. She was very glad to have company tonight. The long walk home alone would have been more than a little nerve-racking.

Half an hour later they reached the tree-lined drive that led to the Harte summer cottage. Rafe walked her to the porch steps and stopped.

"This is as far as I go," he said. "Good night, Hannah."

She went up one step and paused. It struck her that the strange interlude was over. A wistful sensation trickled through her. She stomped on it with all the ruthlessness she could muster. It was okay to have a few romantic fantasies about Rafe Madison. He was the most notorious male in town, after all—at least, the most notorious in her age group. But you couldn't get serious about a guy like this. There was no future in it.

"Thanks for seeing me home," she said.

"No problem. Not like I had anything better to do tonight." In the yellow glare of the porch light his eyes were enigmatic pools. "Good luck with that five-year plan of yours."

Impulsively she touched the sleeve of his jacket. "Think about making some plans of your own, Rafe. Don't screw up your whole life."

He grinned. Without warning he leaned forward and brushed a quick, stunningly chaste kiss across her mouth. "A man's got to capitalize on his strong points, and I'm so damn good at screwing up."

The brief, casual kiss caught her off guard. Heat infused her whole body. It was followed by a tingling sensation. She covered the awkward moment by hurrying up the rest of the front steps.

At the door she paused to dig out her key. Her hand trembled slightly as she unlocked the door. When she finally got into the house, she turned to look back at Rafe. He was still standing there, watching her. She raised one hand in farewell and then quickly closed the door.

THE rumble of voices awakened her the next morning. She opened her eyes and found herself gazing into a wall of fog.

Morning mist was a regular feature of summer and early fall. It would likely burn off by noon, although the cloud cover might last all day. With luck there would be enough scattered sunshine to drive the temperature into the mid-seventies in the afternoon, but that was the most that could be expected. Nobody came to Eclipse Bay to get a tan. Southern California beaches catered to those who liked to fry their bare skin in the glow of the big nuke in the sky. The wild, rugged beaches of the Oregon coast were for people who preferred to put on a windbreaker and brave the morning fog to explore tidal pools and rocky shoreline caves. They were for those who appreciated adventurous walks along high, windswept bluffs and views of seething seawater churning in stony cauldrons at the bottom of steep cliffs.

The voices downstairs grew louder. Her parents were talking to someone in the kitchen. A man. She could not make out the words, but the conversation sounded tense.

She listened for a while, curiosity growing swiftly. Who would come calling at this hour? Then she caught a name. Rafe Madison.

"Oh, damn."

She tossed aside the covers, scrambled out of bed, and hurriedly pulled on her jeans and a gray turtleneck. She stepped into a pair of loafers, ran a brush through her hair, and headed for the stairs.

She found her parents at the kitchen table with a balding, heavy-bellied man she recognized instantly.

"Chief Yates."

" 'Morning, Hannah." Phil Yates nodded in his ponderous fashion. He had been the only law enforcement in town for as long as Hannah could recall, but this was the first time he had ever come to the Harte cottage.

She masked her uneasiness with a bright smile and turned to her parents for an explanation. A single glance was enough to tell her that something was terribly wrong.

Elaine Harte's attractive face was tight with anxiety. Hamilton's jaw was set in a grim line. A formless dread wafted through Hannah. It was as if a ghost had brushed up against her.

"What is it?" she asked with an urgency that made her father's eyes narrow behind his glasses.

"I was just about to come upstairs and wake you, dear," Elaine said quietly. "Chief Yates has some bad news."

For one horrifying instant Hannah had a vision of Rafe lying sprawled on Bayview Drive, the victim of a hit-and-run. He'd had an even longer walk home last night than she'd had.

She went to the table and gripped the back of the empty chair. "What happened?"

"Kaitlin Sadler was found dead at Hidden Cove this morning," her father said in somber tones.

"Oh, my God." Not Rafe, then. He was safe. Hannah sank down into the chair. Then the name registered. "Kaitlin Sadler?"

"Looks like an accident," Yates said. "Apparently she fell from the path above the cliffs. But I've got to ask you a few questions."

Something in his voice got Hannah's full attention. Rafe was okay, but his girlfriend was dead. It didn't take a genius to figure out why Chief Yates had come here today. When a woman died under mysterious circumstances, the cops always came looking for the boyfriend or the husband first. Her brother had told her that.

Hamilton studied her with a troubled look. "There seems to be some confusion, Hannah. Phil says that Kaitlin was on a date with Rafe Madison last night. But Rafe told Yates that he was with you last night at about the time that Kaitlin died."

"We explained to Phil that that was not possible," Elaine said crisply. "You were with that nice young man from Chamberlain College. Perry Decatur."

Yates cleared his throat. "Well, now, I talked to Mr. Decatur. He says that's not quite true."

Hamilton flicked an irritated glance at Yates's broad, patient face. "We also told him that even if you hadn't been with Decatur, you were highly unlikely to have been anywhere near Rafe Madison."

"I'm well aware of the fact that Hartes don't socialize with Madisons," Yates rumbled. "But young Rafe swears he was with Hannah here, and I got to check out his story."

The full implications of what he was saying finally hit Hannah. "I don't understand. You just said Kaitlin's death was an accident. Is there some question about how she died?"

"Can't rule out the possibility that she jumped." Yates wrapped one ham-size fist around a mug of coffee. "That girl always was kind of high-strung."

Elaine frowned. "She comes from an unfortunate family situation, but I never heard anyone suggest that she might be suicidal."

Yates sipped his coffee. "There's another possibility."

They all looked at him expectantly.

"There may have been an argument," Yates said quietly.

"My God," Elaine whispered. "Are you saying she might have been pushed off the path?"

Hannah planted her hands on the table "Wait a second. Are you suggesting that Rafe Madison killed Kaitlin?"

"Could have been an accident," Yates said. "Like I said, maybe they got into a fight."

"But that's crazy. Why would Rafe do such a thing?"

"Word around town is that he didn't like the fact that she was seeing other men," Yates said.

"Yes, but—"

Hamilton looked at her. "Rafe is trying to use you for an alibi, honey. I don't like him dragging you into this one damn bit. But I'll deal with that later."

"Dad, listen to me—"

"Right now you just need to tell Yates where you were last night between midnight and two this morning."

Hannah braced herself for the explosion she knew would follow. "I was with Rafe Madison."

KAITLIN Sadler's death was officially ruled an accident three days later. It took a lot longer for the firestorm of gossip to fade. The news that Hannah had been with Rafe Madison the night Kaitlin died swept through the small community with the force of a tsunami. Few believed for a moment that the pair had engaged only in casual conversation.

The one person who seemed genuinely happy about the fact that Rafe and Hannah had spent two whole hours together on a moonlit beach was Hannah's great-aunt Isabel Harte.

At eighty-three, Isabel was the sole self-avowed romantic in the family. She was a retired professor of English lit who had never married. She lived alone at Dreamscape, the huge three-story mansion her father had built with the fortune he had made in fishing.

It was Isabel who had provided the seed funding for Harte-Madison, the commercial real estate development company founded by Sullivan Harte and Mitchell Madison all those years ago. The bitter feud that had destroyed the firm as well as the friendship between Sullivan and Mitchell was a source of frustration and disappointment to Isabel. She still harbored dreams of ending the rift that had shattered the partnership and ignited the hostility between the two men.

Hannah was very fond of her great-aunt. She was also well aware that her parents had been trying to get Isabel to sell Dreamscape and move into an apartment in Portland. But Isabel refused to budge.

On the fourth day of the seething rumors, Isabel sat with Elaine Harte in the Harte family kitchen.

"It's so romantic," Isabel said, blithely indifferent to Elaine's exasperated expression. "Just like Romeo and Juliet."

"That's ridiculous," Elaine gasped.

"Darn right," Hannah said from the doorway. "We all know what happened to Romeo and Juliet. A very nasty ending, if you ask me."

"This would be Romeo and Juliet with the right ending," Isabel said, unperturbed. "A happy conclusion that would end the long-standing feud between the two families."

Elaine raised her eyes to the heavens. "Sullivan and Mitchell are engaged in a feud, Isabel. The rest of us just ignore each other. Rafe Madison has no real interest in a nice girl like Hannah."

"Gee, thanks, Mom." Hannah went to the counter to pour herself a cup of coffee. "Why don't you just label me boring and be done with it?"

Elaine gave her a repressive look. "You know perfectly well what I meant."

"I sure do, Mom." Hannah made a face. "And you're absolutely right. Rafe doesn't have any interest in me. I'm not his type."

Isabel's vivid blue eyes brightened with interest. "Whatever do you mean, dear?"

Hannah smiled wryly. "Rafe thinks I'm a prim, prissy, goody-goody over-achiever."

"What do you think about him?" Isabel asked quickly.

"I think he's wasting his life. Told him so, too. The only thing we had in common the other night when we ran into each other on the beach was the fact that we both had to walk home after a bad date. Trust me, seduction was the last thing on his mind."

"Unfortunately, almost no one in town believes that," Elaine said grimly. "I'm told that Kaitlin Sadler's brother believes far worse. He's convinced that Rafe really did shove Kaitlin over that cliff and later seduced you in an effort to persuade you to cover up for him."

"I know," Hannah said. "Poor Dell. He's lost his sister, and all everyone can talk about is how Rafe spent the night making wild, passionate love to me on the beach."

Isabel's eyes lit with speculative interest. "I don't suppose that he actually did—?"

"No, he did not," Hannah said brusquely. "I told you, all we did was talk."

Elaine shook her head. "I believe you, dear. And I'm relieved to know that Rafe was nowhere near Kaitlin at the time she died. I just wish that he had found someone else to give him his alibi that night. I'm afraid it's going to be a long time before people stop talking about this unfortunate affair."

"ACTUALLY it's kind of weird when you think about it," Pamela said the next day over veggie burgers and French fries at Snow's Café. "I mean, what are the odds that either you or I would ever spend a couple of hours on a beach with a guy like Rafe Madison?"

Hannah eyed her friend over the top of the bun. Pamela attended Chamberlain College. She had her sights set on a career teaching English literature to undergraduates. She already wore the uniform of the successful young academic: black tights, chunky black shoes, a long black skirt, a slouchy jacket, and glasses with thin frames. Her shoulder-length brown hair was held at her nape with a mock-tortoiseshell clip.

"I admit the odds are not high." Hannah took a mouthful of her tofu burger. "It was just one of those things. I owe it all to Perry Decatur."

Pamela made a face. "So much for your mom's opinion of Perry. She was so sure he was the nice, upwardly mobile type."

"He's definitely committed to upward mobility. Probably go far in the academic world."

"But not a nice guy, huh?"

"Smooth. Slick." Hannah thought back to the scuffle in the front seat and shuddered. "Not nice."

Pamela glanced around the crowded café. Apparently satisfied that no one could overhear, she leaned across the table and lowered her voice. "So what really did happen between you and Rafe Madison?"

"Nothing. I told you, we just talked. That's all."

Pamela's eyes clouded with disappointment. "That's all? Honest truth?"

Hannah briefly considered the insignificant good-night kiss Rafe had given her. "Pretty much."

Pamela flopped back in her chair. "Too bad."

"Think so?"

"Sure. Intelligent, educated, clearheaded women like us know better than to marry guys like Rafe Madison. But that doesn't mean it wouldn't be fun to fool around with one."

"A little hard on the reputation, especially in a town like Eclipse Bay. Trust me, I know this now. After those infamous two hours on the beach with Rafe Madison, my image as a nice girl has plummeted to somewhere in the vicinity of zero."

"The least you could have done for yourself was have a good time on the way down."

RAFE phoned the day he left town. Hannah was alone in the house at the time. When she heard his voice on the other end of the line she had a feeling he knew that her parents had driven into Eclipse Bay together.

"I owe you," he said without preamble.

"No, you do not owe me." She clutched the instrument very tightly. His voice was as sexy on the phone as it was at midnight on a shadowed beach. "I just told the truth, that's all."

"Is everything that simple for you, Miss Voted Most Likely to Succeed? Black and white? True or false?"

"In this case it is, yes."

"You don't care that everyone in town thinks I did a lot more than hold your hand that night?"

She sought refuge in irrefutable fact. "You didn't even hold my hand."

There was a short beat of silence on the other end of the line. She wondered if he was thinking about that meaningless little kiss he had given her just before he sent her into the house. It was certainly on her mind.

"Whatever," he said eventually. "But I still owe you."

"Forget it. No big deal. Besides, to be honest, I owe you."

"How's that?"

"I am no longer known around town as Miss Boring Goody Two-shoes."

There was another beat of silence. "You're definitely not boring."

She was not sure what to say to that. She wrapped the cord around her hand and kept her mouth shut. It was an exercise in self-discipline.

"Hannah?"

"Yes?"

"I meant what I said the other night. Good luck with that five-year plan of yours. I hope things work out the way you want. Hope you do okay with your own business."

He paused. "Hope you find a guy who meets all those requirements on that list, too."

He sounded sincere, she thought.

"Rafe?"

"Yeah?"

"I meant what I said to you that night, too. Get a life."

1

THE long, pearl-studded train of the creamy candlelight-satin wedding gown cascaded in graceful folds behind the bride as she glided to a halt in front of the altar. She smiled demurely at the groom through a gossamer cloud of veil. The organ music trailed off. A respectful hush fell. The minister cleared his throat.

"Well, that's it for me," Hannah murmured to her assistant as they retreated to the portico in front of the church. "I'm out of here. You can handle the receiving line. The limo is ready. Keep an eye on the four-year-old nephew. He'll probably make another grab for the bride's train when she walks back down the aisle. See you at the reception."

"It's so perfect." Carla Groves seized a tissue and dabbed at her eyes. She peeked back into the church. "The flowers, the candles. Everything. The bride looks as if she just stepped out of a fantasy."

"I don't know how to tell you this, Carla, but you aren't going to last long in this business if you weep every time you send a bride up the aisle."

"But she's so beautiful. Practically glowing."

"Uh-huh." Hannah snapped the lock on her briefcase. "Looks even better this time than she did the last time. Probably because her budget was much larger. She did very well in the divorce settlement, you know. Had a great lawyer."

Carla rolled her eyes. "You're such a cynic, Hannah."

"No, I'm not. I agree with you. Jennifer Ballinger does make a lovely bride. And a very profitable one for Weddings by Harte. This is her second marriage with us, and I have every expectation that in a couple of years she'll come back to this firm for her third. Nothing like a repeat customer, I always say."

AT five-thirty that evening, Hannah stepped out of the elevator into a corridor decorated in shades of tasteful beige and walked down the hall toward the door of her apartment. Her footsteps were hushed by the thick, pale carpeting, but the door of the suite next to hers opened before she reached it.

Winston rushed out to greet her with as much enthusiasm as a properly bred Schnauzer considered appropriate to exhibit upon such occasions. As always, the sight of the small, elegant, salt-and-pepper dog hurrying toward her lowered Hannah's stress level by several degrees.

She smiled as she crouched to scratch Winston behind the ears. He gave a discreetly muffled whine, quivered with pleasure, and licked her hand.

"Hello, pal. Sorry I'm late. Been a long day."

Winston looked up at her through a fringe of long, silvery lashes, understanding in his intelligent eyes.

Mrs. Blankenship stuck her head around the edge of the door. "Oh, there you are, dear. Winston was starting to get a trifle anxious. How did the wedding go?"

"Nothing out of the ordinary. The usual number of snafus at the reception. The caterer turned up with a cheese tart instead of the asparagus canapés that the bride had selected. The photographer helped himself to a couple of glasses of champagne and started to flirt with the bartender. The flower girl came very close to getting into a food fight with the four-year-old nephew."

"Just the usual, then." Mrs. Blankenship nodded wisely. She always loved to hear about the weddings. "But I'm sure you nipped all the potential disasters in the bud behind the scenes."

"That's what I get paid to do." Hannah leaned down to pat Winston, who bounced around her high heels. "I think the bride was satisfied. As far as she was concerned, everything went off as if the whole thing had been staged by a computer."

Mrs. Blankenship pursed her lips. "I don't think that's an appropriate image, dear. The thought of a computer-generated wedding is really quite dreadful. It sounds so cold. Weddings are supposed to evoke all sorts of wonderful emotions, after all."

"Trust me, Mrs. Blankenship, behind the scenes, a well-managed wedding has a lot in common with a launch of the space shuttle."

"You know, dear, I hate to mention this, but you've become increasingly cynical ever since you ended your engagement last year. It's so sad to see a young, healthy, vibrant woman like you turn jaded. Maybe you took on too much when you signed up for all those evening classes at the college."

"Mrs. Blankenship—"

"You've been working much too hard for the past year. Perhaps you need a vacation. Go someplace where you can relax and regain your interest in your business and your social life."

"I have no social life to revive, Mrs. Blankenship. And as for my career, nothing will ever make me starry-eyed about my business. The only weddings that I actually enjoy doing are those in which I know for a fact that the couple met through my sister's agency. At least I can feel reasonably confident that those marriages have a good chance of lasting."

"Yes, your sister does have a knack for matchmaking, doesn't she?" Mrs. Blankenship got a dreamy expression in her eyes. "She obviously has a wonderful sense of intuition when it comes to that sort of thing."

"I hate to disillusion you, Mrs. Blankenship, but Lillian uses a computer, not her intuition." Hannah dug her keys out of her massive shoulder bag. "Does Winston need a walk right away?"

"No, dear, we just got back from our walkies," Mrs. Blankenship said.

"Great." Hannah went to her own door and unlocked it, Winston trotting eagerly at her heels. "Thanks again, Mrs. Blankenship."

"Anytime, dear." Mrs. Blankenship paused. "You know, you really should consider taking some time off. Your busy season is finished. You could slip away for a while."

"Funny you should mention that, Mrs. Blankenship. I was just thinking the same thing."

Mrs. Blankenship beamed. "I'm so glad to hear that. You really haven't been quite the same since your engagement ended."

"Several people have mentioned that." Hannah opened her door. "One theory is that I have been possessed by an alien entity."

"I beg your pardon?"

"Never mind. Good night, Mrs. Blankenship."

"Good night, dear."

Hannah stepped into the small hallway, waited until Winston came inside, and then swiftly shut the door. She flipped on the lights.

"Give me a minute to change, Winston. Then I'll find us both something to eat."

In the bedroom she stripped off the jacket and skirt of her blue business suit, then pulled on a pair of black leggings and a cozy cowl-necked tunic and slipped into a pair of ballet-style flats. Pausing for a moment in front of the mirror, she brushed her hair behind her ears and anchored it with a narrow band.

When she was ready, she padded back down the hall into the kitchen and dug one of the expensive, specially formulated dog bones out of a box for Winston. The Schnauzer took it very politely from her fingers.

"Enjoy."

Winston needed no further urging. He set to work on the bone vigorously.

Hannah opened the refrigerator and meditated on the sparse contents for a moment. After a while she removed a hunk of sheep's-milk feta cheese and a nearly empty bottle of Chardonnay.

She arranged her small haul on a tray and carried it into the second bedroom, where she maintained a home office. Winston followed, the remains of his bone wedged firmly between his jaws. Sinking down onto the high-backed chair, Hannah propped her feet on the corner of the desk and munched a cracker with some of the cheese on it.

Winston took up his customary position on the floor beside the desk chair. Muted crunching sounds ensued.

"Brace yourself, Winston." Hannah reached for the phone. "I'm going to check my messages. Who knows what excitement awaits us?"

The automated answering service surrendered three offerings. The first was from a florist, reporting that the orchids Hannah had ordered for the Cooke-Anderson wedding were going to cost more than expected.

"I told the client that they would be expensive."

The second message was from her brother, Nick, letting her know that he had just mailed the manuscript of the most recent addition to his successful suspense series to the editor. "I'm taking Carson to Disneyland, and then we're going on down to Phoenix to see Sullivan and Rachel. Probably be gone for most of the month. You know how to reach me if you need me."

"It's about time he married again," Hannah said to Winston. "Amelia has been gone for three years now. He and little Carson have been alone long enough."

Winston jiggled his brows.

"Yes, I know. I'm a fine one to talk."

She punched the key for the last message . . . and nearly fell off her chair when she heard Rafe Madison's unmistakable, bottom-of-the-sea voice. Her heels came down off the desk with a small thud. She sucked in a half-strangled breath and sat forward abruptly. The Chardonnay sloshed wildly in the glass. Several drops went over the rim and hit Winston between his ears.

He looked up from his bone with a puzzled expression.

"Sorry, Winston." She grabbed a napkin and blotted the wine off the top of his head. "I was a little stunned there for a second, but I don't think I'm going to faint or anything."

She tossed the napkin into the wastebasket, inhaled slowly, and took a steadying swallow of wine.

She had not heard his voice in eight years, and although this time around it was only a recording, it had the same impact on her tonight as it had the last time. Small flashes of electrical energy snapped through her nerve endings. Her stomach seemed to float in midair.

"This is Rafe Madison . . ."

The last conversation she'd had with him flitted through her mind. *Good luck with that five-year plan of yours. I hope things work out the way you want.*

She wondered if he'd ever gotten his act together.

". . . Got the message you sent through your lawyer. The answer is no. Looks like we've got a few things to talk about, and I don't plan to do it through our attorneys. See you in Eclipse Bay."

"No?" The old memories went up in smoke and the present came crashing back. She stabbed the replay key.

". . . The answer is no. . . . See you in Eclipse Bay."

She had not misunderstood. His answer to her offer was loud and clear.

"I think I've got a problem, Winston."

***

SHE dropped the bombshell on her sister the following morning.

"What do you mean, he refuses to sell?" Lillian demanded on the other end of the line. "That house belonged to *our* great-aunt, not his. He can't refuse to sell."

Hannah listened to the muffled sounds of a printer in the background. Lillian was hard at work. She ran her matchmaking firm, Private Arrangements, out of an office in a high-rise located only a few blocks away from the one in which Hannah and Winston lived.

"You were there when Isabel's will was read," Hannah reminded her wearily. "She left the house equally to Rafe and me. The lawyer says he can do whatever he wants to do with his half."

"Hmm. Maybe you didn't offer him enough money."

"The negotiations didn't even get that far. I just sent a message to him through the lawyer telling him that I would be willing to buy out his half of the house. I expected him to come back with a price."

"What on earth do you suppose he plans to do with half of Dreamscape?" Lillian mused.

"Who knows?" Hannah frowned at the array of wedding photos that decorated her office wall. "But I have plans for Dreamscape, and I'm certainly not going to let him stand in my way."

"You're going to meet with him in Eclipse Bay, aren't you?"

"Doesn't look like I've got much choice. I want Dreamscape. Somehow I've got to talk him out of his share of the place."

"We haven't heard much about Rafe in recent years. Just that he got married and divorced."

Hannah thought about her midnight conversation with Rafe. *The men in my family aren't much good when it comes to marriage.* . . . *Figure the odds are against me getting lucky* . . .

"Divorce is a Madison family tradition," she said quietly.

"Unfortunately, it's a very common tradition for a lot of families these days." Lillian made a *tut-tut* sound. "I don't know why so many people refuse to see the obvious. Marriage is a partnership. It should be entered into the same way one would go into any serious business arrangement. All the factors should be examined from every angle before a commitment is made."

"Lillian—"

"There's a staggering amount of scientific evidence that suggests that couples who are properly matched using modern psychological tests and personality inventories are far more likely to succeed at marriage than those who let their emotions—"

"Enough, Lillian. I've heard your professional pitch before, remember?"

"Sorry. You know me. I get a little carried away sometimes." Lillian hesitated. "About Rafe Madison—"

"What about him?"

"Think he's changed?"

"How should I know?" Hannah rose, phone in hand, and went to the window. "Wonder if he achieved his big career objective?"

"Didn't know he had one."

"Oh, he had one, all right." Hannah studied the view of the bridge-studded Willamette River. "His great ambition was to stay out of jail."

"Given the direction in which everyone seemed to think he was headed eight years ago, that would have been a major accomplishment."

"I'm sure we would have heard if he had gone to prison." Hannah tightened her grip on the phone. "That kind of news would have been hot gossip in Eclipse Bay."

"Ah, but as far as we know, he hasn't been back to Eclipse Bay very often since Kaitlin Sadler died. According to Mom and Dad, he makes a couple of short weekend visits to see his grandfather every few months and that's it. How would anyone know if he'd done time?"

"I think he was too smart to end up in prison," Hannah said.

"Smart does not always equate with common sense. We're both in the marriage business. We see smart people do dumb things every day."

"True."

Lillian paused. "You're still serious about your plans for Dreamscape?"

"Very."

"I was afraid of that. My advice is don't let Rafe know you've got your heart set on turning Dreamscape into an inn."

"Why not?"

Lillian made an exasperated sound. "Use your head. If he figures out just how badly you want the place, he'll hold out for a whopping price for his half."

"I'll be careful how much I say. I'm a Harte, remember? I can be cool."

"Do that," Lillian said dryly. "You know, something tells me that it's a good thing that Mom and Dad went on that monthlong cruise. If they knew that you were getting ready to go toe-to-toe with Rafe Madison over Dreamscape, they'd descend on Eclipse Bay like avenging angels."

"Speaking of family interference, I'm counting on you to keep quiet about my decision to go to Eclipse Bay for a while. I want some time to work things out with Rafe. That won't be possible if I'm inundated with helpful Hartes."

"I'll keep quiet." Lillian sighed. "I still can't imagine what Aunt Isabel was thinking. Ever since Rafe used you as his alibi for the night Kaitlin Sadler died, she was obsessed with the notion that the two of you were the Romeo and Juliet of the Harte-Madison feud."

"Rafe didn't *use* me as his alibi," Hannah said. "I *was* his alibi."

"There's a difference?"

"Oh, yes," Hannah said. "There's a difference."

2

THE weird part was that he had never intended to come back for more than an occasional overnight stay, just the obligatory duty visits to check up on Mitchell. Now he was determined to carve out his future here in Eclipse Bay.

Go figure.

Rafe propped one sneaker-clad foot on the bottom rail of the second-story veranda that wrapped around the big house. He braced his elbows on the top rail and watched the sporty little lipstick-red Honda turn into the long drive.

He hadn't had a lot of ambitions eight years ago. He'd only known that he had to stop screwing up. Something of a challenge, given where he was coming from. He'd achieved his primary objective, he thought, as he watched the rakish red car come closer. He'd managed to stay out of jail.

He wondered if Hannah would be impressed.

The crimson vehicle came to a halt next to his silver Porsche. An intense rush of anticipation swept through him. He watched the door on the driver's side of the Honda open.

The first thing he noticed when Hannah got out of the car was that her amber-brown hair was shorter. Eight years ago it had fallen well below her shoulders. Today it was cut in a sleek, sophisticated curve that angled along the line of her jaw.

She didn't look as if she had gained any weight in the intervening years, but there was something different about her figure. The black trousers and snug-fitting black top she wore revealed a fit, lithe body with a small waist, gently flared hips, and discreetly curved breasts. It took him a few seconds to decide that the difference was the sophisticated confidence with which she carried herself. She had seemed painfully young and naïve that night on the beach. Still a girl in some ways. She was a woman now.

She paused, holding the car door open, and leaned down slightly to speak to someone in the front seat. From his vantage point on the upper veranda he could not see who had accompanied her. Sharp disappointment gripped him. For some reason he had assumed that she would be alone. What the hell had he expected? He'd heard that her engagement had blown up a year ago, but that was no reason to think she hadn't gotten serious about someone else in the meantime.

The passenger door did not open. Instead, Hannah stepped back to allow an elegantly trimmed gray Schnauzer to bound out of the car.

Relief whipped through Rafe. Not a boyfriend, after all. Just a mutt. He could handle a dog.

Sensing Rafe's presence on the veranda, the Schnauzer came to a sudden halt and looked up at him. Rafe waited for the little beast to start yapping wildly in typical froufrou-dog style. But the Schnauzer did not bark. Instead, he gazed up at Rafe with an air of watchful stillness.

Okay, so maybe this was not a totally froufrou dog.

Hannah looked up to see what had captured her dog's attention. The light of the late-afternoon sun glinted on her stylish sunglasses.

"Hello, Rafe."

That cool reserve hadn't been in her voice eight years ago, he thought.

"Been a while," he said neutrally.

"Yes, it has," she said. "I've been wondering, did you ever get a life?"

"Depends on your definition. What about you? The five-year plan turn out the way you expected?"

"Not exactly." She moved one hand in a graceful gesture to indicate the big house. "You're going to be difficult about his, aren't you?"

"Yeah."

She nodded. "Had a feeling you would."

She went up the front steps and disappeared into the house. The Schnauzer gave Rafe one last, assessing look and followed Hannah inside.

HE found her standing in the solarium, arms folded beneath her breasts. She smiled coolly, but her shoulders were angled. She was braced for battle. When Rafe walked into the glass-walled room, the Schnauzer glanced up from an exploration of a potted palm.

"Nice dog." Rafe crouched and held out his hand.

"His name is Winston," Hannah said crisply.

"Hello, Winston."

With great dignity, the Schnauzer crossed the tiled floor to where Rafe waited and sniffed politely. Apparently satisfied that the proprieties had been observed, he sat back on his haunches and looked up at Hannah.

Rafe got to his feet. "I think your dog likes me."

She did not look pleased. "Winston is always well behaved. I wouldn't read too much into it if I were you."

"Right. Maybe he's waiting until my back is turned to go for my throat. How long have you had him?"

"A couple of years."

Rafe nodded. "Outlasted your fiancé, huh? Lucky dog."

Her mouth tightened. "I'm not here to talk about Winston or my ex-fiancé."

"Whatever. Want some coffee?"

She hesitated. "All right."

"Don't fall all over yourself."

She trailed after him down the hall into the big, old-fashioned kitchen. Winston trotted briskly at her heels, pausing here and there to investigate a corner or a piece of furniture.

"How did you hear about my engagement?" Hannah asked. Irritation made the question as brittle as thin ice.

"You know how gossip travels between the Hartes and the Madisons."

"In other words, Aunt Isabel told you."

"Yeah." He set the kettle on the stove. "Sent me a note right after the breakup. She seemed delighted. Guess Mr. Right fell a little short in her view."

Hannah watched him intently. "How long have you been here at Dreamscape?"

"Got in late last night." He spooned coffee into the tall glass pot.

She glanced at the French press coffeemaker he was using. "Isabel never made her coffee in one of those. She always used a regular drip machine."

"This is mine. I brought it with me."

"I see." She eyed the gleaming stainless-steel vegetable steamer on the counter. "That's not Isabel's either."

"No."

Frowning, she walked to the pantry and opened the door. He knew what she saw inside. The supplies he had brought with him included several boxes of his favorite brand of dried pasta in a variety of shapes, a bottle of twelve-year-old balsamic vinegar, and a package of capers preserved in salt. There was also a supply of dried herbs and chiles and some French lentils.

Hannah closed the pantry door very firmly. "You've certainly made yourself right at home."

"Why not? Half this place is mine now."

"Lillian was right," she said tightly. "I can't imagine what Isabel was thinking when she made out her will."

He poured boiling water into the pot. "You know damn well what she was thinking."

"Romeo and Juliet."

He set the kettle down. "With a more upbeat ending."

"I am prepared to make you a fair-market offer for your share of Dreamscape."

"Forget it." He smiled slightly. "I'm not interested."

She met his gaze across the width of the kitchen. There was steel in her eyes. "Do you intend to make me an offer for my half?"

He lounged against the counter. "Are you open to one?"

"No. I have plans for Dreamscape."

"What a coincidence. So do I."

She gave him a speculative look. "Looks like we have a problem."

"Think so?"

"How long are you going to stay here in Eclipse Bay?"

He shrugged and turned back to finish the coffee. "As long as it takes."

"You can afford to just drop everything and move back here to Eclipse Bay for an unspecified period of time?"

"Nothing holding me in San Diego."

"That's where you've been all these years?" Her tone was one of unwilling curiosity.

Just had to ask, he thought. As if she couldn't help herself. Good sign. Maybe.

"For the most part," he said easily.

He pressed the plunger down to trap the grounds in the bottom of the pot. Then he glanced at Hannah over his shoulder. She was watching him with an enigmatic expression.

"What about you?" he prodded softly. "How long do you intend to stay here in Eclipse Bay?"

Her brows rose. "For as long as it takes."

"There are three floors. Plenty of bedrooms and baths. Take your pick."

"You're staying here?"

"Sure, why not?"

"Then I think I'll use my folks' place," she said coolly.

What had he expected? That would have been too easy, anyway. Nothing ever came easy to him. He had a talent for doing things the hard way.

"Suit yourself," he said. "But this is Eclipse Bay. You're a Harte and I'm a Madison, and by now everyone knows Isabel left Dreamscape to both of us."

"So?"

"So, people are going to talk, regardless of where you choose to sleep."

She watched him pour the coffee. When he handed her the mug, her fingers brushed against his. He savored the small thrill, wondered if she felt anything at all.

She turned away a little too quickly and paced to the far end of the counter.

"Let's go back into the solarium." He led the way out of the kitchen. "We can sit down out there."

Hannah said nothing, but she trailed after him. He watched her settle neatly onto a cushioned white wicker lounger. Winston sauntered into the sunroom, found a satisfactory place near the window, and flopped down on his belly. He rested his muzzle on his front paws and watched Rafe through feathery brows.

Hannah turned the mug between her palms. "What exactly do you plan to do with Dreamscape?"

"I'm going to open an inn and restaurant."

Her mouth fell open. She stared at him, her eyes widening in astonishment.

"You're going to do *what*?" Somewhere between a screech and a choking sound.

"You heard me," he said mildly.

"You can't be serious," she sputtered. "That's *my* plan. At least, the inn part is my plan." She hesitated, frowning. "I hadn't thought about adding a restaurant."

"You should have thought about it. The reputation of any hotel is greatly enhanced by a high-quality restaurant."

"No offense, but as I recall, your idea of a high-class establishment when you lived here was the Total Eclipse Bar and Grill. I seriously doubt that any place that uses the slogan 'Where the sun don't shine' is going to show up in your better grade of guidebook."

"The Total Eclipse has its place in the grand scheme of things."

"I'll take your word for it." She eyed him. "Just what do you know about running an inn and a restaurant?"

"I worked at a five-star place down in San Diego for a while."

"Terrific." She gave him an icy look. "You've worked in a hotel, so you think you can run one?"

"I'll admit I'm stronger in the food-and-beverage area than I am on the innkeeping side."

"What did you do at this five-star place in San Diego? Wait tables?"

"Among other things," he said. "What about you? Know anything about the innkeeping business?"

"As a matter of fact, I've been taking intensive classes in hotel management for nearly a year. Ever since I got the idea of turning Dreamscape into an inn."

"Is that so? And just where did you get the brilliant notion of converting this place into a hotel?"

She hesitated. "Aunt Isabel and I started talking about it a year ago."

He whistled softly. "What an astonishing coincidence."

"Don't tell me." Hannah's jaw was very tight now. "She mentioned the idea to you at about the same time, right?"

"Right."

Hannah tapped a neatly manicured nail against the side of her glass. "Let me make something very clear. This isn't an impulse or a flash-in-the-pan idea for me. I've done a lot of thinking and planning during the past year. I've made my decision. I'm going to sell Weddings by Harte and open this inn. I'm absolutely committed to this project."

"What a coincidence," he said again.

"Let's get real here. Sooner or later we're going to have to come to some agreement about what to do with Dreamscape."

He settled deeper into his chair and looked out over the bay. "I'm in no rush."

She gave him a frozen smile. "I noticed."

3

SNOW'S Café had changed little in eight years. Whenever she stepped inside, Hannah always felt as if she had entered a time warp. The colorful posters on the walls were always the same—a mix of classic rock band ads and pithy sayings that reflected the conspiracy theories of the owner, Arizona Snow. The large one over the cash register summed up Arizona's worldview. The illustration showed two bug-eyed space aliens in heavy-metal attire. They were armed with futuristic weaponry. The slogan underneath read, "We're from the government and we're here to help."

The café was the main hangout for the faculty and students of nearby Chamberlain College. The Eclipse Bay Policy Studies Institute was not far away, but the think tank staff tended to avoid Snow's. It was no secret that since the day the institute had opened its doors Arizona had viewed the facility with deep suspicion. She was convinced that whatever was going on there constituted a dangerous threat to all those who cherished a free society.

"Over here, Hannah." Pamela's face lit up in welcome. Pamela McCallister was now on the faculty of the English department at Chamberlain, and over the years her upwardly mobile path through the thorny territory of higher education had been marked by subtle but highly significant changes of fashion. She still wore a lot of black, but there was less of the romantic poetess about her now and more of the trendy professional. Her hair was much shorter, marking her shift from student to faculty status. The voluminous bag she carried was made of much more expensive material than the one she had favored eight years ago.

"Sorry I'm late." Hannah gave her a quick hug before sliding into the booth across from her. "I stopped by Dreamscape, and then I had to take my dog and my luggage to my folks' cottage."

Pamela gave her a knowing look. "You're not staying at Dreamscape?"

"Rafe got there ahead of me."

"I heard his car was seen parked in the drive all last night."

"He's definitely taken up residence." Hannah snapped the well-worn, plastic-coated menu out of the slot behind the napkin holder. "I think he's working on the premise that possession is nine-tenths of the law."

"Well, well, well." Pamela looked deeply intrigued. "This is going to be interesting."

"Think so?"

"Yes, indeed. Can't wait to see how it plays out." Pamela's eyes gleamed behind the lenses of her glasses. "And just think, the whole town will be watching."

"I'm glad everyone else finds this mess so amusing." Hannah glanced at the menu and saw that it hadn't changed in eight years, either. It still featured the same eclectic but curiously inspired assortment of vegetarian burgers, French fries, pizzas, quesadillas, and noodle dishes. "I can assure you that from where I'm sitting, there's nothing remotely entertaining about it. Rafe made it clear this afternoon that he's going to be a problem."

"He always was a problem, as I recall." Pamela propped her elbows on the yellow Formica tabletop and rested her chin on her folded hands. "So, tell me. Has he changed much?"

"No. He's driving a Porsche these days instead of a motorcycle, but as far as I can tell, he still has no visible means of support."

"Hmm."

Hannah looked up sharply from the menu. "What does 'hmm' mean?"

"There's been some talk that he might have been dabbling in a few less-than-legal activities during the past eight years."

"Great. You think I'm sharing Aunt Isabel's inheritance with a gangster?"

"No one's really sure, you understand. But you've got to admit the Porsche is a little hard to explain."

Hannah thought about that for a few seconds. "Well, one thing's for certain. Whatever he's been up to in the past few years, he still views me as a prissy overachiever. Not exactly the basis for a lasting relationship."

"Who's talking duration?"

"I refuse to allow you to live out your prurient fantasies vicariously through me, Pam." Hannah sighed. "I guess I'll know soon enough whether or not he's changed. If he starts spending his evenings down at the Total Eclipse, I'll get a very big clue, won't I?"

"I'd say that would be a hint, yes."

"Let's change the subject." Hannah dropped the menu on the table. "Brad and the kids?"

"The kids are great." Pamela's eyes softened and lit up with enthusiasm. "I promised them you'd come to dinner soon."

"I'll be there with bells on. And Brad? Did he get that joint appointment at the institute yet?"

Pamela's smile faded. "We thought we were going to have some excellent news on that front to announce later this month. But now we're not so sure."

"Something go wrong?"

"You could say that. The something is named Perry Decatur. As far as we can tell, he's the one blocking the appointment. He's been jealous of Brad for years. Probably afraid that if Brad joins the staff at the institute, he'll be put in the shade."

Hannah sat back in surprise. "I didn't know Perry worked at the institute."

"I thought I told you. He left his position at Chamberlain six months ago. His title is Vice President of Finance and Administration. Brings in big donors. Everyone assumes he's got his eye on becoming director one of these days."

Hannah shook her head in wry disgust. "Perry always was a fast talker."

<hr />

"NEVER thought you'd come back here for good." Jed Steadman sat forward in the wicker chair and clasped his hands lightly between his knees. "Figured that with the way things were between you and your grandfather, you'd want to stay clear of Eclipse Bay as much as possible."

Rafe stacked his feet on the railing, rocked back in his chair, and took a swallow of beer from the bottle he had brought from the kitchen. "One thing I've learned in the past eight years: Never say never."

"I hear you." Jed watched a seagull ride a current of air above the cliffs. "Life takes some twists and turns sometimes. I thought I'd be long gone by now myself."

"That's right. Your big plan was to get a job as a foreign correspondent with one of the big-city dailies. What happened?"

"A man has to be flexible or he'll miss out on some incredible opportunities. When Ed Bolton said he would sell the *Journal* to me a few years ago, I jumped at the chance. As editor and owner, I get to run my own show."

"A lot to be said for that."

"You got that right." Jed slanted him a sidelong glance. "Judging by the Porsche outside, you've done okay for yourself."

Rafe took another swallow of beer. "Managed to stay out of jail."

Jed gave a short bark of laughter. "Almost forgot. Not doing time behind bars was your big career objective, wasn't it?"

Rafe raised the beer bottle in a mocking salute. "And here I am today, a resounding success in my chosen field. A lesson for wayward youth across this great land."

"Exactly what *is* your chosen field?" Jed's eyes glinted with curiosity. "No offense, but I never heard that you ever actually got yourself what folks like to call a real job."

"I get by."

"I've noticed." Jed watched him intently. "There's talk going around that you maybe found some, shall we say, unconventional ways to accomplish that."

"You're starting to sound like a reporter, Jed."

Jed held up his hands, palms out. "Okay, I get the point. No more questions in that area. Can't blame me for asking. I am in the newspaper business, after all."

They sat in companionable silence for a few minutes.

"Heard you and Connie split up a couple of years ago," Rafe said eventually. "Sorry."

"It was a mistake." Jed glanced down at his clasped hands and then looked up. "She went back to Seattle. Couldn't take small-town life. She's remarried."

Rafe settled deeper into his chair. "I didn't do any better with marriage myself."

"I'm surprised you even gave it a whirl. You always said you wouldn't be any good at it."

"Turned out I was right."

"One thing you should know," Jed said quietly after a while. "Dell Sadler still thinks you pushed his sister over that cliff. You might want to stay out of his way while you're here in town."

"Thanks for the tip."

"Sure. What are friends for?" Jed looked down the length of the broad front porch that encircled the mansion. "What are you going to do with this place?"

"Open an inn and a restaurant."

"Whew!" Jed was clearly impressed. "Talk about big plans! Gonna cost a bundle, though."

"Not a problem," Rafe said.

4

HANNAH stood on the rocky beach below the Harte cottage and watched Winston chase seagulls in Dead Hand Cove. The tide was still out this morning. The five tall, finger-shaped stones that had given the cove its name thrust upward from the wet sand in a pattern that was eerily reminiscent of the outflung hand of a corpse. Or so she and Nick and Lillian had concluded years ago. When the tide came in a few hours from now, all but the very tip of the forefinger would be submerged.

The cove had been a favorite playground for all three Hartes in their youth.

In addition to the macabre rock formation, it boasted an intricate network of small caves in the cliffs that framed the tiny beach. Together with Nick and Lillian, Hannah had spent hours exploring the rocky passages. The caves weren't dangerously deep or convoluted, and they had made excellent hiding places for adventurous children.

Out in the cove, Winston dashed off after another seagull. He was certainly enjoying the stay in Eclipse Bay, Hannah thought. What surprised her was that she was strangely content also, in spite of the looming problem of Rafe Madison.

She and Winston had been here for the better part of a week, but she was no closer to resolving the sticky situation involving Dreamscape than she had been that first afternoon. Rafe refused even to discuss the possibility of selling his share of the mansion. A war of nerves was taking shape. They couldn't go on like this indefinitely, she told herself. Sooner or later one of them would have to make a move toward ending the impasse.

Out on the sand, Winston found a piece of driftwood, seized it in his jaws, and pranced triumphantly back toward Hannah. Halfway across the cove he came to a sudden halt and looked up toward the cliff path.

Simultaneously a whisper of awareness tingled through Hannah. She sensed Rafe's presence just before he spoke.

"Nice to see that Winston doesn't stand on formality all the time," he said.

Hannah braced herself for the little shock of excitement she always got when she first encountered him. She turned and saw that he had reached the bottom of the path. He came toward her with that supple masculine grace that was so much a part of him.

Time had not refined Rafe. The cool, savvy intelligence in his green eyes was more intense and more dangerous—the result of hard experience, no doubt. The bold, sharp planes and angles of his lean face had always had a strict cast, but the years had added an aura of brooding asceticism.

He had left behind the few traces of young manhood that had still clung to him that night on the beach. Nevertheless, for some reason he actually looked better than ever in a pair of jeans. Beneath the tautly stretched fabric of the black, long-sleeved T-shirt he wore, his shoulders seemed broader and stronger. His stomach was still very flat.

What was the matter with her? she wondered. For eight years she had excused herself for her small, youthful, short-lived crush on Rafe Madison. After all, he had been the bad boy of Eclipse Bay, and he had once walked her home after midnight. That was enough to induce a few lusty imaginings in any healthy young woman. But she was far too mature for that sort of romantic nonsense now. Wasn't she?

She had never admitted the crush to anyone, of course—not even Lillian, although she suspected that her sister had guessed the truth. She had a right to her private little fantasies, she told herself. And it wasn't as if she had spent the past few years wondering what she had missed. In fact, she had all but forgotten Rafe Madison until Isabel's lawyer had called to give her the news about the will.

"Good morning, Rafe. Fancy meeting you here. Come to talk about Dreamscape?"

"I make it a policy not to talk business before noon."

"Do you talk about it much after noon?"

"Only if I feel real energetic." He leaned down to greet Winston. "I'm on my way into town to check the mail. Thought I'd see if you and the mutt wanted to go along."

Her first reaction was surprise. This was the first overture of any kind that he had made since the initial confrontation at Dreamscape. Maybe he was going to blink first.

Or maybe she ought to be very, very careful.

On the other hand, sooner or later they had to start communicating.

"I do need to do some grocery shopping," she said warily.

"Might as well go into town together." He gave her an unreadable smile. "Give the good folk of Eclipse Bay a thrill."

She held her blowing hair out of her eyes and peered at him closely. She could not tell if he was joking.

"All right," she said finally.

He startled her with a fleeting grin. "That's one of the things I always admired about you. You were never afraid of the Big Bad Wolf."

She waved a hand toward Winston. "These days I've got my own wolf."

Rafe eyed Winston with an assessing expression. "Five will get you ten that I can take the dog with one hand tied behind my back."

"Don't count on it, tough guy."

AN hour later Hannah emerged from Fulton's Supermarket with a sack in each arm. She looked down the rows of pickups and SUVs parked in the small lot and saw the silver Porsche. Rafe had collected the mail and was waiting for her. He lounged against a gleaming fender, arms folded. A pair of mirrored sunglasses added to the gangster look.

Winston stood on his hind legs in the driver's seat, front paws braced against the edge of the door, nose thrust through the open window. It warmed Hannah's heart to see that he was watching for her return. You could always count on your dog.

She was halfway back to the Porsche when, to her astonishment, Rafe gave her a cool, arrogant smile. Very deliberately he uncrossed his arms and reached out to scratch Winston behind the ears.

It was glaringly evident that Winston did not object. Hannah saw a pink tongue emerge to lick Rafe's hand. Irritation shot through her. Winston never got chummy with strangers, especially male strangers. Winston had standards.

Somehow, during the short time that she had been inside the grocery store, Rafe had co-opted her dog.

"Uh-oh."

She quickened her steps, so intent on the spectacle of Winston and Rafe's buddy-bonding that she never saw the big man who had climbed out of a battered pickup until he was directly in her path.

"Heard you and Madison were back in town," Dell Sadler said. "Come back to screw on the beach for old times' sake?"

Hannah skidded to a halt, barely avoiding a collision. But the abrupt stop sent a shudder through her that dislodged her grip on one of the grocery sacks, and it slipped out of her grasp. She heard an ominously squishy thud. The tomatoes, she thought. Luckily the eggs were in the other bag.

"Hello, Dell," she said quietly.

She knew very little about Dell Sadler other than that he operated a towing service and a body shop on the outskirts of Eclipse Bay. He was a heavily built man in his late thirties with thinning hair and beefy hands. There had always been a grim, morose air about him, as though he had found life to be a serious disappointment and did not expect matters to improve.

"You two got a lot of gall coming back here after what you did."

"If you'll excuse me, Dell—"

He stepped toward her, hands balled into fists. "Think I'd be gone by now? Or that I'd forget what happened to Kaitlin? Or don't you even give a damn?"

"This isn't a good place to talk." With an effort she kept her voice calm and soothing. "Maybe some other time."

"Just because everyone else in this town bought that story about you and Rafe Madison getting it on at the beach the night my sister died, don't think I did. I know damn well he killed her and you lied for him."

"That's not true, and I think that deep down inside you know it." Hannah took a cautious step back, preparing to dart around him. "Please get out of my way."

He thrust his face forward, raised a hand, and stabbed a finger at her chest. "Don't you tell me what to do. Maybe everyone else around here kowtows to you Hartes, but I sure as hell don't. Far as I'm concerned, you and Madison are both scum."

"I'm sorry about what happened to Kaitlin," Hannah said. "Everyone was. But I promise you, Rafe had nothing to do with it."

"He must have screwed you silly to get you to cover for him the way you did."

"Stop it."

"I hear you're back in town on account of that big house. Word is Madison wants the whole place for himself. Probably thinks if he does you long enough and hard enough, you'll turn over your share."

Hannah retreated again, clutching her one remaining sack of groceries. She came up hard against the unyielding fender of a big SUV. Dell closed in on her.

"Get out of my way," she said very steadily, preparing to make a run for Rafe's car.

"When I'm good and ready. I want you to know something. I won't ever—" Dell broke into a yelp as a hand locked on his shoulder from behind.

Rafe used the grip to spin Sadler neatly out of Hannah's path. With seemingly little effort, he pinned the big man to the door of the pickup.

Simultaneously, Hannah heard a low, fierce growl. She glanced down and saw Winston. The Schnauzer stood braced in front of Dell Sadler.

"She asked you to get out of the way, Sadler," Rafe said in a very soft voice.

"Screw you, you sonofabitch. You killed Kaitlin, I know you did."

"I didn't kill Kaitlin. I had no reason to kill her. If you ever decide you want to talk about it, come and see me. But don't bother Hannah again. She had nothing to do with what happened to your sister."

Dell scowled. "Take your hands off me, you bastard."

Rafe shrugged, released him, and stepped back. He scooped up the sack of groceries that Hannah had dropped and took her arm.

"Let's go," he said.

She did not argue. They walked quickly back to the Porsche, Winston marching beside them. When Rafe opened the door, the Schnauzer jumped into the small space behind the seats. He kept his nose close to Hannah as Rafe switched on the ignition.

Hannah was acutely aware of several curious onlookers. "That little scene will keep tongues wagging for a day or two."

Rafe drove out of the small lot onto Bayview Drive. "Told you we'd give the folks a thrill."

A short silence fell. Hannah opened her purse and found her sunglasses. She put them on. Winston licked her ear. She stroked him soothingly.

"Two-timer," she muttered. "I saw you licking Rafe's hand earlier."

Winston rested his chin on her shoulder and sighed in content.

"Your dog and I decided not to duel at dawn after all," Rafe said.

"You both chickened out?"

"We prefer to think of it as a negotiated settlement."

"Huh. Translated, I think that means that neither of you was willing to exert yourself to do battle in my honor."

Rafe glanced at her, his gaze unreadable behind the shield of his sunglasses. "When a guy reaches a certain age, he has to pick and choose his battles. I think it's called getting smart."

"Excuses, excuses." She peeked into the sack that had landed on the pavement. As she had suspected, the tomatoes were little more than pulp inside the plastic vegetable bag. The lettuce and mushrooms looked badly bruised too. "So much for dinner."

Rafe said nothing for a moment. He drove with easy skill, but he seemed to be concentrating on the road with an unnecessary degree of attention.

"Got an idea," he said after a while.

"I'm listening."

"Why don't you and Winston eat at my place tonight? I've got plenty of food."

Another overture? Maybe he really was weakening. She tried not to look too eager.

"Seeing as how there isn't much that's very exciting in the other sack of groceries, I believe I can speak for both Winston and myself when I say that we'd be pleased to take you up on that offer."

"Okay. Fine. It's settled."

She watched him out of the corner of her eye. "You appeared to have some hesitation in putting forth your invitation. Was it such a big deal to ask me over to dinner?"

He flexed his hands on the chunky steering wheel. "Had to work up my courage."

"I beg your pardon?"

"I was afraid you'd turn me down."

"Why would I do that?" She gave what she hoped was a very blasé sort of shrug. "We've got to talk about our mutual business problem sooner or later. Might as well be tonight."

"Wasn't planning to talk about the house tonight."

She stilled. "What do you plan to discuss?"

"Old times, maybe?"

She contemplated that for a moment. Then she gently cleared her throat. "You and I have only one incident between us that could conceivably be classified as old times."

"True. But you've got to admit it was a hell of an incident. I could have gone to jail if it hadn't been for you. That would have really messed up my big career plan. I told you that day I called to say good-bye that I owed you."

"Still feel that way?" She smiled sweetly. "Sell me your half of the house and we'll call it even."

"Not feeling quite that grateful," he said.

***

RAFE walked back into the solarium just as the September sky finally faded all the way to black. Hannah noticed that he did not turn on any lights. Winston, flat on his belly on the floor, looked up hopefully but lost interest when he saw the two snifters Rafe carried.

Rafe lowered himself into the wicker lounger next to Hannah and handed one of the glasses to her.

She watched the darkness settle over the bay and thought about the arugula, beet, blue cheese, and walnut salad and the pasta she had just finished. Rafe had glazed the walnuts with a little sugar and salt and heated them in the oven before adding them to the salad. The pasta had been flavored with an incredibly rich truffle-infused olive oil. A taste of heaven.

"Okay, so you can cook," she said.

"Man's gotta have a hobby."

"I'm with you on that." She took a sip of brandy. "For the record, you can fix dinner for me anytime."

"Thanks. I'll remember that." He cradled his snifter in both hands and gazed out the windows into the deepening night. "Sorry about that scene with Dell Sadler this afternoon."

"It wasn't your fault."

"Depends how you look at the situation, I think. If you hadn't been with me the night Kaitlin died, you wouldn't have had the run-in with Sadler today."

"Well, there is that." She was very conscious of him sitting there, not more than a few inches away. The darkness intensified the sense of intimacy. "About that night—"

He took a sip of brandy and waited.

"We never really talked about it." She drew a breath and took the plunge. "You knew Kaitlin as well as anyone. What do you think happened? Do you think she committed suicide? Or was it an accident?"

He was quiet for a long time. "I'm almost positive that she did not jump."

"What makes you so sure?"

He studied the brandy glass in his hands. "When she kicked me out of her car that night she was pissed as hell. She was angry, not depressed or desperate."

"How angry?"

He tilted his head against the back of the lounger.

"Very. Said she'd had it with Eclipse Bay and everyone in it. Said she couldn't wait to blow this burg."

"Making plans for the future."

"Yes."

"So her death must have been an accident."

Rafe said nothing.

Hannah cleared her throat. "I said, her death must have been an accident."

"That's certainly the most convenient explanation for all concerned."

Shock held Hannah absolutely still for a few seconds. She finally found her breath and let it out very deliberately. "You want to elaborate on that?"

"No point." Rafe sipped his brandy. "Not now."

"You're probably right. I guess we'll never know what really happened that night."

"No."

Rafe was quiet for a while. She had the feeling that he had moved on to some other subject in his mind. Whatever it was, he did not seem to be inclined to discuss it, either.

She tried not to be so acutely aware of him reclining there so close beside her, but it was hopeless. Probably time to go home, she thought. Make that *definitely.* She was about to mention that it was getting late when Rafe spoke.

"Something I've been meaning to ask you."

"Umm?"

"What went wrong with Mr. Right?"

For some reason that was the last question she had expected. She hesitated, not certain how far she wanted to go down that particular road.

"It didn't work out. What about you?" she added quickly to change the subject. "Heard you got married."

"For a while."

"What went wrong?"

"I told you that the men in my family aren't real good at marriage," he said.

"As I recall, I told you that was an excuse."

Without warning, Rafe sat up on the edge of the lounger and rested his forearms on his knees. "Mitchell called today."

Hannah blinked. He could switch topics quickly, too. "Your grandfather?"

"He wants me to come to dinner tomorrow night. Octavia Brightwell will be there. Says he wants me to meet her."

Hannah thought quickly. "Brightwell. The owner of that new art gallery near the pier?"

"Yeah." Rafe set his glass down on the table. "Apparently they're involved, so to speak."

"Good grief. I saw her on the street the other day. She's young enough to be his granddaughter."

"So I'm told." He met her eyes in the shadows. "The thing is, I need a date."

She nearly fell out of the lounger. "You want me to go to dinner at Mitchell Madison's house?"

"Got anything better to do?"

"Well, gee, when you put it like that, I guess not. As you once observed so pithily, the entertainment options in Eclipse Bay are somewhat limited." She paused. "Your grandfather won't be exactly thrilled to see you walk into the house with a Harte."

"Don't worry. He'll be on his best behavior because of his new girlfriend."

"Mitchell Madison making nice with a Harte." She smiled slowly. "Now that should be interesting."

"Well?"

"Okay," she said.

It was his turn to be wary. "You'll do it?"

"Sure. On one condition."

"What's that?"

"You have to promise me that afterward we'll have our little chat about how we're going to handle Dreamscape."

He thought about that for a few seconds. One shoulder rose in a negligent motion. "It's a deal."

She felt a distinct chill all the way down her spine. But it was too late now to wonder if she'd just been had by Rafe Madison.

※

SHE came awake very suddenly, listening to the silence with all of her senses. Her first thought was that an intruder had entered the darkened house. But in the next heartbeat she reminded herself there was no way anyone could have broken in without alerting Winston.

She sat up slowly. "Winston?"

There was no response. She could not feel his weight at the foot of the bed. It struck her that during the past two years she had grown very accustomed to his companionship at night.

She swung her feet to the cold floor and stood. "Winston? Come here, pal."

She did not hear his claws on the hardwood in the hall. Anxiety raised the hair on her arms. She grabbed her robe and stepped into her slippers, listening all the while for the smallest sounds.

Nothing.

She went to the door.

"Winston." Louder this time.

A soft, answering whine came from the foot of the stairs. Winston was in the living room. He did not seem hurt or scared. Instead she thought she caught the unmistakable anticipation of the hunter in the low sound.

The relief was shattering. Not an intruder, after all. Winston had heard some small creature foraging around outside and had gone downstairs to investigate. Here in Eclipse Bay life was rich for a dog who had been raised in a high-rise apartment.

Taking a couple of deep breaths to get rid of the light-headed sensation, she hurried out into the hall and went down the stairs.

Winston was poised in front of the door. He glanced briefly at her and immediately returned his attention to whatever was prowling around outside. He scratched at the wood hopefully.

"It's okay, pal. You're a city dog. You're not accustomed to the kinds of critters that hang around garbage cans out here in the boonies. Trust me—you don't want to actually catch one of them."

She reached out to pat his head. As soon as she touched him she realized that predatory tension was vibrating from one end of his sleek little body to the other. He ignored her hand. Everything in him was concentrated on whatever it was that had awakened him and drawn him downstairs.

Hannah went to the window. She pulled the curtain aside and discovered that sometime during the night a heavy fog had rolled in off the bay. She had left the porch light on, but its glow did not penetrate far into the thick mist that enveloped the house.

She told herself that she ought to go back to bed and leave Winston to his nocturnal amusements. But for some reason that she could not explain, she lingered at the front door and waited for him to lose interest in whatever skulked in the shadows.

It seemed a very long time before Winston relaxed, licked her hand, and led the way briskly back upstairs.

"THINK you can get Bryce to tell you about the trips to Portland?" Gabe asked.

"Not a chance." Rafe propped the phone between his shoulder and his ear, freeing his hands for the job of chopping the onion that sat on the cutting board. "You know Bryce. He takes orders only from Mitchell."

"And Mitchell has told him not to talk about the Portland trips."

"You got it."

Silence hummed briefly on the line. Rafe had a mental image of his older brother at his desk in the president's office at Madison Commercial. It was a good bet that Gabe was dressed in one of his hand-tailored shirts and a pair of expensive trousers. He would likely be wearing a silk tie and Italian leather shoes. He had no doubt arrived at his headquarters at seven-thirty that morning, right after the conclusion of his six A.M. workout at the health club. He would not leave until seven o'clock tonight at the earliest, and when he finally did go back to his austere condominium, he would have a briefcase full of papers with him. Madison Commercial was Gabe's passion. He had devoted himself to it with the sort of single-minded intensity that only another Madison could comprehend.

"It's been more than ten months," Gabe said. "Every Friday. Regular as clockwork."

Rafe finished cutting up the onion and tossed the pieces into the food processor. "I know what you're thinking."

"You're thinking the same thing."

"We might be wrong." Rafe added the pitted olives, three different kinds in all, to the onion. He dumped the rinsed capers and some freshly squeezed lemon juice into the bowl. "But we both know that if he is getting some kind of regular medical treatments, we'll be the last ones to find out."

"Trying to protect us, I guess." Gabe hesitated. "How does he look?"

"Healthy as a bull, except for the arthritis. I'm going to see him tomorrow night at dinner." Rafe paused. "I'll get to meet the new girlfriend."

"Is she really young enough to be his granddaughter?"

"That's what I'm told," Rafe said.

Gabe groaned. "It would be embarrassing if it wasn't so downright amazing."

"Yeah."

"Probably ought to look on the bright side," Gabe said morosely. "If he's able to keep up with her in bed, he can't be at death's door yet."

"There is that," Rafe agreed. He snapped the lid onto the food processor. "Not to change the subject, but how did things go last Saturday night with the lovely Ms. Hartinger?"

"I'd rather not discuss it, if you don't mind."

"Another disaster?"

"I don't like to admit it, but it was excruciatingly clear that she was interested only in my portfolio."

"Thought you said she was perfect."

"I was wrong, okay? Get off my case."

"I still say you're going about this business of finding yourself a wife the wrong way."

"I'm trying to approach it in a non-Madison way. I explained my theory to you."

"I understand what you're trying to do. I'm just saying I don't think it's going to work. It isn't like acquiring a new office tower for Madison Commercial. You can't use the same techniques."

"When did you become an expert?"

"Good point. Forget it." Rafe drummed his fingers on top of the food processor. "I'm taking a date to Mitchell's house tomorrow night."

"Someone local?" Gabe sounded only casually interested.

"You could say that. Hannah Harte."

"*Hannah?* Are you kidding me?"

"No."

"She agreed to go with you?"

"Uh-huh."

"Why?"

"I'm not sure, if you want the truth. Probably thinks it's a step toward getting her hands on Dreamscape."

"You, uh, led her to think that might be the case?" Gabe asked carefully.

"Sort of."

"But you've got no intention of giving up your claim on that mansion."

"No," Rafe said, "I don't."

"What the hell is going on there?"

"I'll let you know when I find out. I've got to go now. Talk to you later."

Rafe hung up the phone and switched on the food processor. He thought about Hannah while the machine turned the mixture inside the bowl into tapenade. An old proverb flickered through his mind, something about bringing a long spoon when you dined with the devil. Madisons had used it to describe the risks of dealing with Hartes for years.

6

RAFE wrapped his hands around the porch railing and gazed out over his grandfather's magnificent garden. A lot of people in Eclipse Bay gardened, but none of them could match Mitchell's spectacular display of lush ferns, herb borders, and rosebushes. A large greenhouse dominated the far end of the scene. Inside it were more horticultural wonders. A vegetable plot occupied a section near the house. Even in early fall when blooms were fading, Mitchell's garden was a work of art.

In the dark months after the death of their parents, Mitchell had taken his two grandsons into the garden a lot. The three of them had spent countless hours there. Mitchell had shown Rafe and Gabe how to prepare the ground, water the tomatoes, and trim rosebushes. They hadn't talked much, but Rafe knew that they had all found some solace in the work of growing things.

Mitchell had lived a turbulent life by anyone's standards. The years had seen the financial and personal devastation brought on by the destruction of Harte-Madison and the ensuing feud with his old army buddy, Sullivan Harte. The turmoil of four divorces and the breakup of innumerable affairs had taken a toll. The loss of his only son, Sinclair, had been a cruel blow. Rafe knew that the unexpected burden of raising two grandsons had come as a shock to a man who, until then, had not worried overmuch about his family responsibilities. But through it all, Mitchell had never lost his interest in gardening.

Gardening was Mitchell's passion. As everyone knew, when it came to a Madison and his passion, nothing was allowed to stand in the way.

Rafe went down the steps. "How'd you meet Octavia Brightwell?" he asked, partly out of curiosity and partly in a bid to find a neutral topic. Conversations between himself and Mitchell were fraught with problems.

For as long as he could remember, he had been at odds with his grandfather. In recent years they had achieved a prickly détente, but that was only because both of them had tacitly abandoned the open warfare that had characterized so much of their earlier communication. Some would say that they had matured, Rafe thought. But he and Mitchell knew the truth. They had both given up butting heads for the most part because it had become obvious that it was a pointless exercise. Which was not to say that they did not occasionally engage in the activity from time to time, just to stay in practice.

They had both been on their best behavior throughout dinner this evening, he reflected. True, things had been a little tense for a few minutes after he walked in the front door with Hannah, but to his credit, Mitchell had recovered quickly. Rafe's theory was that the older man was determined to play the genial host in front of his new girlfriend.

Octavia Brightwell was, indeed, young enough to be Mitchell's granddaughter. She came as a surprise to Rafe. She had proved to be warm, friendly, and intelligent. He could tell that Hannah had liked her on sight. During the course of the conversation at dinner Octavia had explained that the gallery she had opened in Eclipse Bay was her second. The first was in Portland. This summer she had divided her time between the two locations.

"She stuck her head over my garden fence one morning at the beginning of summer and told me that I was handling my roses all wrong." Mitchell snorted. "Told her I'd been dealing with roses since before she was born. She brought me a book on how to grow roses. Told me to read a few pages. I told her the author of the book was a damn fool. You might say we just hit it off."

"I see." Rafe watched Mitchell pause to remove a dead bloom from a rosebush.

Something twisted deep inside him at the sight of his grandfather's hawklike profile. It hit him that the old warrior with whom he had fought so many battles would not be around forever. It was difficult to imagine the world without Mitchell.

The tough, irascible Mitchell had the usual Madison flaws, Rafe thought, but he had been the one solid anchor in his grandsons' lives since the day their father's motorcycle had collided with a truck.

Rafe thought about the mysterious weekly trips to Portland. If there was something seriously wrong, it did not show. Mitchell used a cane, but he still looked strong and fit. He could have passed for a man fifteen years younger. There was a sharp glint in his slightly faded green eyes. The hard lines of his face had softened little with age. There was a slight stoop to his shoulders these days, and he had lost some muscle with the years, but the physical changes were well concealed by his undiminished will and determination to control his world and everyone in it.

"I take it you and Octavia spend a lot of time together," Rafe said as casually as possible.

"Some." Mitchell nipped off another dead rose.

This was not going to work, Rafe decided. If Mitchell did not want to discuss his relationship with Octavia Brightwell, that was the end of the matter. His grandfather had never talked much about his affairs and liaisons over the years. When it came to women, he lived by an old-fashioned code: A man did not kiss and tell. He had drilled that same cardinal rule into both Rafe and Gabe.

Rafe went down the steps and came to a halt on the path beside Mitchell, who was examining a cluster of ferns.

"I understand you've been going into Portland on a regular basis," Rafe said. "To see Octavia?"

"Nope." Mitchell snapped off another dead flower.

Rafe knew that was the end of that conversation. Gabe would have been better at this, he thought.

Mitchell squinted at him. "What the hell are you and Hannah Harte going to do with that damned house?"

"We haven't decided."

"Huh. Just like Isabel to do something crazy like this in her will. She had some romantic notion about you and Hannah patching up the old feud. Told her she was an idiot."

"Telling her that she was an idiot was probably not real helpful."

Mitchell grunted again. "Nobody more contrary than a Harte."

"Except a Madison."

Mitchell didn't deny it. "You look pretty friendly with Hannah."

"I wouldn't say we've reached the friendly stage, but her dog likes me. That's a start."

"Heard she built herself a nice little business in Portland. Organizes weddings or some such nonsense."

"Yeah. She says she gets a lot of repeat clients."

"She's a Harte, and that's not an easy fact to overlook. But I've got to admit that she's got gumption." A thoughtful expression gleamed in Mitchell's eyes. "Never forgot what she did eight years ago. Always felt like we owed her something for the way she backed you up."

"I know."

"There was some nasty talk around town for a while. The folks who believed her when she said she'd been with you on the beach that night assumed you'd seduced her just to score some points against the Hartes."

"I heard that."

Mitchell tapped his cane absently against the base of the sundial. "There are still one or two who think Hannah Harte flat out lied for you that night. They think you really did push Kaitlin Sadler off that cliff."

Rafe felt the tension knot deep inside him. He'd always wondered if Mitchell had been one of those who secretly believed that he had been responsible for Kaitlin's fall.

"Bottom line," Mitchell continued, "is that we're beholden to Hannah Harte."

"Yeah."

"Hate being beholden to a Harte." Mitchell sighed. "Like a bur under a saddle."

Rafe looked at him. "Didn't know it bothered you all this time."

"It did."

"It's not your problem. It's mine."

"You can say that again." Mitchell narrowed his eyes.

"What are you going to do about it? Give up your half of Isabel's house?"

"No."

"Didn't think so." Mitchell started off in the direction of the greenhouse. "Come on. I'll show you my new hybrids."

Rafe glanced back at the screen door. There was no sign of rescue. Reluctantly he trailed after Mitchell.

"I talked to Gabe a few days ago," Mitchell said.

Rafe steeled himself. "Did you?"

"He said he could find a place for you at Madison Commercial." There was not a lot of hope in Mitchell's voice.

"Give me a break. Would you work for Gabe?"

"Hell, no." Mitchell's brows bristled. "He expects everyone to jump when he gives an order."

"That pretty much sums up my problem with him, too."

Mitchell grunted. "Well, it was worth a try."

They walked the length of the garden in silence. Just before they reached the greenhouse, Mitchell launched a salvo in an entirely new direction.

"Don't you think it's about time you got married?" he said.

Rafe felt as if he'd been hit in the head with a ball peen hammer. It took him several seconds to recover. He spent the intervening time with his mouth open.

"Married?" he finally managed. "Are you out of your mind? I tried it once, remember? It didn't work."

"You're going to have to bite that bullet again, sooner or later. You've put it off long enough. If you wait too much longer you'll be so set in your ways you won't be able to adjust to marriage."

"Since when did you become an expert on marriage?"

"I've had some experience."

"You can say that again," Rafe muttered. "For your information, I'm already set in my ways."

"Bullshit. You're still young enough to be flexible."

The door on the back porch opened. Both men spun around so quickly that Rafe was sure they looked guilty of something.

An ethereal-looking woman with a mane of fiery red curls stood in the opening.

"Coffee's ready," Octavia Brightwell called cheerfully.

Rafe did not hesitate. He noticed that Mitchell didn't pause either. He figured his grandfather was just as relieved by the timely interruption as he was.

Side by side, they went swiftly back along the path toward the house.

HANNAH slid her key into the front-door lock. "Not that you've got any reason to consider my opinion on the subject, but I liked Octavia."

Beside her Rafe shrugged. "So did I. So what? She's still way too young for him. Gabe's right. It's embarrassing."

Hannah was amused. "That's almost funny, coming from a Madison. No offense, but the men of your family aren't known for feeling shy or awkward about their sex lives."

"It's different when it's your grandfather's sex life," Rafe said glumly.

Hannah listened to the sound of dog claws prancing madly on the hardwood floor on the other side of the door. "Well, if it's any consolation to you, Octavia told me that she and your grandfather are just friends. I believe her."

"Yeah?"

She gave him a quick, searching glance as she opened the door. He had been in a strange mood since returning from the after-dinner walk in the garden. Rafe had never been an easy man to read, but now there was a dark, brooding aura emanating from him that had not been present earlier in the evening. She wondered what had been said between him and his grandfather.

Winston bounced through the open door, torn as always, between the demands of professional dignity and blatant emotionalism.

"Such a handsome dog." She bent down to pat him. "The finest specimen of Schnauzerhood in the known universe."

Winston glowed.

Rafe watched them with an expression of morbid interest. "He actually believes you when you say that, you know."

"So what? It's true." She stood back to allow Winston to trot across the porch and down the steps. The dog paused briefly to thrust his nose into Rafe's hand, and then he disappeared discreetly into some bushes.

Hannah reached around the edge of the door and flipped a light switch. "I'm probably going to kick myself for getting involved, but I feel compelled to ask. Did things go okay between you and your grandfather out there in the garden?"

"Sure." Rafe glided, uninvited, through the opening into the front hall.

"I see." She was not quite certain what to do with him now that he was inside her house.

She held the door open for Winston. He pranced across the porch and into the hall. He headed straight for Rafe.

Hannah closed the door and leaned back against it. Rafe crouched to scratch the dog's ears. Winston promptly sat down and assumed a blissful expression.

"There was the usual stuff," Rafe said after a moment.

"The usual stuff?"

Rafe kept his attention on Winston, who was clearly ready, willing, and able to absorb an unlimited amount of it. "Mitchell reminded me that it wasn't too late to join Madison Commercial."

"Ah, yes. The usual." She straightened away from the door and walked into the kitchen. When in doubt, make a cup of tea. "And you gave him the usual response, no doubt."

"Well, sure. That's how Mitchell and I communicate. He tells me what I should do, and I tell him I won't do it. We understand each other perfectly."

"Aunt Isabel always said that you and your grandfather had problems from the day you hit puberty because the two of you were so much alike." She filled the kettle and set it on the stove.

"I've heard that theory before." Rafe gave Winston one last pat, got to his feet, and came to stand, in the arched doorway. He propped one shoulder against the frame and crossed his arms. "Neither Mitchell nor I believes it."

She was intensely aware of him taking up space in the kitchen. She could feel his disturbing gaze following her every move as she went about the business of preparing a pot of tea.

"It's true, you know," she said gently. "You're both strong-willed, arrogant, independent, and downright bullheaded at times. The two of you probably have the same motto."

"What's that?"

"Never apologize, never explain."

He contrived to look hurt. "Had it occurred to you that I might have something in common with your dog?"

"Such as?"

He smiled humorlessly. "I might actually believe you when you tell me what you really think about me."

She raised her brows at that. "I can't see you giving much credence to anyone else's opinions."

"Shows how much you know. I'm only human."

"Got proof of that?"

"Okay, I'll accept strong-willed, arrogant, and independent." He gave her a derisive look. "But I object to the last part. What makes you say I'm bullheaded?"

She smiled with cool triumph. "Your refusal to talk about how we're going to deal with the problem of Dreamscape."

"Huh. That."

"Yes, that."

He raised one shoulder very casually. "Well, hell, nobody's perfect."

"Except Winston, of course," she added swiftly, in case Winston had overheard the remark and had started to worry.

There was a short silence.

"Mitchell said something else while we were in the garden," Rafe said eventually.

She glanced at him over her shoulder as she dropped a large pinch of tea into the pot. "What was that?"

He watched her with shuttered eyes. "He told me it was about time I got married."

For some reason her stomach tightened. She hoped it wasn't the grilled salmon they'd had at dinner. It had tasted so good going down, but fish could be tricky.

"Well," she said. "Talk about pressure."

"Yeah."

"I'm sure you responded by telling him to stay out of your personal affairs." She concentrated hard on the teakettle, willing it to boil quickly.

Rafe said nothing.

A tiny shriek rose from the kettle. Close enough, she decided. Grateful for the small distraction, she hastily poured the hot water into the pot.

It was okay, she thought a moment later. She was cool now. But when she turned around with her most polished smile firmly in place, she discovered that Rafe had left the doorway and was now standing less than two feet away.

Much too close.

"I didn't come straight out and say it in so many words." Rafe's eyes never left her face. "But you're right. I made it clear that I'd do what I wanted to do."

"As usual."

"Yeah."

She tried to think of something clever to say in response to that. She wound up clearing her throat instead. "And what do you want to do?"

"Right now I want to kiss you."

7

SHE went very still. The really scary part, she realized, was that she wanted the same thing. She had a hunch that he could see it in her eyes.

She licked her lips and asked the only question that mattered. "Why?"

"Does there have to be a reason?"

"Yes." She could feel the counter pressing against her lower back. She put her arms out on either side and gripped the curved tile edge. "Yes, I think so. Especially given the situation here."

"Situation?"

"You. Me. Dreamscape."

"What happens if I can't come up with any reason except the fact that I want to kiss you?"

"The important thing," she explained very carefully, "the really crucial thing, is that the reason, whatever it is, must have nothing to do with Dreamscape."

He raised his hands and slowly folded them around the nape of her neck. His palms were warm and heavy against her skin. She could feel the strength in him but sensed the control. The combination was electrifying.

His thumbs moved gently just behind her ears. He eased her head back slightly and lowered his mouth to hers.

"This has nothing to do with the mansion," he said against her lips. "You have my word on it."

The kiss was a real one this time, not the chaste, meaningless little brush of the lips he had bestowed on her that night when he had walked her home. And it was just exactly what she had always suspected it would be: devastating.

Excitement sparked along every nerve ending. The effect was not unlike touching a match to extremely dry kindling. The flames erupted without warning, fierce and intense. A liquid heat welled somewhere in the region below her stomach. She was aware of the beat of her own heart. The breathless sensation would probably have warranted a trip to the emergency room under other circumstances.

Rafe deepened the kiss with slow deliberation.

The stuff of teenage fantasies, she thought. Except that no teenager could have appreciated just how good the kiss really was. Only an adult woman who had learned the hard way that real life was seldom this great could savor the finer points and the little nuances here.

Rafe crowded her gently up against the counter. She could feel the unmistakable shape of his erection pressed against her thigh.

Okay, so not all of the nuances here were little.

His mouth slanted across hers. He drew his palms down her throat and covered her breasts. A great urgency went through her. With an effort, she managed to let go of the counter edge. She heard him say something that probably would have gotten him arrested if he had said it in public. He made no effort to conceal his hunger. The knowledge that he wanted her played havoc with the last shreds of her common sense.

Just a kiss, she thought. How much damage could one kiss do?

She heard someone moan softly. Probably her, she decided. Not real cool. It was only a kiss, after all. But at the moment she did not care if she was demonstrating a distinct lack of worldly sophistication. The only thing that mattered was getting her arms around Rafe's neck.

The instant she achieved her goal she heard a husky groan. Not her this time. Rafe.

His hands tightened abruptly. She could feel his control slipping away. She wondered if he was aware of it. Then she wondered what she would do if it vanished altogether. Would she care? Should she care?

The world tilted on its axis. She realized vaguely that Rafe had scooped her up into his arms. A shiver went through her.

He paused briefly to switch off the lights. Then he carried her out of the kitchen into the living room. There he put her down on the aging sofa and lowered himself on top of her. His lips went to her throat. She could have sworn she felt his teeth. Another zinging thrill shot through her. She was shivering now. The weight of his body crushed her into the cushions.

At the sound of dog claws scratching on wood, she opened her eyes for a split second. In the shadows she caught a glimpse of Winston hurrying up the stairs to the second floor. Embarrassed by the unseemly behavior taking place on the sofa, no doubt.

She ought to be embarrassed, too, she thought. And maybe she would be. Later.

In the meantime, her body was singing a fascinating melody. She had caught a few chords of this particular tune from time to time over the years, but she had never experienced the grand finale.

She felt one of Rafe's hands slide beneath her sweater. The clasp of her bra dissolved at his touch. When his thumb lightly touched her nipple she almost screamed. It was as though every inch of her had been sensitized. She was in some never-never land where the line between acute pleasure and pain was murky.

"I've been thinking all day that it would be like this," Rafe muttered into the curve of her shoulder. "I was going crazy waiting to find out."

His hand moved over the curve of her hip. She felt his fingers on the zipper of her slacks. Things were moving swiftly. Much too swiftly. But she could not seem to summon up a lot of good reasons for calling a halt.

She heard Winston on the stairs again. For some reason the knowledge that her dog had returned to the scene cleared some of the fog from her brain.

"I think this is far enough," she managed to get out.

"Not nearly." Rafe peeled up the edge of her sweater and kissed one of her breasts. "I've been wanting you since you got here."

"That's nice."

He went very still. Then he raised his head and looked down at her with gleaming eyes. "Nice?"

"I'm flattered. Honest."

"Flattered," he repeated carefully. "Great. Flattered. Shit."

She swallowed. "I don't want you to think I'm a prude, or anything, but—"

"But you're still Miss Goody Two-shoes, is that it?"

"Not exactly." She was starting to grow annoyed. "It's just that in a lot of ways you and I are strangers."

"You're a Harte. I'm a Madison. The way I look at it, we've known each other most of our lives."

She blinked. "That's certainly an interesting viewpoint. Maybe it's even true in certain ways. But something of an oversimplification, don't you think?"

"Do you always talk like this on a date?"

"That wasn't a date we had tonight. I did you a favor."

His smile was infinitely slow, infinitely seductive. "Well, in that case, allow me to repay it." He started to lower his mouth to hers once more.

She braced her hands on his shoulders to stop him. "My point—"

He gave her a look of polite surprise. "You mean you've actually got one?"

"My point," she continued grimly, "is that, although we've known of each other's *existence* most of our lives, it's stretching things to imply that we've been anything more than distant acquaintances. I still say we're strangers as far as this kind of thing is concerned."

"Shush." He covered her mouth with the palm of his hand.

"Mmmph?" Outraged, she grabbed his wrist and tried to yank his hand away from her lips.

She was so intent on telling him in no uncertain terms that she did not find this kind of stuff a turn-on that it took her a few seconds to realize he was not paying any attention to her. She finally noticed that he was lying much too still, his head turned toward the front door.

She heard a very soft whine. Winston was standing at the door again, just as he had done last night. His alert, watchful tension radiated clear across the room.

"He hears something." Rafe took his hand away from Hannah's mouth. He kept his eyes on the dog as he sat up on the edge of the sofa.

"Probably an animal prowling for garbage." Hannah hastily pulled her clothing back into place. "A skunk, maybe. Or cats."

"Probably." Rafe watched Winston intently.

Hannah sat up slowly. "He did this last night, too."

Rafe got to his feet and crossed the room to where Winston vibrated at the door. He halted at the window and pulled aside the curtain. "Fog's so thick now you can't see past the edge of the porch."

Winston whined softly. He glanced at Rafe and then at the door and then back at Rafe. The message was clear. He wanted to go outside to investigate.

A cold chill went through Hannah. It was the same disturbing sensation she'd experienced last night.

"Whatever it is, it's not coming too close to the house," she said quickly. "Winston would be barking like crazy if there was a critter in the bushes at the edge of the porch."

"Sure." Rafe reached for the doorknob. Winston strained forward, preparing to streak through the crack in the door as soon as it appeared.

Real fear galvanized Hannah. Everything in her was suddenly focused on the danger of opening the front door.

"What, are you crazy?" She leaped to her feet and rushed across the room. She bent down to seize Winston's collar. "You can't send him outside. He was raised in a high-rise apartment in the middle of a city, for heaven's sake. He knows nothing about wild animals. Whatever's out there might be a lot bigger and meaner than he is."

Winston tried to pull free of her grasp. He was trembling with eagerness. His nose did not waver from the crack between the door and the frame.

Rafe glanced down at him. "Okay, city dog. Stay inside and be a sissy. I'll handle this on my own."

"Oh, no, you don't." Exasperated, Hannah released Winston and threw herself in front of the door, arms spread wide. "You're not going out there, either."

Rafe looked amused. "Doubt if whatever is out there is bigger or meaner than me. This is Eclipse Bay, remember? Crime rate around here is almost non-existent."

Winston whined again and bobbed restlessly at Rafe's heels.

Hannah glared at both of them. She did not budge from her position in front of the door. Frantically she searched for a rational, sensible reason for refusing to allow either male outside.

"Cut the raging testosterone, you two. Let's have a little common sense here, shall we? It is entirely possible that there's a skunk outside. Do either of you have any idea of just how long it would take to get rid of the smell if you got sprayed? You'd both have to sleep on the beach for a week."

"Don't think it's a skunk." Rafe looked thoughtful. "A skunk would head straight for the garbage cans. We'd have heard the clatter by now."

"If it's not a skunk, it might be something worse," she said through her teeth. "Maybe somebody's pit bull or Rottweiler got loose. For all you know, there's a whole pack of vicious dogs out there."

"Speaking of common sense," Rafe said mildly, "I think that theory is a bit weak."

"I don't care. It's my theory and I'm sticking to it. Neither of you is going out there and that's final. Besides, you just got through saying that the fog was so thick you couldn't see beyond the edge of the porch. It makes no sense to go floundering around in the stuff."

Rafe looked at her. She realized that he was laughing silently.

"What?" she said.

"Nothing." He pulled the curtain aside again and peered thoughtfully out into the darkness. "Just occurred to me that if you don't let me outside, I won't be able to get home tonight, that's all."

She hesitated. "You can leave after Winston relaxes."

"Can't see a damn thing in that muck."

"You can leave your car here and walk home."

He dropped the curtain. His eyes gleamed.

"*Now* what?" she snapped.

"What if someone drives past your house early tomorrow morning and sees my car parked in front?"

She sighed. "Half the town already thinks the worst, anyway."

"Okay, then what about the pack of maddened Rottweilers and pit bulls I'll have to confront if I walk home?"

She moved just far enough from the position in front of the door to lift the curtain. A single glance outside showed that the fog was an impenetrable barrier. The light from the yellow lamp over the door was reflected back from what looked like a solid gray wall.

She looked at Winston. He was now pacing restlessly in front of the door. Whatever it was that he sensed was still out there. She made an executive decision.

"We'll drink the tea I made," she said. "If nothing has changed by the time we finish, you can sleep on the sofa tonight."

"Okay," Rafe said much too easily.

WINSTON lost interest in whatever lay out in the fog about the same time they finished the tea. But when Rafe checked the view from the window he was pleased to see that the mist had not dissipated. If anything, it was thicker than ever.

Luck was with him tonight.

Hannah came to stand behind him. She peered over his shoulder. "How does it look?"

"Like a great night for mad dogs and skunks."

"Not funny." She hugged herself and rubbed her arms briskly, as though warding off a chill. "I guess you'll have to stay here."

"Don't go overboard with the gracious hospitality routine. I don't mind walking back to Dreamscape. It's not that far."

"No." She turned away abruptly. "You can have the downstairs guest room. I'll get some blankets and a pillow."

He watched her climb the stairs. She had been a little too quick to suggest that he stay here, he decided. The expression in her eyes was wrong, too. He wondered how much of this new, brittle tension derived from the scene on the sofa earlier and how much came from Winston's prowling at the door.

Logic told him that a few kisses wouldn't have rattled her this much. She wasn't a teenager, after all. She was a confident woman who had built a thriving business. It would take more than a sexy tussle on the sofa to throw her. In any event, he was pretty sure that if she really *had* been upset by the small skirmish, she would have been more than delighted to let him walk home in the fog.

Instead, she had insisted that he stay here.

He glanced at Winston. The dog was stretched out on his belly on the rug, nose on his paws, dozing. Hannah had said that it was the second night in a row that he had gone on alert.

Hannah and Winston were both accustomed to life in the city, Rafe reminded himself. They had merely overreacted to whatever small creature had wandered too close to the house. But if Hannah wanted him to stay here tonight, who was he to argue?

AN hour later he was still awake. Arms folded behind his head, he stared up at the deep shadows on the ceiling. He was intensely aware of the fact that Hannah was just out of sight upstairs. He pictured her in a nightgown. Maybe a frilly little see-through number that showed a lot of skin. Fat chance. More likely a sober, long-sleeved flannel thing that fell to her ankles.

Either one sounded interesting, now that he considered the matter. Very interesting, in fact. He was hard as a rock.

Logic told him that a few kisses shouldn't have rattled him this much. He wasn't a teenager, after all. It took more than a sexy tussle on the sofa to throw him.

Right.

8

HE awoke at dawn when a cold nose was thrust against the bottom of his bare foot. The shock brought him to a sitting position in a hurry.

"Sonofa—" He broke off when he saw Winston. "No point in calling you that particular name, is there? You are a son of a bitch. And don't think it hasn't occurred to me that the big dramatic act last night at the door might have been just your deliberate attempt to disrupt the mood of the evening."

Winston gave him a meaningful look.

"Things were going pretty damn good until you showed up and made like Mr. Macho Watchdog."

Winston turned and trotted to the door. There he sat down and stared intently at Rafe.

"Okay, okay. I get the point."

Rafe shoved aside the blankets and got to his feet. He found his trousers and reached for his shirt. After a short search he discovered his low-cut boots fooling around with some dust bunnies under the bed.

"All right, let's go."

He opened the door to a damp, fog-bound morning. Winston stepped smartly outside and headed for the bushes at the edge of the porch. Rafe went down the steps and followed the little path that led to the storage locker used to house the garbage cans. There were no signs of animal tracks in the vicinity and no claw marks on the wooden lid.

Having concluded his personal business, Winston hurried over to see what was going on at the garbage can locker. Rafe watched him closely.

Winston sniffed a bit, but his interest in the locker appeared casual at best. After only a couple of minutes he headed on down the long drive toward the trees that veiled the house and gardens from the narrow road.

Rafe followed, watching to see if the dog paid any unusual attention to any particular point along the way. Winston's progress was slowed by numerous pauses, but none appeared to be any more intriguing to him than another. When he got close to the edge of the property, Rafe decided it was time to call him back.

"Hannah will chew me out but good if she finds out I let you play in traffic." Not that there was much on this quiet road, especially at this hour of the morning.

Winston ignored him, displaying a breathtaking disdain for a clear and reasonable command. Rafe concluded that the attitude was either the result of generations of fine breeding or something that had rubbed off from Hannah. He was inclined to credit the latter.

"Come back here." Rafe walked more quickly toward Winston, intending to grab him before he reached the road.

But Winston stopped of his own accord before he got as far as the pavement. He veered left toward a stand of dripping trees and began to sniff the ground with great authority.

"Just like you knew what you were doing," Rafe said quietly.

Winston flitted briskly from one tree trunk to another, pausing to sniff intently in several places. Eventually he lifted his leg. When he was finished he turned to Rafe as if to say that he was satisfied.

Rafe walked into the stand and took a close look at the tree Winston had marked. He knew that his human senses were abysmally inadequate for the task at hand.

He crouched to get a closer look at the ground at the base of the tree. Unfortunately the pebbles that covered the earth made it impossible to detect any footprints. Always assuming that there were any there to detect, Rafe thought.

He looked at Winston, who was watching him with an inquiring expression. "You know, if one of us had gotten both your nose and my brain, we'd be in great shape."

Winston gave the equivalent of a canine shrug, then turned and went quickly along the drive toward the house.

Rafe straightened. He was about to set off after the dog when he caught a glint of silver foil out of the corner of his eye. A closer look revealed a tightly wadded candy wrapper lying on the ground near the point Winston had marked.

Not exactly a major discovery. A stray breeze could have blown it into the stand of trees. It might have been tossed from a passing car or fallen off the garbage truck.

Or it might have been dropped by someone standing in this very spot about midnight last night.

He picked up the discarded wrapper and went back down the drive to where he had parked the Porsche. He unlocked the door, opened the glove compartment, and rummaged briefly inside. No luck. He looked at Winston, who was waiting, head cocked, on the porch.

"Used to be a time when I carried a spare razor and a few other basic necessities with me for just this sort of occasion," he explained. He shut the door and pocketed the keys. "But I got out of the habit."

His social life had never really picked up again after his divorce, he reflected. Probably because he had not worked very hard to get it up and running. He'd had other interests to occupy him.

He stopped once before he went up the steps and plucked a few sprigs of the mint that were growing beneath the garden's water faucet.

Back inside the house he spent a few minutes in the downstairs bathroom, where he discovered that none of the Harte males had left a razor behind.

"Thoughtless," he told Winston. "But, then, what do you expect from a Harte?"

He listened to the silence upstairs for a moment before he wandered into the kitchen and started opening cupboard doors. He found the usual assortment of aging condiments and spices that tended to get left behind in a vacation cottage. Salt, pepper, sugar, a half-empty bottle of vanilla extract, and an unopened jar of maple syrup. The last item was the real thing, not caramel-colored sugar water, he noted.

He took the vanilla extract and the syrup out of the cupboard and went to check the contents of the refrigerator. The eggs and milk were fresh. The loaf of dense, rustic-style bread baked by the New Age crowd who had taken over the old bakery near the pier was a day old.

Perfect.

The bride's gown was three sizes too big. She tried desperately to pin it into place, but it was hopeless. She knew that no matter what she did the dress would never look right. The client was in tears. The groom kept looking at his watch.

She glanced at the clock and saw that the reception was supposed to start in a few minutes. But the caterers had not yet arrived. None of the tables had been set up. The flowers were limp. She opened a case of the premium-quality champagne that she had ordered and discovered bottles of mouthwash inside. She looked around and realized that the musicians had not yet appeared.

On top of everything else, there was something dreadfully wrong with the room. The reception was supposed to be in an elegant hillside mansion overlooking the city. Instead, she was standing in an empty, windowless warehouse.

The tantalizing smell of something delicious being cooked nearby distracted her from the chaos. She realized that she was very hungry, but she could not abandon the client to go get something to eat. She was a professional, after all . . .

Hannah came awake with a start and found herself gazing into the depths of the impenetrable fogbank that hovered outside the window. For a few disorienting seconds she thought she was still in Portland trying to hold together the unraveling threads of a disastrous wedding reception.

Then she smelled the exquisite aromas from downstairs. Reality returned, jolting her out of bed.

Rafe. He had not vanished discreetly at dawn as she had expected. He was down there making himself at home in her kitchen. She had been so sure that he would be gone by the time she awoke.

She looked at the foot of the bed. There was no sign of Winston. What had become of her faithful pal?

Now that was a really dumb question, she thought. Winston was a truly fabulous dog in many respects. But in the end, he was still a dog. If she wanted to find him, she had only to follow the smell of food.

She staggered into the bathroom, the last wisps of the familiar anxiety dream trailing after her. She'd been plagued by the wedding-reception-from-hell nightmare for months before she had made the decision to sell Weddings by Harte.

She gripped the edges of the white pedestal sink and stared at herself in the mirror. Her hair hung in lanky tangles. There was a sullen, surly look in her eyes, and the flush in her cheeks was unbecoming, to say the least. She could not face Rafe in this condition. Her only hope was a shower.

She whipped the long-sleeved nightgown off over her head and stepped beneath the hot spray. Seizing the shampoo in both hands, she went to work with near-violent determination. It had not been a good night.

When she emerged a short time later she felt infinitely better. She pulled on a sweater and a pair of jeans, brushed her freshly washed hair behind her ears, and anchored it with a headband.

She took another look in the mirror just before she left the room. With dismay she realized that she still looked a little too pink. Probably because of the shower, she decided. All that heat and steam. The effect would surely fade quickly.

She squared her shoulders, opened the bedroom door, and stepped out into the hall.

By the time she got downstairs her mouth was watering. She saw Winston sitting just inside the kitchen doorway. He rose to greet her with his customary gallantry, but it was clear that he was distracted by what was going on in the vicinity of the stove.

Rafe looked just as she had known he would look in the morning. Incredibly sexy, right down to and including the shadow of a beard that gave the hard planes of his face an even more dangerous cast than usual.

It really was not fair. A gentleman would have been gone by dawn. But, then, no one had ever called Rafe Madison a gentleman.

"Right on time." Rafe's eyes gleamed as he surveyed her with one swift, all-encompassing look. He picked up an oven mitt. "You can pour the coffee."

She watched as he removed a pan from the oven. The faint scent of vanilla teased her. "What is it?"

"French toast." He put the pan on the stove and tossed the mitt onto the counter. "Baked instead of fried. Sort of a cross between a bread pudding and a soufflé."

She gazed at it longingly. "It's beautiful. Absolutely beautiful."

He grinned. "Thanks."

So the man could cook. She already knew that. It was not a sufficient reason to fall in love. Lust, maybe, but not love.

She dragged her gaze away from the golden-brown French toast and saw that Rafe was watching her with an odd expression.

"I'll get the coffee." She whirled around and seized the pot.

Rafe arranged the French toast on two heated plates and carried the food to the table. Hannah studied the casually elegant fashion in which the puffy, golden-brown triangles had been positioned. There were little sprigs of fresh mint on top of the toast. The syrup in the small pot in front of her was warm.

She picked up her fork. "You know, there's a theory in some quarters that you turned to a life of crime in order to support yourself after you left Eclipse Bay."

He nodded. "I've heard that theory."

"But after dinner the other night and breakfast this morning, I think the evidence is clear that you went to a blue-ribbon culinary academy instead of jail."

He looked up very quickly.

She paused with a bite of French toast poised in midair. "Good heavens, I was joking. Did you really take cooking classes?"

He hesitated. Then shrugged. "Yes."

She was fascinated. "When?"

"After I got married. In the back of my mind, I think I always had this idea that when you were happily married, you ate at home most of the time. But Meredith wasn't big on cooking, so I took over the job. The better I got at it, the more restless and unhappy Meredith became." Rafe made a dismissive gesture with one hand. "After a while I realized that she wasn't real big on staying at home, either."

She gazed at him in disbelief. "Meredith left you because you're a fantastic cook and because you like to eat at home?"

"Well, those weren't the only reasons," Rafe admitted. "She might have been willing to tolerate my cooking if I had agreed to go to work at Madison Commercial. But I refused, so in the end she gave up on my future prospects and left."

Hannah savored another bite of French toast while she thought about that. "I'm sorry your marriage didn't work out."

"You should be. I figure it's your fault that it bombed."

She nearly dropped her fork. "*My* fault. How in the world can you blame me?"

He met her eyes across the short expanse of the table. His mouth curved slightly. "That night on the beach you told me I didn't have to follow in my father's and my grandfather's footsteps when it came to marriage, remember? So a couple of years later, I figured I'd give it a try. I mean, after all, it was advice from Miss Overachiever herself. How could it be wrong?"

"Now, hold on one dang minute here." She aimed the fork at him. "You can't blame me just because you chose to follow my perfectly good advice and then messed it up by picking the wrong woman."

"I'm a Madison. I was bound to pick the wrong woman."

"That's a cop-out excuse if I ever heard one and you know it. You will not use it again, do you hear me?"

He halfway lowered his lashes. "Yes, ma'am."

She subsided slightly. "It's not like you're the only person on the face of the earth who made a mistake when it came to selecting the right mate, you know. I didn't do any better."

"Yes, you did. You just got engaged. You never got married."

She made a face and forked up another bite of toast. "I'll let you in on a little secret. The only reason I didn't make the mistake of actually marrying Doug was because he very kindly dumped me before we got to the altar."

"What was he like?"

"He's a lawyer, a partner at a very prestigious firm in Portland. We met when I did his sister's wedding. We had lots of things in common."

"He fit all the criteria on the Mr. Right list you gave me that night on the beach?"

She winced. "You remember that list?"

"Never forgot it. Made a profound impact on me."

"Why?"

He picked up his coffee mug and swallowed meditatively. "Probably because I knew I'd never come anywhere near to meeting even half the requirements and specifications on it."

His words blindsided her. "It really bothered you that you couldn't make my Mr. Right list?"

"Uh-huh."

"Good grief, that's crazy. You were never interested in me. To you I was just some naïve, prissy little overachiever. Miss Goody Two-shoes, remember?"

"It wasn't the fact that I personally couldn't make your Mr. Right list that bugged me. It was the fact that there *was* such a thing as a Mr. Right list and you knew all about it."

"I beg your pardon?"

"See, I didn't even know the damn list existed," Rafe explained patiently. "That put me at a serious disadvantage. And when I found out that women like you had one and the kind of stuff that was on it, I knew I was in deep trouble."

She shook her head once, dazed. "I don't get it. What do you mean?"

He exhaled slowly. "I'll tell you something, Miss Goody Two-shoes. That night on the beach you were all those things you just said—naïve and prissy and all that. But I figured you were also an authority on one important thing. You knew what it took to make a good marriage."

"Me? But I'd never been married."

"True, but you'd been raised in a family that looked pretty damn perfect to me. Happily married parents and grandparents. No divorces. No scandals. I assumed that you knew what it took to make it all happen."

Understanding dawned. Rafe had no firsthand knowledge of how a good marriage functioned because, unlike her, he'd never witnessed one close up. Divorce ran as strongly as green eyes in the Madison clan.

"I see. Well, if it makes you feel any better, I have concluded that my original Mr. Right list was flawed," she said.

"Yeah? Why?"

She propped her elbows on the table and rested her chin on the heels of her hands. "I'm going to tell you something that I've never told anyone else. I swear, if this gets out I will throttle you, Rafe Madison."

"Sounds interesting."

"The truth is, Doug had his own list, and I failed to meet all of his specifications and requirements."

Rafe blinked. Then his mouth curved slowly into a grin. "The guy had a Mrs. Right list?"

"Yep. He was decent enough to point out the areas in which I was deficient. He made suggestions for improvement. I got ticked."

Rafe's grin metamorphosed into a chuckle. The chuckle erupted into a full-throated roar of laughter.

She watched him, wondering if he was going to fall out of his chair. Winston, ears cocked, looked intrigued. Rafe's howls filled the kitchen.

It took a while for him to pull himself together. Hannah filled the time by pouring herself another cup of coffee and feeding Winston a scrap of leftover French toast from her plate.

Rafe's shoulders eventually stopped shaking. He sprawled in the chair, one hand on his flat belly, and subsided slowly into a grin.

"Sorry." He didn't sound sorry at all.

"I'm glad you find it so amusing."

"I have to know," Rafe said. "Where did you fall short?"

"Why should I tell you?"

"Because I just cooked breakfast for you."

"Hmm." He had a point. "I fit most of the criteria, you understand. I came from a successful family. I was well educated. I had demonstrated initiative and determination by founding my own business. I was well connected in the community. I shared a lot of Doug's interests."

"But?"

She made a face. "But it turned out that Doug was making long-range plans to enter the political arena. He's a good man. I think he really has something to contribute. But he needed a wife who could handle the sort of social and personal demands that go with that kind of job."

"Hence the list."

"Yes. The more I realized that he was serious about a political career, the more we both came to the conclusion that I couldn't handle being a politician's wife."

Rafe reached for the coffeepot. "Welcome to the select club reserved for those who fail to make the Mr. and Mrs. Right lists."

"Gee, thanks. Is there a merit badge?"

"No. So, tell me, what did you do with your own list?"

She hesitated. "I amended it."

He glanced at her with a strange expression. "You mean you've still got one?"

"Yes. But it's a lot shorter now."

"Huh. What's on it?"

"I really don't think—" She broke off at the sound of a car turning into the drive.

Winston was at the door in a flash. He gave the appropriate warning *woof.* Alert but not yet alarmed. On the job.

The low rumble shattered the fragile intimacy that had enveloped the kitchen. Rafe turned his head to check the drive. Hannah followed his gaze. The fog had burned off enough to allow her to see the vehicle that was approaching the house. A green Volvo.

"Anyone you know?" Rafe asked.

"I don't recognize the car."

"Want me to hide in a closet?"

"Don't be ridiculous." She pushed back her chair and got to her feet. "I'm sure it's just a friend of my folks' who found out that I'm in town and stopped to say hello."

He looked at her. "Whoever it is, he or she will have seen my car by now. Probably recognized it."

"The fact that you are having coffee with me is no one's business."

"Wasn't just coffee," Rafe said as she went past him into the living room. "But who's going to argue?"

She was saved from having to respond because she was already halfway to the front door. She patted Winston, who looked like a ballet dancer, poised and ready on his paws.

"It's okay, pal. I don't think a burglar would arrive in a Volvo."

She opened the door. A polished, good-looking man emerged from behind the wheel of the Volvo. He wore a navy-blue polo shirt, a pair of gray trousers, and loafers. There was a designer logo stitched on the left side of the shirt. The pants appeared to have been hand-tailored, and the loafers had little tassels. She was almost certain that the hair had been styled in a salon located somewhere other than Eclipse Bay.

When her visitor spotted her waiting in the doorway, he gave her a dazzling smile that lit up the foggy morning like a lighthouse beacon.

"Looks like Perry has started bleaching his teeth," she murmured to Winston.

Winston rumbled deep in his throat and trotted after her as she went out onto the porch.

"Hannah." Perry Decatur jogged toward the steps. "Heard you were in town. Great to see you again. You look fabulous."

At the last minute she realized his intention and braced herself. He swept her into an embrace that would have been more appropriate for lovers who had been separated for years by war and star-crossed fates. She felt the breath go out of her lungs as his arms closed around her.

A low growl reverberated across the porch. For one horrible moment, Hannah was not sure if the sound had come from Winston or Rafe.

"Cute dog."

Perry released Hannah, bent down, and thumped Winston lightly on his broad, intelligent head without going through the civilized formality of allowing Winston to sniff his fingers first.

Winston's silvery brows bristled with indignation, but he was too well behaved to make a scene. He did, however, display a discreet glimpse of fang. Could have been an accident, Hannah thought.

Perry straightened quickly. "Dogs love me."

"No kidding." Hannah looked at Winston. "Thank you, Winston. I can handle this. You may go back inside and finish your breakfast."

With a last glare at Perry, Winston turned and stalked back into the house.

"Fine-looking animal," Perry said approvingly. "Do you show him?"

"Show him what?"

"I meant, is he a show dog?"

She stared at him. "Put Winston in a ring and make him perform stunts for a bunch of judges? Are you mad? I wouldn't dream of doing such a thing. He would be mortified."

Perry managed a forced chuckle. "I see. Well, how have you been, Hannah?"

"Fine."

"Great. That's just great." He angled his chin in the general direction of Rafe's car. "I see you've got a visitor."

"We're having coffee."

"Coffee sounds terrific."

She chose to ignore the unsubtle hint. "I'm a little busy, Perry."

The bright light of his smile dimmed a bit. "Hannah, I really need to talk to you."

"Call me this afternoon."

"This can't wait." Perry paused a beat and lowered his voice. "It's important. Not just to me but to a lot of people here in Eclipse Bay."

She wavered. "What is it?"

"It's too involved to explain out here."

He moved past her with a breezy arrogance that made her want to stick out a foot and trip him. She avoided the temptation. If Winston was capable of good manners and restraint in the face of extreme provocation, she could do no less.

She went thoughtfully back into the house and closed the door. Perry was already in the kitchen, introducing himself to Rafe.

"I don't think we've met." He thrust out his hand. "I'm Perry Decatur. I'm with the institute. Sorry to interrupt breakfast. Hannah and I are old friends."

"Rafe Madison." Rafe kept his fingers wrapped around his coffee mug and managed to overlook Perry's outstretched hand. "I know all about your old friendship with Hannah. I was the one who walked her home that night eight years ago when she decided to end her date with you a little early. But I'm sure you heard all about that."

Perry blinked a couple of times and dropped his hand. But if he found the moment awkward, he gave no hint. "What a coincidence, the three of us getting together over coffee after all this time."

"Yeah, life's funny that way, isn't it?" The gleam in Rafe's eyes was diamond-hard. "So, what do you do at the think tank?"

"Vice President of Finance and Administration."

Perry removed a small gold case from his pocket and produced a card. When Rafe did not reach for it, he put it down on the table next to the empty syrup jug. He took one of the chairs, switched it around, and sat down back to front. Very confident. Very much at home in this house. Hannah ground her teeth.

"I'm the guy who deals with the donors and contributors who fund the research projects," Perry said.

"In other words, you hustle cash for the institute," Rafe said.

Hannah raised her eyes toward the ceiling, but there was no help from that quarter.

If Perry was insulted by Rafe's description of his job, he managed to conceal it behind a small chuckle. "It's a bit more complicated than that, but I really don't have time to go into it now."

Hannah dropped down into her chair. "Why don't you tell me exactly why you're here, Perry?"

"Well, I'd like to invite you to attend the reception for Trevor Thornley at the institute tomorrow night," Perry said.

"Thanks," Hannah said, "but I'm not big on political receptions."

"This is an important event," Perry said seriously. "Thornley's going to formally announce his intention to enter the U.S. Senate race."

"So?"

Perry pursed his lips. "Well, the thing is, when I heard that you were back in town, I more or less assured the director of the institute that I could convince you to come to the reception. It would look very good to have a Harte there, if you know what I mean. Your family has always carried a lot of weight here in Eclipse Bay."

Rafe gave a rude grunt and reached for the coffeepot.

Hannah eyed Perry with renewed caution. "You promised your boss that you would produce me tomorrow night, didn't you? And he's going to be annoyed if I don't put in an appearance."

Perry sighed. "I would take it as a great personal favor, Hannah. Tomorrow night is very, very important to me, career-wise."

"Who else is on the guest list?"

Perry appeared briefly surprised by the question. But he switched gears swiftly. "The usual local honchos, of course. Plus all the folks who backed Thornley's previous campaigns. We've also got some heavy-duty movers and shakers from Portland coming in. The big catch of the evening is Tom Lydd."

"Tom Lydd of Lydd-Zone Software?" Hannah asked.

"One and the same." Perry tried and failed to look modest. "I've been courting him for months, trying to get him to endow a research fund at the institute. I don't mind telling you that the fact that he agreed to attend tomorrow night is a very, very good sign. I'll have his name on an endowment agreement by the end of the week if all goes well."

"Big coup for you, I imagine," Hannah said politely.

"Doesn't get any bigger than Tom Lydd." Anticipation glittered in Perry's eyes. "I think it's safe to say that if I land an endowment from him, my position at the institute will be rock solid. I'll be in line to take over as director when Manchester retires next year."

"Wow," Hannah said. She paid no attention to Rafe, who was watching her with a bemused expression.

Perry chuckled. "I think we can agree that 'wow' is the operative word. I've got plans for the institute. Big plans. When I take over I'm going to turn it into one of the most influential social policy think tanks in the country. We'll be able to make or break political candidates. Anyone in the Northwest with an eye on political office will come to us for consulting advice."

"All right," Hannah said. "I'll do it."

Perry patted her hand with the same air of condescending approval that he had exuded when he patted Winston's head. Hannah had the same reaction Winston had had. It was all she could do not to bare her teeth.

She could tell from the glint in Rafe's eyes that he had caught her reaction. Perry, however, did not appear to notice. Goal accomplished, he was already halfway out of his chair.

"I'll be very busy tomorrow evening," he said en route to the front door. "I won't be able to swing by here to pick you up. Why don't you meet me at the institute? Say, eight o'clock? Dressy but not formal attire. I'm sure you know the drill."

"Sure, Perry." She followed him back outside onto the porch.

He paused on the second-to-last step and glanced over her shoulder, evidently assuring himself that he could not be overheard by Rafe. Then he lowered his voice to a confidential tone.

"What's with you and Madison?"

"You must have heard by now that Aunt Isabel left her house to both of us. Rafe and I are discussing how to handle Dreamscape."

A concerned frown furrowed Perry's brow. "Everyone in town heard about that will. Isabel must have been going senile there at the end. Why didn't you let the lawyers work it out?"

"Rafe didn't want to involve lawyers."

"Is that right?" Perry slanted a thoughtful glance at the door. "Probably thinks he can get a better deal on his own. You're lucky that I'm the one who happened to drop by this morning. Anyone else might have taken one look at that domestic little scene in the kitchen and jumped to the wrong conclusions."

"What conclusions?"

"You know what I'm talking about. You, Madison, the breakfast dishes. Hell, it isn't even nine o'clock yet. Looks like the two of you just spent the night together. If that kind of talk got around—"

She folded her arms, leaned one shoulder against the post, and looked at him. "Are you going to spread the rumor that I'm having an affair with Rafe Madison?"

"Of course not. Hell, I'm probably the one person in town who doesn't believe that you let him seduce you on the beach the night Kaitlin Sadler died."

"I appreciate your faith in my virtue. But what makes you so sure I didn't let Rafe seduce me that night?"

Perry chuckled indulgently. "As I recall, you were a bit naïve, not to say, downright inhibited about sex in those days."

"In other words, because I wasn't interested in getting into the backseat with you that night, it's highly unlikely that I fooled around with Rafe Madison later? Is that your logic?"

Perry gave her a knowing look. "As I said, I realize that there's nothing going on between the two of you, but a word to the wise. Eclipse Bay is still one very small town. You'd better be a little more careful about appearances in the future. Someone else might get the wrong idea."

"Thanks for the advice, Perry."

"One other thing you should know." He glanced toward the door behind her again and then leaned forward and dropped his voice still lower. "There's some serious question about Rafe Madison's source of income."

"What exactly are you implying, Perry?"

"I'm not one to make accusations, but there's talk that he may be involved in some less-than-legitimate investments, if you catch my drift."

"You mean he may be a gangster?"

Perry's lips thinned. "I'm just saying he might be skating a little close to the edge of the legal ice. Who knows what he's been up to during the past eight years?"

"Why don't you ask him?"

"None of my business." Perry went hastily down the last step. "Well, got to be on my way. Lots to do before tomorrow night. See you at the reception."

"Don't worry," she said softly. "I wouldn't miss it for the world."

She stayed where she was, lounging against the post, until the Volvo disappeared at the end of the drive. When she finally turned around, she saw Rafe and Winston gazing at her through the screen door.

"You'll be happy to hear that Perry doesn't believe for one moment that anything went on here last night," she said.

"Hell of a relief," Rafe said. "Someone who wasn't quite so high-minded as Decatur might have drawn all the wrong conclusions."

"Yes."

"He's still a jerk," Rafe said.

"Yes."

A speculative look gleamed in his eyes. "Are you serious about going to that political reception?"

"Very serious. Luckily I packed a black dress and a pair of heels. There's just one more thing I need."

"Yeah?" Rafe looked at her. "What's that?"

"A date."

"I got the impression that Decatur thinks he's going to be your date for the evening."

"He couldn't even be bothered to pick me up. I don't count that as a date."

"Got someone else in mind?"

She gave him her brightest smile. "I figure you owe me."

9

"WHAT caused the feud?" Octavia asked after a while.

Mitchell paused in the process of removing dead blooms from the rosebushes. "A woman. What else?"

Octavia folded her arms on top of the fence and rested her chin on her hands. She watched him nip off another faded flower. "What was her name?"

"Her name was Claudia Banner."

"Was she very beautiful?"

Mitchell opened his mouth to say yes, but then he hesitated, thinking back through the years to his first impression of Claudia. "She was fascinating," he said finally. "I couldn't take my eyes off her. But I never really thought of her as beautiful. I just knew that I wanted her so badly that nothing else mattered. Unfortunately, my partner, Sullivan, wanted her, too. For a while."

"What do you mean, for a while?"

Mitchell snorted softly. "Sullivan Harte was always too logical and too cool-headed to let himself be led around by his balls for long. He figured out what Claudia was up to long before I did. I refused to believe him. We fought. End of story."

"How did it happen?"

Mitchell tossed a dead bloom into a sack. "Sullivan and I set up Harte-Madison right after we got out of the army. We had us some mighty big dreams in those days. The plan was simple. We'd pick up a few cheap parking lots in downtown Portland and Seattle and then sit on 'em for as long as it took."

"As long as it took for what?"

"For the boom times to come, naturally. We both knew that sooner or later the Northwest cities were going to be important. What with the Pacific Rim trade taking off, property values were bound to skyrocket. We figured that when the time was right, we'd sell the parking lots to developers and make our fortunes. In the meantime, we'd have income off some very low-maintenance properties in the heart of the cities."

"How did Claudia Banner get involved?"

"Things started happening faster than we expected. We hired Claudia to help us negotiate the first sale. She'd had experience in that kind of thing, you see. Sullivan and I were novices."

"She did the deal for you?"

"Yep." Mitchell moved on to the next rosebush. "And it was a hell of a deal. Sullivan and I were suddenly rolling in dough. Both richer than we'd ever been in our lives. Couldn't wait to sell the next parking lot. Claudia found us a buyer right off the bat. More money fell down out of the sky. We were golden. Couldn't miss."

"What went wrong?"

"Somewhere in the middle of the sale of the third lot, a big one in downtown Seattle, Claudia pointed out that Harte-Madison could structure the deal in such a way that we'd be able to keep a stake in the future profits of the office tower that was slated to be built on the site."

"Uh-oh."

"Yep." Mitchell dropped another dead rose into his sack. "Uh-oh pretty much sums it up. Sullivan and I had financial stars in our eyes. We trusted Claudia. She took us for a ride and then vanished with the company profits on all three parking lots. Harte-Madison got left with a stack of leveraged debt, and the firm was suddenly out of business."

"And you and Sullivan were at each other's throats," Octavia mused.

Mitchell looked at her across the fence, squinting faintly against the weak sun. "I was sure he had somehow seduced Claudia into doing what she did. He figured I was working with her. Sullivan and I cornered each other outside Fulton's Supermarket one day, and the rest, as they say around these parts, is history."

"Did you love her very much, then?"

Mitchell shrugged. "She was my passion. Naturally, I made a fool of myself over her. Making fools out of themselves over females is something Madison men do."

"Is she still your passion?"

Mitchell examined the dead rose he had just pulled off a bush. "I'll let you in on a little secret. When you find yourself within spitting distance of ninety, you start viewing things from a slightly different perspective. If Claudia Banner walked back into my life today, I'd ask for my money back."

"And that's all?"

"Yep." He smiled slightly at the dead rose. "That's all. I've got other passions these days. That's another thing I've learned over the years. If he gives himself a chance, even a Madison can develop a little common sense when it comes to his passions."

Octavia was quiet for a while, watching him work. Eventually she stirred. "You know, if you leave some of the dead blooms on the bush you'll get rose hips. They make a very healthy tonic."

"I can't stand rose hip tea," Mitchell said. He snapped off another dead bloom and stuffed it into his sack. "I've got some good ten-year-old whiskey I use when I need a tonic."

10

AT eight-thirty the following evening, Rafe stood with Jed Steadman at the edge of the crowd and watched Hannah dance with Perry Decatur. Decatur, he was pleased to note, did not appear to be enjoying himself.

The whole scene bordered on amusing. Rafe could almost feel sorry for Thornley and his retinue. The reception was ostensibly in the politician's honor, but most of the guests were too busy sneaking covert glances at Hannah and Rafe to pay much attention to Thornley. That was due to the fact that most of those present were locals, including the mayor and his wife, all of the members of the town council, and the owners of several Eclipse Bay businesses.

Rafe recognized a lot of faces. He knew that the majority of these people had been around long enough to be familiar with the legend of the famous Harte-Madison feud, and virtually all of them had been living in Eclipse Bay eight years ago when Hannah had provided him with his alibi for the night of Kaitlin Sadler's death. In addition, the entire town was no doubt aware of the terms of Isabel Harte's will.

When Rafe and Hannah had walked into the reception together shortly after eight, they had caused any number of heads to swivel and jaws to drop. A ripple of murmurs had spread through the crowd. An amazing number of people had found an excuse to cross the room to greet them and make conversation.

Definitely not a banner night for Thornley, Rafe thought. How could his staff have known that their man's forthcoming announcement of his intention to run for the U.S. Senate seat would take second place to the latest development in the Harte-Madison feud?

Jed munched a cracker slathered in cream cheese and smoked salmon. "Thornley might be the next senator from the great state of Oregon, but he's having a hard time getting anyone's attention tonight."

"Only so far as the locals are concerned. The out-of-town crowd hasn't got a clue about the reason for the buzz."

"True, but almost everyone here is from Eclipse Bay." Jed eyed Perry and Hannah with an assessing gaze. "Decatur certainly doesn't look thrilled. Probably didn't expect you to show up with Hannah."

Rafe watched Perry and Hannah come to a halt on the dance floor. "I'm not real concerned with Decatur's feelings."

"From what I hear, he's got a lot at stake tonight, too. Word is he's trying to position himself to take over the institute next year."

"Not my problem." Rafe picked up a feathered toothpick that had an olive, a bit of cheese, and a mushroom impaled on it. He put the tiny skewer in his mouth and removed the edible portions with his teeth.

Jed shot him a curious look. "So what's up with you and Hannah, anyway?"

"We're conducting negotiations."

Jed looked amused. "Yeah, I heard about that. Your Porsche was spotted at the Harte place night before last. Word is you're doing your negotiating in bed."

Very deliberately, Rafe turned to look at him. He said nothing.

Jed grimaced and put up a hand, palm out. "Sorry. Can't help the curiosity. I'm a reporter, remember?"

"Yeah," Rafe said, "I remember."

"I get the message. No more questions of a personal nature about you and Hannah Harte. But speaking as an old friend, I'll just say that you'd better hope that her family doesn't get wind of the talk that's going around town."

"I'm not worried about the rest of the Hartes. This is between Hannah and me."

"Sure. Whatever you say." Jed reached for another canapé and another topic of conversation. "Some big bucks in this crowd tonight. Just saw Tom Lydd and his new bride arrive. I understand the head of the institute is hoping Lydd will endow a research fund."

Rafe followed his gaze to the man with the boyish face and the techie glasses on the far side of the room. Tom Lydd was not yet thirty, but he was already worth millions. "Very smart guy. Took his company public at the right time. His security software is some of the best on the market. Wouldn't be surprised if there's a buyout on the horizon."

Jed glanced at him. "You follow that kind of business news?"

Rafe shrugged. "It's a hobby."

Jed nodded, satisfied. He turned back to his survey of the crowd. "Not a bad turnout for the institute. A rising politician, a sprinkling of big money, and the right people from the political end of the spectrum. Got to admit, this operation has come a long way since it first opened its doors."

Rafe glanced at the tall, photogenic man talking to Tom Lydd. "And so has Trevor Thornley."

"You can say that again. He'll do okay in Washington. He's got all the right instincts, including good timing."

"You always said that timing was everything."

"It sure as hell is in politics. Thornley is also into long-range planning. Another big asset. In addition, he's smart enough not to neglect his home base here in Eclipse Bay. Pols that take their local support for granted always get into trouble fast."

"The fact that he married Marilyn Caldwell didn't hurt him either," Rafe said dryly.

Jed grunted. "You can say that again. Her father's money has come in real handy. Like I said, the guy knows how to plan."

"He sure pays a lot of attention to the institute."

"With good reason. He was its first important political client, and he's still the most faithful. The higher he climbs, the more prestige and power this place acquires."

"And the more it backs him."

"That's how it works." Jed swirled the wine in his glass. "I remember covering his first public relations events here. I knew even then that he had what it takes to make it big in politics."

Rafe thought about the night he had walked Hannah home. The institute had been ablaze with lights that evening. He had seen them from Bayview Drive. Hannah had mentioned that her parents were attending a reception for a politician named Thornley who had just announced that he was running for the state legislature.

Rafe hadn't paid much attention. Politics had been of little interest to him in those days. In any event, he had been too busy obsessing on Hannah's list of criteria for Mr. Right that night.

The memory made him look around for his date. He spotted her coming toward him through the crowd. The sight of her sparked a thrill of intense awareness deep in his gut. She looked great, he thought. The snug-fitting little black number she was wearing underscored a whole lot of her best assets, including the neatly curved breasts, slim waist, and full hips. Her hair swung in a sleek, gleaming curve every time she moved her head. Her legs were incredibly sexy in dark stockings and black high heels.

The most exciting woman in the room, no doubt about it. At least so far as he was concerned.

He watched her weave her way toward him. She had Decatur in tow, but Perry looked more irritated than ever, so that was okay for now, Rafe concluded. Irritated was good. Irritated meant that Decatur had not liked the fact that Hannah had brought her own date tonight. The jerk had probably counted on taking her home after the reception, maybe even planned to take up where he had left off that night in the front seat of his car eight years ago.

Not bloody likely.

Hannah came to a halt in front of Rafe. She looked flushed and glowing, and there was a sparkle in her eye. He was almost positive that Decatur had nothing to do with the look. She was up to something. He had sensed it when he'd picked her up earlier. She had a scheme cooking tonight. He was content to stand back and watch it unfold.

She smiled.

"We're back," she said.

"Yeah, I can see that," Rafe said.

"You'll have to excuse me," Perry muttered. "Got to say hello to some very big people. I'll catch up with you later, Hannah."

"Yes, you will," she said very sweetly. "I'll look forward to it."

Perry hurried off into the throng.

"He doesn't look real happy," Rafe said. "What did you do? Step on his toes?"

"I'm saving that for later."

Jed looked interested. "That sounds promising. Anything you want to tell the press?"

"Not yet, Jed." Hannah smiled. "But stay tuned."

"If we've got some time before the excitement starts," Rafe said, "may I have the next dance?"

"You may."

"*Hannah!*" A man's voice rose above the din of nearby conversation. "Hannah Harte! Is that you?"

In the next instant, a small knot of people unraveled to allow Tom Lydd to pass between them. He had his wife, a wholesome-looking blonde, in tow. Both were smiling at Hannah with genuine delight.

"What a terrific surprise," the young Mrs. Lydd said. She threw her arms around Hannah and then stepped aside so that Tom could do the same.

"Didn't know that you'd be here," Tom crowed. "This is great. Nice to see a familiar face."

"I'm delighted to see you," Hannah murmured. "Allow me to introduce Rafe Madison and Jed Steadman. Rafe, Jed, meet Tom and Julie Lydd. Fair warning— Jed is the editor of the *Eclipse Bay Journal.*"

"Not a problem. I've got no quarrel with the press. Always been good to Lydd-Zone." Tom pumped the hands of both men with his trademark boyish enthusiasm. "Great to meet you both."

"Any friend of Hannah's." Rafe slanted a quick glance at her. She winked at him. That clarified one thing, he thought. The Lydds were part of whatever plan she had concocted.

"Hannah is more than a friend," Julie Lydd confided. "She was our wedding consultant. A true magician, as far as we're concerned. Tom and I had a vision of what we wanted, but we didn't have the vaguest idea of how to pull it off. Hannah made it all happen."

"Everything went off like clockwork." Tom beamed at his wife. "Isn't that right?"

"It was amazing," Julie agreed. "We wanted the whole thing staged on an alien world, you see. The one Tom created for his first big computer game."

"We're talking waterfalls, lagoons, architectural features, the works," Tom continued. "Did the whole thing on our private island up in the Sans Juans. Hannah was brilliant. You can imagine the logistical nightmare involved. Very impressive organizational talents. After we got back from the honeymoon, I called her up and tried to hire her. There's always room for that kind of management skill at Lydd-Zone."

"I told him that if the bottom ever falls out of the wedding business, I'll take him up on his offer," Hannah said.

"Anytime," Tom assured her genially.

Hannah smiled warmly. "I love doing weddings for couples who are matched by my sister's agency."

Jed cocked a brow. "Your sister's a matchmaker?"

Julie Lydd answered, "Tom and I met through Private Arrangements. That's the name of Lillian Harte's agency. She uses a very sophisticated computer program to make her matches. Not everyone likes that approach, of course. A lot of folks think it takes the romance out of the process. But it appealed to both Tom and me."

Rafe looked at Tom. "I hear you're thinking of endowing a research fund here at the institute."

"Looking into it," Tom agreed. "I'm a big fan of the think tank concept." He turned to Hannah. "You're from this neck of the woods. What's your take on the folks running this place?"

Hannah's smile brightened to a blinding glare. "I'm so glad you asked, Tom. I do have some opinions on this operation. Why don't we find a private place to talk?"

"Great." Tom took his wife's arm. "I noticed a small conference room just outside in the main hall. Doubt if anyone would mind if we used it."

Jed watched the three vanish back into the crowd. He turned to Rafe, his eyes gleaming with interest. "What do you think that was all about?"

Rafe picked up a knife, dipped it into a bowl of what looked like cheese spread, and smeared some on a cracker. "How the heck should I know?"

But he had a pretty good idea, he thought. Hannah was making her move. He couldn't wait to find out what happened next.

"What's wrong?" Jed asked.

Rafe grimaced. "The cheese spread is bland. Could have done with some feta and walnuts."

※

AT ten-thirty Hannah emerged from the rest room in time to see Trevor Thornley take the podium to make his big announcement. The lights dimmed over the crowd. Onstage, the politician stood in the center of a dramatic spot. His wife, Marilyn, stood a little behind and just to the right, glowing with wifely pride.

Hannah had a hunch that Marilyn could take a lot of the credit for the fact that her husband was about to launch a campaign for the U.S. Senate. Marilyn had always been ambitious.

Trevor Thornley raised his hands for silence.

"I want to thank everyone here tonight, starting with the faculty of this outstanding think tank. The cutting-edge work done here at the institute in the areas of social and public policy has had a profound impact, not only on how the pundits discuss the issues, but, more importantly, on how politicians and voters think about the challenges that face our nation today.

"The greatness of this country lies in its people. I have always . . ."

"What the hell do you think you're doing, Hannah?" Perry's voice hissed out of the shadows behind her. His hand closed over her arm. His fingers tightened painfully. He spun her around to face him. "I just got through talking to Tom Lydd."

"Such a nice man. And so smart." She smiled into Perry's fuming eyes. "I like his wife, too, don't you?"

"Lydd just told me that he wouldn't even consider endowing a research fund here at the institute unless Professor Brad McCallister of Chamberlain College received a joint appointment to the faculty."

Hannah widened her eyes. "That shouldn't be a problem. I hear that Brad McCallister has already been nominated by the selection committee. He'll make a terrific addition to your staff."

Perry's face was suffused with an angry red color. "Damn it, you had no business interfering in the professional affairs of the institute."

"But I didn't interfere." Hannah smiled. "I merely told Tom that Brad was brilliant and that the selection committee should be applauded for choosing him."

"Lydd told me that he wants McCallister to run the department created by the endowment." Perry started to sputter. "The whole damn department."

"An excellent idea. Brad is the very soul of integrity. With him in charge, Lydd and the institute will have the satisfaction of knowing that Lydd's money is spent the way he wants it spent."

Perry's face worked furiously. "Pamela McCallister is your friend, isn't she? You knew that Brad was being considered for a joint appointment here."

"I also heard that you were trying to block it because you're jealous of Brad's professional abilities. You're afraid he'll outshine you once he gets on the institute staff, aren't you?"

"That's got nothing to do with it."

"Good. In that case you shouldn't have any problem with the selection committee's choice."

"You planned this. You agreed to come here tonight because you knew the Lydds would be here."

"I believe it was you yourself who mentioned that they had been invited."

"That's beside the point." His voice rose. He grabbed her other arm. Rage flashed in his eyes. "You think you can pull a stunt like this with me just because you're a Harte?"

"Perry, you tried to use me and the Harte name tonight. I let you do it. In exchange, I used the opportunity you dropped into my lap. I'd say we're even."

"You little bitch! You got a kick out of playing the tease eight years ago, and you're still at it, aren't you?"

It occurred to her that Perry had not learned to curb his temper in the past eight years. It flared as quickly and intensely as it had in the old days.

"Let me go," she said coolly. "This scene is starting to remind me of another discussion we had once."

"If you're talking about that night you staged the big drama in my car and then jumped out when I got tired of your cock-teasing—"

Her own temper kicked in. "I'm talking about the night you decided that since you couldn't seduce me into having sex with you, you would try force instead. What were you thinking, anyway? Were you working on the theory that once I discovered what a great lover you were I'd agree to marry you?"

"Damn it—"

"Or did you convince yourself that if I had sex with you, I'd feel that I had to marry you just for the sake of my reputation?"

His eyes narrowed. "If I ever thought you cared a damn about your reputation, you sure straightened me out when you told Chief Yates and anyone else who would listen that you'd spent the night on the beach with Rafe Madison."

Hannah's turbocharger switch suddenly tripped and her temper went into overdrive. "Let me tell you something, Perry Decatur. You are very, very lucky that I did not tell my folks or my brother how you really behaved in the front seat of the car that night. All I ever said was that we'd argued. I never told them how you tried to force yourself on me."

His eyes bulged. "How dare you accuse me of that sort of behavior? No one has done more for women's issues here at the institute than me."

"Forget the political agenda. We both know what you had in mind that night."

"We were on a date." Perry's voice was choked with outrage. "You freaked out when I tried to kiss you. That was all there was to it."

"That's not quite how I remember it." She stabbed her finger against his elegantly knotted white silk tie. "You thought you could coerce me into marrying you."

"You're crazy. Hell, I knew that you were naïve and inhibited in those days, but I didn't think you were *so* naïve and *so* inhibited that you couldn't recognize a grown man's normal, healthy sex drive when you saw it."

"I saw it, but I gotta tell you, Perry, it didn't look normal or healthy to me."

"It was your fault that there was a small misunderstanding."

She gave him an icy smile. "Yes, it was on the small side, but I wasn't going to mention it."

"There's a word for women like you. You can't blame me for trying to take you up on what you were offering."

"I didn't offer you anything, and you know it."

"I cared for you." His jaw jerked a couple of times as if he were on the verge of being overcome by emotion. "I wanted to marry you."

"Sure. But only because I was a Harte."

"That's not true."

"It was true. I wasn't nearly as naïve in those days as everyone seems to think. Do you really believe that you were the first man who latched on to me because he saw it as a way to marry into Harte Investments?"

"I resent the implications of that statement," Perry said furiously. "I'm an academic. I live for the world of ideas, not the world of business."

"Give me a break, Perry. You're a hustler. You always have been a hustler. Eight years ago you saw marriage to me as a quick, easy way to get access to the deep pockets of my father's company. You also figured you'd have a lot of use for the social and business contacts that my family could provide, didn't you?"

"Your parents liked me."

"Mostly because they thought you were bright, charming, and ambitious. Really ambitious. My family admires ambition in a person. Sometimes we admire it a little too much."

"There's nothing wrong with ambition. It's the American way."

"What you seem to have overlooked is that there's a line between ambition and hustling. I'll admit that it can be mighty thin at times, but it's there if you care to check for it." She paused deliberately. "Something tells me that you haven't looked for it in years, Perry."

"You're just as preachy and prissy as ever, aren't you?" His mouth tightened. "Do you know how incredibly self-righteous and officious you sound when you go into your lecturing mode? No wonder your engagement fell apart. What man in his right mind wants to go to bed every night with a woman who can't stop lecturing?"

She caught her breath. Then she glanced very pointedly at the hands he had clasped around her arms. "Let me go, Perry."

He ignored her. His fingers squeezed tighter. "I've got news for you. The Miss Virtue act doesn't work here in Eclipse Bay anymore. You screwed your image eight years ago when you provided Rafe Madison with his alibi. And what do you think will happen when word gets out that the two of you are *negotiating* the details of your aunt's will over cozy little breakfasts at your folks' place?"

"You know, it won't be as easy to knee you in the crotch tonight as it was the last time, because this skirt is much tighter than the one I had on that night. But I think I can manage it, and I will if you don't let me go right now."

He released her and jumped back as if he'd just touched an electrically charged wire. "Bitch!"

"I think this is about where I came in last time," Rafe said from the shadows behind Perry. "But the big difference is that Hannah won't have to walk home tonight. I've got my car."

"*Madison.*" Perry jerked around to face Rafe and then took another hasty step back. "This is a private conversation."

"I got the impression that Hannah didn't want to continue it any longer."

Rafe glided forward with a deceptively lazy movement. His eyes never left Perry's face. "Was I mistaken?"

"This is none of your business." Perry's voice squeaked slightly. "If you touch me, I'll file charges."

Alarmed by the glint of predatory anticipation in Rafe's eyes, Hannah stepped quickly between the two men. "That's enough, Rafe. Everything is under control."

"I know, but it would be sort of fun to bounce him around a little. Please?"

"Rafe, I'm serious." It occurred to her that in her career as a wedding consultant she had honed to a fine art the ability to nip embarrassing public scenes in the bud. Now she was standing in the middle of one that she herself had created. "I do not want anyone hurt here."

"I could take him somewhere else." Rafe looked hopeful. "Pretty quiet down at Eclipse Arch this time of night. No one would hear him squawk."

"You're crazy." Perry backpedaled several more steps. "How dare you threaten me! Do you have any idea of just who is out there in that reception room? There's a future U.S. senator out there. Not to mention a lot of other very important people."

"He's right," Hannah said firmly. "We do not want to cause a disturbance that will only result in embarrassment for all concerned."

"I don't mind a little embarrassment," Rafe assured her. "I'm a Madison."

"Stop threatening me," Perry howled.

"I didn't threaten you." Rafe looked at Hannah. "Did you hear me threaten him, Hannah?"

She seized his arm. "You and I are leaving. Now. The main goal of the evening has been accomplished. Perry has just assured me that he will not stand in the way of Brad's joint appointment at the institute. In fact, he will do everything he can to ensure that it goes through. Isn't that right, Perry?"

"I won't be intimidated," Perry said forcefully. "Furthermore, I am not in charge of the selection committee. You have to remember that."

"Sure, sure, we understand." Rafe winked. "But just among the three of us, Brad McCallister's appointment looks like a sure thing, right?"

Perry cleared his throat and somehow managed to look down his nose even though he was at least three inches shorter than Rafe. "If Lydd goes through with his plans to endow a research fund here at the institute, and if he feels strongly about McCallister's appointment, he will, of course, be able to bring a great deal of influence to bear on the matter."

Rafe glanced at Hannah. "Are you sure you don't want me to bounce him around a bit?"

"Positive. We don't need lawsuits." She tugged on his arm. It was like trying to hoist the anchor of a container ship by hand.

Rafe gave Perry a look of wistful regret. "You know, you're right about one thing, Decatur. When she starts in with the lectures and the good advice, she does sort of take all the fun out of things, doesn't she?"

"That's enough, Madison." Hannah gave up tugging, wrapped her hand around his arm, and leaned forward instead.

"Whatever you say." Without warning, Rafe suddenly reversed course, squeezing her hand against his side.

Hannah, already off balance, with her fingers now trapped under his elbow, had to run a few steps to avoid being dragged.

"*Rafe.*"

"Sorry." He slowed to a normal pace. "You okay?"

"Of course I'm okay." She shoved her hair out of her eyes and yanked hard on her skirt. "Let's get out of here."

"I'm with you. I don't think I'm going to become a big fan of political receptions. The speeches are boring and the food is bad."

For some inexplicable reason she started to laugh.

11

WITH the exception of a few stray chuckles, she had herself under control by the time they got outside. Rafe glanced at her as they walked to the far side of the lot where the Porsche was parked.

"Told you he was still a jerk." He opened the passenger door for her.

"You were right." She slanted him a quick glance. "How long were you lurking there in that hallway outside the rest rooms?"

"Long enough to hear most of the conversation."

She paused, half in and half out of the cockpit. Then she straightened and went up on her toes. Leaning over the top of the car window, she brushed her mouth very quickly against his cheek.

"It really was sweet of you to offer to beat Perry up for me," she said.

He lifted his fingers absently to the place where her lips had touched his skin. In the weak glare of the parking lot lamp his eyes were shadowed, impossibly enigmatic. "That's me, a real sweet guy."

She stepped back quickly and sank into the rich leather upholstery. "But I really didn't need rescuing."

" 'Course not. You're a Harte."

"And Perry is just a jerk with a temper who's always looking for an angle."

Rafe folded his arms on the top of the window frame and looked down at her. "Got news for you. It wasn't you I was trying to rescue back there."

She stilled. "I beg your pardon?"

"I just figured I'd better break up that little one-sided skirmish before you cast any more nasty aspersions on Decatur's masculinity."

She was not quite sure how to take that. "Oh." She narrowed her eyes, trying to see his face against the pale light. "You, uh, care about Perry's fragile male ego?"

"Not particularly. But intimidation is a precious tool. Push a guy like Decatur too hard, and it can backfire on you. He might try to take revenge."

"Hah. There's nothing he can do to me."

"Not to you maybe, but he could sure make life hell at the institute for your friend's husband."

She stared at him for a beat or two as the implications sank in. "You're right. If Brad gets the appointment, he'll have to work with Perry, won't he?"

"Maybe not directly, but he won't be able to avoid him altogether. They'll be colleagues, after all. I'm sure Brad can take care of himself, but why make things any harder than necessary for him?"

"Damn." She drummed he fingers on the edge of the seat and gazed morosely through the front windshield. "I got a little carried away back there, didn't I?"

"Perfectly natural reaction," he assured her. "Victory can make a person giddy."

"Apparently." She frowned. "So how come it was okay for you to threaten to bounce him around, but it wasn't okay for me to make rude remarks?"

He exhaled with an air of long-suffering patience. "Because I'm a man and I was making a direct threat."

"Ah, yes, I get it." She nodded wisely. "Macho challenge stuff."

"A challenge that Decatur was never forced to answer or back down from because you intervened, thus saving both his bacon and his pride."

She thought about that. "You did that on purpose, didn't you? You knew I'd put a stop to anything that looked as if it would turn into real violence."

"Pretty sure, yeah."

"How did you know that?"

He grinned. "Instinct."

"Yours or mine?"

"Yours."

She pursed her lips. "You mean you just assumed that because I'm female I would automatically move to stop a couple of males from getting into a brawl?"

"It had nothing to do with the fact that you're female. Believe me, I've met women who love to watch men fight. But I figured that any successful wedding consultant would have developed finely tuned radar when it comes to scenes. The last thing anyone wants at a wedding is a brawl, right?"

"Well, yes, that's true, of course."

"I figured you'd be good at intervening in a confrontation," he concluded a little too innocently.

"Hmm."

"And you did get in a few zingers," he reminded her. "I heard them. Decatur took some well-placed hits."

She thought about Perry's words. *No wonder your engagement fell apart. What man in his right mind wants to go to bed every night with a woman who can't stop lecturing?* The invisible balloon of her triumph began to deflate.

She exhaled deeply. "Perry got in a few good thumps of his own."

"That's okay. You can handle them. You're tough, aren't you?" He started to close the door. "Hey, you're a Harte."

"Right. I'm a Harte." She continued to gaze out into the darkness on the other side of the windshield. "And what's more, I'm—"

She broke off, startled, when an apparition materialized out of the night directly in front of the car. In the cold glare of the parking lot lamp she saw a figure garbed in black pants, black running shoes, and black gloves. The hood of a black sweatshirt was pulled down over a face smeared with daubs of dark paint.

Rafe glanced over his shoulder, nodded casually. " 'Evening, A.Z. Nice night for recon work."

"Heard you were back in town, Rafe," Arizona Snow said. "Always figured you'd return someday to expose the bastards who tried to frame you for the Sadler girl's murder."

"Well, now that you mention it, that wasn't exactly the reason I came back," Rafe replied. "You see, Hannah and I have this little inheritance problem."

"Dreamscape," Arizona said briskly in a cigar- and whiskey-roughened voice. "I know all about that, too. Isabel was a good friend of mine. If you ask me, it makes a great cover for you." She peered into the Porsche. "Nice to see you, Hannah. Come back to help Rafe flush out the rats?"

Hannah smiled slightly. "Good evening, Arizona."

"My, don't you look fancy tonight." Arizona squinted. "What the devil are you two doin' hanging around with this crowd at the institute? Part of your investigation?"

"Our being back in town has nothing to do with Kaitlin's death, A.Z.," Rafe said gently. "It was an accident. You know that."

"Bulldooky. Suckers here at the institute offed her for some reason. She probably knew too much about somethin' going on up here."

"How would she have known anything about the institute?" Hannah asked curiously.

"Kaitlin slept around a lot," Arizona said. She shot a piercing look at Rafe. "Reckon you know that."

Rafe cleared his throat but did not say anything. Hannah glanced at him, but he deftly managed to avoid her eyes.

"Always figured poor Kaitlin slept with the wrong guy," Arizona continued. "Someone connected to the institute. Probably talked in his sleep. Or maybe she just saw some papers or something. They figured they had to get rid of her. The killers must have panicked when Chief Yates started investigatin', so they decided they needed a fall guy and tried to pin it on you, Rafe. Probably picked you on accounta everyone knew you'd been seeing a lot of Kaitlin that summer."

"An interesting theory," Rafe said neutrally.

"But thanks to Hannah here, the big plan fell apart." Arizona clenched a fist and pumped it into the air. "Once in a while we throw a wrench into the bastards' plans. Gives me hope that someday we'll expose the whole damned pack of weasels."

Rafe glanced at the black plastic binder in her hand. "What are you doing here tonight?"

"Keeping my logbooks up to date, of course." Arizona tapped the binder with one black-gloved finger. "Until the rest of you wake up and smell the coffee, someone has to keep an eye on what goes on up here at the institute. Someday folks will realize that this so-called think tank is a cover for a secret government operation that operates outside the law. When that day comes, everyone's going to be real glad to have my logs."

Hannah leaned slightly out of the car. "Did you put Rafe and me in your log tonight?"

"Honey, I took down the license plate, make, and model of every car in this lot when it arrived, and that includes friends as well as suspects. Got to keep the record accurate."

"Something to be said for accuracy," Hannah agreed.

"I also noted the number of people in each vehicle and, where possible, the identities." Arizona scowled. "Got to admit, I don't always recognize everyone these days. Every year more strangers show up for meetings and parties here at the institute. In the old days I knew just about everyone who came and went. But not anymore. The web is widening daily."

Rafe eyed the logbook. "Are you going to write down the time that we leave?"

"You bet. It's the details that make the difference, you know. When the truth finally comes out, it will be the accumulation of a lot of tiny facts in these logs that will show how the phantom project operated undetected for so long."

Hannah wrinkled her nose. "You don't really think that Rafe and I are involved in the conspiracy, do you?"

Arizona snorted. " 'Course not. You're just a couple of naïve, innocent dupes like most everyone else around here. But I gotta put you in my logs because I gotta have a complete record of all comings and goings. If I start skipping a couple of cars here and there, the government lawyers might try to claim that the logs are incomplete or inaccurate. Can't give 'em any room to squirm when the truth comes out."

Rafe inclined his head in sober acknowledgment of that logic. "Makes sense."

"You better believe it. I've monitored every reception, every meeting, every special event held here at the institute since the day the place opened." She held her log aloft again. "All part of the record."

Rafe glanced at his watch. "Well, you can log us out at precisely ten-forty-three. We're on our way home now."

Arizona's head jerked up and down once in acknowledgment. "Got it." She clicked a black pen and opened her notebook. "You two drive carefully."

"We will." Rafe started to close the passenger door.

"Say, Rafe." Arizona glanced up sharply. "Why don't you stop by the café when you get a chance? About time we updated that menu you worked out when you used to cook for me. The college crowd seems happy enough, but after all these years I'm getting a little tired of fixing the same stuff day in and day out."

"All right, I'll drop by soon," Rafe said.

"Appreciate it." Arizona aimed the pen at Hannah. "You come with him. Always did like the notion of you two gettin' together. Told Isabel so."

Hannah braced one hand against the door to keep Rafe from closing it. "My aunt discussed her intention to leave the house to us with you?"

"Well, sure." Arizona's beefy shoulders rose and fell beneath the black sweatshirt. "Me and Isabel went back a long way. She talked to me about her plans for Dreamscape because she knew that everyone else would think she was crazy for trying to end the feud."

"But not you," Hannah murmured.

"Nope, not me. I told her to go for it. Always knew the feud had been caused by the sonsabitches who opened the institute. The bastards probably wanted to break up Harte-Madison because they knew the company would try to block their plans to establish this damned think tank." Arizona sighed. "Unfortunately, their scheme worked all too well."

"Good night, A.Z." Rafe closed the car door very firmly.

Hannah watched Arizona disappear back into the shadows. Rafe circled around the tail of the Porsche and got in behind the wheel.

"You think we're a couple of naïve, innocent dupes?" Hannah asked.

"Sure, but what the hell." Rafe turned the key in the ignition and put the car in gear. "I'd rather be a happy, carefree dupe who gets to go home at ten-forty-three than an ever-vigilant guardian who has to spend nights running around in black sweats recording license plates."

Hannah glanced at the rows of parked cars as Rafe drove out of the lot. "Still, it's hard to believe anyone could get a lot of satisfaction out of writing down license plate numbers. Just think, she's been doing it for years."

"She's dedicated to the cause of ultimately exposing the secret government conspiracy operating here at the institute. As hobbies go, it probably beats watching television."

Hannah contemplated that as she gazed at the scene spread out below the hillside. There was no fog tonight—at least, there wasn't any yet. The bay was a sweep of midnight velvet ringed and studded with the lights of the town and the pier.

She could make out the neon sign that marked the Total Eclipse Bar and Grill. On the opposite side of the street, the town's single gas station was closed for the night. Near the pier was a row of darkened shops that featured rustic antiques, inexpensive beach souvenirs, and seascapes. The neighboring marina was largely unlit. The boats sheltered there were invisible against the dark expanse of the water.

"Arizona Snow is a nice person in a lot of ways, and she's definitely interesting," Hannah said after a while. "But she's not what anyone would call normal."

"The older I get," Rafe said, shifting gears to negotiate the curving road that led down from the institute, "the more I'm convinced that the only good, working definition of 'normal' is the fact that you're still walking around outside and not locked up in a padded cell."

"Okay, I'll buy that definition. It's as good as any other I've ever heard."

"Thanks. You know, for a guy who never made it through his second year of college, I say some smart stuff sometimes."

She smiled wryly. "And so modest, too."

He shot her a quick glance. "What's with the sudden depression here? Losing the glow of victory so soon?"

"You know the old saying, all glory is fleeting."

"Damn." He accelerated at the foot of the hill. "You *have* lost the sparkle."

"I hate when that happens."

"Me, too. Victory over the jerk should buy you more than a moment of exuberance. But don't worry, I've got a surefire cure for what ails you."

She turned her head on the back of the seat and studied his hard profile from beneath lowered lashes. It felt good to be here with him in the intimate confines of the powerful car. She wondered what her family would say if they knew where she was tonight.

For some reason the answer did not matter at that moment.

"What's the cure?" she asked softly.

A wicked expression, barely visible in the eerie light given off from the instrument panel, flickered across his face. "Come home with me, my sweet, naïve little dupe, and I will show you."

She knew the smart answer to that invitation. The only intelligent, sane, reasonable, logical, suitably Harte-like response was to tell him that she had to get home to her dog.

"Okay," she said instead.

SHE finished the last of the key lime pie and put down her fork with a sigh of mingled satisfaction and regret. The pie had been delicious, tangy and smooth on the tongue, with a flavor that conjured up images of the tropics. The slice had been arranged with artistic precision on the plate and trimmed with a paper-thin almond wafer and a slice of lime.

She looked at Rafe, who was sitting on the other side of the old oak table. He had removed his tie, unbuttoned the collar of his pristine white shirt, and rolled the sleeves up to the elbows. Nothing had changed since that night on the beach, she thought. He wasn't the handsomest man she had ever met, but he was far and away the sexiest.

"The pie was incredible." She tried to focus on something other than sex. It wasn't easy when she was near Rafe, she had discovered. And the problem seemed to be growing worse.

"You don't think I went a little overboard with the lime zest?" he asked.

"You can never have too much zest, I always say."

He nodded. "It's sort of like sparkle, I guess."

"You know, when it comes to cooking, you've got a real talent. Why haven't you ever opened a restaurant?"

"I've been waiting until the time was right."

She put her elbows on the table. "Okay, I can't stand the suspense any longer. If you aren't the owner of a five-star restaurant, how did you finance the Porsche and all this free time you seem to have on your hands?"

He gave her a cryptic smile. "Starting to wonder about all those rumors you've heard concerning my career as a gangster?"

"It never crossed my mind for one second that you might be a gangster."

"Yeah?" He thrust his legs out in front of him, leaned back in the chair, and crossed his feet at the ankles. "Why not?"

"Wrong clothes. Everyone knows gangsters wear shiny suits with big lapels."

"That's East Coast gangsters you're talking about. Out here on the West Coast, your average wise guy prefers a more laid-back look."

"Huh. Well, that blows that theory. So what have you been doing for the past eight years? And don't give me that line about working in a hotel."

"I did work in a hotel. For a while. I've also done a little investing." He paused. "Day trading."

Computer stock trading took nerves of steel and a fine sense of timing, she thought. "I've heard that's an easy way to lose your shirt."

"It is." He shrugged. "But I didn't."

She grinned. "Of course not."

"I'm out of the market now," he said evenly. "I took my profits a few months ago and stuck them into nice, boring bonds and my own portfolio of high techs."

"Stop." She held up a hand. "You're scaring me. It's disconcerting to hear a Madison talk seriously about sound financial planning. Ruins the image of wild, impulsive behavior."

"If you think I'm bad, you ought to talk to Gabe sometime. He's obsessed with making money and doing deals."

She smiled. "A cold-blooded Madison? Hard to imagine."

"Gabe has his share of the Madison hot blood. But he's channeled it into Madison Commercial."

"I'll take your word for it." Hannah hesitated. "Ever cooked for your grandfather?"

He looked genuinely startled. "No. Bryce does all the cooking at Mitchell's house."

"Why don't you invite Mitchell to dinner here at Dreamscape?"

His jaw tightened. "What put that idea into your head?"

"I'm not sure. It just occurred to me that your interest in cooking parallels his in gardening. Creative outlets that you both approach with passion."

"Huh."

"I think you should invite him to dinner."

Rafe contemplated her for a long, brooding moment. "You just can't help yourself, can you?" he said at last. "You can't resist handing out the advice."

She exhaled slowly and sank back into her chair. "You're right. I can't seem to stop. Do you think I should seek professional help?"

"Waste of money. You'd probably end up giving advice to the therapist on your own dime." He got to his feet and stacked the dishes. "Go on into the solarium. I'll bring the coffee out there."

Bemused and feeling oddly flattened, she got up from the table and walked out of the kitchen.

She wandered into the glass-walled room, not bothering to turn on the lights. Drawn by the darkened view, she went to stand at the windows. Rafe was right. She really ought to stop handing out advice to all and sundry. Nobody ever took it anyway.

Morosely she gazed out across the expanse of the curving bay toward the lights of the small harbor and the pier. Music stole softly into the dark shadows of the solarium, curling around her with a lover's touch. It was a slow, sultry number that sounded as if it had been born in a smoky nightclub and had never seen the light of day.

Rafe came through the doorway with a tray in his hands. Without a word he set the coffee and the mugs down on a table. Then he straightened and walked toward her.

A chill of intense awareness swept through her.

So it was dark and there was a torchy tune swirling in the air. So there was a sexy man who could cook like an angel in the immediate vicinity. So what?

Think of Winston.

Rafe came to a stop directly behind her. "Did I tell you how good you look in that dress?"

"Mmm." Noncommittal. That was always a safe way to play it.

He put his hands on her shoulders and turned her slowly around to face him. "You look fantastic in it."

Think of Winston.

Rafe took her into his arms and began to move, very slowly, to the very slow music.

He might as well have been making love to her, she thought. The effect was the same. It felt like things were melting down below. Unable to resist the temptation, she put her head cautiously on his shoulder.

His arms tightened very deliberately around her. His thumb touched the base of her spine.

Think of Winston.

She cleared her throat. "Would you mind if I asked you a purely hypothetical question?"

He put his mouth against her temple. "I live to answer hypothetical questions."

"In your considered opinion, do you think that the average man would be hesitant to become involved in a romantic relationship with a woman who was prone to lecture him in an officious, prissy manner?" She swallowed. "Even though she was right most of the time?"

He said nothing for a moment, dancing in thoughtful silence.

"The average man, maybe," he finally conceded.

Gloom settled on her, darker than fog. "I was afraid you were going to say that."

They danced for another moment or two. Then he brought her to a halt near the window.

"My turn to ask you a hypothetical question," he said. "Do you think I'm average?"

She raised her head very swiftly from his shoulder. "No. No, definitely not. You're a lot of things, Rafe Madison, but you are not average. Not in any way."

She could feel him smiling into her hair.

"Then I don't see that we have a problem here," he said.

He tilted her chin up and kissed her.

She stopped thinking of Winston.

12

SHE wanted him. He could feel it in the way she held him. The fine trembling in her body told him of her gathering excitement. He could not recall the last time a woman had shivered in his arms like this.

He realized his own hands were not completely steady.

Somewhere inside him there was a cloudburst. A hot rain poured down, drenching regions that had been parched and dry for what seemed like forever. Suddenly there was a rain forest where there had been only desert. The raw power, the driving need, and the exquisitely painful anticipation that shafted through him was the pulse of life itself.

He had promised himself that when this moment came he would take his time and savor the experience. He wasn't a kid with his girlfriend in the backseat of a car. He was a man who had some experience. He knew the risks of rushing things. But the urgent hunger was an ungovernable force that threatened to overwhelm his will.

"Rafe?" Hannah speared her fingers through his hair and then tightened them around his neck. "I never intended . . . I mean, I didn't expect to end up like this tonight."

"Are you going to tell me it's too soon?" He kissed her throat. "That we don't know each other well enough?" He counted delicate little vertebrae with his fingertips until he reached the hollow of her back. "Because if you want to stop this, you'd better say something fast."

"No."

He froze, his palm on the curve of her hip, and raised his head to look down at her. "No, you don't want to do this?"

She smiled slowly. "No, I don't want to stop."

He shuddered and pulled her close again. "Don't scare me like that. My heart won't take the shock."

Her laugh was tiny and fraught with nervous energy. It sent sparkles of light through him. In the next moment the small sound transmuted into a sweet, anxious murmur. Her kisses became extravagant, quick, eager. Delicious.

He was tight and hard and edgy now. Every muscle straining. He could no longer think clearly. The fragrance of her body was a disturbing, disorienting incense that clouded his brain. He knew that he was swiftly losing control, but he could not seem to work up any real concern about the problem.

She wanted him.

That was all that mattered.

"Upstairs," he said against her mouth.

"I don't think I can make it that far."

She fumbled with his shirt. Somewhere in the shadows a button bounced and pinged on the tile floor. Her fingers spread across his chest, warm and soft.

"Let's try real hard to make it up the stairs," he said.

Her response was muffled against his bare skin. "Okay."

He guided her toward the door. Simultaneously he found the zipper of her dress and lowered it the length of her back. The top half of the garment fell to her waist. He saw that the manufacturer of her silky little black bra had skimped on fabric. The garment did not cover the top half of her breasts.

Gathering her against his side, he worked feverishly on the clasp of the bra. At the same time he half carried, half dragged her across the hall. It was an awkward process. What the hell was the matter with him tonight? He usually didn't have so much trouble doing two things at once.

The bra finally fell away. He had her as far as the stairs now. He heard a soft clatter and realized that one of her high heels had come off.

She lost the second one just as he got them both to the third step.

"Oh, yes." Her hands gripped his shoulder, small nails tattooing his skin. She kissed him wildly. *"Yes."*

Slowly, he worked his way up the stairs with Hannah in his arms. It wasn't easy. She wasn't helping him. He missed a step when she sank her teeth lightly into his bicep. She nearly lost her balance when he retaliated by kissing one taut nipple. Both of them grabbed the banister to keep from falling.

Hannah was quicksilver in his grasp. She slipped and slithered around him. He groaned aloud when he felt her hand on the buckle of his belt. Halfway to his goal, he looked up at the landing. It was lost in distant shadows.

"Not much farther," he said hoarsely. He was lying to both of them, he thought. The top of the stairs was in another universe.

"Close enough." She had his belt undone now. Her fingers were on his zipper.

"Better wait until we get upstairs," he whispered.

"Can't wait." One nylon-clad foot glided up his leg.

He felt the heat from the inside of her thigh and sucked in his breath. They were never going to make it at this rate. It was time to take unilateral action.

He picked her up, settled her across his shoulder, and clamped one arm across the back of her legs to hold her there.

"Rafe."

He ignored her breathless, sensual laughter. With total determination he took a firm grip on the banister and hauled them both to the top of the stairs. There he turned right and went down the hall to the bedroom he had chosen the day he arrived. It was a big one, with a sweeping view of the bay.

He went swiftly through the doorway and dumped her onto the quilt that covered the old-fashioned four-poster. She lay there amid the pillows, then reached for him with both arms. He fell on top of her.

He kissed her throat while he rummaged with one hand in the drawer of the nightstand. He knew the box of condoms was in there somewhere. He had put it there this evening before leaving the house. Optimism had been riding high at that point. Probably because he had had several engaging fantasies in the shower and had emerged semi-erect. A man was always at his most optimistic when he had a hard-on.

When he couldn't immediately locate the condoms, alarm set in.

"What the hell . . . ?"

"What's wrong?" Hannah's eyes widened. "Are you all right?"

Mercifully his fingers closed around the box. A sense of victory soared through him. "Yeah, sure. I'm fine. Nothing's wrong."

"Good."

"Very good," he whispered. "Excellent, in fact."

She slid her hands inside the wings of his unbuttoned shirt. Her palms were silken on his skin. Breathing took serious effort now.

By the time he was ready, most of their clothing had magically disappeared. He lowered himself between her legs. She raised her knees and tightened her thighs around him.

He cupped her with his hand. She was wet and hot and swollen. When he used the pad of his thumb on the small bud, she quivered violently. His own body nearly exploded in response.

"Now," she ordered, clutching furiously at him. "Now, please, yes. Do it now."

He needed no further urging. If he didn't do it now, it would not get done at all.

He fitted himself to her and started to enter her carefully. She was snug and tight and damp. He tried to take it slow, but when she lifted herself against him, he abandoned all attempt at sophistication and restraint.

There was nothing sophisticated or restrained about how he felt at this moment.

He thrust deeply into her, losing himself in a world of intense sensation. He heard her soft, exultant cry and felt her body grip him with fierce satisfaction. Her head tipped back. Her lips parted in a soundless scream.

She climaxed immediately. He wanted to indulge himself in the pleasure of her release before he surrendered to his own, but he had only a few seconds to enjoy the experience. The small shivers that went through her were more than he could stand. He tried to swallow his own roar of triumph and exultation, but he did not succeed.

※ ※

SHE did not doze, but she was vaguely aware of a sense of detachment from time and reality. It was a pleasant interlude that she knew would not last forever. Nevertheless, she was reluctant to emerge from it.

Rafe sprawled on his back beside her, big and warm enough to heat the whole bed to a cozy temperature. He had one arm behind his head, the other around her. She opened her eyes partway and studied him in the shadows. He looked as relaxed as a large cat after a successful hunt. She raised her head for a better look. Her glance fell on the green numbers of the radio clock.

"*Winston.*" She sat up quickly.

"Huh?" Rafe slitted his eyes. "What's wrong?"

"I've got to get home to Winston." She shoved aside the quilt and scrambled off the bed. "He'll be worried."

Rafe looked amused. "You think your dog worries when you're a little late coming home?"

"Okay, so maybe he won't be worried, exactly." She spotted her panties on the floor and dove for them. " 'Concerned' might be a better word."

"I doubt it."

"Well, he'll certainly need to go outside by now." She stepped into the panties and looked around for her bra. It was nowhere to be found. "He's been cooped up in that house for hours."

"Take it easy." Rafe thrust aside the quilt and got up from the edge of the bed. "I'm sure Winston is fine. He's probably sound asleep."

He was right, she thought. This panicky sensation nibbling at her insides had nothing to do with Winston. She was experiencing some sort of bizarre reaction to what had just happened here in this room. What in the world was wrong with her?

"Have you seen my bra?" she asked. She was glad the lights were still off. She could feel the heat in her cheeks.

He paused in the act of fastening his trousers and reached out to turn on the bedside light. He swept the room with a deliberate look. "Nope. Must have left it back there on the stairs."

She shot him a suspicious glare, almost certain that he was teasing her. She glanced down and saw the toe of her panty hose sticking out from under the bed. Even from here she could see the massive run in the foot of the stocking. With a sigh she shimmied into her dress and groped wildly for the zipper.

"I'll get it for you." Rafe's voice was softer now. He walked across the room to stand behind her. His fingers caught hold of the zipper tab and raised it straight to the base of her neck in a single motion.

"Thank you." Her voice sounded stiff and prim, even to her own ears.

"Sure. Anytime."

She did not dare look at him now. Instead she began to hunt for her shoes.

Rafe shrugged into his shirt. He did not bother to button it. Folding his arms, he lounged against the bedpost and watched her frantic search.

"I don't think your shoes made it upstairs, either," he offered eventually.

"Good grief." She straightened quickly, shoved the hair out of her eyes, and bolted for the door.

He followed her at a more leisurely pace. She ignored him, horrified by the sight of bits and pieces of her clothing strewn on the stairs and in the hall. What had come over her? She didn't do things like this. She must have lost it, big time.

By the time Rafe got downstairs she had retrieved her shoes and her bra and had the door in sight. Clutching her lingerie in one hand, she focused intently on the only thing that mattered at that moment: escape from the scene of her wild, frenzied, totally uncharacteristic passion.

Rafe's voice stopped her cold just as she was about to twist the knob.

"You want to tell me what's wrong, Hannah?"

For a second she could not breathe. She looked down at her trembling fingers. "I think I'm having an anxiety attack."

"Yeah, I can see that. The question is, why?"

His laconic tone chased away some of the panic. Anger rushed in to fill the empty space. This was all his fault. If he hadn't fed her that incredible key lime pie, if he hadn't turned on the music, if he hadn't danced with her in the darkness . . .

If . . .

She whirled around, hands behind her on the knob, and glowered at him.

"Panic attacks happen," she said grimly. "Not my fault."

He studied her for a long, brooding moment. "Second thoughts already?" he finally asked.

She drew a deep, steadying breath. A semblance of reason returned. She could not blame any of this on him. She was the one who had gone crazy here. *Act like a grown-up.*

She cleared her throat. Her fingers tightened on the doorknob. "Sorry. I'm not being real cool, am I?"

"No, but that's not the problem. Nobody ever said you had to be cool." He did not move, just stood there in the hall, watching her. "But for the record, I'd really like to know what went wrong."

"I'm not sure." She released her death grip on the doorknob and shoved her fingers through her hair. She met his eyes. "No, that's not right. Rafe, I need to ask you a question, and you have to tell me the truth."

"What's the question?"

"This." She swept out a hand to indicate the searing passion that had begun in the solarium and ended in his bedroom. "What just happened between us. It didn't have anything to do with Dreamscape, did it?"

His eyes narrowed. "You tell me."

She flinched. "What's that supposed to mean?"

"You've had your wicked way with me, and now you're trying to leave as quickly as you can. Some dumb excuse about a dog, I think. I'll bet you're not even going to call me in the morning, are you?"

"Damn it, Rafe—"

"What the hell am I supposed to think?"

She stared at him, stunned. "Do you really believe that I just . . . I just—" She broke off because her voice was threatening to get lost in a squeaky soprano. She swallowed and tried again. "You think that I just *seduced* you in order to manipulate you into selling your half of this place to me?"

He let her wait a beat. She felt perspiration between her shoulder blades.

Then he smiled slightly. "No."

She sagged back against the doorjamb. "I should hope not. Good Lord, I don't do things like that."

"Neither do I," he said simply.

She looked at him for a long time. Gradually the tension inside her began to seep away. She had gone mad, she thought.

"No. No, of course not." She rubbed her brow. "I don't know why I freaked. I guess I'm just a little stressed."

"You've had a busy night."

"You can say that again." She straightened away from the door, composed herself. "Speaking of which, I think it's time you took me home."

"All right." He fished keys out of a pocket. "On one condition."

She jerked back around. "What condition?"

He walked past her and opened the door. "You gotta promise to call me in the morning."

He was gone, out into the night, before she could think of an appropriate response. She heard the less than civilized growl of the Porsche engine. The lights came on, blinding her.

A vivid mental image of a hapless deer paralyzed by the beams of an oncoming car galvanized her into action.

She slammed the front door shut behind herself. Hand held high to shield her eyes from the merciless glare of the lights, she rushed toward the passenger side door.

WINSTON greeted her with a yawn and his customary good cheer. He bestowed an equally enthusiastic welcome on Rafe. Then he trotted across the porch, went down the front steps, and disappeared into the privacy of the bushes. It was obvious that he was in no great rush to use the facilities.

Rafe looked at her, eyes gleaming. "You're in luck. He doesn't look like he's been worrying too much."

She felt the heat rise in her cheeks. "You've made your point."

"You think so?"

"I've already admitted that my little panic attack back there was an over-reaction to stress."

"Stress, huh? Sounds like another excuse."

"Good night, Rafe."

He caught her chin on the heel of his hand and kissed her very deliberately. He stopped just as she felt the breathlessness setting in again.

"Good night," he said. His eyes were shadowed and intense in the yellow porch light. "You've got my number at Dreamscape and my cell phone number. Call me if Winston goes into his alert mode again tonight, okay? I can be here in less than ten minutes."

"His alert mode?" She had forgotten all about Winston's nocturnal prowling. "Oh, right. That's very kind of you, but I really don't think—"

"I know you're having trouble thinking tonight. You've already explained that." He went down the steps. "Just call me if he does the sentry thing."

She held the door open for Winston. Rafe waited until they were both inside the house before he drove away into the darkness.

Twenty minutes later she emerged from the bathroom clad in her primmest nightgown. It was a Victorian number, pure white, with long sleeves, a ribbon-trimmed neckline, and a hem that fell to her ankles. She glanced once at herself in the mirror and was satisfied with the demure gown. It was definitely not the sort of nightwear favored by women who were in the habit of leaving their undergarments strewn on the staircase while they indulged themselves in a mad, passionate fling with the most exciting man in town.

Make that the most exciting man she had ever met.

An aberration. That was what it had been. It had been much too long since she'd had anything resembling a normal sex life. Aberrant behavior was to be expected under such circumstances.

With a sigh, she switched off the lamp. Winston was already in position at the foot of the bed. He raised his head from his paws when she went to the window that overlooked the bay. She could feel him watching her as she opened the drapes.

"Weren't you even a little bit concerned about the fact that I was so late getting home?" she asked.

He did not dignify that with a response.

"I was afraid of that."

She padded through the shadows to the side window and pulled the curtains wide. She was about to turn back to the bed when she glimpsed the sheen of moonlight on metal between two trees.

"What in the world?"

She gripped the window ledge and peered more closely at the glint. A closer look verified her first impression. There was a car parked in a stand of trees near the road. In that position, whoever was in the vehicle had a clear view of the house and the entrance of the long drive.

She glanced at Winston. He had his muzzle on his paws. Not in alert mode. She closed the drapes again, switched on the light, and picked up the phone.

She punched in one of the numbers she had jotted down on the pad beside the bed.

Rafe answered on the first ring.

"What are you doing out there in the bushes?" she asked.

"Nothing for which I could get arrested."

A small thrill of pleasure rippled through her at the sound of his voice; low, sexy, and just rough enough around the edges to bring back some very recent, very heated memories.

She turned off the light again. Carrying the phone, she went back to the window and opened the drapes a second time. She gazed out into the darkness, searching for the metallic gleam of the Porsche's fender.

"Are you sure about that?" she asked.

"Positive."

Talking to him now on the phone was a lot easier than facing him after that interlude in his bedroom, she discovered. There was a strange intimacy to the experience, but at the same time the distance allowed her to finally relax.

"You're keeping watch, aren't you?" she asked. "Waiting to see if whatever alarmed Winston shows up again."

Silence hummed briefly on the other end.

"Just thought I'd stick around for a few minutes," he said.

"That's not necessary. I told you I'd call if Winston starts prowling. Go home, Rafe. We'll be fine, honest."

"I'll only hang around for a little while. Whatever it is showed up between midnight and two the last couple of times, right?"

"Yes."

"It's almost two. I'll leave soon."

"Rafe—"

"Go to sleep," he said softly.

She clutched the phone more tightly. "Rafe, about tonight—"

"What about it?"

"I apologize for acting like a complete idiot. Asking you whether or not what happened between us was all about Dreamscape was inexcusable. I knew better than that."

"Whatever is going on between you and me, it's not about the house."

She hesitated. "A lot of people in town will think it is."

"Everyone in Eclipse Bay thinks that I seduced you on the beach eight years ago, too." The dismissive shrug in his voice was loud and clear. "Do you really care what people think?"

She contemplated the question for a long moment. "No."

"Neither do I."

"Rafe?"

"Yeah?"

"If what happened tonight wasn't about Dreamscape, what was it about?"

"Good question. When you figure out the answer, let me know."

"Rafe?"

"Yeah?"

"Sometimes you remind me an awful lot of Winston when it comes to communicating."

"Probably a guy thing."

"Good night, Rafe."

"Don't forget to call me in the morning."

She hung up the phone and climbed into bed. She did not even attempt to close her eyes until she heard the muted purr of his car's engine recede into the distance sometime later. She glanced at the clock. It was two-fifteen.

At the foot of the bed, Winston was sound asleep.

13

THE next morning she waited until ten o'clock to call.

"Don't want to look too eager," she told Winston as she punched out the number on the kitchen cordless. "Guys sense it if you're too eager."

Winston looked bored. He went to the door and looked back at her with an expectant expression.

"You've already been out twice this morning." She listened to the phone ring on the other end. "I think you're getting addicted to the beach."

It was true, she thought. Winston's approval of their new lifestyle was evident. He loved running around in Dead Hand Cove with its myriad smells and odd inhabitants. He clearly delighted in his off-leash freedom.

Rafe finally answered the phone.

"This is Madison." He sounded impatient, as if his attention was on something vastly more interesting than a phone call.

She frowned briefly at the instrument in her hand and then held it to her ear again.

"Sorry if I'm interrupting anything important," she said dryly. "I thought you were expecting my call."

" 'Morning, honey." Rafe's voice warmed measurably. "I'm a little busy at the moment. Can I get back to—hang on a second." He broke off abruptly and spoke to someone else. "Take a good look at the wiring in that panel, will you, Torrance?"

"Honey?" Hannah pondered the simple endearment. Rafe had never called her honey, not even last night in the middle of making love to her. Of course, he had not made a lot of conversation in bed.

"Hell, there should be insulation in that wall," Rafe continued in a muffled voice. "Yeah, I can see the pipes. That's why I want insulation in it. Who wants to listen to every flush and shower?"

"Pipes?" Hannah stopped trying to tease out the little nuances of "honey" and focused on the more disturbing word. "Rafe, what's going on there? Is something wrong?"

"I'm getting an assessment of the condition of the plumbing and wiring," he said casually. "The good news is that Isabel had it all brought up to code a few years ago." He paused to speak to someone else again. "Is that copper?"

"Rafe, who are you talking to?"

"The Willis brothers are here," he said into the phone. "I'm having them go over the place from top to bottom."

"You've got Walter and Torrance Willis there?" She shot up from the kitchen chair. "Why?"

"Just getting together some preliminary estimates to see how much it will cost to put in the inn and restaurant," he said with breathtaking innocence.

"You can't do that." She grabbed her keys and broke into a run, heading to the door. "Not without my permission, damn it."

"We both agreed we wanted to open an inn here at Dreamscape."

"We haven't even decided how we're going to deal with the legalities of ownership. Don't you dare touch a thing until I get there."

Winston saw her heading for the door. He started to bounce a little.

"I told you, I'm just getting some preliminary figures together," Rafe said.

"I am coming over there right now. You listen to me, Rafe Madison. I own half of that house. Don't you dare touch a single thing until I get there. And don't let the Willis brothers touch anything, either."

"It's a little late to call them off," Rafe said reflectively. "They're already pretty deep into the plumbing."

"I don't believe this."

She tossed the cordless phone down on the hall table and rushed outside to the car. Winston followed. He leaped into the passenger seat and sat back with an air of anticipation.

"I knew last night was all about Dreamscape," she told him.

SHE sailed through the front door of the big house a short time later, ready for battle. Winston trotted in right behind her, greeted Rafe briefly, and began a tour of the kitchen.

Rafe glanced at his watch as Hannah came to a seething halt in front of him. "Six minutes and twenty-two seconds. You made good time."

She planted her hands on her hips. "What is going on here?"

Rafe was saved the necessity of responding to the question by the small, neatly made man who chose that moment to wander out into the hall.

Compact and completely bald, Walter Willis had always reminded Hannah of an android. There was a mechanical precision about his movements that lacked the casual human element. His speech was clipped and crisp. The starched creases in his work clothes never softened. It was as if he had been designed and constructed under controlled, sterile conditions in a high-tech manufacturing plant.

"Hannah." Walter wiped his hands on a spotless rag that dangled from his belt. "Good to see you again. Heard you were back in town."

Hannah was amazed by her self-mastery. She managed to veil the fuming expression she knew had been blazing in her eyes. She even summoned up what she hoped looked like a genuinely pleasant smile of greeting.

"Hello, Walter," she said. "It's been a while."

"Certainly has." Walter turned his head and called to his brother over his shoulder. "Torrance, come on out here and say hello to Hannah."

Torrance stepped out of the laundry room. His expression brightened instantly. He hoisted a pipe wrench in greeting. "Hey there, Hannah. Welcome back."

The Willises were identical twins, but it was easy to tell them apart because, sartorially speaking, they were polar opposites. If Walter had been engineered to precise specifications on a futuristic, computerized assembly line, Torrance had been someone's home-garage project.

Rather than shaving off what little hair he still possessed as Walter did, Torrance wore his thin, scraggly locks in a ponytail that stuck out through the opening at the back of his cap. The trailing end of a snake tattoo slithered out below one sleeve. His coveralls were stained with what looked like several eons' worth of grease, grime, and pizza sauce. The only things that were clean and shiny about him were the tools in the wide belt that he wore low on his hips.

"Isabel always said the two of you would come back for good someday." Torrance turned to Walter. "Didn't she say exactly that?"

"She sure did," Walter agreed. "If she said it once, she must have said it a hundred times. I believe the last time was the day she had us out here to install the washing machine in the laundry room."

Torrance nodded. "Believe it was." He winked at Hannah and Rafe. "Told us she wanted to leave everything in good working order for you two."

Willis shook his head indulgently. "That Isabel. Always did have a real romantic streak."

Hannah narrowed her eyes. "Don't you two have some plumbing you should be looking at?"

"Plumbing. Whoa. Almost forgot. You heard the lady," Torrance continued. "Reckon we better get back to work."

"Right." Walter's head jerked once in a mechanical nod. "Plumbing. Listen, you two, don't pay any heed to the talk that's going around town these days. Bound to be some for a while, given what happened the night the Sadler girl died and all and now this business with Isabel leaving you the house. But it'll fade quick enough."

"Let's hope so," Hannah said.

Torrance clapped Rafe on the shoulder. "Just want you both to know that me and my brother here never once thought you'd had anything to do with Kaitlin Sadler's death."

"I appreciate that," Rafe replied.

Walter pursed his lips. "Torrance and I always suspected that she got killed by some sex maniac from Seattle. Isn't that right, Torrance?"

Torrance bobbed his head several times. "Yup. That was how we figured it, all right. Not that Chief Yates paid any attention to us."

"Yates just wanted to close the case as fast as possible," Walter said somberly. "He was getting ready to retire. Last thing he wanted to do was leave behind a nasty unsolved murder. Would have spoiled his record."

"Murder." Hannah met Rafe's eyes for a few seconds. He gave her an enigmatic look. She turned back to Walter. "Are you serious? Do you really think Kaitlin was murdered by a sex maniac?"

Walter traded glances with Torrance. "Can't blame us for wondering, given what we found the day we fixed her washer. Right, Torrance?"

Torrance's head went into nodding mode again. "Right. Gotta wonder."

Rafe looked at Walter. "What exactly did you find the day you fixed her washer?"

To Hannah's astonishment, Walter blushed a bright shade of red.

"Kinky stuff," he muttered.

"What kind of kinky stuff?" Rafe asked.

Something in his voice made Hannah glance sharply at him. But she could read nothing in his expression.

Torrance rolled his eyes. "You know. Frilly undies."

Hannah thought about the little demi-bra she had lost on the stairs last night. When her gaze collided with Rafe's, she knew he was thinking about it, too.

"What's so kinky about a woman wearing frilly underwear?" she demanded.

"Well, the stuff we found wasn't exactly little," Torrance said. "Big enough to fit a man."

"Definitely a heck of a lot bigger than Kaitlin," Walter confided. "She was real petite, if you recall."

"There was also a sexy nightgown that was much too big for her," Torrance continued. "And some really large sparkly high heels."

"Don't forget those videotapes," Walter added.

Hannah stared at him. "You found all that stuff inside her washer?"

"Not exactly inside the washer." Torrance hesitated.

"Well, see, once we got goin' on the washer, we realized that her dryer exhaust hose probably hadn't been cleaned in a long time."

"Dangerous things, exhaust hoses," Walter put in seriously. "If they get clogged with lint, they can cause fires. Anyhow, we figured we'd do Kaitlin a favor, so after we finished with the washer, we pulled out the dryer to check the exhaust hose. That was when we found the large-sized undies and the videos and all."

"*Behind* the machine?" Rafe asked carefully.

Torrance nodded violently. "Someone had cut out a big chunk of drywall and stuffed the videos and the ladies' things into the space between a couple of studs."

"Knew right off the female stuff didn't belong to you, Rafe," Walter assured him hastily.

"What was your big clue?" Rafe asked. "Wrong size?"

Torrance guffawed with laughter. "Heck, everyone knew you'd been seein' a lot of Kaitlin that summer. But me and Walter never figured you for one of them transistors."

"Transvestites," Rafe corrected mildly.

Torrance nodded. "Never figured you for one of them."

"You were right about my taste in underwear. I'm a pretty traditional kind of guy."

Torrance's laughter faded. "Anyhow, after Kaitlin died, Walter and I remembered that stuff we found in the wall. That's what made us think she'd been done in by some out-of-town sex maniac."

"From Seattle," Walter concluded.

"Why Seattle?" Hannah asked.

Torrance snorted. "Not the sort of thing they do in Portland."

Hannah looked at Rafe.

He shrugged. "The man has a point. You know what they say about those folks up in Seattle."

She turned back to Walter and Torrance. "You said you told Chief Yates about the videos and the lingerie?"

"Yup, figured it was our civic duty," Torrance said. "But he told us to keep our mouths shut. Said there was enough gossip goin' around as it was. Town didn't need any more."

"Besides, the stuff was gone when we took the chief to Kaitlin's house to show it to him," Walter added. "I don't think he believed us."

Rafe frowned. "The lingerie and videos weren't there when you went back?"

"Nope." Torrance sighed. "That's the main reason Walter and me didn't talk too much about what we'd found. Didn't have any proof, and Chief Yates said we could get in a lotta trouble if we started spreadin' false rumors. Right, Walter?"

"Right," Walter said crisply. "We're not blabbermouths. But we always thought Kaitlin was murdered by that sex maniac she must have been seein'." He looked at Rafe.

"No offense, but everyone knew she was fooling around with other men."

"Yes." Rafe did not look at Hannah. "Even I figured it out. Why do you think the guy who was into the lingerie murdered her?"

"Who knows?" Torrance said.

"Maybe he didn't like the fact that she had those videos," Walter said. "Could be they were films of him dressed in the lingerie."

Rafe's gaze went to Hannah. She saw the glint of curiosity in his eyes. She didn't blame him. She was reluctantly fascinated, herself.

"You think this guy from Seattle went back to Kaitlin's house after he murdered her and stole the lingerie and videos?" Rafe asked.

"Makes sense, doesn't it?" Walter asked. "He wouldn't want to leave any evidence around that might point back to him."

"It's certainly an interesting theory," Hannah allowed cautiously.

"That's all it'll ever be now," Walter said. "Kaitlin's been dead and buried for a long time. No one's going to reopen that old case. Probably for the best." He turned with military precision. "Well, you'll have to excuse us, we've got work to do. Don't we, Torrance?"

"Yup." Torrance's head bobbed up and down half a dozen times with great enthusiasm. "Turnin' this place into an inn with a restaurant attached is gonna be a big project. But you know, it makes a lotta sense. What with the institute and the college and the plans to renovate the old pier and put in more shops, Eclipse Bay is attractin' a lotta visitors these days. Don't have many nice places for 'em to stay. Just the motel out on the highway. Way it is now, folks have to drive on up the coast to find a classy place."

He swung around and lumbered off after his brother.

Hannah waited until both Willises were out of sight. Then she looked at Rafe.

"A sex maniac from Seattle?" she said softly.

"I have a hunch that everyone in town has a personal theory of what happened that night."

"Frilly lingerie in sizes big enough to fit a man?"

"Don't look at me." He held up both hands, palms out. "I never saw any of that stuff."

"What about the videos?"

He shook his head. "Nope. No videos. Hannah, I only went out with Kaitlin a few times before it became real obvious that she was just amusing herself with me while she hunted for her real meal ticket. I never got to know her well enough to learn about her little quirks and eccentricities."

"Hmm. You do realize what this means, don't you?"

He leveled a finger at her. "Nothing. It means absolutely nothing. We only have the Willis brothers' word on what they found in the wall behind her dryer. And no offense to either Torrance or Walter, but they're not the most sophisticated guys to come down the pike. I doubt if they've been any farther than Portland in their entire lives. What looked like kinky clothing and dirty videos to them might be nothing more than a little late-night entertainment to other folks."

"Kaitlin wasn't exactly shy about her own sexual activities. I can't see her going out of her way to protect the reputations of the men she dated, either. If she went to the trouble of hiding that lingerie and those videos to protect a boyfriend, she must have had big plans for the poor guy."

Rafe hesitated. "Kaitlin's supreme goal in life was to marry someone with enough money to help her escape Eclipse Bay."

"So, maybe this particular boyfriend had money. Maybe she saw him as a hot prospect for marriage."

"Why hide the undies and the tapes?"

"Who knows? Maybe he was already married. Maybe she wanted to protect him because she was hoping he'd get a divorce and marry her. Maybe—"

"Whoa," Rafe said. "Lots of maybes here."

She made a face and planted her hands on her hips.

"You're right. Got a little carried away there for a minute, didn't I?"

"Imagination is a wonderful thing. But in this case it's wasted. It's been eight years. We'll never know for sure what happened to Kaitlin that night. Like Walter said, that's probably just as well."

Reluctantly she pulled her thoughts back to the matter at hand. The instant she refocused on her chief problem, her irritation returned.

"Let's get something clear here," she said. "You're not going to do anything to Dreamscape until you and I have come to some agreement about how to handle the legal aspects of Isabel's inheritance."

Rafe pondered the view of the hall. "I could open the restaurant in my half of the house."

"That's crazy. There's no way you can turn half of this place into a restaurant. How would we divide the kitchen? What about all the people who would use *my* half of this hall to get to *your* restaurant? And who gets the solarium?"

"I thought it would make a nice dining room. In the summer I'll set up tables outside on the veranda, too."

"Not without my permission, you won't. Rafe, you just can't run roughshod over the legal technicalities of this inheritance. We're talking several hundred thousand dollars worth of mansion here. We have to settle things first. You know that as well as I do."

"Well," Rafe said a little too casually, "speaking of settling the minor details, I've got a suggestion."

Sensing danger, she went very still. "What is it?"

"How about a partnership?"

She stared at him, momentarily speechless.

"You?" she managed at last. "Me? Partners in Dreamscape?"

"You don't think it would work?"

"What about last night? Are you just going to pretend it never happened?"

"What's last night got to do with it?"

Suddenly she could no longer breathe. "*Everything.* How can you talk about a business partnership after—" She waved a hand, unable to finish the sentence.

"Ah." Understanding lit his eyes. "You're worried about us mixing business with pleasure?"

There was a distant ringing in her ears now. Was that all it had been to him? A pleasant interlude? She struggled to regain her composure.

"Aren't you?" she asked in as cold a voice as she could manage.

"Well, sure," he said far too readily. "Naturally I'll have a problem with it because I'm a Madison. Madisons always have problems when they get their financial affairs mixed up with their sexual affairs. But it shouldn't be a stretch for you. You're a Harte. You can compartmentalize."

He was goading her, she thought. She had to get out of here before she lost it. Hartes did not do that kind of thing. Not in public, at any rate.

"You're right," she said. "I could probably handle it. But as you just pointed out, you're a Madison. You'd screw it up for sure."

She spun on her heel and walked swiftly outside. Winston, ever faithful, trotted out of the kitchen to follow her. Together they went down the front steps without a backward glance.

She yanked open the car door. Winston bounded inside and took up his post on the passenger seat. She got in behind the wheel and slammed the door shut.

The last thing she saw in her rearview mirror was Rafe lounging against the porch railing watching her roar out of the driveway. He had enjoyed seeing her come so close to the edge, she realized. He had deliberately pushed her, just to see what would happen.

A wave of uncertainty swept through her. All of her grandfather's warnings about Madisons flashed through her mind. What kind of game was Rafe playing?

14

RAFE brought the Porsche to a halt in the drive, switched off the engine, and sat for a while, staring at the front door of Mitchell's house.

Asking his grandfather to come to dinner was a crazy idea. If he had any sense he would fire up the engine and drive straight back to Dreamscape. But then he would have to explain to Hannah why he had chickened out.

The thought of going through another scene with her after the one that had taken place this morning when she had arrived to find the Willis brothers hard at work was not appealing. He had taken a chance, pushed his luck, and, predictably enough, things had exploded in his face. He would be more cautious next time. Who said a Madison couldn't learn from his mistakes?

He climbed out from behind the wheel and walked toward the porch steps.

The front door opened just as he raised his hand to knock. A cadaverously thin figure with a buzz cut and a face that looked as if it had been hewn out of the side of a mountain stared at him.

Bryce had worked for Mitchell for nearly ten years. No one knew where he had come from. He had started out as a part-time handyman and had gradually carved out a position as full-time majordomo. If Bryce had a last name, it had been lost in the mists of time. As far as Rafe knew, he had no close relatives. Bryce had brought order to the chaos of Mitchell's household. He was unswervingly loyal to his employer. Beyond that, he was a mystery.

"Hello, Bryce."

"Good afternoon."

"I'm looking for Mitchell."

"Your grandfather is out in the garden."

"Thanks."

Rafe nodded in a friendly manner and walked off down the porch. No point exchanging further pleasantries. Bryce was not one for extended conversations.

Rafe opened the gate and entered the lush wonderland. When he didn't see Mitchell, he took the narrow gravel path that led toward the greenhouse at the far end of the garden.

He found his grandfather inside the opaque structure, tending to a tray of plants. Mitchell had a long-spouted watering can in one hand and a small spade in the other.

Rafe took a breath and stepped into the humid atmosphere of the greenhouse. He recalled Hannah's comment. *Your interest in cooking parallels his in gardening. Creative outlets that you both approach with passion.*

The idea of having something in common with Mitchell was a hard concept to digest.

"Lookin' good in here," he said. He told himself Hannah would have been proud of him for trying to start things off on a civil note. Then again, maybe not. She was pretty pissed at him right now. "You ever think about opening a commercial nursery?"

"Hell, no. Last thing I want to do is turn a good hobby into a business. Ruin all the fun." Mitchell set down the watering can with a *thunk* and scowled ferociously. "Speaking of business, what's this I hear about you opening an inn and a little restaurant out there at Dreamscape?"

"Word gets around fast."

"If you wanted to keep it a secret, you shouldn't have called the Willis brothers out to give you an opinion on the condition of the plumbing and wiring in that old place."

"You're right." Rafe examined a row of tiny pots containing small green plants with glossy leaves. "On the other hand, not much point trying to keep the plan a big dark secret here in Eclipse Bay."

Mitchell gave him a sharp glance from beneath bushy brows. "You're serious about opening an inn?"

"Yeah." Rafe moved on to a tray of feathery ferns. "Been thinking about it for a year now."

Mitchell whistled softly. "Well, shoot and damn. Why the hell didn't you ever say anything?"

"Got to work things out with Hannah first."

"Huh. That's a fact."

Rafe looked up from the ferns. "Aren't you going to tell me that turning Dreamscape into an inn and restaurant is just about the dumbest idea any Madison has ever had?"

"Dumb is beside the point. Madisons don't concern themselves with dumb. They concentrate on what they want." Mitchell's eyes crinkled at the corners as he squinted at Rafe. "You really want this?"

"Yes."

Mitchell studied him for a long moment. Then he nodded once and stripped off a garden glove. "Go for it."

"I beg your pardon?"

"You heard me. If you want it that bad, there's no point in me trying to talk you out of it. You're a Madison. Nothing's going to get in your way. Hell, you've got a better chance of pulling off an inn out there at Dreamscape than most folks."

Rafe was thunderstruck. He stared at Mitchell until he finally got his jaw back in place.

"Are you telling me you think opening an inn and a restaurant is a *good* idea?" he finally managed.

"Didn't say that." Mitchell tossed the glove down on the workbench. "Don't know if it's a good idea or not, to tell you the truth. Just said I could see that nothing was going to stop you. You've got a good head for business when you choose to use it. You could make this inn-restaurant thing work."

Rafe lounged back against a waist-high potting bench, slightly shaken. This was the first time that Mitchell had ever given even halfhearted approval for any idea that did not involve going to work for Madison Commercial.

"Where does Hannah Harte fit into this big plan of yours?" Mitchell asked.

Rafe did not move. He did not even blink. "What do you mean?"

"Last I heard, she still owned half of that old house. Has she agreed to let you buy her out?"

"No."

"Then what the hell are you going to do with her?"

Rafe examined the hibiscus next to him. "I've suggested to her that we form a partnership to operate the inn and restaurant."

"A *partnership*?" Mitchell's face worked in astonishment. "With Hannah Harte? Have you lost every damned marble you've got?"

So much for getting Mitchell's unqualified support.

"You don't have to shout," Rafe said. "I can hear you just fine."

"Now you listen to me. You're a Madison. You can't have a business partnership with a Harte. It'll never work. Never in a million years."

"Okay, so it might be a little more complicated than the usual business partnership," Rafe said.

"Well, shoot and damn." Mitchell grabbed a pair of pruning shears. "The rumors are true, aren't they? You are foolin' around with her, aren't you?"

"We have started what some people might call a relationship. Sort of."

"A relationship?" Mitchell went to work on the hibiscus with the shears. "That mean you're shacking up together?"

Rafe realized that he was standing closer to the hibiscus than was comfortable. He moved a couple of steps aside to give Mitchell and his shears plenty of space.

"I don't think I'd use that term."

Mitchell snipped off a straggling branch and glared. "Well, just what term would you use?"

"Like I said, the situation is a little complicated at the moment."

Mitchell aimed the shears at Rafe. "Pay attention for once in your life. What I got to say is important. That woman put her reputation on the line for you eight years ago. Saved you a lot of grief."

"I know that."

"You can't fool around with her. It's not right."

"I'm not fooling around with her." Rafe searched for the right words, but they eluded him. "Whatever is going on, it's serious."

Mitchell frowned at him for a long, considering moment. "It sure as hell better be serious." Abruptly, he turned back to his pruning. "Why'd you come here today?"

"Came over to see if you want to have dinner with Hannah and me tomorrow night." Rafe hesitated. "Feel free to bring your friend Octavia with you, if you want."

"Octavia's gone back to Portland."

"Invitation still stands."

"Huh." Mitchell clipped off another small branch. "Hannah Harte can cook?"

"I don't know. She's never done any cooking around me. I'll be doing the cooking."

"Should be interesting," Mitchell said.

"Does that mean we can expect you for dinner?"

"I'll be there. Be a change of pace from Bryce's grub."

Rafe exhaled slowly. "Okay. Fine." He straightened and headed for the door. He felt as if he had just weathered a storm. "See you around six."

"Should be *damned* interesting," Mitchell muttered again.

Waste of time, Rafe thought. But what the hell. Maybe Hannah would cut him some slack. He should get some points out of this. After all, it had been her suggestion to invite Mitchell to dinner.

He wondered if it was a bad sign that he was trying to please her.

RAFE paused in the office doorway and studied the scene. There was a computer on the desk. The telephone had several lines. The hardware was nearly buried amid piles of notebooks, photos, and newspapers. The bookcase was crammed with volumes. Several framed front-page editions of the *Eclipse Bay Journal* hung on the walls. One of them featured a photograph of Trevor Thornley standing with the former owner and editor of the newspaper, Ed Bolton, and his smiling wife, Bev.

"I always wondered what a newspaper editor's office looked like," Rafe said.

Jed grinned and leaned back in his chair. "This is what this particular newspaper editor's office looks like. Have a seat."

"Thanks." Rafe cleared a heap of out-of-town newspapers off a chair and sat down.

"Want some coffee?" Jed gripped the arms of his chair as if about to push himself up and out of it. "One thing we've got a lot of around here is caffeine. Part of the mystique."

"No, thanks." Rafe glanced at the computer. The screen showed a page of text. He glimpsed the words. *"Thornley stated that he will run for the Senate on a platform that calls for social and personal responsibility."*

"You got a one-on-one interview with Trevor Thornley?" Rafe asked.

"Did it this morning before he left for Portland. I'm writing an editorial for tomorrow's edition."

Rafe settled back into the chair. "What's it like talking to a future U.S. senator?"

"Not a whole lot different than it was talking to a future member of the state legislature eight years ago. Only he's much more polished these days. But it's still tough to get a straight answer out of him."

"Probably why he's come so far, so fast."

"Probably. Well, like they say, he may be a sonofabitch, but he's our sonofabitch. I think Eclipse Bay can count on him to remember his roots even when he winds up in Washington, D.C." Jed propped his elbows on the chair arms and linked his fingers across his small paunch. "What brings you here today?"

"Idle curiosity."

"The best kind, I always say. That's what makes good reporters." Jed chuckled. "What are you curious about?"

Rafe steepled his fingers. The decision to pay a visit to the offices of the *Eclipse Bay Journal* had seemed a spur-of-the-moment thing. He'd been on his way back to Dreamscape when it struck. But now that he thought about it, he realized that it had been nibbling at the back of his mind all morning, ever since Walter and Torrance Willis had voiced their theories about Kaitlin Sadler having been murdered by a sex maniac from Seattle.

"I've got a favor to ask," he said. "I want to take a look at some old editions of your paper."

Jed's eyes darkened with sudden interest. "How old?"

"Eight years."

Jed whistled tunelessly. "Well, I'll be damned. You want to see the coverage of Kaitlin Sadler's death, don't you?"

"Is that a problem?"

"Hell, no." Jed's chair squeaked as he sat forward abruptly. He fixed Rafe with an intent look. "What's up?"

"Nothing. I told you, I'm just curious, that's all. I didn't pay any attention to the stories that appeared in the paper at the time. I was too busy trying to keep from getting arrested. As soon as I was cleared, all I wanted to do was get out of town."

"An understandable reaction." Jed picked up a pen and absently tapped the edge of the computer keyboard. "Sure you're not looking for something in particular?"

"I'm sure."

"Hey, this is your old buddy, Jed Steadman, boy reporter and pool pal, remember? If you've got a line on what really happened that night, the least you can do is fill me in."

"Think it would still be news after all this time?"

Jed raised his eyebrows. "If you've got anything to indicate that what happened to Kaitlin was something other than an accident, yes, it sure as hell would be news. No one here has forgotten that incident." He paused. "We've only had one real murder in Eclipse Bay in the past decade, and that was when a couple of tourists got into a quarrel out at the RV park and one of them shot the other."

"I don't have a line on Kaitlin's death," Rafe said swiftly. "Just a couple of questions."

"Such as?" Jed paused ever so briefly. "I hate to remind you, but this is my newspaper now."

"I could try the public library."

Jed's grin came and went. "Yes, you could. All right. I've stuck with the agreement." He got to his feet. "Come on, I'll dig them out for you. Can't blame me for trying to find out if you've got an angle on that old story, can you?"

"Guess not." Rafe shoved himself up out of the chair and turned to follow Jed through the doorway. "I'll tell you what I'm looking for, if you'll promise to keep it quiet."

Jed raised one hand as he went down the hall. "Word of honor."

"I want to see if whoever covered the story mentioned the fact that Kaitlin Sadler was seeing someone other than me that summer."

Jed came to a halt in another doorway and gave Rafe a quizzical frown. "Everyone knew she was seeing other men. Hell, *you* knew it. It was no big secret that she was running around."

"I just want to see if the names of any of the other men she dated came up in the course of the investigation."

"Aha." Jed's hand tightened on the edge of the doorjamb. He gave Rafe a knowing look. "You want to see if there were any other serious suspects besides yourself, don't you? What is this? You think maybe one of her other boyfriends really did push her off the cliff that night?"

"I haven't got a single thing to go on here, Jed. I'm curious, that's all. Are you going to let me see those old papers or not?"

"Sorry. Force of habit. Come on, I'll get you set up on the machine."

A short time later Rafe found himself seated in front of a microfilm reader, scanning eight-year-old editions of the *Eclipse Bay Journal.* He paused when he came to the front-page headline that had been printed the morning after Kaitlin's death: LOCAL WOMAN FOUND DEAD AT HIDDEN COVE.

"That's it." Jed hung over his shoulder, one hand gripping the back of Rafe's chair. "I didn't cover the story. I was busy writing up the piece on Thornley's reception at the institute."

Rafe glanced at the byline. "Did you know Ben Orchardson well?"

"No one knew him well, but I learned a few things from him. He was a halfway decent reporter in his day. Worked for a couple of the big-city dailies for several years. But he had a problem with the bottle. Wound up here at the *Journal* for a while, but Ed had to let him go after a few months."

"Is Orchardson still around?"

"Are you kidding? He was sixty-three when he covered the Sadler story. He retired and moved away just before I married Connie. Haven't heard from him since he left Eclipse Bay. I remember him saying something about heading for Mexico or maybe Costa Rica where he could live like a king on his Social Security check while he wrote the great American novel. Doubt if he ever sobered up long enough to buy a computer and go to work, though."

Rafe read through the first story that had appeared, searching for names other than his own. The first one that leaped out was Hannah's. He paused to study the short paragraph that had covered his alibi.

Hannah Harte, daughter of longtime Eclipse Bay summer visitors Hamilton and Elaine Harte, stated that she had been with Raphael Madison at the time of Sadler's death. "We met on the beach near Eclipse Arch a few minutes after midnight," she said. "We talked for a while. Then he walked me home. It was a long walk. We arrived shortly before two."

The words were simple enough, but they had cost Hannah a lot at the time, Rafe reflected. He could imagine what her parents had had to say about the events of that night. But that was Hannah for you. Not a woman to stay silent when she had something to say.

Jed leaned closer. "Something I've always wondered about . . . ?"

The story jumped to an inside page. Rafe advanced the film. "Yeah?"

"Is talking really the only thing you and Hannah Harte did that night on the beach?"

Rafe leaned back and met Jed's eyes. "Yes."

Jed straightened quickly and took a step back. He cleared his throat. "Hey, just a reporter's natural curiosity, you understand."

Rafe turned back to the article and continued reading.

Yates said that he is still investigating Sadler's movements on the night of her death. "No one seems to know where she went or what she did after Madison got out of her car near the Arch. No one has any idea why she was on Hidden Cove Trail at that hour of the night. The trail is closed at sunset. There are no lights . . ."

"Whatever happened to Chief Yates?" Rafe asked as he went on to the next story. "Is he still around?"

"Didn't you know? He died of a heart attack a couple of years ago."

"Wonder if there's any way of getting a look at his old file on the case?"

"The new chief of police is named Sean Valentine. He's a solid guy. He'll probably let you look at the old files, but I doubt that you'll find anything. Orchardson went through them thoroughly at the time. I remember him saying that with you in the clear, there was no other viable suspect. He said he was fairly sure Kaitlin's death had been an accident or suicide."

"I don't buy suicide," Rafe said.

Jed shrugged. "Neither do I. But I can see her having a few drinks and losing her balance on that trail."

"But what was she doing there on the trail in the first place?"

Jed considered for a moment. "Think maybe she went there to treat herself to a couple of beers after she ditched you?"

"I don't know. She didn't have any booze in the car when she dropped me off at the Arch, I can tell you that."

"She could have picked someone up after she left you."

"Yeah." Rafe studied the article on the screen. "Maybe. But Kaitlin was not a big drinker."

Jed crouched down behind the chair and rested an elbow on the back. He eyed the screen over Rafe's shoulder. "You're serious about this, aren't you?"

"Curious, not serious."

"There's a difference?"

"I'm not sure," Rafe admitted. He went back to the front page of the story he had been reading. He paused when he saw a night shot of the brightly lit facade of the Eclipse Bay Policy Studies Institute. "I see Thornley's big event at the think tank that night got squeezed below the fold."

Jed made a face. "Don't remind me. My first big story, and I lost the lead because of the Sadler piece."

Rafe followed the reception story to an inside page and found a photo of the crowd that had attended the Thornley reception. "Looks like most of Eclipse Bay was there."

"Everyone in town was invited, but it was understood that if you went you were expected to donate to Thornley's campaign. That limited the guests to the upwardly mobile among us, the local movers and shakers, and the hustlers who felt they had a stake in getting Thornley elected."

Rafe smiled slightly. "Not a lot of guys like me there, I take it?"

"Not that I recall." Jed grinned. "I was the youngest person there, and the only reason I attended was because I was covering it for the paper."

Rafe leaned back in the chair, thinking. "What time did the reception end?"

"I don't remember precisely. It ran late because Thornley was a little long-winded in those days. And because there was plenty of free booze."

The lights had still been on at the institute when he walked Hannah home along Bayview Drive, Rafe thought. "So, it would probably be safe to say that everyone who attended the Thornley reception that night has a reasonably solid alibi."

Jed slanted him a speculative glance. "Yes. I could probably dig up the old guest list if you want to look at it. As the only representative of the local media at the event, I'm sure I got a copy. It might be in my files. But Kaitlin didn't move in those circles, Rafe. Why would anyone from that crowd want to kill her?"

"Good question." Rafe thought about the oversized lingerie, the high heels, and the videos that the Willis brothers claimed to have discovered behind Kaitlin's dryer. No point in mentioning them, he thought. He had nothing hard to go on yet. "You're right. There's nothing here, Jed. Sorry I wasted your time."

"No problem," Jed replied. "Keep me in mind if you get any other wild hairs, okay? This is a slow news town. I wouldn't mind a big exposé on the Sadler death, especially if it involves an eight-year cover-up. Pulitzers have been won on less."

"Don't worry," Rafe said. "If I get any more brainstorms, you'll be the first to know."

15

"IT was one of the more embarrassing moments of my life." Hannah propped her heels on the ottoman, sank deeper into the brown leather sofa, and sipped glumly on the hot green tea Pamela had given her. "I couldn't believe that I was standing there in the front hall of Dreamscape, yelling at him. I know the Willis brothers were listening to every single word. The story will be all over town by now."

Pamela, ensconced in the big recliner on the other side of the coffee table, curled one leg under herself. She wrapped her hands around her own mug and smiled wryly. "Very un-Harte-like."

"Very."

"One could almost call it outrageous. For a Harte, at any rate."

A searing vision of her black bra lying on the staircase at Dreamscape flashed before Hannah's eyes. If Pamela only knew, she thought, just how outrageous she had been in the past twenty-four hours.

"I'm glad you find it so amusing," Hannah muttered into her tea. "I'd like to remind you that half of Dreamscape belongs to me. I had a right to scream some when I realized what he was doing."

"Of course you did."

"You're not taking this seriously, are you?"

Pamela raised one brow in a very knowing fashion. "I'm waiting for the other shoe to drop, as it were."

Both shoes had dropped last night before she even got upstairs, Hannah recalled. "What's that supposed to mean?"

"You're involved in a sticky situation with a Madison," Pamela said. "So far, all you've done is yell at him in front of witnesses. That may be a big scene for a Harte, but I doubt if it even ruffled Rafe Madison's hair. The question here is, what happens next?"

Hannah swallowed more tea and submerged herself deeper into the pool of gloom. "He's proposed a partnership in an inn and restaurant."

"A partnership?" Pamela's eyes widened behind the lenses of her glasses. "You and Rafe Madison? Oh, my."

"It's impossible, of course."

"Of course."

"It would never work."

"Never in a million years. I can't even begin to imagine what your family would say about the notion of you and Rafe opening an inn together."

"I prefer not to think about it."

Pamela looked as though she was attempting to suppress a smile.

"What?" Hannah demanded.

"I'll say one thing about you and Rafe Madison," Pamela murmured. "You two don't get together often, but when you do, it's never dull."

The sound of a vehicle in the drive saved Hannah from having to come up with a response to that observation. Two small whirlwinds, both dressed in jeans, T-shirts, and miniature running shoes, blew into the front room. They flew toward the door. A massive beast that went by the wholly inappropriate name of Kitty followed in their wake.

Kitty was the reason Winston had remained at the cottage that afternoon. Kitty did not care for Winston. Hannah was fairly certain that the feeling was reciprocated. On the one occasion when Winston and Kitty had been introduced, she had caught Winston eyeing Kitty with a peculiar gleam in his eye. It was the same gleam that he got when he chased seagulls on the beach. For her part, Kitty had hissed and growled and generally made it clear that she was not a dog lover.

"Daddy's home, Daddy's home," the whirlwind named Rose chanted happily as she stretched both hands overhead and tried to seize the doorknob.

Mark, Rose's older brother, grabbed the knob before she could get a grip on it. "I get to show him my new maze before you make him look at your stupid drawing."

"My drawing isn't stupid." Rose looked at Pamela for confirmation of her artistic ability. "It isn't stupid, is it, Mom?"

"It's beautiful," Pamela assured her. "We're going to hang it on the refrigerator with the others just as soon as you finish it."

Rose whirled back to her brother. "Told you so, you big dummy. You don't know what you're talking about."

Pamela gave Hannah an amused glance. "I think she takes after me. Not at all reticent about standing up for herself."

Hannah grinned. "It's so thrilling to see the genes pass down to another generation."

"Ever think about producing your own little bundle of Hannah genes?"

Hannah watched the two children battle over who got to open the door for Brad. A pang of deep longing twisted through her. She gazed at Mark and imagined a little boy with Rafe's eyes. For the first time she wondered if her growing restlessness this past year had something to do with her ticking biological clock.

"Funny you should ask," she said softly. "Of course, there's one small problem. I need more than just Hannah genes to create the final product."

The front door opened, and Brad walked into the hall. He was a fair-haired man with earnestly intelligent eyes framed by wire-rimmed glasses. There was a deceptively quiet, deeply thoughtful way about him that belied a quick, razor-sharp brain. He was fashionably rumpled in what passed for academic chic. His button-down shirt and khaki trousers were both wrinkled. The loud, awkwardly knotted tie, scuffed leather shoes, and bulging book bag accented the young, professorial look.

He barely had time to wave a hand toward Hannah before the two whirlwinds and Kitty descended on him.

"Daddy, wait until you see the maze I built."

"Daddy, Daddy, I want to show you my picture."

Brad crouched to greet his children and the family cat. There was genuine pleasure on his face.

Hannah watched the intimate little family ritual of greeting daddy and was horrified when she detected a hint of dampness on her own lashes. She blinked hurriedly and looked away. What was wrong with her today? At this rate she would soon be an emotional basket case. She had to get a grip on herself. Pamela was watching her with gathering concern.

"Are you okay?" Pamela pitched her voice below the hubbub taking place in the front hall. "Something wrong?"

"No, of course not. I'm fine." Hannah took a long, reviving swallow of tea. "I've been a little tense since the scene with Rafe this morning, that's all. I've got to do something about the problem of Dreamscape, Pam. The situation is a mess. It has to be resolved."

It was Brad who responded. He wandered into the living room, Rose and Mark bobbing around his legs. "From what I heard this afternoon, Rafe Madison has his own plans for Dreamscape. What's going on? Are you going to sell him your half of the house?"

"He isn't offering to buy it," Hannah said dryly. "He's proposing a partnership."

Brad considered that. "Maybe he can't afford to buy out your half."

"From what I can tell, money is not a problem for Rafe," Hannah said.

Brad met her eyes. "Then what's the issue? Pamela has told me something about the history of the Hartes and the Madisons. I got the impression that there was no love lost between the two clans."

"I'll admit that we haven't socialized much in the past three generations."

"Why would Rafe Madison want to get involved in a business partnership with you?" Brad asked.

"Beats me." Hannah decided it was time to change the subject. "How's tricks with you, Brad?"

"As a matter of fact, I have some good news. I got a call from the director of the institute this morning. He offered me the joint appointment. I start the first of the month."

"*Yahoo!*" Pamela leaped off the recliner and threw her arms around Brad. "Congratulations! I knew you'd get it."

Brad grinned at Hannah over Pamela's head. "I think I may have had a little help from my friends. Rumor has it that Perry Decatur mysteriously withdrew his objection to the appointment."

"That little S.O.B." Pamela made a face. "I knew he was the one who was holding up the process. He's jealous as all get-out. He's afraid you're going to show him up for the lightweight he is once you're on the faculty there. Which you will, of course. Wonder what made him back off?"

"Why don't you ask Hannah?"

Pamela swung around, a hundred questions in her eyes. "What's going on?"

"Not much," Hannah said mildly. "Perry asked me to attend the Thornley reception last night. He wanted to impress everyone at the institute with his contacts. You get the picture."

"Got it," Brad said. "The Hartes are one of the most important families in town. Having a representative from the family there last night would have been a coup for Decatur."

"As it happened," Hannah continued, "I discovered that a former Weddings by Harte client was also scheduled to attend the reception. Perry was angling to get him to endow a research fund at the institute."

"Tom Lydd," Brad said.

Hannah nodded. "You are good. Something tells me you'll go far at the institute."

"And you had a word with Lydd, I take it?"

"All I did was mention that I knew the institute's selection committee had your name under consideration for a joint appointment and that you would make a wonderful addition to the faculty. Tom Lydd took it from there."

Brad exhaled deeply. "Decatur must have blown a gasket."

Pamela slapped a palm across her own mouth and then exploded with laughter. "A classic Harte tactical maneuver. Your folks would be so proud of you."

"I owe you," Brad said to Hannah. He looked serious.

"No, you don't." She grinned, feeling somewhat cheered for the first time since the scene at Dreamscape that morning. "Perry Decatur owed me for something that happened eight years ago. It was payback time."

Brad shook his head. "You Hartes sure do have long memories."

Hannah wasn't sure that he meant it as a compliment.

⁂

SHE drove back to the cottage later that evening after sharing dinner with the McCallister family. The meal, with all its noise and chaos, had done wonders to improve her mood, she realized.

Maybe she could finally do some clearheaded thinking tonight. She needed to put things in perspective. Not that it was easy to gain any sort of real perspective on Rafe Madison. But the good news was that she was no longer feeling as unsettled as she had for the better part of the day. She was a Harte. As Pamela had reminded her, she was supposed to be good at strategic planning and tactics. Hartes did not allow themselves to get tangled up in messy emotions when it came to business. That was a Madison characteristic.

She had to start concentrating on the business aspects of Dreamscape. She could not allow Rafe to muddy the waters again.

Something told her that would be easier said than done. Madisons were very good at muddying things, she reflected as she pulled into the driveway in front of the darkened house.

She switched off the engine, climbed out from behind the wheel, and started toward the front door with a vaguely wistful sensation. She didn't have a loving husband and a couple of lively kids waiting to greet her, but at least she had Winston.

Faithful, loyal, lovable Winston.

She put her key in the lock and waited for the muted sounds of doggy welcome. But there was no muffled scratch of toenails on hardwood, no happy whine.

The first tingle of unease shot through her. Winston was an alert dog. His hearing was almost preternatural. Surely he had caught the sound of the car in the drive.

Quickly she unlocked the door, opened it, and stepped into the hall.

"Winston?"

There was no response.

"Winston? Where are you? Here, Winston. Look, I'm sorry about Kitty. I admit that I patted her on the head a couple of times, but that was all, I swear it."

Winston did not come trotting around the corner.

She switched on a light and walked into the kitchen. Most of the water she had left in one of the twin stainless-steel bowls on the floor was untouched. The expensive chewing bone had been abandoned under the table.

Unease turned to concern that was only a little shy of panic. Something was wrong.

"Winston?"

She hurried back into the living room and started up the stairs. Perhaps he had gotten himself trapped in a bedroom or a bathroom when a door had accidentally closed. Frantically she tried to think of reasons why an inside door would suddenly swing shut. A draft? But if Winston was locked in an upstairs room, why wasn't he barking furiously to let her know where he was?

By the time she reached the top of the stairs, she was running. A single glance down the hall showed her that all of the doors stood wide open.

She darted from room to room, checking under beds and inside closets. There was no sign of Winston.

It occurred to her that he must have somehow gotten out of the house on his own and wandered off. It was a very un-Winston-like thing to do, but for all his canine cleverness he was still a dog and dogs were born explorers.

She went slowly back downstairs and came to a halt once more in the hall, pondering the mystery of how he might have escaped the house. The front door had been locked when she returned. That left the kitchen door and the mudroom door.

A quick check in the kitchen revealed that that door, too, was still securely locked. With mounting trepidation she walked back out into the hall and turned right. Automatically she switched on lights as she went toward the rear of the house.

The small mudroom was swathed in darkness. She hit the light switch and glanced quickly around the neat clutter. Rain gear, umbrellas, beach shoes, and a stack of old towels filled most of the space. Two brooms and an aged mop stood in the corner.

She studied the door. It was closed, but it was unlocked. She could not have forgotten to lock up before she left for Pamela's earlier in the day, she thought. It simply wasn't possible. She had lived alone in the city too long to neglect such simple precautions.

Even if she had left it unlocked, how had Winston gotten it open? He was a brilliant dog, but he had paws, not hands. It was pushing credibility much too far to believe that he had somehow managed to twist the doorknob and open the door. A specially trained dog might have accomplished the feat, but Winston had never been taught to do fancy tricks.

It was hard to believe that she had left this door not only unlocked but ajar. But she must have done just that. It was the only conceivable way that Winston could have gotten out of the house.

Despair engulfed her. Winston was somewhere outside in the darkness, possibly lost and terrified. If he reached the road, he might get hit by a car.

She whirled around, yanked open a cupboard, and grabbed a flashlight. She would need it. Although there was a moon, the fog was thickening rapidly.

She seized a faded windbreaker from a wall hook, pulled it on, and opened the mudroom door. She stepped out onto the rear porch and switched on the flashlight.

"*Winston.*"

A faint bark sounded in the distance. It was barely audible above the muted rumble of the light surf at the base of the cliffs, but her heart leaped in relief. Winston was in Dead Hand Cove.

She plunged down the steps and entered the ghostly tendrils of gathering fog. The beam of the flashlight infused the surrounding mist with an unearthly light. With the ease of long familiarity, she made her way toward the path that led down the rocky cliff to the beach.

"Winston. Talk to me. Where are you?"

This time she got a series of hard, sharp, excited barks. They definitely emanated from the cove, but they did not sound as if Winston was moving toward her. She wondered if he had somehow managed to trap himself inside one of the small caves at the base of the cliff.

At the top of the path she paused to shine the flashlight down on the rocky beach. The beam pierced the mist in places, revealing a wide swath of damp sand. The tide was coming in, but it had a ways to go before the water filled the cove. She could still make out the tips of the five fingers. But sprays of foam were already dampening the rocky monoliths. In another hour or so the water would cover all but the tallest of the stones.

Winston barked again, louder this time. She was definitely getting closer to him, she realized. But he was not making any headway toward her.

She started cautiously down the pebble-strewn path that led to the tiny beach. Only the fact that she had used the trail for years and knew it better than she knew the streets of Portland made it possible to navigate it at night with some confidence. The foggy darkness and the slippery rocks made for slow going. Twice she lost her footing and had to grab at a stony outcropping to save herself from a nasty fall.

She was breathing hard by the time she reached the rough beach. Immediately she shone the light along the dark voids that marked the caves.

"Winston!"

Another series of barks sounded in the mist. Behind her now. But how could that be? Fresh alarm swept through her.

She turned quickly to face the fingers. Aiming the flashlight toward the thumb, she started cautiously across the damp sand.

Spray dampened the front of her windbreaker. A wave broke at the entrance to the cove. Cold seawater swirled around her feet. Should have taken time to put on a pair of boots, she thought.

More loud, demanding barks punctuated the mist. Winston was getting impatient. Perhaps he had bounded up onto a finger before the tide returned and was now reluctant to jump down because he would get wet. But that didn't make any sense. Winston wasn't afraid of a few inches of water. She gasped when another swirl of cold foam lapped at her ankles.

She started toward the nearest finger and aimed the beam of the flashlight at the top. There was no dog there. Methodically she shone the light on the next monolith. The spray had thoroughly dampened her hair and face now. She would take a hot shower when she got back to the house. She definitely did not need a case of hypothermia.

It was getting harder to see through the ever-thickening fog, but she managed to make out the shape of the second finger. There was something wrong about it.

Another string of tense barks echoed in the fog. Definitely coming from the vicinity of the second finger.

She hurried forward, ignoring the cold water now swirling around her calves. The beam of the flashlight fell on a large square animal cage perched atop the monolith. Winston was inside.

"Oh, my God, Winston! What happened?" She sloshed toward him through the slowly deepening water. "Who did this to you?"

She found the door of the cage and yanked it open. Winston exploded into her arms. He was damp and trembling. She staggered backward under the impact, slipped, and barely managed to keep her footing. Winston lapped happily at her face. The flashlight beam arced wildly in the darkness as she clutched at him.

"After this little incident, I'm going to have more gray hair than you do," she whispered into his wet fur. "What on earth happened here?"

But Winston had no answers for her.

She carried him quickly toward the beach. "I'm going to call the police. This is a small town. The chief will know which one of the local punks would pull a vicious trick like this. I'm going to press charges. I swear it."

Winston licked her ear.

She set him down at the water's edge. "Come on, let's get you home and dried off. I wonder how long you were out there on that rock? I can't wait to get my hands on whoever did this. I'll—"

Winston interrupted her with a low, startlingly savage growl. She flashed the light down at him and saw that his whole attention was focused on the darkness that cloaked the cliff path. The tension in him was the only warning she got.

"Winston, no!" She grabbed his collar just as he leaped forward. "No. Winston, stay."

He obeyed instantly, but she could feel him quivering with predatory urgency. There was someone in the vicinity of the cliff path. Someone Winston did not like.

Fear crashed through her. She had to assume that whoever was on the trail was the same person who had caught Winston and set him out on the monolith to drown.

At the same instant it occurred to her that although she could not see the person watching from the shadows, he could certainly see her. The flashlight in her hand made a very effective beacon.

She turned off the beam and crouched down beside Winston. "Hush." She closed her fingers lightly around his muzzle. She did not think his low growls could be heard above the sound of the incoming tide, but if he started barking again, he would give away their location.

Winston shuddered under her hands. His attention never wavered from the cliff path.

One thing was certain, Hannah thought as she waited for her eyes to adjust to the new level of darkness. They could not go up the path. They would run straight into whoever waited there. Nor could they just stay here in the cove like sitting ducks.

Keeping her fingers around Winston's muzzle, she tugged on his collar to guide him.

"This way," she whispered. "Heel, or whatever it is dogs are supposed to do at times like this."

If Winston was offended by the command, he was gracious enough not to complain. He paced obediently along beside her. She bent low, not daring to take her fingers off his muzzle as they made their way toward the dense darkness of the cliff caves. She relied on the sighs and splashes of the returning seawater to cloak whatever noise she made as she scrambled over the rocks with Winston.

The biggest danger would come from tide pools that littered the cove. At night, without a flashlight, each one was a potential trap. Things slipped and slithered under her feet, but Winston detoured safely around the edges of the pools.

The deeper darkness of a cave entrance loomed in her path. The scent of rotting seaweed enveloped her. But for once Winston showed no interest in the fascinating odors that assailed his nostrils. He was alert and focused. She did not dare release her grip on his muzzle.

"Hush," she said again. "Please, hush."

He gave a low, almost inaudible whimper and quivered tensely.

She put out one hand and felt for the wall of the cave. When her palm made contact with the damp rock she started cautiously forward. Winston must have sensed her intention or perhaps he was merely responding to some ancient den-seeking impulse. Whatever the reason, he willingly took the lead as they made their way deeper into the convoluted cavern.

As soon as they rounded the corner, they lost what little fog-reflected moon-light there was coming through the mouth of the cave. The quality of the dark-ness took on a deeper, thicker feel. Hannah could see nothing now. She stumbled awkwardly along, blindly following Winston. But after she bumped her head on a rocky outcropping and scraped a knee, she decided to risk the flashlight again.

She kept the beam pointed straight down toward the rising floor of rock. Winston trotted forward through the sandy rubble that littered the bottom of the cavern. He no longer seemed inclined to bark. Cautiously, she released his muzzle.

The path led through a series of small, damp chambers. She stumbled over the remains of an old pink-plastic sandal. Probably one that she or her sister had lost when they had come here to play years ago, she thought.

The cavern branched off in several directions. Some of the tunnels were too narrow for any human to pass through, although Winston could have made it. She selected a passage she had often used in the past. Her brother, Nick, had marked it with an **X** painted in red. Here in the endless gloom the paint had faded little over the years.

Winston strained forward more eagerly now, perhaps sensing the fresh air that wafted in from the far end of the twisted passage. They rounded a bend. There was a difference in the density of the light at the far end of the cavern. She realized she was looking at night and fog now, not at rock wall.

Hastily she doused the flashlight beam again and allowed Winston to draw her quickly toward the exit. His mood had altered. He was still eager, but he seemed excited and cheerful, no longer the hunter confronting danger.

"Hannah."

The shock of hearing her name called loudly just as she and Winston emerged from the cavern sent a jolt through her. The realization that it was Rafe's voice that echoed in the mist brought a nearly paralyzing sense of relief.

"Over here, Rafe."

Winston whimpered and bounded up the slope that led to the top of the cliff. She rushed after him. They were both running now.

Hannah did not slow down when she saw Rafe silhouetted against the glare of the flashlight. She kept going at full speed, straight into his arms.

16

AN hour later Rafe heard her stalk back into the kitchen behind him. He removed the pan of steaming cocoa from the stove and glanced over his shoulder.

She had washed and dried her hair and tucked it back behind her ears. A thick white toweling robe was belted around her narrow waist. Her face was pink and flushed. He knew that the high color in her cheeks was not from the hot shower she had just taken. She was still fuming.

He hadn't entirely recovered from the roller coaster of emotions he'd been through in the past hour either, he realized. Hannah and Winston had been through a bad experience, but the whole event had not been a picnic for him. He'd endured his own private ordeal.

First there had been the nightmare images he had envisioned when he knocked on the front door of the house and received no answer. Given the fact that Hannah's car was in the drive, he'd started out with the worst-case scenario—that she was upstairs in her prissy little bedroom with another man. When he'd finally climbed out of the dark pit into which that vision had cast him, he'd summoned up some common sense and logic. Even if Hannah had been engaged in passionate sex upstairs, he reasoned, Winston would have come to the door.

Winston had not come to the door. Ergo, Winston and Hannah had gone for a walk. Given the fog and the late hour, however, that conclusion had induced other, equally disturbing scenarios. The tide was coming in. It was a damfool time to go walking on the beach.

When he'd finally spotted them coming toward him from the vicinity of the caves, the relief that had flashed through him had been stunning. Then Hannah had launched herself into his arms, and he'd realized that she was scared and shivering. Her clothes and hair were wet.

She'd told him the full story on the way back to the house, and he'd been chilled to the bone by the tale. A hundred variations on disaster had assailed him. She could have been swept up in the churning waters of the cove while attempting to rescue Winston. What if whoever she thought had watched her from the path had pursued her and the dog into the caves?

After the visions had come the questions, the primary one being, what the hell was going on? He'd made the cocoa partly as therapy for himself. Cooking always centered him and allowed him to think more clearly.

He'd done a lot of thinking while he stirred the hot chocolate and waited for Hannah to come back downstairs. He'd even managed to reach a few conclusions. He was calm and cool again, he told himself. He was back in control.

"Sit down," he instructed. "I'll pour you a cup of this stuff. Winston has already had his treat."

She looked at Winston, who was flopped under the table. Rafe had dried him off and fluffed his fur with some of the old towels in the mudroom. He looked none the worse for his ordeal. In typical dog fashion, he appeared to have forgotten the entire experience.

The same could not be said of Hannah, Rafe thought.

"I still can't believe that that twit at the police station actually said they could not spare an officer to investigate what happened to Winston tonight." She dropped into a chair at the kitchen table. "The woman acted as if I had phoned in a complaint about some stupid childish prank."

"Try not to take it personally." Rafe poured the cocoa into a mug and put it on the table. "This is a small town, remember? There aren't many officers on the force. The dispatcher explained that they were all busy out at Chamberlain tonight because of the big rally."

"I *am* taking it personally. Winston would have drowned if I hadn't found him in time."

"Maybe, but once you told the dispatcher that you and the dog were okay and that there was no sign of forced entry here at the house, you lost your status as an emergency."

"I know, I know." She heaved a sigh and then, frowning slightly, she sniffed. She looked down at the mug of cocoa he had put in front of her. "That smells good."

"Drink it."

Obediently she took a sip. "Just what the doctor ordered. Thanks."

"You're welcome." He sat down across from her. "I went back to the edge of the cliffs and looked for that cage or animal trap or whatever it was. But it's gone."

"Knocked off the finger by the incoming waves, no doubt." She took another sip. "Maybe it will get washed ashore or left on the sand when the tide goes out tomorrow. I'll watch for it. It's the only evidence I've got."

"Even if you find it, I doubt if it will prove useful. There won't be any fingerprints left on it by the time the sea gets finished with it."

She looked dismayed. "You're probably right."

Rafe glanced down at Winston. "Someone must have opened the back door and enticed him into the trap."

"Probably wouldn't have been too hard." Her mouth tightened. "A nice chunk of raw steak would have gotten his attention."

"The real question is, how did the mudroom door get unlocked?"

She pursed her lips. "I've been thinking about that. It's no secret that Mom and Dad leave a spare key with a realtor here in town who looks after the place when no one in the family is using it. It's not too much of a stretch to imagine someone stealing the key or copying it."

He thought about it. "Maybe. But it seems like more trouble than the average kid would go to just to play a nasty prank."

She looked at him with troubled eyes. "You think this was something more than a vicious stunt?"

He shoved his hands into the front pockets of his trousers. "If you put this incident together with the possibility that someone may have been watching your house at night on and off this past week, you've got the makings of a stalker scenario."

She shuddered. "That occurred to me while I was in the shower. But it would have to be someone who had followed me from Portland, and I honestly can't think of anyone there who is obsessive about me."

"The ex-fiancé?"

She looked genuinely taken aback by the suggestion. Then she shook her head with grave certainty. "No, definitely not Doug. He's not the type."

"I'm not sure the type is always obvious."

"Our engagement ended a year ago. Why would he start stalking me now? And why follow me here to Eclipse Bay to do it? He doesn't know his way around this town. Whoever trapped Winston and stuck him out on that finger knows a lot about this place."

"Good point. Got to be someone from Eclipse Bay. Someone who knew about the fingers and the tides in Dead Hand Cove. Someone who knew how to get a key to this house."

"What are you thinking, Rafe?"

"I'm thinking Perry Decatur."

"Perry?" She sat back, startled. "Oh, no, that's ridiculous. Why would he do something like that?"

"To get even for the way you finessed his move to keep Brad McCallister off the faculty at the institute?"

She chewed on her lower lip for a few seconds and then shook her head again. "I suppose it's possible. But I don't think so. Not his style. Perry's a convincing little twerp, but I don't see him pulling a stunt like this."

"Why not?"

"Well, for one thing, whoever carried that cage out to the finger had to get wet and dirty doing it. Perry isn't the type to get wet and dirty if he can help it. Plus there was a real risk of getting caught in the act if I came home early. Perry doesn't take risks if he can avoid them. He prefers to maneuver behind the scenes."

Rafe was unconvinced. "I don't know. He was plenty pissed last night."

She exhaled heavily. "It just doesn't feel like the kind of trick he would pull. More likely it was a local kid. A budding little sociopath who has graduated from setting fires to torturing animals."

Rafe said nothing.

"You've got a problem with my logic?"

"I'm just thinking," he said.

"I can see that. And it makes me nervous."

"Me, thinking, makes you nervous? Why?"

"Because the last time you did some serious thinking you decided to make us partners in Dreamscape."

"That's different."

"Bull."

"It's going to work. You'll see, partner."

She pointedly ignored that. "What, exactly, are you thinking about what happened tonight?"

He hesitated and then decided there was nothing to be gained by keeping silent. "I'm thinking that whatever is going on here might not be about you."

"Not about me? That was my dog out there on the finger."

"What I meant was it might not be about you alone." He paused. "It might be about us."

"Us? You mean someone doesn't like the idea that we're——" She broke off and made another run at it. "Someone doesn't like the rumors that are going around about us? But why on earth would anyone care if we're, uh——"

"Sleeping together?" he offered helpfully.

"One time," she said swiftly. "There was only one time. That does not exactly constitute a flaming affair."

For some reason he found that observation both extremely irritating and strangely depressing. "Can't argue that."

She sipped her cocoa for a moment, then put the mug down. "I just had a thought. Maybe whoever did this is one of your old flames. A jealous lover from your misspent past?"

"Doubt it."

She was undeterred. "Good grief. If I'm right, we've got more suspects than we can count."

His incipient depression vanished in the heat of a sudden, fierce anger. He sat forward quickly, flattening his palms on the table. "My reputation in this town was always a hell of a lot more exciting than the reality."

She blinked. "Now, Rafe——"

"Trust me on this. I was there."

She cleared her throat. "Well, yes, of course you were, but everyone knows about your reputation in those days."

"This may come as a stunning surprise to you, but contrary to popular opinion, I don't have a legion of old flames hiding in the bushes here in Eclipse Bay."

"I don't believe I used the word 'legion.' "

"Close enough. For the record, virtually all of my dates——and there were not as many of them as everyone seems to think——were weekend or summer visitors who came here for the beach, the boardwalk, and a good time. They knew what they were doing and so did I. There was nothing serious with any of them, and I've never seen any of them again."

Her jaw clenched visibly. "There was Kaitlin Sadler."

"Yes. There was Kaitlin Sadler. She was a year older than me, experienced, and she could take care of herself."

"I never implied that you took advantage of her. No one ever said that."

"I didn't have a lot of rules for myself in those days, but I had a few and I stuck to them. I never got involved with anyone who was married or too young or too naïve to know the score. Hell, you ought to know that better than anyone else."

"Me?" She gripped the edge of the table. "Why should I know anything about the history of your love life?"

"Because I never laid a hand on you eight years ago, that's why."

For the space of two or three heartbeats she simply stared at him in utter astonishment. Then she pulled herself together with an obvious effort. "Of course you never touched me. I wasn't your type. You wouldn't have looked twice at me if we hadn't been stuck out there at the Arch together that night."

A cold, mirthless amusement shafted through him. "You weren't my type, and you were squarely in the 'don't touch' category as far as I was concerned, but that doesn't mean that I didn't look twice."

Her eyes widened. "Because I was a Harte? Was I some sort of challenge?"

"The fact that you were a Harte had nothing to do with it."

"Then why did you look twice?"

"Damned if I know. Pure masochism, probably, because I sure as hell knew that you'd never look twice at me."

"That's not true." She shot to her feet. "I had a crush on you. Every girl in Eclipse Bay did."

"That's supposed to thrill me?" He was suddenly on his feet, too, although he had no recollection of getting out of his chair. "To know that for you I was just the interesting bad boy with the bike and the leather jacket and the dangerous rep? The kind of guy your parents always warned you about? The kind of guy it might be amusing to fool around with but definitely not the kind you would ever marry?"

A fresh tide of hot color rose in her face. He could have sworn he had embarrassed her. Good. Served her right. But her gaze did not slide away from his.

"How did you know what kind of man I'd marry?" she asked evenly.

"You told me that night, remember? You were only nineteen and you already had your damned list of requirements for a husband made out."

"I was twenty, not nineteen, and I swear, if you mention that list one more time—"

He reached for her. He closed his hands around her shoulders and hauled her up against his chest. "As far as I'm concerned, I don't care if I never hear about that damned list of yours again for as long as I live. Furthermore, I'm not real keen on hearing about your new, updated version of it, either."

"Uh, Rafe, you're acting a little weird here. Maybe the stress—?"

"Yeah. Maybe."

He covered her mouth with his own, letting the fierce tension that was eating him up inside pour into her. She made a soft, muffled sound, and then her arms closed tightly around him and she was kissing him back with all the passion that had infused her anger a few seconds earlier.

"My God," he muttered against her throat. "Do you have any idea of the scare you gave me tonight?"

"Scare?" Her own voice was muffled because she was frantically kissing his jaw. "Why were you scared?"

"First, because I thought maybe the reason you weren't answering the door was that you were with some other man."

"No. Really?" She went very still. Then she pulled back slightly and looked at him with wide, fascinated eyes. "You were actually afraid that I might be in bed with another man? Did you think that I might have a few old flames of my own here in Eclipse Bay?"

"Let's not go there." He refused to be sidetracked again by that possibility. "My other big fear was that you'd gone for a walk with Winston and fallen on the rocks."

"Like Kaitlin Sadler?"

"I wasn't thinking of Kaitlin," he said bluntly. "All I could think about was you." He wrapped his fingers around the back of her head. "Lord help me, I haven't been able to concentrate on anything else except you since I got that letter from the lawyer."

"Don't give me that." Fresh outrage erupted. "If you've been concentrating on me, it's because I'm connected to Dreamscape. You have to deal with me before you can get your hands on my property. *That's* why you suddenly started focusing on me. Admit it."

He cast about briefly for the words he needed, but he could not find them.

"We both want the same thing for Dreamscape," he said finally. "We ought to be able to work together."

"And sleep together?"

"We both want that, too. I really don't see the problem here, Hannah."

"Probably because you're thinking like a Madison."

"You know something?" he said through his teeth. "I've had it with you implying that just because I'm a Madison, I can't handle a sexual relationship and a business relationship simultaneously."

"I've had it with you classifying our relationship as *sexual.*"

"Well, what would you call it?"

She stilled. "I don't know."

"Fine. Great. That's a lot of help."

She raised her chin. "I just know that for me there has to be more than sex."

That stopped him cold. "More?"

"And don't you dare tell me that a business partnership will fill in the empty places," she added icily.

He was annoyed. "I wasn't going to say that. That sounds like something a Harte would say, not a Madison."

"If I'm not allowed to insult your family, you can't insult mine."

"Sure, right. Take all the fun out of the argument. Damn it, Hannah, I've had enough of this. You know that what we've got is more than just a sexual thing. I want you. I think you want me. Can't we just go with that for now?"

She put her hands on his shoulders as if to steady herself. "I don't understand what's happening here. But I do know that adding sex to the mix complicates things."

"In the most interesting way," he muttered against her throat.

"Rafe—"

"Give whatever we've got going for us a chance, okay?" He drew his finger down the curve of her neck. "That's all I'm asking."

"I really don't think that's a good idea, Rafe."

He cradled her chin in his palms. "Tell me something."

She searched his face. "What?"

"Do you ever stop talking?"

"Not as long as I have something to say."

"Just wondered." He kissed her again.

For a few seconds she hesitated and then, with a tiny sigh, she softened.

Maybe she no longer had anything to say, he thought. A man could always hope.

Afraid to risk any more conversation, he kept his mouth on hers as he maneuvered her through the kitchen door. When they went past the light switch, he reached out and flipped it to the off position. Heavy shadows descended. The only light now was a dim, welcoming glow at the top of the stairs. He started toward it with Hannah tucked safely against his side.

His breathing was heavy and ragged by the time he got both of them to the bedroom at the end of the hall. He did not turn on the lamp, but the light from the corridor was sufficient to allow him to see that the room, with its white wicker furniture, white bedspread, and bleached wooden floors, was just as he had imagined it all those years ago: a pristine retreat for an untouchable princess. He felt like the intruder he was.

Not that that was going to stop him, he thought.

Exultation raced through him. Nothing could stop him as long as he knew that Hannah wanted him as badly as he wanted her. The passion between them was mutual. He could work with passion. He was a Madison.

He stopped beside the bed and untied the belt that bound the robe around her waist. She wore a longsleeved, high-necked, prim white gown underneath it. Womanly armor, he thought. Did she know the challenge it presented?

She mumbled something against his mouth as he slipped the robe off her shoulders. He did not catch the precise words, but he had no trouble at all understanding the meaning. She was as swept up in the moment as he was.

Her arms tightened fiercely around his neck when he started to unfasten the tiny little buttons of the flannel nightgown. She smelled so good. He knew that when he threaded his fingers through the triangle of hair at the apex of her thighs she would be moist. He could hardly wait.

She unbuttoned his shirt and spread her palms across his chest. "I love the feel of you," she whispered.

He was already hard, but her touch and the sultry desire in her words made him absolutely rigid. Electricity flashed through his senses.

He released her long enough to sit down on the edge of the white bed and remove his running shoes. When he looked up he saw that she was watching him with hungry attention, as if every move he made fascinated her.

He rose and lowered the flannel gown to her waist. It slipped low on her hips but it did not fall all the way to the floor. He caressed the tips of her small breasts. Her nipples were stiff and full. He closed his eyes briefly against the torrent of need that threatened to drown him.

She undid his belt, and then she lowered his zipper. When her fingers closed lightly around him he stopped breathing for a few seconds. The sensations tearing through him were so intense that he was sure he could live without oxygen for a while.

She slid her hands beneath the waistband of his trousers and pushed slowly downward. The pants hit the floor at his feet.

"Rafe."

He stepped out of the trousers and quickly sheathed himself in the condom he took from his back pocket. Then he grabbed her around the waist and fell back across the white bedspread with her. She sprawled atop his chest and thighs, the bottom of her gown tangling in his bare legs.

She rained kisses on his flesh. Her fingers circled his upper arms. He shuddered under the gentle assault. Then he rolled her onto her back, leaned over her, and tore the gown off altogether. It vanished into the darkness below the bed.

He curved his hand around her hip and kissed the gentle swell of her belly. She trembled beneath him and reached for him.

"No," he said. "Not yet."

He found the tight, hot place between her legs. And she was wet, just as he had anticipated. He inhaled the secret scent until he could no longer think clearly. Then he separated her thighs and kissed the exquisitely soft skin he found there.

She shivered again. Her nails dug into his shoulder as she tried to pull him up along the length of her. But he was not yet ready to be lured into the climax.

He drew a fingertip along the tight nub hidden in the silky thatch of hair and felt her quiver in response. She was clawing at him now.

He bent his head and touched the tip of his tongue to her full, taut clitoris. She tensed.

"Rafe." It was a plea and a protest. "Wait. Don't do that."

"Come for me."

"I can't. Not like this. It's too—*Rafe.*"

"Come for me." He kissed her again, intimately, and simultaneously eased two fingers into her, stretching her gently.

Her hands twisted in the sheets. "No, wait. I want—"

"Come for me."

"I . . . Oh, no. Oh, yes. *Yes!*"

He felt her climax take her. The sensation was so intoxicating he nearly went with her.

He held himself together until the tremors had begun to subside. Only then did he shift his position to lie on top of her.

"Open your eyes," he whispered. "Look at me."

Languidly she raised her lashes and smiled at him, a dreamy smile that was somehow smug and all-knowing and filled with invitation.

He plunged into her body, driving himself to the hilt. She closed around him and took him deeper still, straight down into uncharted depths and unknowable waters.

"Come for me," she said into his mouth.

He gave himself up to the tides of a mysterious sea.

A long time later he roused reluctantly from the cocoon of warmth that enveloped them, levered himself up on his elbow, and looked down at her.

"I just want to know one thing," he said.

She raised her lashes halfway and yawned. "What?"

"Are you sleeping with me because you've got some kind of kinky thing about finding out what it's like to do it with the kind of guy your parents would hate?"

"That would be extremely immature."

"Yeah."

"Hartes do not act out just for the hell of it, nor do we take risks merely for the sake of novelty. We are not immature. We're the logical, reasonable, rational ones, remember?"

"Yeah." He kissed her breast. "So why are you sleeping with me?"

She studied him with an enigmatic expression. "You had all the answers earlier."

"Earlier I was trying to talk you into bed."

She punched him lightly on the arm. "We are not amused, Madison."

"I'm serious. I know why I'm sleeping with you. I want to know why you're sleeping with me."

She searched his face. "Is it that important to you?"

Anger stirred deep inside him, dissolving much of the warm afterglow that had enveloped him. "Hell, yes, it's important. You think I'd be trying to get through a stupid conversation like this if the answer wasn't important?"

"Well, I'll tell you one thing," she said. "I'm certainly not doing this because I still have a teenage-type crush on you or because you're the guy my parents always warned me about."

He rolled onto his back, put one hand behind his head, and gazed moodily up at the dark ceiling. "So what's the reason?"

She rose partway off the bed and leaned over him in the shadows. When she spoke, her voice was low and steady.

"I am sleeping with you because, among other things, I am a mature, un-attached adult who happens to be physically attracted to you and also because—"

An eagerness that bordered on desperation swept through him. Get a grip, he thought. "And also because—?"

He sensed that she was on the verge of saying something crucial. But in the next heartbeat the intense, important thing disappeared beneath a breezy smile.

"And because my dog likes you, and I trust Winston's judgment implicitly," she said demurely.

So what the hell had he expected her to say? He wondered. "Sonofabitch."

"Yes, but we do not refer to him in those terms in his presence."

"Huh."

"In my experience, Winston is never wrong in these matters."

He thought about that for a while. "Winston didn't like the ex-fiancé, I take it?"

"Winston was civil, but he never warmed up to Doug." Hannah paused. "There was an unfortunate incident one evening toward the end of the relationship that more or less summed up his opinion."

"What sort of incident?"

She cleared her throat. "Winston mistook Doug's leg for a fire hydrant."

"Winston and I are pals," Rafe said. "I don't think he'd make the same mistake with me."

"He seems to like you very much."

"Guess that'll have to do. For now."

She tilted her head slightly. "I guess so. For now."

He lay there unmoving, intensely conscious of the warmth of her hip where it rested against his thigh and the elegantly sensual curve of her shoulder. He could not shake the feeling of destiny that rippled through him. It was the same sensation that had come over him the day he opened the letter from Isabel's lawyer.

"What are you thinking?" she asked.

Don't let the feeling run away with you, he warned himself. Stay on top of it. Stay in control. Don't think about the future. Stay with the present.

But the future was so important now.

He inhaled slowly, centering himself. "I was thinking about the subject that we were discussing before we were so delightfully interrupted."

"I believe you were holding forth on a theory that whoever tried to murder Winston might have been attempting to express his displeasure over our relationship."

"You don't have to say it in that tone of voice. It's a good theory. But I never got a chance to explain the finer points."

"I'm listening."

"I didn't mean to imply that whoever tried to off Winston did so because he was pissed about the fact that you and I are sleeping together. What I was going to suggest was that he or she might be worried about something else altogether."

"Such as?"

"Think about it," he said patiently. "Ever since we arrived here in Eclipse Bay, there has been talk. It hasn't all been focused on the speculation that one of us is trying to screw the other out of Dreamscape."

She winced. "What a delicate way to put it."

He ignored her. "There's also been gossip about what happened eight years ago."

"Oh, for pity's sake. You actually think that some people still care whether or not we had sex on the beach that night?"

"No. The conversations have circled around the subject of Kaitlin Sadler's death. You heard the Willis brothers. Others are talking, too. I overheard a couple of folks in the vegetable aisle at Fulton's chatting about how no one was really sure what happened that night. One of them suggested that Yates might have closed the case a little too quickly, for lack of suspects."

Hannah's lips parted as understanding struck. "Kaitlin died a long time ago. Who would care if there was fresh talk going around about an old tragedy?"

"Someone who thinks that I really did murder Kaitlin might care. A lot."

She froze. "Dell Sadler. But why would he try to harm my dog?"

"As far as Dell is concerned, you covered for me that night. You're involved."

"You think he would have tried to harm Winston as a way of taking some revenge?"

"I think," Rafe said deliberately, "that we'd better talk to him."

17

THE faded sign over the gate read SADLER'S AUTO REBUILD. Beneath it, in slightly smaller letters, were the words 24-HOUR TOWING. And below that was the phrase SPECIALIZING IN INSURANCE WORK. But the chain-link fence that enclosed the metal carcasses of ruined automobiles and the big dog with the massive head sprawled in front of the trailer sent a slightly different message. This was a junkyard.

Hannah took one look at the huge dog and decided to leave Winston in the car. "Whatever you do, don't let him out," she said as Rafe opened the door on his side.

Rafe eyed the animal lying in the shade of the tattered awning that shielded the trailer door. "Have a little faith. We're talking brains versus brawn here. My money's on Winston."

"We are not going to put that to the test." Hannah looked at Winston through the two-inch crack she had left between the window and the top of the car-door frame. "Don't do anything to provoke that beast, understand?"

Winston whined softly. His rear legs were planted on the seat she had just vacated, his front paws braced against the door. Ears alert, nose quivering, he stared through the window, his whole attention concentrated on the other dog.

Hannah shuddered at the thought of what might happen if Winston got out of the car. She checked the passenger door to make certain that it was firmly shut and then sent Rafe a warning glance over the low roof of the Porsche.

"Be sure you close that door firmly."

"You worry too much," Rafe said. He gave the Porsche door a rather casual push. "Winston's smart. He can handle that guy."

She watched the big dog heave his bulk to his feet. "I'm sure I'm a lot smarter than that monster, too. But I wouldn't want to get into a fight with him."

"Okay, okay. Winston stays in the car." Rafe walked to the gate and leaned on a grimy button.

A few seconds later the door of the trailer opened. Dell Sadler appeared, silhouetted in the gloom. He gazed at Rafe and Hannah, his face shadowed by the brim of a greasy billed cap. After a while he apparently came to a decision. He started toward the gate. The dog paced stiffly after him, moving with the painfully awkward stride of an animal who was either very old or had been badly injured.

Dell crossed the yard, weaving his way between piles of tires, crumpled fenders, and assorted mutilated auto parts. When he reached the gate he made no move to open it. He stared balefully at Rafe through the chain links. The dog came to a halt beside him and stared, too. Dell did not look down, but he put his hand on the creature's head in a gesture that was at once calming and absently affectionate. The bond between man and beast was evident.

"It's okay, Happy," Dell said.

Quite suddenly Hannah found it difficult to believe that this man had tried to murder Winston last night.

"What d'ya want?" Dell asked gruffly.

"We need to talk to you, Dell."

"What about?"

"Kaitlin."

Dell's shoulders stiffened visibly. He hesitated for a long time. Then he reached for the latch. "You better come inside."

The gate swung open. Dell led the way through the piles of dead automobiles.

The tidy interior of the trailer was a surprise. Hannah glanced surreptitiously around as she sat down on the worn vinyl-covered couch. There was a good reading lamp on the built-in end table. A pile of magazines bearing recent dates was stacked beside it. A new mystery novel by a familiar author lay on the miniature coffee table.

Dell hovered in the little kitchen. He appeared nervous, uneasy, as if he was not sure how to handle guests. "You want something to drink? I got some soda and beer."

"Soda's fine," Rafe said. "Whatever's handy."

"Soda sounds great," Hannah said gently.

"Sure." Dell opened the refrigerator and hauled out two cans. He carried them into the living room portion of the trailer and set them on the table in front of Rafe and Hannah.

Hannah glanced through the screen door of the trailer, studying the dog sprawled outside. "What happened to your dog?"

"Happy got run over by some drunk bastard on the highway while we was out on a tow job one night. Messed up his rear legs pretty bad. Vet told me I oughta put him down, but I just couldn't do that. Cost me a fortune, but what was I gonna do? Me and Happy are partners, y'know?"

"I know," Hannah said. Definitely not a dog killer, she thought. But if Dell Sadler wasn't the one who had put Winston out on the rocks in Dead Hand Cove, who had? "Someone tried to kill my dog last night."

"Why would anyone wanna kill a dog?"

"We think it may have been meant as a warning of some kind," she said quietly.

"Shit. That's why you're here, isn't it? You think maybe I tried to hurt your dog on accounta what happened to Kaitlin?"

"It crossed our minds," Rafe admitted. "You're the only one I can think of who might have wanted to avenge Kaitlin's death."

"Shit," Dell said again. He sank down onto a threadbare chair and stared at the logo on the can in his hand. "I wouldn't hurt no dog. That little pooch of yours didn't have anything to do with what happened to my sister."

"You're right." Rafe leaned forward, legs spread. He held the can of soda loosely in his fingers between his knees. Serious but nonthreatening. Man-to-man. "I'll come to the point, Dell. I know you think I killed Kaitlin. I didn't. That's the God's honest truth. You'll believe what you want to believe, but in the meantime, I really need to know why you're so sure I'm guilty."

Dell turned the can between his hands. Eventually he looked up. "I always figured it was you because you were the last one with her that night. Everyone said you were pissed that she was playing around."

Hannah stirred. "But why were you always so sure that it was murder in the first place? Why couldn't it have been an accident?"

"Because they found her in Hidden Cove. Said she must have been up on the path in the middle of the night. Doesn't make sense. Why would she go out there?"

"To meet a man?" Hannah suggested gently.

Dell gave her a derisive look. "She had her own house. And a car, too. She didn't have to go to someplace like Hidden Cove to fool around."

"Unless she didn't want to be seen with whoever she met there," Rafe said bluntly. "Which lets me out. She sure didn't mind having people see her with me."

Hannah pursed her lips, thinking. "Maybe she didn't go out there to meet anyone. Maybe she just went there to meditate."

"Meditate?" Dell looked at her as if she had lost her mind. "Kaitlin wasn't into that kinda weird stuff."

"Everyone needs to get away to a quiet place to think about their future once in a while," Hannah persisted. But she noticed that Rafe was now looking at her strangely, too. Obviously neither of these two considered Kaitlin to be the thoughtful, introspective type.

"Not Kaitlin." Dell took a swallow from his can of soda and wiped his mouth with the back of a stained sleeve. "She had her future down cold. Didn't need to do any meditating on it. Kaitlin always had big plans, y'know?"

A tingle of expectation shot through Hannah. She and Rafe exchanged nods. She turned back to Dell.

"Why do you say that Kaitlin didn't have to do any meditating on her future?" she asked carefully.

"She already knew what she was going to do. Called me that night." Dell studied his soda can intently. "Said she'd had enough of this town. She was gonna leave first thing in the morning and never come back."

"Are you telling us that you spoke with Kaitlin just before she died?" Rafe asked.

"Yeah. Like I said, she called me. Woke me up. She was still really mad at you, y'know? Said she'd had it with everyone here. 'All losers,' she said."

"How did she plan to finance this final exit?" Rafe asked.

Dell sucked in a deep breath and took another swallow of soda. He lowered the can slowly and peered into the middle distance. Looking into the past. "She told me that she was going to use her nuclear option."

Rafe did not move. "What the hell was that?"

Dell hesitated. "I'm not sure, to tell you the truth. She never was real clear about it. I got the feeling that she had some cash stashed away. Figured one of her boyfriends had given it to her. Or maybe someone gave her a piece of fancy jewelry she thought she could sell."

Hannah's mouth went dry. She said nothing.

"Let me get this straight." Rafe sounded as if he was choosing his words with exquisite care. "You're saying that she left me on the beach that night, went home, and called you to tell you that she was going to go nuclear and then leave town?"

"The next thing I know," Dell said dully, "Yates is pounding on my door. Come to tell me Kaitlin's dead."

"And you told him you were pretty sure I'd killed her—is that it?"

"Well, yeah," Dell muttered.

"Follow your own logic for a while here," Rafe said. "How did I know she was headed for Hidden Cove?"

"I figure you went to her place. You killed her there and then dumped her body in Hidden Cove."

Rafe groaned. "Well, it's a theory. I'll give you that much."

"Kaitlin wasn't like me," Dell pleaded to Hannah. "She wanted to get out of this town. Be someone. She had dreams, y'see? Lots of 'em. Big ones."

"I understand," Hannah said.

"But none of 'em ever worked out for her." Dell gave a sad sigh. "Seemed like everything always went wrong. I was her brother, y'know, but there was never anything I could do to fix things for her."

Rafe frowned. "It wasn't your fault you couldn't straighten out her problems, Dell."

"Maybe. But it just seemed like I shoulda been able to do something, y'know?"

"Yeah," Rafe said. "I know. Sometimes you've just got to live with the fact that there wasn't anything you could do."

Dell nodded bleakly. "Thought I'd put it all behind me. Told myself it was finished. Then you two showed up in town together. Made it clear you planned to hang around awhile. People started talking about what happened that night again."

Rafe looked at him. "When Yates came around asking questions, did he say whether or not he had searched Kaitlin's house?"

"He went through the place real thoroughly. Her car, too. I was with him when he did it," Dell said morosely. "Said he was looking for a suicide note, but he tore that place apart, y'know? Why would he do that if he was just lookin' for a note? I mean, if she'd left one, she would have put it in plain sight, don't you think? Why leave a note if you don't want it to be found?"

"You're right," Rafe said. "She'd have left it in plain sight."

Hannah gripped the edge of her chair very tightly. "Do you recall whether or not Yates pulled out her washer and dryer to check behind them?"

Dell nodded. "And the refrigerator, too. Like I said, he really went through her stuff. But I know she didn't jump off that cliff. There was no note. I told him she wasn't the type to commit suicide. Asked him what he was really looking for."

Hannah watched him. "What did he say?"

"Said he'd know it if he found it. But he didn't find anything."

They all sat in silence for a time. After a while Dell sighed heavily and drained the last of his soda. "I didn't try to kill your dog, Hannah."

"I believe you," Hannah said. "You wouldn't hurt an innocent animal."

Dell nodded and said nothing.

"There's something else," Hannah said. "Rafe didn't kill Kaitlin. I really was with him that night on the beach near the Arch. There was no way he could have followed your sister home, let alone kill her and take her body to Hidden Cove. You have my word on it."

Dell did not move for a long time. Then he looked at Rafe. "If it wasn't you, who was it?"

"Good question," Rafe said.

❦

BACK in the car, Winston draped the front half of his body over the back of the seat and nuzzled Hannah's shoulder. She scratched his ears and glanced at Rafe.

"Are you thinking what I'm thinking?" she asked.

"About that lingerie and the videos the Willis brothers found hidden behind Kaitlin's dryer?" Rafe steered the Porsche in a tight circle and drove down the dusty, rutted road that led away from Sadler's Auto Rebuild. "Yeah, that's what I'm thinking. Maybe those videos were her nuclear option."

"Blackmail material?"

"Maybe," Rafe said again. "And maybe Chief Yates suspected something. Maybe that's why he tore her place apart that night."

"But he didn't find anything."

Rafe turned right onto the main road. "Which means that whoever killed Kaitlin managed to recover the videos and the lingerie."

Hannah shivered. "Do you realize what we're saying here?"

"We're saying that Dell Sadler was right all along. Kaitlin didn't die in an accidental fall. And she sure as hell didn't jump off the Hidden Cove path. She was murdered by someone she was attempting to blackmail."

Hannah took a breath. "We're making some huge assumptions here."

He shrugged. "After what almost happened to you and Winston last night, I'm willing to take some very big leaps."

"If we're right, someone murdered Kaitlin because she had possession of compromising videos."

"The question is, who in this burg would have committed murder just to keep her quiet about an affair involving some frilly lingerie? Cross-dressing isn't that big a deal."

"Come on, Rafe. You want possibilities? How about some desperate assistant professor at Chamberlain who might have been afraid that his chance at tenure was about to go up in smoke because of those videos? Or try a minister at a local church who would lose his congregation if his taste for ladies' underwear became public knowledge. And then there's the crowd up at the institute. Arizona Snow has always been convinced that there are some very unsavory characters up there. Maybe she's right."

Rafe sank deeper into the leather seat. "You're right. A long list of possibilities."

"Then there's the Willis brothers' theory that the killer was someone from out of town. Which gives us an even longer list."

Rafe's dark brows met above his shades in a thoughtful frown. "Don't think so. Her decision to 'use her nuclear option,' as Dell put it, was apparently an impulse. Her victim had to be someone she could reach on the spur of the moment that night. Not someone who had to be summoned from Portland or Seattle or Salem."

"Makes sense." Hannah pondered for a minute. "Okay, let's try this from another angle. Surely not everyone in Eclipse Bay is into ladies' lingerie. And not everyone here who is into women's underwear would commit murder to keep a blackmailer quiet."

"Your point?"

"All we need to do is find out who fits the profile, as the cops say. Someone who is into female undies and who would also be willing to kill to get his hands on the compromising videos."

"To do that we need to talk to someone who knows this town better than you and I do."

"Got a name in mind?"

Rafe's mouth curved in a humorless smile. "As a matter of fact, I do. Our dinner guest tonight."

18

R AFE rinsed the red radicchio leaves under running water and dropped them gently into the colander on top of the arugula and cilantro. Mentally he ran through his plans for the meal. Three carefully chosen ripe avocados sat in a bowl at the far end of the counter. He would cut them in half just before serving, spoon balsamic vinegar into the hollows and sprinkle them with some coarsely grated sea salt. The pasta would be a straightforward dish using olives and tomatoes and goat cheese.

When he finished rinsing the lettuce for the salad, he went to work on the hummus. He tossed a sizable quantity of cooked garbanzo beans into the food processor and added tahini, lemon juice, and a bit of garlic.

He snapped on the lid, flipped the switch, and thought about what Dell Sadler had said while he listened to the pleasant sound of garbanzos being pulverized. *Kaitlin had intended to use her nuclear option.*

A killer who had thought himself in the clear for the past eight years might have reason to worry now that the old gossip was being dredged up and rehashed all over town. What if someone remembered something important after all this time? What if someone put two and two together in a way that hadn't been done eight years ago? What if someone had seen something that night and belatedly realized that it was a clue?

A murderer who had struck once to keep his secret might be willing to strike again.

A cold feeling closed in on Rafe. The dread that he had been holding at bay all day broke through the dam, and he was suddenly dealing with a nightmarish river. The question he had not raised with Hannah, the one that had been plaguing him for hours, could no longer be avoided.

That question was horrifyingly simple: What if Winston had not been the main target last night? Maybe the attack on the dog had never been intended as a warning. Maybe the Schnauzer had been set out on the finger as bait to lure Hannah into danger. If she had arrived home as little as half an hour later, rescuing Winston would have put her in great jeopardy. The force of the incoming tide could have swept her feet out from under her, perhaps dashed her against the rocks.

He thought about how she had taken Winston into the caves because she had sensed someone watching her from the cliff path. What if the killer had been hanging around, watching to see if his plans were going to work out as he'd intended? What if he had waited on the cliff path with the intention of making certain that Hannah and Winston never made it back from the cove alive?

What if?

Rafe switched off the food processor and removed the lid. He could not afford to take any more chances, he thought as he scooped out the fragrant hummus. Tonight he would have to take drastic steps. He would never be able to sleep if he didn't.

AT six-thirty that evening, he picked up the tray of hors d'oeuvres. Winston, who had been supervising the final kitchen preparations with an expression of mingled wistfulness and lust, got to his feet.

"Here you go, mutt." Rafe tossed him a slice of pita bread slathered in hummus. "Chef's privilege."

Winston gnawed happily on the tidbit as he hurried after Rafe. Together they crossed the hall toward the sunroom, where Hannah and Mitchell were sharing a glass of wine and the view of evening fog moving in over the bay.

Rafe glanced at the bowl of hummus and pita toast points arranged on the tray, double-checking the visual appeal of the hors d'oeuvres. The trickle of uneasiness he felt was disconcerting. He was usually confident of his cooking. He knew he had a keen sense of how to blend flavors into intriguing combinations and a flair for presentation. He had planned this meal with great care. He knew everything was perfect. It was the first time he had ever cooked for Mitchell, and he did not want any screwups.

Mitchell's low growl stopped him just as he was about to enter the room.

". . . Don't you worry. Rafe will do right by you," Mitchell said. "I'll see to it."

Rafe froze in the doorway. Winston stopped, too, cocking his head with an inquiring look.

"What the heck does that mean?" Hannah sounded baffled and more than a little wary. "Are you going to force him to give up his claim on this house?"

"Never could force that bullheaded boy to do anything he didn't want to do, and I'm pretty sure he won't give up Dreamscape. Seems to have his heart set on turning it into an inn and a restaurant."

"He certainly does." Hannah's voice was clipped.

"When a Madison's got his heart set on something," Mitchell warned with gruff gentleness, "it isn't easy persuading him to change course."

"That's what I've heard."

"He's got the cash to make it happen. Made himself a bundle in the market, you know." Mitchell sighed. "Always did have a head for business."

"Apparently." Hannah's tone was becoming grim.

"Barring a tsunami or an earthquake or a volcanic eruption that wipes out this section of the coast, I reckon Rafe will see his plans through." Mitchell paused. "Thing is, he's a lot like me when it comes to going after what he wants."

Hannah was quiet for a time. Rafe realized that his hands were clenched around the handles of the hors d'oeuvres tray. He could not seem to move through the doorway. He was waiting for something, but he was not sure what that something was.

"So what did you mean when you said you'd see to it that he would do right by me?" Hannah asked eventually.

"Lord above, woman, don't play dumb with me. There isn't any such thing as a dumb Harte, and we both know it. I'm talking about marriage, naturally."

"*Marriage!*" Hannah's voice rose to a shrill squeak. "Rafe and me?"

"Well, sure. What did you think I was talking about?"

"Are you out of your mind?"

"Hear me out, now, Hannah. I've been doing a lot of thinking about this, and I'm pretty sure I can swing it."

"Pretty sure? *Pretty sure?*"

"Okay, damn sure. Pardon my language. Not quite the same thing as making him give up Dreamscape, of course. That would be a real case of hitting my head against a brick wall. But this fear of marriage that he's got, that's just a case of bad nerves."

"Nerves," Hannah repeated in a dazed voice.

"Right. He's convinced that Madison men have a bad time with marriage."

"Well, you do have a history of disastrous marriages in your clan," Hannah muttered. "And Rafe has already screwed up once."

"Okay, so he made one little mistake."

"Little?"

"These things happen."

"You ought to know," Hannah said much too sweetly. "How many times have you been married, Mr. Madison?"

"Don't go tagging Rafe with my lousy track record. I admit that for a long time after Claudia Banner took off with the assets of Harte-Madison, I didn't think real clearly when it came to women. Had a few problems."

"That's putting it mildly, from what I understand."

Mitchell made a rude sound. "Can't blame you for your opinion. You've been brought up to think the worst of me. I know that Sullivan has fed you a lot of wild stories over the years. What I'm trying to tell you is that Rafe and I are alike in a lot of ways but not in every way."

"If you say so."

"If that isn't just like a Harte," Mitchell said heatedly. "Throw a man's mistakes back in his face and don't bother to give him a chance to put things right. You got a lot in common with your granddad, young woman."

"I think we're straying from the point here."

"Look, that divorce wasn't Rafe's fault. Don't hold it against him. He learned from it."

"Uh-huh. From what I can gather, he learned that he doesn't want to get married again," Hannah said dryly.

"Exactly what I'm trying to tell you," Mitchell said quickly. "Like I said, I've been doing a lot of thinking, and I've figured out Rafe's problem. He's got some sort of phobia about marriage, see."

"You've concluded that he's afraid of marriage?" Hannah's voice was oddly weak.

"Right." Mitchell sounded pleased that she had grasped the point so readily. "The way some folks are scared of spiders or snakes."

"A charming analogy."

"I can sort of see how it happened," Mitchell continued earnestly. "I got to admit I didn't set a good example for Sinclair, and things trickled on down to Rafe. But I figure I can get him past it. Figure I owe him that much, since it was me who was responsible for this phobia thing in the first place."

"How do you intend to do that?" Hannah's voice was stronger now, infused with morbid curiosity. "Get out your shotgun and march him to the altar?"

Rafe felt as though he'd been turned into a block of solid marble.

"Is that what you want?" Mitchell asked ingenuously.

"Good grief, *no.* Of course not."

Rafe winced. Did she have to sound so positively negative about the idea?

"It might take a little push from me," Mitchell allowed reflectively. "When it comes to phobias, sometimes you've got to force folks to face up to 'em."

"You just told me that force didn't work well with Rafe."

"I'm thinking more in terms of applying a little pressure in the right spots."

"As it happens," Hannah said, sweet, sharp steel in every syllable, "I'm in the business of getting people married, and I can tell you that making a marriage work is hard enough when both parties go into it enthusiastically. Any marriage forged by outside pressure would be doomed before the vows even got said."

"You're too young to be so pessimistic," Mitchell complained.

"Mitchell, I'm sure you mean well, but the very last thing I want to do is marry a man who doesn't want to get married. Are we clear on that?"

"Now don't let Rafe's bad nerves put you off the notion," Mitchell replied. "It's true the Madison men have a lousy track record when it comes to marriage, but the right woman could change all that."

"Why do you want to change it?" Hannah demanded, thoroughly exasperated now. "What is this all about, anyway? Why do you want Rafe and me to get married?"

Still stuck in the doorway, Rafe waited for the other shoe to drop.

"Because it's the right thing to do," Mitchell snapped, evidently out of patience himself. "It's the only way to stop people from talking."

"Since when did you start worrying about local gossip?" Hannah asked.

"There's gossip and there's gossip," Mitchell declared. "Everyone in town is saying he's carrying on with you because he wants to get his hands on the other half of this place. That's a damned lie. Reminds me of the talk that went around town the night Kaitlin Sadler died. All those rumors about how he'd seduced you just to get himself an alibi. Pure garbage."

"They certainly were," Hannah said quietly.

"Hell, I know that." Mitchell's voice rang with conviction. "Rafe had nothing to do with that poor girl's death. Madison men got problems when it comes to dealing with the opposite sex, but no Madison man has ever laid a hand on a woman in anger. No man in this family would ever assault a female, by God. And no Madison would seduce an innocent girl like you to cover his own tracks, and that's a fact."

A loud silence gripped the sunroom.

"I know that," Hannah said quietly.

Rafe remembered to take a breath.

"I'm not saying Rafe might not have argued with Kaitlin Sadler," Mitchell continued. "He's a Madison. He's got a temper. But if he had been with Kaitlin that night and if there had been some terrible accident, he'd have gone for help and then he'd have told the flat-out truth about what happened."

"I know that, too," Hannah said again. Her voice was very even. "I'm a Harte, remember? Lord knows that we're well aware that Madisons have their faults, but no one in my family has ever accused anyone in your clan of lying."

"Damn right," Mitchell agreed.

Rafe glanced down at the tray of hummus and pita bread points he held. Mitchell had believed him all those years ago. The old man disapproved of just about everything he'd ever done in his life, but he had never doubted Rafe's word about what had happened the night Kaitlin Sadler died.

Rafe discovered that he could move again. He walked into the sunroom and set the tray down on a table. He noticed that Hannah's cheeks were flushed. She avoided his eyes. He knew she was wondering how much of the conversation he had overheard.

"The hummus looks wonderful," she said a little too brightly.

"Thanks." Rafe picked up the small glass pitcher of very good, very expensive olive oil that sat on the tray. He poured a liberal stream of the rich, fruity oil over the hummus.

"What's that?" Mitchell studied the hummus with curiosity. "Some kinda bean dip?"

"Yeah," Rafe said. "Some kind of bean dip." He set down the pitcher of olive oil. He pulled the bottle of Chardonnay out of the ice bucket and poured himself a glass. "Glad you left some for me. I need it."

Hannah and Mitchell gazed at him as though he were charming a snake. Both were uneasy. Neither wanted to make any sudden moves. He took his time, savoring the perfect balance of oak and fruit and the elegant finish of the wine.

When he was done, he set the glass down on the table very deliberately and looked at Hannah and Mitchell.

"I hear that wine is good for the nerves," he said.

TWO hours later, Mitchell put down his fork with a sigh of satisfaction. Just a few slivers of buttery pastry was all that remained of the kiwi tart.

"Where the hell did you learn to cook?" he asked Rafe. "Sure didn't get it from me. The best I can do is throw a salmon steak on the grill."

"Took some classes," Rafe said. "But mostly I just spend a lot of time fooling around in the kitchen."

"Well, if this inn of yours doesn't work out, it won't be because the food is bad."

Rafe caught Hannah's attention. He knew that they were both aware of what had just happened. Mitchell had bestowed his approval, not only on the food but on the entire inn project. She was probably thinking that she had just lost a lot of ground in her battle to claim his half of the inn. She was right.

"I need to talk to you about something important, Mitchell." Rafe settled back in his chair and contemplated his grandfather across the remains of the meal. "Last night someone tried to drown Hannah's dog."

Mitchell blinked in astonishment. Then he looked at Winston, who was dozing peacefully on the rug beneath the table. "Who the hell would do a thing like that?"

"I don't know," Rafe admitted. "But I intend to find out."

"What's going on here?" Mitchell demanded.

Nobody ever accused Mitchell of being slow, Rafe thought. "I don't know that, either, but we've concluded that it might be connected to what happened to Kaitlin Sadler."

Mitchell gazed at him for a very long time. "You're serious, aren't you?"

"Very. There's some stuff I need to tell you before this conversation goes any further." Rafe gave Mitchell a brief summary of events, including the talk with Dell Sadler.

When he had finished, Mitchell whistled softly. "You realize what you're saying?"

"That it's possible Kaitlin Sadler really was killed, just as Dell Sadler has always believed. And that the reason she was murdered was because she tried to blackmail someone here in Eclipse Bay."

"Well, shoot and damn." Mitchell sounded thoughtful now. "Yates was so damn sure it was an accident."

"Maybe not quite so certain as he let everyone think," Rafe said. "In addition to asking a lot of questions, he did a thorough search of Kaitlin's house and car that night. He must have had a few suspicions."

Mitchell shrugged. "Yates was a good cop in his time."

Hannah sipped coffee from a small cup. She regarded Mitchell very steadily. "We need a little help."

"From me? Now, see here, just what are you two thinking of doing?"

"We're going to try to find out who Kaitlin was blackmailing," Rafe said.

Mitchell frowned. "You want my advice? Don't go poking a stick in a hole. There might be a real nasty varmint inside."

"The problem," Rafe said deliberately, "is that the varmint has already crawled out of the hole. I don't think Winston was the real target last night. I have a hunch that whoever put him out there on that finger may have intended for Hannah to get caught by the incoming tide."

Hannah snapped her head around in surprise. "Rafe, what are you saying? You never told me you thought that someone had tried to—" She broke off.

"I'm not sure that someone did try to hurt you last night. Winston may have been just a warning. But I'm not taking any chances."

"What do you mean?"

"Never mind. We'll deal with that later."

"Deal with what later?" She slammed her coffee cup down onto the saucer. "Now just one damn minute. I want an explanation."

Rafe met Mitchell's gaze and talked over the top of Hannah's simmering words. "If I said to you ladies' underwear in sizes big enough to fit a man, big high heels, Kaitlin Sadler, and some compromising videotapes that were bad enough to serve as blackmail material, what would you say?"

Mitchell's face worked. For a moment Rafe thought that he was going to explode with outrage. But abruptly the ire metamorphosed into something else. Curiosity, or reluctant interest, Rafe decided.

"We're talking eight years ago, aren't we?" Mitchell said thoughtfully.

Rafe watched him. "One way or another, you've been connected to this town for more than fifty years. Any names come to mind?"

"No," Mitchell said immediately. "But that's no big surprise. I never paid much attention to other people's sex lives. The only one that ever interested me was my own." He paused. "But there was someone who did keep track of that kind of thing, along with every other damn secret in this town."

Hannah groaned. "I hope you're not going to tell us that person was Arizona Snow. It's hopeless trying to get anything out of her. She might know some secrets, but she filters them all through her conspiracy theories."

"Wasn't thinking of Arizona," Mitchell said. "I was talking about Ed Bolton. Owned the *Eclipse Bay Journal* for more than forty years until he sold out to Jed Steadman. Ed knew everything about everyone in this town."

Disappointment coursed through Rafe. "I heard that Ed Bolton died four or five years ago."

"He did," Mitchell said in an oddly neutral voice. "Heart attack. But his widow, Bev, is still around. Lives in Portland now."

"Do you think that Bev Bolton would know the secrets that Ed knew?" Hannah asked.

Mitchell nodded slowly. "Bev and Ed were together for a long time. Fine woman. Good marriage, from all accounts. Yeah, I reckon she'd know what Ed knew."

Somewhere in the back of Rafe's brain something went *click*.

"How do you know so much about Bev Bolton's marriage?" he asked Mitchell.

"Bev and I get together once in a while," Mitchell said very casually. "Talk over old times. You know how it is."

Rafe flopped back in his chair. "Damn. How long have you and Bev Bolton been having an affair?"

Mitchell's brows bunched and quivered in annoyance. "See here, my private life is none of your business."

"Right. Sure. Your business."

"Bev and I go back a long ways." Mitchell paused. "A couple of years after Ed died, I asked her to marry me."

Rafe was astounded. "No kidding? What happened?"

"Turned me down flat," Mitchell admitted.

"I see." Rafe said.

"As I was saying," Mitchell went on, "Bev and I get together whenever I go to Portland."

"I understand." Rafe recalled the conversation with Gabe concerning Mitchell's frequent trips to Portland. "And you've found a reason to go nearly every week for the past ten months."

"What the hell business is it of yours? A man's got a right to his personal life."

Rafe started to smile. The smile turned into a grin before he could control it, and then, without warning, he was laughing so hard he feared he might fall off his chair.

Winston roused himself to thrust his nose inquiringly into Rafe's hand. Rafe scratched him behind the ears and laughed even harder.

Hannah and Mitchell frowned.

"What's so funny?" Hannah asked with a bewildered expression.

Mitchell glowered. "If there's a joke here, you'd better share it."

"The joke is on Gabe and me," Rafe said, subduing the laughter to a wide grin. "We thought all those trips to Portland you've been taking for the past year were to get medical treatment. We were afraid you had some terrible, lingering disease you were hiding from us."

"Huh." Mitchell blinked, and then his eyes gleamed with secret amusement. "One of those trips last year was to see a doctor. But it wasn't because I had come down with anything serious."

"Just a checkup?" Rafe asked.

"You might say that," Mitchell said with a benign smile. "Happy to tell you that everything is in pretty fair working order, considering the mileage I've put on this body."

"Glad to hear it." Rafe realized he felt a lot lighter.

"Unless you do me in with your cooking," Mitchell said, "Dr. Reed tells me I'm likely to be around to pester the rest of you for quite a while yet. Now, then, as I was saying before I was so rudely interrupted, I was planning to go to

Portland at the end of the week. No reason I can't drive in with Bryce in the morning instead."

BRYCE arrived to collect Mitchell shortly after ten that night. Hannah stood on the front porch with Rafe and Winston, her arms folded, and watched the big SUV lumber off down the drive. It turned left onto the road, and the headlights disappeared into the night.

She braced herself. She had managed to relax midway through the meal, and later when the conversation had turned to the subject of Kaitlin Sadler's death, she had almost forgotten the awkward moments she'd experienced earlier in the evening. But now that she was alone again with Rafe, she could feel the uneasiness stealing back over her.

The unsettling question returned in a rush. Just how much had Rafe overheard of Mitchell's vow to make his grandson do right by her?

"Well, I'd call the evening a resounding success," she said briskly. She turned away and walked back toward the open front door. "Mitchell liked your cooking, and he seems genuinely interested in helping us figure out what's going on around here. Can't ask for more than that."

"As a matter of fact," Rafe said, "there is one more thing."

"You want help with the dishes?" She paused in the doorway. "No problem."

He leaned against the railing and studied her in the yellow glow of the porch lights. "Thanks. I'll take you up on that. But I wasn't referring to the dishes. I've been doing some thinking."

She realized that her heart was beating much too quickly. Maybe she shouldn't have had that cup of strong coffee after dinner. "What exactly have you been thinking about?"

"I said earlier that I think there's a possibility that whoever stuck Winston out on the rock last night was after you, not your dog."

She felt the world drop away from beneath her feet. "Are you saying that you think someone actually tried to kill me last night?"

"I don't know. Maybe he just hoped there would be a convenient accident. All I know for sure is that I don't think we should take any chances."

She chilled. "You're leaping to a very wild conclusion, Rafe."

He straightened away from the railing and crossed the porch to stand in front of her. He gripped her shoulders with both hands. "Listen, I didn't want to scare you like this, but I couldn't come up with any other way to convince you."

"Convince me of what?"

"That you can't stay alone in your folks' house any longer."

"I'll think about it," she said.

"I'm trying to be real rational and logical here. The way I see it, we've got two options. You and Winston can move in with me here or else I can pack a bag and settle in at your place. Take your pick. Either one is fine by me, but I think you'd be more comfortable here. There's more space. Hell, you can have the entire third floor to yourself if that's what you want."

For a split second she was on the verge of a very primitive sense of panic. It was one thing to spend the occasional night together while they charted their way through uncertain waters in a relationship that might easily founder. It was something else again to actually pack up and move in here with him. She wasn't sure just what the nature of that difference was, but she knew that it was important. She tried to stall while she sorted out the implications.

"People will talk," she said. It was weak. She knew it was weak even before she saw his brows lift.

"People are already talking," he said dryly. "I doubt if the gossip will get any more exciting if you move in here. You can always say that you're just trying to stake your claim to your half of Dreamscape."

It was a perfectly reasonable, eminently pragmatic suggestion she told herself. And there were more bathrooms and more space here. What if someone really had intended for her to drown last night? And she did own half of this place.

"Okay," she said, trying to sound very cool. "I'll go back to the house and pack my things. But I think we need some ground rules here."

"I was afraid you'd say something like that. Let me guess what you mean by ground rules. Separate bedrooms, right?"

"I think it would be best," she said very primly. "This thing is getting very complicated."

"And sharing a bedroom with me on a routine basis makes it even more complicated?"

She narrowed her eyes. "An occasional night of . . . of—"

"Wild passion?" he offered helpfully.

She stiffened. "As I was saying, an occasional night together is one thing. But sharing a bedroom feels more like . . . like—"

"Like a commitment?" he supplied with an air of amusement.

"Yes," she shot back, goaded. "Like a commitment. Which, I might add, neither of us has made."

"The subject has not arisen."

"That's not the point." She could hear the waspish edge in her own voice. "If I'm going to stay here, it will be on my terms, and that means separate bedrooms."

He moved his hand in a suspiciously careless manner. "Whatever you say. I'll drive you back to your place and give you a hand with the packing."

"That's not necessary."

"It's the least I can do if you're going to help me with the dishes."

Suspicion flickered briefly. He was being entirely too cooperative, she thought. But when she searched his gaze she saw nothing but mocking amusement.

MUCH later that night she awoke quite suddenly, aware that something was wrong. She stared at the ceiling for a while before she realized that she could not feel Winston's familiar warmth at her feet.

There was a soft whine in the darkness. Alarm zapped through her. She sat straight up in bed and switched on the light.

Winston was sitting in front of the bedroom door. He looked impatient to get out.

"Oh, damn." She shoved aside the covers, grabbed her robe, and hurried toward the door. "What is it? Is there someone out there watching us here at Dreamscape? I thought we left that problem behind when we moved out of the cottage."

Winston scratched politely at the base of the door. She flung it open for him. He trotted out into the unlit hall. She followed quickly.

On the second floor landing she paused. "We should wake Rafe. He'll want to be involved in this, whatever it is."

Winston ignored her. He trotted down the next flight of stairs to the first floor and disappeared. Hannah peered over the railing to look for him and saw a glow coming from the kitchen. Rafe was already awake.

She hurried downstairs, crossed the hall, and walked into the kitchen. She stopped when she saw Rafe standing in front of the counter with a knife in his hand. He had taken the time to pull on a pair of jeans, but that was all. His sleek shoulders gleamed in the kitchen light. His bare feet looked strong and supple and very sexy.

There was a chunk of leftover feta cheese on the plate that sat on the drainboard. Winston was positioned at Rafe's feet, looking expectant.

Hannah came to a halt in the doorway. "What's going on here?"

"Couldn't sleep," Rafe said. He dropped a bit of the cheese into Winston's waiting jaws. "Came down here to get a bite to eat." He held up the knife. "Want some?"

"No, thanks." She was torn between the urge to let him drop a bite of cheese into her mouth and the knowledge that if she had any sense she would hurry back upstairs. As was so often the case when she was caught between two equally opposing forces, she did nothing. "I was afraid that Winston had heard a prowler outside."

"Nope." Rafe ate some more cheese. "He must have heard me come downstairs a few minutes ago. How about you? Sleeping okay up there on the third floor?"

"I was sleeping just fine until Winston decided to follow you down here."

Rafe studied her with an unreadable expression as he munched cheese. "Hey, that's just great. Lot of people don't sleep well in a strange environment, you know? Sometimes they just lie there staring at the ceiling and think about things."

"Things?"

"Yeah." He sliced off another bit of cheese. "Things."

"Right. Things." The dangerously enigmatic shimmer in his eyes was starting to worry her. It was definitely time to retreat, she decided. She gripped the lapels of her robe and took a step back. "Well, as long as everything is okay down here, I'll go back to bed."

"You ever do that, Hannah? Just lie in bed and think about things?"

She hesitated. "Sometimes."

"I've been doing it a lot lately."

"Is that so?"

He put some cheese on a cracker and then popped the whole morsel into his mouth. "Aren't you going to ask me what kind of things I think about?"

She took another wary step back, not trusting his odd mood. "None of my business," she said crisply.

"Don't be so sure of that. Tonight, for instance, one of the things I was thinking about was who, besides Bev Bolton, might be able to give us a few insights into the bedroom lives of our friends and neighbors here in Eclipse Bay. I had an idea."

She folded her arms and propped one shoulder against the doorjamb. "Don't tell me one of your buddies is the local Peeping Tom?"

"He would be highly offended at the suggestion. I always had the impression that he sees himself as a lone crusader for freedom, privacy, and the First Amendment."

"I assume we are not talking about the head of the public library."

"Nope." Rafe ate more cheese. "I'm going to talk to my potential informant tomorrow while Mitchell is in Portland."

"I'm probably going to regret this, but I want to be there when you talk to this person." She paused delicately. "Who is it we're going to see?"

"Virgil Nash."

She winced. "I don't suppose there's any way we can talk to him without someone finding out."

"Doubt it. Still want to come with me?"

She decided to be philosophical about the situation. "Ah, well. It's not as if I have anything but a few tattered threads left of my reputation here in Eclipse Bay, anyway. What do I care if the whole town finds out that I was seen entering the local porn dealer's shop with you?"

"That's the spirit," Rafe said with enthusiasm. "Virgil's Adult Books and Video Arcade is just the kind of place folks would expect me to take a nice girl like you."

"Nobody ever said you didn't know how to show a lady a good time." She turned away to seek the safety of the third floor.

"I was thinking about something else besides Virgil Nash," Rafe continued in a conversational tone. "I also thought a lot about phobias."

Her mouth went dry. So he had overheard her awkward conversation with Mitchell. An ominous sensation rolled through her. She turned very slowly in the doorway to face him.

"I was afraid of that," she said.

"You know, my grandfather may be right. Perhaps the best way to get over a phobia is to confront it head-on. Just do it, you know?"

She cleared her throat. "I'm no expert on phobias, but it seems to me that that approach would be likely to trigger severe panic attacks."

"Hadn't thought of that."

"I suggest you do think about it. Now, if you'll excuse me, I'm going back to bed."

"Hannah?"

She looked back unwillingly. "Now what?"

"If I'm the one with the phobia, how come you're the one who looks panicked?"

"Good night, Rafe." She fled toward the stairs.

WINSTON did not return to the third-floor bedroom right away. When he finally did come back upstairs, his fur was cool and damp. Hannah realized that Rafe had taken him outside for a late-night walk.

"What did you two talk about out there?" she whispered.

Winston did not reply. He settled into position at the foot of the bed and promptly went to sleep.

"Guys always stick together."

She tried to go back to sleep. It was hard work. For a long time, she just stared at the ceiling and thought about things.

19

VIRGIL'S Adult Books and Video Arcade was located less than a hundred feet beyond the official boundary of the town of Eclipse Bay. When he had established his business fifteen years earlier, Virgil had been careful to select a location that was just outside the reach of local reformers, civic activists, and members of the town council who saw running the local porn store out of town as a sure ticket to reelection.

"It's the old law of real estate," Virgil had once explained to Rafe. "Location, location, location."

While convenience had been of paramount importance, Virgil had also realized that most of his clientele would also appreciate a measure of privacy while they made their purchases. With the aim of providing customers with that treasured commodity, he had placed the small parking lot behind the shop rather than in front, where familiar vehicles might be noted by neighbors, business acquaintances, and parents who happened to drive past.

"I can't believe I'm taking my dog into a place like this." Hannah scowled at the sign over the shop's rear entrance as she snapped the leash onto Winston's collar. "I can only hope that he doesn't realize what sort of business this is."

Rafe took the keys out of the ignition and unbuckled his seat belt. "It was your idea to bring Winston along."

"I refuse to leave him home alone until we find out who tried to murder him." Hannah glanced swiftly around the nearly empty parking lot. "Thank goodness there aren't too many customers here at the moment."

"There aren't *any* other customers here," Rafe said. "That van in the corner belongs to Virgil."

"Oh. Hard to see how he stays in business. It's two o'clock in the afternoon and there's no one here."

Rafe cracked open his door. "Virgil doesn't get busy until after dark."

"How do you know that?"

"Everyone knows that." He got out of the car and closed the door very quickly before she could think of any more questions.

Hannah opened her own door and climbed out warily. "All right, Winston, let's go. But whatever you do, don't touch anything. Understand?"

Winston sprang lightly out of the car. And immediately paused to sniff curiously at a small plastic wrapper that lay on the pavement.

Hannah glanced down to see what had caught his interest. She gave a half-strangled shriek of dismay. "Good grief, that looks like a used condom. Didn't you listen to me, Winston? I said, *don't touch anything.*"

Rafe watched her drag Winston away from his investigations. "Are you two going to fool around out here all afternoon?" He opened the rear door of the shop. "We've got business to do."

Hannah gave him a ferocious glare. She stalked toward him with Winston in tow. "You certainly seem to know your way around the premises."

"Spent some extremely educational afternoons here when I was a young man."

"I'll bet."

"Virgil always was a pioneer in the field of sex ed."

"Sex ed, my left pinkie. Virgil sells dirty books and movies. I refuse to dignify his profession by referring to him as an instructor in the field of sex education."

"Suit yourself." Rafe led the way into the shop. "But I think you'll like Virgil once you get to know him."

"I doubt if I'll be coming back here much in the future," she said austerely. She followed him into the shop and let the door slam shut with a reverberating bang.

"Okay, be that way," Rafe said.

She did not dignify that with a response. Her attention was on Winston, who was busily sniffing around a display of what looked like small bottles of whipped cream. Rafe glanced at the sign above the display. PASSION CREAM. FOUR EROTIC FLAVORS.

Winston appeared to be particularly fascinated with the cherry pie flavor.

"Winston, leave that alone."

Rafe had a feeling that Hannah was going to be saying that a lot while they were in the shop.

"Rafe." The elegantly modulated voice emanated from the far side of the shop. "Heard you were back in town. Good to see you again."

Rafe turned around and greeted the thin, slightly built man seated in the large wing chair near the window. "Hello, Virgil. Been a while."

"It has indeed." Virgil put down the book he had been reading and stood up. "And judging from the latest gossip, I assume that the charming lady at your side is Hannah Harte?"

"Hannah, meet Virgil."

Hannah managed a smooth, brittle smile. She did not give Virgil her hand to shake. Instead she managed to make it appear as though she had all she could do to hang on to Winston's leash and her purse at the same time.

"You haven't changed a bit, Virgil," Rafe said. "I think I recognize that vest."

Virgil's gray eyes twinkled a little behind the lenses of his reading glasses. He glanced down the front of the frayed green sweater vest that he wore over a plaid shirt. "You may be right. Can't even recall when I got this. Probably a birthday gift from some dead relative whose name I have apparently forgotten. Where does the time go, eh?"

There was an oddly ageless quality about Virgil. His background was as cloaked in mystery as Arizona Snow's. No one knew where he had come from or what he had done before he set up the porn shop just outside the town limits. With his gaunt frame, neat silver goatee, slightly stooped shoulders, and thick glasses, he had the look of an absentminded professor who had spent too much time indoors with his books.

The scholarly impression was not far off the mark, Rafe thought. Somewhere along the line Virgil had acquired a fine classical education. Virgil's personal library, a sophisticated collection of history, literature, and philosophy, was extensive. Rafe knew that because he had spent a lot of time in it.

Virgil was not anyone's idea of a porn dealer, but he considered himself a professional in a sadly underappreciated line of work. He had once told Rafe that he had dedicated himself to the business of selling what he liked to call erotica years ago and had never wavered from his career choice.

Virgil glanced from Rafe to Hannah and back again. His silver brows rose inquiringly. "I am delighted that the two of you found time to pay me a visit. I've heard all about your plans for an inn and a restaurant out there at Dreamscape. I think it's a wonderful idea."

"Those plans have not been finalized," Hannah said brusquely.

"I'm sure everything will work out." Virgil smiled at Rafe. "Heard you did all right for yourself."

"Didn't go to jail," Rafe said.

"Had a hunch you would turn out okay."

"I understand Rafe spent a lot of time here in the old days," Hannah offered.

"Yes, indeed," Virgil said with paternalistic pride. "I sold him his first condom. Taught him how to use it properly, too, before he left the store."

"I see."

Rafe winced. "Now, Hannah, it wasn't like I came in here every week. Besides, none of the guys wanted to risk buying condoms at the local drugstore. The word would have been all over town by nightfall. Here at Virgil's there was a lot more privacy."

Hannah raised her eyes to the ceiling. "I'd rather not hear too many details about your past, thank you very much."

Virgil chuckled. "Looks like your aunt Isabel was right all along. The two of you were obviously meant for each other."

Hannah stared at him. "You knew Aunt Isabel?"

"Yes, indeed. We had some mutual interests."

"I find that difficult to believe."

Virgil arched a brow. "Did you know that she collected eighteenth-century erotica?"

"Uh, no." Hannah cleared her throat. "She never mentioned it."

"Yes, indeed. I helped her build her collection. I have some excellent contacts in the rare book business, you see. I'm sure you'll run into Isabel's old books and prints when you two start going through her things at Dreamscape. Whatever you do, don't toss or sell any of those books and things until you check with me. Some of those volumes are worth several thousand dollars."

"Good grief," Hannah said weakly. "I'm suddenly getting a whole new picture of my aunt."

Rafe tried not to laugh. It wasn't easy. The bewildered, bemused expression on Hannah's face was priceless.

Virgil crouched and held his hand out to Winston. "Lovely dog."

Hannah frowned as Winston trotted forward to sniff politely. When the dog appeared satisfied, she hesitated and then said, "Thank you."

She still sounded stiff, but Rafe could tell she was softening. Virgil put his hand in the small of his back and straightened with great care.

"Arthritis," he explained. "Or the old war wound. I can never tell the difference."

"Which war?" Hannah asked warily.

"Does it matter? They're all the same, aren't they? At least, they all look the same when you're standing in the middle of one." He looked at Rafe. "What can I do for you? Something tells me that the two of you are not here to purchase the latest issue of *Fetish* magazine or to rent *Alice Does Wonderland*."

Rafe leaned back against a counter stocked with rainbow-colored, plastic dildos arranged in order of size. He shoved his hands into his front pockets and plunged straight into the tale.

"This is about what happened the night Kaitlin Sadler died," he said. "Hannah and I have some reason to think that her death might not have been an accident."

Virgil nodded somberly. "Yes, of course."

Hannah shot him a quick, frowning glance. "You don't look surprised, Mr. Nash."

"Why should I be surprised? I've heard the rumors."

"Exactly what rumors have you heard?" Rafe asked.

Virgil raised his thin shoulders in a small shrug. "Everyone knows that the two of you went to see Dell Sadler yesterday. Given his history with you, Rafe, there could be only one reason why the pair of you would sit down and talk after all this time."

"Okay," Rafe said, "I'll cut to the chase. A few things have happened lately that make us think that someone doesn't want the old investigation reopened."

Virgil said nothing. He just waited.

"We've picked up some indications," Hannah added, "that Kaitlin Sadler may have been blackmailing someone in town. If it's true, it might mean that same someone killed her to silence her."

Glittering curiosity flared without warning in Virgil's gaze. "You don't say."

"We don't have anything solid to go on yet," Rafe said. "But it looks like the blackmail material might have had something to do with someone's sex life."

"It often does." Virgil paused. "But in this day and age, it would have to be a particularly interesting sex life to be worth blackmail payments or murder."

"That's why we came to you," Rafe said. "Know any men in town who like to wear ladies' underwear?"

"At least half a dozen names come to mind," Virgil said without missing a beat. "If that's all you've got, you'll be at this investigation for a very long time."

"You're kidding," Hannah said. "You know half a dozen men in Eclipse Bay who have a penchant for female underwear?"

"The fetish for women's undergarments is not all that rare or unusual." Virgil adopted a professional tone as he warmed to his lecture. "It is generally considered a harmless quirk, as these things go. Indeed, the history of prominent men dressing in lingerie goes back for centuries. There have been kings, generals, presidents, statesmen—"

"But of the six men here in Eclipse Bay who like to wear lingerie which one would be seriously horrified if the news got around?" Rafe asked before Virgil could get sidetracked by his professional interest.

"I imagine that they would all be embarrassed, to varying degrees."

Hannah looked at him. "Think any of them would be so humiliated that he would pay blackmail or kill to keep the secret?"

Virgil stroked his goatee while he pondered that. In the end, he shook his head decisively. "Frankly, I don't see any of them in the role of murderer. But one never knows, does one?"

"Six men," Rafe repeated.

"Those are just the ones who come to mind immediately because I have had some contact with them over the years," Virgil said. "There are no doubt several others who don't shop at my store."

Hannah sighed. "It's hopeless. Sounds like we can't even get a complete list, let alone verify the whereabouts of all the men on it for the night Kaitlin died."

"You don't need to find all of them," Virgil pointed out. "Just the ones who knew Kaitlin intimately."

"From what I've heard, that would still be a mighty long list." Hannah shot Rafe a dark glare.

"Don't look at me," Rafe said calmly. "I prefer lingerie on ladies."

"And he is the only suspect who had an ironclad alibi that night," Virgil reminded her. "Thanks to you."

"I know." Hannah scowled. "Still, there must be some way to narrow the list."

"For starters, I imagine that you can eliminate any man who wasn't reasonably affluent at the time," Virgil said. "After all, no point blackmailing someone who can't afford to pay."

Rafe was intrigued. "You're right. That might cut the list down a little."

Hannah frowned. "If he was rich enough to pay blackmail, chances are he would have been wealthy enough to be invited to the political reception up at the institute that night. But if he was there, he's also got a solid alibi."

"I'm not so sure about that," Rafe said slowly. "The institute was crowded that evening. Everyone who was anyone in Eclipse Bay was there. Someone could have slipped away long enough to murder Kaitlin and then returned to the reception with no one the wiser."

"I don't see how you could possibly ascertain that information," Virgil said quietly.

Rafe glanced at Hannah. He knew they were both thinking the same thing.

"There just may be a way to do that," he told Virgil.

"Indeed?" Virgil looked intrigued. "Fascinating. You do understand that under normal circumstances I would not even consider providing you with this list. But given what you say may have been an attempt on your life, Ms. Harte, I will try to help. There is just one thing I would like for you both to keep in mind."

"What's that?" Rafe asked.

"When it comes to blackmail," Virgil said very seriously, "there are sometimes others besides the victim who have a motive to kill the blackmailer."

Hannah's brows snapped together. "Such as?"

"Such as anyone who has a great deal invested in the victim," Virgil said.

Rafe looked at him. "Hell, do you think maybe we should be looking at all the *wives* of these guys you know who like to run around in lacy unmentionables?"

"Never forget the old saying about the female of the species being just as deadly as the male. The wife of a prominent, wealthy, or powerful man who could be brought low by blackmail would certainly have reason to get rid of a potential threat to her future income and position."

They all pondered that for a moment. Then Virgil turned away and walked to the counter. He picked up a pen and started to write names down on a sheet of yellow paper.

Hannah moved closer to Rafe and lowered her voice. "Are you thinking what I'm thinking about how to figure out who might have left the reception and returned between midnight and two?"

"A.Z.'s logbooks."

"Yes." Hannah watched Virgil. "You know her better than I do. Think she would let us look at them?"

"I might be able to talk her into it."

"But, Rafe, even if we come up with a good suspect, what can we do with the information? Officially there was no murder, and we don't have anything that resembles proof."

"We'll work on that part after we get the good suspect."

They stood in silence for a while, waiting for Virgil to finish his list. After a time Rafe got restless. He wandered over to a pile of padded leather handcuffs. He picked up one and examined the Velcro fastener.

Hannah gave him the same sort of look she had given Winston when he tried to investigate the condom wrapper out in the parking lot.

"Don't even think about it." she said.

MITCHELL settled into the overstuffed easy chair with a familiar sense of contentment. The chair had been new and a little stiff a year ago when he had first started visiting Bev on a regular basis. But he had spent a lot of time in it during the past months, and the leather upholstery had shaped itself to his body. It was comfortable and welcoming. Sort of like Bev herself, he thought.

But there was a lot more to Bev than warmth and comfort. There was stimulation, both mental and physical. He loved to argue with her. Loved to play cards with her. Loved to go for long walks along the river with her. She made him feel good in ways that no other woman ever had, not even in the wild years following the breakup of Harte-Madison when he'd chased the illusion of passion the way other men had chased wealth or fame, or adrenaline.

Bev walked into the living room with the coffee tray. He turned away from the view of the river to look at her. A deep pleasure reverberated somewhere inside. There was wisdom and warmth and laughter in her eyes. Her own personal standards were high, always had been. But unlike some folks he knew who had made it this far in life, himself included, she was not inclined to judge others harshly. She accepted people as they were.

A fine figure of a woman, he thought, watching her pour the coffee. Bev was a great believer in vitamins and exercise, and the results were obvious. There was a healthy, energetic aura about her. She had not magically escaped the common chronic problems that came with the years. Six months ago he'd noticed the bottle of blood pressure pills in the kitchen cupboard above her sink. There was another bottle of tablets for the relief of arthritis in her bathroom, the same brand his own doctor had prescribed for him. But Bev's natural optimism and zest for living subtracted years from the calendar.

She had always had an instinct for style. Today her silver hair was swept back from her forehead in a short, sophisticated bob. She wore a good-looking black-

and-white pantsuit that accented her healthy figure. Little silver rings dangled from her ears.

She smiled and handed him a cup of coffee. "How are things going over there in Eclipse Bay? Are you and Rafe getting along okay?"

"As well as we ever did." Mitchell sipped the coffee. Just enough sugar and a splash of milk. Bev knew how he liked it. "Better, maybe. But he's still one stubborn, muleheaded son of a gun."

Bev took her seat and crossed her legs in a graceful, unconsciously feminine movement that sent a whisper of anticipation through him. A few months back, his doctor had written another prescription for him, one that worked hydraulic marvels. He and Bev had gotten a lot of use out of it lately.

"Sounds like a chip off the old block," Bev said.

"Why the hell does everyone keep saying that?"

"Probably because it's true."

He bristled a little. "Well, I'm working on seeing to it that Rafe doesn't make all the same mistakes I did."

Bev chuckled. "A worthy project. Good luck."

"Thanks. I'm gonna need it." He frowned. "He's carrying on with Hannah Harte."

Bev's brows rose in surprise. "Carrying on, as in having an affair with her?"

"That too. It's Isabel's fault. If she hadn't left that damn house to both of 'em none of this would have happened."

"What exactly has happened?"

"I just told you—they're sleeping together."

"Are you sure?"

"Hell, everyone in town knows it."

"Hmm." Bev tilted her head slightly to the side as she contemplated that information. "I wouldn't worry about it too much if I were you. Isabel was a very, very smart woman. She probably knew what she was doing when she drew up that will."

Mitchell grunted. "Maybe yes, maybe no. Either way, it all comes down to the same thing. Rafe's carrying on with Hannah, and her family hasn't got a clue. When Sullivan Harte finds out, he's gonna shit . . . uh, he's gonna blow his top."

"Rafe and Hannah aren't kids anymore. They're full-grown adults. They'll make their own decisions."

"Huh. Far as I'm concerned, Rafe's already made his, and he's by God gonna follow through if I have anything to say about it. Hannah's a nice young woman, even if she is a Harte. If he thinks he can fool around with her and then walk away, he's got another thing coming."

Bev peered at him with a mixture of amusement and curiosity. "Are you saying you feel Rafe ought to marry Hannah?"

Mitchell balanced the cup and saucer on the broad leather arm of the big chair. "Yep. That's exactly what I think."

"Since when did you become such a zealous believer in old-fashioned morality?"

"Since I started watching the two of 'em together. You ought to see the way he looks at her, Bev. Damn near painful."

"What about Hannah?"

"She looks at him the same way. Thing is, they're scared to death of each other."

"You think you can play Cupid?"

"Figure it's my responsibility to straighten things out." Mitchell looked at the river. "I put my son, Sinclair, through hell when he was a boy. Set a real bad example. Sure enough, he turned right around and did the same thing to Rafe and Gabe. I figure it's up to me to stop this cycle before it goes on to another generation."

"And you're going to do it by marrying Rafe off to Hannah?"

"If I can." Mitchell paused to take another swallow of coffee. "But before I can see about getting Rafe to the altar, I've got to help him and Hannah fix another little problem that's come up."

"What's that?"

Mitchell looked at her. "Rafe has convinced himself that someone may have tried to kill Hannah and her dog a couple of nights ago."

Bev's shock left her mouth hanging open for a few seconds.

"Are you serious?" she finally managed.

"On the surface, it looks like some bastard tried to drown her dog, but Rafe thinks it may have been an attempt to get Hannah, too. He's sure it's got some tie back to what happened to Kaitlin Sadler."

"But that's ridiculous," Bev sputtered. "Kaitlin's death was an accident. Everyone knows that. And if it had been something worse, heaven forbid, why would the killer make a move against Hannah now?"

"Ever since Rafe and Hannah returned to Eclipse Bay to sort out the business with Dreamscape, there's been talk. Some of it is about the fact that they're carrying on together, naturally. But some of it is about the past. Rafe and Hannah have started asking questions themselves, and now, what with the incident involving the mutt, they're beginning to dig a little deeper." Mitchell met her gaze. "To tell you the truth, I'm afraid they just might uncover some old bones that would probably be better off left buried."

"But Rafe, being Rafe, won't listen to your advice to leave well enough alone, is that it?"

Mitchell shrugged. "He never did listen."

"So you've decided to help him look into the matter?"

"That's about the size of it."

Bev studied him for a long moment. Then she gave him a knowing smile. "You're enjoying yourself, aren't you? I think you like the idea of playing Dr. Watson to Rafe's Sherlock Holmes."

"Be the first thing Rafe and I have done together since he was a kid." Mitchell was aware of an oddly wistful feeling. "We got along pretty good for a few years after he and Gabe came to live with me. But from the day Rafe hit his midteens, he and I locked horns. It's been a little better in the past few years, but it's like we're walking on eggshells. Doesn't take much for either one of us to set the other off. My fault, I reckon."

"Don't be too hard on yourself, Mitch. You did all right by your grandsons. Sinclair wasn't much of a father to his boys."

Mitchell gripped the mug hard. "That's because he had me for an example."

"The point is that after your son's death, you stepped in and did what you had to do. You stopped your running around—"

"Well—"

Bev chuckled. "All right, let's just say you cut way down on your running around. You paid attention to the job of raising Rafe and Gabe, and neither one of them has screwed up his life. I'd say you did okay."

Bev always had a way of making him feel better about things, Mitchell thought. She had a way of giving him a slightly different perspective.

"Let's get back to the reason you're here." Bev put her coffee aside and sat forward. "You say you want to help Rafe find out what really happened to the Sadler woman. But what if there isn't any conspiracy to uncover? What if Chief Yates was right about her death being an accident?"

Mitchell shook his head. "I started into this thinking that Rafe and Hannah were going off the deep end. But now I'm not so sure. Bev, you knew everything that Ed knew about the goings-on in Eclipse Bay, and Ed knew a hell of a lot. If I said that there's a possibility that Kaitlin Sadler might have been having an affair with someone who wanted to keep it a big, dark secret, do any names come to mind?"

"Kaitlin got involved with more than one married man." Bev made a face. "She was not very popular with the ladies of Eclipse Bay, I can tell you that."

"How about if I throw in some dirty movies and some female underwear in a man's size? Does that narrow the list a bit?"

Bev angled her chin. "Hmm," she said thoughtfully.

Mitchell waited.

"Unfortunately," Bev said slowly, "there is one name that does come to mind. Ed once told me about some rumors he'd heard shortly before Kaitlin's death. Naturally he ignored them. Ed was an old-fashioned kind of journalist. Unlike this modern bunch, he didn't believe in printing the details of people's sex lives on the front page of a family newspaper."

Mitchell could feel himself getting revved up. This investigating business was fun. He was starting to understand why Rafe was so eager to poke a stick into this particular varmint hole. "Can I have the name of this guy Ed didn't want to put on the front page?"

Bev hesitated. "I'll give it to you, but it won't do you any good. He has an ironclad alibi for that night."

"How do you know that?"

"Because I can vouch for his whereabouts that evening, as well as the whereabouts of most of the rest of the good, upstanding citizens of Eclipse Bay."

"Well, shoot and damn." Disgust replaced the anticipation Mitchell had been savoring. "Don't tell me you saw him at that reception up at the institute that night?"

"I'm afraid so," Bev replied. "Still want the name?"

"Sure." A thought struck Mitchell. "You never can tell. Maybe he ducked out long enough to murder the Sadler woman. In a crowd of that size, he might not have been missed for a while."

"Trust me, he would have been missed if he had vanished for any period of time longer than what it would take to go to the men's room," Bev said. "The name is Trevor Thornley. Soon to become Senator Thornley, if all goes according to plan."

Mitchell groaned. "Well, shoot and damn."

20

"TREVOR Thornley? In lingerie and high heels?" Hannah sank back into the depths of the wicker chair. "There's an image I could have done without."

Rafe paced back across the solarium. "But it makes sense. Dell told us that Kaitlin had claimed that she was going to score big. None of the names on Virgil's list would qualify as big scores. She might have pried a few bucks out of some of them, but not enough to finance a fresh start outside of Eclipse Bay."

"But a politician with a bright future in front of him might have looked very tempting to her," Hannah said quietly.

"Sure would be embarrassing as all get out if Kaitlin actually had movies of him running around in ladies' undies," Mitchell said. "Thing like that would have cost him the election eight years ago. Seeing as how he was the conservative on the ticket and all."

Rafe continued his pacing. "Might have been worth murder to Thornley."

"Never did trust him," Mitchell said.

Rafe was almost amused. "Big deal. You've never trusted any politician in your life."

"It's a grand theory, gentlemen." Hannah picked up her wineglass. "But let's not get too carried away here. As Bev pointed out to Mitchell, Thornley is the one person who could not have disappeared from the reception without being missed that night."

Rafe came to a halt and rested a hand on the windowsill as he contemplated the steel-colored waters of the bay. "Remember what Virgil told us. In a blackmail case there are others besides the victim who have a motive to kill. Anyone with an investment in the person being blackmailed might be moved to do something drastic to stop the extortionist."

Hannah swirled the sauvignon blanc in her glass. "Are you suggesting Thornley's wife might have murdered Kaitlin?"

Rafe thought about it. "Marilyn Thornley is as dedicated to her husband's career as he is. A decade ago she had a reputation for getting what she wanted. Doubt that's changed much in the last few years."

"I won't ask how you know that," Hannah grumbled.

Rafe shrugged. "Don't give me that look. Marilyn never wanted me. She knew I wasn't headed for big things."

Hannah frowned. "So how do you know that she had a way of getting what she went after?"

It was Mitchell who answered. "He knows because for a while Marilyn wanted Gabe."

"Aha." Hannah pondered that fact. "Did she, uh, get him for a while?"

"You know, I never came right out and asked him," Mitchell said laconically. "But to tell you the truth, if they did have a fling, it wouldn't have meant much to him. The only thing he cared about in those days was reviving Madison Commercial. Still is, come to that. I swear, if that grandson of mine doesn't figure out that there's more to life than doing deals and making money, he's gonna wind up missing all the stuff that really matters."

Rafe shot him a narrow-eyed look. "Gabe resurrected Madison Commercial for you, Mitchell."

"You don't have to tell me that. I admit I steered him in that direction. But I never meant for him to make the damn company his entire life."

Rafe shrugged. "The company's his passion. What did you expect?"

"We all know what happens with a Madison once he's fixated on his great passion in life," Hannah murmured into her wine.

"You make it sound like Gabe doesn't have time for a wife, but that's not true," Mitchell continued. "The only reason he hasn't married is because he's got a problem with women."

Hannah was interested. "What kind of problem?"

"He expects them to work the same way his company works." Mitchell's voice dripped with disgust and frustration. "Don't know where he got the notion that women operate like an accounts receivable department or that you could treat one of 'em like a branch of the head office. Certainly not from me."

"We're getting a little off track here," Rafe said. "Why don't we get back to the problem at hand?"

Hannah straightened in her chair. "Right. Okay, let's see what we've got so far. We think that Trevor Thornley might have been Kaitlin's blackmail target. But we also know that he couldn't have killed her that night because he was the star of the institute reception. That leaves us with the extremely weak possibility that someone who didn't want Thornley compromised might have gone out to meet Kaitlin and silence her."

"Makes sense to me," Mitchell said. "What do we do next?"

Rafe turned the glass in his hands. "We talk to Arizona Snow. See if she'll let us look at her logbooks for that night."

"Let's just hope she wasn't home sick with the flu that evening," Hannah said.

"Thank you, Miss Optimism," Rafe growled.

"Well, to be honest, I keep wondering what we can do even if we do come up with a really terrific scenario for the murder of Kaitlin Sadler. It's not like we can hope to find any proof after all this time. Say that we're successful. What are our options?"

Rafe hesitated. It was Mitchell who sat forward, determined and eager.

"I'll tell you what you do," he said. "You blow the whole damn story wide open so there are no more secrets to be kept. You go to Jed Steadman down at the *Journal* and give him the facts. He always wanted to be a real investigative reporter. This is his big chance, and I'm betting he'll take it. If he runs with it, you can pretty much guarantee that every paper in the state will start digging into the Sadler woman's death."

"He's right," Rafe said. "Jed might not find hard proof, but the entire Thornley camp will be on the defensive. Hell, the lingerie rumors alone will be enough to keep them fully occupied. Whoever's behind this will be too busy proving Thornley's innocence on both counts to bother with any more attacks on you or Winston."

Hannah looked at each man in turn. The same ice-cold intent glittered in both pairs of sea-green Madison eyes. She shook her head. "And you two wonder why everyone says you're so much alike."

AFTER dinner Rafe walked out onto the porch with Mitchell. Winston padded along at their heels. Together the three of them gazed at the big SUV lurking in the shadows of the drive, looking for all the world like some modern-day *Tyrannosaurus rex* waiting for prey. Probably hoping some slow-witted, herbivorous little compact would wander within range, Rafe thought. The silhouette of Bryce's figure behind the wheel was just barely visible in the gathering shadows. The dinosaur's brain.

"Well, thanks for dinner," Mitchell said.

"Sure. Anytime."

"Still can't get over the fact that you can turn out first-rate grub like that."

"Maybe you've just been eating too much of Bryce's cooking."

"Could be. But I'm used to it."

Rafe leaned against a post. "I haven't thanked you for the information you brought back from Portland."

"No problem." Mitchell tapped the end of his cane on the edge of the step. "Sort of interesting, if you want the truth. Haven't ever done anything along those lines."

"Neither have I. Lucky for us, you and Bev Bolton are such good friends."

"Uh-huh."

There was another short silence. Winston yawned.

"Sure hope to hell we know what we're doing here," Mitchell said after a while. "If we're right, we're talking about blowing apart the campaign of a hot-shit candidate for the United States Senate. Lawsuits could be the least of our worries when this is over."

"Since when did a Madison ever let the small stuff get in the way?"

Mitchell nodded. "You've got a point there."

"The important thing is that we put a stop to whatever is going on around here." Rafe folded his arms. "Hannah's safety comes first."

"Can't argue that one," Mitchell said. "What's a political campaign compared to protecting a lady? Speaking of Hannah—"

Rafe braced himself. "Were we?"

"We sure as hell were. I didn't want to say anything in front of her, but we both know the two of you can't stay shacked up here like this indefinitely."

"Shacked up?" Rafe managed a politely blank expression. "I don't believe I'm familiar with the term."

"Bullshit! You know damn well what I'm talkin' about. When are you going to do the right thing by that girl?"

"When are you going to do the right thing by Bev Bolton?"

Mitchell's face tightened. Rafe was startled to see a flash of pain in his grandfather's eyes. The expression vanished swiftly behind glittering outrage.

"I'd marry Bev Bolton tomorrow if I thought she'd have me," Mitchell said ferociously. "But I've got a reputation to live down. She doesn't think I know how to make what she likes to call a commitment."

Rafe looked at him, saying nothing.

Mitchell blinked once or twice. The outrage faded to dawning chagrin. "Well, shoot and damn. You're in the same leaky boat, aren't you, son?"

"I don't think Hannah bought that story you gave her about my bad nerves," Rafe said. "She's got the same problem with me that Bev Bolton has with you."

"Your checkered past?"

"Yeah. But in my case it's not only my own that I've got to live down. I've got yours and Dad's in the way, too."

"Well, shoot and damn." Mitchell gazed unhappily at the tip of his cane, then at Rafe. "Don't suppose you've got any good ideas on what to do about this problem Madisons seem to have with females?"

"No."

"Well, shoot and damn."

"Yeah," Rafe said. "Shoot and damn."

"No sense asking Gabe. He's no better with women than we are."

"Apparently not."

Mitchell glanced at Winston. The Schnauzer cocked his head in polite inquiry.

"No point asking him for advice, either," Rafe said. "Hannah had him neutered."

The night coalesced swiftly around them, deepening the somber atmosphere.

"I think there's some irony here somewhere," Rafe said eventually. "But I can't be sure, because I never finished college."

"Told you you'd regret dropping out."

"I know. Look at me now. Doomed to go through life without knowing about stuff like irony and postmodernism. It's almost enough to make a man regret a misspent youth." Rafe paused. "But I'll probably get over it."

Mitchell nodded. "Fix yourself a whiskey and soda and take a long walk on the beach. Always worked for me." He roused himself and went down the steps. "Tell you one thing," he said over his shoulder as he strode toward the waiting SUV.

"What's that?"

"You may not have finished college, but you're a Madison."

"So?"

"So, no Madison ever let anything stand in his way once he made up his mind to go after what he wanted. Remember what I said. You can't shack up with Hannah forever. It's not right. You've got to come up with a fix for this mess. Hear me?"

"I hear you."

Mitchell opened the passenger-side door of the SUV and climbed in. Rafe and Winston watched the monster vehicle lumber off down the drive.

When the taillights disappeared, Rafe looked down at the dog. "You know, Winston, one of the reasons you and I get along so well is that you never hand out unsolicited advice."

Winston yawned again, rose, and ambled back inside the house.

❦

MITCHELL peered at the road through the windshield. "I think those two need a little kick in the right place to get them moving in the right direction."

"My advice is to stay out of the matter, sir," Bryce said. "The conduct of close interpersonal relationships is not your strong point."

"I don't pay you for advice."

"You have made that clear many times over the years."

"Never seems to stop you from interfering."

"That's why you keep paying me, sir."

"Hmmph."

"I hate to ask," Bryce said, "but do you have a plan to apply this kick you seem to feel your grandson and Miss Harte require?"

Mitchell drummed his fingers on the dash, thinking furiously. "I'm working on one."

Bryce nodded. "I was afraid of that."

❦

RAFE was brooding. Hannah could feel the vibes. He had been in a strange mood since he came back into the house after seeing Mitchell off. She had helped him with the dishes. There had been very little conversation. The few words that had been exchanged had been centered on speculation about what they might or might not learn from Arizona Snow.

"She's so weird," Hannah said. "Lord only knows what those logs of hers will look like, assuming she'll even let us see them."

"I think she'll let me have a look at them." Rafe finished drying a pan and shoved it into a cupboard. "She and I always got along pretty good in the old days."

"I know." Hannah glanced at him. "Why did the two of you hit it off so well, anyway?"

"I don't know why she liked me, but I can tell you why I took to her."

"Why?"

"She was the only one who never tried to tell me what I should do with my life."

Hannah winced. "Okay, I can see the appeal there. Did she ever tell you anything about her past?"

"Nope."

"Ever wonder about it?"

"Sure." Rafe shut the cupboard door. "Everyone in town wonders about her past. Most people figure she's just one hundred percent bonkers."

"When I was younger," Hannah said slowly, "I imagined that she was an ex–secret agent who was forced to retire after her mind cracked under the strain of undercover work."

"That's as logical as any of the other theories I've heard over the years."

When they finished the dishes they wandered out into the darkened solarium. Rafe put two glasses on the table between a pair of wicker loungers and filled each with gently steaming water. He picked up a bottle of orange liqueur and splashed some into two balloon glasses. Then he cradled the bowls of the balloon glasses over the hot water to warm the liqueur.

When he was finished, he lowered himself into one of the loungers and handed one of the balloon glasses to Hannah.

She accepted the pleasantly warm glass and took a sip of the sultry liqueur. Winston stuck his head over the edge of the lounger. She stroked his ears. An air of doggy bliss emanated from him.

The darkness grew heavier. So did Rafe's mood. Hannah resisted the urge to break the silence. She was determined that he would be the one to do that. If he wanted to brood, that was his business. It wasn't like she was his wife or even a close friend, she reminded herself. It wasn't her job to cheer him up when he was down or jolly him out of a bad temper. Sure, they had made love a few times, but that didn't mean they were lovers.

Instead of rallying her, that thought lowered her own spirits.

Wonderful. Now she was brooding, too.

For a while she thought Rafe might not speak at all. She was telling herself that she was getting accustomed to the silence when he finally started talking. The first words out of his mouth startled her so much that she was the one who was momentarily speechless.

"Ever since the night Kaitlin died," he said, his voice seeming to come from a distant place, "I've always wondered whether or not Mitchell believed that I might have killed her."

Hannah opened her mouth and then closed it again. She was so taken back she could not think of an appropriate response. Maybe there wasn't one.

"He never said a word." Rafe turned the heated glass between his palms. "But that didn't mean anything. His first loyalty is to Gabe and me. I've always known that. Even when we were going toe-to-toe about everything from my lousy job prospects and the motorcycle to my choice in girlfriends, I knew that he would stand by me no matter what. He might disapprove. He might be disappointed. He might be furious. But he would be on my side in a fight. Just like Gabe."

Hannah stared at him. "You actually thought that all these years Mitchell has been wondering what really happened that night? You weren't sure he believed your story?"

"I was never certain." Rafe's jaw tightened. "And I was too damn proud to confront him and ask him straight out."

She pondered that for a moment. "Maybe you were afraid of the answer."

He looked out at the lights on the far side of the bay. "Maybe. Or maybe I just didn't want him to be put in the position of having to pretend that he never doubted me. Mitchell and I have had our problems, but we've always been straight with each other. Didn't want that to change."

She thought back to what Mitchell had said about Rafe the first night they had invited him to dinner. *He's a Madison. He's got a temper. But if he had been with Kaitlin that night and if there had been some terrible accident, he'd have gone for help and then he'd have told the flatout truth about what happened.*

"Your grandfather knows that you had nothing to do with Kaitlin's death," she said. "He never doubted you."

"I know that now."

Hannah exhaled slowly. "Well, if nothing else good comes from this situation, it sounds like you and he are working out some sort of long overdue reconciliation. That's worth something."

Rafe gave her a laconic, sidelong look. "Why do you care whether or not Mitchell and I patch up our differences?"

"I live to bring joy and happiness to those around me."

"Try again."

She made a face. "Don't pin me down."

"Right." He took another swallow of the liqueur.

She gave him a few seconds. When he did not volunteer anything further in the way of conversation, she tried another tack.

"I promised myself I wasn't going to ask what happened between you and Mitchell outside on the porch a while ago, but my curiosity has gotten the better of me."

"No surprise there."

She ignored that. "Look, you just told me that you're no longer worried that

Mitchell might be harboring some deep, dark suspicions about what happened on the night of Kaitlin's death. And the two of you have decided that you'll work together on our little investigation. Heck, you're even having your grandfather over for dinner these days. Obviously your relationship is improving rapidly. So what went wrong out there on the porch?"

"Nothing went wrong."

"Don't give me that baffled, befuddled male stare. I'm not buying it."

He sank deeper into his lounger and wrapped his long-fingered hands around the balloon glass. "I thought I was pretty good at doing baffled and befuddled."

"Not funny, Madison. When you went outside you were in a reasonably good mood. You came back in a lousy mood. You can't blame me for wondering what transpired on the front porch."

For a moment she thought he would not answer. Then he tilted his head against the back of the lounger and closed his eyes. "Mitchell made it clear that he didn't like the fact that you and I are, and here I quote, '*shacking up* together.' "

"*Shacking up?*" Hannah sucked in an outraged breath. "He actually used that term?"

"He did, yes."

"Ridiculous. No one uses that phrase anymore."

"I mentioned that."

"It's old-fashioned. Downright archaic. It implies an outdated value system that demeans and insults two rational, intelligent adults who choose to make their own decisions in an extremely private area of life."

"Damn right."

"It's a stupid phrase implying low morals and a complete disregard for societal norms."

"You can say that again—I think."

"It takes absolutely no allowance for alternative lifestyles, freedom of association, and the right to life, liberty, and the pursuit of happiness."

"Well, Mitchell never was what anyone would call politically correct, even on his good days."

"Besides," Hannah concluded, "it's not even true."

"Sort of hard to explain the facts to Mitchell."

"We are *not* shacking up." She batted at the air with one hand while she fumbled for words. "We're not even sharing the same floor here at Dreamscape, let alone the same bedroom."

"Believe me, I am well aware of that."

"We haven't even *done* anything," she raced on wildly. "Not since I moved into Dreamscape, at any rate."

"That fact has not escaped my notice, either." He sounded disappointed.

"I own half this house." She gripped the arm of the lounger. "If I want to use part of it, that's my business."

"You're entitled, all right."

"Furthermore, it was *your* idea for me to move in here."

"I take full responsibility," Rafe said piously.

"Oh, stop being so bloody reasonable about it." She flopped back in the lounger in disgust. "You're a Madison. You're not supposed to be reasonable."

21

"YOU want the logbook from the night Kaitlin Sadler died?" Arizona Snow squinted her eyes against the smoke that rose from her cigar. She regarded Hannah and Rafe across the expanse of the wide table that dominated the space she fondly called her war room. "Well, now, isn't that an amazing coincidence?"

Hannah tensed. She felt Rafe, sitting beside her, do the same. Winston, apparently sensing the suddenly charged atmosphere, paused in the act of sniffing around the base of a metal file cabinet. They all looked at Arizona.

"Okay, you've got our attention, A.Z.," Rafe said. "What's with the crack about a coincidence? Are you saying that someone else has been here asking for that particular log?"

"In a manner of speaking." Arizona shoved her hands into one of the half dozen pockets of her khaki cargo pants. She chewed thoughtfully on the fat stogie she had stuck between her thin lips. "But he didn't exactly ask politely. The institute sent an agent to break into my place a week or so after Kaitlin's death. Took only one thing. Give you two guesses what that one thing was."

Hannah leaned forward, stunned. "The log that covered that particular night?"

"You got it," Arizona said. She removed one hand from a pocket and slammed the table with the flat of her palm. "I knew right then and there something big had gone on that evening. But the next morning the only thing everyone in town could talk about was Kaitlin Sadler's so-called accident and the possibility that Rafe, here, might have offed her. Now, don't that tell you somethin'?"

Rafe studied her warily. "You still think Kaitlin was killed by someone up at the institute?"

Arizona gave him a grimly triumphant look. "The way I figure it, there's only two possibilities. Either that poor gal was murdered by an agent in order to create a distraction for whatever the hell they were doin' up there at the institute—"

"Or?" Hannah prompted cautiously.

Arizona lowered her voice to a whisper laden with portent and dark implication. "Or like I said the other night, the Sadler girl saw somethin' she wasn't supposed to see. Either way, it's obvious that the institute got rid of her before she could spill the beans, and then they set Rafe up as the fall guy. If it hadn't been for you, Hannah, he might have gone to prison."

Hannah's heart sank. She did not dare meet Rafe's eyes. They had both known that it would be difficult to talk to Arizona Snow. But neither of them had allowed for the fact that her logbook for the fateful night might have gone missing.

"You got any ideas of who might have taken your log?" Rafe asked.

"I just told you who took it. One of the institute agents."

"Huh." Rafe flicked a glance at Hannah.

She smiled encouragingly at Arizona. "I don't suppose you remember any cars that left the institute parking lot that night sometime around midnight and returned before the reception ended?"

Arizona shook her head regretfully. "Been eight years now. All I recall is that there was an awful lot of activity up there that night. The parking lot was full most of the evening. Lots of coming and going. There was the media, some out-of-town institute agents, and all the innocent dupes of Eclipse Bay who paid good money to cheer for Thornley."

Rafe sat back. "Damn. Told you years ago that you should start entering your data on a computer, A.Z."

Arizona gave a snort of disgust. "Can't trust computers. Any kid can break into them and help himself to anything he wants."

"Filing your information in hard copy sure didn't do us much good," Rafe muttered.

Arizona raised one massive shoulder in a shrug. She regarded her guests with a crafty gleam in her eyes.

Hannah turned to Rafe. "Got any more bright ideas?"

"Let me think." He rubbed the back of his neck. "Jed Steadman mentioned that he might be able to dig up an institute guest list for that night."

"Checking the whereabouts of everyone on the list for that two-hour window would take days and days of work," Hannah said. "Even assuming it could be done at all. And we couldn't ever be sure of the accuracy. Like Arizona said, it's been eight years. No one's going to recall many details."

Rafe studied the large topographic map of Eclipse Bay and the surrounding vicinity that was laminated to the surface of the war room table. "Jed might be able to help us out there, too. He covered the reception. He might still have his notes."

Hannah thought about that approach and shook her head. "He might have some old notes regarding the most newsworthy people in attendance. But he certainly wouldn't have kept tabs on everyone in the crowd."

"If we're right, we're looking for someone who may have been newsworthy, or at the very least, attached to the Thornley campaign." Rafe rose from his chair. "It's just barely possible Jed will be able to help us. Worth a try."

"Well, it's not like we have anything else to go on." Hannah started to rise. "Without Arizona's log for that night—"

"Didn't say there wasn't a log for that night," Arizona drawled.

Halfway to her feet, Hannah paused. "What?"

Rafe planted both hands on the laminated map and leaned across the table. "A.Z.? You told us that log was missing from your file."

A deep, hoarse chuckle rumbled through Arizona. "The original was stolen, like I told you."

"Original?" Rafe waited.

"I didn't just fall off the turnip truck," Arizona said with cool satisfaction. "I've been in this business a long time. First thing I do when I get back from a recon job is make a copy of my log."

Rafe started to grin. "I should have guessed."

Hannah felt a small flicker of hope. "Where's the copy of your missing log, Arizona?"

"Hidden in the bunker along with all the other copies." Arizona glanced at the massive multifunctional steel watch on her wrist. "Take a couple of hours to drive to the site, dig out the log, and get back to town. What d'ya say we meet up out at Dreamscape at 1100 hours?"

"We'll be waiting." Rafe straightened. "Thanks, A.Z. I really appreciate this."

"Sure. Any time." Arizona gripped the arms of her desk chair and shoved herself to her feet. "Just glad to see some folks from around here finally start paying attention to what's going on up there at the institute."

"Innocent dupes of the world, arise," Hannah murmured. "You have nothing to lose but your innocence."

Rafe took her arm and headed toward the door. "We'll keep you informed of everything we discover, A.Z."

"You do that." Arizona hesitated, concern furrowing her forehead. "And you two take care, hear? You're tangling with the institute crowd now. That means you're dealing with some ruthless types. Someone up there ordered the Sadler girl's death to cover up something. Whoever did it might be willing to kill again."

A chill went through Hannah. She cleared her throat. "Well, on that cheerful note—"

"By the way," Arizona interrupted rather casually, "how long are you two gonna shack up together out there at Dreamscape?"

Anger surged, temporarily submerging the little thrill of dread Hannah had felt a few seconds ago. She jerked to a halt, spun around, and glared at Arizona.

"We are *not* shacking up."

Rafe tightened his grip on her arm. "Hannah, this isn't the time to go into it."

"The heck it isn't." Hannah grabbed the edge of the door as Rafe tried to haul her forcibly out into the hall. "I want to set the record straight before we leave. Listen, Arizona, Rafe and I are *sharing* Dreamscape until we negotiate a way out of the mess Isabel left us in. We are not shacking up there."

"Sorta hard to tell the difference," Arizona answered through a cloud of smoke.

"Not from where I stand," Hannah retorted. "We're sleeping on separate floors."

"Sounds uncomfortable," Arizona said.

HANNAH was a bundle of simmering outrage. Rafe could feel her vibrating on the seat beside him. Winston had draped himself over the back of the seat and licked her ear repeatedly in an effort to console her, but she refused to be restored to a more reasonable mood.

Rafe tried distraction first.

"A.Z.'s got a strange view of the world, but she doesn't make things up out of thin air," he said. "She thinks that logbook was stolen. I'm inclined to believe her."

"It's been eight years. She probably misplaced it."

"Not A.Z. She's one well-organized conspiracy theorist. Trust me." He down-shifted as he drove past the pier. "Makes you wonder, doesn't it?"

"I'll say it does. It was bad enough when people suspected that we were having an affair. But now the whole town apparently thinks that we're living together openly out there at Dreamscape."

"We are. Sort of."

"Doesn't it bother you?"

"Well, no, not really. Hannah, I'm trying to hold a rational conversation here. We were discussing the missing logbook, if you will recall."

"It bothers me. I realize that you Madisons are accustomed to being gossiped about here in Eclipse Bay. But we Hartes try to avoid being the subject of idle rumors and speculation."

She was tight and wired, Rafe realized. Her arms were crossed beneath her breasts. Her face was pinched with irritation.

"People have been talking about us since the day we arrived," he said evenly. "It didn't seem to bother you so much at first. Why are you going ballistic now?"

"I'm getting tired of it." She looked out at the bay. "I thought everything would be settled by now. It all seemed so simple back at the beginning. I would buy out your share of Dreamscape and start work on my inn. But things just keep getting more complicated."

"By 'things,' " he said carefully, "I assume you are talking about our rela-tionship, not the possibility that we may have awakened a sleeping murderer?"

"Yes, I am talking about our relationship."

He gripped the wheel and braced himself. "Okay. You want to discuss that instead of the missing logbook?"

"No."

He drew a deep breath. He should be feeling relieved, he thought. But for some reason, he was vaguely disappointed.

"Well, that simplifies matters," he said. "Let's get back to the logbook."

"Why bother? There's nothing we can do until Arizona finds her copy."

He flexed his hands on the wheel. "Whatever you say. I need gas."

"So? Get some."

"Yes, ma'am."

He drove past the library and the small park next to it, then turned the corner into the town's main shopping area. Chamberlain College and the institute had had an impact here. For years the post office, together with the hardware, drugstore, and grocery store had formed the core of Eclipse Bay's tiny business district. But lately a smattering of new shops, including a bookstore and a restaurant, had appeared to cater to students and faculty.

He pulled into the Eclipse Bay Gas and Go, stopped at the first pump, and switched off the engine. He realized that his own temper was starting to fray.

"I wish you'd stop that," he said.

"Stop what?"

"Stop fuming. You're starting to make Winston and me tense."

"I'm angry. I've got a right to be angry. I intend to stay angry for as long as it suits me."

That did it. He turned halfway around and flung his arm over the back of the seat. "What the hell is going on here, anyway? I don't know why you're letting a simple crack about us shacking up together upset you like this."

"I hate that term."

"Shacking up?" He shrugged. "You've got to make allowances for the older generation."

"Now you're starting to say it, too. For the last time, we are not 'shacking up.' "

"Okay, okay, take it easy." Rafe watched a vaguely familiar figure garbed in grease-stained coveralls emerge from the garage and amble toward the car. "Son of a gun. Is that Sandy Hickson?"

The question got Hannah's attention for a moment. She peered through the windshield, "Yes, I think so."

Rafe popped the door. "He sure hasn't changed much, has he?"

"No." Hannah's mouth thinned. "He still looks like the kind of guy who checks out rest room walls for the names of potential dates."

"A man has to use whatever resources are available." Rafe climbed out from behind the wheel and closed the door. He braced one hand against the roof of the Porsche and leaned down to look at Hannah through the open window. "Better stop glaring at me like that. Sandy might come to the conclusion that we've having a lovers' spat. If you think the gossip is unpleasant now, just imagine what it will be like if word gets out that we're fighting."

Hannah chose to ignore him.

"Hey, Rafe."

Rafe straightened and nodded at Sandy. "Sandy."

"Heard you were back in town. How's it hangin'?" Sandy leaned down to speak through the open window. "Hi there, Hannah."

"Hello, Sandy."

Sandy gave Rafe a keenly interested glance. "What can I do for you?"

"I just need gas. What have you been up to, Sandy?"

"Doin' okay." Sandy beamed proudly. He hoisted a rubber-bladed scraper out of a bucket of dirty water and went to work on the front window of the Porsche. "Bought the station from old man Carpenter a couple years ago."

"No kidding?" Rafe noticed the sign that pointed customers toward the rest rooms. He thought about what Hannah had said a moment earlier. "That's gotta be convenient."

"What's that?"

"I said, Congratulations. I'll bet you do pretty good during the summer months."

"You can say that again." Sandy winked. "Looks like you're doin' all right for yourself, too."

"Getting by." A dark cloud of premonition settled on Rafe. Maybe stopping for gas had not been such a swell idea.

But it was too late to change course. Sandy's grin was only a decimal point away from a leer. He dropped the wiper back into the bucket and moved closer to Rafe. He lowered his voice to a conspiratorial whisper.

"Heard you and Hannah were having yourselves some good times together out there at Dreamscape."

"I heard that, Sandy Hickson," Hannah shouted through the open window. "It's not true. Furthermore, if you repeat that one more time I will wrap one of those gas hoses around your throat. Do you hear me?"

Sandy blinked and took a quick, startled step away from the fender. "Hey, Hannah, I didn't mean nothin', honest. Just passin' the time of day."

"Bull," she said. "Just because you own your very own rest rooms now and have access to an unlimited source of phone numbers, don't think that everyone else gets involved in the same kind of limited, one-dimensional relationships you apparently prefer."

"Sure, sure." Sandy threw Rafe a desperate look.

"What do I owe you, Sandy?"

"Uh, eleven-fifty," Sandy said.

A classic finned Cadillac pulled into the neighboring aisle. A petite woman with a helmet of steel-gray curls got out. "Is that you, Rafe Madison?"

"Yes, ma'am, Mrs. Seaton." Rafe grabbed his wallet. Speed was of the essence.

Edith Seaton examined him from head to toe with an expression of frank feminine admiration. "My, my, you did fill out nicely, didn't you?"

Rafe could feel the sudden heat in his face. He had a nasty feeling that he was turning a dull red. There wasn't much that could make him blush, but Mrs. Seaton had managed the trick.

"Nice to see you again, Mrs. Seaton." Damn. He didn't have fifty cents in change. He concentrated on plucking a ten and two ones from his wallet. "I see you've still got the antique shop on the corner."

"Oh, yes. Wouldn't know what to do with myself if I didn't have the shop." Mrs. Seaton glanced into the car. "Is that you, Hannah?"

"Yes, Mrs. Seaton." Hannah's voice sounded strained and slightly muffled.

"Thought so. Heard all about you and Rafe inheriting Dreamscape. I talked to Isabel shortly before she made her transition, you know. She was very excited about the whole notion of leaving that place to the two of you." Mrs. Seaton winked. "She was always such a romantic at heart."

"Uh-huh," Hannah said. Her voice dripped icicles.

The crowd was growing rapidly. Across the street the door of the Total Eclipse Bar and Grill opened, and two of the patrons emerged. They stood for a few seconds beneath the neon letters that spelled out the bar's slogan, "Where the sun don't shine." Then, curiosity obviously aroused, they jaywalked toward the gas station to see what was happening.

A familiar green Volvo rolled up to a pump. The window on the driver's side was down. Perry Decatur, dressed in a slouchy jacket and dark glasses, sat behind the wheel. His head swiveled toward the car.

The audience continued to swell. It was definitely time to leave. Rafe tossed the gas money at Sandy. "Here you go. Keep the change. See you later." He reached for the door handle.

But escape eluded him. A battered white pickup pulled up to the pump just ahead of the Porsche, and a burly man dressed in denim jeans held up by a belt fastened below his belly got out. He adjusted the billed cap that covered his thinning hair.

"Rafe Madison." The big man's eyes crinkled with genuine pleasure. "Long time no see."

"Hello, Pete."

Pete Levare hitched up his jeans and screwed his features into a good-natured expression of avid curiosity. "Heard you and the Harte girl each got a chunk of Dreamscape. What the hey's going on out there, anyway? Is it true the two of you are—"

He never got to finish the sentence. The passenger door of Rafe's car flew open.

"That does it." Hannah erupted, Mount St. Helens fashion, from the Porsche's cockpit. Sensing an exciting new game, Winston leaped to follow her.

Together dog and woman whipped around the front of the car and started toward the hapless Pete. A sense of impending disaster settled on Rafe. It was like watching a film in which events are spinning out of control. All he could do was stand there and wonder how bad it would get.

"Whoa." Pete held up both hands, palms out, and backpedaled furiously toward the safety of his pickup. "Calm down, Hannah. What did I say? What did I say?"

"It's not what you said, it's what you were about to say," Hannah yelled as she charged toward him. "You think Rafe and I are shacking up together, don't you?"

"Shacking up? No, no, I never said that. Did I say that, Rafe?" Pete cast a helpless, beseeching glance at Rafe.

Rafe ignored him. He was too busy admiring the sight of Hannah in a full-blown temper. Invisible waves of energy shimmered in the air around her. The stylish acid-green scarf she wore around her throat snapped in the breeze. Who would have thought a Harte would demonstrate so much passion in public?

Winston pranced at her heels, his little legs moving so rapidly that all that could be seen in the vicinity of his paws was a silvery blur.

It was a thrilling sight, but one that he knew would have some repercussions. Rafe cleared his throat. "Uh, Hannah—"

She paid him no heed. He groaned, folded his arms, and lounged against the car door. He'd tried. Later, when she was pissed at him for having caused this scene, he would remind her of that singular fact. Whatever was about to happen here was definitely not his fault.

"Pay attention, Pete." Hannah came to a halt in front of the big man and planted her hands on her hips. "Rafe and I are not—repeat, *not*—shacking up together at Dreamscape. Is that clear?"

"Sure, you bet," Pete said quickly. "Right. Not shacking up."

Mrs. Seaton looked fascinated. "I heard the two of you are planning to get married."

"What?" Hannah whirled around to stare at her. "Where did you hear that?"

"At the post office this morning," Mrs. Seaton said brightly. "Ran into Mitchell collecting his mail. He said he thought you and Rafe made a wonderful couple. Said you'd probably have something to announce any day. Is that true?"

"No!" Hannah's voice rose. "There will be no announcements."

Rafe kept his mouth shut.

Everyone looked expectant.

"Are you sure?" Mrs. Seaton asked.

"I am absolutely positive," Hannah ground out between set teeth. "Rafe and I have never discussed marriage."

From out of nowhere a lightning bolt of anger sizzled through Rafe. He stirred against the side of the car. "Strictly speaking, that's not true."

Hannah swiveled to pin him with a dangerous look. "What are you talking about?"

"I'm just saying that subject has come up between us."

"The hell it has," she shouted.

"I'll agree that we haven't come to any definitive conclusions yet, but you can't say that we haven't talked about it."

"Don't you dare get cute on me here, Rafe Madison." She took a step toward him. "You have never once asked me to marry you."

"You know what Mitchell said about my phobia."

"Don't give me that stupid excuse about having a phobia. You're the one who said the best way to deal with a phobia was to confront it head-on. I haven't noticed you trying that approach."

"Okay." He felt his stomach clench. "I'm asking."

For a second or two he didn't think he would get an answer. He heard Mrs. Seaton catch her breath. The others gazed with rapt attention. Even Perry Decatur was staring, transfixed by the scene.

Hannah pulled herself together with a visible effort. She glanced hurriedly around, as though finally coming to her senses. Rafe saw the gathering dismay and anger in her eyes.

"That was not a real proposal." There was a strange edge to her voice now. "That was a joke. At my expense. I don't appreciate it, Rafe."

"No joke," he said softly. "The proposal was real to me." He held her complete attention. "Do I get an answer?"

She stared at him, her face frozen. And then, to his horror, he saw the glint of moisture in her eyes. Her lips parted, trembled ever so slightly.

"Oh, shit." He knew instinctively that if she burst into tears in front of all these people she would never forgive him.

He pushed away from the car door and wrapped one arm around her waist. "Sorry, folks. We've got an appointment."

He got her around the hood of the car and into the passenger seat before anyone had quite realized what was happening.

"Winston," he said firmly.

Winston scrambled nimbly into the car. Rafe closed the door behind him, circled back around the front of the Porsche, and got behind the wheel. He twisted the key in the ignition, wrapped one hand around the gearshift, and pulled out of the station onto Bay Street before the crowd could react.

When he checked the rearview mirror, he saw a row of excited faces. He knew only too well that the news about his gas station proposal would be all over town by five o'clock that evening.

He glanced uneasily at Hannah. She was blinking rapidly and dabbing at her eyes with a hankie, but she appeared to have the potential flood of tears under control. Winston rested his muzzle on her shoulder.

"Sorry about that," Rafe said eventually.

"Oh, shut up."

He tried to look on the positive side. At least she hadn't said no.

22

THE letdown was far worse than the anger or the tears. It bordered on outright depression, Hannah thought. She retreated to the upstairs veranda as soon as she was inside the house. Rafe did not try to stop her.

Half an hour later, stretched out in a wicker lounger, with Winston hovering loyally beside her, she tried to sort out her mangled emotions and jumbled thoughts. She gazed at the restless surface of the bay and told herself that she had overreacted. She had, in fact, come unglued in a way that was most unusual for her.

Obviously she had been under more stress lately than she had realized.

She had every right to be furious with Rafe for that scene at the Eclipse Bay Gas and Go, she decided. But why had she let events get to her like that? She had been screaming at Pete Levare. She had nearly burst into tears in front of all those people.

What was the matter with her?

The answer was out there, but she knew she did not want to deal with it. She almost welcomed the sound of Rafe's footsteps behind her. Anything was better than looking at the hard facts of her situation.

"You okay?" he asked.

She took some satisfaction from the fact that he sounded worried.

"I'm pissed," she said.

"Yeah. I know." He handed her a glass of iced tea. After a second's hesitation she took it from him. He seemed relieved. He lowered himself onto a wicker chair and rested his elbows on his knees. "It was my fault."

"We've already established that." She examined the glass in her hand. The tea was not ordinary black tea over ice. It was a luscious green-gold in color. There was a sprig of mint draped artistically over the rim and tiny little mint leaves frozen inside each ice cube. A crisp straw poked over the edge of the glass. An impossibly thin slice of lemon floated in the crystal-clear depths. "There's no little paper umbrella," she said.

He examined the glass critically and then shook his head once, decisively. "An umbrella would have been over the top."

"Just like that scene at the gas station." She sipped the tea through the straw. It was perfect. Cold, strong, and invigorating. "Why did you do it?"

"Do what?"

"Ask me to marry you in that dumb, tacky way."

"You sure you want to reopen that conversation?"

"I want an answer."

He looked out at the silver surface of the bay. "All right. I wanted to marry you the day you got out of the car here at Dreamscape, but I knew you wouldn't take a chance on me. At least, not right away."

Tea sloshed over the side of her glass. She sputtered wildly, "You *what* . . . ?"

He did not respond to her interruption. Instead he plowed ahead with a sort of dogged determination. She got the feeling that having launched himself on this venture, he was bound to see it through to the conclusion, even if that conclusion was ill-fated.

"During the past few days I thought maybe we were getting closer. Making progress."

"Having sex, you mean."

He nodded agreeably. "That, too. But I didn't want to push it."

"The sex?"

"The relationship."

"Oh, that." She scowled. "Why not?"

"Mostly because I figured you'd get nervous and back off."

"Me? You're the one who claims to have a deep-seated fear of having inherited a genetic tendency to screw up relationships."

"I had every right to play my cards close to the chest. I wasn't sure what I was dealing with. After all, you told me you'd drawn up a new list of qualifications for a husband. Hell, you wouldn't even tell me what was on the revised version."

She dropped her head against the back of the lounger. "That stupid list."

"Yeah. That stupid list. Worrying about it has been a real source of stress for me, Hannah."

Her hand stilled on Winston's head. "It has?"

"That damned list has driven me nuts. At any rate, this afternoon at the gas station when you started to tell everyone that the subject of marriage had never even come up between us, I guess I got a little irritated. Hell, I lost my temper." He paused. "And whatever common sense I've got."

She slowly lowered the glass. "Are you serious?"

He turned his head back to look at her. "Dead serious."

"You've been thinking about marriage since I first got here?"

"Before that, if you want the truth." He looked down at his loosely clasped hands for a moment. When he raised his head again his eyes were bleak. "Maybe since I got the news about Dreamscape from Isabel's lawyer and realized that you were still single."

"I don't understand," she whispered. "What put the notion of marriage into your head? Did you have some crazy idea that it would be the simplest way to deal with our inheritance?"

"Hell, no. Marriage is not a simple way of handling anything. I know that better than anyone."

"Then why?" Her voice was rising again. She'd have to watch that. She was a Harte, after all.

Rafe's jaw tightened. "It's hard to explain. It just seemed right somehow. When I got the letter from the lawyer things started to fall into place. For the first time in my life I knew exactly what I wanted. It was as if I'd been groping my way through a fog bank for years and suddenly the fog evaporated."

"What, precisely, do you want?"

He spread his hands. "Nothing too bizarre. You. The inn and the restaurant. A future."

She waited for him to add undying love and mutual devotion to the list. But he didn't. "I see. Some people would say that a marriage between a Harte and a Madison would definitely qualify as bizarre."

He watched her intently. "Look, I don't know what's on this new list of yours, but I've done some changing during the past eight years. I still don't meet all the requirements you gave me when you were nineteen—"

"I was twenty that night, not nineteen."

"Whatever. The thing is, I do meet at least some of those specifications, and I'm willing to work on the rest."

"Why?" she asked bluntly.

He leaned forward, intense and earnest. "You're a Harte. You ought to see the logic in us getting married. Hey, we'd be going into this deal with our eyes wide open. We know a hell of a lot more about each other than most people know about their potential spouses. We've got some history together. Three generations of it. We'd have Dreamscape to work on together. Sharing a business enterprise is a very bonding experience."

"You think so?"

"Sure." He was warming to his theme now. "For my part, I can guarantee that this wouldn't be another typical Madison marriage."

She sipped her tea, reluctantly fascinated. "In what way?"

"I just told you." He spread his hands in a gesture of exasperation. "It won't be based on some wild, romantic fantasy of endless lust."

"No lust at all?" she asked around the straw.

His jaw locked. "I'm not saying I don't find you attractive. You know I do. We're sexually compatible. That's important in a marriage."

"Sexual compatibility is nice," she agreed.

"Right. Real important."

"But what you're proposing here is a marriage of convenience."

"What I'm proposing," he said, his voice tightening, "is a marriage based on the sort of things that are supposed to appeal to a Harte, the kind of crap that was on that original list of yours: Mutual goals. Shared interests, et cetera, et cetera."

The edge in his voice made her look at him quickly, but his face was an unreadable mask.

"Right." She jiggled the straw among the ice cubes. "Crap."

He drew a breath. "Okay, 'crap' was not a great word. Look, what I'm trying to say here is that I think we've got a shot at making a marriage work. Hannah, you told me once that I didn't have to repeat the same mistakes my father and my grandfather made. I haven't been one hundred percent successful, but I have managed to avoid some of the larger disasters. And I did meet the goal I set for myself eight years ago."

"You didn't end up in jail."

"Doesn't that count for something?"

"Huh."

"It's taken me a while to find out what I want in life, but I've got it straight now. I need to know if you can stretch your new list of requirements in a husband to accommodate me."

"Depends." She steeled herself. "You see, the new edition of my list is extremely short, at least compared to the old one. Only one requirement is on it."

He watched her the way Winston watched seagulls. Hope and determination burned in his eyes, but so did the knowledge of potential defeat.

The roar of a sturdy truck engine rumbled in the drive on the opposite side of the house. Winston removed his head from under Hannah's hand and hurried off around the corner to investigate. Rafe frowned, clearly annoyed by the interruption. Then he realized who it was and surged to his feet.

"That will be A.Z.," he said. He started after Winston.

Hannah glared at his back. "So much for declaring undying love and devotion." But she said it very softly so that he would not hear her because it was entirely possible that he did not have either to declare.

Who would have guessed that a Madison would have ever settled for a marriage based on mutual interests and shared goals?

Who would have guessed that a Harte would have hungered for a little wild passion and romantic love?

The noise of the truck engine ceased abruptly. Hannah got up from the lounger and followed Rafe and Winston around the corner.

"THIS here's the log for that night." Arizona opened the black leather-bound volume on the kitchen table and swiveled it around so that Rafe and Hannah could look at the entries. "That first Thornley reception was a big event. Lots of folks there, including some from Portland."

"We're looking for a record of a car that left the parking lot and returned between midnight and two." Rafe slid the log closer to get a better look at the tiny, meticulously made notations. "I assume you stayed until the reception ended, A.Z.?"

"Until the last car pulled out of the lot," she assured him. "No point keeping a half-assed record, I say."

Hannah flipped pages. "There are a lot of entries here. It's going to take a while to go through them."

"Take your time." Arizona shoved herself to her feet. "Reckon I'll go out into the sunroom and relax while you two conduct your little investigation. Mind if I pour myself some more of your coffee, Rafe?"

"Help yourself." He reached for a pen and the lined tablet he had set out on the table.

"Thanks." Arizona reached for the pot. "Been a while since I sat in Isabel's sunroom. Miss those visits. Isabel always had something interesting to say."

The sad, faintly wistful note in Arizona's voice caught Hannah off guard. She looked up quickly.

Arizona headed for the kitchen door, chunky mug in hand. "I could talk to her, you know? She understood when I told her about the goings-on up at the institute. Didn't laugh the way some folks do."

Arizona ambled out into the hall and disappeared in the direction of the solarium. Hannah gazed after her for a moment, aware of a glimmer of curiosity.

"I wonder just how close Arizona and Aunt Isabel actually were," she said quietly. "As far as I know, neither of them ever married. They were friends for a long time. You don't suppose—?"

"None of our business." Rafe wrote down a license plate number. "This will go faster if you take the notes while I read the entries."

"All right." She took the pen from him and positioned the yellow tablet. "Go."

It was a discouraging process. Arizona's log was more than a simple list of license plates, names, and times. It was complicated by extensive notations. Rafe read some of them aloud.

> . . . *Member of the Inner Circle?*
> . . . *Claims to be from Portland but spotted a copy of the* New York Times *on the backseat . . .*
> . . . *Showed up for last Tuesday's secret meeting at the institute. Probably on the inside . . .*

"She's crafted a fantasy world for herself," Hannah whispered. "It's amazing."

"I'm not so sure it's any more amazing than the fact that we're sitting here going through her fantasy world logbooks because we think we can use them to solve an eight-year-old murder."

"Okay, you've got a point." Hannah tapped the pen against the table. "I can see where some people might conclude that we're as far out in left field as Arizona herself."

It took nearly half an hour to get through the log for the night of Kaitlin Sadler's death. Hannah was privately on the verge of conceding defeat when Rafe paused at a license plate number.

"Huh," he said.

She looked up quickly. "What?"

"We've been concentrating on plates and vehicles connected with the Thornley campaign."

"So?"

Rafe sat back slowly and shoved his hands into his back pockets. He studied the open logbook. "None of them left and returned during that two-hour window. Maybe we've been coming at this from the wrong angle."

Hannah did not like the dark excitement in his voice. "You think maybe whoever left to meet Kaitlin borrowed someone else's car?"

"Maybe." Rafe hesitated. "But there's another possibility. From what we can figure out, Kaitlin was acting on impulse that night. She had made up her mind to leave town in the morning. She needed cash in a hurry. We've been going on the assumption that she tried to sell the blackmail tapes to someone from Thornley's camp. But there was another potential market for those tapes."

"What market is that?"

"The media."

"Well, sure." Hannah tossed aside the pen. "But why would anyone in the media murder her after agreeing to buy the incriminating tapes? The last thing a journalist would want to do is get rid of his source. He'd want backup for his story."

"Not if," Rafe said slowly, "he planned to use the tapes to blackmail Thornley himself."

Hannah drew a breath and let it out carefully. "The news of Thornley's interest in lingerie never appeared in the media. You think that's because some journalist who attended the reception that night kept the tapes and has been using them to blackmail Thornley all these years?"

Without a word, Rafe took one hand out of his back pocket and rotated the logbook so that she could see the entry he had marked.

"Not *some* journalist," he said quietly. "One Kaitlin knew well enough to call in a hurry that night. One she had reason to believe might be interested in handling a sleazy story about Thornley. An old acquaintance she thought she could trust."

Hannah looked down at the name written next to a license number. Stunned, she glanced quickly at the notes she had been making. The vehicle had left the reception shortly after midnight. It had returned at one-forty-seven A.M.

"A journalist," Rafe went on very quietly, "who might have known that Arizona Snow had a habit of hiding in the shadows to make notes about events at the institute. One who might have decided that even though no one in town ever paid any attention to A.Z.'s conspiracy theories, it would probably be a good idea to steal the log for that evening."

A chill of disbelief numbed Hannah. "You think Kaitlin tried to sell the tapes to Jed Steadman?"

AN hour later Hannah paused halfway across the sunroom to glare at Mitchell, Rafe, and Arizona. All three of them glowered back at her.

"What the heck are we supposed to do now?" she demanded. "The big idea was to take the evidence to Jed Steadman and let him run with the story. Now it looks like he's the chief suspect."

Arizona shook her head and made a *tut-tut* sound. "Should have guessed the local media were involved in covering up institute actions. Explains a hell of a lot, if you ask me. No wonder they've been able to maintain a cloak of secrecy over their activities up there."

"If we're right, this has nothing to do with the institute," Hannah said with a patience she did not feel. "It's a simple case of blackmail and murder. It looks like Kaitlin called Jed that night. He went to meet her on the path above Hidden Cove. Maybe she offered to cut him in on the blackmail deal. Or maybe she simply wanted to sell the tapes to him outright. Either way, he saw a golden opportunity to cash in on the compromising videos."

"But he figured he'd better get rid of Kaitlin," Mitchell said. "Probably didn't trust her to keep her mouth shut. Or maybe he didn't want to split the potential profits two ways."

Rafe massaged the back of his neck. "The bottom line here is that we don't have any hard evidence for any of this."

"You got my logs," Arizona reminded him.

"No offense, A.Z., but we need more than that to take this to the police."

"We've still got the option of turning the story over to the media," Hannah reminded him. "Not the *Eclipse Bay Journal,* obviously. But maybe one of the Portland papers will be interested."

"Maybe. Maybe not." Rafe tapped his finger on the arm of the wicker chair. "I was counting on Jed going with the story and doing the basic legwork because it was a hometown scandal. He had the best reason to get excited about it."

"He'll get fired up about it, all right," Mitchell said morosely. "Probably sue us."

Hannah looked out over the bay. "I wish we had a little more to go on here. Rafe is right. We don't have any hard evidence."

There was a short, stark silence behind her.

"You know who you're looking at now," Mitchell said eventually. "If nothing else, you ought to be able to use what you've got to scare the hell out of Jed Steadman. Make sure he knows that if he makes one false move, a lot of folks will be watching. That should keep him in line."

Arizona grunted. "Why not call up the Thornley crowd and tell them we know who's been blackmailing their candidate all these years? That would stir things up a mite."

"I'm not so sure Jed has been blackmailing Thornley," Rafe said thoughtfully.

Everyone looked at him.

He sat forward and folded his arms on his knees. "When you get right down to it, there's no evidence that Steadman has been living above his income. If he's getting cash out of Thornley, where has the money been going?"

Another silence greeted that observation.

"Well, shoot and damn," Mitchell muttered. "Why would he commit murder for the tapes and then sit on them for eight years?"

A cunning light appeared in Arizona's eyes. "Why waste time prying a few bucks out of a small-time state pol when you can hold your ammunition and use it on a genuine U.S. senator?"

Hannah heard a collective intake of breath.

"You know something, A.Z.?" Rafe's smile held no humor. "For a professional conspiracy theorist, you sometimes make a lot of sense."

"She's got a point, all right." Mitchell whistled softly in admiration. "Everyone knew from the start that Thornley would probably go all the way to Washington." He glanced at Rafe. "You know Steadman better than anyone. Think he's into that kind of long-range planning?"

"Maybe," Rafe said thoughtfully. "He always likes to talk about the importance of timing and planning."

Hannah clasped her hands behind her back. "If Jed has been sitting on those tapes all this time, he must be getting a little antsy now that the big payoff is almost within reach. No wonder he freaked when Rafe and I returned to Eclipse Bay and people started to talk about the past."

"The question is, what do we do with all this guesswork?" Mitchell asked of the room at large.

Rafe looked out over the bay. "We get a little more information, if we can."

Hannah swung around in alarm. "What are you going to do?"

"There's a town council meeting tonight. They're going to be discussing the pier renovations. Jed will cover the session. It will probably run late."

Understanding hit her. She took an urgent step toward him. "You're going to search his house, aren't you? Rafe, you can't take that risk. What if a patrol car goes past his place while you're inside and you're spotted? If you get caught you'll be arrested for breaking and entering. You could end up in jail."

"Now that would be ironic," Rafe said. "Be the fulfillment of a long-standing prophecy."

"That is not amusing." She whirled around to face Mitchell. "I'm sure you don't want him to take this kind of risk. He's your grandson. Help me out here."

Mitchell stroked his chin. His expression of wolfish anticipation was uncomfortably familiar. "Well, I sure wouldn't want him to take such a dumb risk on his own. Reckon I'd better go with him to keep him out of trouble."

Hannah looked from his face to Rafe's and back again. She groaned. "Well, shoot and damn. This is a fine time for the two of you to decide to bond."

MITCHELL studied the big house from beneath the branches of a dripping tree. Jed Steadman's home stood dark and silent in the fog-drenched gloom. "You thought about what we're going to do if we set off an alarm?"

"Doubt if there is one," Rafe said. "Not many people here in Eclipse Bay are worried about crime."

"If we're right about Steadman, he isn't exactly a typical resident of our fair town. You and Hannah have made him nervous lately. He might have put in an alarm. All I want to know is if you've got a backup plan in case we run into one."

"You think I'd do something dicey like this without figuring all the angles first?"

"Just tell me what we're supposed to do if we trigger an alarm."

"We run like hell."

Mitchell nodded. "I was afraid of that."

"You want out before we go inside?"

"Hell, no. Haven't had this much fun in years."

Rafe smiled slightly to himself. "I was afraid of that."

Getting inside was easy. Maybe a little too easy, Rafe thought as he slid the unlocked bedroom window open. He eased one leg over the sill and paused for a few seconds, listening to the silence.

"What's the matter?" Mitchell demanded.

"Nothing." Rafe got the other leg over the sill and stood inside the bedroom. He was conscious of an eerie stillness in the house. A lonely quality permeated the darkness around him. He was only too well acquainted with this bleak, melancholy sensation. He had been aware of the emptiness collecting in his house in San Diego for a long time before he had made the decision to move to Eclipse Bay. Maybe this was how any man's home felt when there was no woman in it to soften the edges and warm the shadows.

"Now what?" Mitchell whispered after he climbed through he window.

"You take this room. Look for a wall safe. I'll go see if I can find a study or a home office. Got your gloves?"

"Sure, but we're not exactly experts at this kind of thing. What if he realizes later that someone went through his belongings?"

"Give him something more to worry about," Rafe said. "If we don't turn up those tapes, giving him a good scare may be the only tactic we've got to use against him."

He left Mitchell in the bedroom and went swiftly down the hall. He stopped in the doorway of another bedroom and clicked on his penlight. The room was beyond spartan in its bareness. It looked as if no one had ever slept in it. He opened a closet door. A mound of old camping equipment was piled inside.

He closed the door and went on down the hall to the next room. A quick glance revealed that Jed used it as an entertainment center. A massive television set took up a large section of one wall. Several thousand dollars' worth of speakers and other electronic equipment were positioned around a large recliner cushioned in black leather.

A wastebasket sat next to the recliner. Rafe glanced inside and saw a small heap of trash. A little square of yellow paper and a bit of foil clung to the side of the basket.

Rafe aimed the penlight closer to the candy wrapper. It looked identical to the one he had discovered beneath the tree at the end of the Harte cottage drive. It wasn't conclusive proof that it had been Jed who had kept watch on the house that night, but the evidence was mounting.

"Rafe." Mitchell's voice echoed softly from the other bedroom. It was husky with urgency. "You better take a look at this."

Rafe swung around and hurried back down the hall. "What is it?" He rounded the corner and aimed the penlight at Mitchell, who was standing in front of a chest of drawers. "Find something?"

"It's what I didn't find." Mitchell waved a hand at three open drawers. "There's nothing in here. Cleaned out."

"Are you sure?"

"Have a look for yourself."

Rafe went to the closet and yanked it open. Three shirts hung limply in the far corner. A pair of worn slippers sat on the floor. The rest of the space was empty. The door of a small safe built into the closet wall hung open. There was nothing inside.

"Looks like he packed up and left." Mitchell hooked his thumbs on his belt. "Maybe he figured out we're on to him."

"How could he have known?"

Mitchell shrugged. "Small town. He might have seen Arizona's truck parked at Dreamscape this afternoon. Wouldn't take much for him to put two and two together. He's got to know you're one of the few people who takes her seriously. Maybe he figured out that she was helping you look into the Sadler girl's death. Wouldn't be a real big leap for him."

"No." Rafe thought about it. "Not if he was already paranoid about that possibility. Maybe he planned for the possibility that someone would come around asking questions someday."

"One thing's for certain." Mitchell turned toward the open wall safe. "If Steadman has cleared out for good, you can bet he didn't leave those tapes behind for us to find."

23

RAFE was brooding again. Hannah tolerated it as long as she could stand it, but by ten o'clock that evening she was starting to climb the walls. She tracked her quarry down in the solarium, where he was sitting in the shadows. He had one hand on Winston's neck, rubbing the dog absently behind the ears.

"I vote we all take Winston for his evening walk on the beach," Hannah said from the doorway.

At the sound of his name included in the same sentence as the word "walk," Winston moved smartly out from under Rafe's hand and bounced toward the door.

Rafe's hand paused in midair over the place where Winston's ears had been a second earlier. "It's dark, in case you haven't noticed."

Hannah lounged in the doorway, arms folded. "There's no fog. The moon is out. All we need is a flashlight."

"It's late."

She looked at the back of his head. "Just a little past ten. The first time you and I walked on the beach it was after midnight."

There was a short, stark silence. Without another word, Rafe levered himself up out of the lounger.

They went out of the big house through the French doors that opened onto the lower veranda. Rafe clicked on the flashlight, but Winston ignored the beam. He bounded ahead, zipping down the steps and heading toward the shadowy beach path with the ease of a creature who relies on a variety of senses to get around.

Rafe and Hannah followed in the dog's wake.

The evening was cool but not cold. The bay was a dark mirror beneath the icy white moon. A swath of silver streaked the surface of the deceptively still water. In the distance the lights of the pier and the streets of the small downtown section of Eclipse Bay glittered. Hannah could see the glow of Chamberlain College and the institute on the hillside.

Everything about the night brought back memories of her first walk on the beach with Rafe. She wondered if he was remembering that same evening and if so, what he thought about it.

When they reached the sand they followed Winston toward the rocky pools uncovered by the low tide.

"This is about Jed Steadman, isn't it?" Hannah asked after a while. "I know it must have been hard for you to discover that he may have been the one who murdered Kaitlin. He was your friend, after all."

"Jed was just a guy I knew a long time ago," Rafe said distantly. "Someone I could shoot a game of pool with on a dull night."

She peered at him. "I thought you two were quite close in the old days."

"I hardly thought about him in the past eight years, let alone picked up the phone to call him. And he sure as hell never bothered to get in touch with me. We weren't buddies. Just a couple of guys who did some stuff together on long summer weekends because we had one big thing in common."

"What was the big thing? Kaitlin Sadler?"

"No. The big thing was that neither of us had a father anywhere in the picture."

Hannah shoved her hands into the pockets of her sweater jacket. "I can see where that would have been a bond of sorts."

"I envied him a little, if you want to know the truth. I always figured he was the lucky one. He seemed like he knew what he was doing. Had a plan for his future. Knew where he was going. The kind of guy who wouldn't screw up."

Halfway down the beach, Winston paused to investigate a hunk of driftwood. Rafe aimed the flashlight at him and then let the light slide away toward the foam at the water's edge.

"I was wrong about Jed, you know," Rafe said after a while.

"What do you mean?"

"He wasn't the lucky one. I was. I had Mitchell after my parents were killed. Gabe and I both had him. I went off track for a while, but at least I knew there was a track, thanks to him."

Hannah nodded. "I understand."

"I don't think there was ever anyone there for Jed. His father drank a lot, and one day he just disappeared. His mother remarried two or three times."

"Hmm," Hannah said.

"What's that supposed to mean?"

"Let's not go too far into let's-feel-sorry-for-poor-Jed-who-came-from-a-dysfunctional-family territory. I'm sure it's all true, but I can't believe that he didn't know a few of the rules. The night he murdered Kaitlin Sadler in order to get his hands on those blackmail tapes he broke those rules. I'm sure he was well aware of what he was doing."

"You know, Hannah, that's one of the things I like about you." For the first time that evening there was a trace of wry amusement in Rafe's words. "I can always count on you to cut right to the heart of the matter."

Hannah sighed. "All right, if you're not brooding because of Jed, do you mind telling me why you've been in such a foul mood all evening?"

"I've been thinking."

"No offense, but I'm not sure it's good for you."

"I appreciate the positive feedback."

"Okay, okay. I don't want to argue."

"But you're so good at it."

She tightened her hands inside the pockets of her sweater jacket. "Let's start over. Tell me what you've been thinking about this evening."

He was silent for a couple of heartbeats. She had the impression that he was gathering himself for a big jump.

"I've decided to sign over my half of Dreamscape to you," he said.

For a few seconds she thought she had misunderstood. She reran his simple statement twice through her brain before she finally decided she had gotten it right the first time.

She came to a sudden halt on the beach and swung around to face him. "You're going to do *what?*"

"You heard me." He stopped and looked at her. "Dreamscape is Harte property. It's always been Harte property. I know your aunt had some romantic notions, but the truth is, I don't have any real claim on the place. It's yours. I'm not going to fight you for it."

Panic seized her. She jerked her hands out of her pockets and grabbed fistfuls of his black pullover. "I thought we had a deal."

"You didn't seem interested."

"I never got a chance to respond." She stood on tiptoe and leaned closer. "Arizona Snow arrived with her logbook in the middle of our business discussion, if you will recall. Then came our big deductions concerning Kaitlin Sadler's death."

"Hannah—"

"That was followed by you and your grandfather deciding to engage in a bit of breaking and entering. The next thing we know, Jed Steadman has left town and you're brooding. All in all, it's been a somewhat hectic day. I haven't had a chance to get back to you on your business offer."

"I've known for a long time now that my claim on Dreamscape was the only thing I could use to hold you. I don't want to use it."

"Excuse me if I got this wrong, but I was under the impression that you saw me and Dreamscape as a sort of package deal."

"I can build my restaurant somewhere else."

"Your dream of a restaurant is your passion. Dreamscape is the best possible location for it, and you know it. You can't give it up."

"Got news for you, Hannah. The restaurant is important, but it's not my greatest passion."

"Rafe—"

"I don't want you and the restaurant in a business deal."

"You're the one who made the offer."

"I was getting desperate."

Hope soared within her. Grimly she tamped it down, forcing herself to keep things in perspective. "But now you've changed your mind? You don't want me anymore?"

He closed his free hand around one of her fists. "I want you, Hannah, but it's no good unless you want me. Tonight I realized that taking Dreamscape out of the equation is the only way to find out how you really feel about me."

She couldn't keep the lid on the tide of hope any longer. It surged through her. "You want to know how I feel? I'll tell you how I feel. I love you, Rafe Madison. I want to stay here in Eclipse Bay with you. I want to open a five-star inn and restaurant at Dreamscape with you. I want to have babies and a future with you."

For an instant he did not move. Then he abruptly wrapped one arm around her and pulled her hard against his chest. "Are you sure?"

She snuggled against him. The heat and strength of his body enfolded her. He was her future.

"I'm sure."

"I love you," he said into her hair. "You're my passion, not the restaurant. You know that, don't you?"

"I do now." Relief and joy washed through her. Once a Madison was committed to his passion, nothing else was allowed to get in the way.

"What about your new list?" he asked quietly. "Do I qualify?"

She smiled against his throat. "There was only one item on it. I wanted to marry someone I could love with all my heart. Someone who loved me the same way in return."

"No problem. I meet all the qualifications." He tightened his hold on her. "We'll make it work. You and me. Dreamscape. The future. We'll make it all work. I swear it."

"With your dreams and my brains, how can we miss?"

He raised her chin on the edge of his hand. "That night on the beach I told myself I could never have you, but I knew even then that I would never be able to forget you."

"I told myself the same thing about you."

He smiled against her lips. "You and your damned list were always there, somewhere in the back of my mind. You want to know the truth? Part of me wanted you to be happy. But another part hoped like hell that you would never find a man who met all those specifications for a husband."

"You and your big career objective to stay out of jail were always in the back of my mind. The thought of so much potential going to waste was extremely annoying."

"Sounds like we've been a constant source of irritation for each other all these years."

"I can't think of a better basis for a marriage."

He grinned. "Neither can I."

The beam of the flashlight splashed across the sand when his mouth came down on hers. Hannah reveled in the kiss. A singing happiness exploded inside her.

Winston's sharp, harsh bark broke the spell.

Rafe reluctantly raised his head. "I don't think your dog approves of us making out on the beach."

"He'll just have to get used to it."

Winston left the piece of driftwood he had been worrying and dashed toward them. He barked again, louder and more urgently this time. Not a request for attention or an invitation to romp.

A surge of alarm shot through Hannah. "I think something's wrong."

Winston did not stop when he reached the place where Hannah and Rafe stood. He sped on down the beach toward the path that led back to Dreamscape. He was barking furiously now.

"What the hell?" Rafe swung around to follow the dog with the flashlight beam. "Oh, shit."

He broke into a run.

Hannah looked toward the mansion. Shock seized her. The background rumble of the restless bay behind her blotted out any sound that might have drifted down the cliffs from Dreamscape. But she did not need to hear the crackle and hiss of the fire. She could see the flames leaping into the night quite clearly.

SHOULD have taken the cell phone with me, Rafe thought as he raced toward the house. But the possibility that the fire could still be handled with the garden hose was too tempting to allow for a detour into the house to call 911.

He leaped the steps and ran the length of the veranda. Winston was a short distance ahead of him. The dog was in full charge mode. He was no longer sounding the alarm with short, warning barks. The porch lights glinted on bared teeth and flattened ears.

He had been right about Winston the first time he saw him, Rafe thought. Definitely not a froufrou pooch.

"I'll call the fire department," Hannah shouted.

"Right." He did not look back as he rounded the corner of the veranda.

Winston's growl was the only warning he got before he glimpsed the figure silhouetted by the flames. The man was attempting to flee, but the dog had closed his jaws around a pant leg.

Rafe saw Winston's victim raise the gasoline can in his hands and prepare to smash it down hard on the Schnauzer's skull.

"Goddamn dog," Jed yelled.

Rafe slammed into him. The can sailed out onto the grass, away from the flames. Jed went down hard on the wooden boards. He opened dazed, angry eyes. Hatred and rage flared hotter than the crackling fire.

Winston tried to get a better grip on Jed's leg.

"Let go, Winston."

The dog released the trouser cuff and looked at Rafe.

"You sonofabitch," Jed roared. "I had it all planned. Waited all this time. But you had to come back and ruin everything."

He heaved himself upward, hands stretched out for Rafe's throat.

Rafe saw the madness in his eyes and moved back out of reach. "It's over, Jed."

"Why did you have to come back here and screw up everything? Why, god-damn you?"

"It's over," Rafe said again.

In the distance sirens wailed. Winston pranced in agitation and started to bark again. Hannah rounded the corner, the fire extinguisher from the kitchen cupboard in her hands.

"Oh, my God." She halted at the scene in front of her.

"I had it made until you came back." Jed's face crumpled in fury. "Everything was in place. After all these years, everything was in place. And then you came back."

He launched himself wildly across the short space that separated him from Rafe.

Rafe sidestepped the charge and stuck out one foot. Jed tripped over it and fetched up against the wall of the mansion. He clung there a few seconds and then slid slowly to a sitting position.

When he opened his eyes this time, the rage was gone. In its wake was a bleak awareness of abject failure.

"I had it all planned," he whispered.

24

"WINSTON was the hero of the hour." Hannah looked proudly at her dog, who was gnawing on a chewing bone. "Thanks to him, the fire damage was minimal. The Willis brothers assured us they could have things in great shape in a couple of weeks."

"I'd allow more like a couple of months, if I were you," Mitchell said. "Con-struction work never gets done on time, especially when the Willis brothers are handling things."

"Maybe it's just as well," Hannah said. "We wanted to make some major modifications to that wing, anyway. We can incorporate them into the repairs."

"Makes sense." Mitchell leaned back in his chair and cast an assessing glance the length of the veranda. "Got your work cut out for you here. But I think, in the end, you'll have yourselves a nice little inn and restaurant."

"Five stars," Rafe said. His voice was soft with certainty.

"Don't doubt it for a minute." Mitchell chuckled. "Always knew you could do anything you set out to do. Just a matter of applying yourself."

Hannah grinned. "Gee, what a coincidence. I once told him the same thing."

Rafe stacked his heels on the railing and took a swallow from the beer bottle in his hand. "How could I miss with both of you telling me what to do with my life?"

"Took you long enough to live up to expectations, but you finally made it." Mitchell cradled his beer in one fist and squinted into the dying light. "Any more news on Jed Steadman?"

"Just that everything went down pretty much as we figured." Rafe looked out over the bay. "Except, of course, that Jed is claiming through his lawyer that Kaitlin's death was an accident."

"The result of a quarrel over the tapes," Hannah explained.

"Yeah, yeah," Mitchell muttered. "Reckon it's a given he'll end up facing only a manslaughter charge. But what happened to the tapes?"

"Jed claims they went over the cliff with Kaitlin and were swept out to sea. Says he never even viewed them."

"Ha." Mitchell grimaced. "And if you believe that, I've got some waterfront property in Arizona I can sell you."

"I don't think anyone actually believes his story," Hannah said slowly. "But if those tapes don't surface, no one will be able to prove otherwise. The Thornley camp is taking the line that the incident had nothing to do with their man. But there's a rumor going around that Trevor Thornley met Kaitlin when she worked for his first campaign."

"Wonder how many copies there are of those tapes," Mitchell mused.

"Not our problem," Rafe said. "Thornley's the one who has to worry about opening a tabloid someday and finding a picture of himself modeling lingerie inside. We've got other things to occupy us."

Mitchell cocked a brow. "Such as?"

"Such as planning a wedding," Hannah said smoothly.

For a split second Mitchell looked stunned. In the next instant delight exploded across his weathered features. He gave a whoop that made Winston drop his chewing bone, get up from the floor, and pad over to his chair to see what all the excitement was about.

"Well, shoot and damn," Mitchell said when he finally got his exuberance under control. "I knew you two would get around to doing the right thing. You just needed a little kick in the you-know-where."

"Don't know how we could have managed without your help," Rafe said dryly. "Telling everyone at the post office that Hannah and I were planning to get married was certainly an inspiration for us. Wasn't it, Hannah?"

"Definitely inspirational," Hannah said.

Mitchell was clearly having trouble containing his delight. "Least I could do. Wait'll Sullivan and the rest of those uptight, upright Hartes hear about this. Your family is going to have a combined hissy fit, Hannah."

Hannah winced. "I expect there will be some fireworks when Rafe and I tell them the good news."

"Gonna light up the sky," Mitchell agreed cheerfully. "Sure would like to be there when you spring it on 'em."

"Forget it," Rafe muttered. "You're not going to be anywhere in the vicinity."

"Ah—"

"Speaking of family reaction," Hannah said firmly, "I'll be planning this wedding. I've had a certain amount of experience in the field, but I must admit this particular event presents some unique challenges."

Mitchell chortled. "Worried about a brawl in the church?"

Hannah gave him a repressive look. "I expect some cooperation, restraint, and civilized behavior from everyone. Is that clear?"

"Don't look at me like that." Mitchell contrived to appear deeply offended. "We Madisons aren't going to cause a ruckus."

"Damn right," Rafe agreed. "If there's trouble it won't start on the Madison side."

Hannah gave both men a steely look. "It better not finish there, either."

THE wedding was held two months later, in the Eclipse Bay Community Church. Everyone in town was invited, and virtually everyone came. In spite of several ghoulish predictions of carnage, the ceremony went off without a hitch.

Halfway through the reception, which was held at Dreamscape, Mitchell could no longer restrain himself. He sought out Sullivan in order to gloat.

He found his old partner and rival on the veranda. Sullivan stood alone near the railing, a glass of champagne in one hand, a cane in the other.

Well, shoot and damn, Mitchell thought. He's lost as much hair as I have. Seemed like he was taller back in the old days, too. Guess we've both shrunk.

Looking at Sullivan was a little like looking into an old mirror. What had he expected? That they would stay young and dynamic forever? *At least I'm not the only one here with a cane.*

"Hey, Sullivan." He came to a halt a few paces away. "What do you think of your new grandson-in-law?"

Sullivan turned slowly around to face him. Mitchell relaxed a little. His ex-partner might be showing some wear and tear, but a savvy gleam still burned brightly in his eyes. This was the same man who had fought at his side in a long ago military action that no one except those who had been involved in it even remembered. This was the same man who had saved his life in that miserable jungle and whose life he had saved in return.

This was the same man he had teamed up with to risk everything in a financial gamble that had made them both rich for a while. The same man whose teeth he had tried to knock out in front of Fulton's Supermarket.

He met Sullivan's eyes and knew that they were both aware of the truth. The bonds that joined them would never dissolve.

Sullivan glanced down the length of the veranda to where Rafe stood with Hannah. "He'll do. Always said he had potential."

"I sure as hell never heard you say that."

"We haven't talked much for a long time, Mitch."

"Nope. Sure haven't."

"You did okay by Rafe and Gabe."

Startled, Mitchell glanced quickly at him and then turned just as swiftly away. "Can't take all the credit."

"No, but you can take some of it."

They stood together for a while, watching the crowd. Mitchell noticed that Sullivan made no effort to walk away.

"Looks like we're going to be seeing a lot of each other again," Mitchell offered finally. "I hear you Hartes are big on family gatherings."

"Yes." Sullivan looked at him. "We're very big on that kind of thing. How do you feel about your new granddaughter-in-law?"

Mitchell smiled. "She'll do."

"This better work out, Mitch. I swear to God, if Rafe doesn't treat her right—"

"Don't sweat it." Mitchell watched Rafe slide a protective arm around Hannah's waist. "She's his passion. You know how it is with Madisons and their passions."

"Yes." Sullivan sounded satisfied. "I know how it is with Madisons and their passions. Nothing gets in the way."

25

One month later . . .

THE phone rang, shattering the moment. Rafe paused in the act of leaning over to kiss Hannah. She looked up at him from the pillow.

"The phone," she said.

"I knew I should have switched off the ringer before we went to bed tonight."

The instrument warbled insistently.

"You'd better answer it. Might be your grandfather."

"All the more reason to ignore it." Reluctantly he picked up the phone. "This better be important," he said to whoever was on the other end of the line.

"Am I interrupting anything?" Gabe asked politely.

"Yes. Our one-month wedding anniversary."

"It's only nine o'clock."

"Us old married folks go to bed early."

"I've heard that," Gabe said. "Actually that brings me to what I wanted to talk about."

Rafe groaned and flopped back on his pillow. "I really do not want to talk about your thwarted love life tonight."

"I haven't got a love life to thwart."

"Another date go south?"

"Big time."

Rafe glanced at Hannah, who raised one brow. "Told you this idea of using a businesslike approach to finding a wife wasn't going to work very well."

"No, I know I'm on the right track. I just need to fine-tune the strategy. I realized tonight that what I have to do is approach this the same way I would approach a merger or an acquisition. I need to hire a professional consultant."

A premonition of disaster shot through Rafe. "I hope you aren't going to tell me what I think you're going to tell me."

"I'm going to call Hannah's sister first thing in the morning and sign up with her matchmaking agency. I understand she's fully computerized."

Rafe shut his eyes. "This is a bad dream. I know it is."

"I spoke with Lillian briefly at the wedding. She said she's got a very high success rate."

"Gabe, I don't think this is a good idea."

"Why not?"

"Well—" Rafe hesitated. "I don't know. It just feels sort of dicey for some reason."

"What have I got to lose?"

"Uh, well—" Rafe felt a tug on his wrist. "I'm going to hang up now, Gabe. I want to go back to celebrating my one-month anniversary."

"Give Hannah my best. If things work out with the Private Arrangements agency, I'll be celebrating some anniversaries myself one of these days."

"Something tells me it won't be that simple," Rafe warned. "You're a Madison, remember? We don't do simple when it comes to marriage. We always do things the hard way."

DAWN IN ECLIPSE BAY

This one is for Don and Joan:
May you live happily ever after!

"FIRE me?" Gabe Madison came to a halt in the center of the carpet. Disbelief warred with outrage on his hard face. "You can't fire me. I'm a client. You don't fire clients."

"I do." Lillian Harte sat very stiffly behind her sleek Euro-style desk, her hands clasped firmly atop the polished glass surface. She struggled to hold on to what was left of her temper. "I've been downsizing for the past few months."

"Downsizing is for getting rid of employees, not customers. What's the matter with you? You're supposed to be running a matchmaking business here." Gabe swept out a hand to indicate the expensively furnished office and the skyline of the city of Portland, Oregon, beyond. "You need clients. You want clients. You don't fire them."

"Some clients are more trouble than they're worth."

He narrowed dangerously green eyes. "And I'm one of them, is that it?"

"I'm afraid so." She unclasped her hands and leaned back in her chair. "Look, I'm sorry about this. Really."

"Oh, yeah, I can see that." His smile was cold.

"This was a mistake, Gabe. I told you that when you talked me into letting you sign on with Private Arrangements. I explained that it probably wouldn't work out well. But you refused to take no for an answer."

Which was hardly a major shock, she thought. It was a good bet that Gabe had not overcome his wild Madison family legacy to build Madison Commercial, a very successful venture capital firm, by taking no for an answer. Only a Harte, such as herself, could fully appreciate the magnitude of his accomplishment. Only a Harte knew just how far Gabe had had to go in order to live down three generations of spectacularly failed potential to rebuild an empire.

Her father had frequently speculated that Gabe had been successful because he had mastered the art of self-discipline, a rare accomplishment for a Madison. But in the few weeks that he had been a Private Arrangements client she had begun to suspect that Gabe had done more than merely learn how to control the notoriously hot blood that ran in his veins. He had subdued it with such ruthlessness that she suspected he had also crushed a lot of perfectly normal emotions along with it. As far as she could tell, he did not allow himself any strong feelings. She was convinced that he had paid a far higher price for his personal triumphs than anyone had realized.

Gabe smiled with relative ease, but he didn't laugh out loud. He didn't seem to know how to have fun. She had seen him annoyed, as he was now, but she had never seen him lose his temper. Her feminine intuition told her that he was very definitely attracted to women, but she was pretty sure that he did not permit himself to cross the line that separated physical satisfaction from mind-spinning passion. She was willing to bet that Gabe Madison had never allowed himself to take the risk of falling in love.

And he had expected her to find him a wife? Not a chance.

"It wasn't a mistake on my part," Gabe said. "I knew exactly what I was doing and what I wanted when I signed on with you. You're the one who made the mistakes. Five of them, so far."

"The fact that all five of the dates that I arranged for you went bad, should tell both of us something," she said, trying for a soothing note.

"It tells me something, all right. It tells me that you screwed up five times."

She had known that this would be a difficult conversation but she had not expected him to be quite so rigid about the matter. After all, it was obvious that the project had not been a success. One would have thought that he would have been content with merely demanding that his money be refunded.

His icy determination not to be dismissed from her client roster was starting to make her a little uneasy. Belatedly it occurred to her that Gabe was accustomed to fighting for what he wanted. She should have known that he would not abandon a goal without a battle.

She propped her elbows on the desk and balanced a capped pen between her forefingers, buying herself a little time to compose her arguments. Nothing was ever simple between a Madison and a Harte, she reminded herself. The younger members of the two families liked to pretend that the old feud that had erupted between their grandfathers and destroyed a thriving business empire all those years ago didn't affect them. But they were wrong. The fallout had echoed down through three generations. Gabe was living proof that the past had the power to haunt.

"I feel I have lived up to my part of the arrangement," she said. "I have sent you out on five dates in the past three weeks."

"Big deal. Five dates. I paid for six."

"You have complained about all five dates. In my opinion a sixth date would be a total waste of everyone's time."

"Those five bad dates were your fault." His jaw tightened. "Or maybe the fault of your computer program. Doesn't matter. The point is, they weren't good matches."

"Really?" She gave him a small, brightly polished smile. "I can't imagine how they could have been anything but perfect matches. According to my computer analysis the women I paired you with met over eighty-five percent of your requirements."

"Only eighty-five percent? Well, there's your problem." He grinned humorlessly. "The real issue here is that you and your computer aren't doing a very good job. You haven't found me any one hundred percent matches."

"Get real, Gabe." She put the pen down very precisely using both fingers. "There is no such thing as a one hundred percent perfect match. I use a computer program, not a magic wand."

"So, go for ninety-five." He spread his hands. "I'm flexible."

"Flexible?" She stared at him, completely nonplussed for two or three seconds, and then she swallowed a laugh. "No offense, but you're about as flexible as one of those steel beams they use in high-rise construction projects."

And just as tough, she thought. His hallmark uniform—expensive steel-gray suits, charcoal-gray shirts, silver-and-onyx cuff links, and striped silver-and-black ties—had taken on near-legendary status in the Northwest business community, which tended toward a more relaxed look. But the classy attire was poor camouflage for an iron will that had been forged in a strong fire.

The evidence of that will was plain to see. At least, it was obvious to her. It was there in the way he moved with the unconscious grace of a natural hunter. It was clear in the way he held himself and in the cool, remote, watchful expression in his eyes. Always on the alert, even when he appeared to be relaxed. There was a centered quality to him that was so strong it formed an invisible aura around him. This was a man who did nothing on impulse. A man in control.

What worried her the most, she admitted silently, was that she found him both compelling and fascinating.

In one sense she had known Gabe all of her life. He hailed from Eclipse Bay on the coast of Oregon where her family had always maintained a summer and vacation home. Growing up she had encountered him from time to time in the small town—but he was a Madison. Everyone knew that Madison males were trouble. Nice girls might indulge a few fantasies, but they didn't date Madisons. That, coupled with their complicated family history and the fact that he was five years older than she, had formed a huge barrier. The stone wall had not been breached until the wedding of her sister, Hannah, to his brother, Rafe, a few months ago. The event had shocked and delighted the entire town, leading to much speculation about whether or not the infamous Harte-Madison feud had finally ended. The question was still unanswered in most quarters.

Meeting Gabe at the reception had left her unsettled and unaccountably restless. She had told herself she would get over it. But when he had walked into her office a few weeks later she had realized that, on some level, she had been waiting for him. She could not explain her anticipation but it had come as a cold shock to learn that he was there on business. His only goal had been to sign up as a client.

Still, she had allowed herself a few interesting daydreams.

Then, of course, he had filled out the lengthy questionnaire she used to feed client data into her program and she had realized just how hopeless it all was. *No arty types.* It was, she reflected, one of the few places on the form where she was pretty certain he had been completely candid in his responses.

"It's not my fault you picked five bad matches in a row," he said.

"I picked five excellent matches." She raised one hand, fingers bunched into a loose fist. "They were all college educated." She extended one finger. "They were all within the age span that you specified." She extended a second finger. "They all had successful careers and were financially independent." Another finger. "They were all comfortable with the idea of helping you entertain your business clients." A fourth finger went up. "And, as you stipulated, not one of them could even remotely be described as the *arty* type."

"All five made less than subtle inquiries about my portfolio."

"Why shouldn't they have shown an interest in it? You certainly showed great interest in *their* financial status. You made a huge deal about it, in fact. You wanted someone who was clearly financially well-situated."

"Only because I don't want to be married for my money." He turned and started to prowl the room. "Another thing, all five acted offended when I brought up the subject of a prenuptial contract."

"You should have known better than to bring up a subject like that on a first date, for heaven's sake."

He ignored that. "All five talked about extended vacations in the south of France and second homes on Maui. I don't take monthlong vacations."

"Do you take *any* vacations?"

"I've got a company to run, damn it."

"Uh-huh." No vacations. A real fun guy. But she refrained from voicing that observation aloud.

"And another thing." He turned back around to face her. "All five of those women looked very high-maintenance to me."

"And you're not high-maintenance?"

He appeared genuinely startled that she would even suggest such a possibility. His expression darkened. "Of course not. I just told you, I'm a very flexible man."

She sat forward abruptly. "Pay attention here, Gabe. According to the feedback I got from the five women I sent you out with, you showed distinct signs of being bored and impatient within half an hour after each date began."

He shrugged. "That was approximately how long it took each time before I realized that you had picked another bad match."

"Did you have to start sneaking glances at your watch before the entrées arrived?"

"I wasn't *sneaking* glances. So I checked my watch occasionally. So what? Time is money."

"There was also a general consensus among all five women that you do not have a romantic bone in your body."

"Those dates weren't about romance." He sliced one hand through the air in a quick, thoroughly disgusted arc. "They were business meetings as far as I was concerned."

"Business meetings," she replied, keeping her tone very neutral. "Oddly enough, the women I matched you with did not view the dates in quite the same light."

"I'm looking for a wife, damn it. Not a girlfriend."

"I see." She cleared her throat delicately. "All five of the women reported that when they did manage to get a conversation going with you, it went nowhere because you are clearly paranoid about being married for your money."

"You'd be paranoid, too, if every person you dated wanted to know how much you had invested in high-tech stocks and how much in bonds and real estate." He broke off, looking thoughtful. "Maybe I should have adopted an alias for the dates."

"Oh, sure. Lying about your identity is a great way to start a long-term relationship. And for your information, I have had more than one date with men who took what I considered an unpleasant interest in my finances. I'm a Harte, remember?"

"Oh, yeah. Right. Harte Investments."

"Exactly. Anyone who knows me well understands that my brother and sister and I will each inherit a large chunk of my family's company. In addition, I haven't done badly with Private Arrangements."

He surveyed the well-appointed office. "I've heard that your client list is very high-end. And you sure do charge high-end fees for your services."

She gave him a cool smile. "In short, my balance sheets look very appetizing to a certain type of man. But I don't allow that fact to color my view of the entire male population. I'm not totally paranoid that every guy who asks me out is hoping to marry into money."

"Nice for you," he muttered. "But a little naïve, don't you think?"

She could feel her teeth starting to clench together. "I am not naïve."

He shrugged and went to stand at the window that looked out across the rain-swept city toward the Willamette River. She followed his gaze and saw that lights were coming on all over town. The late winter day was ending swiftly. Here in the Northwest there was a price to be paid for the long, long days of summer. That fee came in the form of very short days at this time of year.

"Okay, maybe I am a little paranoid about being married because of Madison Commercial," Gabe said quietly. "I've had a couple of close calls."

"Give me a break. Are you telling me that the reason you've never married is because you're afraid that every woman you meet is after your money?" She did not bother to keep the skepticism out of her voice. "I find that a little tough to swallow. You haven't always been wealthy and successful. Far from it. I know exactly where you came from, remember?"

He contemplated the mist that shrouded the darkening city. "During the time when I didn't have any money I was too busy with Madison Commercial to get seriously involved with anyone."

"Now that I do believe."

There was a short silence.

"It isn't just caution that kept me from getting married."

"No?"

"I wasn't in any hurry to follow the Madison tradition."

She watched him narrowly. "Which tradition, exactly, would that be?"

"Messy relationships and divorce run in my family. We're not real good at marriage."

She straightened in her chair. "Sorry, you can't use that excuse anymore. Your brother put an end to that famous Madison tradition when he married my sister. Rafe and Hannah's marriage is going to work out brilliantly."

"You sound very sure of that."

"I *am* sure of it."

He glanced at her over his shoulder, intense curiosity gleaming in his eyes. "Why? You didn't run them through your computer program to see if they were a good match. How can you be so certain that their marriage will work?"

"You can feel it when you're with them," she said quietly. "There's a bond. I don't think either of them will ever look at anyone else as long as they have each other."

"You can *feel* it, huh?"

"Call it female intuition."

"Intuition is a funny word coming from a woman who uses a computer to match people. Wouldn't have thought you would be real big on intuition."

She stiffened. "Every woman likes to think she has good intuition." This was getting into dangerous territory. "Don't you believe their marriage will work?"

"Oh, yeah," he said with stunning casualness. "It'll work."

The absolute conviction in his words took her back for a second or two. "I beg your pardon? You just accused me of relying on intuition. What makes you so sure their marriage will hold up?"

"It sure as hell isn't my intuition."

"What is it?"

"Simple logic. For starters, it's obvious that Hannah is Rafe's passion. You know what they say about us Madisons."

"Nothing gets between a Madison and his passion," she recited evenly.

"Right. In addition, your family has a reputation for being good at marriage. I've never heard of a Harte getting a divorce. I figure that makes for a winning combination for Rafe and Hannah."

"I see." Time to change the topic. "Well, we seem to be in agreement on that point. Why are we arguing about it?"

Gabe turned away from the window and resumed prowling the room. "We're not arguing. I just wondered how you could be so sure of your conclusions when you hadn't run Rafe and Hannah through your computer, that's all."

She glanced uneasily at the laptop on her desk. She was not about to explain that in the past few months she had been forced to admit to herself that her computer program was not the sole secret of her success as a matchmaker. But the truth was too disturbing to discuss with anyone else, let alone a Madison. She was having a hard enough time dealing with it herself.

The realization that she was relying on her intuition and a hefty dose of common sense combined with the computer's analysis to get successful matches was fraught with disturbing implications. She was, after all, assuming a huge responsibility with each client. She guided and assisted them in making one of the most important decisions of their lives. The possibility of making a mistake weighed more heavily on her with each passing day. Although nothing awful had happened yet, lately she'd had the uneasy sensation that she was on extremely thin ice.

The time to get out was now, before disaster struck.

She was ready to switch careers, anyway. While her rapidly accumulating qualms about the risks of the matchmaking field were not the main reason she had decided to close down her business, they definitely constituted an added incentive to shut her doors. Fast.

She was not looking forward to announcing her intentions to her family. She knew only too well that the news would not be greeted with wild enthusiasm in the Harte clan. But she had made her plans. The only thing standing between her and her new profession was Gabe Madison. He was the last client left on her active list.

Unfortunately, getting rid of him was proving more difficult than she had anticipated.

Gabe came to a halt in front of her desk, shoved aside one edge of his sleekly cut jacket and hooked his thumb in his belt.

"Let's get to the bottom line here," he said. "You want to ditch me because I'm a Madison and you're a Harte."

She raised her eyes to the ceiling, seeking patience and forbearance. When she got no help from that direction, she took a deep breath instead.

"That's got nothing to do with this," she said. "I don't give a darn about the family feud. Even if I did, I could hardly use it as a reason to drop you from my list now that your brother and my sister are married."

"Just because Rafe and Hannah got together doesn't mean that you've changed your opinion about the rest of us Madisons."

"Oh, for heaven's sake, Gabe, it was our grandfathers who started the feud. I couldn't care less about that old nonsense."

"Yeah?" He gave her a razor-sharp smile. "You mean that you really believe that I'm capable of making a long-term commitment?"

The sarcasm was too much. She had been through a lot since the day Gabe had shown up here in her office, demanding to sign on as a client. The way he had demolished her private fantasies was the least of it.

"I think you're perfectly capable of a long-term commitment," she said. "But it looks to me like you've already made it."

"What the hell are you talking about? I'm not in a relationship."

"Yes, you are. You've got a very serious, very committed, one hundred percent exclusive relationship with Madison Commercial."

"Madison Commercial is my company," he said. "Of course I'm committed to it. That's got nothing to do with getting married."

"That company is your passion, Gabe. You've devoted your entire life to building that business."

"So what?"

"You're a Madison," she said, thoroughly exasperated now. "As you just pointed out, nothing comes between a Madison and his passion."

"Damn, this *is* about me being a Madison." He jerked his thumb out of his belt and planted his hands flat on her desk. "You *are* biased against me because our families have a history."

"It's not our family history that is the problem here." She could feel her temper rising. She had a nasty suspicion that her face was flushed. Probably an unpleasant shade of red. "*You're* the problem."

"Are you telling me that just because I'm running a successful corporation, I can't commit to a wife?"

That gave her pause.

"I wouldn't go that far," she said carefully. "But I do think that you're going to have to refocus if you want to make a relationship work."

"Define refocus."

She sighed. "You're going about this all wrong, Gabe."

"I'm trying to use a logical, rational, scientifically based technique to find a wife. I would have thought you, of all people, would appreciate that approach."

"Why? Because I'm a Harte and you Madisons think all Hartes have ice water in their veins?"

"You do own and operate a computerized matchmaking firm, don't you? Some people would say your line of work requires a pretty cold-blooded approach to marriage."

Damn. She would not allow Gabriel Madison to make her feel awkward right here in her own office. She was a Harte, after all. Hartes did not put up with this sort of behavior from Madisons.

"There's a difference between going about the process of finding a mate in an intelligent, logical manner and going about it in a cold-blooded fashion," she said evenly.

"And I'm being cold-blooded, is that it?"

"Look, you're the one who filled out the questionnaire that I fed into my computer program, not me."

There was a beat or two of silence. He watched her with a shuttered look.

"What was wrong with the way I filled it out?" he asked a little too softly.

She tapped the printouts in front of her. "According to these results, you want a robot for a wife."

"That's crazy." He straightened and shoved his fingers through his dark hair. "If that's the conclusion your idiotic program came up with, you'd damn well better see about getting some new software."

"I don't think the program is at fault here."

"A robot, huh?" He nodded once. "Maybe that's what went wrong on those five dates you arranged for me. Maybe you sent me out with five robots. Come to think of it, they were all a little too thin and there was something very computerlike about the way they tried to grill me on the subject of my portfolio."

"You got exactly what you said you wanted, according to the questionnaire," she said very sweetly. "There was no strong emotion in any of your responses except when it came to the importance of not being matched with what you call *arty* types and your insistence on a prenuptial agreement."

"What's the problem with the lack of strong emotions?"

"For one thing, it makes it extremely difficult to find a match for you."

"I would have thought taking emotion out of the equation would have made it easier to match me, not harder."

"Don't get me wrong," she said. "I'm a big believer in approaching marriage logically. I've built this business on that premise. But you've gone to extremes. You're hunting for a wife as if you were interviewing a potential employee for an executive slot at Madison Commercial. It won't work."

"Why not?" His eyes were emerald hard. His voice fell to an even softer pitch. "Because I'm a Madison and Madisons can't do anything without getting emotional?"

"That does it." She powered down the laptop. "It has nothing to do with the fact that you're a Madison. You can't expect me to find you a proper match when you insist on concealing your true feelings on certain matters."

"Concealing my true feelings?"

"Yes." She closed the lid of the laptop, reached down, opened a drawer and removed her shoulder bag.

"Just a minute. Are you accusing me of having deliberately shaded a few of my answers on that questionnaire?"

"No." She straightened and slung the strap of the bag over her shoulder. "I don't think you *shaded* a few of your responses. I think you lied through your teeth about everything except prenuptial agreements and arty types."

"Why the hell would I lie on that stupid questionnaire?"

"How should I know? You'd need to discuss that with a trained therapist. I can give you the name of one, if you want to pursue the matter. He's right here in this building. Three floors down. Dr. J. Anderson Flint."

Gabe's expression hardened. "His name certainly popped up in a hurry in the course of this conversation."

"Probably because he's on my mind at the moment." She glanced at the roman numerals etched on the jade green face of her watch. "I'm on my way to his office."

"You're seeing a therapist?"

"In a manner of speaking." She went to the small closet behind the desk, opened it and removed the hooded, ankle-length rain cloak inside. "Anderson is doing research for a book. He wants to interview me."

"Why?"

"Because he specializes in treating people who have problems in their, uh, physical relationships with their partners."

"In other words, he's a sex therapist?"

She could feel herself turning red again. "I believe sex therapy constitutes the major portion of his practice, yes."

"And he wants to interview you. Well, now, that would certainly raise a few eyebrows back in Eclipse Bay."

"Try to get your mind out of the gutter." She scooped the laptop off her desk and stuffed it into a waterproof case. "I've got a very high success rate here at Private Arrangements. Anderson feels my computer program is the key. He is looking for ways to incorporate the principles of that program into a useful guide for couples seeking committed relationships."

"You sure can't prove your very high success rate by me."

"No." She picked up the case containing the laptop and walked around the corner of her desk. "I admit you are a glaring failure. Most of my clients, however, are satisfied with the results they get here at Private Arrangements."

And I intend to quit while they all feel that way, she thought, heading for the door.

Gabe grabbed his black trench coat off the coatrack. "Your matchmaking program sucks in my opinion."

"You've made your feelings on the subject quite clear." She opened the door. "And that is why I'm releasing you from your contract with Private Arrangements."

"You're not releasing me, you're firing me."

"Whatever." She flipped the bank of wall switches, plunging the office into stygian gloom.

"What the hell? Hold on, damn it." Gabe hoisted the monogrammed leather briefcase sitting on the floor near the coatrack. "You can't just walk out on me like this."

"I'm not walking out, I'm closing my office." She stepped into the hall and jangled her keys in a pointed fashion. "I just told you, I'm on my way to see Dr. Flint."

He shrugged into his trench coat, leaving it unbuttoned. "You're certainly in a rush to keep the appointment. A sex therapist. I still can't believe it."

"I don't have an appointment. I'm just going to drop by his office. I need to tell him something important. Not that it's any of your business. Furthermore, I don't like the sarcastic tone of your voice. I'll have you know that Anderson is a thorough-going professional."

"Is that so? A professional sex therapist." Gabe moved out into the hall. "Guess I should show some respect. They do say it's the oldest profession. No, wait, maybe I've got that mixed up with another line of work."

She would not dignify that with a response, she thought. She locked the office door with a quick twist of her hand and dropped the keys into her shoulder bag. Whirling around, she strode toward the elevators.

Gabe fell into step beside her. "Don't forget, you owe me another date."

"I beg your pardon?"

"I only got five dates, remember? The contract guarantees six matches."

"Don't sweat it. I'll refund one-sixth of the fee you paid me."

"I don't want my money back, I want my sixth date."

"Better take the money." She came to a halt in front of the bank of elevators and stabbed the call button. "It's all you're going to get."

He flattened one hand on the wall beside her head, leaned in very close and lowered his voice to a low, dangerous pitch that made tiny chills chase down her spine.

"Trust me," Gabe said very deliberately. "You don't want a lawsuit over this."

She spun around to face him and found him standing much too close.

"Are you trying to intimidate me?" she asked.

"Just making an observation."

She gave him a frigid smile. "I can see the headlines now. *President of Madison Commercial Threatens Lawsuit over Cancelled Date.* Talk about looking ridiculous."

"You owe me that date."

"Back off, Gabe. We both know you're not going to sue me. You'd look like a fool in the press and that's the last thing you'd want. Just think of what the publicity would do to the image of your company."

Gabe said nothing—just looked at her the way Roman gladiators had no doubt studied each other before an event in the arena. Behind her the elevator doors opened with a soft sighing hiss. She turned quickly and got into the cab.

Gabe got in behind her.

She punched the floor number she wanted and then, without much hope, she also selected the lobby button. Maybe Gabe would take the hint and remain in the elevator when she got off on Anderson's floor.

She stood tensely near the control panel, watching the doors close. She was very aware of Gabe at her shoulder, dominating the small space, using up all the oxygen so that she could hardly breathe.

"Admit it," she said when she could no longer stand the silence. "You lied on that questionnaire."

"The questionnaire has nothing to do with this. You owe me a date."

"You didn't enter the truth when you made your responses. You put down what you thought the truth should be."

He quirked one brow. "There's a difference?"

"Night and day in most cases."

The elevator doors opened. She walked quickly out into the hall.

Gabe glided out after her. So much for hoping he would stay on board and descend to the lobby.

"What do you think you're doing?" she said. "I told you, I'm on my way to talk to Dr. Flint."

"I'll wait until you're finished."

"You can't do that."

"Why not? Doesn't he have a waiting room?"

"I don't believe this."

"I'm not leaving until you guarantee me a sixth match."

"We'll talk about it some other time. Give me a call tomorrow."

"We'll talk about it today."

"I refuse to let you push me around like this."

"I haven't touched you," Gabe said.

She would not lower herself to his level, she thought. She was a mature, sophisticated woman. More to the point, she was a Harte. Hartes did not engage in public scenes. That was more of a Madison thing.

The only option to yelling at Gabe was to pretend he was not right here, shadowing her down the hall. It was not easy.

Obviously she had pushed her luck with Private Arrangements, she thought morosely. She had waited a little too long to go out of business. If only she had stopped accepting clients the day *before* Gabe had walked into her office.

She reached the door marked DR. J. ANDERSON FLINT, opened it and walked into the waiting room. Gabe flowed in behind her, Dracula in a very expensive black trench coat.

The first clue that the situation had the potential to deteriorate further came when she noticed that Anderson's secretary, Mrs. Collins, was not behind her desk. She realized that she had been counting on the woman's presence to ensure that Gabe behaved himself.

She glanced quickly around the serene, vaguely beige room hoping to spot the secretary somewhere in the shadows. There was no one in sight.

The muffled strains of some loud, hard-core, sixties-era rock music reverberated through the wooden panels of the closed door that separated Anderson's inner office from the waiting room.

Her sense of foreboding increased for some unaccountable reason.

"It looks like Anderson's secretary has gone home early today," she said. "He's probably working on his notes."

"Sounds like rock music."

"Anderson enjoys classic rock."

"You know him pretty well, huh?"

"We met last month in the coffee shop downstairs." She knocked lightly on the inner door. "We have a lot in common. Similar professional interests."

"Is that right?" Gabe said. "You know, I don't think he can hear you above the music. He's really got it cranked up in there."

The music was loud and getting louder and more intense by the second.

She twisted the knob and opened the door.

And stopped short at the sight of J. Anderson Flint stretched out on his office sofa. He was naked except for a pair of very small, very red bikini briefs that did nothing to conceal his erection. His hands were bound at the wrists above his head. A blindfold was secured around his eyes.

A solidly built woman dressed in a skintight leather catsuit, long black leather gloves, and a pair of five-inch stiletto heels stood over him. She had one leg balanced on the back of the sofa, the other braced on the coffee table. Her back was to the door but Lillian could see that she held a small velvet whip in her right hand and a steel-studded dog collar, in her left.

Neither of the room's occupants heard the door open because the music was building to its crashing finale.

Lillian tried to move and could not. It was as if she had been frozen in place by some futuristic ray gun.

"Similar professional interests, you say?" Gabe murmured into her left ear.

His undisguised amusement freed her from the effects of the invisible force field that held her immobile. With a gasp, she managed to turn around. He blocked her path, his attention focused on the scene taking place on the sofa. He smiled.

"Excuse me," she croaked. She put both hands on his chest and shoved hard to get him out of the way.

Gabe obligingly moved, stepping aside and simultaneously reaching around her to pull the door shut on the lurid scene.

The music thundered to its rousing climax.

Lillian fled through the tasteful waiting room out into the hallway. She did not look back.

Gabe caught up with her at the elevator.

An eerie silence gripped the corridor for the count of five.

"Dr. Flint obviously believes in a hands-on approach to sex therapy," Gabe remarked. "I wonder just how he plans to incorporate your computer program into his treatment plans."

This could not be happening, she thought. It was some kind of bizarre hallucination, the sort of thing that could turn a person into a full-blown conspiracy theorist. Maybe some secret government agency was conducting experiments with chemicals in the drinking water.

Or maybe she was losing it. She'd been under a lot of stress lately, what with making the decision to close down Private Arrangements and change careers. Having Gabe as a client hadn't helped matters, either.

No doubt about it, stress combined with secret government drinking water experiments could account for what she had just seen in Anderson's office.

"I think you need a drink," Gabe said.

2

OUTSIDE on the sidewalk the weird afterglow of the rainy twilight combined with the streetlamps to infuse the city with a surreal atmosphere. It was as if he and Lillian were moving through a dream sequence, Gabe thought. It was easy to believe that they were the only real, solid beings in a world composed of eerie lights and shadows.

In the strange, vaporlike mist, Lillian's flowing, iridescent rain cloak glittered like a cape woven of other-worldly gemstones. He wanted to reach out and pull her close against his side, feel the heat of her body, inhale her scent.

It was getting worse, he thought. This gut-deep awareness had hit him hard when he had first experienced it at Rafe's wedding. He had told himself it would fade quickly. Just a passing sexual attraction. Or maybe a little fevered imagination brought on by the monklike existence he had been living ever since he had turned his attention to the business of finding himself a wife.

The decision to go celibate after the end of the affair with Jennifer several months ago had seemed like a good idea at the time. He had not wanted something as superficial as lust to screw up his thinking processes while he concentrated on such an important matter. To avoid complications, he had deliberately opted to put his sex life on a temporarily inactive status.

Within about six seconds of seeing Lillian after all those years of living in separate universes, he had been inspired to revisit that particular executive decision, however.

Thankfully, he'd had enough common sense still functioning at that point to convince himself that an affair with her was probably not a brilliant idea. She was a Harte, after all. Things between Hartes and Madisons were always complicated. He had come up with a compromise solution. Instead of asking her out on a date, he had signed up as a client of Private Arrangements. He had spent an inordinate amount of time convincing himself that using a professional matchmaking firm was actually a terrific plan. What better, more efficient way to find a wife?

But things had rapidly gone from dicey to disastrous. He had endured five seemingly endless evenings with five very attractive, very successful women. He had spent each of the five dates tormenting himself with visions of how much more interesting things would have been if Lillian had been the woman seated across the candlelit table.

The uncanny part was that he had never been aware of her as anything other than a Harte kid while he had been growing up in Eclipse Bay. But then, in all fairness, the only thing that had held his attention in those days was his dream of rebuilding the financial empire that had been shattered by the Harte-Madison feud.

The fact that the Hartes had resurrected themselves after the bankruptcy and gone on to prosper while his family had floundered and pretty much self-destructed had added fuel to the fire that had consumed him.

He had left Eclipse Bay the day after he graduated from high school, headed off to college and the big city to pursue his vision. He had not seen Lillian at all during the years of empire-building. He had not even thought about her.

But ever since the wedding he had been unable to think about anything else.

If this was lust, it was anything but superficial. If it was something more, he was in trouble because Lillian was not what he had pictured when he set out to look for a wife. For the first time since he had decided to get married he wondered if he should put the search for a wife on hold for a while. Just until he got this murky situation with Lillian cleared up and out of the way. He needed to be able to concentrate and she was making that impossible.

He realized they had halted at a crosswalk.

"Where are we going?" he asked.

"I don't know where you're going, but I'm walking home." Her voice was slightly muffled by the hood of her cloak.

"What do you say we stop somewhere and get you that drink I suggested? I have to tell you that after watching your colleague work with a patient, I could use one, myself."

"Don't start with me on that subject, Madison."

He smiled and reached out to take her arm. "Come on, I'll buy."

He steered her toward the small café in the middle of the block.

She peered fixedly through the glass panes into the cozily lit interior.

"You know what?" she said. "I think you're right. A glass of wine sounds like an excellent idea."

She pulled free of his hand and went toward the door with quick, crisp steps. She did not look around to see if he was following.

He made it to the door a half a step ahead of her and got it open. She did not thank him, just swept past him into the café.

The place was just starting to fill up with the afterwork crowd. A cheerful gas fire cast an inviting glow. The chalkboard listed several brands of beer from local microbreweries and half a dozen premium wines by the glass. Another hand-lettered menu on the wall featured a variety of oyster appetizers and happy-hour specials.

He knew this place. It was only a few streets over from the office tower that housed the headquarters of Madison Commercial. He stopped in here occasionally on his way home to his empty apartment.

"Come here a lot?" he asked as they settled into a wooden booth.

"No." She picked up the miniature wine menu and studied it intently. "Why?"

"Portland is a small town in a lot of ways. It's a wonder our paths haven't crossed before," he said, trying for a neutral topic of conversation.

She frowned at the little menu. "I haven't lived here much in recent years."

"Where have you been since college?"

"You really want to know?"

"Sure." He was suddenly more curious than he wanted to let on.

She shrugged and put down the menu. Before she could answer his question, however, the waiter arrived to take their orders. She chose a glass of Chardonnay. He asked for a beer.

When the waiter left, there was a short silence. He thought he might have to remind Lillian of the question. Somewhat to his surprise, however, she started to talk.

"After I graduated from college I worked in Seattle for a while," she said. "Then I moved to Hawaii. Spent a year there. After that I went to California and then back to Seattle. I didn't return to Oregon until I decided to open Private Arrangements."

"Were you running matchmaking businesses in all those different places?"

She eyed him with a wary expression. "Why do you want to know?"

"Been a while. Just catching up."

"You and I don't have any catching up to do. We hardly even know each other."

That was almost funny, he thought.

"I'm a Harte and you're a Madison," he said. "My brother is now married to your sister. Trust me, we know each other."

The waiter returned with their drinks and disappeared once more. Lillian picked up her Chardonnay, took a sip and set the glass down very precisely on the little napkin. He got the feeling she was debating how much to tell him about herself.

"The official Harte family version of events is that I've spent the last few years trying to find myself," she said.

"What's the unofficial version?"

"That I'm a little flaky."

Definitely not wife material, he thought. Probably not good affair material, either. He did not date flakes. He didn't do business with flakes, either. If he had known Private Arrangements was run by a flake, he would never have signed on as a client.

Then again, who was he kidding?

Damn. This was not a good idea. If he had any sense he would run, not walk, to the nearest exit. Some lingering vestige of self-preservation made him glance toward the door.

What the hell, he thought, turning back to Lillian. Plenty of time to escape later.

"Didn't realize any of you Hartes had to find yourselves," he said after a while. "Figured you were all born knowing where you wanted to go in life and how you would get there."

"You're thinking of everyone else in the family." She wrinkled her nose. "I'm the exception."

"Yeah? How exceptional are you?"

She studied the wine in her glass. "Let's just say I haven't found my niche yet."

"From all accounts you've been extremely successful with Private Arrangements."

"Oh, sure." She raised one shoulder in dismissal. "If you're talking business success."

He went blank.

"There's another kind?" he asked.

Irritation gleamed in her eyes. "Of course there's another kind."

He leaned back in the booth. "This isn't about finding yourself and inner peace through work, is it?"

"You've got a problem with the concept of work as a source of happiness and personal fulfillment?"

"I've got a problem with people who think work is supposed to be entertainment. Work is work." He paused. "Probably why they call it work instead of, say, fun. A lot of folks don't seem to get that."

"You ought to know," she said.

"What's that supposed to mean?"

"You've been working night and day since you were a boy to build Madison Commercial." She smiled wryly. "Folks back in Eclipse Bay always said that you were a different kind of Madison."

"Different?"

"One who might actually make a success of himself. You certainly proved them right, didn't you?"

How the hell had the conversation turned back on him like this?

"All I proved," he said carefully, "is that you can get someplace if you want to go there badly enough."

"And you wanted to get where you are now very, very badly, didn't you?"

He did not know what to make of her in this mood, so he took another swallow of beer to give himself time to come up with a strategy.

"Tell me, Gabe, what do you do for fun?"

"Fun?" The question put him off stride again. He was still working on strategy.

"As far as I can tell, all you do is work. If work isn't fun for you, where do you go and what do you do when you're looking for a good time?"

He frowned. "You make it sound like I never get out of the office."

"Do you?"

"I'm here, aren't I? This sure as hell isn't my office."

"You're right. This isn't your office. So, tell me, are you having fun yet?"

"I didn't come here to have fun. We're here because you received a severe shock back there in Dr. J. Anderson Flint's office. I figured you needed a glass of wine for medicinal purposes."

"The only reason you're still hanging around is because you're trying to figure out how to get your sixth date. Forget it. Never happen."

"We'll see."

"Pay attention, Madison." She leaned forward and narrowed her eyes. "It will never happen because Private Arrangements is closed."

"So? We'll talk about my sixth date when you reopen on Monday."

"I meant closed for good. Today was the last day of business. As of five o'clock this afternoon, my firm ceased operations. Get it?"

She was serious, he thought. "You can't just shut down a moneymaking enterprise like that."

"Watch me."

"What about your clients?"

"You are the last one." She raised her glass in a mocking little toast. "Here's to you. Good luck finding yourself a robot."

"A wife."

"Whatever." She took a sip of the wine.

"Why the hell would you want to go out of business? You're a huge success."

"Financially, yes." She sat back. "That isn't enough."

"Damn. You really are into this work-has-got-to-be-a-transcendent-experience thing, aren't you?"

"Yep." She propped one elbow on the table and rested her chin in her hand. "Let's get back to you and fun."

"Thought you just got through implying that the two don't belong in the same sentence."

"Well, let's talk about your relationship with Madison Commercial, then."

"Relationship? Are you suggesting that the company is my mistress or something?"

"That's certainly what it looks like to me."

He was getting irritated. "Is that your *professional* opinion?"

"I'm a matchmaker, remember? I know a good match when I see one. Tell me, what, exactly, do you get out of Madison Commercial?"

He was wary now. "What do I *get* out of it?"

She gave him a bright-eyed, innocently inquiring look. "Do you think your relationship with the company is a substitute for sex?"

She was a Harte, he reminded himself. Damned if he would let her goad him.

"Got news for you. In case you don't know, Ms. Matchmaker, there is no substitute for sex. What I get out of Madison Commercial is a lot of money."

"And power," she added a little too helpfully. "But, then, the two usually go together, don't they?"

"Power?" he repeated neutrally.

"Sure. You have a lot of clout here in Portland. You mingle with the movers and shakers. You're on the boards of some of the major charitable organizations. You know the players in business and politics. People listen to you. That's called power."

He thought about it and then shrugged. "I do get stuck with a lot of board meetings."

"Don't try to pretend you don't know what I'm talking about. I can't believe you would have worked so hard to make Madison Commercial such an important and influential company if you weren't getting something very personal out of it. Something besides money."

"You know," he said, "this kind of conversation isn't my forte."

"Really? I would never have guessed."

"My turn," he said. "Just what were you doing in all those different places you were living in for the past few years?"

"You want my whole résumé?"

"Just hit the high spots."

She put the tips of her thumbs and forefingers together, forming a triangle around the base of her glass and looked down into her wine.

"Well, let's see," she said. "After I graduated from college, I worked in a museum for a few years."

"Why did you quit?"

"The public never seemed to be compelled by the same art that fascinates me and the whole point of a successful museum is to attract the attention of the public. I wasn't very creative with the exhibitions and displays."

"Because you were not real interested in the subjects you were supposed to make attractive to the public."

"Probably. After that I worked in various art galleries. I had no problem figuring out what would sell, but I wasn't personally attracted to the art that most of the clients wanted to buy."

"Hard to stay in business when you don't want to give your customers what they want to buy."

Her mouth curved ruefully. "Oddly enough, that's what the gallery owners said."

"What came next?"

She turned the base of the wineglass slowly between her fingers. "I switched to a career in interior design. It was okay for a while but then I started getting into arguments with my clients. They didn't always like what I thought they ought to have in their homes and offices."

"Nothing worse than a client with his own personal opinion, I always say."

"Very true. I decided to get out of that field, too, but before I did, I introduced one of my clients, a software designer, to a friend of mine. I thought they made a good match and I was right. After the wedding, my software client got enthusiastic about the whole idea of designing a matchmaking program. It sounded interesting, so I agreed to work with her on it. We consulted with some experts. I designed the questionnaire. She did the technical part. When it was finished, I bought her out."

"That's how you got into the matchmaking business? You just sort of fell into it?"

"Chilling, isn't it?"

He exhaled slowly. "Well, yeah, as a matter of fact, it is."

"You're not the only one who has pointed that out recently. I never set out to get into the business, you understand. After my ex-client finished the program, I tested it. More or less as a lark, I tried it on some acquaintances and got lucky a couple of times. People went out on dates, had a good time. An engagement or two was announced. All of a sudden, I was in the matchmaking business."

"Damn." He rubbed his jaw. "Are you sure that's legal?"

"Got news for you, Madison, anyone can set up in business as a matchmaker."

"Sort of like the sex therapy business, huh?"

"Don't." She leveled a warning finger at him. "Mention that subject again."

"Hard to resist."

"Try." She gave him an evil smile. "Now that you know the gruesome truth, that you placed your entire future in the hands of an amateur, maybe you'd like to rethink your insistence on that sixth date you say I owe you."

"No way." He picked up his beer, tilted it to his mouth and took a long swallow. Then he put the bottle down again. "I paid for it. I want it."

She made a face. "Anyone ever told you that you've got a real stubborn streak?"

"It's a Madison thing." He studied her across the table. "What are you going to do next? After I get my sixth date and you shut down Private Arrangements, that is?"

"Gee, I don't know. Maybe I'll apply for an executive position at Madison Commercial."

"Don't bother. Something tells me you wouldn't last long there, either."

"You're probably right," she said. "I'm what you'd call a self-motivated type. I don't like working for other people. I prefer to make the decisions and set the agenda. It would be inevitable that sooner or later I would start telling you how to run your company."

"At which point I would have to can you."

"Of course." She waved a dismissive hand. "Another career path down the tubes."

"How important is Flint to you?"

"I told you not to mention his name to me again." But there was no heat in her words this time.

He decided to take a chance and push a little harder.

"If the two of you had something serious going on, I can see where the sight of all the leather might have been a little traumatic."

"Anderson and I don't have anything serious going on," she said very steadily. "Not in the way you mean. I won't say I didn't enjoy his company on a few occasions but I knew from the start that he wasn't interested in me personally."

"Just your program."

"Yes."

"Are you going to help him out with his book?"

"No," she said.

"Was it the scene in his office that made you change your mind?"

"No." She went to work on the little paper napkin that had accompanied the glass of wine, folding and creasing it in an abstract pattern. "I changed my mind several days ago. That's what I was going to tell Anderson this afternoon when I went downstairs to see him."

"Why back out of the project?"

"I've got my mind on other things right now."

He had been through too many negotiations, played too many games of strategy and brinksmanship not to know when an opponent was being evasive. But he had also had enough experience to know when to push and when to let things ride.

"As long as we're here," he said. "We might as well have dinner."

She looked up from her origami project. "Dinner?"

"We both have to eat. Unless you've got other plans?"

"No," she said slowly. "I don't have any other plans."

HE walked her back to a handsome brick building and saw her to her front door on the top floor. When she turned in the doorway to say good night, he looked past her through a small foyer into the living room of her apartment. He could see warm yellow walls, white moldings near the ceiling and a lot of vividly patterned velvet pillows heaped on a brilliant purple sofa. The curved arm of a scarlet wingback chair was visible near the window. The edge of a green, yellow, and purple patterned rug peeked out from beneath an abstract, glass coffee table.

The strange combination of colors and designs should have looked garish but for some reason it all went together perfectly. That was a disturbing sign but it was not what really worried him.

What bothered him the most were the glimpses he caught of the paintings hanging on the yellow walls. There were a number of them. Not framed reproductions or posters. Lillian bought originals, apparently. A real bad sign. She obviously cared enough about art to have formed her own opinions.

From where he stood in the doorway, he could not get a good look at any of the pictures but he got an impression of strong light and dark, edgy shadows. He thought back to the conversation in the café, the part where she had detailed her job history working mostly in museums and art galleries.

A sense of deep gloom settled on him. He could no longer deny the evidence of his own eyes. Lillian was into art big-time.

"Thank you for the drink and for dinner," she said politely.

He pulled his attention back from the ominous scene inside her apartment. Realized that she was watching him closely, maybe reading his mind.

"Sure," he said. "My pleasure."

She gripped the door with one hand, preparing to close it. A speculative expression crossed her face. "You know, when you think about it—"

"Forget it," he said.

"Forget what?"

"You aren't going to get away with calling that dinner we just had my sixth date. I'm not letting Private Arrangements off the hook that easily."

Her mouth tightened. "You have been a difficult client from day one, Madison."

"People say stuff like that to me all the time. I try not to take it personally."

3

LILLIAN watched Octavia Brightwell's expressive face while she examined the painting. Rapt attention radiated from the gallery owner.

Octavia stood in the center of the studio, her red hair aglow in the strong light cast by the ceiling fixtures. Her slender frame was taut with concentration; she seemed lost somewhere inside the picture propped in front of her.

Or maybe she hated the painting and didn't know how to deliver the bad news, Lillian thought.

She berated herself for the negative thinking. She considered herself to be a positive, glass-half-full kind of person under most circumstances, but when it came to her art she knew she was vulnerable.

Octavia was the first and, thus far, the only person from the art world who had seen her work. Until recently, she had allowed only the members of her family and a very few close friends to view the paintings.

She had always drawn and painted. She could not remember a time when she had not kept a sketchbook close at hand. She had been fascinated with watercolors and acrylics and pastels since childhood. She picked up her brushes as easily as other people picked up a knife and fork. Her family considered her painting as nothing more than a hobby but she knew the truth. It was as necessary to her as food and water and fresh air.

She had been born into a family of financial wizards and entrepreneurs. It was not that art was not respected in the Harte clan. Some of the members of her family actively collected it. But they treated it as they would any other investment. Hartes did not establish careers as artists. She'd dreamed her dreams of becoming an artist but she'd kept them to herself.

Until now.

The time had come to turn her dreams into reality. She could feel it. She was ready. Something inside her had changed. She sensed new dimensions in her work, new layers that had not been there in the past.

She was sure of her decision to try her hand at painting full-time, but she did not know if her work had a market. She had enough Harte business instincts to understand that in the real world, art was a commodity like any other. If there was no consumer demand for her work there was no possibility of making her living as an artist.

The route to financial success as an artist required the support and savvy marketing of a respected dealer. The decision to show her paintings to Octavia Brightwell first had been based entirely on intuition.

Octavia owned and operated an influential gallery, Bright Visions, here in Portland. She had also opened a branch in Eclipse Bay.

"Well?" Lillian prompted when she could no longer stand the suspense. "What do you think?"

"What do I think?" Octavia appeared to have trouble dragging her gaze away from the painting. "I think it's absolutely extraordinary, just like the others in your *Between Midnight and Dawn* series."

Something inside Lillian relaxed a little. "Good. Great. Thanks."

Octavia turned back to the painting. "I'm pulling out all the stops for your upcoming show. I want maximum impact."

"I don't know how to thank you, Octavia."

"Don't bother. We're both in this thing together. I have a feeling that it isn't just your career that will take off when I hang your work in my gallery. Mine is going to get a real shot in the arm as well."

Lillian laughed. "Sounds good to me. I'll leave you to do your job. I'm off to Eclipse Bay on Wednesday."

"You're really going to do it? You're going to close down Private Arrangements?"

"Yes, but keep it to yourself for a while." Lillian folded her arms and studied the paintings that lined the studio wall. "I'm still working on figuring out how to break it to the family gently."

"I suppose it will come as a shock."

"Well, it won't be quite as much of a blow as it was when Nick announced that he was leaving Harte Investments to write mysteries full-time. After all, my grandfather had counted on him taking over the company when my father retires. But no one is going to be real thrilled when I announce that I intend to paint full-time. Hartes don't become artists. They're businesspeople."

HALF an hour later, the laptop under her arm, the hood of her rain cloak pulled low over her face, Lillian walked quickly through the misty rain toward the building that housed the offices of Private Arrangements. Her thoughts were on the conversation with Octavia. She did not see the big man until he stepped right into her path.

"You're Lillian Harte, aren't you?" he said fiercely.

The anger in his voice made her mouth go dry. She came to a halt in the middle of the busy sidewalk, fervently grateful for the fact that she was surrounded by a large number of people.

The man looming in front of her appeared to be in his mid-forties, big, heavily built with blunt features and thinning, short-cropped hair. She could not see his eyes. They were concealed behind a pair of dark sunglasses. Not real useful on a cloudy, rainy day, she reflected, but they certainly added a note of menacing drama.

"Do I know you?" she asked cautiously.

"No." His heavy jaw jerked. "But I know you, lady. You're the matchmaker, aren't you?"

She clutched the laptop very tightly. "How do you know that?"

His mouth twisted. "I've been watching you for the past couple of days."

A blast of stark fear left her palms damp. "You *followed* me? You had no right to do that. I'll report you to the police."

"I didn't do anything illegal." He looked disgusted. "I just wanted to be sure."

"Sure of what?"

"Sure you were the woman who runs that matchmaking outfit, Private Arrangements."

"Why do you care who I am?"

He moved in closer. "You're the one who took Heather away from me. You hooked her up with someone else, didn't you? I called her a couple of days ago. Thought I'd give her another chance, y'know? That's when she told me that she planned to marry this guy you set her up with. She thinks she's in love. I think you messed with her mind."

Ice touched Lillian's spine. "Are you talking about Heather Summers?"

"Heather was with me before you tricked her into thinking I was no good for her. She left me because of you."

It took everything Lillian had to stand her ground. "Who are you?"

"My name's Witley." He took another step toward her, his face clenching with anger. "Campbell Witley. Heather and I were together before you came along. You ruined everything."

She glanced quickly around again, reassuring herself that she was not alone here on the sidewalk. Then she looked very steadily at Campbell Witley.

"Please, calm down, Mr. Witley. I did match a woman named Heather but when she filled out the forms I gave her she stated that she was not currently seeing anyone. I always insist that my clients be single and unattached when they sign up with my firm."

"I don't care what Heather said on your damned forms." He tapped his wide chest with a stubby thumb. "She was with *me*."

Lillian remembered Heather very well. She was a shy, nonconfrontational type who would have found it extremely difficult to deal with an aggressive man like Witley.

She also recalled that Heather had been a different woman after her first date with Ted Baker. Baker was the quiet, studious sort, very much a gentleman. He and Heather had attended the opera together. It had been love at first sight.

"Out of curiosity," Lillian said, "do you enjoy the opera, Mr. Witley?"

"What business is it of yours?"

"Heather loves the opera. I just wondered if you shared her interests."

Witley's mouth creased into a thin line. "Are you saying I didn't have anything in common with her just because I wouldn't go to the damned opera? That's bullshit. Heather and I had a lot in common. We went to ball games. I took her camping. We went white-water rafting. We did lots of stuff together."

"Those were all things that you enjoyed. But it doesn't sound as if you did many things that she liked to do."

"How do you know what she liked?"

"She was very specific on the questionnaire I had her fill out. She is really quite passionate about the opera, you know. And she likes to attend film festivals."

"I took Heather to the movies. We saw *Battle Zone* twice."

This was hopeless, Lillian thought. Campbell Witley would probably never understand, much less care, that he and Heather had had no common interests.

"I'm sorry about your personal problems, Mr. Witley, but I assure you, I had nothing to do with the breakup of your relationship," she said.

"The hell you didn't. If it hadn't been for you, Heather would be with me now."

"When did she end your relationship?"

Witley scowled furiously. "The night we went to see *Battle Zone* the second time. When I took her home that evening, she said she didn't want to date me again. Why?"

"You say that she broke up with you after you took her to back-to-back screenings of *Battle Zone*. As I recall, that film came out early last fall. I remember the ads were everywhere."

"So what?"

"Heather didn't register with Private Arrangements until December. I matched her in January."

"Who cares when she registered with your damned agency?"

"I'm trying to explain that my firm had nothing to do with the end of your relationship with Heather," Lillian said patiently. "She didn't come to me until after the two of you had stopped seeing each other."

"Don't try to weasel out of this. She'd have come back to me by now if you hadn't fixed her up with someone else."

"I don't think so," Lillian said as gently as possible. "It doesn't sound like the two of you were a good match. You need an outdoorsy type. Someone who likes to camp and hike. Someone who isn't afraid to argue with you."

"That just shows how much you know. One of the things I really liked about Heather was that she never argued with me."

"Guess there wouldn't have been much point."

His face worked. "What's that supposed to mean?"

"I get the feeling you didn't listen to her very well, Mr. Witley."

"That's a damned lie. I listened to her."

"Can you honestly say that Heather never once indicated that she preferred attending the opera to camping?"

Witley grimaced. "She may have mentioned the opera crap a couple of times but I told her to forget it. That highbrow stuff is boring. No beat to it, y'know?"

"In other words Heather did everything you wanted to do but you didn't do any of the things she liked. You don't see that as a problem in a relationship?"

"I told you, Heather and I had a great relationship." Witley's voice got louder. "And you wrecked it. What gives you the right to play games with other people's lives, Lillian Harte? You can't get away with treating folks like lab rats."

She held the laptop in front of her as if it were a shield. "I don't treat them that way."

"Using a damned computer to figure out who people should date and marry? You don't think that isn't treating them like rats in a maze? Hell, you're like some mad scientist in a movie or something. Like you know what's best for everyone else."

"Mr. Witley, I can't discuss this with you. Not while you're in this mood." She made to step around him but he blocked her path.

"You can't mess up my life like this and then just blow me off," he said. "You took Heather away from me. You had no right to do that. You got that? No right, damn it."

"Excuse me, I've got to go now," Lillian said.

She whirled abruptly to the left and plunged through the glass doors of the large department store that occupied most of the block. There would be security staff inside if she needed help, she thought.

But Campbell Witley did not follow her into the store. She paused in front of a cosmetics counter and glanced over her shoulder to see if he was still on the sidewalk outside.

There was no sign of him.

She stared down through the polished glass at a display of elegantly packaged face creams. Her pulse was beating too rapidly. Her stomach was doing weird things.

What gives you the right to play games with other people's lives, Lillian Harte? You can't get away with treating folks like lab rats.

She could not blame this queasy, slightly panicky feeling entirely on the scene with Campbell Witley, as unpleasant as it had been. She had been getting little foretastes of this nasty sensation for several weeks. It was one of the reasons why she knew she had to shut down Private Arrangements.

"Can I help you?" a solicitous voice asked from the other side of the counter.

Lillian looked up and saw immediately that the saleswoman was not offering to summon medical assistance. She was looking to make a sale.

"Uh, no." Lillian pulled herself together with an effort. "No, thanks. Just browsing."

The clerk's smile slipped a little the way clerks' smiles always did when you used the magic words.

"Let me know if I can be of service," she said and moved off toward another potential customer.

"Yes. Thanks. I'll do that."

Lillian turned away. She wove a path through the remaining cosmetic counters, angled across accessories and shoes and exited the store through the doors on the cross street.

Outside on the sidewalk she glanced uneasily in both directions. Campbell Witley was gone.

But he had followed her home the other night. He knew where she lived.

This was scary stuff.

She took a steadying breath and walked purposefully toward her office building. She had definitely made the right decision when she had made up her mind to close down Private Arrangements.

A short while later she stepped off the elevator. Halfway down the hall she saw a familiar figure waiting for her in front of the door marked PRIVATE ARRANGEMENTS. J. Anderson Flint.

She was immediately hit with a full-color flashback to the scene in Anderson's office on Friday afternoon. Every lurid detail was there, including the red bikini briefs. One of the drawbacks to having an artist's eye, she thought. You sometimes remembered things that you would just as soon forget.

It was all she could do to resist the urge to leap back into the elevator before the doors closed.

She made herself continue moving forward. There were things that had to be done before she left town. She could not avoid Anderson. Running away was not going to solve anything. Sooner or later she had to deal with the man.

Anderson did not notice her immediately. He was too busy checking the time on his very elegant black and gold wristwatch.

"Good morning, Anderson."

He turned slightly at the sound of her voice and smiled. It struck her, not for the first time, that he could have played the part of the wise, understanding, all-knowing therapist in a soap opera. He certainly had the cheekbones and the jaw for television. He also had the eyes. They were very, very blue and filled with what looked like insight. He was in his late thirties but he projected an image of wisdom and maturity far beyond his years. His thick, precision-cut, prematurely silver hair and the precision-trimmed goatee added to the impression.

Anderson was dressed more conventionally this morning than he had been the last time she had seen him. He wore a gray chunky-weave turtleneck sweater, dark tailored trousers, and loafers. He had explained to her once over coffee that a formal business suit and tie made patients tense and uncomfortable. She tried not to think about whether he had on the red bikini briefs.

"Lillian." He looked relieved to see her. "I was getting a little worried. It's nearly eleven o'clock. I called your office several times this morning. When there was no response I thought I'd come up here and see what was going on."

She jammed the keys in the lock and opened the door with a single twist of her hand. "I didn't have any appointments today so I used the time to take care of some personal business."

"Of course."

She flipped on the lights and went toward her desk. "Was there something you wanted?"

Anderson followed her into the office. "I thought we might have dinner tonight."

"Thanks, but I'm afraid that won't be possible." She gave him an apologetic smile and put the laptop down on her desk. "I'm going to be busy all day and I have a lot to do tonight."

"You just said you didn't have any appointments."

"I'm getting ready to leave town for a while."

"You never said anything about planning a trip."

"I'm not going on vacation. I'm changing careers."

"Changing—?" he asked with concern. "What's going on here? You're not making any sense, Lillian. You seem tense. Is something wrong?"

"Nothing's wrong, Anderson. I'm going to stay at my family's place in Eclipse Bay for a while, that's all."

"How long will you be gone?"

"A month."

He stared at her. She doubted that he could have looked any more dumbfounded if she had just told him that she intended to join a cloistered order of nuns.

"I see." He pulled himself together with a visible effort. "I hadn't realized. Can you take that much time off from Private Arrangements?"

"I can take all the time I want, Anderson. Private Arrangements went out of business Friday afternoon."

His jaw dropped a second time.

"I don't understand," he said, looking genuinely baffled. "What do you mean?"

"You heard me. I've closed my doors."

"But that's impossible," he sputtered. "You can't just walk away from Private Arrangements."

"Why not?"

"For one thing, you've got too much invested in it." He swept out his hand to indicate their surroundings. "Your office. Your program. Your client list."

"My lease is up next month. I made back my investment in the program several times over a long time ago. And I've whittled my client list down to one." She waved one hand. "I admit I'm having a small problem getting rid of him, but I'm sure that situation will soon be resolved."

"What about our book project?"

"That's another thing, Anderson. I'm sorry, but I've decided not to get involved in helping you with your book."

He went very still. "Something is wrong here. This isn't like you. Your behavior is very abnormal. It's obvious that you've got some issues."

She propped herself on the edge of the desk and looked at him. "Anderson, a very unpleasant thing happened to me this morning. A man named Campbell Witley stopped me on the street. He used to date one of my clients. You know what? Mr. Witley was really, really mad at me because I'd helped his girlfriend find someone else to date."

"What does this Witley have to do with your decision to shut down your business?"

"He pointed out in no uncertain terms that I had no right to use my computer program to meddle in other people's lives."

"That's ridiculous."

"As it happens, I tend to agree with him."

Anderson stared at her, clearly appalled.

"What do you mean?" he asked sharply. "Why do you say that?"

She eyed the closed laptop and wondered how to explain things to him. He probably wouldn't believe her if she told him that the program only worked in conjunction with her intuition and a dose of common sense. She hadn't wanted to believe it, herself.

She needed a more technical-sounding excuse with which to fob him off.

"The program is flawed," she said finally. In a way, that wasn't really far from the truth, she thought.

"*Flawed.* Are you certain?"

"Yes."

"I don't understand. You've been so successful. You've attracted so many high-end clients."

"Dumb luck, I'm afraid." She shrugged. "Keep in mind that I don't have any long-term statistics yet because I haven't been in business long enough to obtain them. It's possible that over time my matches won't prove any more successful than the ones people make on their own in the usual ways."

Anderson gave her a long, considering look. "I think I see the problem here."

"The problem," she said very deliberately, "is that Campbell Witley has a point. I don't have the right to fiddle with other people's lives. Besides, it's too stressful."

"Stressful?"

"Lately I've begun to wonder—what would happen if I screw up badly someday and put the wrong people together? Oh, sure, I do a comprehensive background check on all of my clients to make certain they don't have a criminal record or any history of serious mental disorders. But what if I miss something? Don't you see? There's a very real potential for disaster."

Anderson nodded soberly. "I agree."

"You do?"

"Yes." He shoved his hands into his pockets and rocked a little in his tasseled loafers. "To be perfectly frank, I had been meaning to broach the subject, myself."

"You were?"

"Yes. But I wanted to get to know you a little better before I raised such a delicate question. After all, Private Arrangements is your business."

There was something distinctly patronizing about his smile, she decided.

"What delicate question?" she asked carefully.

He looked at the laptop. "As you know, I have been deeply intrigued by your program for some time now, but I must admit that the fact that you have been using it without professional guidance has worried me more than somewhat."

She waited a beat. "Professional guidance?"

"Let's be honest here, Lillian. You don't have a background in psychology. You have no training or experience in clinical therapy or counseling techniques. It says a great deal for your program that you've been as successful as you have thus far. But I agree that in using it for real-life matchmaking, you assumed an enormous responsibility and a degree of risk. Obviously such a sophisticated program should be used only by a professional."

"I see. A professional. Like you."

"Actually, yes. If you're serious about getting out of the business, I would like to make you an offer for the program and the related files that you've developed in the course of your work."

That stopped her momentarily. She hadn't bargained on this. The last thing she wanted to do was sell the program to Anderson. If he used it, he would soon discover that it didn't work very well on its own. No telling how many mistakes he might make before he realized that it was not magic.

"No," she said. "I told you, it's flawed."

"You mean there are bugs in the program?"

"Not technical bugs," she said, trying to keep things vague. "It just doesn't work very well."

He chuckled. "I'm sure that I have the professional background necessary to fix any small problems that might come up. I'll make you a fair offer. We can work out mutually satisfactory terms. Perhaps a licensing agreement?"

"The Private Arrangements program is not for sale."

"Lillian, be reasonable."

"I'm sorry, but I've made my decision."

He frowned. "Obviously that confrontation with Witley was traumatic. Your state of generalized anxiety is extremely high. But I think that when you have a chance to calm down you'll see that you're overreacting."

She straightened away from the desk, walked to the door and yanked it open. "If you don't mind, I have a lot of things to do here today, Anderson. I want to leave town the day after tomorrow. That means I don't have time for this conversation."

He hesitated and then apparently decided that further argument would get him nowhere. "Very well. We'll discuss this later."

Don't hold your breath, she thought. But she managed what she hoped was a civil smile.

He hesitated and then took the hint and walked out into the hall. He paused. "Lillian, perhaps—"

"Goodbye, Anderson." She shut the door very firmly in his face.

It felt good.

Probably overreacting, but what the heck. She had a right to overreact. Between Gabe, Witley, and Anderson she'd had a very difficult week.

She went back to the desk, picked up the phone and called a familiar number. Nella Townsend answered on the second ring.

"Townsend Investigations."

"Nella, it's me."

"Hi, Lil. What can I do for you? Got a new client you want me to check out?"

"Not exactly. I want you to get some background on a man named Campbell Witley."

"Not a client?"

"No. Ex-boyfriend of one."

There was a short, distinct pause on the other end of the line.

"A problem?" Nella asked.

"I don't know. That's what I want you to find out for me."

"Okay, what have you got?"

"Not much. All I know is that until sometime last fall he was seeing Heather Summers, a client, on a regular basis. You did a check on her when she signed up with Private Arrangements."

"Got it. This shouldn't take long. He'll probably pop up in her file. I should have a preliminary report ready for you by the end of the day."

"Great. I'll pick it up on my way home. Thanks, Nella. I really appreciate this."

"No problem. Got any plans for tonight?"

"I'll be packing."

"Packing takes energy. You need to eat. Why don't you have dinner with Charles and me?"

"I'll bring the wine."

AT five-thirty that afternoon, Lillian sank into a deeply cushioned chair in the living room of Nella's apartment and kicked off her shoes.

"I'm exhausted. It took an entire day to pack up that office. I thought I'd be finished by two o'clock. How can a person accumulate so much stuff in an office?"

"One of the great mysteries of life."

Nella picked up the blue folder lying on the table and carried it across the room. She wore jeans and a deep yellow blouse with a spread collar. The gold necklace at her throat gleamed against her dark brown skin. She wore her black hair cut close to her head in a style that showed off her excellent bone structure.

She took the chair that faced Lillian's, curled one leg under her and opened the folder.

"I thought you told me all of your files were stored on the hard drive of your computer," she said.

"The client files are on the computer along with the program, but that still leaves a lot of paper. Receipts, correspondence, notes to the janitorial staff, messages from the company that leased me the space, you name it. I had to go through every single item and make a decision about whether to keep it or toss it." Lillian exhaled deeply. "But it's done and Private Arrangements is no longer in business."

"Congratulations," Nella said. "Feel good?"

"Yes, but I'll feel even better after you assure me that Campbell Witley is not a serial killer."

"He looks squeaky clean to me." Nella glanced at some of her notes. "Witley was in the military at one time, as you guessed. He received an honorable discharge. After leaving the service he took over his father's construction business and has been very successful. He was married for six years. Divorced. No children. No record of arrests, no outstanding warrants, no history of violence or abuse."

"Just what I wanted to hear," Lillian said.

"I also managed to get hold of his ex-wife. She said Witley was the domineering type and inclined to get a little loud at times, but she sounded shocked at the suggestion that he might turn violent. She said he was, and I quote, 'harmless.' "

"Excellent."

Nella closed the file and looked seriously at Lillian. "None of this means that he might not be dangerous under certain circumstances, you understand."

"I know. But I suppose you could say that about any man."

"True." Nella pursed her lips. "This was a fairly superficial check. I didn't have time to go deep. Want me to continue looking in the morning?"

"No, I don't think it's necessary. If his ex-wife vouched for him, I'm satisfied. Thanks, Nella. I really appreciate it. I'll sleep better tonight."

The sound of a key in the lock interrupted her.

Nella uncoiled from the chair. "That'll be Charles. Time to pour the wine."

Lillian twisted in the chair to give Nella's husband a welcoming wave. Charles came through the door, a long paper sack with a loaf of bread peeking out of the top in one arm, a briefcase in his hand.

He was a slender black man with serious dark eyes framed by gold-rimmed glasses and the air of an academic. He kissed his wife and released the bread to her custody. She disappeared into the kitchen.

Charles turned his slow smile on Lillian while he removed his jacket. "I hear we're celebrating the closure of Private Arrangements tonight."

"Yep, I finally took the big step. I am now officially a full-time painter. Or officially unemployed, depending on your point of view."

He nodded gravely. "This is going to put a dent in Nella's business, but I've told you all along, that matchmaking business of yours was nothing but a lawsuit waiting to happen."

Nella walked out of the kitchen with a tray of wine and cheese. She wrinkled her nose. "You're a lawyer, Charles. To you, just walking down the street is a lawsuit waiting to happen."

"Dangerous places, streets." Charles took one of the wineglasses off the tray and lifted it in a toast. "Here's to art."

4

"I love what you've done with the guest rooms," Lillian said. "Very spacious and airy." She opened the French doors of the corner suite and stepped out onto the balcony. "Fabulous views, too."

Her sister, Hannah, glanced around the suite with satisfaction and then followed Lillian outside into the chilly evening.

"It wasn't cheap getting plumbing into all of the rooms," she said. "And installing balcony doors in each one was a major project but I think it will be worth it. Considering what we plan to charge for an overnight stay here at Dreamscape, Rafe and I have to be able to provide our guests with privacy and a sense of luxury."

Lillian wrapped one hand around the railing. "You and Rafe are going to do it, aren't you? You're going to make this inn and restaurant idea work."

Hannah looked amused. "You had doubts?"

"No, not really. You're both so committed to making a success of this venture that I knew you couldn't fail."

"We owe it all to Great-Aunt Isabel." Hannah smiled. "Although I must admit that when I first learned that she had left a half-interest in Dreamscape to Rafe in her will, I didn't feel quite so grateful."

Lillian looked out across the bay. Night was closing in rapidly. The wind was picking up, bringing with it the unmistakable scent of rain off the sea. Another storm was approaching. She had always loved this time of year here on the rugged Oregon coast. The stark contrasts of the season appealed to the artist in her. The dark, blustery storms drove away the summer tourists, leaving the town to the locals.

The shops on the pier and the handful of small, casual eateries geared down for the long, quiet months. In summer the establishments were crowded with vacationers from Portland and Seattle. But when you went out to dinner in winter, you usually knew the folks sitting at the next table. If you didn't recognize them, they were probably students at nearby Chamberlain College or visitors attending a seminar at the Eclipse Bay Policy Studies Institute. The think tank and the school were both located on the hillside overlooking the tiny town.

When they blew ashore, the wind-driven rains of winter churned the waters of the bay, created boiling cauldrons in the coves and lashed the weather-beaten cottages on the cliffs. The squalls were often separated by periods of bright, chilly sunlight and crisp, intensely clear air. There was an energy in winter that was very different from the moody, atmospheric, fog-bound summers, she thought.

The evening was still clear. From her perch on the balcony she could see straight across the curving expanse of the semicircular bay to where a cluster of lights marked the location of the small town and the marina. Another string of lights identified the pier.

The sweeping arc of Bayview Drive followed the edge of the rocky beach. The road started just outside of town near Hidden Cove, which marked the northern tip of the bay. It linked the tiny community to the beach houses and cottages scattered loosely about on the bluffs. It continued past her parents' summer place and beyond Dreamscape to terminate at Sundown Point, the bay's southern boundary.

It was a familiar landscape, Lillian reflected, one she had known all of her life. She had not spent a lot of time here in recent years, but that did not affect the strong sense of connection that had swept through her earlier this afternoon when she drove into town.

For three generations Hartes had been a part of this community. Their roots went deep here, as deep as those of the Madison men.

She hugged herself against the brisk night air. "Aunt Isabel knew all along that you and Rafe were meant for each other."

"If that's true, she was certainly the only one who knew it." Hannah shook her head. "Personally, I think it's far more likely that she just hoped to goodness we were meant for each other. It was her dream to resolve the feud. She saw Rafe and me as Romeo and Juliet with the right ending. She left us Dreamscape in an effort to make her fantasy of reconnecting the Hartes and the Madisons come true."

"Either way, it worked out for you and Rafe."

"Maybe she had a touch of your gift for matchmaking," Hannah said lightly. "Could be it runs in the family."

"I don't think so."

"Okay, Lil, what's going on here? Don't get me wrong, I'm delighted to see you. I think it's great that you've decided to take some time off from work. But this is your sister, Hannah, remember? I know you haven't given me the whole story."

There was no point trying to evade the questions, Lillian thought. Hannah knew her too well. They had always been close even though they were different in so many ways. Hannah was nearly two years younger but she had always been the more levelheaded and goal-oriented of the two. Hannah was the one who had always known where she was going; at least that had been the general opinion in the Harte family until she had stunned everyone by announcing that she intended to marry Rafe Madison and turn Dreamscape into an inn.

True to form, however, even that uncharacteristically wild decision had turned out to be a sound one. It was obvious that Rafe and Hannah were happy together and that they would make a success of the inn.

"I closed Private Arrangements," Lillian said.

Hannah looked bemused. "For a few days? A couple of weeks? A month?"

"For good."

Hannah took a long moment to absorb and process that announcement.

Then she gave a low, soft, tuneless whistle.

"Oh, my," she said.

"I know."

"Just when Mom and Dad were getting used to the idea of you being a professional matchmaker."

"I'm not sure they would ever have come around completely, anyway." Lillian sighed. "They still have a hard time telling their friends what I do for a living. In their minds my matchmaking enterprise was always a little suspect. Not nearly as respectable as that wedding consultant agency you owned before you decided to go into the inn business."

"Okay, I'll agree that Mom and Dad thought the whole thing was a little flaky, but you were *successful.* They couldn't deny that. You have an impressive list of clients. All those new, wealthy software folks love the idea of computerized matchmaking. You were turning a serious profit and that counts for a lot in this family."

"If Mom and Dad think matchmaking is flaky, I can't wait to hear what they'll say about my next career move."

"Well?" Hannah tilted her head slightly. "Don't keep me in suspense."

"It's a long story."

"I want to hear every word of it." Hannah paused when a set of headlights turned into the drive that led toward Dreamscape. "But I'm afraid the tale will have to wait. Here comes dinner."

The low growl of a powerful, finely tuned engine rumbled in the gathering night. Lillian watched the sleek Porsche prowl down the drive.

The vehicle came to a halt near the inn's main entrance. The engine went silent. The door on the driver's side opened. Hannah's husband, Rafe, got out, moving with the easy masculine grace that characterized all the Madison males.

A dapper salt-and-pepper Schnauzer jumped out of the open car door after him. The dog paused and looked up toward the balcony.

"Hello, Winston," Lillian called down. "You're as handsome as ever."

Winston bounced a little in refined appreciation of what he obviously considered no more than his due. Then he trotted briskly up the steps and disappeared under the overhanging roof.

Rafe retrieved two grocery sacks from the interior of the car.

"About time you guys got home," Hannah said to him. "We were starting to wonder if the two of you had stopped off at the Total Eclipse for a beer and a fast game of pool."

Rafe nudged the door of the Porsche closed and looked up. He gave Hannah and Lillian the patented Madison smile, all rakish charm and a promise of trouble to come.

"Sorry we're a little late," he said. "Ran into an old pal who just happened to show up in town late this afternoon. I invited him for dinner. Hope you don't mind."

"Who is he?" Hannah asked curiously.

"Just some guy I know."

Rafe turned to look back toward the far end of the drive. Lillian followed his gaze and saw a second set of headlights coming toward the inn.

A dark-green Jaguar glided down the drive and stopped next to the Porsche.

A sudden premonition sizzled through Lillian. She gripped the railing very tightly and leaned forward to get a better look.

"No," she muttered. "Surely he wouldn't—"

Hannah glanced at her in surprise. "What's wrong?"

Before Lillian could answer the Jag's door opened. Gabe climbed out. His gaze went straight to the balcony.

"Hello, Lillian," he said much too easily. "I see you got invited to dinner, too. Isn't this an amazing coincidence?"

"There are no coincidences," Lillian said darkly.

"I've heard that."

She was intensely aware of Rafe and Hannah watching the little scene. They both looked amused and intrigued. "What are you doing here? And don't try to tell me that you just decided to take a mini-vacation this weekend."

"One thing you should know about me." Gabe walked around the front of the Jag, making for the front steps. "I never do anything on a whim. You're probably thinking of Rafe, here. He's been known to get a little wild and crazy at times."

"Hey, don't look at me," Rafe said quickly. "I'm a married man now. I've settled down. I only get wild and crazy with Hannah." He gazed up at the balcony. "Isn't that right, honey?"

"If you know what's good for you, it is," Hannah said. There was warmth and laughter in the words.

Gabe stopped at the foot of the steps and looked at Lillian. "You didn't really believe that I was going to let you skip out on me, did you?"

She dug her fingers into the rail. "I offered to repay your money."

"I don't want a refund. I want what I paid for."

"I don't believe this," Lillian said.

Rafe paused, one booted foot on the bottom step, and gave his brother an inquiring look. "What's this all about? Sounds interesting."

"She owes me a date," Gabe explained. "I paid for six. I only got five."

"That is not true," Lillian said loudly.

"It is true," Gabe assured Rafe and Hannah. "I've got a signed contract to prove it."

Aware of Rafe's and Hannah's thinly veiled amusement, Lillian felt called upon to defend herself. "He lied on the questionnaire."

"You're just saying that to cover up the fact that you did such a lousy job of matching me. Bottom line here is that I've got another date coming."

"Lots of luck," she shot back. "Nobody gets any more dates from Private Arrangements. The company is out of business. You'll have to get your last date somewhere else."

Gabe started up the steps. "Nobody takes my money and leaves town without delivering the goods."

"For crying out loud." Lillian leaned a little farther out over the rail. "This is ridiculous. You can't possibly be serious about one lousy date."

"When it comes to business, I'm always serious." He disappeared into the house.

"That's my brother for you," Rafe said, mockingly apologetic. "Could have written the book on how not to get screwed in a business deal. He fixates, you know?"

Before Lillian could tell him what she thought about Gabe's business style, Rafe, too, vanished beneath the overhang.

"Well," Hannah said thoughtfully. "This is an interesting turn of events."

"This isn't interesting, it's seriously aberrant behavior." Lillian continued to look uneasily over the railing into the now-empty drive. "You think maybe Gabe's gone a little nuts or something in the years since he left Eclipse Bay? Maybe the stress of building his business empire has been too much for him."

"I don't think it's the empire-building that's making him act weird," Hannah said. "I think it's the fact that he's a Madison."

"I was afraid you were going to say that."

"Something tells me there's more to this story than your failure to live up to your end of a business contract."

"Believe it or not, things started out fairly normally when Gabe signed up with Private Arrangements. I had stopped taking new clients but he seemed serious and determined. I figured okay, he's not exactly an old *friend* of the family, but he certainly qualifies as a longtime acquaintance, and we *are* sort of connected because of you and Rafe and all. I thought, what the heck? I still had the names of several nice women in my files."

"What went wrong?"

"What can I say?" Lillian held out both hands, palms up. "Gabe became the client from hell."

"WE'VE got no choice but to move out for at least three weeks," Hannah said an hour later. She passed a large ceramic bowl across the table to Lillian. "The Willis brothers have sent us straight into remodel hell. It was bad enough when they were doing the plumbing."

"They kept shutting off the water without warning and we had to cope with a stack of bathroom fixtures in the front hall for ages," Rafe said. "I started having nightmares featuring endless mazes of gleaming porcelain commodes."

"We keep assuring each other that we're lucky to have the full attention of the Willis brothers," Hannah said. "There's a new wing being built up at the institute and we were worried for a while that the folks up there would lure Torrance and Walter away. Fortunately they called in outside contractors."

"We made it through the endless commodes phase," Rafe concluded, "but there's no way we can live here while they refinish the wood floors and paint the rooms."

"I can see the problem." Lillian gripped the bowl in one hand and served herself a large helping of Rafe's dill-and-yogurt-laced cucumber salad. "The dust and fumes would be bad for Winston."

"Wouldn't do us much good, either," Rafe said dryly. "Besides, we need a vacation before we open for business. We're going down to California to tour some wineries in the Napa Valley. It will be a good opportunity to finalize my selections for the wine list that we'll be using in the restaurant."

"Another astounding coincidence." Gabe dipped the edge of a wedge of sourdough bread into the fragrant curried potato stew on his plate. "I've decided to take some time off, myself."

Rafe raised a brow. "Good idea. About time you grabbed a few days off. It's been a while since you got out of your office."

"So they tell me," Gabe said noncommittally.

Lillian stilled. "You're going to be here in Eclipse Bay for three or four days? That's all?"

Rafe chuckled. "Don't worry, Lillian, he won't loiter long in the vicinity, if that's what's worrying you. He can stay at Mitchell's place for a couple of days, at least until Mitchell gets back from Hawaii. But after that he'll be on borrowed time. I can safely predict that after forty-eight hours the two of them will be at each other's throat."

"Really? Just two days?"

"Sure. Take it from me. Mitchell will start in with his usual lectures, telling Gabe how he's become too obsessed with M.C. Gabe will tell him where to get off. Next thing you know, Gabe will be packing his bags."

Lillian allowed herself to relax. Rafe had a point. Everyone knew that the three Madison men were notoriously stubborn and hardheaded. The trait no doubt made it next to impossible for any two or more of them to share a house for an extended period of time.

"You're right." Gabe raised one shoulder in easy acquiescence to Rafe's pre-diction. "A day or two of sharing a house with Mitchell would be about all I could take."

Rafe winked at Lillian. "Told you so."

"Lately he's been getting worse with the lectures, if you can believe it," Gabe continued. He shook his head sadly. "In hindsight, giving him a computer was a major mistake."

"Are you kidding?" Rafe chuckled. "He loves that thing. Took to it like a duck to water."

"He's got an aptitude for it, all right," Gabe said. "But he's not using it the way I thought he would."

Lillian paused, her fork in midair. "How did you expect him to use it?"

"For good, wholesome, educational purposes. I figured he'd wile away many happy hours checking out senior porn sites. Instead, he's gotten into the habit of e-mailing me every day."

Rafe grinned. "Bet I can guess the content of those e-mail notes."

"They cover a variety of topics but they all come down to his opinion of how I'm running my business and my personal life."

Lillian cleared her throat. "I take it he doesn't approve of how you're handling either one?"

The strong emotion in Gabe's voice startled her. Whatever was going on between Gabe and his grandfather was more than just annoying to Gabe. It was generating some real pain.

"No," he said quietly. "He doesn't approve."

"I'm sorry if you were planning to stay with us," Hannah said gently. "As you can see, things are a mess. No one can be in here while the floors are being redone."

"I know." Gabe added some of Rafe's homemade tomato chutney to his curry.

Rafe watched him expectantly. "So, how long, exactly, do you think you'll stay with Mitchell?"

"I won't be staying with him at all." Gabe waited a beat. "I rented the old Buckley place."

"For how long?" Lillian asked warily.

"A month."

There was a moment of acute shock.

"You're actually going to take off an entire month?" Hannah asked in dis-belief.

"I'll have to make a couple of trips back to town for some events that I couldn't scrub from my calendar," Gabe said. "I'm scheduled to deliver the in-troduction at a banquet to honor one of my former college professors, for instance. But otherwise I don't see any reason why I can't handle anything that might come up at Madison Commercial from here. I brought my computer and my fax machine and there's always the phone."

"I don't believe it," Lillian said flatly. "Something weird is going on here."

"She's right," Rafe said. "This is weird. I don't care how good you are at telecommuting. You'll have withdrawal symptoms, probably get the shakes or something if you try to stay away from your office for a whole month."

Gabe said nothing, just kept eating curry.

"Damn." Rafe looked intrigued now. "You're serious about this, aren't you?"

A sardonic look gleamed in Gabe's eyes. "You've known me all of your life. Ever known me when I wasn't serious?"

"No, can't say that I have."

An ominous sensation drifted through Lillian. She studied Gabe more closely. Something dangerous moved beneath the cool, controlled surface he presented to the world.

"This isn't about getting your sixth date out of Private Arrangements, is it?" she asked. "You were just teasing me with that nonsense. You're here because you really do want to get away for a while."

Gabe shrugged again but he did not argue the point.

Hannah turned to Gabe. "Is everything okay at Madison Commercial?" she asked hesitantly.

Lillian was startled by her question. She understood Hannah's concern. Anyone who knew anything about Gabe, even indirectly, was aware of how much the company meant to him. Impending trouble at Madison Commercial would certainly account for odd behavior on his part.

But she was very sure that if there was a problem with his business he would be living at his office twenty-four hours a day, seven days a week while he worked to fix it. He would not take a month off and head for the coast in the face of impending disaster.

"Things are fine at M.C." Gabe ate more curry.

"But?" Rafe prompted.

Gabe swallowed, put down his fork and leaned back in his chair.

"But, nothing," he said. "I need a little time to concentrate on something else, that's all. I hate to admit it, but Mitchell might have a point. Maybe I have been a little too focused on business for the past few years."

"Burnout," Lillian said quietly.

They all looked at her. Gabe and Rafe had the baffled, blank expressions that were common to the male of the species when psychological explanations for behavior were offered. But Hannah nodded in immediate agreement.

"Yes, of course," she said. "Makes sense. Lil's right. Sounds like burnout."

"Sounds like psychobabble to me," Gabe said. "What's this about burnout?"

"Think about it," Lillian said patiently. "You've expended an enormous amount of physical and mental energy on Madison Commercial for years. It's no secret that you've driven yourself very hard to make your company successful. That kind of intense focus over a long period of time takes its toll."

"How would you know?" he asked. The words were spoken in deceptively silky tones. "From what you've told me about your checkered job history, you haven't stuck with anything long enough to burn out on it."

The blatant rudeness crackled in the solarium like sheet lightning. To Hannah and Rafe, the sharp retort must have appeared to come out of nowhere.

Afraid that Rafe was going to say something to his brother that was probably better left unsaid, Lillian moved to defuse the situation.

"You're right about my job history," she said to Gabe. "Guess some of us are just born to be free spirits. Funny, isn't it?"

"What's funny about it?" Gabe asked.

"Most people would have assumed that you would have been the one who wound up with the spotty employment record."

"Because I'm a Madison?"

"Yes." She gave him a steely smile. "Whereas I am a stable, steady, long-range-planning Harte." She turned to the others. "I suggested to Gabe that he might want to hire me into an executive position at Madison Commercial, but he declined on the basis of my erratic résumé."

Gabe rested an arm along the back of his chair. He did not take his eyes off Lillian. "That wasn't the reason I said I wouldn't hire you."

"What was the reason?" Hannah asked curiously.

"She pointed out that within a very short time she would probably be trying to tell me how to run my company. I said if that happened, I'd have to fire her. We both agreed there was no point even starting down that road, given the foregone conclusion."

"As you can see," Lillian said, "the decision not to hire me at M.C. was mutual. The last thing I need is another short-term position on my résumé."

The tension that had cloaked the dining room lightened as she had hoped. Hannah took her cue and shifted deftly to the new topic.

"But you are looking for a new job, I take it, now that you've closed Private Arrangements?" she asked.

"Well, no," Lillian said.

"You're going to apply for unemployment? That'd be a first for a Harte," Gabe mused.

"I'm not going on unemployment."

Rafe raised one brow. "Accepting a position with Harte Investments?"

"Never in a million years. It's not just that I can't work for my father. The main problem is that I'm not the corporate type."

Gabe sat forward and folded his arms on the table. "Okay, I'll bite. What are you going to do next?"

"Paint."

"You've always painted," Hannah replied.

"I'm going to do it full-time now. I'm turning pro."

All three of them contemplated her as if she had just announced that she intended to go to work in a carnival sideshow.

Hannah groaned. "Please don't tell me that you've closed Private Arrangements so that you can devote yourself to art."

"I've closed Private Arrangements so that I can devote myself to art."

"Mom and Dad are going to have a fit." Hannah flopped back in her chair. "To say nothing of Granddad."

"I know," Lillian said.

Rafe reached for the coffeepot. "Got any reason to think you can make a living painting?"

"I'll find out soon enough whether it will work. Octavia Brightwell is going to put on a show of my work in her Portland gallery in a few weeks."

Rafe smiled wryly. "I'd give you the standard advice about not quitting your day job. But I guess it's too late."

"Much too late," she agreed.

GABE stood at the rail of the inn's broad front porch and watched the taillights of Lillian's car disappear down the drive. Rafe leaned against a nearby post. Winston was stretched out at the top of the steps, his paws dangling over the edge, ears and nose angled to take in the sounds and scents of the night. Hannah had disappeared back into the warmth of the kitchen.

"If you're going to be here in Eclipse Bay for a whole month, maybe I'd better fill you in on some of the local news," Rafe said after a while.

"Save your breath. I'm not real interested in gossip."

"This concerns Marilyn Thornley."

Gabe took a moment to rummage around in his memory for some images of the woman he had dated for a time in those first years after college. She had been Marilyn Caldwell in those days, the daughter of one of the wealthiest men in the region. The Caldwells' home was in Portland but, like the Hartes, they had always kept a second home in Eclipse Bay. They also had a third in Palm Springs.

Marilyn had excellent instincts when it came to selecting winners. Gabe knew that while she had viewed him as having long-term potential, Trevor Thornley had looked like more of a sure thing. She had taken a long, hard look at the two men and chosen to cast her lot with Thornley.

There had been no hard feelings on his part, Gabe reflected. He certainly couldn't fault her decision. It had been a sensible, businesslike move. Trevor had been on the fast track in the political world. It was obvious even back then that he had the charisma, the glibness and the looks required to grab and hold the media's and the public's attention. It was clear that, barring some major disaster, he would go far, maybe all the way to Washington, D.C. All he required was money. Lots of it. Marilyn's family had supplied the missing commodity. Everyone had agreed that it made sense to invest in a son-in-law who was on his way to becoming a major political powerhouse.

There had been an unexpected bonus for Thornley in the arrangement. Marilyn had proven to be a brilliant campaign strategist. With the help of the politically astute staff of the Eclipse Bay Policy Studies Institute, she had orchestrated every step of Trevor's career. Under her guidance, he had moved up steadily through the political ranks. Last fall, he had announced that he was making a bid for the U.S. Senate.

To everyone's surprise, he had pulled out of the race shortly before Thanksgiving. The only explanation Gabe had seen in the papers was the ubiquitous *personal reasons.*

"What about Marilyn?" Gabe asked.

"Haven't you heard? She and Thornley have filed for divorce. She moved into her folks' summer place here in town last month. She's got an office at the institute."

"A staff position?"

Rafe shook his head. "She's getting set to launch her own career in politics."

"Huh. Doesn't surprise me. She was born for politics."

"Yeah. Just one problem."

"What's that?" Gabe asked.

"Word is she burned through a big pile of her family's money financing Thornley's career. Apparently her folks have declined to invest any more cash in politics for a while. Rumor has it they won't be backing her. At least not until she's proven that she can win."

"In other words, she needs money."

"Yeah. Lots and lots of it," Rafe said knowingly. "I mention this because it occurs to me that you have what she wants. Expect you'll be hearing from her as soon as she learns that you're back in town."

"Thanks for the heads-up. But don't worry about it. One thing I can spot real quick is a woman who's after my money."

Rafe looked out over the dark bay. "The two of you were once an item."

"That was a long time ago."

"Sure." Rafe shoved his hands into his front pockets. "Consider yourself forewarned."

"Okay."

There was another pause. Gabe could feel his brother shifting mental gears.

"You really rented the old Buckley place for an entire month?" Rafe asked after a while.

"Yes."

"Got to admit, it does seem a little uncharacteristic for you to do something like that. You think maybe Lillian is right? You burned out or something?"

"Madisons don't do burnout. You ever heard of a Madison burning out?"

Rafe thought about that. "No. Heard of one or two exploding. Couple have imploded. Of course you've got your occasional cases of spontaneous combustion in the family. But never heard of any burnout."

"Right."

"What's with you and Lillian, anyway?"

"What makes you think there's anything between us?"

"I'll be the first to admit that I'm not the most sensitive, intuitive, perceptive guy around."

" 'Course not. You're a Madison."

"But even I could see that every time you looked at Lillian tonight you had the same expression you get when you've got a major deal going down at Madison Commercial."

"Like you said, you're not real sensitive, intuitive, or perceptive."

"I'm not real stupid, either," Rafe reminded him. "I've never seen that particular look when you were with any other woman."

"Lillian's not a business deal."

"Hold on to that thought, because I've got a hunch that if you treat her like you would an M.C. investment you're gonna have some serious problems."

Gabe looked at Winston. "My brother, the advice columnist."

Winston cocked his head and looked intelligent. It was an expression he did very well.

Rafe contemplated the empty drive. "Always figured you'd go off the rails someday."

"Being a Madison and all."

"Probably inevitable. Question of genetic destiny or something. You know, I'm a little sorry Hannah and Winston and I are leaving town tomorrow. Would have been interesting to see it."

"What?"

"The train wreck."

5

THE storm came and went during the night. The morning dawned bright and mild for the time of year. The temperature was somewhere in the high fifties.

Gabe came to a halt at the top of the small bluff and looked down into Dead Hand Cove. The tide was out, exposing the five finger-shaped rocks that had given the cove its name. There were a number of dark holes and voids in the base of the cliffs. They marked a series of small caverns and caves that nature had punched into the rock.

He saw Lillian perched on one of the carelessly strewn boulders near the water's edge. The winter sun gleamed on her dark hair. The keen edge of expectation that shafted through him heightened all his senses. He felt the now-familiar tightness in his lower body.

She wore a pair of snug black leggings that emphasized the neat curve of her calves and trim ankles. The neckline of an orange-gold sweater was visible above the collar of a scarlet jacket. Her hair was coiled into a knot at the back of her head.

She was bent intently over an open sketchbook propped on her knees.

Last night at Rafe and Hannah's he had learned the terrible truth. She wasn't just an arty type. She was a for real artist.

He watched the deft, economical movements of her hand as she worked on the drawing. There was a supple, controlled grace in the way she wielded the pencil that fascinated him. A sorceress at work on a magical spell.

A gull screeched overhead, breaking the trance that held him still at the top of the short cliff.

He pulled the collar of his black-and-tan jacket up around his ears and went down the pebbled path, moving quickly, perversely eager to get closer to his own doom. Probably a Madison thing, he thought.

She became aware of his presence when he reached the rocky patch of ground that formed the tiny sliver of beach. Lillian looked up quickly, turning her head to watch him. She seemed to go very still there on the rock. Sorceress caught in the act. He could sense the cool caution in her.

Maybe she was right to be wary of him. He sure as hell didn't understand what was happening here, either. He forced himself to move more slowly as he neared her perch, trying for the laid-back, easygoing, nonthreatening look.

"How long were you standing up there spying on me?" she asked.

"You sure know how to make a man feel welcome."

"I thought I was alone. You startled me."

"Sorry. I usually work out in the mornings. There's no gym in the vicinity so I thought I'd take a long walk, instead."

"You just decided to walk in this direction?"

He smiled. "Is it me or do you always wake up in this charming mood?"

She hesitated and then returned his smile. "My turn to apologize. I shouldn't have snapped at you. I've been feeling a little edgy lately."

"What a coincidence. So have I."

"I'm not surprised." She looked wise and all-knowing. "Probably the burn-out."

"You've got me all analyzed and diagnosed, don't you?" He lowered himself onto a nearby rock. "Are you on edge because I'm here in Eclipse Bay?"

"No," she said.

"Liar."

She shot him an irritated look. "It's the truth. I'm on edge for a lot of reasons that have nothing to do with you."

"Such as?"

"You want a list?"

"Let's hear it."

Her mouth firmed. "Well, let's see. There's the fact that I'm not currently employed because I just closed my business."

"Your own fault."

"Thank you for reminding me. I'm also nervous about how well my show at the gallery will be received."

He couldn't think of anything to say to that so he let it go.

"Also, I had a couple of rather unpleasant scenes before I left Portland. I've been worrying about them. Wondering if I handled them properly."

"What kind of scenes?"

She looked out toward the five finger rocks. "Anderson came to see me. He did not take it well when I told him I didn't want to work on his book."

"I'll bet he didn't. Did you mention that you had seen him in his red underwear?"

"Of course not."

"Just as well. I wouldn't worry too much about that scene, if I were you. What was the other one?"

"A man named Campbell Witley stopped me on the street to tell me that I had no business messing around in other people's lives."

Something in the tone of her voice made him look at her more closely. "This Witley guy scared you?"

She hesitated. "Maybe. A little."

"Who is he?"

"The disgruntled ex-boyfriend of one of my clients. He didn't like the fact that I had matched her with someone else, even though it's obvious that Witley and Heather were not meant for each other."

He searched her face. "Did he threaten you?"

"No."

"I'll have him checked out." He reached for the cell phone in the pocket of his jacket. "Madison Commercial keeps an investigation agency on retainer."

"Thanks, but that's not necessary. I had Townsend Investigations run a quick background check. Witley has no history of violence or abuse."

"You're sure?"

"Yes. It's okay, really. Nella Townsend knows what she's doing. The guy was just mad. I think what bothered me the most is that he had a point."

"Bullshit."

"He accused me of messing around with people's lives and that's exactly what I did. As a professional matchmaker I assumed a massive responsibility. What if I had made a terrible mistake? I could have seriously impacted someone's future negatively."

"Stop beating yourself up over this. You were a consultant. People paid you for advice. You gave it. They made their own decisions. A simple business transaction. You have absolutely no reason to feel guilty."

She was silent for a moment, considering his words. Then her voice brightened.

"You do have a way of boiling things down to the bare essence, Madison."

"One of the things I'm good at." He leaned a little to get a look at the drawing on her lap. "Can I see what you're working on there?"

She handed the sketchpad to him without comment.

He examined the drawing for a while and discovered that the longer he studied it, the more he wanted to look at it.

It was a picture of Dead Hand Cove but it was the cove as he had never really seen it, at least not consciously. There was a riveting intensity about Lillian's rendering of this small chunk of nature—a dark promise of potent, primordial power. It called to something deep within him—made him aware that he was forever linked on the cellular level to these wild forces of life.

Damn. All that in a simple sketch. It was worse than he had thought. She was good. Very, very good.

"One thing's for sure," he said finally. "You were wasting your time in the matchmaking business. You're an artist, all right. This is your calling."

"Doesn't mean my work will sell," she said.

"No." He handed the sketchpad back to her. "It also doesn't change the fact that this is what you were born to do. Can I ask you a question?"

"What is it?"

"Could you stop doing your art?"

"Stop? You mean, just call it quits?"

"Say someone came along and said he'd give you a million bucks if you agreed to never draw or paint again. Could you take the money and keep your promise?"

"No." She looked down at the sketch. "Sooner or later, I'd have to go back to it. It's a compulsion, not a choice."

"That's what I figured." He exhaled deeply. "So you'll keep doing it, even if you have to get another day job."

"Yes."

"You're an artist."

"Yes," she said again. "I guess so."

She sounded a little startled. Thoughtful. As if he had surprised her.

He listened to the seawater tumble in the cove. The tide was returning. Soon only the tips of the fingers would be visible.

"Madison Commercial must have been like that for you all these years," Lillian said slowly. "A compulsion. Something you had to do."

"Maybe."

"Why?"

"Who knows?" He picked up a small stone and sent it spinning out into the foaming water. "Maybe I just wanted to prove that a Madison could do what you Hartes seemed to do so well."

"What's that?"

"Not screw up."

She looked toward the point where the stone had disappeared into the water. "Are you telling me that everything you've accomplished, all your success, happened just because you felt a sense of competition with my family?"

He shrugged. "That was part of it. At least at first. I grew up knowing that you Hartes were smart enough not to make the mistakes we Madisons have always been so good at. Your businesses prosper. Your families are solid. Hell, your parents were actually married. What a concept."

She did not respond to that. There was no need. They both knew each other's family histories as well as they knew their own. His father, Sinclair, had been a sculptor with a passion for his art and his model, Natalie. Gabe and Rafe had been the result of that union.

The relationship between his parents had lived up to the expectations of everyone familiar with the Madison clan. The long-running affair had been fiery and tempestuous. Sinclair had never seen any reason to burden himself with the petty strings of marriage. Gabe was pretty sure his parents had loved each other in their own stormy fashion, but family life had not been what anyone could call stable, let alone normal.

He and Rafe had each learned to cope in their own ways with their erratic, eccentric, larger-than-life father and their beautiful, temperamental mother. Rafe had chosen to pretend to himself and everyone else that he did not give a damn about his own future. "Live for the moment" had been his motto, at least until he'd come within a hair's breadth of getting himself arrested for murder.

Gabe knew that he, on the other hand, had probably gone to the other extreme. Control and a sense of order had been his bulwarks against the shifting tides of fortune and emotion that had roiled his childhood. In putting together Madison Commercial he had done everything he could to carve his own future out of granite.

"What's the rest?" Lillian asked.

"The rest?"

"I don't believe you could have accomplished so much just because you were inspired by a sense of competition with my family."

He shook off the brooding sensation that had settled around him like an old, well-worn coat. "I'm not the introspective type."

"Oh, yes that's right. How could I forget? You made that fact very clear on the questionnaire that you filled out for Private Arrangements."

"Probably."

"As I recall," she continued, "on the portion of the form reserved for 'other comments,' you wrote that you considered yourself pragmatic and realistic by nature. You instructed me not to waste your valuable time with any elitist academics or fuzzy-brained New Age thinkers."

"Uh-huh."

Lillian closed the sketchpad with a snap. "You also noted that you did not want to be matched with what you called *arty types*."

Well, hell.

"Correct me if I'm wrong," Lillian said, "but I got the impression that the 'other comments' section of the questionnaire was one of the few places on the form where you were actually more or less truthful in your responses. Or did you shade those answers, too?"

Definitely time to change the subject.

"You got anything to eat back in your cottage?" he asked.

She blinked and refocused. "You're hungry?"

"Starving. I woke up this morning and realized I didn't have any coffee in the house. Nothing to eat, either. Forgot to stop at a grocery store last night."

"You expect me to feed you breakfast?"

"Why not? Be the neighborly thing to do. If I had coffee and toast and maybe some peanut butter, I'd invite you to my place."

"Peanut butter?"

"Be amazed at what you can do with peanut butter."

"I see. Well, sorry to disappoint you, but I didn't pick up anything yesterday, either. I'm planning to drive into town in a few minutes to get something from that bakery Rafe raved about last night."

"Incandescent Body?" He got to his feet. "Good idea. My brother knows food."

SHE was not sure why she had allowed herself to get talked into accompanying Gabe into town. Something to do with the odd mood she was in, no doubt. But when she walked through the doors of the bakery a short time later, the heavenly fragrance of freshly baked bread quickly resolved any doubts about her decision. She suddenly realized that she was ravenous.

No one knew much about the group of New Age types who had moved into town a year ago and opened Incandescent Body near the pier. They dressed in long, colorful robes, wore a lot of jewelry that appeared to have been inspired by ancient Egyptian and Roman artifacts, and seemed a little too serene to be real. They called themselves Heralds of Future History.

The initial reaction of the townsfolk had been one of acute disgust and, in some quarters, outright alarm, according to Rafe and Hannah. The town council had expressed deep concerns about the possibility that Eclipse Bay had a genuine wacko cult in its midst. The *Eclipse Bay Journal* had run an editorial that had advised the authorities to keep a close watch on the new crowd.

But in a town in which the only bakery had been closed for nearly three years, the Heralds of Future History soon proved to possess one major redeeming feature. They baked like angels.

It was going on ten o'clock when Lillian and Gabe arrived. A number of people were sprinkled around the handful of tables. The customers were primarily a mix of local residents, a couple of rare winter tourists, and some young people in denim and khaki who looked like students from Chamberlain College.

The heads of the locals swiveled immediately toward the door when Lillian walked in with Gabe on her heels. Lillian could guess their thoughts. Hannah and Rafe's marriage a few months ago had thrilled and fascinated the entire town. And now here was another Harte woman with a Madison male. Would wonders never cease?

"Maybe this wasn't such a good idea," she whispered to Gabe.

"Don't be ridiculous." He came to a halt at the counter and studied the artfully arranged breakfast pastries behind the glass. "The only other place open at this hour is the Total Eclipse. You don't want to eat breakfast there, trust me."

"Good point. Any restaurant that uses the motto 'Where the sun don't shine' probably isn't a terrific breakfast spot."

"Right. Besides, those corn bread muffins look incredible. I'm going to have two. What do you want?"

"People are staring at us."

"Yeah?" He glanced around curiously, nodded civilly at the people he recognized and then turned back to the croissant display. "So what? You're a Harte. I'm a Madison. Put the two together in this town and you're bound to get a few stares."

"It doesn't bother you?"

"Nope."

"Of course, a few stares don't bother you," she muttered. "You're a Madison."

"You got that right."

He approached the middle-aged woman dressed in a long, pale robe standing behind the counter. She wore a white scarf over her graying hair and a pristine white apron. A crescent-shaped amulet hung from a chain around her neck.

"May the light of future history be with you," she said politely.

"Thanks," Gabe said. "Same to you. I'll have a couple of those corn bread muffins and a cup of coffee, please." He looked over his shoulder. "Decided what you want, Lillian?"

She hurried forward. "A croissant, please. And green tea."

"For here or to go?" the woman asked.

"For here," Gabe said.

"Say, I recognize those voices," boomed a whiskey-and-cigar voice from the other side of a curtained doorway.

Lillian suppressed a small groan and summoned up a smile for the husky, robust woman dressed in military fatigues and boots who appeared in the opening. Arizona Snow had long since passed the age that officially placed her in the senior citizen category but she had enough energy for a far younger person. She also had a cause.

"Well, now, I call this perfect timing," Arizona Snow said with evident satisfaction.

"Morning, A.Z." Gabe said. "How's the conspiracy business these days?"

"Those bastards up at the institute laid low for a while after your brother and Hannah managed to put a spoke in their wheel, but things are heating up again." Arizona beamed at Lillian. "Good to see you back in town."

"Nice to see you, too," Lillian said. She waved a hand to indicate the bakery. "What are you doing here?"

"Regular weekly briefing with the Heralds." Arizona lowered her voice to what she no doubt thought was a confidential level. "Instituted the routine a couple of months ago after I got to know 'em better and discovered that they're not naïve dupes of the agency like most everyone else around these parts. They understand what's happenin'."

"Glad someone does," Gabe said.

Arizona leaned a little farther out the doorway, swept the outer room with a quick glance and then motioned to Lillian and Gabe. "Come on back. I'll bring you up to date, too."

"Uh, that's okay, Arizona," Lillian said hastily. "We're a little busy this morning. Aren't we, Gabe?"

"Don't know about you." Gabe put some money down on the counter. "But I'm in no rush."

"You're *not?*" In her wildest flights of imagination she would never have envisioned him willingly going down the rabbit hole into the alternate universe that was Arizona Snow's world.

He glanced at her, brows raised. "What?" he asked amused.

"Don't you, uh, have some telecommuting to do?" she asked weakly.

"It'll keep."

Arizona gave Lillian a knowing look, squinting slightly. "Hannah and Rafe weren't real interested in what was going on up at the institute, either, until it was damn near too late."

Lillian knew when she was beaten. She tried and failed to come up with an excuse but nothing came to mind. The bottom line was that the Hartes and the Madisons owed Arizona Snow. She was more than a little eccentric but a few months ago it had been her meticulously kept logbooks that had provided the clues Rafe and Hannah had needed to identify a murderer.

"I suppose we can stay for a few minutes," Lillian said.

"Forewarned is forearmed." Arizona held the curtain aside.

"Can't argue with that," Gabe said. He picked up his muffins and coffee and went around the counter.

Lillian reluctantly collected her croissant and tea and trailed after him.

Arizona let the curtain fall behind them. Lillian stopped at the sight of the three men and two women grouped around a large, floured worktable. All were dressed in Herald-style attire, complete with robes and ancient-looking jewelry. Their ages were varied. The youngest was a man whose long hair was neatly bound up in a white sanitary cap. Lillian thought he was probably in his midtwenties. The oldest was a woman with silver hair and a matronly figure. A tall man with a shaved head and a stately air appeared to be the authority figure in the group.

The Heralds regarded Lillian and Gabe with serenely polite expressions.

Arizona took up a position at the head of the table and fixed everyone in turn with a steely look.

"Gabe, Lillian, meet Photon, Rainbow, Daybreak, Dawn, and Beacon." She gave the Heralds a pointed look. "Gabe and Lillian are friends of mine. Take it from me, you can trust 'em. Fact is, in this town, you can trust anyone with the last name of Harte or Madison."

Lillian nodded, determined to be polite. "Good morning."

Gabe inclined his head in an easy greeting. He set his mug down on a nearby table and took a bite of one of the muffins on his plate.

"Great corn bread," he said.

Photon, the man with the shaved head who seemed to be in charge, said, "Thank you. We do our best to introduce the light of future history into all our products. But we're only human. Sometimes our negative thoughts get into the dough in spite of our best efforts."

"Light's your secret ingredient, huh?" Gabe picked up the remaining portion of the muffin. "Works for me." He took another bite.

Arizona picked up a large rolling pin and rapped it smartly on the table to get everyone's attention.

"Enough with the chitchat," she said. "Got a briefing to get through here. Not like we have time to waste. The future of this town, not to mention the whole country, is hanging in the balance."

Everyone obediently moved a little closer to the table.

Arizona cleared her throat loudly.

"Now, then, as I was sayin' before I heard Lillian and Gabe out front, I've put the evidence together and it's become real clear why they're building the new wing at the institute. Official word, of course, is that it's supposed to be additional office and conference space." She broke off to give everyone at the table a meaningful look. "But I think everyone here knows that's just another one of their lies."

Lillian studied the map spread out on the table. It showed the hillside above town where the Eclipse Bay Policy Studies Institute was located. A handful of photos that looked as if they had been snapped with a long-range lens were scattered around the edges. They were pictures of what was obviously a construction zone at the institute. She could make out a truck and something that looked like electrical equipment.

Gabe leaned over the photos. "Good long-range recon shots, A.Z."

"Thanks." A.Z. allowed herself a proud smile. "Took 'em with my new surveillance camera. A genuine VPX 5000. Latest model. Replaces the old 4000 series. Telephoto lens, sniper grip shutter release trigger. Half a dozen filters for day and night photo work. And a real nice leather carrying case."

"I hate to sound like just another naïve, innocent dupe," Lillian said, "but what makes you think they aren't adding office and conference space?"

"Number of factors." Arizona motioned toward the map with the rolling pin. "First, increased volume of traffic in this sector during the past six months."

"Are we talking out-of-town traffic?" Gabe asked.

"We are, for sure," Arizona said.

"Huh." Gabe took another bite of the muffin. "That's suspicious, all right."

"For heaven's sake," said Lillian. "Everyone knows the institute has been growing rapidly for some time now. They give seminars, receptions, and political theory retreats on a regular basis. In addition, they provided the springboard for Trevor Thornley's campaign. It's only natural that there would be a lot of traffic."

Arizona squinted. "Cover, is what it is. All that political think-tank stuff and those seminars and such make good camouflage for concealing what's really goin' on up there. Furthermore, the traffic volume didn't fall off for long after Thornley pulled out of the campaign. No, sir. There was a brief lull, but by the end of November, there were more vehicles than ever going in and out of there."

"Sounds serious, all right," Gabe concurred. "What other factors besides increased traffic point to a clandestine operation?"

"Oh, geez," Lillian muttered. No one paid any attention.

"Most of the construction work on the new wing is being done by contractors who aren't from around here," Arizona said ominously.

"Heard something about that." Gabe examined another photo. "My brother said the Willis brothers didn't get a chunk of the construction action."

"No, they didn't and that tells us a lot, doesn't it?" Arizona said.

"Uh, what, exactly, does it tell us?" Lillian asked cautiously.

"That they didn't want no one from around here getting a close look at what's going on up there," Arizona announced. "That's what it tells us."

"Probably knew the Willis brothers couldn't be bribed to keep their mouths shut if they saw something suspicious," Gabe said. "Everyone knows how Walter and Torrance talk."

Lillian had an urge to stomp hard on the toe of his large running shoe. She managed, with an effort, to resist.

"Stands to reason they would bring in outside contractors when you think about it," she said quickly. "Hannah and Rafe have been keeping the Willis brothers busy for months turning Dreamscape into an inn. They wouldn't have had time to work on the new wing."

They all ignored her. So much for being the voice of reason, she thought.

"Volume of overnight and regular freight deliveries has picked up recently, too," Arizona droned on. "I staked out the loading dock for a couple of days. Took a whole series of shots with the VPX 5000. Amazing how much equipment and material is being moved into that place."

"High-tech stuff?" Gabe asked.

"You bet. Tons of it."

Gabe looked up from the photos. "What about heavy-duty heating, ventilation, and air-conditioning equipment?"

Lillian glared at him. He paid no attention. He was really getting into this, she realized with a shock. Enjoying himself.

Arizona gave him an approving look. "They started unloading HVAC crates last week. Got 'em on film."

Gabe shook his head. "Not good."

The Heralds murmured among themselves, obviously agreeing with that conclusion.

"What do you mean, it's not a good sign?" Lillian knew her voice was rising but there was nothing she could do about it. She was getting desperate. "Any large, modern business structure needs a lot of computers and commercial-grade heating and air-conditioning equipment."

This time she was totally ignored.

"I'd estimate their security level as Class Three at the moment," Arizona said. "Fences have gone up around the construction perimeter."

"Perfectly normal," Lillian said. "The last thing the institute would want is a lawsuit filed by someone who happened to trip and fall over a pile of pipes."

"Guards on the premises?" Gabe asked.

"Yep. Disguised as low-profile security, though," Arizona said. "Didn't see any weapons. Probably knew that would attract too much attention in a small town like this where there's not much of a crime problem. Expect they'll wait until after the big move before they go to Class Two status and arm the guards."

Lillian clutched her untouched croissant. "What are you talking about? What big move?"

"We all know what's happening up there," Arizona said. "Problem is, we've got no hard evidence yet. I'm stepping up my surveillance work, though. I'll try to get us some pictures that we can take to the media."

"You're a true hero, Arizona." Photon looked at her with unconcealed admiration. "If it hadn't been for you, we wouldn't have had a clue. Who knows how long Project Transfer would have gone undetected?"

Lillian was amazed to see Arizona turn pink.

"Just doin' my duty."

"It's people like you who keep this country safe for democracy," Gabe said.

"Excuse me." Lillian held up her hand. "As the sole representative of the naïve, innocent dupes of Eclipse Bay, I would like to ask a question."

"Go right ahead," Arizona said.

"What, precisely, do you think is going on up at the institute, A.Z.? What is this Project Transfer you mentioned?"

Arizona made a *tut-tut* sound.

The Heralds shook their heads sadly at Lillian's failure to grasp the obvious.

Out of the corner of her eye she saw Gabe hide a quick grin behind his coffee mug.

"Thought it was as plain as the white lines out on the highway," Arizona said. "The secret gov'mint agency in charge of Roswell and the Area 51 facility has decided it's attracting too much attention. The Internet was what did 'em in, I reckon. After those satellite images of the old test site went online, they knew they had a real problem. That's probably when they started making plans."

Gabe nodded knowingly. "Had a feeling those mysterious fires in New Mexico a while back weren't accidental."

"You got that right," Arizona said. "No such thing as an accident where this bunch is concerned."

"Plans to do *what*?" Lillian demanded.

Arizona rocked back and forth in her boots and looked grim. "Pretty clear they're gonna transfer the bodies of those extraterrestrials they've got in deep freeze in Area 51 along with the remains of their spaceship and all that alien technology right here to Eclipse Bay."

6

GABE got into the passenger side of Lillian's car and closed the door. "Makes sense when you think about it."

"What makes sense?" Lillian turned the key in the ignition and checked the rearview mirror.

"Transferring those frozen aliens and their UFO equipment here. Who'd ever think to look for them in Eclipse Bay?"

"I *knew* it. You were enjoying yourself back there, weren't you? You were actually encouraging A.Z. in her idiotic conspiracy theories."

"Not like anything I said would have *discouraged* her. Everyone knows she lives in her own parallel universe."

"Doesn't it worry you that she's glommed on to the Heralds?" Lillian snapped the car's gearshift into reverse and backed out of the parking space. "It was one thing when she was the lone conspiracy theorist in town. But now she's got a bunch of enthusiastic assistants."

"You're right," Gabe intoned darkly. "I don't like the sound of this."

"Oh, for pity's sake." She turned the wheel and drove out of the parking lot. "You're determined to make a joke out of it, aren't you?"

"Look at it from my point of view."

"What is that?"

"Pondering the possibility that some secret gov'mint agency is getting ready to transfer dead space aliens and their technology to Eclipse Bay makes an interesting change."

"Change from what?"

"From thinking about that sixth date you owe me."

"Hmm." She concentrated on the curving sweep of Bayview Drive. "Hadn't thought of that. Dare I hope that you might sign up with A.Z.'s happy little band of conspiracy buffs and forget about trying to make me fulfill the terms of that contract you signed with Private Arrangements?"

"Well, no. Thing is, I never forget about getting what I paid for."

She gripped the wheel. "Gabe, I told you I'd refund your money."

"It's not the money."

"Hah. With you, it's the money. You've made that very clear from the start. I've never known anyone as paranoid about being married for his money as you are."

"I am not paranoid."

"The heck you aren't. On this particular subject, you're as bad as A.Z. is when it comes to secret government conspiracies."

He settled deeper into the seat and looked out over the gray waters of the bay.

"I'm not that bad," he said.

The dry, sardonic amusement that had infused his voice a moment ago was gone now. She shot him a quick glance, trying to read the shift in his mood. But his head was turned away from her. She could discern nothing from the hard angles of his profile.

─────※─────

SHE turned off the main road a short time later and went down the narrow, rutted lane that led to the old Buckley place. The weathered cottage was hunkered down on a windswept bluff overlooking a rocky stretch of beach. It looked as if it had not been lived in for a long time. The trees grew right up to the edge of the tiny yard. The blinds in the windows were yellowed with age. The porch listed a little to the right. The whole structure was badly in need of a coat of paint.

The only sign of life was Gabe's gleaming Jaguar parked in the drive.

She brought her compact to a halt in front of the sagging porch.

"Thanks for the lift into town." Gabe stirred and unfastened his seat belt.

"You're welcome."

He opened the car door and paused, gazing straight ahead through the windshield.

"You really think I'm a full-blown paranoid?" he asked quietly.

This was not good. No doubt about it, Gabe was sinking deeper into a very strange mood.

"Let's just say I think you're a little overly concerned about the issue of being married for your money," she said gently.

"Overly concerned."

"That's how I would characterize it, yes."

"And you're not."

"Not what?"

"Paranoid. About being married because of your connection to Harte Investments."

She took a deep breath. "I won't say that I don't think about the possibility once in a while. As I told you, I have dated a few men who gave me some cause for concern. But I try to employ my common sense in the matter. I don't obsess on the idea that every man I meet is only interested in me because of my family's company."

"Can't help noticing that you still haven't married, though."

She felt her jaw tense. "The fact that I'm still single has nothing to do with being secretly paranoid about being married for my inheritance."

"So, why are you still single?"

She frowned. "Why do you care?"

"Sorry. None of my business." He pushed the door open and got out. "See you later."

"Gabe?"

"Yeah?" He paused and leaned slightly to look at her.

"Are you, you know, okay?"

"Sure. I'm swell."

"What are you going to do today?"

"Don't know. Haven't decided. Maybe take another walk on the beach. Check my e-mail. Do some research." He paused. "What are *you* going to do?"

"Paint. That's why I came here."

"Right." He made to close the door.

She hesitated, trying to resist the impulse that had just struck her. She failed. "Gabe, wait a second."

"What now?"

This was stupid, she thought. Just because Hannah was married to Rafe, it did not follow that she herself had to assume any responsibility for members of the Madison family. Gabe was perfectly capable of taking care of himself. If she had any sense she would keep her mouth shut.

But she could not get past the feeling that something was not as it should be with Gabe. The way he had tried to amuse himself with Arizona's conspiracy theories and now this swing to another, darker mood did not seem right. He was definitely not in a good place.

Burnout was a form of depression, she reminded herself.

"What about dinner?" she asked before she could give herself any more time to think.

"What about it?"

"I'm going to drive back into town later this afternoon to do some serious grocery shopping. If you don't have any plans for tonight, I could pick up something and bring it over here. We can fix it together."

"I'm no gourmet chef like Rafe," he warned.

"Few people can cook as well as Rafe, but I can find my way around a kitchen. What about it? You interested? Or do you have other plans?"

"One thing I do not have is other plans," he said. "By the way, if you're going to the grocery store, could you pick up some peanut butter?"

"I suppose so."

"Make it chunky style. See you for dinner."

He closed the car door with a solid-sounding *kerchunk,* went up the steps and disappeared into the lonely-looking house before she could figure out how to climb back out of the hole she had just dug for herself.

HE heard the sound of a car's engine in the driveway just as the early winter twilight descended. A gut-deep sense of pleasurable anticipation rippled through him. He powered down the laptop computer, closed the lid and got to his feet.

He peered out the window, checking the weather. He could almost feel the weight of the heavy clouds moving in off the ocean. The storm would hit later tonight.

Perfect timing.

He crossed the threadbare carpet, opened the front door and went out onto the porch. The little rush of excitement faded at the sight of the vehicle coming toward him. It was a late-model Mercedes. Not Lillian's Honda.

The Mercedes halted in front of the steps. The door on the driver's side opened. An attractive, athletic-looking woman with stylishly cut honey-brown hair got out. She wore a pair of expensively tailored trousers and a pale silk shirt. Silver gleamed discreetly in her ears. A designer scarf in a subdued mauve print framed her long neck.

Marilyn Thornley hadn't changed much since she had been Marilyn Caldwell, he thought. If anything, she had become more striking and more self-confident with the years. There was an invisible aura of authority and importance about her. When she walked into a room, you knew it.

She saw him watching her from the porch and gave him a glowing smile.

He did not take the smile personally. Marilyn always glowed like this when-ever they occasionally encountered each other at one of the social events they both were obliged to attend. As Rafe had reminded him, he had a lot of what poli-ticians loved most. Money. Marilyn had been a tireless fund-raiser for Trevor Thornley for years. Now she was firing up her own campaign.

Under the circumstances, he was not real surprised to see her.

"Gabe." She came around the front of the Mercedes with long, purposeful strides. "I heard you were in town for a while."

She was moving more quickly now, coming up the steps, heading toward him.

Belatedly he realized her intention and took a step back. But he didn't move fast enough. She had her arms around his neck, her face tilted for a welcoming kiss before he could dodge. Reflexively, he turned his head at the last instant. Her lips grazed his jaw.

The mouth thing caught him off guard. It was the first time she'd pulled that stunt. But then, this was the first time he'd seen her since she and Thornley had announced their intention to divorce.

She released him, giving no indication that she had even noticed his small act of avoidance. Politicians had thick skins.

"You look wonderful," she said.

"You're looking great yourself."

She gave him an arch look. "You mean for a woman whose husband humil-iated her by withdrawing from a senatorial campaign and who is in the midst of a nasty divorce?"

"You've had a busy year."

"You can say that again. Talk about stress. Life's been a little rough lately." She opened the front door of the house. "Come on, let's go inside. It's cold out here. Another storm's coming."

He checked his watch. "I've got company scheduled to arrive at any minute."

"Lillian Harte?"

Should have known, he thought.

Marilyn gave a throaty laugh. "Don't look so surprised. It's all over town that you walked into Incandescent Body bakery with her first thing this morn-ing."

"It wasn't first thing."

"How serious is it? You two sleeping together?"

The ease with which she asked such a personal question was a forcible re-minder of just how personal their own relationship had once been. He found himself wanting to protect Lillian from some vague menace that he could not quite define. Or maybe it was just the residual effect of Mitchell's notion of early-childhood education kicking in. Madison men did not kiss and tell. Mitchell had drummed that basic principle of proper masculine behavior into Rafe and Gabe early in life.

Besides, he had nothing to kiss and tell about, Gabe reminded himself.

"No," he said. "We just happened to come out here to the coast at the same time. Found ourselves at loose ends today. We both wanted some company for breakfast. No big deal."

Marilyn winked. "Don't worry, I won't cramp your style. I just wanted to say hello to an old friend."

She swept through the door of the cottage.

He glanced once more back along the drive. There was no sign of Lillian's car. Reluctantly he followed Marilyn into the small house.

"Good lord, couldn't you find a better rental?" Marilyn surveyed the dilapidated interior with a grimace. "Not exactly your style, is it?"

"Until Rafe and Hannah get Dreamscape open there isn't a lot of high-end rental housing available around Eclipse Bay. You know that as well as I do. It was either here or my grandfather's house." He allowed the door to close slowly behind him. "Knew that wouldn't work so I picked this place. It's got everything I need."

"Like what?"

"Privacy."

"Okay, I get the point. You've got a hot date with Lillian Harte and I'm in the way." She settled on the arm of the shabby sofa with a regal grace. "I won't stay long, I promise. I need to talk to you, Gabe."

He did not sit down. He didn't want to encourage her. Instead, he propped one shoulder against the wall and folded his arms. "What's this all about, Marilyn?"

"Do I have to have a special reason? You and I go back a long way. We have a history."

"History was never my best subject. I was a business major in college, remember?"

"I hear you signed up with Lillian's matchmaking agency."

"Who told you that?"

"Carole Rhoades. I got to know her when she did a little fund-raising for Trevor at her law firm last year."

He identified the name immediately. Carole Rhoades was one of the five women Lillian had matched with him.

"Portland sure is a small town in some ways, isn't it?" he said. "Almost as small as Eclipse Bay."

"It's not the size of the town, it's the size of the universe in which you move." She swung one long leg. "People who run companies like Madison Commercial tend to circulate in certain limited spheres."

"I can see I need to get out more. Broaden my horizons."

She chuckled. "I hear the date with Carole was a bust."

"And here I thought we'd had a very pleasant evening."

"She said she was home by ten o'clock and you didn't even try to invite yourself in for a nightcap. She said it was obvious that you would much rather have been at your desk."

"Damn. Women talk about stuff like that?"

"Of course they do."

"I'll have to keep that in mind." He turned his wrist slightly to check his watch. "You want to tell me why you're here?"

Her smile stayed in place but he thought he saw it tighten a notch or two.

"You make it sound as though the only thing that might bring me here is business."

"Whenever we've run into each other during the past few years, you've usually hit me up for a campaign donation for Trevor."

"Which you have always declined to give."

"Madisons aren't real big on political campaign contributions."

"I realize that you never supported Trevor but things have changed—"

A brisk knock on the back door interrupted her before she could finish the sentence.

Gabe straightened away from the wall. "Looks like my guest decided to walk instead of drive this evening."

He went through the ancient kitchen and opened the back door.

Lillian stood inside the glass-enclosed rear porch, a large, well-stuffed grocery bag in her arms. She wore the hooded iridescent rain cloak he'd seen in Portland, although it had not yet begun to rain. The cloak was unfastened, revealing the black turtleneck and black trousers she had on underneath. The tunic-length top was slashed with a lightning bolt of intense turquoise.

"I thought you were going to drive over," he said.

"Walking seemed faster."

"It's almost dark."

"So what? This is Eclipse Bay, not the big bad city."

"Listen, tough lady, you ought to know better than to run around an unlit, sparsely inhabited stretch of coastline after dark."

"You want to help me with this grocery sack or would you rather stand there and lecture me for a while?"

"Give me the damn sack."

"My, you're in a swell mood tonight."

"Uninvited company." He took the sack from her and stood back. "Marilyn Thornley. She won't be staying long."

"That's good, because I didn't bring enough food for three."

The weight of the grocery sack belied that claim, but he did not argue the point. He set it on the counter without comment.

Marilyn appeared in the kitchen doorway. She gave Lillian the same glowing grin she'd used on Gabe.

"Lillian. It's been ages. Good to see you again."

"Hello, Marilyn. Been a while," she responded sweetly.

"I didn't mean to intrude on your little dinner party," Marilyn said. "I heard Gabe was in town. Thought I'd stop in and say hello."

"Doing a little fund-raising?" Lillian asked smoothly. "Rumor has it that you're going into politics on your own, now that Trevor is no longer in the picture."

There was a short, brittle silence during which neither woman's smile faltered.

"Gabe and I were just talking about how fast word travels in this town," Marilyn said with a slight edge on her voice.

"I ran into Pamela McCallister at Fulton's Supermarket this afternoon," Lillian said. "Her husband, Brad, is on the faculty at Chamberlain but he has a joint appointment at the institute. He says you've already got your campaign staff organized and that you've put Claire Jensen in charge."

"You know Claire?"

"Yes. I haven't seen much of her in recent years but we worked together at a local restaurant one summer when we were both in college. She always said she wanted to go into politics."

"Claire worked very hard on Trevor's staff. She's had a lot of experience. I think she's ready to head up a campaign."

"I hear you've got your sites on a seat in the U.S. Senate."

There was another brittle pause. Gabe helped Lillian with her rain cloak.

"Yes," Marilyn said.

"Expensive," Lillian murmured.

"Yes," Marilyn said again. "Politics is an expensive pursuit."

Lillian went to the counter, reached into the grocery sack and removed a plastic bag containing a head of dark-green broccoli. "Probably not a lot of money left over after Trevor bowed out of the race last fall."

"No."

"The Thornley campaign did a lot of media, as well. The television commercials must have cost a fortune."

"You're right," Marilyn said in a low voice. "The ads wiped out most of the war chest. We knew going in that they would be expensive, but you can't win elections without television." She paused. "There were also some additional, unplanned expenses toward the end."

The sudden anger in her voice made both Gabe and Lillian look at her.

"We were so close. So damned close," Marilyn said bitterly.

"I'm sorry it all fell apart," Lillian said quietly. "I know it must have been a blow."

"You don't have to pretend that you don't know what happened," Marilyn said. "I'm sure you heard the rumors about the videos."

Gabe exchanged a glance with Lillian. They were both aware of the story behind the videos that had disappeared when the former editor of the *Eclipse Bay Journal* had been arrested a few months ago. The missing films purported to show Trevor Thornley cavorting in high heels and ladies' undergarments.

"I heard that those tapes, assuming they ever actually existed, were destroyed," Gabe said neutrally. "No one I know has ever seen them."

"That bastard, Jed Steadman, lied about having destroyed them without looking at them. He made copies." Marilyn's voice roughened with tightly controlled rage. "He blackmailed Trevor from jail. Said he needed the money for his trial."

Gabe exhaled slowly. "That was the unexpected additional campaign expense you mentioned? Blackmail payments to Jed Steadman?"

"Steadman was too smart to approach me," Marilyn said. "He contacted Trevor. And that idiot *paid* him off. I couldn't believe it. When I discovered that he was actually making blackmail payments I knew the campaign was finished. But Trevor thought he could keep it all hushed up. He did not even begin to comprehend what we were up against."

"You walked out and Trevor was forced to quit the race," Lillian said.

"There wasn't any other viable option. It was obvious that Trevor was going down, but that didn't mean that I had to go down with him." Marilyn looked at Gabe. "Politics is a lot like any other business. You have to know when to cut your losses."

"Sure," Gabe said, keeping his voice very even. "I can see the parallels."

Marilyn blinked rapidly once or twice, realizing she'd gone too far. "So much for catching up on my personal news. It's getting late. I'll leave you two to your private little dinner party. Nice to see you both."

She turned away from the kitchen and started toward the front door.

Gabe looked at Lillian. She raised her brows but said nothing.

"I'll walk you out to your car," he called to Marilyn.

He caught up with her and together they went out onto the porch. The fast-moving storm clouds had cut off what little was left of the sunset's afterglow. He switched on the porch light. The wind had grown stronger while they had been inside the cottage. The limbs of the fir trees at the edge of the drive were stirring briskly.

Marilyn put up a well-manicured hand to keep her hair in place. She looked at her Mercedes, not at him.

"Do you ever wonder how things might have worked out for us if we hadn't broken up?" she asked in a pensive voice.

" 'Never look back' is about the closest thing we Madisons have to a family motto."

"You've never married."

"Been busy for the past few years."

"Yes, I know. So have I. Sure wish I could adopt your family motto." Her mouth twisted sadly. "When I think of all the time I invested in Trevor's career, I feel almost physically ill. Looking back, I can't believe I made such a huge mistake. How could I have been so stupid, Gabe?"

"We all make the best choices we can with the information we have available at the time we have to make them. None of us ever has enough information to be absolutely sure we're making the right choice."

"We've followed separate paths for a while," she said. "But now we seem to be circling back toward each other. Strange how life works, isn't it?"

"Strange, all right."

She unfolded her arms and reached up to touch his cheek very lightly with her fingertips. "Enjoy your dinner with Lillian."

"Thanks. I will."

"You know, if anyone had suggested a few days or months or years ago that you might find her attractive, I would have laughed. But now that I'm going through the breakup of my marriage, I view male-female relationships in a different light."

"Light is funny. Did you know that if you put it into corn bread dough, it makes terrific muffins?"

"I understand the appeal that Lillian has for you, Gabe."

"You might want to take it easy on the way back to the main road. The rains must have been heavy last month. They washed out a chunk of the drive."

"Your family and hers have a very tangled history."

"I think I hear my cell phone ringing." He patted his pockets.

"Don't forget, I know you well from the old days. I remember very clearly how you measured your own success against that of Harte Investments. I can only imagine how tempting it would be for you to marry Lillian and graft a third of her family's company onto Madison Commercial. In a way, it would be the ultimate triumph for you, wouldn't it?"

"Must have left the damn thing in the house."

He took a step back toward the partially opened door.

"I know you probably aren't interested in any advice from me," Marilyn said. "But for the sake of the past we share, I'm going to give you some, anyway. Don't marry just to prove something to yourself or because you think it would be worth it to add a chunk of Harte Investments to your empire. I married Trevor for reasons that had nothing to do with love. It was the biggest mistake of my life."

She went down the steps, got into the Mercedes and drove away.

He watched the taillights until they disappeared, listening to the wind, aware of the oncoming storm.

"Going to donate to her campaign?" Lillian questioned.

He turned around slowly, wondering how long she had been standing there on the other side of the screen door.

"Don't think so." He opened the door and walked into the warmth of the house. "Ready to work on dinner?"

"Sure. I've worked up quite an appetite. Spent the day setting up my studio in the spare bedroom at the cottage. I'm starving."

She turned and disappeared into the kitchen.

Had she overheard Marilyn's crack about marrying her to get a chunk of Harte Investments?

He went to stand in the doorway of the kitchen. A variety of vegetables, including the broccoli, stood on the counter. A wedge of parmesan cheese wrapped in plastic and a package of pasta were positioned nearby.

"Looks like some assembly required," he said.

"We're both smart people. I think we can get this done." She picked up a small knife and went to work on a yellow bell pepper. "Why don't you pour us a glass of wine? Probably make things go more smoothly."

"Good idea." He moved out of the doorway, opened a drawer and removed a corkscrew.

Lillian concentrated on the bell pepper.

He should probably say something, he thought. But he wasn't sure what she expected from him. How much had she overheard?

"Marilyn just showed up a few minutes before you got here," he said. "Out of the blue."

"She'll be back. You've got something she wants."

"I know. Money. You're not the first one to warn me."

Lillian dumped the sliced pepper into a bowl. "It's not your money she wants."

"Sure it is. She needs cash to fuel her campaign."

"I'm not saying that she wouldn't find your money useful. But what she really wants is someone she can trust completely, a man who will support her ambitions. She wants someone who will add strength and influence to her power base. Someone whose goals won't conflict with hers and who will not try to compete with her."

The cork came out of the bottle with a small pop. "You could tell all that in the five minutes you spent talking to her?"

"Sure. I'm a former matchmaker, remember?"

"Oh, yeah, right. I keep forgetting about your famous matchmaking intuition."

"Go ahead, mock me at your own peril. But I'm here to tell you that you've got a lot of what she's looking for in a husband." Lillian paused, head tipped slightly to the side. "And you know what?"

"What?"

"She's got a lot of what you stated you wanted on the Private Arrangements questionnaire. Say, maybe you were a tad more honest in your responses than I thought."

He poured two glasses of the cabernet, grimly pleased that his hand remained steady. "Marilyn and I already tried the couple thing. It didn't work out."

"I'm serious." Lillian put down the knife and picked up one of the wineglasses. "Marilyn meets a lot of the requirements you listed. There's money in her family. Even if they have cut off her campaign allowance for the moment, she'll inherit a nice bit of the Caldwell fortune someday. She's not an elitist academic or a fuzzy-brained New Age thinker." She paused a beat. "And she's not the *arty* type."

He leaned against the refrigerator and swirled the wine in his glass. "So, do you think she and I would be a good match if we gave it another try?"

She reached for the box of pasta. "No."

"Decisive. I like that in a matchmaker. Why don't you think she and I would be a good match?"

"Because you lied on the questionnaire."

"In your opinion."

"Mine is the only one that counts here," she said coolly. "I'm the professional, remember?"

7

THE storm crashed ashore shortly after ten o'clock. Time to go, Lillian thought. The edgy intimacy that had been thickening the atmosphere all evening was getting to her. She could no longer ignore the vibes. If she hung around any longer she might embarrass herself by making a pass at Gabe.

She put down her cards. "Gin."

"Damn. Not again." Gabe tossed his cards onto the cushion between them. He sprawled against the back of the sofa and regarded her with a malevolent expression. "Didn't realize you were the competitive type."

"I'm a Harte, remember? We're all competitive in some ways. Besides, it was your idea to play gin rummy."

"I wasn't concentrating. Had my mind on other things."

"Yeah, sure. They all say that when they lose to me." She looked out the window into the heavy darkness. "I'd better be on my way. That rain is going to get worse before it gets better."

He uncoiled from the depths of the sagging sofa. "I'll drive you back to your cottage."

He didn't have to sound quite so eager to get rid of her, she thought. But it was probably for the best. At least his mood seemed lighter now. Her mission of mercy was accomplished.

"Thanks." She rose quickly, a sense of urgency pulsing through her.

She had left it too long, she thought. It was *past* time to leave. She was not sure when or how it had happened but she was suddenly, intensely aware of the heavy blanket of sensual awareness that enveloped her. It had settled around her slowly and lightly over the course of the evening, the warm, thick folds practically weightless until now.

She wondered if Gabe felt anything at all. If he did, he was doing a terrific job of concealing it.

He was already at the door, her rain cloak in his hand. Obviously she was the only one who could feel the energy of the storm gathering here inside this room.

The smartest thing she could do tonight was leave right now and go straight home to her own bed.

She touched the back of a chair briefly to steady herself, took a deep breath and walked deliberately toward him.

"One thing I've been meaning to ask you," he said when she reached the place where he waited with her cloak.

She turned her back to him so that he could help her into the garment. "What's that?"

"Did you invite yourself over here tonight just because you thought I needed cheering up or did you have something else in mind?"

She froze, her hands slightly raised to take the edges of the cloak from him.

"Not that I don't appreciate the neighborly gesture," he said.

"We were both at loose ends this evening." She was irritated now. "And we *are* neighbors. Sort of. And you did seem a little moody this morning. Dinner together sounded reasonable. If you've got a problem with that, I'll make sure it doesn't happen again."

"Ouch. You've got teeth, don't you?"

"I'm a Harte."

"Right. I just wanted to let you know that I don't need any do-gooder nurturing. I'd much rather you had another agenda."

He draped the cloak around her shoulders. When he was finished he did not release her and step back. Instead he stayed there, so close that she could feel the heat of his body. He rested his hands on her, letting her feel the weight and strength of them.

"Another agenda?" She twitched the cloak into place, fussing with it a bit to cover her awkwardness. "Such as exploring various strategies we can use to help A.Z. prove that a secret government agency is planning to move frozen space aliens into the institute?"

He tightened his hands on her shoulders. "I was thinking more along the lines of you seducing me."

She opened her mouth. And closed it immediately when she realized she did not know what to say.

"You know, just to help lift my mood." His voice roughened a little. Getting dangerous. "Wouldn't be too much different from inviting yourself over for dinner so that I wouldn't be alone. Just another little act of charity."

"I already gave at the office."

"So much for small acts of random kindness."

He lifted her hair aside and kissed the nape of her neck. Electricity went down her spine. The room dissolved into a thousand different hues. She was inside the rainbow.

"Gabe."

"And here I thought you felt sorry for me," he said against her nape. "I thought you were genuinely concerned about my burnout problem."

"Look, Gabe—"

"Got another question for you," he said.

"Forget it."

"Can't. It's been eating at me for weeks. I've got to know. Did you ever fill out one of your own questionnaires and run it through your computer program to see if you could find the perfect match for yourself?"

The question blindsided her. It caught her up with the force of a heavy wave, sweeping her off her feet and roiling her senses. She pulled herself together with an effort.

"You're very chatty all of a sudden, aren't you?" she muttered.

"You didn't answer my question."

She felt the heat rise in her face. *Damn.* "I don't owe you any answers."

"Ah. So you *did* try to match yourself. I had a hunch you might have done it. Who could resist? There you were with your program and all those potential dates. What happened? No good candidates on your list of clients? Hard to believe."

"I told you," she whispered, "the program is not fool-proof."

"Maybe not, but it's got a very high degree of accuracy. You assured me of that when I signed on. What went wrong? Didn't like the matches it selected for you?"

She put out her hand and closed her fingers around the doorknob. "Take me home, Gabe."

"Or did you lose your nerve? It's one thing to use intuition and the results of a questionnaire to help other people make a decision that will affect them for a lifetime." He turned her slowly around to face him. "It's another thing altogether to use them to make a choice that will affect your own life."

"Gabe—"

"Maybe your mistake was in looking too far ahead," he said softly. "Hell, maybe I was making the same mistake. Maybe we should both stop obsessing on the long term and focus more on the short term."

She swallowed. "How short a term are we talking about here?"

"Let's start with tonight." He kissed her throat. "We'll reassess matters in the morning."

She stiffened. "I don't do one-night time frames."

"There you go, trying to think too far ahead again."

"Goading me will not work," she said. "I do not respond to taunts or dares."

"Of course you don't. You're a Harte." He leaned his forehead against hers. His thumb moved along the line of her jaw. "What *will* work?"

She took a deep breath, inhaled some of the dancing storm energy that swirled around them and used it to fortify herself.

"You have to admit that you cheated on the Private Arrangements questionnaire," she said.

"What the hell does that damned questionnaire have to do with what's happening between us?"

"I ran the one you filled out through my program. Compared it with one that I had filled out on myself. If you were completely honest in all your responses on that form, I have to tell you that we are definitely not a good match, Gabe. Not even in the short term."

For the space of two or three heartbeats, he went utterly motionless.

"And if I did shade some of the answers?" he asked.

"Then the conclusions were invalid, of course."

He smiled slowly. "I lied through my teeth on most of them."

She touched the tip of her tongue to her lower lip. "Honest?"

"I swear it on my honor as a Madison," he said against her mouth.

"I *knew* it." Satisfaction unfurled within her. She put both arms around his neck. "I was sure of it. Even the one about—?"

His mouth closed on hers before she could finish the question. He kissed her, long and hard and deep; so deep that she forgot everything else.

The colors of the rainbow that surrounded her grew brighter, becoming almost painfully intense. She had to close her eyes against the shattering brilliance.

She kissed Gabe back, full on his warm, hard, incredibly sexy mouth. She gave it everything she had, moving into the moment the way she did when she was painting all out; flying with the vision, trying to get it down on the canvas before it evaporated.

Rain pounded on the roof of the cottage. Wind lashed at the windows. Electricity arced in the atmosphere. The night was alive and so was she.

She was vaguely aware of the rain cloak sliding off her shoulders. And then she realized that her feet no longer touched the floor. Gabe had picked her up in his arms.

She turned her face against his chest, savoring the scent of his body and the strength of his arms. She spread the fingers of one hand across the expanse of his chest. Beneath the fabric of his pullover, he was hard and sleek.

He carried her into the cottage's tiny bedroom and tumbled her down onto the old-fashioned four-poster. Her shoes thudded softly on the old rug. He straightened, peeled off his pullover in a single, sweeping motion and tossed it carelessly aside. It caught on a bedpost.

He never took his eyes off her as he stripped off his trousers and briefs. His hands were quick and ruthlessly efficient. The sight of his heavily aroused body elicited an immediate reaction far inside her. She was suddenly aware of a liquid heat pooling in her lower body.

He paused long enough to open a drawer in the nightstand. She heard foil tear in the darkness.

And then he was on the quilt with her, looming over her, caging her between his arms. The ancient bed squeaked beneath his weight. If she had tried to sketch him at that moment, she knew the result would have been a picture composed of dark light, strong shadows, and fathomless pools of mystery.

He tugged the tunic off over her head. Unfastened the satin bra. Excitement sent another flood of brilliant colors through her when he touched her breasts. She could hardly breathe. All of her senses sharpened and focused.

Gabe slid one leg between her thighs. He shifted his mouth back to hers in a heavy, drugging kiss.

She gripped his shoulders, digging her fingers into his bare skin. His hard body cut off what little light came through the doorway from the main room. She could hear the storm swirling outside the cottage, weaving a magic force field that held the rest of the world at bay. At least for now.

His hands moved on her again. Her trousers disappeared. They were soon followed by her panties.

He moved his hand across her stomach and down to the place where she was hot and wet and full. He stroked her as if he were now the painter, applying colors with lavish passion and precision. Getting into his art.

She wanted to tell him to slow down. She needed time to adjust to this unfamiliar level of raw, physical sensation; time to savor the sweep and nuance of the hues of this amazing rainbow.

But time was out of her control, along with everything else tonight. When he found her again with his fingers, she screamed. It was too much.

Her body clenched violently. The rainbow pulsed. Neon brights, effervescent blues and glorious, eye-searing reds filled the shadows with light. She could not think; could not sort out impressions or emotions.

He surged into her at that moment, spilling a whole new palette across the canvas. These were the mysterious, unnamable hues that she had seen only in her dreams.

She felt the rigid tension in the muscles and bone beneath his skin and knew that he was no longer in control either. His release crashed through both of them.

THE first thing she noticed when she awoke a long time later was that she could not move. Gabe had her pinned to the bed with one heavy arm wrapped around her midsection and a muscular leg thrown across her thigh.

The second thing she became aware of was that the storm winds had died down. She could still hear gentle rain on the roof, and the darkness on the other side of the window remained immutable. But the world outside was a much quieter, calmer place than it had been earlier.

She lay still, partly because she knew that if she tried to move she would awaken Gabe and she was not at all certain she wanted to do that. Not yet, at any rate. She had things to think about and she needed to think without distractions.

Now that the chaos of passion had resolved itself, the first thing she ought to do was take a cold, hard look at what had happened between herself and Gabe. Life had suddenly become extremely complicated.

But she could not bring herself to focus just yet on her new problems. First she would allow herself the pleasure of absorbing the myriad impressions she had not been able to catalog and enjoy in the heat and turmoil of what had happened earlier. She was entitled.

Memories and impressions stirred her senses. Sex with Gabe had been as disorienting, thrilling, and ultimately as disturbing as that flash of recognition that sometimes struck while she was in the process of trying to translate a vision onto a canvas. In those rare moments of acute awareness she could *see* the whole picture in her mind. But the images came so swiftly, so relentlessly, that it was impossible to paint fast enough to keep up with them. She had learned to concentrate on the critical elements, the core of the vision, knowing that she could go back later to fill in the less essential parts.

Now she tried to do just that, calling up the little details that she had missed during the passionate encounter. The way his fingers had closed around her thigh. The way his teeth had grazed a nipple. The way his tongue—

"You awake?" Gabe asked.

"Yes."

He shifted a little, settling her more comfortably into the curve of his body. "What are you thinking about?"

She smiled into the pillow and said nothing.

He nibbled gently on her shoulder. "Tell me."

"I was just wondering why you lied on the Private Arrangements questionnaire."

"Can't let it go, can you?"

"Nope."

"Going to throw it in my face again and again, aren't you?"

"Yep."

"Okay, why do you think I lied?"

She propped herself up on one elbow and looked down at him, trying to read his expression in the shadows. Impossible. "I think you fiddled with the responses because subconsciously you didn't want me to find you a perfect match. You set things up so that failure was the only option."

"Huh. Why the hell would I do that after paying you all that money for some good matches?"

She put her hand on his bare chest. "Probably because, when crunch time came, your Madison genes just couldn't tolerate the idea of applying such a sensible, logical, rational approach to an intimate relationship with a woman."

"Screwed by my genetic predisposition to do things the hard way, you think?"

She drew her fingertips through the crisp, curling hair. "Madisons are known for doing things the hard way."

"True." He stroked the curve of her head. "There's just one point I want to make before we get up in a few hours and fix breakfast."

"And your point is?"

"Tonight does not qualify as my sixth date."

For an instant, she did not understand. Then the meaning of his words shot through her brain, charring the semi–dream state she had been enjoying.

She sat bolt upright. His arm slid down to her hips. Aware that she was nude, she grabbed the sheets and held them to her breasts.

"I've got news for you," she said, "we had dinner and sex. If that doesn't qualify as a date in your book, I'd like to know what does. It's certainly a heck of a lot more than any of my other dates have involved in a very long time."

"You came over here tonight because you felt sorry for me, remember? Being neighborly doesn't qualify as a date."

Anger, pain, and outrage slammed through her without warning. She found herself teetering on an invisible emotional cliff that she had not even noticed a few seconds ago.

"I certainly didn't sleep with you just to jolly you out of your brooding mood."

"It worked, though." He closed his palm around her hip, squeezing gently. "I'm feeling a lot more cheerful than I did earlier."

"Damn it, Gabe, don't you dare imply that having sex was no different than . . . than playing gin rummy together. One is a game. The other is not."

There was a short silence. Was he actually having to think about her comment? She went cold. Maybe he didn't believe that there was any major difference between sex and gin rummy. Maybe to him they both ranked as nothing more than casual pastimes.

Maybe she had been a complete fool.

"One is a game, the other is not," Gabe repeated very deliberately. "This is a test, right?"

"Yes," she said through her teeth. "And if you get it wrong, you're a doomed man."

"Okay, okay, just give me a minute." He sounded as serious and intent as a game show contestant who had a hundred thousand dollars riding on the outcome. "One is a game. The other is not. One is a game. The other—"

"Gabe, so help me—"

"I'm thinking, I'm thinking."

There was an odd ringing in her ears now. Surely she could not have been dumb enough to go to bed with a man who treated sex as entertainment for a rainy night in a small town where there was very little in the way of nightlife. She could not have misjudged Gabe Madison so badly. She was a professional matchmaker, for heaven's sake.

He moved his warm palm up over her hip, along the curve of her waist, and pulled her down across his chest. One of her legs lodged between his thighs. She felt a familiar pressure and knew that he was getting hard again.

He cupped her buttock in one hand. "I'm ready."

The sensual laughter in his voice jolted her back to reality. He was teasing her. She was overreacting. Time to get a grip. Act mature and sophisticated.

With an act of will she forced herself to step back from the invisible emotional precipice. Her ears stopped ringing. She took a deep breath and managed a cool smile.

"I'm waiting for your answer," she said.

"Gin rummy is the game, right?"

"Congratulations. Right answer."

He slipped his fingertips along the rim of the cleavage that divided her derrière. Without warning, he rolled her onto her back and came down on top of her.

"What do you think you're doing?" she whispered.

"Collecting my prize."

A long time later she stirred again and leaned over him.

"You know," she said, "there was another reason I decided to stay tonight."

He smiled in the darkness. His hand moved in her hair.

"What was that?" he asked.

"I was curious to see what you do with the peanut butter."

"I'll show you."

"Now?"

"This is as good a time as any. I seem to have worked up an appetite."

8

THE sound of a heavy engine lumbering down the drive toward the house woke him. He opened his eyes. The gray light of a rainy morning illuminated the window. Beside him, Lillian did not stir.

What he wanted most in the world at that moment, he thought, was to stay right where he was with Lillian's beautifully curved bottom nestled against his midsection. But the rumble outside made that a non-option.

With deep regret, he eased himself cautiously away from her warmth. She wriggled a little, as though in protest. He leaned over and kissed her shoulder. She sighed and snuggled deeper into the pillow.

He studied her as he rose and reached for his pants. She looked very good lying there in his bed. Like she belonged there.

Outside, the large vehicle had come to a halt. The motor shut down.

He made himself go out into the hall, pausing long enough to close the bedroom door firmly. Then he went into the main room.

He glanced around quickly on his way to the front door, checking to see if there was any evidence of Lillian's presence. A glimmering pool filled with shifting lights on the floor caught his eye. He scooped up the iridescent rain cloak and crammed it into the hall closet.

By the time he got the front door open and saw the familiar SUV hulking in the drive, his grandfather was already on the porch.

"What the hell is going on here?" Mitchell roared. He thumped his cane on the boards for emphasis. "Just what are you up to, Gabe Madison?"

Damn.

Gabe reassessed the situation quickly. Lillian had walked to his place. Her car was not in the drive. Mitchell could not possibly know that she had spent the night here.

Could he?

Small towns had some serious drawbacks when it came to privacy issues.
When in doubt, stall.

"Good morning to you, too," he said easily. "When did you get back into town?"

"Last night. Late."

"Where's Bev?"

Bev Bolton, the widow of a former editor of the *Eclipse Bay Journal,* was the woman Mitchell had been seeing for several months She had accompanied him to Hawaii. Bev lived in Portland. Mitchell had been so discreet about the relationship that for several extremely uneasy weeks Gabe and Rafe had both feared that his frequent trips to the city had been for the purpose of seeing a specialist. They had leaped to the conclusion that he was suffering from some dire medical condition that he was trying to keep from them. The truth had come as an enormous, if somewhat startling, relief.

"Bev went on down to California to visit her grandkids," Mitchell said. "Now tell me what's happening here."

"Not much." He yawned and absently rubbed his chest. It was cold out here. Should have grabbed a shirt out of the closet. "Been raining a lot."

"Don't try to change the topic. This is me, your grandfather, you're talking to. I had coffee in town at the bakery. Must have been at least half a dozen folks who couldn't wait to tell me that Marilyn Thornley's car was seen turning into your driveway last night around suppertime."

Gabe drew a slow, deep breath. Relief replaced some of the tension that had tightened every muscle in his belly. Mitchell didn't know about Lillian. He was here because of Marilyn's car.

"Well, it's gone now, isn't it?" Gabe said.

He moved farther out onto the porch, pulling the door closed behind him. Rain dripped steadily from the edge of the porch roof. The temperature had to be in the very low fifties. Maybe the high forties. He tried to ignore the chill. How long did it take to contract a case of hypothermia?

He'd just have to tough it out. He could not risk going back inside to get more clothes. Mitchell would follow him into the hall and the commotion would awaken Lillian. She would probably come out of the bedroom to see what was going on and all hell would break loose. A real doomsday scenario, if ever there was one.

He needed to think and he needed to do it fast.

Priorities, priorities.

The first order of business was to get rid of Mitchell.

He glanced at the SUV and raised a hand in a casual salute to Mitchell's faithful factotum, Bryce, who waited stoically behind the wheel. Bryce nodded once, acknowledging the greeting with a military-style inclination of his head.

Gabe turned back to Mitchell. "So, how was Hawaii?"

"Hawaii was fine." Mitchell scowled. "Hawaii is always fine. I didn't come here to talk about my vacation."

"I was trying to be civil."

"Bullshit. You're trying to slip and slide around this thing. Don't waste my time. I didn't just fall off the turnip truck yesterday. I want to know what's up with you and Marilyn Thornley."

"Absolutely nothing of any great interest to anyone, including me." Gabe folded his arms. Nothing like a clear conscience when dealing with the old man.

The tension that simmered between the two of them lately was a new element in their relationship. Gabe could not pinpoint when it had first begun to emerge. Sometime during the last two years, he thought. It had grown remarkably more acute since Rafe's marriage, however.

In the old days, after he and Rafe had gone to live with Mitchell following the death of their parents, there had been relatively few conflicts between Gabe and his grandfather. Rafe had been the rebel, the one who had gone toe-to-toe with Mitchell at every turn.

But looking back, Gabe knew that he had taken the opposite path, not because he had wanted to please Mitchell but because he was committed to his future goal. All he had cared about was his dream of proving that a Madison could be a success. In high school he had charted a course that he had calculated would enable him to achieve his objective and he had stuck to it. He had been the one who had gotten the good grades, stayed out of trouble and graduated from college because he could see that was how the Hartes did things. They had been his role models. It was clear to him, even as a boy, that the traditional Madison approach to life led to poor outcomes.

In the end, he had achieved his objective. He had put together a business empire that rivaled Harte Investments. One of these days, it would be even bigger than Harte.

He knew that now, although he had not built Madison Commercial with the conscious intention of pleasing his grandfather. Mitchell's approval had been one of the satisfying side effects of success. He had taken it for granted for some time.

The realization that nothing he had accomplished seemed to matter to Mitchell anymore left him with a peculiar, empty feeling deep inside. This morning, for the first time, he realized that anger was seeping in to fill the void.

What right did the old man have to give him advice on how to run his life?

Mitchell squinted, searching Gabe's face. Whatever he saw there appeared to reassure him somewhat.

"Marilyn didn't hang around?"

"Not for long," Gabe said mildly.

"She and Thornley are calling it quits, you know," Mitchell said.

"I heard."

"Word is, she's got her own plans to go into politics."

Gabe dropped his arms and wrapped his hands around the wet railing. Damn, it was cold. In another few minutes his teeth would probably start to chatter. "She told me that much yesterday when she stopped by to see me. Probably do okay."

"You know what she's after, don't you?"

"Sure. Don't worry, Mitch, I didn't just fall off the turnip truck either. It's obvious that Marilyn is looking for someone to help finance her political career."

"I hear her father is a little pissed because she blew so much cash on Thornley's campaign. They say Caldwell isn't real eager to pump more money into another political race, even if it is his daughter who is running this time."

"The Caldwells will come around. Eventually. They always do for Marilyn."

Mitchell nodded. "That woman always did have a way of getting what she wanted, even when she was a little girl. Still, no politician ever has enough cash. She could use a rich husband with connections. Looks like you're back on her radar scope."

"I'm not interested in being married to a politician. If she doesn't know that already, I think she'll figure it out real quick. Marilyn is smart."

"The two of you had something going there for a while. Maybe she figures she can relight some old flames."

Gabe shrugged. "Whatever we had was over a long time ago."

"Don't count on her giving up easily."

"Okay, I won't count on it."

Mitchell's hawklike face tightened in a shrewd expression. "You know, things would be a whole lot simpler if you got married."

Gabe gripped the railing and said nothing.

"Marilyn Thornley wouldn't be hanging around here at suppertime if you had a wife," Mitchell said.

Gabe looked at him. "Don't start."

"A man your age oughtta be married. Hell, I was married at your age."

"Would that have been Alicia or Janine? No, wait, Alicia was number three, wasn't she? So was it Susan? It can't have been Trish because I'm sure you told me once that Trish was number one. Must have been Janine."

Mitchell hammered the cane against the boards. "The point is, I was married."

"And divorced. A couple of times, at least at that point. Two down and two more to go."

"So I screwed up once or twice."

"Four times in all."

"Shoot and damn." Mitchell's voice went up a few decibels. "You're supposed to learn from my mistakes."

"Madisons never learn from their mistakes. Family tradition."

Mitchell raised the cane and leveled it at him as if it were a rapier. "You know what your problem is? You're going about this marriage business all wrong."

"You're certainly an authority on the subject."

Mitchell snorted. "Should have known you couldn't go after a woman the way you go after investment prospects for Madison Commercial."

"I did manage to figure that out. That's why I signed up with Private Arrangements."

"What the hell kind of results do you expect from a computer?" Mitchell shot back. "I'm not saying Lillian Harte isn't a smart lady. No such thing as a stupid Harte. And I'm not saying she doesn't know how to run her business. But the fact is, you aren't going to have any luck finding a wife with a computer."

"Why not?"

"Because you're a Madison, that's why not. When it comes to women, a Madison relies on his gut, not his brain."

"And look where it's gotten us," Gabe said. "Three generations of screwed-up relationships."

"Rafe broke that jinx." Mitchell lowered the cane with grim dignity. "I expect you to do the same, by God. But you're gonna have to stop fooling around with Madison Commercial for a while and pay attention to what's important."

That did it.

Gabe felt his Madison temper flash through him with all the stunning heat of summer lightning. It crackled and flared, surging forth from the windowless vault where he kept it locked and chained in the name of establishing total control.

He released the railing and turned on Mitchell.

"Fooling around with Madison Commercial? Is that what you call what I've been doing all these years? *Fooling around with Madison Commercial?*"

Mitchell blinked. Then the lines at the corners of his eyes creased in wary concern. "Simmer down, son. Just trying to have us a reasonable discussion here."

"Fooling around with Madison Commercial? Is that what you call building a major venture capital company that did a few hundred million dollars' worth of business last year?"

"Now, see here, Gabe, this isn't what—"

"Maybe it has slipped your mind that your stock in Madison Commercial is the primary source of your retirement income."

"Shoot and damn, this isn't about money."

"Not about money? All I ever heard from you when I was growing up was how Harte-Madison had been destroyed because you and Sullivan Harte went to war over a woman. How many times did you tell me how you'd been financially ruined because Claudia Banner made fools out of you and Harte? A couple of thousand, maybe?"

"What happened to Harte-Madison all those years ago has got nothing to do with this."

"The Hartes recovered financially because they had the brains and the determination to concentrate on business. You could have done the same thing, but you didn't, did you, Mitch? You preferred to get married. Over and over again."

"This is your grandfather you're dealing with here. Show some respect."

Gabe flexed his hands at his sides. "I proved to you and the whole damn world that a Madison could be as successful as a Harte."

"I'm not saying you haven't been successful with Madison Commercial. But the fact that the company's making a profit isn't what's important here."

"Tell me that the next time you cash your quarterly dividend check."

"Stop talking about money." Mitchell whacked the cane against a post. "We're talking about getting your priorities straight."

"Madison Commercial is a success because I've had my priorities straight all along."

"If you'd had 'em straight, you'd have been married by now. I'd have me some grandkids."

"Don't tell me how to run my life, Mitch."

"Someone's gotta do it."

"And you think you're qualified?"

The door opened.

Gabe went still. He was vaguely aware that Mitchell did the same.

"Good morning, gentlemen," Lillian said from the other side of the screen. "Lovely day, isn't it?"

Gabe shoved his hand through his hair. Just what he needed.

There was nothing but acute silence from his grandfather. He wondered how he was going to take this turn of events.

Mitchell stood transfixed. He gazed at Lillian as if she were a mermaid who had just appeared at the edge of the bay.

Gabe switched his attention back to Lillian and did a quick assessment. She was dressed in the black trousers and the turquoise-slashed sweater she had worn last night. A little dressy for day wear but it just might pass, especially with Mitchell, who didn't pay attention to the nuances of fashion. Her hair was caught up in a neat twist. She wasn't wearing any makeup, but there was nothing unusual in that. In his experience she never wore much.

With luck Mitchell would assume that Lillian had just walked over from her place to join him for breakfast.

She looked out at the two silent men with an expression of amused interest.

"Am I interrupting anything?" she asked politely.

Neither said a word.

"It's a little chilly out there," she said. "Why don't you both come inside? I'm making coffee." She turned away from the screen. "Don't forget to bring Bryce with you," she called over her shoulder.

꧁ ꧂

BRYCE collected his cup of coffee with a short, brusque "Thank you, ma'am" and went back out to the SUV.

"Bryce isn't real keen on socializing," Mitchell said.

Lillian sank down onto the sofa. "I can tell."

Nonchalantly she watched Gabe where he stood at the window, his mug gripped in both hands. He had disappeared into the bedroom while she had poured coffee. When he reappeared a few minutes later he wore a dark flannel shirt with the sleeves rolled up on his strong forearms. The neckline of a black crew-neck tee was visible at his throat. Must have been a little chilly out there on the porch, she thought.

The tension in the tiny front room was charged with remnants of the quarrel she had interrupted.

When she had awakened to the sound of the heated argument, her first instinct had been to get dressed and slip out the back door. She was fairly certain that was the course of action Gabe would have preferred.

She might have done just that, sparing everyone, including herself, this awkward scene. But halfway down the hall she had overheard Gabe. *Fooling around with Madison Commercial? Is that what you call what I've been doing all these years?*

The frustration and stark pain in his words had stopped her in her tracks, canceling all thought of disappearing out the back door.

Mitchell studied Lillian. "Heard you were in town. Going to be here for a while?"

She took a sip of coffee. "Yes."

"Your family's place isn't far from here."

"No. A short walk along the bluffs."

A speculative gleam appeared in Mitchell's eyes. "So, you walked on over here for coffee, is that it?"

"I walked over here, yes," Lillian said.

At the window, Gabe tensed a little, as though preparing himself for battle.

Lillian pretended to ignore him. What she had told Mitchell was the truth as far as it went. Admittedly, it was the truth unencumbered by pesky little details such as those pertaining to the exact time and day she had made the trek, but that was not her problem. Mitchell had obviously decided to play inquisitor, but he was a Madison and she was a Harte. She was under no obligation to tell him everything he wanted to know.

Mitchell angled his chin toward the gray mist outside the window and looked concerned. "Pretty wet out there to be taking a walk."

"Yes, it is quite damp this morning," she agreed. "But what else can you expect this time of year?"

Gabe took a swallow of coffee. He did not speak, but she knew that Mitchell's blunt questioning was stoking the flames of his anger. She could only hope that he would have enough sense not to lose his temper again.

"A real coincidence, you and Gabe both deciding to take a little vacation here in Eclipse Bay at the same time, isn't it?" Mitchell said.

"Just one of those things," Lillian said.

"How long you going to be here?" Mitchell asked.

Gabe turned around at that. "What business is it of yours how long she intends to stay here?"

Mitchell glowered. "Just trying to make polite conversation."

"Sure," Gabe said. "That's you, all right. Polite."

Lillian cleared her throat. "As a matter of fact, I'm going to be here for quite a while. I've closed my business in Portland."

Mitchell's attention snapped back to her. "You shut down your matchmaking operation?"

"Yes."

Mitchell looked thoughtful. "So you're the one."

"I beg your pardon?"

Mitchell shrugged. "The one your dad's going to groom to take over Harte Investments. Never figured it would be you. No offense, but you always seemed to be a little on the flaky side."

"And here we thought my flakiness was a closely held family secret."

Mitchell ignored that, busy with his own logic. "Well, makes sense, when you think about it. I reckon you're the only choice left now that Hannah's fixin' to open the inn with Rafe, and your brother quit the company to write those mystery novels."

"As a matter of fact, I'm not going to go to work for my father. I closed Private Arrangements so that I could paint full-time."

"Paint what?" Mitchell looked nonplussed. "Houses? Cars?"

"Pictures."

"Pictures." If he had looked nonplussed a moment ago, he was clearly floored now. "You mean real paintings? The kind they put in museums?"

"I should be so lucky." Lillian drummed her fingers on her mug, aware that Gabe was watching her with an odd expression. "Octavia Brightwell is going to give me my first show in Portland in a few weeks."

Mitchell shook his head. "Well, shoot and damn. If that don't beat all. Bet your folks and your grandfather are climbing the walls about now. Bad enough having a writer in the family. Now they've got themselves a real live artist."

"I haven't told them yet that I plan to paint full-time," Lillian said carefully. "In fact, they don't even know that I've closed Private Arrangements."

"Don't worry, they won't hear it from me," he said. "But I sure would pay big bucks to be a fly on the wall when you tell 'em that you're going to quit working to paint pictures."

Lillian stiffened. "They'll understand."

"They may understand, but they sure as hell aren't going to be real thrilled about it." Mitchell was almost chortling. "Sullivan sweated blood putting Harte Investments together after our company went under. And your father has worked in the business his whole life. Everyone figured one of you three kids would take over and manage it for another generation. Now, one by one, you're all peeling off to do your own thing."

He was right, she thought. But she didn't need the guilt trip this morning.

"Nick's son, Carson, may develop an interest in the business when he gets older," she said.

Mitchell snorted. "Your brother's boy is only, what? Four? Five?"

"Five."

"It'll be twenty years at least before he's even ready to think about taking on a job like running Harte Investments, assuming he wants to do it in the first place." Mitchell squinted. "Your dad's in his early sixties. He can't wait that long to turn the company over to the next generation."

"It's no secret that Dad plans to retire sometime in the next couple of years," she admitted. "He and Mom want to establish a charitable foundation aimed at teaching disadvantaged young people how to run a business."

"If he wants out, he'll have to sell or merge the company." Mitchell pursed his lips. "Probably make a truckload of money, but for all intents and purposes, Harte Investments will come to an end with this generation."

"It's just a business," Lillian blurted.

"Just a business, my left, uh, foot." Mitchell took another sip of coffee and lowered his mug very slowly. "This is Harte Investments we're talking about."

Lillian became aware of the fact that Gabe had turned away from the window. He was watching her intently. She looked at him and then back at Mitchell. Both pairs of green eyes were identical. It sent a chill down her spine.

It occurred to her that the success of Harte Investments over the years had been more of a thorn in the sides of the Madison men than anyone in her family had ever fully understood.

TEN minutes later, Gabe stood with Lillian on the front porch and watched Mitchell climb into the SUV. Bryce put the behemoth into gear and drove off toward the main road.

They watched the rain fall for a while.

"I'm thinking about giving you a break," Gabe said.

Lillian folded her arms. "What kind of a break?"

"You know that sixth date you owe me?"

"That sixth date is a figment of your obsessive imagination. It will never happen."

"I'm serious."

"So am I."

He watched the SUV disappear into the trees. "I need a date for that banquet in Portland I mentioned the other night at dinner. The one scheduled to honor a former professor of mine. Are you free?"

She turned halfway around, searching his face with an unreadable expression. "This is your idea of a real date? A rubbery-chicken business dinner complete with long, boring speeches?"

"I'll be giving one of those long, boring speeches. Do you want to come with me or not?"

"I'll think about it."

"Think fast. I'm going to drive into Portland Monday morning so that I can get some time in at the office before the dinner. I plan to stay overnight and drive back here Tuesday."

"Hmm."

"What does that mean?"

She shrugged. "Going into Portland for the night would give me a chance to stop by my studio and pick up some odds and ends that I left behind. Yes, I can see where the trip might be marginally worthwhile for me."

"Okay, I get the point. It wasn't a real romantic invitation, was it?"

"I can live with the unromantic part. Just so we're clear that this is not to be considered as your sixth, contractually arranged, bought-and-paid-for Private Arrangements date."

"Call it whatever you want."

"I'll do that," she said curtly and opened the screen door. "And another thing you should know before we drive into Portland for this big evening on the town."

"What's that?"

"I feel that we both need to give ourselves a chance to evaluate the future direction of this relationship."

He stilled. "What the hell does that mean?"

"In simple terms?"

"Yeah, I do best with simple terms."

"It means no more sex, at least not for a while. I want some time to think about what's going on here. I believe that you should do some thinking about it, too."

He said nothing. Just looked at her.

"Is that a problem for you?" she asked.

"Hell, no. I can think. Do it all the time. Sometimes I have two or three whole thoughts in the course of a day."

"I thought you could probably handle it."

"What I'm thinking now is that this decision not to have any more sex for a while has something to do with that scene that just took place with Mitchell."

She hesitated. "Maybe his sudden appearance on the doorstep first thing this morning did help to put some things into perspective. But don't blame him. They were things that I should have thought about last night."

"Like what?"

"Do you have to get obsessive about this, too?"

"I just want some answers."

She put one hand flat on the screen. "I want us both to be sure that we know what we're doing."

"Does that mean you don't know what you're doing? Or that you don't think I know what I'm doing?"

"I came here to Eclipse Bay to paint. You came here to recover from a bad case of burnout. Neither of us planned to get involved in a relationship."

Understanding hit him.

"What happened between us last night scared the hell out of you, didn't it?" he asked softly.

Her nails made little indentations in the screen.

"Maybe we should both be a little scared, Gabe."

"If it's Mitchell you're worrying about, forget it. I'm pretty sure he bought that story you gave him about walking over here for coffee this morning. He doesn't know you spent the night."

She looked down the long drive to the place where Mitchell's SUV had disappeared.

"He knows," she said.

"WHERE'S that damn cell phone?" Mitchell asked.

Bryce took one hand off the wheel long enough to reach into the small space between the seats. He picked up the phone and handed it to Mitchell without comment.

Mitchell found his reading glasses, fished a notebook out of his pocket, flipped it open and located the number he wanted. He carefully punched the digits on the phone, peering carefully at the display to make sure he'd struck the right ones. It wasn't easy. The arthritis made some things harder than they had been in the old days.

"Why do they make these buttons so damn tiny?" he asked.

"People like small phones," Bryce said. "Small phones require small buttons."

"That was what they call one of them rhetorical questions." Mitchell listened to the phone ring. "You weren't supposed to actually answer it."

"You ask me a question, you get an answer," Bryce said.

"You'd think I'd know that by now."

"Yes, sir, you would think that."

The phone rang a third time.

"Shoot and damn," Mitchell said. "He'd better be there. I don't have time—"

The fourth ring was cut short.

"Hello?" Sullivan Harte said.

Mitchell grunted with satisfaction at the sound of the cool, graveled voice. He and Sullivan hadn't had much to do with each other in the years since the destruction of Harte-Madison and the infamous brawl in front of Fulton's Supermarket. They hadn't even had a civil conversation until Hannah and Rafe's wedding a few months ago. But some things you didn't forget, he reflected. The voice of the man who had fought alongside you in the green hell of jungle warfare was one of those things.

"This is Mitch."

"What's wrong?" Sullivan asked immediately.

"Your granddaughter is shacking up with my grandson."

There was a short silence.

"Got news for you, Mitch." Sullivan chuckled. "It's okay now that they're married."

"I'm not talking about Hannah and Rafe."

There was another brief pause.

"What the hell *are* you talking about?" Sullivan no longer sounded amused.

"Lillian and Gabe."

"Sonofabitch," Sullivan said very softly.

"You referring to me or my grandson?"

"Sonofabitch."

"You've made your opinion real clear," Mitchell said. "Point is, what are you gonna do about it?"

"Gabe is *your* grandson."

"And Lillian is *your* granddaughter. I fixed things last time. It's your turn."

"You *fixed* things? What the hell do you mean, you—"

Mitchell punched the button to end the call, cutting Sullivan off in mid-sentence.

He looked at Bryce and grinned.

"This," he said, "is gonna be downright entertaining."

9

CLAIRE Jensen dropped an overstuffed leather briefcase onto the vinyl seat and slid into the booth across from Lillian. She was flushed and a little breathless.

"Sorry I'm late," she said. "Marilyn wanted to go over some talking points for an interview she's doing tomorrow and we had to make some last-minute changes in the schedule for the Leaders of Tomorrow open-house event. Hey, you're looking great, Lil."

"Thanks. So are you. It's good to see you again. Been a while."

"Too long."

Claire laughed and Lillian felt the years fall away. Claire had always been fun. She was a bright, high-energy woman who bubbled with personality and plans.

"You're right," Lillian said. "Much too long. Where did the time go?"

"Life happens. Not like we both haven't been busy for the past few years."

They had met when Claire had been a student at Chamberlain College. Lillian had been attending a college in Portland but she had always spent her vacation breaks with her family in Eclipse Bay. She and Claire had both gotten jobs as waitresses at a pier restaurant one summer. Claire had needed the money. Strictly speaking, Lillian had not needed the income but she had needed the job. The Harte family believed very strongly in the work ethic. All Harte offspring were expected to work during summer vacations.

Initially she and Claire had had little in common, but the long hours spent dealing with stingy tippers and rude tourists had forged a bond between them. They had hung out together after work and talked a lot about the important things: guys and the futures they were planning for themselves.

Claire was the first person and, for a long time, the only person to whom she had confided her dream of becoming an artist. In what some would call typical Harte fashion, she had been very focused on her goal but, acutely aware of her family's opinion on the subject of art as a career, she hadn't discussed it much. It had been exciting to share her secret with someone who understood an impractical dream.

Claire had had some very impractical dreams of her own in those days. She had wanted to go into politics.

"This place certainly hasn't changed much, has it?" Claire commented. "Snow's Café looks just like it did when we used to come here back when we were in college."

The décor of Snow's Café had always reflected Arizona Snow's unique view of the world, Lillian thought. The walls were hung with a mix of faded rock band posters and enlarged satellite photos of the terrain around Area 51 and Roswell, New Mexico. The clientele consisted mostly of students from nearby Chamberlain College.

"What about the menu?" Claire asked. "Is it still the same?"

"Let's see." Lillian plucked the plastic laminated menu out from its position between the napkin holder and the little carousel that held the condiments. She surveyed the offerings. "Still heavy on veggie burgers, french fries, and coffee drinks."

"The three basic food groups for college students. Arizona knows her clientele," Claire mused. "I'm so glad you called. How did you know where to find me? I didn't even know that you were in town."

"I saw Pamela McCallister in Fulton's Supermarket. She mentioned that you were up at the institute, plotting Marilyn Thornley's campaign. How's it going? Think she can step into Trevor's shoes?"

"No problem," Claire assured her. "One thing's for certain, she'll look a whole lot better in them than he did."

"I beg your pardon?"

"Didn't you hear the rumors that went around after Trevor pulled out of the running?" Claire leaned forward and lowered her voice. "Word has it that Trevor liked to have sex in high heels and women's lingerie."

"Oh, *those* rumors."

Claire sat up and settled back against the seat. "Gossip among the campaign staff has it that he was forced to quit the race because he was being blackmailed with some old videos that showed him prancing around in frilly underwear. It was a shock, you know?"

"The campaign staff never had a clue?"

Claire sighed. "Of course not. The staff is always the last to know."

"What made Marilyn decide to become a candidate?"

"She's always been extremely ambitious. But I think that until recently she saw herself in the role of the candidate's wife. The power behind the throne, as it were."

"I heard she put a lot of her family's money into Trevor's campaign."

"True." Claire made a face. "Between you and me, when Trevor imploded, she was absolutely furious. I've never seen anyone in such a rage. I overheard a massive fight between the two of them one afternoon. She told Trevor that she could do a better job of running for office herself and that she was going to prove it. Said a lot of things about how much time she had wasted on him. She dropped the divorce announcement on the staff the next day."

"How did you end up as her campaign manager?"

"I was in the right place at the right time. She and I had worked together a lot in the course of Trevor's campaign. She knew me. Knew what I could do. Most of all she wanted someone she could trust to head up her campaign. When she offered me the job, I jumped at the chance. That woman is going places."

"And you're going to go with her, is that it?"

Claire laughed. "You got it." Her grin faded to a thoughtful expression. "You know, it's funny. Back at the beginning, when I used to dream about getting into politics, I pictured myself as the dynamic female senator from the great state of Oregon. Then I found out how much cash it takes just to run for dog catcher, let alone to get a shot at a state or national office. Short of marrying money, the way Trevor did, there aren't a lot of options. So I decided to carve out a career behind the scenes."

"Still dream of becoming a candidate?"

Claire shook her head decisively. "Not anymore. I love what I do. There's real power and a real rush in running a good campaign. And there's very little downside if it fails. The candidate may disappear from the face of the earth after a big loss but a good strategist just moves on to another campaign."

"I'm glad things worked out for you, Claire."

"You and me both. What's up with you? How long will you be in town?"

"I'm here for a month."

"A whole month?" Claire asked in surprise.

"I've made the big move. I closed down Private Arrangements. I'm going to devote full time to my painting and see what happens."

Claire's lips parted on a silent *wow.* "Good for you. No risk, no glory, I always say. Staying at your folks' cottage?"

"Yes."

"Funny how you Hartes and Madisons keep coming back to Eclipse Bay, isn't it?" Claire commented. "Hannah and Rafe are full-time residents now."

"They love it here."

"I'll tell you one thing, those of us up at the institute can't wait until they get Dreamscape open. As it is now, when people come for seminars and receptions like the Leaders of Tomorrow event, we're forced to put them up in one of those low-budget motels out on the highway."

"They're planning to open in the spring. Assuming the Willis brothers co-operate, of course."

Claire grinned. "What a pair. I practically had to get down on my knees and plead with them to come out to my place a couple of weeks ago just to unclog a toilet. They charged me a small fortune. I didn't have any choice but to pay it, of course, and they knew it."

10

GABE dropped Lillian off at the entrance to her apartment building shortly before ten o'clock on Monday morning.

"I'll pick you up at seven," he said when she made to slide out of the Jag.

She stood and looked at him through the open door. Tension coiled in the pit of her stomach. He was dressed for business once again in the legendary Gabe Madison war armor: steel-gray jacket and trousers, charcoal-gray shirt secured with silver-and-onyx cuff links, silver-and-black striped tie. When he moved his hand on the wheel, the dark-gray edge of his shirt cuff shifted, revealing the gleaming stainless-steel watch on his left wrist.

He looked good, she thought. Exciting. Powerful and predatory and wholly in control. You'd never guess that he was suffering a bad case of burnout. But, then, what did burnout look like?

"Fine," she said. "I'll be ready."

She hurried toward the building's secured entrance and punched in the code. Gabe waited until she was safely inside the lobby before he drove off in the direction of his downtown office.

He was wrong to accuse her of being nervous about their relationship, she thought a few minutes later when she twisted the key in the lock of her apartment door. She had spoken the truth the other morning when she had tried to explain herself to him. They both needed to think things through. Neither one of them could trust their own judgment at the moment.

A man dealing with burnout was certainly not in the best position to make sound decisions regarding his personal relationships. As for herself, she had arrived at a major turning point in her life. Getting involved in an affair with a man who was going through his own emotional crisis was the last thing she needed.

Probably be best to write off that night at his cottage as an ill-advised one-night stand.

It all sounded so logical. Why did she feel depressed by her own clear reasoning?

She opened the door and walked into the apartment. They had made good time on the long drive from Eclipse Bay this morning. She had most of the day ahead of her to tidy up some of the loose ends that she had left dangling when she had rushed out of town a few days ago. She had a number of things on her agenda, not the least of which was deciding what to wear to the dinner tonight.

The atmosphere of the apartment had the closed-up feeling that accumulates quickly when a residence has been uninhabited for a few days. She walked through the rooms, cracking open windows to allow fresh air to circulate.

She did the living room first and then went down the hall to her bedroom. At the entrance, she paused. A tingle of eerie awareness drifted through her.

There was something different about the room. Something wrong.

She looked around with her artist's eye, noting the small details. The bedding was undisturbed. The closet doors were firmly closed. The dresser drawers were shut.

The closet doors were closed. Completely closed.

Her attention snapped back to the mirrored closet. She stared at it for a long time.

She was certain that she had left it partially ajar because of the way the slider got hung up when it was pushed fully closed.

Almost certain.

She had been in a hurry the other morning when she had left for Eclipse Bay, she reminded herself. Perhaps she had forced the door closed without thinking about it.

She crossed the room, gripped the handle and tried to open the slider. It stuck. Just as it had been sticking for the past two months. She took a firmer grasp, braced herself and forced it open.

The slider resisted for a few seconds and then reluctantly moved in its track. She stood back and surveyed the interior of her closet. The clothes on the hangers seemed to be in the same order they had been in when she had packed. The stack of plastic sweater boxes on the shelf looked untouched.

This was ridiculous. She was allowing her imagination to get carried away.

She reached for the handle of the slider again, intending to close the door. She went cold when she saw the smear on the mirrored glass at the far end next to the metal frame.

She allowed her hand to hover over the smear. It was right where the heel of a palm would rest if one were to take hold of the frame at the far end in an attempt to force the slider closed. But the mark was a little higher than one she would have left if she had grasped the frame.

Right about where a man or a woman a couple of inches taller than herself might put his or her palm.

She stepped back quickly.

Someone had been in this room.

Take deep breaths. Think about logical possibilities.

Burglary.

She whirled around, examining the scene once more. Nothing appeared to be missing.

She rushed back out into the living room and threw open the doors of the cabinet that housed her entertainment electronics. The expensive equipment was still safely stowed in place on the shelves.

She went cautiously down the hall to the small second bedroom that she used as a study. Halting in the doorway, she studied the interior. The most valuable item in this room was the art glass vase her parents had given her for her birthday last year. It glowed orange and red on the shelf near her desk.

She was definitely overreacting here. Maybe she was on edge because of the tension of dealing with Gabe.

More deep breaths. Other logical possibilities.

The cleaning people.

She had canceled the weekly appointments until further notice. But there could have been a mix-up about the dates. The cleaners had a key. Perhaps they had come in last Friday on the usual day.

It made sense. One of them might have tried to close the closet door. But surely a professional housecleaner would have wiped off the smear on the mirror?

Then again, perhaps the cleaner had been in a hurry and hadn't noticed the smudge.

The light winked on the phone, snapping her out of her reverie. Belatedly it occurred to her that she hadn't checked her messages during the time she had been away in Eclipse Bay. She pulled herself out of the doorway, crossed to the desk and punched in the code.

There had been two calls. Both had been received the night before last between ten and eleven o'clock. In each instance the caller had stayed on the line long enough for the beep to sound. But no one had left a message.

A shiver went through her. She listened to the long silence before the hangup and fancied she could hear the unknown caller breathing.

Logical possibilities.

Two wrong numbers in a row. People rarely left messages when they dialed a wrong number.

This was crazy. She needed to get a grip and fast.

She grabbed the phone and dialed the number of the agency that cleaned regularly. The answer to her question came immediately.

"Yes, we sent the crew in last Friday," the secretary said apologetically. "Sorry about the mix-up. We'll give you a free cleaning when you restart the service."

"No, that's all right. I just wanted to know if you had been into the apartment, that's all."

She put the phone down and waited for her heart to stop pounding. It took a while.

SHE did the little black dress bit for the dinner. The darkened hotel banquet room was filled to capacity with members of both the business and academic worlds. She sat at the head table, next to the wife of the guest of honor, and listened, fascinated, to Gabe's introductory remarks. She had known this event was important to him but she had not been prepared for the deep and very genuine warmth of his words.

". . . Like so many of you here tonight, I, too, was profoundly influenced by Dr. Montoya . . ."

He stood easily in front of the crowd, hands braced on either side of the podium frame, speaking without notes.

". . . I will never forget that memorable day in my senior year when Dr. Montoya called me into his office to discuss my first five-year plan, a plan which, in all modesty, I can only describe as visionary . . ."

Laughter interrupted him for a moment.

". . . 'Gabe,' Dr. Montoya said, 'with this plan, I sincerely doubt that you could attract enough venture capital to put up a lemonade stand . . .' "

The audience roared. Beneath the cover of applause, Dolores Montoya, a lively woman with silver-and-black hair, leaned over to whisper in Lillian's ear. "Thank goodness the committee chose Gabe to make the introduction. At this kind of event half the crowd is usually dozing by the time the guest of honor gets to the podium. At least he's keeping them awake."

Lillian did not avert her attention off Gabe. "Trust me, he won't let anyone fall asleep. This is important to him. I hadn't realized just how important until now."

"My husband has told me more than once that Gabe was the most determined student he ever had in the classroom," Delores told her.

At the podium, Gabe continued his remarks.

". . . I'm happy to say that I finally got my lemonade stand up and running . . ."

This understatement was greeted by more chuckles from the crowd. Likening Madison Commercial to a lemonade stand was somewhat on a par with comparing a rowboat to a nuclear submarine, Lillian thought.

". . . in large part because of what I learned from Dr. Montoya. But looking back, I can see that it wasn't just his nuts-and-bolts advice on how to survive market down-turns and nervous investors that I took with me when I left his classroom." Gabe paused for a beat. "He gave me something much deeper and more important. He gave me a sense of perspective . . ."

The crowd listened intently.

". . . Dr. Montoya gave me an understanding not only of how business works in a free country but of what we who make our living in business owe to our communities and our nation. He showed me the connections that bind us. He gave me a deep and lasting appreciation of what it takes to maintain the freedoms and the spirit that allows us to succeed. He taught me that none of us can make it in a vacuum. And for those teachings, I will always be grateful. I give you now, Dr. Roberto Montoya."

The gathering erupted once again as Dr. Montoya walked to the podium. This time the applause was led by Gabe. It metamorphosed into a standing ovation. Lillian got to her feet and clapped along with everyone else.

No wonder Dr. Montoya was important to Gabe, she thought. This was how a kid from a family that could not provide any successful male role models became one of the most successful men in the Northwest. He found himself someone who could teach him how to get ahead and he had paid attention.

"I'm the one who's supposed to be crying." Dolores handed her a tissue.

"Thanks." Lillian hastily blotted her tears, grateful that the lights were all focused on the podium.

The applause died away and the members of the audience took their seats again. The spotlight focused on Roberto Montoya. Gabe made his way back through the shadows to the chair beside Lillian. She felt his attention rest briefly on her profile and sensed his curiosity. She hoped he hadn't seen her dabbing at her eyes with the tissue.

He started to lean toward her, as if about to ask her what was wrong. Fortunately his attention was distracted a moment by Dr. Montoya, who had just launched into his own remarks.

"Before I get to the boring parts," Dr. Montoya said, "there is something I would like to clarify. I taught Gabriel Madison many things, but there is one thing I did not teach him." He paused to look toward the head table. "I did not teach him how to dress. That, he learned all on his own."

There was a startled silence and then the crowd howled with delight.

"Oh, hell," Gabe muttered, sounding both resigned and amused.

Dr. Montoya turned back to the audience. "Five years ago when I approached Gabe to try to talk him into participating in a program that would place college seniors in local businesses during their final semesters, he said—and I recall his exact words very clearly—he said, 'What the hell do you expect me to teach a bunch of kids about business that you can't teach them?' "

There was a short pause. Montoya leaned into the microphone.

" 'Teach 'em how to dress for success,' I said."

When the fresh wave of laughter had faded Montoya continued. "He took me seriously. Every semester when I send him the current crop of business students, he takes them to meet his tailor. What's more, he quietly picks up the tab for those who can't afford that first all-important business suit. Tonight, some of his protégés have prepared a small surprise to thank him for what he taught them."

The spotlight shifted abruptly to the far end of the stage. Two young men and a woman stood there. All three were dressed in identical steel-gray business suits, charcoal-gray shirts, and black-and-silver striped ties. All three had their hair combed straight back from their foreheads. Three sets of silver-and-onyx cuff links glinted in the light. Three stainless-steel watches glinted on three wrists.

The Gabe Madison clone on the right carried a box wrapped and tied in silver foil and black ribbon.

They walked forward in lockstep.

The audience broke out in another wave of laughter and applause.

Gabe dropped his face into his hands. "I will never live this down."

The young woman in the Gabe suit assumed control of the microphone. "We all owe Mr. Madison a debt of gratitude for the opportunities he provided to us during our semester at Madison Commercial. Most of us came from backgrounds where the unwritten rules of the business world were unknown. He taught us the secret codes. Gave us self-confidence. Opened doors. And, yes, he introduced us to his tailor and offered us some advice on how to dress."

One of the young men took charge of the microphone. "Tonight we would like to show our gratitude to Mr. Madison by giving him a helping hand with a concept that he has never fully grasped . . ."

The clone holding the silver foil box removed the lid with a flourish. The young woman reached inside and removed a scruffy-looking tee shirt, faded blue jeans, and a pair of well-worn running shoes.

". . . The concept of casual Fridays," the clone at the microphone concluded.

The banquet room exploded once again in laughter and applause. Gabe rose and walked back to the podium to accept his gift. He flashed a full laughing smile at the three clones.

It struck Lillian in that moment that Gabe looked like a man at the top of his game—a man who enjoyed the respect of his friends and rivals alike, a man who was comfortable with his own power in the business world, cool and utterly in control.

He sure didn't look like a man who was going through a bad case of burnout.

11

AN hour later Gabe bundled her into the Jag and made to close the passenger door. Impulse struck. She gave into it without examining the decision.

"Would you mind if we stopped at my studio on the way back to the apartment?" she said. "I forgot a few things this afternoon when I went there."

"Sure. No problem."

He closed the door, circled the car and paused long enough to remove his jacket. He put it down in the darkness of the backseat and got in behind the wheel. She gave him directions but she had the feeling that he already knew where he was going. He drove smoothly out of the parking garage and turned the corner.

A short time later he stopped at the curb in front of the brick building in which she rented studio space.

"This won't take long," she said.

"There's no rush."

He got out of the car and opened her door for her. She walked beside him to the secured entrance. He waited while she punched in the code.

They went up the stairs to the second-floor loft in silence. When she inserted her key into the lock she realized that her pulse was beating a little too quickly. A sense of anticipation mingled with unease quickened her breathing.

Why had she brought him here? she wondered. Where had the urge come from? What was the point of showing him the studio tonight? He was a businessman with no use for arty types.

She opened the door and groped for the switches on the wall to the right.

She flipped two of the six, turning on some of the lights but not all, leaving large sections of the loft in shadow.

Gabe surveyed the interior.

"So this is where you work." His voice was completely uninflected.

"Yes." She watched him prowl slowly forward, examining the canvases propped against the walls. "This is where I paint."

He stopped in front of a picture of her great-aunt Isabel. It showed her seated in a wicker chair in the solarium at Dreamscape, looking out to sea.

Gabe looked at the painting for a long time.

"I remember seeing that expression on Isabel's face sometimes," he said finally. Absently he loosened the knot in his tie and opened the collar of his shirt. He did not take his gaze off the picture. "As if she were looking at something only she could see."

Lillian crossed to the large worktable at the far end of the room, propped one hip on the edge and picked up a sketchpad and a pencil. "Everyone has that look from time to time. Probably because we all see something a little different when we look out at the world."

"Maybe."

He removed the silver-and-onyx cuff links and slid them into the pocket of his trousers. Again, his movements were casual and unself-conscious; the easy actions of a man relaxing after a formal evening.

He moved on to the next picture, rolling up the sleeves of the charcoal-gray shirt as he crossed the space, exposing the dark hair on the back of his arms.

She watched him for a moment. He looked rakish and extremely sexy with his tie undone and his shirt open at the throat. But what compelled her was the way he looked at her paintings. There was an intensity in him that told her that he made a visceral connection with the images she had created. He might not like the arty type but he responded to art. Unwillingly.

She began to draw, compelled by the shadows in her subject.

"You meant everything you said about Dr. Montoya tonight, didn't you?" she asked, not looking up from her work.

"He was the closest thing I had to a mentor." Gabe studied a picture of an old man sitting on a bench in the park. "I was a kid from a small town. I didn't know how to handle myself. Didn't know what was appropriate. I had no polish. No sophistication. No connections. I knew where I wanted to go but I didn't know how to get there. He gave me a lot of the tools I needed to build Madison Commercial."

"Now you repay him by allowing him to send some of his students into Madison Commercial every year."

"The company gets something out of it, too. The students bring a lot of energy and enthusiasm with them. And we get first crack at some bright new talent."

"Really? I've heard my father talk about what a nuisance student interns are for a busy company. They can be a real pain."

"Not everyone is cut out to work in a corporation."

Her pencil stilled for an instant. "Me, for instance."

He nodded. "You, for instance. And apparently your sister and brother, too. You've all got strong, independent, entrepreneurial streaks. You're all ambitious and you're all talented but you don't play well with others. At least not in a business setting."

"And you think you're so very different? Give me a break. Tell me something, Gabe, if you were only a vice-president instead of the owner, president, and CEO of Madison Commercial, would you still be on the company payroll?"

There was a short pause.

"No," he said. Flat and final.

"You said that not everyone is cut out to work in a large corporation." She moved the pencil swiftly, adding shadows. "But not everyone is cut out to run one, either. You were born for it, weren't you?"

He pulled his attention away from a canvas and looked at her down the length of the studio. "Born for it? That's a new one. Most people would say I was born to self-destruct before the age of thirty."

"You've got the natural talent for leadership and command that it takes to organize people and resources to achieve an objective." She hunched one shoulder a little, concentrating on the angle of his jaw. Going for the darkness behind his eyes. "In your own way, you're an artist. You can make folks *see* your objective, make them want to get there with you. No wonder you were able to get that initial funding you needed for Madison Commercial. You probably walked into some venture capitalist's office and painted him a glowing picture of how much money he would make if he backed you."

Gabe did not move. "Talking her out of the venture capital funds I needed wasn't the hard part."

She glanced up sharply, her curiosity pricked by his words.

"Her?" she repeated carefully.

"Your great-aunt Isabel is the one who advanced me the cash I needed to get Madison Commercial up and running."

She almost fell from her perch on the worktable.

"You're kidding." She held the point of the pencil in the air, poised above the paper. "*Isabel* backed you?"

"Yes."

"She never said a word about it to any of us."

He shrugged. "That was the way she wanted it."

She contemplated that news.

"Amazing," she said at last. "Everyone knew that it was her dream to end the Harte-Madison feud. Hannah figures that's the reason she left Dreamscape equally to her and your brother in the will. But why would she back you financially? What would that have to do with ending the old quarrel?"

"I think she felt that the Madisons got the short end of the stick when Harte-Madison went into bankruptcy. She wanted to level the playing field a little for Rafe and me."

"But when Harte-Madison was destroyed all those years ago, everyone lost everything. Both the Hartes and the Madisons went bankrupt. That's about as level as it gets."

"Your family recovered a lot faster than mine did."

He concentrated on the painting in front of him. "I think we both know why. So did Isabel."

She flushed. There was no denying that the tough, stable Harte family bonds, not to mention the Harte work ethic and emphasis on education, had provided a much stronger foundation from which to recover than the shaky, shifting grounds that had sustained the Madisons.

"Point taken," she agreed. "So Isabel, in her own quiet way, tried to even things up a bit with money."

"I think so, yes."

"What was the hard part?"

"The hard part?"

"You said that getting the backing from her for Madison Commercial wasn't the hard part. What was?"

His mouth curved reminiscently. "Structuring the contract so that Isabel got her money back plus interest and profit. She didn't want to do things that way. She wanted me to take the cash as a straight gift."

"But you wouldn't do that."

"No."

Madison pride, she thought, but she did not say it out loud. She went back to work on her drawing. Gabe moved on to another picture.

"I was wrong about you, wasn't I?" She used the tip of her thumb to smudge in a shadow.

"Wrong?"

"Watching you at the banquet tonight, it finally hit me that I had leaped to a totally false conclusion about you. And you let me do it. You never bothered to correct my assumption."

He gave her his enigmatic smile. "Hard to imagine a Harte being wrong about a Madison. You know us so well."

"Yes, we do. Which is why I shouldn't have been fooled for even a minute. But I was."

"What was the wrong conclusion you leaped to about me?"

She looked up from the sketch and met his eyes. "You aren't suffering from burnout."

He said nothing, just watched her steadily.

"Why didn't you set me straight?" She returned to her sketch, adding more depths and darkness. "Because it suited your purpose to let me think you were a victim of stress and burnout? Did you want me to feel sorry for you?"

"No." He started toward her down a dim aisle formed by unframed canvases. "No, I sure as hell did not want you to feel sorry for me."

"What did you want?" Her pencil flashed across the paper, moving as though by its own volition as she worked frantically to capture the impressions and get them down in all the shades of light and dark.

He came to a halt in front of her. "I wanted you to see me as something other than a cold-blooded machine. I figured that if you thought I was a walking case of burnout, you might realize that I was human."

She studied the sketch for a moment and then slowly put down the pencil. "I've always known that you were human," she said.

"You sure about that? I had a somewhat different impression. Must have been all those comments you made about how I wanted to date robots."

He reached for the sketchpad. She let him take it from her fingers, watching his expression as he looked at the drawing she had made of him.

It showed him as he had appeared a few minutes ago, standing in front of one of her canvases, his hands thrust easily into the pockets of his trousers, collar and cuffs undone, tie loose around his neck. He stood in the shadows, his face slightly averted from the viewer. He was intent on the painting in front of him, a picture that showed an image that only he could see. Whatever he saw there deepened the shadows around him.

She watched his face as he studied the drawing. She knew from the way his jaw tightened and the fine lines that appeared at the corners of his mouth that he understood the shadows in the picture.

After what seemed like an eternity, he handed the sketch back to her.

"Okay," he said. "So you do see me as human."

"And you saw what I put into this drawing, didn't you?"

He shrugged. "Hard to miss."

"A lot of people could look at this sketch and not see anything other than a figure standing in front of a canvas. But you see everything." She waved a hand at the canvases that filled the studio. "You can see what I put into all of my pictures. You pretend to disdain art but the truth is you respond to it."

"I spent a lot of the first decade of my life in an artist's studio. Guess you pick up a few things when you're surrounded by the stuff during your impressionable years."

"Yes, of course. Your father was a sculptor. Your mother was his model." She put the sketch down on the worktable. Guilt and dismay shot through her. "I'm sorry, Gabe. I know you lost your parents when you were very young. I didn't mean to bring up such a painful subject."

"Forget it. It's a fact, after all, not something you conjured up out of your imagination. Besides, I thought I made it clear that I don't want you to feel sorry for me. Sort of spoils the Harte-Madison feud dynamic, you know?"

"Right. Wouldn't want to do that." She hesitated. "Gabe?"

"Yeah?"

"When you stated on the Private Arrangements questionnaire that you didn't want any arty types, you were telling the truth, weren't you?"

"I thought we'd decided that I pretty much lied through my teeth on that questionnaire."

"I don't think you lied on that issue. Did you make a point of not wanting to be matched with so-called arty types because of your parents? Everyone knows that they didn't give you and Rafe what anyone could call a stable home life."

He was silent for a moment.

"For years I blamed most of what wasn't good in my childhood, including my parents' deaths, on the fact that they were both involved in the world of art," he said finally. "Maybe, in my kid brain, the mystique of the wild, uncontrolled, temperamental, artistic personality was convenient. Better than the alternative, at any rate."

"What was the alternative?"

"That we Madisons were seriously flawed; that we couldn't manage the self-control thing."

"But you've proved that theory wrong, haven't you? I've never met anyone with more self-control."

He looked at her. "You don't exactly fit the image of the temperamental, self-centered artist who has no room in her life for anything except her art, either."

"Okay. I think we've successfully established that neither of us fits whatever preconceptions we might have had."

"Why did you bring me here tonight, Lillian? I know it wasn't because you needed to pick up some supplies."

She looked around at her paint-spattered studio. "Maybe I wanted to find out how you really felt about arty types."

He raised one hand and traced the cowl neckline of her black dress. His finger grazed her throat. "Let's see where we stand here. We've established that you don't think I'm a machine."

She caught her breath at his touch. "And you don't think I'm typical of what you call the arty type."

"Where does that leave us?"

"I don't know," she whispered.

He lowered his head until his mouth hovered just above hers. "I think we ought to find out, don't you?"

"Sex is probably not the best way to explore that issue."

He kissed her slowly, lingeringly. When he raised his head she saw the hunger in him. She felt her blood heat.

"Can you think of a better way to explore it?" he asked.

She swallowed. "Not right at the moment."

He put one hand on her knee just beneath the hem of the little black dress. He smiled slowly and eased the skirt higher. She caught the ends of his silk tie in her hands and drew him closer.

He took the invitation the way a shark takes prey: smoothly and swiftly, leaving her no time to consider the wisdom of moving back into shallower waters.

Between one heartbeat and the next, he was between her knees, using his thighs to part her legs and open her to him. The black dress was up to her hips now, leaving only a scrap of midnight-colored lace as a barrier to his hand. It proved woefully inadequate to the task. She felt the silk grow damp at his touch.

She gripped the ends of the necktie and hung on for the ride.

HE roused himself a long time later, sated and content. For the moment, at any rate. He sat up on the edge of the worktable. Beside him Lillian was curled amid scattered sheets of drawing paper, brushes, and tubes of paint. Her hair had come free from the sleek knot in which it had been arranged earlier in the evening. The little black dress that had looked so elegant and tasteful at the head table was now crumpled in an extremely interesting, very sexy and no doubt less-than-tasteful manner. But it looked terrific on her that way, he thought.

His tie was now looped around her throat instead of his own. He grinned, remembering how it had gotten switched in the middle of the lovemaking.

She stirred. "What are you staring at?"

"A work of art."

"Hmm." She nodded once in appreciation. "A work of art. That was pretty quick, Madison."

"Pretty quick, you mean for a man who is still recovering from a truly mind-blowing experience?"

"Gosh. Was that your mind?" Her smile was very smug. "I didn't realize."

He grinned. "I handed you that line on a platter. Admit it."

"I admit it. You're good, you know that?"

"At the moment, I'm a lot better than good." He leaned down to kiss her bare hip. "I'm terrific. What about you?"

"I think I'll survive." She hauled herself up on her elbows and surveyed herself. "But the dress is dead meat."

"I'm sure there are plenty more where it came from."

"Probably. Department stores are full of little black dresses." She noticed the tie around her neck and frowned. "How did that get there?"

He eased himself off the table, stood and stretched. "Some questions are better left unanswered."

He studied a canvas propped against the wall directly across from him as he zipped his trousers and buckled his belt. It was another one of her unique, riveting creations, all hot, intense light and dark, disturbing shadows. He felt it reaching out to pull him into that world, just as her other works did. He had to force himself to look away from it.

He turned his head and saw that the sensual, teasing laughter that had gleamed in her eyes a moment ago had evaporated. She was watching him in the same way that he had looked at the painting, as if she were wary of being sucked into his universe.

"Does this mean we're having an affair?" she asked.

Curious. Polite. Very cool. Just asking.

Her deliberately casual air wiped out a lot of the satisfaction that he had been enjoying. Whatever was going on here was a long way from settled.

"Yes," he said. "I think we'd better call this an affair. I don't see that we have any real choice."

She sat up slowly and dangled her legs off the edge of the worktable. "Why is that?"

She had small, delicate ankles and beautifully arched feet, he noticed. Her toenails were painted scarlet. And here he'd never considered himself a foot man.

He walked back to the table, fitted his hands to her waist, lifted her and set her on her feet. He did not release her. "Be sort of awkward to have to admit that we're into one- and two-night stands, wouldn't it?"

"Might make us both look extremely shallow and superficial."

"Can't have that," he said easily. "Come on, let's go back to your apartment. We need some sleep. Got a long drive back to Eclipse Bay tomorrow morning."

12

A deceptively bright sun supplied light but very little heat to Eclipse Bay. Small whitecaps snapped and sparkled on the water. The brisk breeze promised another storm soon. They drove through the community's small business district on the way back to the cottage. Lillian noticed that the handful of men standing around a truck at the town's only gas station were huddled into goose-down vests and heavy windbreakers.

Sandy Hickson, the owner of the station, spotted Gabe's car and waved a casual greeting. His companions turned to glance at the vehicle. Even from where she sat, Lillian thought she could see the open speculation in their eyes.

A Harte and a Madison could not even drive through Eclipse Bay together without drawing interested gazes.

"Small town," Gabe said. He sounded completely unruffled by the attention.

"Very."

"Not like there's a heck of a lot to do around here in the middle of winter. It's almost like we've got a social obligation to bring a little excitement to town."

"Since when did Madisons worry about their social obligations?"

"Since we started hanging out more with you Hartes. You're a bad influence on us."

She noticed the illuminated message indicator on the answering machine when she walked into the Harte family cottage a short time later.

Gabe saw it, too. "Got a hunch Mitchell ratted us out."

"Looks that way. Probably my mother. Great." She put down the carton of painting supplies she had carried in from the car. "I'll deal with it later."

"Thought you said your folks were on a business trip in San Diego."

"They are. But you know as well as I do that gossip travels fast among the Hartes and the Madisons, especially since the wedding."

"Well, we both knew we wouldn't be able to keep this a secret. And it's not as if we're not all adults here."

He sounded a little too philosophical, she thought. Downright upbeat, in fact. As if the prospect of explaining away a red-hot affair between a Harte and a Madison was no big deal. Just a walk in the park.

"Yeah, right," she said. "We're all adults here."

He set her suitcase in the hall and looked at her, brows raised in polite inquiry. "Need backup?"

"From a Madison? That would be like pouring oil on a burning fire."

"We Madisons are good at that."

"I'll remember that the next time I'm trying to start a blaze instead of putting one out."

"This is going to be a tough fire to put out," he said softly.

She did not know if she ought to take that as a warning or just another teasing remark. Upon brief reflection, she decided it would be best to assume the latter.

"I'm an adult," she said. "I make my own decisions. My parents know that."

"Uh-huh." He looked unconvinced but he turned to walk toward the door. "Well, if you don't need my assistance in pacifying your mother, I'll be on my way. See you for dinner."

He said it with such breathtaking casualness, she thought. Taking the concept of dinner together for granted. The unspoken expectation of spending the night was very clear. He was moving right into her daily routine, making himself comfortable.

Well? They had both agreed that they were starting an affair, hadn't they? Why the sudden qualms?

But the answer was there in the next heartbeat. For all her fine talk of being a grown-up, the bottom line here was that getting involved with Gabe was a dangerous business.

"Why don't we go out tonight?" she said on sudden impulse.

Dining out in public would be more like a date. She could handle a date with him. Dates were more structured, more ritualized. They were not infused with quite the same degree of casual intimacy as cooking dinner together and eating it at the kitchen table. A date allowed her to keep a little distance. So what if they went back to his place later and made wild, passionate love. Some people did that after a date. Or so she had heard.

"Fine."

Something told her that he had guessed what was going through her mind. But he did not argue. Instead, he walked out onto the porch.

"I'll pick you up. Six-thirty okay?"

"I can meet you at your place." She went to stand in the doorway. "It's a short walk."

"No. It'll be dark. I don't want you walking alone after dark."

"There's nothing to worry about. We're not exactly crime central around here. Especially in the dead of winter."

"Eclipse Bay isn't the same town it was when you and I were kids. It's not just the summer tourists who cause trouble around here now. Chamberlain College is expanding and so is the institute. I'd rather you didn't stroll around on your own after the sun goes down."

She propped one shoulder against the door frame, amused, and crossed her arms. "Are you always this bossy?"

"I'm cautious, not bossy."

"And maybe a tad inclined to be overcontrolling?"

"Sure, but hey, isn't everyone?" He brushed his mouth across hers. "Humor me, okay?"

"Okay. This time."

He nodded, satisfied, and went down the steps. "See you later. Good luck with your painting."

"What are you going to do this afternoon?"

He paused and looked back over his shoulder. "I'm going to go online to do some deep background research on a potential Madison Commercial client. Why?"

She made a face. "Have fun."

"I thought I explained to you that what I do at M.C. is called work, not fun." He gave her his slow, sexy Madison smile. "Fun comes later, after work. I'll show you."

He walked to the Jag, opened the door and got behind the wheel.

Back at the beginning she had made the mistake of assuming that he was a victim of burnout because he claimed that running Madison Commercial was not fun for him. In one sense, she thought, he was right. But work wasn't the correct label, either, although it was the one he preferred. The truth was, Madison Commercial was his passion.

Passion wasn't fun. Passion was serious stuff.

She had always understood that distinction intuitively when it came to her painting. Now she was starting to understand it about her relationship with Gabe, as well. Serious stuff.

She went back into the house, closed the door and crossed to the phone to listen to her messages. There were two, she noticed. The first was, as she had expected, from her mother.

Might as well get this over with fast. She braced herself and dialed the number of the hotel room in San Diego.

We're all adults here.

Elaine Harte answered on the second ring. In typical maternal fashion, she did not take long to come to the point.

"What in the world is going on up there in Eclipse Bay?" she asked without preamble.

"Long story."

"Your grandfather phoned yesterday. He and your father talked for a very long time. It was not what anyone would call a cheerful, lighthearted conversation. I haven't heard those two go at it like that in years. Sullivan says that you've closed Private Arrangements for good. Is that true?"

"Yes."

"But, darling, why?" Elaine's voice rose in that practiced wail of dismay that is unique to mothers around the world. "You were doing so well."

Elaine did not actually add *at last* but it was there, silently tacked on to the end of the sentence.

"You know why, Mom."

There was a short silence, then Elaine sighed.

"Your painting," she said.

The whining tone had vanished from her voice as if by magic, Lillian noticed. Smart moms also knew when to abandon a tactic that no longer worked.

"I've been thinking about this for a long time, Mom. I need to see if I can make it happen."

"Can't you keep Private Arrangements going while you find out if you can make a living with art? You've always painted in the evenings and on weekends."

Lillian flopped down on the sofa and stacked her heels on the coffee table. "I feel that the time has come to put my art at the top of my agenda. I need to concentrate on it. The fact is, after a full day at Private Arrangements, I'm tired, Mom. I don't have a lot of energy left for my work."

My *work*. She was using the word, herself, she realized, mildly astonished. The same way Gabe used it, to describe the important thing that she did. Painting wasn't a hobby. It wasn't fun. It wasn't entertainment. It was her passion.

"And if the painting doesn't go well?" Elaine said. "Will you reopen Private Arrangements? You still have your program and your client list, don't you?"

"I can't think about that now, Mom. I have to stay focused."

"You sound just like your father and your grandfather when you say things like that." Elaine hesitated and then probed further. "Sullivan told your father something else. He said that you and Gabe Madison are seeing each other . . . socially."

Lillian laughed in spite of the tension. "I'll bet he said a lot more than that."

Elaine cleared her throat. "I believe he used the phrase 'shacking up together.' "

"I *knew* it." Lillian took her heels off the table and sat up on the edge of the sofa. "Mitchell Madison did squeal to Granddad. Interesting that he went straight to Sullivan with the news, isn't it? I wonder why he did that."

There was another brief pause.

"So it's true?" Elaine asked, her voice grim.

"Afraid so." Lillian hunched around the phone in her hand. "But I prefer the phrase 'seeing each other socially' to 'shacking up together.' "

"Men of Mitchell's and Sullivan's age have a different view of these matters. And a different vocabulary to describe them."

"Guess so."

"If you don't mind my asking, how does Gabe describe your, uh, relationship?"

We're all adults here.

"I haven't actually asked him that question. Not in so many words. Look,

Mom, I know you mean well, but this conversation is getting a bit personal. I'm perfectly capable of handling my own private life."

"When Hartes and Madisons get together in Eclipse Bay, there is no such thing as a private life," Elaine said.

"Okay, I'll give you that. But I'm still capable of dealing with things here."

"You're sure?"

"Of course, I'm sure. Mom, I'm not in high school anymore. Or even college, for that matter. I've been getting by out there in the big bad world all on my own for quite a while now."

"You haven't had to deal with the complications of having a Madison in your life."

"Gabe is a different kind of Madison, remember? He's the one who made it through college and built a very successful business. When I was a kid, I recall Dad saying that Gabe was the one Madison who proved the exception to the rule that all Madisons were bound to come to a bad end."

"Yes, dear, I know." Another short silence hummed on the line. "But between you and me, Gabe was the one I worried about the most."

That stopped Lillian cold. "You did?"

Elaine was quiet for a moment. Lillian could almost hear her thinking about the past.

"I wasn't the only one who was concerned about him," Elaine said eventually. "Isabel and I discussed him often. Even as a little boy, Gabe always seemed too self-contained, too controlled. He never lost his temper, never got in trouble at school. Always got good grades. It just wasn't natural."

"You mean for a Madison?"

"No, I mean for a little boy. Any little boy."

"Oh."

"It was as if he always had his own private agenda. Looking back, I can see that he must have been driven, even then, by his vision of building a business empire."

"I think you're right," Lillian said. "He needed to prove something to himself. But he accomplished his goal."

"People who are compelled by a lifelong ambition do not change, even after it appears to everyone else around them that they have achieved that ambition. In my experience they remain driven. It's a deeply imbedded characteristic."

A Madison and his passion.

"Mom, listen, I really don't—"

"I don't want to intrude on your personal life, but I *am* your mother."

"I know." Lillian sighed. "You gotta do what a mom's gotta do."

"I think you should assume that nothing has changed with Gabe."

"What?"

"Madison Commercial was always the most important thing in his life. It still is. If anything, all that single-minded determination and willpower he used to get to where he is today has only become more honed through the years."

"Meaning?"

"Meaning," Elaine said bluntly, "that if he has decided to see you socially, as you call it, he very likely has a reason."

She felt her stomach tighten. "Is this where you tell me that the only thing Gabe wants from me is sex?"

"No." Elaine paused. "To be frank, I expect that, given his money and position, Gabe can get as much of that as he wants."

Lillian winced. She had a feeling her mother was right. "Please don't tell me that you think he's getting some sort of perverse satisfaction out of having an intimate relationship with a Harte. I refuse to believe that he's so warped or so immature that he sees seducing me as a form of one-upsmanship."

"No."

She felt her stomach unknot. "He wouldn't stoop to such a thing just to score points off a Harte. Heck, his brother is married to one now. Even Granddad couldn't possibly believe——"

"No," Elaine said again, soothing now but firm. "I don't think Gabe would seduce you just to score points in that ridiculous old feud. He's a long-term strategist, not a short-term opportunist."

She let herself relax a little more. "So, what are you trying to say, Mom?"

"I just want you to be careful, dear. Your father and I have been talking a lot lately. It is clear that Harte Investments will have to be sold or merged when Hamilton retires in a couple of years. None of you three kids wants to take over the company, nor does your father want you to feel that you must."

"I know. He's been great about not pressuring us."

"Lord knows he experienced enough pressure when he was your age. He refuses to put any of you through it, regardless of what Sullivan wants."

"What?" Lillian froze. "Are you telling me that the only reason Dad took over Harte Investments was because Granddad pressured him to do it?"

"In the years following the breakup of Harte-Madison, your grandfather put everything he had into building Harte Investments. It was always understood that Hamilton would be his heir apparent. Your father went along with Sullivan's dreams but they were never really his dreams."

"I see."

Lillian got to her feet and stood in front of the window, the phone clutched very tightly in her hand. She looked out at the white ripples on the bay and knew a strange sense of sudden understanding. It was as if a veil had been pulled back. She had just gotten a fleeting glimpse of a piece of family history that she had never even suspected existed.

"Hamilton did not want any of you three to feel you had to live someone else's dreams," Elaine said. "He made that clear to your grandfather years ago."

"Dad took the heat for us? I always wondered why Granddad didn't make a bigger issue out of the fact that none of us showed much interest in Harte Investments. We all thought that Sullivan had just mellowed with the years."

"Fat chance." Elaine gave a soft, ladylike snort. "Your father went toe-to-toe with Sullivan more than once over that issue. He warned your grandfather that he would not permit any of you three to be coerced into turning the company into a family dynasty. Hamilton wanted each of you to feel free to choose your own paths in life."

"But Dad never felt that he, himself, had that option?"

"Not in the early days," Elaine said. "But things have changed. Hamilton and I agree now that life is simply too short to spend it maintaining someone else's vision. Your father has plans for his future and he's going after it with both hands. Sullivan has called the shots in this family long enough. He can do whatever he wants with Harte Investments. Hamilton and I are cutting loose."

There was no mistaking the steely satisfaction and determination in her mother's voice. This was, Lillian thought, a whole new side of Elaine.

"You're talking about the charitable foundation you two plan to set up, aren't you?" Lillian asked.

"Yes. Your father can't wait to get started on it."

"I see." Lillian blinked away the moisture that was blurring her view of the bay. "Guess Hannah and Nick and I all owe Dad big-time for keeping Sullivan off our backs, huh?"

"Yes, you do," Elaine said pointedly. "But that's not the issue here. What I want you to understand is that Gabe Madison is one very smart, very savvy CEO. Rumors travel like wildfire in his world. He has to be aware of the situation at Harte Investments. He must know very well that the company probably won't continue as a privately held family business much longer."

"So what?"

"I suspect he's working on the assumption that H.I. will either be merged or sold soon. But if he marries you—"

"*Stop.*" Lillian could hardly breathe. "Stop right there. Don't say it, Mom. Please don't tell me that he's sleeping with me just because he thinks he can get his hands on a third of Harte Investments that way."

There was a heavily freighted pause on the other end of the line.

"He'd have to do more than sleep with you to get his hands on a large piece of the company," Elaine said finally. "He'd have to marry you to accomplish that goal, wouldn't he?"

Through the window Lillian could see that another new storm was moving in quickly. The winds were snapping and snarling beneath the eaves of the cottage. An ominous haze was forming out on the bay. The water was turning steel gray.

"Look on the bright side, Mom. Gabe hasn't said a word about marriage. I have it on good authority that, when you get right down to it, I'm not his type."

SHE went through the motions of making a pot of tea while she dealt with the floodtide of restless thoughts that cluttered her brain after she hung up the phone. By the time the water boiled, she had managed to regain some perspective.

Get a grip, she told herself as she poured the brewed green tea into a cup. What she had said to her mother was true. Gabe had not even hinted at marriage.

He seemed quite satisfied with the prospect of having an affair with her, but that appeared to be his only goal.

On the other hand, she did not have a great track record when it came to applying her intuitive abilities to Gabe Madison. For some reason, her normally reliable sensors always seemed to get scrambled when it came to analyzing his vibes. Until last night, for example, she had been laboring under the assumption that the man was suffering a severe case of burnout.

She wandered into her studio, mug in hand, and looked at the blank canvas propped on the easel. She had come here to Eclipse Bay to paint, but thus far she had done little more than unpack her paints and brushes. She had made some sketches but she had not done any serious work. The relationship with Gabe was proving to be a huge distraction.

She fiddled with a pencil for a while, doing a little drawing, trying to get into the zone where the vision of the picture took shape around her, forming an alternate universe.

But she couldn't concentrate, so she headed back toward the kitchen to refill her tea mug.

She saw the light on the telephone answering machine when she was halfway across the living room. Belatedly she remembered that there had been two messages. She had only listened to the one from her mother.

She changed course to play the second message.

". . . This is Mitchell Madison. We gotta talk."

Just what she needed to round out her day and ensure that she got absolutely no painting done whatsoever.

THAT afternoon, she walked into Mitchell Madison's garden and looked around with interest. She had heard about this fantasyland of lush ferns, exotic herbs, and exuberant roses for as long as she could recall. For years it had been generally accepted in Eclipse Bay that Mitchell's garden was far and away the most spectacular in town. Even now, in the heart of winter when all of the blooms had disappeared, it was an earthly paradise. But, then, they said gardening was Mitchell's passion and everyone knew how it was with a Madison and his passion.

She followed the graveled path that led past banks of thriving ferns and through a maze of exquisitely maintained plant beds. The recent rains had released rich scents from the ground. At the far end of the walk a large greenhouse loomed. She could see a shadowy figure moving behind the opaque walls.

She opened the door and stepped into the fragrant, humid warmth. Mitchell was working intently over some clay pots arranged on a waist-high bench. He had a pair of small shears in one hand and a tiny trowel in the other. The pockets of his heavy-duty, dirt-stained apron were filled with gardening implements. He appeared to be totally engrossed in his plants.

"I got your message, Mr. Madison," she said from the doorway.

Mitchell looked up quickly, gray brows bristling above his fierce, aquiline nose. "There you are. Come in and close the door. It's cold out there today."

She stepped farther into the greenhouse, allowing the door to swing shut. "You made it sound urgent. Is something wrong?"

"Shoot and damn, 'course there's something wrong." He put down the shears and the trowel and stripped off his gloves. "I turned this thing over to Sullivan but as far as I can see, he hasn't done a blame thing to straighten up this mess. Looks like I'll have to take a hand."

"Situation?"

"First things first. You serious about Gabe or are you just havin' yourself some fun?"

She came to an abrupt halt. This was going to be worse than she imagined. For an instant she was afraid the thick air would suffocate her. With an effort of will, she managed to resist the temptation to flee back outside.

"I beg your pardon?"

"Don't play games with me, young woman. You know what I'm talkin' about here. If you're fixin' to break Gabe's heart, I want to find out now."

"Me? Break Gabe's heart?" From out of nowhere, anger surged through her. "What makes you think that's even a remote possibility?"

Madison gave a muffled snort. "You've got him in the palm of your hand and you know it. Question is, what are you gonna do about it?"

"That's ridiculous. Just because we're seeing a lot of each other—"

"Seeing each other? Huh. Appears to me that the two of you are doin' a heck of a lot more than just lookin' at each other. You think no one would notice if you just up and ran off to Portland together for a night? Shoot and damn, you aren't even trying to keep things a secret."

"You know as well as I do that you can't control gossip here in Eclipse Bay."

"When I was your age most folks had the common decency to do their foolin' around out of sight."

He was genuinely irate, she realized, as if this mess were somehow all her fault. His bad temper only served to inflame her own.

"That's not what I hear, Mr. Madison. The way my folks tell it, you were more than a little obvious about your fooling around back in the good old days. In fact, Madisons in general are notorious for keeping the gossip mills humming here in Eclipse Bay."

"Times change. Things are different now."

"The fact that things are different now doesn't change the past."

"We're talking about Gabe." Mitchell planted his hands on his hips. "He's a different kind of Madison."

"People keep saying that, but how do I know if it's true?"

"You're gonna have to take my word for it."

She smiled coldly. "Now why would I do that?"

"Look, I can see where you might not be able to figure him out. Gabe's a little complicated."

"A *little* complicated. That's putting it mildly."

"The important thing here is that I don't want him hurt. If you're not serious about him, I want you to break it off now before he gets in any deeper."

"Just because we're *seeing* each other," she said through her teeth, "it does not necessarily follow that your grandson is in love with me."

"If the two of you were just bouncing around together in a bed in Portland, that would be one thing. I wouldn't pay any attention. But Gabe left Madison Commercial to follow you here to Eclipse Bay. That means he's serious."

"Good grief, you make it sound like the company's his wife and I'm the other woman."

Mitchell nodded. "That's not too far off, when you think about it."

"Look, for the record, Gabe did not leave Madison Commercial for me." She spread her hands. "He's just taking a little vacation, that's all."

"Bullshit. 'Scuse my language. Gabe doesn't take vacations. Leastways, not monthlong ones. He walked out on M.C. because he lost his head over you. That's the only explanation."

"A very romantic notion but that's not what happened. Furthermore, there are any number of people around these parts and several in my own family who will be only too happy to tell you what they believe is the real reason he took a month off from Madison Commercial."

"And just what the heck do they figure that real reason is?"

"I'm sure you've heard the talk. The gossip in certain quarters is that Gabe wants to marry me in order to get his hands on a large piece of Harte Investments."

Mitchell stared at her in astonishment. He looked genuinely thunderstruck. "Are you crazy, woman? Madisons don't marry for money."

"Maybe most Madisons don't marry for money. But everyone has always claimed that Gabe is a different kind of Madison."

Mitchell snorted. "Not that different."

"Look, we all know that Madison Commercial is the most important thing in Gabe's life. It's his creation. Over the years, he has sacrificed for it, fought for it, nurtured it. Why wouldn't he be attracted to someone who could add significantly to his empire?"

"If he'd been the type to marry for money, he'd have married Marilyn Thornley all those years ago. Her family has plenty of cash."

She frowned. "I was under the impression that they broke up because Marilyn ditched him for Thornley, not because Gabe didn't want to marry her."

"Shoot and damn. Can't you figure it out for yourself? They split on accounta Gabe made it clear that Madison Commercial was more important to him than she was. That woman likes to be number one."

"So do I, Mr. Mitchell."

"You're a Harte. You understand about business coming first."

"No, as a matter of fact, I do not."

"Sure you do. Look, you know damn well you've got Gabe's full, undivided attention and that means things are dead serious. At least they are for him. What I want to know is, how do you feel about Gabe? You willing to get married?"

She took a step back and groped for the doorknob with one hand. "Mr. Madison, this discussion is purely hypothetical. For your information, the subject of marriage has never come up between Gabe and me."

"Looks like it will. And pretty damn quick, too, if I know Gabe. He didn't get where he is by letting grass grow under his feet."

"I really don't think so, Mr. Madison." She found the doorknob and wrapped her fingers around it very tightly, using it to steady herself. "For the record, Gabe has made it very clear that he does not want to marry what he refers to as an arty type. If you will recall, I'm an artist. That sort of takes me out of the running, don't you think?"

"Nah. Not with a Madison. Madisons aren't that logical when it comes to love."

She had to get out of here. She was ready to explode. "Let me make something clear. If, and I repeat, if, Gabe ever brought up the subject of marriage, I would want to know that I was more important to him than just another addition to his empire."

"And just how the hell is he supposed to prove that?"

"Beats me. That's not my problem. It's Gabe's. Assuming you're right, of course, which is highly doubtful."

"Shoot and damn, if that isn't just like a Harte. Askin' for hard evidence when it comes to something that's downright impossible to prove." Mitchell leveled a finger at her. "Know what I think? I think you've just decided to play with him a little. You're havin' yourself some fun, aren't you? You're not serious about him."

She had the door open now but something in his voice made her pause on the threshold. "You're really worried about him, aren't you?"

"Got a right to worry about him. He's my grandson, damn it. I may not have done the best job of raising him and Rafe after their parents died, but I did what I could to make things right. I got a responsibility to Gabe. I got to look out for him."

She searched his face. "He has the impression that you don't care that he's made a success of Madison Commercial."

" 'Course I care," Mitchell roared. "I'm proud of what he's done with that company. He proved to you Hartes and the whole damn world that a Madison can make somethin' of himself. He proved that a Madison who sets his mind to it can get his act together, that being a member of this family doesn't mean you're doomed to screw up everything you touch the way I did and the way his father did."

There was a short, hard silence.

"Did you ever tell him that?" Lillian asked softly. "Because I think he needs to hear it."

Mitchell's mouth opened again but this time no words emerged.

She turned and walked out into the garden.

GABE dunked a clam strip into the spicy red sauce. "Heard you went out to the house to see Mitchell this afternoon."

Lillian started a little. The fork in her hand trembled slightly. She clenched her fingers around it and stabbed at the mound of coleslaw on her plate.

"Who told you that?" she asked.

Stalling, he thought. Why? What the hell was going on here?

This morning when they had left Portland together he had been feeling good. More settled. Like he finally had a handle on this relationship. He had assured himself that various issues had been clarified.

He and Lillian were having an affair. They both agreed on that. Couldn't get much simpler or more straightforward than that.

But now that they were back in Eclipse Bay, everything was starting to get complicated again.

He pondered that while he listened to the background hum of conversations and the clatter of dishes and silverware. The Crab Trap was a noisy, cheerful place. Until Rafe and Hannah got Dreamscape open, it was the closest thing to fine dining that Eclipse Bay could offer. It boasted a view of the bay, actual tablecloths and little candles in old Chianti bottles. On prom night and Mother's Day it was always fully booked.

It had seemed the obvious choice for dinner tonight.

A little too obvious, he had realized a few minutes ago when Marilyn Thornley had walked in with a small entourage and occupied the large booth at the rear.

"Ran into Bryce at the gas station." Gabe put the clam strip into his mouth, chewed and swallowed. "He mentioned you'd been out to the house. Not like Bryce to say anything about a casual visit. He doesn't talk much. Must have figured it was important."

Lillian hesitated and then gave a tiny shrug. "Your grandfather left a message on my answering machine while we were in Portland. Said he wanted to see me. I drove over to his place. It seemed the polite thing to do under the circumstances."

"What did he want?"

"Seemed to think that I was exerting my feminine wiles on you. Weaving a net of seduction in which to trap you, et cetera, et cetera. Evidently he's afraid that I might break your heart."

He managed to swallow the clam strip without sputtering and choking but it was not easy.

"He said that? That he's worried you might break my heart?"

"Uh-huh."

"Well, shoot and damn."

"He said 'shoot and damn' a lot, too."

"This is a little embarrassing."

"He wanted to know if my intentions were honorable," Lillian said without inflection.

Gabe made himself pick up another clam strip. "What did you tell him?"

"I told him the same thing that I told my mother today when she asked me about our relationship."

Definitely getting more complicated by the minute.

"And what was that?" he asked.

She picked up her water glass. "That the subject of honorable intentions had not arisen and that it was highly unlikely to arise."

"You told both of them that?"

"Yes. Well, it's true, isn't it?"

"Want to talk about 'em now?" he asked.

She flushed and glanced hurriedly around, apparently making certain that no one had overheard him. "That is not funny."

"Wasn't trying to make a joke."

"For heaven's sake, Gabe, keep your voice down."

"It is down. Yours is starting to get a little loud, though."

"You know, I don't need this. I've had a difficult day. I came here to work. Thus far I have accomplished nothing. Absolutely zilch."

"Painting not going well?" he asked.

"What painting? I'm starting to think I'll have to go back to Portland to get anything done."

"Take it easy. You seem a little tense tonight."

"I'm not tense," she muttered.

"Okay, if you say so, but I gotta tell you that you look tense."

She lowered her fork very deliberately. "If this is your idea of a relaxing evening, I—" She broke off, stiffening in her chair. "Oh, damn."

"What's wrong? Is it Marilyn? I saw her come in earlier. Don't worry about her, she's busy with her staff in the booth at the back. I don't think she'll pester us tonight."

"Not Marilyn." Lillian stared past him toward the door. "Anderson."

"Flint? Here? What the hell?" He turned to follow her gaze. Sure enough, J. Anderson Flint stood in close conversation with the hostess. "Well, what do you know? Almost didn't recognize him in his clothes."

"What on earth could he possibly be doing in Eclipse Bay?"

"I'd say that was obvious." Gabe turned back to his food. "He followed you here."

"There is absolutely no reason for him to do that."

"I can think of one."

She frowned. "What?"

"He wants to buy your matchmaking program, remember?"

"Oh. I forgot about that. But I told him I didn't want to sell."

"Probably thinks he can talk you into it."

"Damn. I did not need this."

Gabe turned his head to take another look at Flint. At that moment Anderson caught sight of Lillian. His smile was the sort a man bestows on a long-lost pal. He made a never-mind gesture to the hostess and started across the restaurant.

"He followed you, all right," Gabe said.

Lillian crushed a napkin in one hand. "I can't believe he wants my program that badly."

"You made a lot of money with that program. Why wouldn't he want to do the same?"

Her brows came together in a sharp frown. "You really are paranoid when it comes to money, aren't you?"

"I'm not paranoid, I'm cautious."

"Cautious, my—"

"Lillian." Anderson came to a halt beside the table before Lillian could finish her sentence. He leaned down with the clear intent of kissing her lightly in greeting. "What a pleasant surprise."

Lillian turned her head slightly, just enough to avoid the kiss. "What are you doing here?"

"I'm attending a conference at Chamberlain College. Arrived this afternoon. I'm staying at a motel just outside of town. I remember your saying something about taking some time off here in Eclipse Bay. We'll have to get together while I'm here." He extended his hand to Gabe. "J. Anderson Flint. I don't believe we've met."

"Gabe Madison." He rose slowly and kept the handshake perfunctory. "We haven't been formally introduced but I did see you once. Don't think you would remember the occasion, though. You were a little busy at the time."

"Gabe Madison of Madison Commercial? This is, indeed, a pleasure. Are you one of Lillian's clients?"

"As a matter of fact—"

"We're friends," Lillian interrupted crisply. "We both have roots here in Eclipse Bay. My sister is married to his brother. Our families go back a long way together."

"I see." Anderson kept his attention on Gabe. "How long are you going to be in town?"

"As long as it takes," Gabe said.

There was a stir at the front of the restaurant. He was conscious of a change in the atmosphere of the room. At the door an attractive woman was in heated conversation with the hostess.

"That's Claire Jensen." Lillian sounded concerned. "Marilyn's new campaign manager, remember? Looks like something's wrong."

She was right, he thought. Even from here he could see that Claire's face was tight with fury.

He also noticed that Marilyn had left her booth and was making her way swiftly toward the front of the restaurant. Her mouth was compressed into a tight, determined line.

"Uh-oh," Lillian said. "I don't like the looks of this."

Claire's voice rose above the hubbub. "Get out of my way, I said." She tried to push the hostess aside. "I have something to say to that bitch and I'm not leaving until I've said it."

Marilyn reached the hostess's podium. She gripped Claire's arm.

"I'll take care of this," she said to the hostess.

"Let go of me, you bitch," Claire raged. "Take your hands off me. I'll have you arrested. You can't do this."

But Marilyn already had her halfway through the door. Within seconds both women disappeared outside into the rainy night.

A hush fell over the restaurant. It lasted for all of five seconds. Then the room erupted in a buzz of excited conversation.

"Was that Marilyn Thornley?" Anderson sounded awed. "The wife of the politician who quit the senate race?"

"Soon to be ex-wife." Lillian watched the closed doors at the front of the room. "And something tells me that Claire Jensen is now an ex-campaign manager. Poor Claire. I wonder what happened? I thought everything was going so well for her in her new job."

The front door opened again a short time later. Marilyn strode back into the room, looking cool and unruffled by the skirmish. She paused to speak quietly to the hostess. Then she walked straight toward the table where Gabe sat with Lillian.

"You know her? You know Marilyn Thornley?" Anderson asked urgently.

"Her family has had a summer place here in town for years," Lillian explained. "Gabe is much better acquainted with her than I am, however."

Gabe gave her what he hoped was a silencing glare. He got one of her bright just-try-to-shut-me-up looks in return.

Marilyn arrived at the table.

"Sorry about that little scene," she said. "I had to let Claire go today. She didn't take it well."

"Terminations are always so stressful, aren't they?" Anderson's voice throbbed with compassion. "May I say that you handled that unfortunate scene very effectively. You took complete control before things got out of hand. That's the key. Complete control."

"Someone had to do something before she interrupted everyone's dinner." Marilyn smiled and extended a graceful hand. "Marilyn Thornley."

Anderson looked dazzled. "J. Anderson Flint. In town for a conference at Chamberlain. I'm delighted to meet you, Mrs. Thornley."

"Please, call me Marilyn."

"Yes, of course."

This was getting downright sticky, Gabe mused.

"Got a new campaign manager lined up?" he asked.

"I'm putting together a short list," Marilyn said. "I intend to announce my selection as soon as possible. This problem couldn't have come at a worse time. I can't afford to lose any momentum."

Anderson glanced toward the door, a concerned expression knitting his brows. "I trust your former manager won't cause you any trouble. Disgruntled employees can sometimes be dangerous."

"Claire will behave herself if she knows what's good for her," Marilyn declared. "It was a pleasure to meet you, Mr. Flint. Any friend of Gabe's and Lillian's is welcome at the institute. Please feel free to drop by while you're in town and pick up some of my campaign material."

"I'll do that," Anderson said immediately.

Marilyn inclined her head. "Wonderful. Now I'll let you two get back to your meal. Have a nice evening."

She walked away toward the booth at the rear. Anderson did not take his eyes off her.

"A very impressive woman," he breathed. "Very impressive. So forceful. Dynamic. Authoritative. We need more people like her in public office."

Lillian caught Gabe's eye. She looked amused.

"A perfect match," she murmured beneath the hum of background chatter.

He grinned. "Are you speaking as a professional?"

"Absolutely."

HE knew before she started making excuses that she wasn't going to spend the night with him.

"I really need to get some sleep," Lillian said when they walked out of the restaurant some time later. "I want to get up early tomorrow morning and try to do some work."

"Here we go again. It's those conversations you had with your mother and Mitchell, isn't it?" He opened the door of the Jag with a little more force than was necessary. "They messed with your mind."

She slid into the dark cave that was the front seat. "It's got nothing to do with them. I just need some quiet time."

"Sure. Quiet time."

"I told you earlier that I haven't gotten any real painting done since I got here. If I go home with you tonight, I probably won't get to work until noon or later."

"Wouldn't want to interfere with your best painting time."

He closed the door. With a little more force than was necessary.

13

"IT'S just a business," Hamilton said on the other end of the line.

"The hell it is." He'd had enough of the familiar argument, Sullivan decided. He ended the call abruptly with a sudden punch of a button.

He ought to be used to this feeling after so many years of butting heads with his stubborn son. It was always like this whenever the subject of the future of Harte Investments arose. Hamilton had done a brilliant job with the company, but he flatly refused to be concerned about what happened to it in the next generation. As if it didn't matter a damn.

It had taken him a long time to realize that, to Hamilton, Harte Investments was just a business. Running the company was nothing more than a job to him. He had done it extraordinarily well but he could walk away tomorrow and never look back.

In fact, walking away from H.I. was precisely what Hamilton planned to do. Sometime in the next two years. Sullivan swore under his breath and reached for his cane. He still could not believe that after having worked so hard to take the company to another level, his son was looking forward to retiring so that he could start a charitable foundation.

As far as he was concerned, Sullivan thought, charity began at home.

Just a business.

What the hell was the matter with everyone else in the family? Didn't they understand that a company like Harte Investments was a work of art? It had required vision and sweat to bring it to life. It was the result of a lot of carefully calculated risks and farsighted strategy. It had heart. It had struggled and fought and survived in a jungle where other businesses, large and small, got eaten alive.

And now, because none of his grandchildren had any interest in the company, it would be sold or swallowed up by some other, larger, predator.

He rapped the tip of the cane sharply against the cool terra-cotta tiles of the living room floor. The small gesture did nothing to release his pent-up frustration.

Just a business.

He stopped at the bank of floor-to-ceiling French doors that overlooked the pool.

Rachel was on her last lap. He watched her glide through the turquoise water and felt some of his anger fade. He became aware of the quiet sense of connection that he always experienced when he saw her. It calmed him and gave him a centered feeling that he could not explain. The older he got, the more he realized that Rachel helped define him. A great deal of what he knew about himself he had learned from living with her all these years.

He opened one of the glass-paned doors and went out onto the patio. It was late afternoon. The long rays of the desert sun were blocked by the walls of the house. The pool lay in comfortable shadow. In the distance the mountains were very sharp against the incredibly blue Arizona sky.

He selected two bottles of chilled springwater from the small refrigerator he had installed near the outdoor grill and lowered himself onto a lounger. He unscrewed the cap of one of the bottles, took a long swallow, and waited for Rachel to emerge from the jeweled pool. Talking to her always helped him put things into perspective.

She reached the steps and walked up out of the sparkling water. He watched her peel her swim cap off her short, silver-blond hair and admired her figure in the black-and-white bathing suit. After all this time he still felt the quiet heat of sexual attraction. She was only five years younger than he but somewhere along the line she had stopped aging, at least to him. He would want her until the day he died. And probably after that, too.

Her mouth curved as she walked toward him across the patio. "I can see that the discussion with Hamilton did not go well."

"I don't know where he gets that stubborn streak."

"Certainly not from you."

She picked up her white terrycloth robe, wrapped it around herself and sat down beside him. He handed her one of the bottles of cold water. She removed the cap and took a sip. They sat and watched the sunlight on the mountains. Sullivan relaxed into the lounger.

"Hamilton and Elaine think that Gabe will try to marry her in order to get his hands on a chunk of Harte," he said after a while.

"What do you think?"

"No Madison I ever knew had enough common sense to marry for money."

"Good point. But everyone says that Gabe is a different kind of Madison. His company is his passion. He built it to prove something to himself and everyone else. It's as important to him as Harte Investments is to you."

"I know." Sullivan grimaced. "Just wish one or two of my grandkids felt the same way about H.I. It's Hamilton's fault that none of them ever showed much interest in the company."

"He didn't want them to feel the same kind of pressure he got from you when he was growing up."

"Pressure, hell. I just guided him a little, that's all."

"You groomed him for Harte from the day he was born. Made him think he owed it to you and that he had to prove he wouldn't turn out to be the same kind of wastrel Mitchell's son was. Hamilton took over the firm to please you and you know it."

"What's wrong with that? He's done a damn fine job of growing the company. He couldn't have run it that well if he hadn't had a talent for business."

"Hamilton has a talent, all right. But he wants to use it to set up that foundation of his. He's had enough of H.I. and he doesn't want any of our grandchildren to be forced into running it when he steps down."

Sullivan groaned. "I knew Hannah and Lillian probably wouldn't take on H.I. But I had hopes that Nick would take the helm eventually. Why he had to go off on his own to write mysteries is beyond me. Don't know why anyone as smart as he is would want to waste time writing novels when he could be running a company the size of Harte Investments."

"All three of them have followed their own stars and that's the way it should be." Rachel patted his shoulder. "Besides, you enjoy Nick's mysteries and you know it."

Sullivan brooded on that for a moment. "Little Carson may show some interest in business in a few years," he said hopefully. "He's a bright kid."

"For heaven's sake, he's only five years old. It will be ages before Carson can even think of assuming such a responsibility. You certainly can't expect Hamilton to hold the reins for another two decades on the off-chance that your great-grandson might someday want to take over the business."

Sullivan leaned his head against the back of the lounger and considered the problem.

"You're always telling me what people will do and why," he said eventually. "Do you think Gabe Madison would marry Lillian just to get his hands on Harte?"

To his surprise, Rachel hesitated briefly. A troubled frown creased her forehead.

"It's a legitimate concern, under the circumstances," she said finally. "Of the two boys, I think Gabe was more affected by all the baggage Mitchell carried because of the blowup of Harte-Madison. Proving to himself and everyone else that he could compete with a Harte has been a fierce source of motivation for Gabe for years. In addition, H.I. is one of his competitors."

"Only occasionally. H.I. and M.C. have carved out different territories for the most part."

"My point is that if he saw a chance to control a portion of Harte Investments he might not be able to resist for both emotional and business reasons."

"The ultimate revenge for a Madison, hmm?"

"I'm not saying that it would be a deliberate act of revenge on his part. More of a subconscious motivation."

"Subconscious, my sweet patoot." Sullivan took a swig of his springwater and lowered the bottle. "When it comes to business, Gabe Madison knows exactly what he's doing."

Rachel stretched her legs out on the lounger. "That stupid feud. I can't believe that it's still affecting both our family and the Madisons, too."

Sullivan said nothing.

Rachel studied the pool for a while. "Do you ever think about her?"

When Rachel spoke in that quiet, thoughtful tone he paid attention. It meant that she was very serious.

"Who?" he asked, groping to refocus on whatever this new issue was.

"Claudia Banner. The woman who destroyed Harte-Madison and ruined your friendship with Mitchell. I've always assumed that she was very beautiful."

He summoned up an image of the Claudia he had known all those years ago, contemplated it for a few minutes and then shrugged.

"She was a pretty little redhead. Sharp as a tack, too. Mitch and I were fresh out of the service and eager to make our fortunes. She showed us how to do it. That combination of qualities can make a woman seem pretty damn attractive."

"Were you in love with her?"

He sensed a minefield.

"Thought I was for a time," he said. "Changed my mind real fast when she disappeared with the total assets of Harte-Madison and dumped the company into bankruptcy. But poor Mitch had fallen for her hook, line, and sinker. He refused to believe she'd conned us. He was convinced that I had somehow used her to grab his share of the firm."

"Hence the infamous knock-down-drag-out fistfight in front of Fulton's Su-permarket and the start of the legendary Harte-Madison feud."

"It was a long time ago, Rachel. Mitch and I were young men. Young men do dumb things."

"You said you thought you were in love with Claudia Banner."

"For a time."

"Don't you know for certain whether or not you loved her?"

He gazed out at the mountains. "I now know for sure that whatever the hell I felt for Claudia Banner was not love."

"How can you be so certain of that?"

"I didn't know what love was until I met you."

She turned her head very quickly, obviously startled.

Then she laughed softly, leaned across the small space that separated the two loungers and kissed him lightly.

"Good answer," she said.

"Thanks. I thought it was pretty good, myself."

It was also the truth, he thought. But after all these years he was certain she knew that.

14

HE dressed carefully before he went to see her, wanting to strike precisely the right note. So much hung in the balance. He contemplated the limited range of clothing in the closet. Unfortunately he had left many of his best shirts and ties behind in Portland. He hadn't expected to need them here on the coast. But he was not entirely unprepared. He was never entirely unprepared. He wanted her to know that.

After due consideration he went with a pale-blue shirt that matched his eyes and an Italian knit sweater that made his shoulders appear a little broader. The trousers and loafers worked well with the sweater.

He stood in front of the mirror studying the effect. Not quite right. He took off the sweater and went back to the closet for a tie and the corduroy jacket. The tie showed respect. The cord jacket said he was a deep thinker.

Satisfied, he left the room and went outside to the parking lot. He got into the car and drove the short distance to the Eclipse Bay Policy Studies Institute.

Ten minutes later he was standing in front of her secretary's desk.

"I'm here to see Mrs. Thornley," he said.

The secretary looked skeptical and apologetic at the same time. It was prob-ably a natural-born talent.

"Do you have an appointment?"

"No, but please give her this card. I think she'll see me."

The secretary examined the card and the note he had jotted on it. She got to her feet, went to the closed door behind her desk and opened it.

He waited until she disappeared inside before checking his reflection in the highly polished chrome base of her name plaque.

He straightened quickly when the door opened again.

"Mrs. Thornley will see you, Dr. Flint."

"Thank you."

He took a deep breath, preparing himself for acute disappointment in case he had gotten the wrong impression about her last night. The scene in the restaurant had happened so quickly.

He went through the door, closed it firmly and stood looking at his fate.

She studied him from where she sat behind her desk, a vision in a fitted red knit jacket that was accented with gold buttons and well-defined, padded shoulders. She toyed with the small card he had sent in a moment earlier.

He gave the office a quick once-over, checking the quality of the furnishings. First-class all the way. The lady had style and taste. The room was spacious with a view of the town and the bay spread out below in the distance.

There was another door on the far side of the office. It stood open a crack. Someone was moving around in the adjoining room. Probably an assistant or a speech-writer. He heard a desk drawer slam.

"Please sit down, Dr. Flint," Marilyn said. Cool, self-possessed authority rang in the words.

He felt his blood heat. He had not been wrong. She was magnificent. A goddess.

He lowered himself into one of the sleek black leather chairs.

Marilyn rose, crossed the room to the door that separated her office from the smaller one on the far side of the room and closed it very firmly. She smiled at him.

Absolutely magnificent.

"We need to talk," Anderson said.

⚜

"I found out that she had an affair with Trevor," Marilyn said. She went to stand at the window of the cottage and looked out over the bay. "I could hardly keep her on as my campaign manager after I learned the truth."

"Guess it would be a little awkward," Lillian admitted. She glanced at her watch. Another morning's work shot. The last thing she had needed today was to open the front door and find Marilyn Thornley on her front porch. *Why me?* she wondered. She did not relish being a politician's confidant.

"I knew that he was probably screwing someone but I just assumed it was one of his perky little campaign workers. Someone unimportant. Lord knows, it wouldn't have been the first time. Trevor and I had an understanding, you see. As long as he was reasonably discreet about it, I could ignore it."

Marilyn looked different this morning, Lillian thought. No longer the battlefield general with antifreeze running in her veins. More like a woman who has learned the name of her ex-husband's lover. Hurt. Angry. Resentful.

"I've heard about understandings like that," Lillian said neutrally.

Marilyn's mouth twisted. "You sound very disapproving."

"Let's just say I wouldn't want a marriage based on that kind of unwritten contract."

"You'd rather be married for your family's company, is that it?"

It wasn't easy but Lillian managed to hold on to her temper. "I don't know why you came here this morning to tell me this, Marilyn. It's none of my business."

"Don't you understand? I had to talk to someone. I don't know anyone else I can trust here in town. Not with something this personal. I certainly can't talk to anyone on my staff. I would look weak and emotional." Marilyn took a deep breath and exhaled, making a visible effort to compose herself. "I'm sorry. I shouldn't have made that crack about being married for Harte Investments. That was uncalled for."

Lillian lounged back against the counter. "Forget it. Not like you're the first person to leap to the conclusion that Gabe is only interested in me because of Harte."

"Still, it wasn't right. I apologize. I'm not at my best this morning. The thing is, even though I knew Trevor was sleeping with someone, I never dreamed it was Claire."

"You're sure it was Claire who had the affair with Trevor?" Lillian asked.

"Yes."

"How did you find out?"

"Pure accident. I was going through some old expense account statements the other day, gathering data for my divorce attorney. I came across records of some reimbursements Trevor had made to Claire. At first I thought they were legitimate expenses associated with the campaign. Something made me dig a little deeper. Turned out the expenses were incurred at a series of cheap hotels over a period of several months. In each case Trevor and Claire had registered as Mr. and Mrs. Smith. Can you believe it?"

"Tacky."

"Very. Once I started looking, I turned up a few other unusual receipts. When it comes to sex, Trevor has his little, uh, eccentricities. Apparently Claire catered to them."

"I see. What did Claire say when you confronted her?"

"She denied it, of course. Claimed Trevor must have been with some other woman, not her."

"But you didn't believe her."

"No." Marilyn rubbed her temples in a gesture of weariness that seemed uncharacteristic. "Naturally I had to let her go. Wouldn't you have done the same?"

"If I was absolutely sure of my facts."

Definitely should not have answered the door, Lillian thought. At the very least, she ought not to have invited Marilyn inside. But it had been impossible to ignore the bleak pain in the other woman's eyes. The sisterhood thing.

"I really shouldn't have come here," Marilyn said. "I had no right to dump this on you. But I woke up this morning needing to talk to someone and I couldn't think of anyone else. You and I have a common bond."

"I beg your pardon?"

"Gabe."

"*Gabe?* That's stretching the definition of a common bond a bit far, don't you think?"

Marilyn rested a hand on the windowsill. "Don't worry, I'm not even going to try to take him away from you."

"Oh, hey, thanks. I appreciate that."

"I'm a pragmatic woman," Marilyn said. "I don't waste time beating my head against stone walls. You don't have to think of me as your competition."

"Well, as a matter of fact, I hadn't thought of you in quite those terms."

"When I saw you two together that night at the old Buckley place I knew that I had no chance of ever resuming my relationship with him. You can offer him something I can't."

Lillian felt her insides tighten. "I suppose you mean Harte Investments?"

"I'm sure it's not just the company," Marilyn said. "He probably finds you attractive, too."

"Gosh. You really think so?"

Marilyn sighed. "You want to know a little secret? I used to blame your family and Harte Investments for the breakup of my relationship with Gabe."

Lillian stilled. "I see."

"A part of me will always wonder what would have happened if he hadn't been so obsessed with competing with you Hartes. Who knows? Maybe he and I could have had something lasting together."

Enough with the sisterhood thing, Lillian thought. She had done her politically correct duty. She straightened away from the counter.

"If you don't mind, I have a lot of things to do this morning, Marilyn."

Marilyn regarded her with an apologetic expression. "Yes, of course. Forgive me. I didn't mean to get into old history."

"Didn't you?"

"No. I just wanted to talk to someone." Marilyn blinked rapidly and wiped moisture away from the corner of her eye with a fingertip. "Things have been a little rough lately, what with the divorce and getting my campaign organized and now finding out that my campaign manager had an affair with Trevor."

Lillian hesitated. "You've been under a lot of stress. Maybe you need to take some time off. Go somewhere quiet and relax before you start your big push for office."

"I can't afford to take that kind of time. Not at this juncture." Marilyn squared her shoulders. "I intend to go to Washington, D.C., one of these days, so I'd better get used to dealing with stress, hadn't I? But I shouldn't have come here. It wasn't fair to you."

"Forget it. That's certainly what I intend to do." Lillian went past her and opened the front door. "Good luck in the campaign, Marilyn."

"Thank you." Marilyn walked out onto the porch and went down the steps to the Mercedes. She paused just before getting behind the wheel. "I hope you'll vote for me."

Lillian watched her drive away and then slowly closed the door. She walked to the table, picked up her mug and carried it into the second bedroom. She looked at the blank canvas propped on the easel.

For a long time she sipped tea and contemplated the empty white space, trying to get back into that alternate reality where she stood within the vision. But it was hopeless. Too many real world thoughts barred the way.

"*. . . You want to know a secret? I used to blame your family and Harte Investments for the breakup of my relationship with Gabe.*"

After a while she gave up trying to get into the zone. She went into the kitchen and took a bottle of wine and some cheese out of the refrigerator. She put both into a paper sack.

She went upstairs to her bedroom, opened a drawer, selected a nightgown and a change of underwear, and put them into a leather tote. In the bathroom she quickly packed the basics into a small, zippered case and dropped the case into the tote.

Carrying the tote in one hand, she went back downstairs, collected the sack with the wine and cheese inside and a jacket. She left the cottage through the mudroom door.

Outside she was met with a brisk, bracing wind and the roar of the surf down in Dead Hand Cove. The day was already darkening into night.

She walked across the top of the bluffs to the old Buckley place.

Gabe opened the back door just as she raised her hand to knock. He looked at the bulging tote bag.

"Looks like you plan to stay awhile."

"Thought I'd spend the night if it's okay with you."

He smiled slowly, emerald eyes warm and sensual.

"Oh, yeah," he said.

She walked into the kitchen.

"Don't want to push my good luck but curiosity compels me to ask." He took the tote and the sack from her. "Why the change of heart?"

"Marilyn came to see me today. You know, it's one thing for my mom and your grandfather to mess with my mind. They're family. They got a right, I guess. But having your ex-girlfriend try the same trick is going too far. Got to draw the line somewhere."

He closed the door and looked at her. "Marilyn paid you a visit today?"

"Uh-huh."

"Why?"

"Among other things, she said she needed to talk to someone about the real reason she'd fired Claire."

"And that reason is?"

"She thinks Claire had an affair with Trevor."

"She *thinks* that or she knows it?"

"Let's just say she's convinced of it." She unfastened her cloak. "At any rate she doesn't trust Claire anymore. So she canned her."

Gabe took the cloak. It spilled from his hand in an iridescent waterfall.

"What's the big deal?" he said. "Marilyn is divorcing Thornley. Their relationship was obviously based on Trevor's electability, not true love. Why worry about an affair with Claire that may or may not have happened?"

"For heaven's sake, Gabe. Would you want to employ someone as your close, personal assistant who had slept with your wife?"

He didn't miss a beat.

"I'd destroy any man who slept with my wife."

The absolute finality of that statement made her catch her breath. "I see."

"But I'm not a politician," Gabe continued. "Politicians are different."

She thought about Marilyn's disturbed behavior. "I'm not sure that they're so very different."

"Marilyn mention me?"

"Oh, yes."

"What did she say?"

"What everyone else seems to be saying. Something about your interest in me probably being linked to an obsessive interest in Harte Investments."

He watched her with unreadable eyes. "And that observation is what made you decide to come over here this afternoon?"

"I'm here because I want to be here."

"Glad to hear that. You do realize that you probably won't get home until noon tomorrow."

"Not like I'm getting much work done here in Eclipse Bay, anyway."

15

SHE did not return to the cottage until after lunch the following day, just as Gabe had warned. He walked her back across the bluffs and left her at the front door with a long, lingering kiss.

"I know you need to paint this afternoon," he said. "Why don't I come over here for dinner tonight? I'll bring the wine this time."

She went into the house and smiled at him through the screen. "That'll work."

He raised a hand in casual farewell and went down the steps. She watched him walk away across the bluffs, hands shoved deep into the pockets of his jacket, his dark hair ruffled by the wind. A dark squall line hung across the bay, moving swiftly toward shore.

Memories of last night's lovemaking ignited hot little sparklers of pleasure deep inside her. But there was something else burning down there, too, a long fuse that promised a painful explosion sometime in the future when this very adult relationship blew up in her face.

Don't look too far ahead. Just take it one day at a time. That's all you can do for now. That's all you dare to do now.

Gabe was right. She needed to paint.

She hung her jacket in the closet and started toward the hall that led to her makeshift studio. Halfway across the living room she noticed the light on the answering machine and changed course. She went to the table where the phone sat, and punched up the message.

She was startled to hear Arizona Snow's harsh whisper.

". . . Being tailed by an institute spy. Bastard's too smart to get close enough for me to get a look at him but I know he's out there somewhere, watchin' me. I can feel him. Must've seen me doin' recon and knows I'm on to the plans for the new wing.

"I called you on accounta I don't know Gabe's number. I'm at a pay phone at the pier. Can't risk leaving all the details on that machine of yours. When I leave here, I'll head for my place and hole up there.

"I got to talk to you and Gabe. Heard you two are shackin' up together so if this message gets to you, I figure it'll get to him, too. My place is the only safe house in the sector. Appreciate it if you two would come on out as soon as you can. Things are getting hot around here.

"Gotta go. Bye."

There was a muffled crash on the other end of the line. Arizona had hung up in a hurry.

Lillian glared at the answering machine. "You know," she said to the universe at large, "I came out here to find a nice, serene place to do some painting."

She picked up the phone and dialed Gabe's cell phone. He answered on the first ring.

"Madison here."

She could hear the muffled sound of the wind and the surf. He was probably halfway back to the old Buckley place.

"Doing anything important?" she asked.

"Depends how you define important. I'm thinking about a proposal from a small startup company that needs five million in cash. That strike you as a weighty matter?"

"Five mil? Sounds like penny-ante stuff to me."

"Appreciate your consulting opinion."

"My bill is in the mail." She watched the dark shadow of the squall line moving across the bay. "Would you like to do something more exciting?"

"Such as?"

"Help defend Eclipse Bay against the spies up at the institute?"

"Does this involve frozen extraterrestrials?"

"Probably."

"Well, it's not like I've got anything else to do now that you've taken all the fun out of my puny little five-mil deal. I'm almost back to the house. I'll get my car and come pick you up."

THE squall struck just as he geared down to take the steep, rutted path that led through the woods to Arizona's cabin. He did not want to think about what the rough road was doing to the Jag's expensive alignment.

"She said she was being followed?" he asked.

"Yes."

"Did she give you a description?"

"No." Lillian watched the narrow road. "Just said she thought it was an institute spy. But she sounded nervous, Gabe. That's what worried me. In all the years I've known A.Z. she's always seemed very cool and somehow in full command of her crazy conspiracy theories. I've never heard her sound genuinely scared or even uneasy."

"Maybe she's slipped another cog. Sunk a little deeper into her fantasy world."

"Gone from being seriously eccentric to seriously crazy, you think?"

"It's a possibility."

Lillian folded her arms tightly beneath her breasts. Her body was tense. She was concerned and she appeared to be getting more so as they got closer to Arizona's cabin.

"Take it easy, we both know there's nothing really wrong here," he said.

"It's A.Z's state of mind I'm worried about. I wonder if getting involved with that crowd at the bakery is responsible for pushing her over some psychological edge."

"If she has cracked up big-time," he said, "you're right. We've got a big problem on our hands. I doubt if we'll be able to talk her into checking into some nice quiet psych ward for observation."

"She'd never trust a psychiatrist or a sanitarium."

"Probably not." He negotiated another sharp bend in the road. "There's not much you can do for someone who won't go for help unless she is a clear danger to herself or others."

"Let's try to keep some perspective here. We're talking as if A.Z. has gone off the deep end. We have no evidence of that yet. Keep in mind that she hasn't ever hurt anyone in her life."

"That we know of."

She shot him a swift, searching glance. "What do you mean?"

"Just that no one around here knows anything about her past before she showed up in Eclipse Bay. I remember asking Mitchell about her once when I was in high school. He just shrugged and said that she was entitled to her privacy so long as she didn't do anyone else any harm."

"That's the whole point," Lillian said. "To the best of our knowledge or anyone else's she's never done any damage to people or property."

He navigated the last tight curve in the road and saw the cabin. Rain and wind slashed the heavy limbs of the trees that loomed over the weather-beaten structure. Arizona's ancient truck was parked in the small clearing.

He eased the Jag to a halt behind the truck and switched off the engine.

"Well, at least she's here and not out prowling around the new wing of the institute with her VPX 5000," he said.

He unfastened his seat belt and reached into the back seat for Lillian's rain cloak and his jacket.

"She said something about holing up for a while." Lillian put her arms into the sleeves of her cloak and pulled the hood up over her head. "That's not like her, either, when you stop and think about it. She's always out doing recon and surveillance. Says she likes the bad guys to know she's keeping an eye on them."

"True."

He shrugged into the jacket, tugged the hood up over his head and opened the door. Rain driven by rough winds dampened his hair when he got out.

Lillian did not wait for him to come around to her side of the car. She already had her own door open. A few seconds later she joined him at the front of the Jag.

They both went quickly toward the shelter of the porch. Gabe took the steps two at a time and came to a halt at the front door. Dripping rain from her sparkling cloak, Lillian stopped beside him.

There was no doorbell. Gabe banged the brass eagle knocker a few times.

There was no response. No surprise, he thought. No right-thinking paranoid would open a door without verifying the identity of the person on the other side.

"A.Z.? Gabe and Lillian out here," he called.

The door did not open. He glanced at the nearest window. It was covered with what looked like blinds fashioned from metal slats.

"I got your message." Lillian rapped her knuckles on the blank window. "Are you okay in there?"

The wind-driven rain whipped around the cabin. He knew Lillian was getting more agitated. He had to admit that the utter silence from inside the cabin was starting to bother him, too.

He tried the heavy, steel-braced screen door. It was locked.

"She's not a young woman," Lillian said. "I hope something hasn't happened."

"Like what?"

"A heart attack or stroke. Or maybe she fell."

"Calm down. I'm sure she's fine. Probably locked in her war room and can't hear us."

"Let's try the back door." Lillian turned and disappeared around the corner of the porch.

"Hang on, not so fast, damn it." He went after her, moving quickly. "The woman's a full-blown conspiracy theorist, remember? Paranoid as hell. No telling how she's got this place booby-trapped."

"I just want to see if I can find a window that isn't covered with those steel blinds. I don't understand why she isn't—"

She broke off on a strangled gasp. He saw the crumpled body lying on the porch at the same time.

"A.Z." Lillian rushed forward. "Oh, my God, Gabe, I was afraid of this. She's had a heart attack."

She went to her knees beside Arizona, feeling for a pulse at the throat.

He looked at the blood on the wooden boards beneath Arizona's head and went cold.

"Not a heart attack." The cell phone was in his hand. He didn't remember taking it out of his pocket. He punched in the emergency number.

Lillian followed his gaze. "You're right. It wasn't her heart. She fell and hit her head." Her fingers moved gently on Arizona's throat. "She's breathing but she's unconscious. The bleeding doesn't seem to be too bad."

"Better not move her."

Lillian nodded. She stripped off her cloak and arranged it snugly around Arizona's chunky frame while he gave a terse account of the situation to the 911 operator.

He saw the overturned plant stand lying nearby just as he ended the call. The stand was made of wrought iron.

Lillian bent intently over A.Z. "Arizona? It's me, Lillian. Help is on the way. You're going to be okay. Can you hear me?"

Arizona groaned. Her lashes fluttered. She squinted up at Lillian.

"What happened?" she mumbled.

"It looks like you slipped and fell. How do you feel?"

"Bad."

"I'll bet you do," Lillian said gently. "But you're going to be okay."

Arizona closed her eyes again. She mumbled something.

"What did you say?" Lillian asked.

"Said I didn't fall."

"You probably don't remember much," Lillian said soothingly. "I think that's pretty normal when you've had a blow to the head. Don't worry about it."

Arizona's hand moved a little in a small, agitated gesture, but she did not speak again.

Lillian looked up and saw Gabe watching her. She frowned.

"What?"

"I don't think she fell, either," he said.

"Why in the world do you say that?"

"I'm no cop, but it looks to me like someone used that plant stand to hit her on the back of the head."

16

THEY were standing in the busy hallway outside Arizona's hospital room. Monitors beeped and pinged. Lights winked on computer screens. High-tech equipment gleamed. Eclipse Bay Community Hospital had moved with the times, Gabe thought.

He noticed that everyone around him who wore a name tag and a stethoscope appeared purposeful and competent and a little high on adrenaline. Those who were not decked out with a name tag and a stethoscope looked worried. Civilians, Gabe thought. He and Lillian fit into that category. Definitely worried.

Sean Valentine, Eclipse Bay's chief of police, on the other hand, fell into some middle zone. He had the same purposeful, competent air that marked the members of the hospital staff, but he didn't look as if he were enjoying an adrenaline rush. There were deep lines around his eyes and mouth. The marks weren't caused by Arizona's problems. Sean always looked as if he anticipated the worst. Gabe figured the permanently etched expression was a legacy of his days as a big-city cop in Seattle.

"Probably came home and interrupted some SOB who was trying to break into her cabin," Sean said. "The bastard must have grabbed the first available heavy object and used it on the back of her skull."

"Whoever he was, he can't be from around here," Gabe said. "Everyone in town knows that it would take an armored tank and a battering ram to break into A.Z.'s cabin."

"Could have looked like a challenge to some dumbass kids from Chamberlain who'd had a few beers," Sean speculated. "Or maybe a transient found the place and didn't realize it was actually a small fortress."

"He could have killed her." Lillian's anger vibrated in every word and in every line of her body. She was very tightly wound at the moment.

"The blow was a little off," Sean said. "Fortunately for A.Z. She's concussed but they say she should be okay. They're going to keep her here at the hospital for a couple of days for observation."

Lillian looked at him. "Are you sure we shouldn't take that message she left on my machine seriously?"

"I take everything seriously," Sean said. "Way I'm made, I guess. But I gotta tell you that a call from A.Z. claiming that she was being tailed by an institute spy does not give me a whole heck of a lot to work with. In her world, institute spies are everywhere and they're all trying to follow her."

"There is that," Lillian agreed reluctantly.

"Another thing," Sean added. "There's a small flaw in A.Z.'s logic here. Assuming the institute actually employed spies, none of them would need to tail her in order to find out where she lives. Everyone in town knows where her cabin is located. All anyone looking for her would have to do is ask a few questions down at Fulton's Supermarket or the video rental shop."

"Nobody ever said A.Z.'s logic holds up well under scrutiny," Gabe said.

Sean's face twisted briefly in a wry smile. "Nope."

Lillian gave them both a quelling glance. "A.Z. operates in a parallel universe but within that universe, her reasoning is consistent and logical."

Sean looked wary. "Meaning?"

"Meaning that something scared her enough to make her use a telephone and leave a message on an answering machine. She would never willingly do that if she could avoid it. She's convinced that all phones are tapped. She doesn't even have one in her house."

"Tapped by institute spies?" Sean asked politely.

Lillian exhaled unhappily. "Yes."

"I think I'll go with my theory of an interrupted burglary in progress for now, if you don't mind. But if you get any more useful information from her when you talk to her, let me know."

He nodded to Gabe, then turned and walked off down the hospital corridor. Lillian watched him until he turned a corner and disappeared. Then she looked at Gabe.

"He's probably right, isn't he?" she said.

"Probably." Gabe hesitated. "You have to admit, it's a simpler explanation than one involving vast government conspiracies. When it comes to this kind of stuff, cops prefer simple because most of the time that's the right answer."

"I know. And we are dealing with A.Z. here. Whatever the answer is, it can't possibly be as mysterious as she thinks it is. Come on, let's go see how she's doing."

"Sure."

He walked beside her to the doorway of the hospital room. Arizona was stretched out on a bed. She looked so different in a hospital gown, he thought. In all the years he had known her he had never seen her in anything except military camouflage and boots. She had always seemed curiously ageless, sturdy and vigorous. But now, bandaged and helpless, her gray hair partially covered with a white bandage, she looked her age. A wave of anger swept through him. What kind of bastard would hit an elderly woman on the head with a wrought-iron planter?

A nurse wearing a tag inscribed with the name Jason leaned over A.Z., taking her pulse. When he was finished he lowered her wrist very gently to the sheet and moved toward the door. Behind him, Arizona stirred restlessly but she did not open her eyes.

"Are you family?" Jason asked quietly.

"No." Lillian looked toward the bed. "I don't think she has any family. We're friends. How is she doing?"

"She's got a nasty headache and she's confused and disoriented. Pretty much what you'd expect after a severe blow to the head."

"A.Z. always seems confused and disoriented to people who don't know her well," Gabe said. "Has she said anything?"

Jason shook his head. "Just keeps talking about something called a VPX 5000."

"Her new camera," Lillian said. "She was very excited about it."

On the bed, Arizona moved slightly. She turned her head on the pillow. Her face was drawn with pain. Her cheeks were slightly sunken. "Lillian? Gabe?"

"Right here, A.Z." Lillian went to the bed and patted Arizona's hand. "Don't worry about anything. You're going to be fine."

"My VPX 5000." Arizona's voice had lost its usual hearty timbre. She sounded a thousand years old. "I can't find it."

"Don't worry about it," Lillian assured her. "You'll find it when they let you go home."

"No." Arizona gripped Lillian's hand with gnarled fingers. "They said someone hit me. Probably the institute spy. I'll bet he took my VPX 5000. Gotta get it back. Can't risk having it fall into the wrong hands. Pictures. Of the new wing. They'll destroy 'em."

Gabe went to stand at the bed. He leaned on the rails. "Tell you what, A.Z., Lillian and I will go back to your cabin and see if we can find the camera. Maybe you left it in your truck."

"Gotta find it." Arizona's eyes fluttered closed. "Can't let the bastards get it."

⌇⌇⌇

AN hour later, after a fruitless search of the interior of Arizona's aging pickup, he closed the door on the driver's side and pocketed the keys. He watched Lillian come down the cabin's porch steps and start toward him.

"Any luck?" she asked.

"No. What about you?"

"I went over every square inch of the porch and checked the flower beds around it. It's gone, unfortunately. I hate to have to give her the bad news. She was so thrilled with that camera."

"She may be right. Whoever hit her probably stole it. Maybe he figured he could get a few bucks for it."

"If he's got any sense, he won't try to unload it anywhere near Eclipse Bay," Lillian said. "Sean Valentine will be watching for it and so will everyone else in town."

"I'll do some research online," Gabe said. "Maybe I can find another one to replace it for her."

Lillian flashed him a grateful smile. "That would be wonderful."

He liked it when she smiled at him like that, he thought. He liked it a lot. That smile had a very motivating effect on him. He took a long, slow breath and then he took her arm.

"It's getting late," he said. "Be dark soon. Let's go back to your place and get some dinner."

ANOTHER squall struck just as Gabe halted the car in front of the cottage. Lillian pulled up the hood of her cloak, opened the door, leaped out and made a dash for the front porch. Gabe was right behind her. She stopped in front of the door, shook rainwater off her cloak and rummaged in her purse for her keys.

When she got the door open, she headed straight for the mudroom, intending to hang up her cloak so that it could drip dry.

Gabe followed, stripping off his jacket. When they reached the mudroom she did not bother to switch on the overhead light. There was enough illumination from the hall to see the row of metal clothes hooks beneath the window.

"I don't know about you," she said, "but I'm starving."

"I'll open the wine. You can do the salad tonight."

"It's a deal." A damp draft sent a chill through her. "It's cold in here. Why don't you start a fire before you—" She broke off abruptly.

"What's wrong?"

"No wonder it's cold in here. The back door is open. I can't believe I forgot to lock up. But I've been distracted a lot lately."

She crossed the small space to push the door closed.

"Wait," Gabe said quietly, pointing to the door.

He reached out to switch on the mudroom light and then moved past her. She watched him lean forward slightly to examine the door frame.

"Damn."

"What is it?" She moved closer. "Something wrong?"

"Yeah. Something's wrong, all right. Looks like A.Z. wasn't the only one who got hit by a burglar today."

She didn't answer him, just stared, disbelieving, at the deep gouges in the wooden door frame and the broken lock.

"YOU sure there's nothing missing?" Sean Valentine asked for the second time.

"No, not as far as I can tell," Lillian said.

Gabe leaned against the kitchen counter and watched her answer Sean's questions. She sat hunched on the kitchen stool, knees drawn up, feet propped on the top rung.

"I went through the whole house," she added. "Nothing looks as if it's been touched. Of course, we don't keep anything really valuable here because the cottage is empty for weeks, sometimes months, at a time. Still, there's the old television and the new answering machine. And all the stuff I brought with me from Portland. My painting supplies. Some clothes."

"Nothing that would bring a burglar a lot of fast cash, though." Sean looked down at what he had written. "You know, these guys aren't known for neatness. They usually leave the place in a mess. Maybe he got scared off before he could get inside. A car coming down the drive would have done it. Or someone taking a walk along the bluff with a dog."

Gabe considered that. "Think that after he got nervous here, he went looking for another, more isolated house to break into? A.Z.'s place?"

"And got surprised again. Hit Arizona and took off with her fancy camera." Sean nodded. "Makes sense." He flipped the notebook closed. "I've been interviewing people all day. So far no one has noticed any strangers acting suspiciously. But that still leaves a bunch of college kids and unknown transients. The camera is my best hope. If someone turns up with it, I'll have a lead."

"Otherwise, zip, right?" Lillian asked morosely. "I've heard that these kinds of burglaries often go unsolved."

"That's true in big cities but not so true in a small town where you've got a more limited group of suspects." Sean stuffed the notebook into the pocket of his jacket and started toward the door. "I'll let you know if I come up with anything useful. Meanwhile, get that back door fixed."

Lillian nodded. "I'll ask the Willis brothers to come over here tomorrow and take care of it."

Sean paused at the door. "Folks are usually a little nervous after a break-in." He angled a brief, meaningful glance at Gabe. "Nice for you that you won't be here alone tonight."

Lillian gave him a basilisk stare from her perch on the stool. She did not say a word.

Sean did not move. But, then, that was only to be expected, Gabe thought. A basilisk could turn a man to stone with the power of her gaze.

"I mean, you'll be a lot more comfortable with Madison here," Sean muttered. "Not nervous or anything."

Lillian continued to glare.

"Right, she won't be alone." Gabe pushed himself away from the counter. "I'll walk outside with you."

He did not know why he felt obliged to rescue Sean. A guy thing, maybe. Or maybe he just didn't like the way Lillian had reacted to Sean's assumption that she was sleeping with him. She looked ticked. For some reason that irritated him.

Sean cleared his throat. "Sure. Got to get going. Things to do."

Gabe crossed the kitchen in a few long strides. He had the front door open for Sean by the time the police chief reached it.

He moved out onto the porch after Sean and closed the door behind them. They stood in the yellow light and looked at the cars parked in the drive.

"Guess I stepped in it back there," Sean said.

"Yeah."

"Sorry about that."

Gabe braced a hand on the porch railing. "Not like it's a big secret."

"Secrets like that are a little hard to keep here in Eclipse Bay. Especially when a Harte and a Madison are involved."

"I know," Gabe said.

Sean looked thoughtful. "Folks in town are sort of assuming that you're planning to marry her in order to get your hands on a piece of Harte Investments."

"Dangerous things, assumptions."

"You can say that again. I generally try to avoid them in my work, but once in a while I slip up." Sean zipped his jacket and went down the steps. "I'll be in touch."

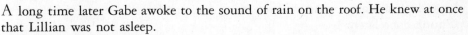

A long time later Gabe awoke to the sound of rain on the roof. He knew at once that Lillian was not asleep.

"You okay?" he asked.

"Yes."

"What's wrong?"

"I'm not sure."

"I was afraid of this." He levered himself up on one elbow and reached for her. "Are you upset because Sean Valentine guessed that we're sleeping together? Honey, this is a small town and we haven't exactly tried to hide."

"It's not that." She locked her hands behind her head and stared up into the shadows. "I mean, I'm not real thrilled with the fact that Sean and everyone else in town thinks you're trying to sucker me into marriage so that you can get your hands on a third of Harte Investments—"

"Valentine didn't say that. He just sort of observed that you and I are having an affair."

"It's what he was thinking. But, to tell you the truth, I'm getting used to people thinking that."

He wondered if that was a good thing. Did he want her thinking that their affair was fine just as it stood? "So, the gossip isn't what's keeping you awake?"

"No."

"All right, why can't you sleep? The break-in?"

"Yes."

He flattened his hand on her soft, warm belly. "There's nothing to worry about. I wired the mudroom door shut, remember? Besides, if the guy didn't find anything worth stealing the first time, he's not likely to come back."

"I know."

He did not like the disquiet that threaded her words. "What is it?"

"Something like this happened to me in Portland."

He stilled. "A break-in?"

"I discovered it when we went into town for the Montoya dinner. I got the feeling that someone had been inside my apartment."

He sat up very fast. "Why the hell didn't you tell me? Did you call the cops?"

"No. There was no evidence. My door hadn't been forced open the way it was here. Nothing was missing."

"You're sure?"

"Yes. I figured it was the cleaning people. I called them and I was right. A schedule mix-up. But there was a smear on the bedroom closet mirror and well—"

"Well, what?"

"I guess that after what happened tonight, I can't help wondering, that's all."

"Remember what I said about the simple answer usually being the right one. Sounds like whoever cleaned your apartment left a smear. It happens. As long as there was no sign of forced entry or theft, I think we can assume that the break-in here had nothing to do with the cleaning day mix-up in Portland."

"I'm sure you're right. Guess I'm just a little nervous after what happened, that's all. You know, what with one thing and another, I'm not getting a lot of painting done lately."

He lay back against the pillows and gathered her against him. She snuggled close. He stroked her slowly, his hand gliding down her spine to the curve of her hip, letting himself enjoy the warmth and the sensual curves of her body.

"What you need is some artistic inspiration," he whispered.

"You may be right." She put an arm around him. "Unfortunately, it isn't always easy to find."

He moved his hand on her again, savoring the shiver that went through her. Then he eased her onto her back and came down on top of her. "Luckily for you, I am prepared to give my all to art."

17

SHORTLY before noon the next day, Lillian stood in the opening that separated the mudroom from the back hall and watched Gabe and the Willis brothers. The three men huddled around the broken lock with a solemn air. Their expressions were grave, their voices hushed and serious. A guy thing, she thought. You saw it whenever the male of the species was in the presence of a nonfunctioning piece of hardware or machinery.

"Looks like the work of an amateur." Torrance Willis bent low to make a closer examination of the gouges in the door frame. "A real pro would have slipped right through this old lock without leaving a scratch. What d'ya say, Walt?"

Walter stooped to get a better look. "Yep. An amateur, all right."

Lillian hid a grin. The Willis brothers were identical twins but in style and appearance they were opposites. With his completely shaved head, precisely pressed work clothes, and neat, mechanical movements, Walter always made her think of an efficient little robot. In contrast, Torrance was a genial slob. His long, straggly hair was cinched in a ponytail at the nape of his neck. His clothes were stained with what looked like several years' worth of oil, paint, grease, and some orange-red stuff that might have been pizza sauce.

"For what it's worth, Sean Valentine agrees with you." Gabe studied the gouges. "Not that it tells us much."

"If whoever broke in here is the same rat who hit Arizona on the head, I reckon he's long gone," Walter said. "Be a damn fool to hang around Eclipse Bay now that the heat is on."

"I hope you're right," Gabe said. "But the important thing is to get something solid on this door. I don't want Lillian spending another night here with a busted lock."

"No problem." Torrance absently scratched the snake tattoo that slithered out from beneath the sleeve of his grimy work shirt. "After you called us this morning, we stopped off at the hardware store. Picked up just what we need. We'll have this fixed in no time."

Walter selected some tools from a polished metal box. "Won't take long. We can fill in those gouge marks and paint 'em out for you, too."

"That would be great," Lillian said. "I really appreciate this. I know how busy you are with Dreamscape."

"Rafe and Hannah would be the first to tell us to take care of this for you," Walter said. "But I got to admit, they're keeping us real busy over there at the inn."

"You got that right," Torrance agreed. There was a groan of metal and wood as he leaned into the task of removing the broken lock. "Walt and me didn't even bother to bid on any of the work on the new wing of the institute. Knew we wouldn't have time."

"Not that we was invited to bid, mind you." Walter removed the new lock from its packaging. "Perry Decatur is runnin' things up there now. Doesn't like dealin' with local business if he can avoid it. Made it real clear he wanted to bring in out-of-town contractors. Said they were more *competitive*."

"Like money's the most important aspect of a good job," Torrance scoffed. "No respect for fine craftsmanship these days."

"So you two didn't even get a slice of the project?" Gabe asked.

"Nope." Walter positioned the new lock. "Not to say we don't get some work on the side from time to time. Lot of the folks employed up there are local. They know us. They call us when they got a plumbing problem or need a hot-water tank replaced. Those fancy out-of-town contractors aren't interested in the small jobs."

"Claire Jensen mentioned that she had you take care of a clogged toilet for her," Lillian said.

"Yep, she did, as a matter of fact." Walter exchanged a meaningful look with Torrance. Both men smirked.

"What's the joke?" Gabe asked.

"Nothing much." Torrance readied a drill. "Just that while Walt and me was in Claire's bathroom we couldn't help noticing that she had some birth control pills and a box of condoms under the bathroom sink."

Lillian frowned. "Don't you think it's a little tacky to snoop in people's bathroom cupboards when they hire you to fix their plumbing?"

Walter had the grace to blush. "You're right. We shouldn't have said nothin' about it."

"Why not?" Torrance said. "Not like it's news. That woman always did have what you'd call an active social life, even back in the old days. Remember how she used to sneak around with Larry Fulton?"

"Sure do," Walter said. "The two of 'em used to crawl into the back of his dad's delivery van and go at it like a couple of bunnies."

Lillian straightened in the doorway. "She ran around with Larry Fulton? But he's married."

"This was back before he married Sheila Groves and took over his dad's grocery store," Walter assured her. "Way back when he was still in college. That sound right to you, Torrance?"

"Yep, sounds about right. Way I hear it, Claire hasn't changed much over the years."

"I think that's enough gossip about Claire," Gabe said.

He spoke quietly, but Walter and Torrance immediately changed the subject. Lillian smiled to herself. Everyone knew that whatever else you could say about the Madison men, they didn't kiss and tell. Apparently, they didn't listen to other masculine gossip about women either. That kind of old-fashioned chivalry was an extremely endearing trait in a man.

18

THE following morning Arizona held her security briefing from her dimly lit hospital room. She certainly looked the part of the heroically wounded warrior, Lillian thought. The bandages around A.Z.'s head gave her a dashing air. It was clear from the glittering determination in her eyes that she was recovering rapidly.

Lillian was quite relieved to see Arizona looking so much better this morning. She and Gabe had received the phone call summoning them to A.Z.'s bedside half an hour ago, just as they were finishing breakfast.

The only other attendee present today was Photon from the Incandescent Body bakery. He stood in the corner, serene and silent in his strange robes and jewelry. His shaved head gleamed green in the light of a nearby monitor. Could have passed for a space alien, Lillian thought.

"Way I figure it," Arizona said, "the institute spy followed me home because he spotted me taking my routine sector surveillance photos. I cover the whole town right out to the boundaries three mornings a week, you know. Check up on the institute daily, of course. I must have caught something on film that they didn't want anyone to see. When he saw his chance he knocked me out and stole my VPX 5000."

"Don't worry about it, A.Z.," Gabe said. "You can replace the camera and get back to your daily recon work in no time."

"Forget the camera," Arizona said. "Now that we know for sure that we're on to something, we've got to get inside."

That sounded ominous, Lillian thought.

"Inside?" she repeated cautiously. "Inside what?"

"The new wing, of course. Listen up here." Arizona's voice lowered. "Got no choice now. We need to get a firsthand look at whatever is going on in there. My guess is they've made the big move."

Dread settled on Lillian. "Oh, I really don't think they've had time—"

"Probably brought 'em in with the HVAC equipment," Arizona said.

"If that's the case," Photon murmured, "whoever goes inside will have to search for a large freezer compartment somewhere in the new wing."

"Right." Arizona adjusted her position on the pillows, checked the door and then lowered her voice again, this time to a raspy whisper. She motioned with one hand. "Move in as close as you can. The institute probably has spies out there in the hall. Be easy enough to disguise them as orderlies or janitors."

Lillian suppressed a sigh and obediently leaned over the bed. Gabe and Photon followed suit.

"We all know that they'll never let me or one of the Heralds step foot inside the institute." Arizona gave Lillian and Gabe a meaningful look. "That leaves you two."

Lillian gripped the bed rails. "Wait a second here, A.Z. We're not, uh, trained in this kind of work."

"Don't worry, I'll give you a few pointers before you go in."

"How do you plan to get us inside?" Gabe asked, looking interested.

Lillian frantically tried to get his attention but he pretended not to see her.

"I figure the Leaders of Tomorrow open-house event will give you both the perfect opportunity," Arizona said. "Easy for you to get invites because one of you is a Harte and the other is a Madison. Perry Decatur and the folks who run the institute will fall all over themselves to get you there. You're both potential donors."

Phonton nodded somberly. "An excellent plan."

"Just might work, A.Z.," Gabe said.

"But the new wing won't be open yet." Lillian struggled to bring some common sense to the situation. "We won't be able to get in there."

"Shouldn't be too hard," Gabe said. "Everyone will be busy with the reception. Don't see why we can't slip out at some point and take a look at the area under construction."

"It's settled then." Arizona gave them a thumbs-up. "You two will go in the night of the open house."

"What about a camera?" Lillian said quickly. "I don't have one and I doubt if Gabe has one either."

"Could always get one of those little throwaway cameras they sell at the pier," Gabe said helpfully.

"One of those gadgets won't do it," Arizona said. "I'll give you my old VPX 4000. Fine piece of equipment. Lacks a few of the features of the 5000 but it'll get the job done. Remember, we need hard proof that they've stashed those frozen extraterrestrials in that new wing."

19

GABE gave up trying to work, closed the laptop, grabbed a jacket and went down to the beach. He walked for a long time, trying to make sense of the screwy dream that had awakened him in the middle of the night. It had featured broken locks and the grinning faces of the Willis brothers. Not quite a nightmare but close enough.

He stopped at the edge of the water and watched a gull angle into the offshore breeze. Normally he didn't pay much attention to dreams. He didn't believe in intuition, premonitions, or the like.

But he had a healthy respect for his own hunches. They had served him well in business.

Something J. Anderson Flint had said the other night at the restaurant was running through his brain again and again this morning.

"Disgruntled employees can be dangerous."

When he added it to the dream he got a very uneasy feeling.

What if Lillian's first intuitive suspicion had been correct? What if the break-in at her cottage had nothing to do with what had happened to Arizona but was, instead, linked to her fear that someone had intruded into her Portland apartment?

THE knock on her front door interrupted her just as she was about to mix some paint. She put down the palette knife with a sense of deep resignation. What had ever made her think she would get some work done today?

She opened the door warily.

Gabe stood there, one hand braced on the door frame. There was no sign of his car. He was dressed in a black-and-tan windbreaker, jeans, and running shoes. His dark hair was tousled from the wind and a little damp from the mist-heavy air.

"We need to talk." He walked into the hall and shrugged out of his jacket.

His cold, grim expression silenced whatever comment she had been about to make on the subject of interruptions.

"What's wrong?" she asked.

"I've been thinking about something Flint said about Claire."

She took the jacket from him. "What was that?"

"He mentioned that disgruntled employees could be dangerous. It occurred to me that maybe disgruntled boyfriends of former clients might fall into the same category."

She stared at him, the jacket clutched in her hand. "Are you talking about Campbell Witley?"

"Yeah." He disappeared into the kitchen. "Got any coffee?"

She draped the jacket over the hanger, jammed it into the closet and hurried to the doorway of the kitchen.

"What are you thinking?" She watched him fill the coffeemaker with fresh water. "That Witley might be responsible for the break-in here?"

He removed the lid of the coffee canister. "It would explain the incident at your apartment."

"Assuming there was an incident."

He nodded. "Assuming that."

A shiver went through her. "But that would make Witley a stalker."

"I know." He finished spooning ground coffee into the filter and switched on the machine. "I don't want to scare you. Sean Valentine probably got it right when he concluded that whoever conked A.Z. on the head was a transient who had tried to break in here, first. But there is a remote possibility that the two incidents are related. Which, in turn, means that the break-in here could be connected to what happened in Portland."

"It would explain why nothing was taken. A stalker probably wouldn't be interested in stealing stuff."

He crossed the kitchen and cradled her face in his hands.

"Look, this should be easy enough to check out," he said. "All we have to do is find out where Witley was when someone here in Eclipse Bay was breaking into your mudroom. Shouldn't be too hard to see if he's got an alibi. If he can account for his whereabouts during that time period, we can go back to Valentine's theory of a transient burglar."

She swallowed. "I never considered the possibility of a stalker."

"Neither did I until I got to thinking about Flint's comments."

"I can call Nella Townsend, the investigator I used to check out my clients. She might be able to verify Witley's alibi."

"Fine. Call her. I'll speak to Valentine, too. Let him know what's going on. But from what I've read, stalkers can be very slick. Very devious. It's hard to prove that they're doing anything illegal."

She bit her lip. "I know."

"I want to see this guy myself."

"*What?*"

"I want to meet Witley face-to-face. Ask him some questions," Gabe said.

"No." Alarm washed through her. "You can't do that."

"Take it easy, honey. I've done a lot of deals with a lot of people who have things to hide. I'm good at knowing when I'm being lied to."

"Are you nuts?" she yelped. "You can't confront Witley on your own. What if he really is a stalker? He could be very dangerous."

Gabe looked first surprised and then pleased. "Worried about me?"

"Of course I'm worried. No offense, Gabe, but this is not one of your more brilliant ideas."

"I'm just going to drive into Portland and meet the guy. Don't worry, if he is a stalker, I doubt that he's a danger to me. Stalkers are obsessed with their victims, not other people."

"Listen, I don't want you handling this on your own. If you insist on going to Portland to see him, I'll go with you."

"No." There was no give in the single word. "I don't want you anywhere near him."

"Witley is a big man. He's had military training. He works in construction. Get the picture?"

"You think he might beat me to a pulp. Gee. You really don't have much faith in my manly skills, do you?"

"Your manly skills are not the issue here," she said. "I don't want you to take that kind of risk on my account. I mean it. You can't do this by yourself and that's final."

He hesitated. "I guess I could take along some backup."

That stopped her for a heartbeat or two.

"Backup?" she repeated cautiously.

"A guy I know. He's big. Had some military training. Worked construction for a while."

"Do I know this man?"

"Yeah."

❦

"TELL me again why we're going to drive all the way into Portland to see this guy, Witley," Mitchell said, buckling his seat belt.

"Long story." Gabe put on his dark glasses and turned the key in the ignition. "It's just barely possible that Witley is stalking Lillian. She's going to have an investigator check out his movements in the past few days, but I want to talk to him myself. Lillian made it clear that she didn't want me meeting him alone. I refused to take her along. You're the compromise."

"Well, shoot and damn," Mitchell said cheerfully. "This sounds like fun. Any chance of a fight?"

"Probably not. But there's always hope."

20

SHE stared at the blank canvas, knowing that she was even less likely to get into the zone now than she had been earlier in the day when Gabe had interrupted her.

All she could think about was that he and Mitchell were on their way to Portland together to confront Witley.

The phone rang in the living room. She turned away from the canvas and went to answer it.

"Lillian? This is Nella. I got your message. What's up?"

"Thanks for calling me back." She sank down onto the arm of the sofa. "I've got a little problem here. Remember that guy Witley I asked you to check out?"

"Sure." Nella paused. "Something happen?"

"Maybe. Maybe not. Can you find out if he left town sometime during the past few days?"

"Shouldn't be too difficult. What's going on, Lil?"

"I'm not sure." She gave Nella a quick rundown of events.

"I'll get right on it," Nella said. "Meanwhile, watch yourself, okay? These guys tend to escalate."

"What do you mean?"

"The incidents get more serious. It's a progressive thing. Do me a huge favor. Lock all your doors and windows and keep them locked until your friend Madison gets there or until I give you the all-clear. I'll get back to you as soon as I have something solid."

"Thanks."

Lillian ended the call, put down the phone and went back into the studio.

The blank canvas might as well have been sitting in another universe, a place where she could not go today.

⁓◦⁓

A red compact pulled into the drive just as she was about to pour herself another cup of tea. Her fourth that afternoon. She went to the window and saw Claire Jensen, dressed in a navy blue shirt and a pair of jeans, get out from behind the wheel and walk up the front steps.

Just what she needed. Another interruption. She put down the cup and went to open the front door.

"Hi." Claire looked and sounded as if she had not slept much in recent days. "I need to talk to someone. Mind if I come in for a few minutes?"

More sisterhood stuff. How much of this kind of thing was a woman supposed to do to retain her politically correct status?

"No, of course not." Lillian held the door open. "I made tea. Want some?"

"That would be nice. Thanks."

Claire walked into the front hall, took off her coat and gave it to Lillian to hang in the closet.

"Come on into the kitchen," Lillian said.

"I assume you know that Marilyn fired me."

"I heard."

"It's not exactly the end of the world." Claire folded her hands on the table and looked out the window. "Campaign managers get canned a lot. Goes with the territory."

"I'm sure you'll find another position."

"Sure. Something will turn up. That's not what's bothering me. It was the scene in the Crab Trap. It's all over town. I have never been so embarrassed in my life. The worst part is that I have no one to blame but myself."

Lillian took another cup down out of the cupboard. "It'll all blow over in a few days."

"I still don't know what made me track her down at the restaurant and confront her like that. I guess I was just so angry that I wasn't thinking straight. She actually accused me of sleeping with Trevor, can you imagine?"

Lillian poured tea. "I take it you didn't have an affair with him?"

"Are you kidding? I admired Trevor's political agenda, but that was as far as it went. I'm a pro. I don't sleep with my clients."

Lillian set the cup down in front of her. "Probably a good policy in your line of work."

"You bet." Claire blew on her tea. "Besides, according to the rumors, Thornley likes to dress up in women's lingerie and prance around in high heels. Don't know about you, but personally I don't find that type of thing a real turn-on."

"I can see where the lingerie and heels might be a little off-putting. What happens now?"

"I'll be leaving town in a couple of days. I plan to go to Seattle and regroup. I've got contacts there. But I didn't come here to whine today. Well, maybe just a little."

"Why did you come here?"

Claire put down her cup. "Marilyn has always been a little overcontrolling and a bit paranoid. I never worried about it too much. You expect that in a strong candidate. But I have to tell you that after those crazy accusations about Trevor and me, I'm starting to wonder if maybe she's gone off the deep end. If that's the case, I think you should be careful."

"Me? Why should I worry?"

"Because I've noticed that she's become a little fixated on your relationship with Gabe Madison. Maybe it's because she's divorced now. But I think there's more to it than that."

The phone rang. On the off chance that it might be Nella reporting back with the all-clear, Lillian lunged for it.

She heard the muffled noise of a car in motion.

"Hello?"

"Witley is gone." Gabe's voice was very even. Too even. "He told some friends that he was taking a vacation. He's not at his house. No one has seen him for a few days. Heard from your investigator yet?"

"No." Lillian clutched the phone very tightly. "Where are you?"

"We're on our way back to Eclipse Bay. It's almost four o'clock. We should get there around seven."

"I'll hold dinner for you both."

"Now that we know for sure that Witley has disappeared, I don't think it's a good idea for you to be there alone. We don't know where he is or what he's doing."

"I'll be fine until seven tonight, for heaven's sake. Claire Jensen is here with me now, as a matter of fact, so I'm not alone."

There was a murmur of conversation in the background. Lillian realized that Mitchell was speaking to Gabe.

Gabe spoke into the phone again. "Mitchell wants to send Bryce over to baby-sit until we get back."

"That's not necessary." Lillian checked her watch. "Look, I'm going stir-crazy here. I need to run into town and pick up some groceries for dinner. I'll leave the house right after Claire. I'll do the shopping and then I'll stop and see A.Z. at the hospital. That will keep me busy and I won't be alone. Call me at the hospital when you get into town and I'll meet you back here at the cottage. That way I won't be alone for any extended period of time."

Gabe hesitated. "All right. But don't take any long walks on the beach by yourself, okay?"

"I thought you didn't want to scare me."

"I've changed my mind. I figure if you're scared, you'll be careful."

"Don't worry, I won't wander off by myself."

"Good. See you soon."

Lillian ended the call and put down the phone.

Claire gave her a quizzical look. "Something wrong?"

"To tell you the truth, I don't really know. There have been a couple of small incidents lately. Someone broke in here the other day while I was at the old Buckley place with Gabe."

Claire frowned and slowly lowered her cup. "Anything taken?"

"No. Sean Valentine thinks it's the same guy who tried to burglarize A.Z.'s place."

"I heard about that. It's all over town. They're saying it was a transient."

"I know. But the thing that's worrisome is that there was another possible break-in at my apartment in Portland. Nothing taken there, either. Gabe leaped to the conclusion that the culprit might be a guy named Witley."

"Who's he?"

"A former boyfriend of one of my clients."

"But why on earth would he break into your apartment and this place?"

"The theory is that he blames me for ruining his relationship with his girl-friend."

"You mean because you matched her with someone else?"

"Yes."

"Uh-oh. Are we talking stalker here?"

"It looks like a possibility. A remote one, I hope. You know, a friend told me I was courting a lawsuit in the matchmaking business. But I never considered this kind of thing."

"We worry about stalkers when we plan security for candidates. There are always a few nutcases running around. But I must admit, I never thought about it in your line of work."

"My *former* line."

Claire blew out a deep breath. "And I thought I had problems."

"A matchmaker's life is never dull."

"I can see that." Claire got to her feet. "Well, at least you've got Gabe Madison looking out for you. Things could be worse."

"There is that."

"I'd better be on my way. I can see you've got other things to worry about than my little scene in the Crab Trap. Promise me you'll be careful."

"Don't worry, I will." Lillian rose and followed her out into the hall. She got Claire's coat out of the closet and handed it to her. "You said you had something you wanted to tell me."

"What? Oh, yeah." Claire shrugged into her coat. "But it seems a little petty compared to this stalker business."

"What was it?"

"It's about Marilyn. I'm no shrink, but like I started to tell you before Gabe phoned, I really do think she may be a bit paranoid. When you add that to the fact that she's a very determined woman who always gets what she wants, well, I just think you might want to watch your step around her, that's all."

"Why?"

"Because you've got something she wants," Claire said.

"What's that?"

"Gabe Madison."

⁂

"WELL, shoot and damn." Mitchell watched Gabe disconnect the phone. "We've got ourselves a problem here, don't we?"

"Maybe. I sure don't like the fact that Witley has disappeared."

Mitchell watched him for a moment. He'd seen that same look of focused determination back when Gabe had been a twelve-year-old kid doing his home-work at the kitchen table. Nothing had changed, Mitchell thought. Gabe was a different kind of Madison. But not that different.

"Wasn't talking about Witley," Mitchell said. "We'll get that sorted out. Meant this situation between you and Lillian."

"Situation?"

"Way it looks to me, you're in up to your neck and sinking deeper by the minute."

Gabe navigated a turn, accelerating smoothly on the far side. "What are you talking about?"

Mitchell absently massaged his arthritic knee. He tried to remember if he had taken his anti-inflammatory medication. Things had been a little busy today.

"Had what you might call a chat with Lillian," he said.

"I heard about that. Stay out of this, Mitch. My relationship with Lillian is none of your business. You don't have the right to interfere."

"I'm your grandfather. 'Course I've got the right."

Mitchell watched the road. There was very little traffic now that they had left the city behind. The last of the daylight was evaporating. The white lines on the pavement marked the path into the darkness.

He braced himself for the old memories. No matter where he was or what he was doing, they always came back to haunt him for a while at this time of day; the point when the oncoming night could no longer be ignored. He knew from long experience that once the transition to full dark was made, the specters would fade. They would not return for another twenty-four hours.

When he was home it was his custom to handle the ghosts with a shot of whiskey. But tonight he had nothing to take the edge off. He would just have to deal with it. Wouldn't be the first time.

From out of the depths the phantoms arose, right on schedule. The scene was a twilight-shrouded jungle drenched with the smell of death and gut-wrenching fear. The worst part had been knowing that the night was inevitable and that there was no hope of rescue until dawn.

He and Sullivan had made it through that hellish night together because they had both understood that their survival depended on staying in control of the panic. They had both understood the need for absolute silence and absolute stillness. Side by side in the unrelenting darkness, they had somehow managed to reinforce that grim knowledge in each other without words or movement of any kind. And without words or movement they had managed to keep each other from slipping over the edge into that place where the fear took over and got you killed.

At dawn, he and Sullivan had still been alive. A lot of the others had not been so lucky.

He wondered if Sullivan went through the same ritual every evening. Waiting. Knowing the night was inevitable.

"What, exactly, did you say to Lillian?" Gabe asked.

Mitchell watched the light disappear, unable to look away. "Just told her flat-out that it looked to me like you were fallin' for her in a big way and that I didn't want her to stomp all over your heart."

"Those were your exact words?"

Mitchell thought back to the conversation in the greenhouse. "Pretty close."

"Did Lillian imply that she intended to, uh, stomp all over my heart?" Gabe asked.

What the hell was it about this time of day? The shift from day to night always seemed to take forever.

"In a manner of speaking," he said.

Gabe gazed steadily at the road unwinding in front of the car. "Doesn't sound like something Lillian would say. What were her precise words, Mitch?"

"Well, she got irritated when I told her that I didn't want you gettin' hurt. Said something about how she was the one who stood to get stomped on account of everyone was so sure you were after her because you wanted a chunk of Harte Investments."

Gabe nodded. "I can see where she'd get that impression. Lot of people have been saying that lately."

"Natural assumption, under the circumstances."

"Probably."

"I told her that was garbage. Said you were a Madison and Madisons never marry for money. Not that practical, when you get right down to it."

"Good point." Gabe waited a beat. "So, how did she respond to that observation?"

"She reminded me how everyone said that you were a different kind of Madison. I told her you were different, but not that different."

"What else did she say?"

"Well, let's see. I believe I may have pointed out that Madison Commercial is your passion and that when it comes to a Madison and his passion—"

"Nothing gets in the way. Yeah, right, I've heard that. She say anything else?"

The transition to night was complete at last. The phantom images receded into the darkness.

Mitchell exhaled slowly. "Seemed to think I'd maybe given you the wrong impression."

"About what?"

"About what you've done with Madison Commercial."

Gabe's hands tightened a little on the wheel. "For the past year and a half you've been telling me that I've spent too much time fooling around with the company. Maybe you were right."

Mitchell had to swallow twice to keep from sputtering. "Shoot and damn, son, you built that company from the ground up. You sweated blood to prove something to the whole damn world."

"What did I prove?"

"You know what you proved. Hell, after you created Madison Commercial no one could say that every Madison who came along was doomed to screw up everything he touched."

"You consider that a major accomplishment?"

"Damn right, I do." He stared at the road. "More important than you'll ever know."

"How so?"

"Because after Madison Commercial, folks had to quit sayin' that I had screwed up both my grandsons' lives the same way I had messed up your father's life."

A crystalline silence enveloped the front seat of the car.

"Did people really say that?" Gabe asked after a while. "To your face?"

"Some said it to my face. Most folks said it behind my back. They were all pretty much agreed that I wasn't fit to raise you and Rafe after Sinclair killed himself and your mother on that damn motorcycle."

"Huh."

"They said I set a piss-poor example for a couple of young boys." He rubbed his jaw. "To tell you the truth, they were right. But what the hell was I gonna do? Not like there was anyone else around to take over the job."

"You could have walked out. Disappeared. Let the social workers deal with us."

"Bullshit. You don't turn your grandkids over to the state to raise."

"Some people would."

"Madisons don't do stuff like that."

Gabe smiled slightly. "Got it."

Mitchell suddenly realized that he wanted to explain things, but he didn't know how to go about it. He wasn't good at this kind of situation. He groped for the right words.

"The point I'm trying to make," he said, "is that you were smart enough not to follow my bad example. You made something of yourself, Gabe. When you built M.C. you broke the Madison curse or jinx or whatever that made us all failures."

"No."

"What the hell do you mean? That's exactly what you did and don't you ever forget it."

"It wasn't me who broke the jinx," Gabe said. "It was you."

"*Me?*"

"Don't you get it? You're the one who changed after Dad's death. And when you changed, you altered the future for Rafe and me."

21

LILLIAN stopped the car in the drive, opened the door and checked her watch in the weak overhead light. Just after seven. There was no sign of Gabe and Mitchell yet but they would be here any minute. Gabe had called her from the outskirts of town a short while ago.

She had left the porch light on as well as several lamps inside the house. The cottage was illuminated with a warm, welcoming glow. Keys in hand, she collected the two sacks of groceries she had picked up at Fulton's Supermarket and went up the porch steps. With a little jockeying, she managed to get the front door open without having to put down one of the grocery bags.

She walked into the front hall, kicked the door shut and wrestled her burdens into the kitchen. The house felt unaccountably cold.

She was certain she had left the thermostat set at a comfortable temperature.

An uneasy feeling drifted through her. There had been a cold draft in the mudroom the night someone had broken in.

She went to the door and studied the living room. Nothing appeared to be disturbed. Maybe she had left an upstairs window open a crack.

But the draft was not coming from the staircase. It emanated from the downstairs hall.

Her studio.

Galvanized, she rushed toward the guest bedroom. As soon as she turned the corner she saw that the door stood partially ajar, just as she remembered leaving it earlier. But through the narrow opening she could see that something was very wrong inside her studio.

A chill that had nothing to do with the draft of cold air went through her. With a sense of deep dread, she pushed the door open wide.

The studio was in chaos. The blank canvas on the easel had been ripped to shreds. Rags, brushes, and knives were scattered across the floor. There was paint everywhere. The contents of several tubes of paint had been smeared across one wall and the floor. Her palette lay upside down on the bed. Pages of drawings had been ripped from her sketchbook and crumpled into balls.

She finally identified the source of the cold draft. It came through the broken window.

GABE felt everything inside him turn to stone when he saw Sean Valentine's SUV parked in the drive.

Then he saw Lillian standing on the front porch talking to Valentine, and allowed himself to start breathing again.

He hit the brakes and switched off the engine. "Something's wrong."

"Yeah, I figured that." Mitchell surveyed the scene on the porch. "Not like Sean to be running around at this time of night unless there's trouble."

Gabe got the Jag's door open. He loped toward the steps. Sean and Lillian looked at him.

"What happened?" Gabe asked.

"Looks like Lillian had another visit from whoever broke in the other night," Sean said.

"He vandalized my studio this time," Lillian said shakily.

Mitchell came up the steps with his cane. He frowned at Lillian. "You okay?"

"I'm fine." She smiled wanly. "But he made a mess. The floor, the bedspread, the wall. Everything's covered in paint."

Sean looked serious. "Didn't think too much of your idea that this guy Witley might be stalking her, Madison. But after seeing what he did to that bedroom, I'm inclined to agree with you. Let's go inside and see what we've got."

"WE'VE got jack squat, that's what we've got," Mitchell announced an hour later when they finally got around to dinner. He squinted at Lillian. "How the heck did you get into so much trouble running a matchmaking business?"

"Darned if I know." She picked up her wineglass. "Friend of mine told me that the business was a lawsuit waiting to happen. But no one warned me about stalkers."

"Well, don't you worry about it too much." Mitchell tackled his stir-fry vegetables with gusto. "One thing to be a stalker in Portland where no one notices a guy hanging around places he shouldn't be hanging around. Another thing to do your stalking here in Eclipse Bay where a stranger gets noticed, especially at this time of year."

"He's right," Gabe said. "If Witley's in town, Sean Valentine will find him quickly."

"Meanwhile, you'll be okay," Mitchell added. "Gabe here will watch over you."

Lillian looked at Gabe.

He gave her his sexy grin. "Won't let you out of my sight."

She contemplated the wine in her glass. "The thing is, even if Sean does find Witley, what can he do? I've heard it's tough to prove a charge of stalking."

Gabe and Mitchell exchanged silent looks.

She frowned. "What?"

Gabe shrugged. "Don't worry about Witley. If Sean can't do anything, Mitch and I will think of something."

Her hand tensed around the glass. "Such as?"

"Us Madisons are pretty creative," Mitchell assured her cheerfully.

She looked at each of them in turn. Another small chill wafted through her. They were both smiling, easy, laid-back Madison smiles. Probably trying to re-assure her. But there was something very different going on in their eyes. Something very dangerous.

SHE did not argue when Gabe suggested that they go back to his place after dinner. The idea of leaving the cottage undefended made her uneasy but the notion of actually spending the night there gave her the jitters. She knew that she would not sleep.

When she emerged from the bathroom she found him standing at the bedroom window, gazing out into the night. He wore a pair of jeans but nothing else. The sleek, muscled contours of his bare back and shoulders made her fingers itch for a pencil and some drawing paper. Other parts of her were tingling, too, she noticed.

"What are you thinking?" she asked.

"I had an interesting conversation with Mitch on the way back to Eclipse Bay this evening." He did not turn around. "Apparently Madison Commercial is more important to him than he likes to admit."

"Oh." She tightened the sash of her bathrobe and sank down on the end of the bed. "I could have told you that."

"He said it was proof to the world that he hadn't screwed up completely with Rafe and me."

She thought about it. "I can see where he might view your success as a sign that he hadn't botched the job of raising you. What did you say?"

Gabe let the curtain fall and turned around to face her. "That he was the reason Rafe and I made it at all."

"Ah, yes."

"It's the truth. I've known it for years but I don't think I ever told him."

"Madison Commercial is important to your grandfather, but you and Rafe mean a lot more to him than the company does."

Gabe sat down beside her, leaned forward and clasped his hands loosely between his knees. He contemplated their images in the mirror above the chest of drawers.

"He really is afraid you'll break my heart," Gabe said.

She managed a soft little laugh. "Did you assure him that's not very likely?"

Gabe said nothing.

She stilled. "Gabe?"

"What?"

"You didn't allow him to think that I could really break your heart, did you?"

"Well, sure." He said it carelessly, easily, casually. As if it were an incontrovertible fact. "I'm a Madison."

She stopped breathing altogether for the space of a couple of heartbeats. With concentration she managed to drag some oxygen into her lungs.

"Is this your subtle, roundabout way of telling me that you see our relationship as something more than just a short-term affair?" she whispered.

"It's been something more than just an affair for me right from the start."

She could hardly speak. "But I thought we had agreed that we aren't a good match."

He shrugged. "You Hartes probably worry about things like that more than we Madisons do."

"You're supposed to be a different kind of Madison."

He straightened and reached for her, pushed her gently down onto the bed. He leaned forward and kissed her throat.

"Not that different," he said.

THE following morning they went back to the cottage together to clean up the studio. There was a message from Nella on the answering machine. It was short and to the point.

"Call me."

Lillian grabbed the phone and punched in the number.

"What have you got?" she asked without preamble.

"Where have you been? I've been trying to reach you since six o'clock this morning."

Lillian glanced at Gabe. "Out. I was out."

"Is that so?" Nella sounded amused. "Wouldn't have thought there was enough going on in Eclipse Bay to keep a jaded city girl out all night."

"Nella—"

"I found Witley," Nella said, brisk and businesslike now. "He has a rock-solid alibi for the entire time that you've been in Eclipse Bay."

"What is it?"

"He and a pal are down in the Caribbean doing some diving. They're registered at a hotel on Saint Thomas. I checked with some of the local dive shops and I called his room. He was there, Lil. No way he could have flown back to Oregon, driven to Eclipse Bay yesterday and then returned to the island this morning in time to take my call."

"I see." Lillian looked at Gabe, who was listening intently to her side of the conversation. "I'm not sure if that's good news or bad news because it means we have to start from scratch. But thanks for checking him out."

"Sure. By the way, apparently whatever you said to him on the street that day made an impact. I had a long conversation with him. He said he realized that maybe you'd been right about how he needed an outdoor type, not one of those highbrow arty types."

Lillian groaned. "He used the term *arty?*"

"Uh-huh. He now agrees with you that he and Heather Summers were not made for each other after all."

"Well, what do you know."

"Anything else I can do for you?"

"Not just yet, but stay tuned."

Nella hesitated. "Can you think of anyone else besides Witley who might want to harass you? Any old boyfriends hanging around?"

"No."

"You're sure?"

"You know better than anyone else what my social life has been like for the past year, Nella. Boring doesn't even begin to describe it."

Gabe raised a brow. She ignored him.

"We in the investigation business have a saying," Nella continued. "When the picture doesn't make sense, draw a new one. Maybe you should look at these incidents from another perspective."

"Problem is, I can't see any other angle here."

Nella hesitated. "You know, if it weren't for the trashing of your studio yesterday, I'd say that someone had broken into your apartment and your cottage to look for something."

"I can't imagine what it could be. I told you, nothing was taken."

"The pieces of this puzzle aren't fitting well together, Lil. Be careful."

22

THE darkened hallway was lined with office doors fitted with opaque glass. Gabe could hear the din of muffled voices in the distance. The noise came from the large reception room in the intersecting corridor. The Leaders of Tomorrow openhouse event was in full swing.

Lillian stood beside him in the shadows. Her hair was pinned into a sleek, graceful knot at the back of her head. She wore a close-fitting, midnight-blue dress made out of a stretchy, slinky fabric that moved when she did and a pair of sexy, strappy heels.

He could think of a couple of other things he would rather do with her tonight than hunt for frozen space aliens. But duty called.

He checked the bulky camera Arizona had given him. "We're all set."

"I still say this is a really bad idea," Lillian muttered. "What if we get caught prowling through the new wing?"

"If anyone stops us, which is highly unlikely given that they're all very busy with the reception, we'll say we were curious about the new construction. Big deal. You really think anyone would arrest a Harte and a Madison who just happened to wander into the wrong hallway here at the institute?"

"You never know."

"It's a lot more likely they'd ask us for a contribution. Stop worrying. You're a little tense tonight."

"I've had a very difficult week and now I'm getting ready to look for frozen aliens. I've got a right to be tense. I'm supposed to be devoting myself to art, remember?"

"Take it easy," he said. "Think of this as performance art."

"Yeah, right. Performance art."

"We'll get in, take a few shots of empty offices and get out. Tomorrow we'll turn the pictures over to A.Z. and she can weave whatever conspiracy theories she wants. That will be the end of it for us."

"How do we explain the camera if we're stopped by a guard?"

"No problem," Gabe said. "We'll say we wanted some souvenir photos of the reception."

"It's a high-tech spy camera, for heaven's sake. No one's going to buy that story."

"Trust me. I can fake it if necessary."

"All right," she said with annoyance. "Let's get it over with and get back to the open house."

She started off down the hall toward the new wing with long, determined strides. He fell into step beside her, marveling at how well she could move in the sexy shoes. Together they prowled deeper into the bowels of the institute. The sounds of the open house faded into the distance behind them.

At the far end of the dark passage a temporary door fashioned out of plywood had been installed to separate the uncompleted wing from the main building. A band of loosely draped construction zone tape barred the way. Gabe ducked under the tape and found the partition unlocked.

"We're in luck." He eased the plywood door open and stood aside to allow Lillian to enter. "Ready to boldly go where no Harte or Madison has gone before?"

She moved into the unpainted hall and stopped.

"Shouldn't you start taking pictures?" she said in a low voice.

"Right."

He walked to the nearest door and opened it. There was enough light filtering through the window from the parking lot lamps to reveal the bones of an empty room that was clearly intended to serve as an office.

"No frozen aliens in here," he announced.

"Big surprise." She leaned around the edge of the door. "Hurry up and take a picture. We've got a whole bunch of rooms to cover."

He raised the heavy VPX 4000 and snapped off a shot. The flash flared, brilliantly illuminating the small space for an instant. Darkness closed in again almost immediately.

"Great," Lillian said. "Now I can't see a thing."

"This thing really puts out some wattage, doesn't it?" He blinked a few times to get rid of the dark spots. "Next time close your eyes when I take the picture."

He went to the door across the hall, opened it, and took another picture of an empty, partially painted interior. When he finished, he moved to the next door and repeated the procedure.

After a while, it became routine. Open a door, take a photo of a bare office, close the door. Go to the next room.

"I don't think A.Z. is going to be real thrilled with these pictures," Lillian said halfway down the hall. "She has her heart set on finding proof that the government has secretly moved frozen extraterrestrials here to Eclipse Bay."

"Don't worry about A.Z. She's a professional conspiracy buff, remember? A pro can always find a way to spin the facts into a new theory."

He opened the next door in line, raised the VPX 4000 and fired off a shot.

A woman yelled at the same instant the flash exploded. Not Lillian, he realized. Someone else. This room was inhabited. Not frozen aliens. Warm bodies.

Two figures were illuminated in the intense light. A man with a serious erection dressed in a pair of red bikini briefs and a woman in a black leather bustier and high-heeled black boots.

J. Anderson Flint and Marilyn Thornley.

"Holy cow," Gabe said. "A.Z. was right. But it's worse than she thought. Wait'll she hears that they've thawed out two of the frozen alien life-forms."

For two or three seconds everyone stared at everyone else. Marilyn, demonstrating the well-honed instincts of a natural-born politician, recovered first.

"Give me that camera," she shouted.

"Sorry, it's not mine to give away." Gabe took a quick step back toward the door. "Private property, you know. A bulwark of our constitutional republic. Wouldn't be right."

"I said give me that damned camera." Marilyn lunged toward him.

"Give her the stupid camera, for heaven's sake," Lillian said.

She grabbed the heavy VPX 4000 out of his hand and hurled it toward Marilyn the way you'd hurl garlic and a silver cross at a vampire.

"Let's get out of here." She seized his arm and hauled him out of the doorway. "Right now."

She broke into a run. Gabe had to stretch a little to keep up with her. He admired her form as they went down the corridor.

"I didn't know a woman could move that fast in high heels," he said.

By the time they reached the main building he was laughing so hard he accidentally went through the construction zone tape, severing it. The ends fluttered to the floor.

"A.Z. was right," he managed to get out between howls. "Strange things going on in the new wing."

Lillian stopped and turned to look at him. She was breathing hard from her recent exertion. She watched him for a long moment, a strange expression on her face. You'd think she'd never seen a man doubled up with laughter, he thought.

"I'd give anything for a picture of you right now." She stepped forward and brushed her mouth lightly against his. "And to think that I once thought you were a walking case of burnout."

THE following morning Lillian was still trying to figure out how to deliver the bad news to Arizona. She stood at the kitchen counter in Gabe's house watching him slather peanut butter onto two slices of toasted Incandescent Body sourdough bread, and went through the possibilities.

"We could say we lost her VPX 4000," she said. "Or maybe imply that it was stolen out of the car."

Gabe did not look up from his task. "Could tell her the truth."

"Don't be ridiculous. No one, not even A.Z., would believe it."

"You've got a point." Gabe put the peanut butter toast on a plate. "Some things defy description."

"Some things are also actionable. The last thing we need is a lawsuit from Marilyn's campaign." Lillian poured coffee. "We have to come up with a reasonable story or A.Z. will invent another new conspiracy theory to explain a second missing camera."

Gabe picked up a slice of peanut butter toast and took a bite. "You have to admit that it's pushing coincidence a bit."

"I beg your pardon?"

"Think about it. Two missing spy cameras. One stolen by force. One confiscated by a politician in a black leather bustier. Both cameras belong to a woman dedicated to uncovering the truth about a clandestine government project housed at the Eclipse Bay Policy Studies Institute. I mean, what are the odds?"

"You find this all very entertaining, don't you?"

He grinned and took a swallow of coffee. "Most fun I've had in a long time."

"Great. Wonderful. I'm glad you're amused. But what the heck are we going to tell A.Z.?"

"Leave it to me. I'll handle it. I think I'll go with the truth. By the time A.Z. gets through twisting it, no one will recognize it, anyway."

Lillian took a bite of toast. She chewed on it for a while and then swallowed.

"Something I've been meaning to ask," she said.

"Yeah?"

"Did Marilyn wear black leather bustiers a lot when the two of you were an item?"

"It's been a long time," Gabe said. "My memory isn't so good when it comes to some things. But I'm pretty sure the black leather gear is new. Probably a political fashion statement."

"Probably." She looked at the unfinished portion of her toast. "You're good with peanut butter, you know that?"

"It's a gift."

"MARILYN Thornley confiscated the camera?" Arizona slapped a big hand, palm down, fingers spread, on the laminated map that decorated the table of her war room. "Damn. I was afraid of this. She's either working with them or she's one of their dupes."

Lillian suppressed a groan. This was not going well. The good news was that Arizona appeared to be back to her old self. She still wore a small bandage but there was no sign of any other physical problems resulting from the blow to her head.

"Personally," Gabe said, "I'd vote for the dupe possibility. I can't see Marilyn getting involved in a conspiracy to cover up dead space aliens and high-tech UFO secrets. She's too busy working on the launch of her campaign."

Arizona squinted a little while she considered that angle. "Guess you know her better than anyone else around here does."

"Guess so," Lillian agreed brightly.

"I doubt that she has changed much," Gabe said deliberately. "She's devoted to one cause and that cause is Marilyn Thornley."

"She's been involved in politics for the last few years, though," A.Z. mused. "Makes for strange bedfellows."

A vision of Anderson in his red bikini briefs flared briefly in Lillian's mind. "You can say that again."

"We'll replace the camera, A.Z.," Gabe said. "In the meantime, you have our full report. The bottom line is that there was no sign of heavy-duty lab equipment in the new wing and we found no evidence of frozen extraterrestrials. If those alien bodies were moved into the institute, they've got them well hidden."

"Figures." Arizona nodded sagely. "Should have known it wouldn't be this easy. We'll just have to keep digging. Maybe literally, if they've hidden the lab underground."

"A scary thought," Lillian murmured.

"My work will continue," Arizona assured them. "Meanwhile, thanks for the undercover job. Couldn't have done it without you. Unfortunately, you'll never get the public recognition you deserve because we have to maintain secrecy."

"We understand," Gabe said.

Arizona nodded. "But I want you to know that your names will be legend among the ranks of those of us who seek the truth about this vast conspiracy."

"That's certainly good enough for me," Lillian said quickly. "How about you, Gabe?"

"Always wanted to be a legend in my own time," Gabe said.

"We don't want any public recognition," Lillian added, eager to emphasize the point. "Just knowing that we did our patriotic duty is all the reward we need. Isn't that right, Gabe?"

"Right." Gabe got to his feet. "Publicity would be a disaster. If our identities as secret agents were exposed, it would ruin any chance of us helping you out with future undercover work."

Lillian was almost to the door. "Wouldn't want that."

"True," Arizona said. "Never know when we might have to call on you two again."

SHE knew that something was bothering Gabe. The amusement that had carried him through last night's investigation and this morning's debriefing with Arizona had vanished. When she had called him to suggest a walk on the beach a short while ago, he had agreed, but she could tell that his thoughts were elsewhere.

He had met her at the top of the beach path. She had noticed immediately that the cool, remote quality was back. At least she had finally figured out that the withdrawn air did not automatically indicate major depression or burnout. It meant that he was doing some heavy-duty thinking.

At last. Progress in the quest to understand the deeper elements of Gabriel Madison's enigmatic nature.

He moved easily beside her, his jacket collar pulled up around his neck, his hands shoved deep into his pockets. She recognized this brooding mood, she suddenly realized. She had experienced it often enough herself. It came upon her at times when she was struggling to find the key to the inner vision of a picture. She wondered why she had never understood the similarity before.

She did not try to draw him out of whatever distant space he was exploring. Instead she contented herself with setting an energetic pace for both of them. The tide was out, exposing small, rocky pools. She picked a route through the driftwood and assorted debris that had been deposited by the last storm.

Gabe did not speak until they had almost reached Eclipse Arch, the rock monolith that dominated the beach.

"How well do you know Flint?" he asked without any preamble.

The question took her by surprise.

"Anderson?" She came to a halt. "Not well at all. He moved into the same office building in Portland about six months ago. Like I said, we had some conversations of a professional nature. That's about it."

"You told me that he wanted to buy your matchmaking program."

She shrugged. "And I explained to him that it wasn't for sale."

"Maybe he figured he could get it another way," Gabe said.

"What other way is there?" Then it hit her. "Good grief. You don't really think Anderson would try to . . . to steal it, do you? But—"

"I checked with the college public affairs office this morning. There is no conference of any kind scheduled at Chamberlain this week or next. Flint lied when he said that he was in town to attend a professional seminar."

"Are you absolutely sure?"

"Yes."

She started walking again, mulling over the possibilities. "Okay, maybe he made up the story about being here for a conference. I can see where he might have followed me to try to talk me into selling him the program. But it's hard to envision him actually breaking into my apartment and the cottage."

"Why? You've got something he wants. You refused to sell it to him. In his mind that might not leave a lot of options."

"Yes, but—" She trailed off, trying to sort out the logic. "Anderson is a sex therapist, for heaven's sake."

"He hasn't been one for long."

That stopped her in her tracks. "I beg your pardon?"

"After I called Chamberlain, I talked to some people I know in Portland and went online for some research. The institution that issued Flint's professional credentials is a mail-order outfit."

"What do you mean?"

"It's a paper mill. You pay them money, they give you a fancy piece of paper."

"In other words, his credentials are bogus?"

"Let's just say that his alma mater is not real rigorous when it comes to academic standards."

She thought about the women she had seen in Anderson's waiting room. A shudder went through her. "Talk about a lawsuit waiting to happen. And I thought I was on dangerous ground."

"Funny you should mention the word 'lawsuit.' "

"Why?"

"Turns out that Flint reinvented himself as a sex therapist after he got into legal troubles in his former profession."

She groaned. "I'm afraid to ask but I can't help myself. What did he do before he went into the field of sex therapy?"

"He headed up a consortium that invested heavily in some Internet ventures that disappeared into thin air."

"Are you telling me Anderson is a complete fraud?"

"No. From what I could learn this morning, it appears that no one has as yet managed to prove that. Flint appears to have a talent for staying inside the gray area between legal and illegal activities. But a guy like that might not have any qualms about trying to steal a computer program."

"Great." She took her hands out of her pockets and spread them wide. "What are we supposed to do now?"

"I think," Gabe said, "that we should have a conversation with J. Anderson Flint."

THE motel was typical of many that dotted the winding coast road that led to and from Eclipse Bay, a little down at the heels and mostly empty at this time of year. The rooms all opened directly onto the outside sidewalk. There were three cars parked in front of three doors. Two of the vehicles were mud-splattered SUVs. The third was a sparkling-clean late-model Lincoln.

Gabe brought the Jag to a halt at the far end of the parking lot and studied the blue Lincoln.

"What do you want to bet that's his car?"

Lillian followed his gaze. Tension angled her shoulders.

"If you're wrong, this could be a little hard to explain," she said.

"I told you to let me handle this on my own."

"I can't do that and you know it. Anderson is my problem."

"Correction." He cracked open the door and got out. "He's *our* problem."

He closed the door before she could argue.

She emerged from the Jag without another word. Together they walked to number seven.

Gabe knocked twice. Anderson opened the door immediately. He wore gray trousers and a blue sweater that matched his car and his eyes. He did not look at all surprised to see them standing outside his room.

"I wondered when you two would get here," he said.

Lillian looked at him unhappily. "We came to talk to you, Anderson."

"Obviously." Flint held the door open. "You might as well come inside. I trust this won't take long. I've got a meeting with Marilyn in an hour."

Lillian entered the room warily. "A meeting?"

"I'm going to be taking over as her campaign manager."

"I don't understand." Lillian hesitated for a moment. "You're taking Claire's place?"

"Marilyn made her decision last night," Anderson said.

"Is that what she was doing?" Gabe moved into the small room. "Selecting a new campaign manager? I wondered."

"Save your pathetic little jokes for someone else." Raw anger sharpened the lines of Anderson's face. He closed the door with sudden force. "I don't have time for your crude humor."

"Congratulations, Anderson," Lillian said quietly. "I didn't know you were interested in politics."

"I wasn't until I met Marilyn." An odd light appeared in his eyes. "It's obvious that she needs me."

He means it, Gabe thought. What the hell was going on here?

Lillian watched Anderson closely. "Why do you say Marilyn needs you?"

"She's a brilliant candidate but it's clear from the way she fired Claire Jensen on impulse that she lacks maturity and experience. I can bring those strengths to her campaign."

"I see," Lillian said.

Gabe leaned against the closed door and folded his arms. He took stock of the room. From the thin bedspread to the faded flower-print curtains, it fit in with the rest of the establishment. A bit on the seedy side. He had a hunch it was not a J. Anderson Flint kind of place. But, then, Flint hadn't had a lot of choice when it came to accommodations here on the coast. Too bad Dreamscape wasn't up and running. Hannah and Rafe could have made some money off him.

"If you're going to join Marilyn's campaign, can we assume that you'll be giving up your practice in Portland?" Lillian asked.

"Yes, of course." Anderson sounded impatient.

"What about your clients?" Lillian said. "Are you just going to abandon them?"

"There are other sex therapists. I'm sure they'll be fine."

"Probably no worse off, at any rate," Gabe said.

Anderson scowled. "There are priorities here. The transition to a new campaign manager has to be made without delay. Any loss of momentum at this juncture could be disastrous for Marilyn."

"Sure," Gabe said. "Gotta have a seamless transition. I understand that. Hell of a sacrifice on your part, though."

"Marilyn's candidacy is far more important than my personal business affairs."

"If you say so."

"She has a great deal to give to this country." Anderson's rich voice was laced with what sounded like genuine fervor. "I can help her achieve her full potential."

"Your patriotic duty to get her elected, is that it?" Gabe asked.

Anderson's expression tightened. "I don't have time for this. There's no point expecting you to comprehend what's at stake here. Let's get down to business."

Lillian cleared her throat. "We didn't actually come here to talk about business."

Anderson made a disgusted sound at the back of his throat. "I wasn't born yesterday. I know why you're here. You came to bargain for access."

Lillian looked baffled. "Access to what?"

"To Marilyn, of course." Anderson did not look at her. He kept his attention on Gabe. "We all know that when she's elected, she'll have a great deal of power. You want me to guarantee that you'll have access to her, isn't that right, Madison? A man in your position likes to have friends in high places."

Lillian stared. "You don't understand."

"Of course I do." Anderson flicked a quick glance at her. "What's the matter, didn't Madison tell you how he intended to use those pictures?"

"But we don't have any photos," Lillian said. "Marilyn took the camera, remember?"

"Don't give me that crap. I know you had two cameras last night."

"Why do you say that?" Gabe asked.

"You were too quick to turn the first one over to Marilyn when she demanded it." Flint moved his hand in a small arc. "There's only one reason why you would do that. You knew you had backup."

"That's not true." Lillian was indignant.

"The double-camera routine is as old as the hills." Anderson cut off her protest with a patently bored look. "It buys the photographer some time to escape an unpleasant confrontation. The victim thinks she's confiscated the incriminating film and doesn't realize until too late that there is another set of photos."

"You sound familiar with the technique," Gabe said.

"I didn't tell Marilyn because I knew it would upset her. Now that I'm her manager, it's my job to handle this type of incident. I certainly don't intend to allow her to be destroyed by the same type of cheap blackmail that ruined her husband's campaign."

"How dare you imply that we would do something like that?" Lillian was furious now. "We didn't come here to blackmail Marilyn."

Anderson paid no attention to her. "Just tell me what you want, Madison, and I'll see to it that you get it, provided that you destroy those photos."

"What we want," Gabe said evenly, "are some answers."

Anderson's brows came together in a puzzled scowl. "Answers to what?"

"Did you break into Lillian's apartment in Portland?"

For an instant Anderson appeared frozen in place. Then he came up out of the chair. He was practically vibrating with outrage.

"Are you out of your mind?" he hissed. "Why would I do such a thing?"

"To look for her computer program," Gabe said. "You can save the act. It's good but it's not that good."

"I did not break into her apartment." Each word was pronounced with unnatural precision.

"And what about her cottage here in Eclipse Bay?" Gabe said. "I assume that was you, too, but I'll admit that incident is a little confusing because of the assault on Arizona Snow."

"I don't even know anyone named Arizona Snow," Anderson gritted.

"Maybe that was an unrelated event, after all," Lillian said to Gabe.

He shook his head. "I don't know. I can't get past the coincidence thing."

"Coincidences happen," she pointed out.

Anderson swung around to face her. "Stop it. Both of you. You can't make false accusations like this. You can't prove a damn thing."

"You're right about not being able to prove anything," Gabe said.

Anderson settled himself, relieved. "I knew it."

"That's why we came here instead of going to the cops. Of course, if you'd rather we went to Marilyn, we can do that. She might be interested to hear about your legal problems back in the days when you were selling online investments."

Shock flashed on Anderson's face. "Marilyn would never listen to you."

"Don't bank on it," Lillian responded. "She and Gabe have a history. They go back a long way. I think Marilyn would listen to him if he told her that he didn't believe that you were a good choice for campaign manager."

"You can't do that," Anderson stammered. "You have no right. Nothing was ever proven."

"All we want is confirmation that you went through Lillian's things looking for her matchmaking program," Gabe demanded.

Anderson abruptly turned away toward the window. He gazed bleakly out at the motel parking lot.

"I did not break into Lillian's apartment or the cottage," he said eventually, again enunciating each word with care.

"Let's not quibble over the details." Gabe watched him closely. "Maybe you didn't *break* into her apartment. Maybe you let yourself inside with keys that you either duplicated from her key ring or conned out of the housekeeping staff or the manager."

Lillian flashed him a startled look. Her mouth opened but she closed it quickly without saying a word.

"The cottage was a problem," Gabe went on, "because you didn't have a key so you had to pry open the door. The second time you smashed a window. By then you had heard about our theory that Lillian was being stalked. Word of that kind of thing gets around fast in a small town. You trashed her studio hoping to keep us looking in that direction. You didn't want us thinking there might be another motive for the break-ins."

"*I am not a stalker.*"

"I didn't say you were," Gabe said. "But I think it's pretty clear that Marilyn can't afford to be connected to a campaign manager who goes around imitating stalkers. Or one who breaks into apartments and cottages, for that matter. Bad for the image, you know."

"It's a lie. I didn't trash Lillian's studio. You can't do this to me."

"All we want is the truth," Gabe said.

"Damn it, I won't let you ruin this for me."

Without warning, Anderson spun away from the window and flung himself at Gabe.

"Anderson, no," Lillian called. "Stop. This won't solve anything."

But Anderson was beyond reason. Gabe managed to sidestep the initial charge but Anderson wheeled with startling speed and came at him again. This time Gabe found himself trapped in the corner, the television set on one side, a lamp on the other.

He took the only way out, going low to duck Anderson's swinging fist. Anderson's hand struck the wall where Gabe had been standing a second earlier. A shuddering jolt went through him. Gabe heard him suck in an anguished breath.

He caught Anderson by the legs and shoved hard. The momentum toppled both of them to the rug. They went down with a stunning thud, Anderson on the bottom. He struggled wildly, fighting back with a reckless fury, completely out of control. He hammered the floor with his heels and managed to slam a fist into Gabe's ribs. He twisted violently, trying to lurch free.

Gabe finally pinned him to the rug, using his weight to force him to lie still.

Trapped, Anderson stared up at him. Gabe felt him go limp as the hurricane of violence dissipated as suddenly as it had appeared.

"I don't want her hurt, do you understand?" Anderson's voice was ragged. "I'll do whatever you want—just don't hurt her."

"Listen to me, Anderson, no one wants to hurt Marilyn. We just want the truth." Gabe tightened his hands on Anderson's shoulders. "Tell me about the break-ins."

"All right. Okay. I did go into Lillian's apartment. But I didn't break in, damn it. I went in with the cleaning people."

"It was that easy?"

Anderson nodded. "It was that easy. Just told them I was there to check out some electrical problems. People trust you when you wear a uniform with your name on it."

Lillian moved closer. Gabe sensed the shock that gripped her. He caught a glimpse of her hands. They were clenched so tightly that her knuckles were white. But her voice was surprisingly steady.

"Did you want the matchmaking program that badly, Anderson?" she asked. "I told you, it wasn't magic. Just a standard personality inventory analysis program that I used together with a dose of common sense."

Anderson looked up at her. "It wasn't the damned matchmaking program I wanted, you little fool. It was the data on your clients."

"My *clients.*"

"Don't you get it?" He made a disgusted sound. "Hell, you really don't know what you've got, do you? Don't you have any concept of what that client database is worth? You've got detailed background information on some of the wealthiest, most successful, most powerful people in the city. Hell, in the whole damn state."

"But what would you do with it?"

"Why don't you ask your boyfriend, here. I'm sure he understands what that kind of information is worth these days."

"A fortune." Gabe released Anderson and got to his feet. "Good client data is one of the most valuable commodities on the market today. Businesses, investors, politicians, charitable organizations, you name it, they all want it. They'll all pay big bucks for solid background on people who have a lot of money to spend."

Lillian looked at Anderson. "You never were interested in collaborating on a book, were you? You were after my client roster all along. Who did you plan to sell my files to?"

He sat up slowly, wincing. "I hadn't finalized my list of prospects. I was still working on it when you announced that you intended to close down Private Arrangements. When I realized you were serious, my first thought was to salvage the data. I offered to buy your program, thinking I'd get the client list with it. But you refused to sell."

"So you tried to steal it."

"I didn't intend to steal the damned files." Anderson actually looked offended. "I just wanted to take a copy for myself."

"You don't call that theft?" Lillian asked.

His jaw clenched. "It wasn't like you had any use for that data."

"When you didn't find her files in Portland, you followed her here to Eclipse Bay," Gabe said. "That night in the restaurant you encountered the perfect prospect for the client info. Marilyn Thornley. A politician badly in need of a rich donor list."

Some of the fierceness returned briefly to Anderson's expression. "She needs those names and the background on those people."

Lillian opened her mouth. Gabe didn't know what she planned to say but quite suddenly he had had enough. He shook his head once. She got the message and remained silent.

"Let's get out of here," he said.

She glanced once more at Anderson and then walked to the door.

"Just a minute." Anderson gripped the edge of the television set to steady himself. "What are you going to do? You can't involve Marilyn in this. She had nothing to do with it."

"Don't worry, Flint." Gabe opened the door. "We're not going to do a damn thing. I told you, all we wanted was the truth. It stops here, provided you leave Lillian alone. But if you make another move to get her computer, I'll take the story straight to the cops and to the press."

Anderson looked horrified. "Marilyn's campaign couldn't survive that kind of scandal at this stage. Things are too delicate."

"I know," Gabe said. "You have my word that if you leave Lillian alone, this won't go any further."

"I swear I won't bother her again." Anderson sounded frantic. "I promise."

"It's a deal," Gabe said.

He ushered Lillian through the door and out onto the sidewalk. A chill, damp wind was blowing bits of litter around the parking lot.

"Lillian, wait." Anderson came to stand in the doorway. "If you change your mind, my offer to buy those client files is still good."

"Forget it, Anderson. The files are gone."

"I don't believe you destroyed them. They're too valuable. Think about my offer. You've got in-depth information on guys like Tom Lydd of Lydd-Zone Software and Madison, here. That data is worth a lot of money."

"I don't know about the Lydd information," Lillian said quietly. "But the data on Gabe certainly wouldn't do anyone any good."

Anderson scowled. "What the hell do you mean?"

"Most of it is false," Lillian explained. "He lied through his teeth on the questionnaire that he filled out for Private Arrangements."

23

GABE needed a place to think. And a cup of coffee. So he drove to the nearest restaurant, Snow's Café. They found a booth at the back. Lillian ordered tea. He went for the hard stuff, a double espresso.

There was a sprinkling of Arizona's customary clientele around them, primarily students and faculty from Chamberlain College, but no one bothered them. Arizona was not behind the counter today. Gabe figured she was probably at home in her war room, devising strategy to uncover the secret, underground labs at the institute.

"Do you really think he'll leave me alone now?" Lillian asked after a while.

"Yes."

"He didn't believe me when I told him that I had destroyed the client files."

Gabe sipped the supercharged espresso and lowered the small cup. "Did you?"

"First day I got here. I couldn't figure out how to be absolutely certain that my clients' privacy would be protected as long as the data concerning them was stored in my computer. So I removed the hard drive and tossed it into Dead Hand Cove at high tide. I left the rest of the computer in the trunk of my car. It's still there as far as I know."

"The only copy of those files was on that hard drive?"

"Yep."

"Guess that took care of the privacy issue."

"That was the whole point." She sighed. "Looking back, I suppose I should have realized sooner that Anderson was after those files. But he kept talking about the program so I assumed he wanted to go into matchmaking. It seemed like a logical extension of his sex therapy business."

"He could hardly admit that he wanted the background info on your clients. He knew how strongly you felt about guarding their privacy."

"One thing bothers me," she said slowly. "He acknowledged that he went into my apartment in Portland. Why didn't he admit that he broke into the cottage here in Eclipse Bay, too?"

"He's smart enough to know that he left no proof of illegal entry in your apartment. Like he said, he just walked in disguised as a repairman and looked around. Nothing was taken. No damage done. Hell, he's got witnesses that he didn't steal anything. Your cleaning people will vouch for him. And you never even filed a report with the cops. He had nothing to lose by telling us about that incident."

"But here in Eclipse Bay, he left obvious signs of forcible entry and I did file a report with Sean Valentine."

He nodded. "In addition, everyone knows that Valentine is investigating the assault on A.Z. and that he's working on the assumption there may be a link to at least one of the break-ins at your place. Flint didn't want to take the risk of admitting that he was ever inside your cottage."

"Must have been him, though. He was the only one who knew about the files on my computer."

Gabe contemplated the espresso cup. "And after meeting Marilyn, he wanted those files very, very badly."

"He probably made the deal with her right after he met her and then had to deliver the goods quickly. So he took some chances and used force to get into the cottage."

"Yeah." Absently he touched his side, feeling the sore place around his ribs.

Her gaze followed the movement of his hand. Sudden alarm tightened her expression. "Are you all right?"

"Yes."

"Good heavens, did Anderson hurt you?"

"I told you, I'm fine, Lillian." He put his hand back down on the table.

"You're sure?"

"I'm sure."

"Do you think you should have a doctor check out your ribs?"

"No."

"Okay, okay, no need to snap at me. I was just worried about you."

"Thanks." He took another swallow of coffee.

"It was a little scary there for a while." She shivered. "To tell you the truth, I was completely taken off guard when Anderson turned violent. I never expected him to attack you that way. He seemed the type who would try to talk himself out of trouble."

"People change when they fall in love."

"In *love*." She set her cup down hard on the table and fixed him with a dumbfounded expression. "*Anderson?* Are you crazy? Who in the world could he possibly—? Good grief, not Marilyn Thornley."

"Yeah."

"But he just met her."

"Happens that way sometimes."

She flopped back against the vinyl cushions. "It boggles the mind. J. Anderson Flint in love with Marilyn Thornley."

"You're the one who said they were a perfect match."

"Yes, but I was joking. Sort of."

"It's no joke."

She looked thoughtful. "You may be right. He was very protective of her, wasn't he? I wonder if she cares about him?"

"I don't know. But if she's smart, she'll keep him on as her campaign manager. He's committed. She'll have his complete loyalty."

"Nice qualities in a campaign manager. And in a husband. Be interesting to see what happens there."

"Yes."

She smiled at him across the table. "Weird, when you think about it."

"Their relationship?"

"No, the fact that you picked up on it first. I'm supposed to be the expert in that department. What tipped you off?"

"Male intuition." He drained the last of the espresso and put down the cup. He certainly wasn't going to tell her the truth. Not yet at any rate. He had problems enough dealing with it, himself.

"It bothers you, doesn't it?"

"What?"

"The fact that you found his weak spot and you used it to apply pressure to get him to confess."

He looked up, surprised. "No."

"Are you sure?"

"Let's get something clear here." He pushed aside the empty espresso cup and folded his arms on the table. "Protecting you is my only priority. I don't give a damn about Flint's finer feelings."

She searched his face. "I see. But if that's true, then why are you acting so weird?"

"I'm not acting weird." He started to extricate himself from the booth. "Are you finished? Let's go."

She reached across the table and covered one of his hands with her own. He went very still, intensely aware of the warmth of her fingers.

"Gabe, I'm sorry. I know you've been through a lot because of me. I'm very grateful."

Anger heated his blood, just as the violence had earlier. He clamped down on the fierce surge of emotion, seeking refuge in that inner space to which he always retreated when things threatened to get out of control.

"The last thing I want is your gratitude," he said.

She recoiled, her hand coming off his so swiftly an onlooker would have thought she had gotten her fingers burned.

"I didn't mean it that way," she said tightly.

He made himself breathe. "I know." He got to his feet and reached for his wallet. "I'll take you home."

"Sure." She slipped quickly out of the booth and hurried toward the front door without looking back.

He watched her rush away. *Nice going, Madison, you really screwed that up, didn't you?*

24

GABE was thinking of shutting down the computer and walking to Lillian's cottage to join her for lunch when he heard the sound of a car in the drive.

He opened the front door and saw a large black Lincoln come to a halt in front of the steps. The man behind the wheel wore a dark, inexpensive suit and a single gold earring. A hired driver.

The rear door of the vehicle opened. Sullivan Harte got out of the car.

This did not look promising.

Sullivan said something to the driver and then started toward the front porch.

"I didn't know you were in town," Gabe said.

The tip of Sullivan's cane hit the first step. "We need to talk."

"I was afraid you were going to say that." He held the door open. "Is this where you tell me that if I manage to sucker Lillian into marrying me you will make certain that she never inherits a dime's worth of Harte Investments?"

"Not quite."

Sullivan went past him into the house.

Gabe glanced at the limo. The driver had pulled out a paperback novel and appeared to be content to remain where he was.

Gabe followed his uninvited guest inside and let the door close behind him. "Coffee?"

"I could use a cup." Sullivan surveyed the desk where Gabe had left the laptop and a stack of papers. "You really trying to run Madison Commercial from here?"

"I'm not trying to run it. I am running it from here. Technology is amazing." Gabe went into the kitchen.

"How long can you afford to stay away from the office?" Sullivan demanded.

"Long as I want." Gabe poured a cup of coffee and carried it into the living room. "Did you come here to talk about the wonders of modern techniques for long-distance management?"

"No."

"Didn't think so," Gabe said.

MITCHELL slammed the newspaper down with such force that the little table vibrated on its spindly legs. He scowled at Bryce, who had just walked into Incandescent Body with the news.

"What the hell do you mean, Sullivan Harte is in town?"

"Saw him sitting in the back of a limo a few minutes ago," Bryce said. "Passed me while I was at the gas station. Must have flown into Portland and hired a car and driver there. Thought you'd want to know."

"Damned right I want to know." Mitchell grabbed his cane and levered himself to his feet. "Where was he headed?"

"Took Bayview Drive. Could be on his way out to the Harte cottage."

"Or he could be headed toward the old Buckley place where Gabe is staying." Mitchell tossed some money on the table. "What do you want to bet that he came here to try to scare off my grandson?"

"Forget it. I never take bets on Hartes and Madisons. Too unpredictable."

LILLIAN studied the fresh canvas propped on the easel while she finished cleaning the last of her brushes. It was the start of a portrait of Gabe based on the sketch she had made of him in her Portland studio. All brooding shadows and hard, bright light, it was the first real work she had done since she had arrived in town. She was pleased with it. She had been in the zone this afternoon. About time.

She set the brushes in a holder to dry and looked at her watch. She was startled to see that it was nearly two o'clock. Gabe had said he would come over around noon for lunch. As usual, she had lost all track of time while she was in that other place where the vision reigned supreme.

Maybe he had been delayed by business or a phone call.

She looked out the window. There were whitecaps on the bay and no rain in sight. She could use some fresh air after such a long stretch of work. The over-stimulated sensation that always followed a particularly good session in the studio was making her restless. She needed to get out and work it off. A walk along the bluffs would do the trick. She would probably run into Gabe on his way here.

She indulged herself in a brief, romantic picture of herself flying into his arms on the top of a windswept bluff. Gulls would be wheeling overhead. His dark hair would be ruffled by the crisp breeze. She would be sexy and free-spirited in a gossamer dress and bare feet.

That image made her wonder if she ought to take time to change out of her paint-stained jeans and long-tailed denim shirt. Then she remembered that it was only about fifty-three degrees outside and that there was a lot of rough gravel on the bluff path. Forget the gossamer dress and bare feet.

She put on a pair of scuffed running shoes, took a black denim jacket out of the hall closet and left the house through the mudroom door.

Outside, the scene on the bluffs was very much as she had envisioned it, blustery and invigorating. The bay was a dramatic sweep of quietly churning seawater. The town was picturesque in the distance. The air was clear and bright. The only thing missing was Gabe. There was no sign of him on the path.

An uneasy feeling coiled around her, pushing aside the zesty anticipation. By the time she emerged from the trees and found herself near the back porch of the old Buckley place a dark foreboding had settled on her.

She walked around the side of the house to see if Gabe's car was in the drive. It was. So was another vehicle, a dark limo complete with a driver behind the wheel. The chauffeur did not notice her. He was deep into a paperback.

She told herself to relax. Obviously business from out of town had caught up with Gabe. But for some obscure reason the anxiety didn't dissipate. Things felt wrong.

She returned to the back door, opened it quietly and moved stealthily into the kitchen. If Gabe was wheeling and dealing with an important client she did not want to interrupt.

The low rumble of voices from the other room made her stop short. She knew those voices. Both of them.

Suddenly everything made sense. Outrage flared. She rushed to the doorway.

Sullivan and Gabe were seated on the sofa. A leather-bound binder and a stack of computer printouts were arrayed on the low table in front of them.

"Granddad, how dare you?"

Sullivan looked up swiftly, peering at her through a pair of reading glasses. She could have sworn that he turned red.

"Lillian."

Gabe said nothing. He took one look at her and lounged back into the corner of the sofa, one arm stretched out along the top of the cushions.

She ignored him. Her entire attention was focused on Sullivan.

"What in the world are you doing?" Her voice cracked. "No, don't bother explaining. I know exactly what you're doing."

Sullivan blinked owlishly behind the spectacles. "You do?"

"It's as obvious as those papers on the table." She walked a few steps closer. "You're here to try to buy off Gabe. Or maybe you want to scare him off. Which is it?"

"Now, honey," Sullivan said in placating tones.

She was vaguely aware of the sound of a large vehicle arriving in the drive. She ignored it.

"You think he wants to marry me so that he can get his hands on a chunk of Harte, don't you? What are you offering him to get out of my life? Or are you threatening him?"

The front door crashed open. Mitchell stormed into the house.

"Who's threatening my grandson?" he roared. He came to a halt, brows bristling, jaw clenched, and glowered at Sullivan. "What do you think you're doing, Harte?"

"Things aren't quite the way they look," Sullivan said.

"I don't believe that for one minute," Lillian declared. "You've been talking to Mom and Dad, haven't you? They told you I was seeing Gabe and you just leaped to the conclusion that he was after me because of H.I."

"Speaking of leaping to conclusions," Gabe said mildly.

She glared at him. "Stay out of this. It has nothing to do with you. This is between me and Granddad."

"And me." Mitchell jabbed a thumb at his own chest. "Don't forget about me. I'm involved in this thing, too."

"Sure," Gabe said dryly. "Don't know what I was thinking."

Lillian whipped her attention back to Sullivan. "I realize you feel you're acting in my best interests. I know everyone believes that Gabe is after a piece of Harte. But that is absolute nonsense."

All three men stared at her.

"Nonsense?" Sullivan repeated carefully.

"Yes. Nonsense." She swept out a hand. "He would never marry for business reasons. He's a Madison. They don't do things like that."

Sullivan cleared his throat. "Always heard that Gabe, here, was a different kind of Madison."

"Not that different," she shot back. "And what's more, you can't buy him off or scare him off. Madisons don't work that way."

"She's right," Mitchell said. "If Gabe wants to marry her, you won't be able to get rid of him with money or threats."

"Which brings up a very crucial issue," Lillian said. "As I told Mom on the phone, Gabe has never asked me to marry him. Isn't that correct, Gabe?"

"Correct," Gabe said.

"What's this?" Sullivan grabbed the handle of his cane and used it to haul himself up off the sagging sofa. He turned on Gabe with a thunderous expression. "I was under the impression that you were serious about my granddaughter. If you think I'm going to stand by while you shack up indefinitely with her, you can think again."

"Wasn't planning to shack up indefinitely," Gabe said.

Mitchell beetled his brows. "Just what are you doing here, Sullivan?"

"Before we were so rudely interrupted," Sullivan said, "I was presenting a business proposition to Gabe. Of course, that was when I was still under the impression that he intended to marry Lillian."

Mitchell eyed him with deep suspicion. "What kind of business proposition?"

Gabe looked at Lillian. "Your grandfather was outlining the financial advantages of marriage to you. You come with one-third of H.I, you know."

"The *advantages*?" Lillian stared at Sullivan. "You mean you're trying to *bribe* him to marry me?"

"I just wanted him to understand that we'd be happy to have him as a member of the family," Sullivan said mildly.

"Well, shoot and damn." Mitchell whistled softly. "Got to hand it to you, Sullivan. Didn't think you had that much common sense."

Lillian was aghast. "You weren't trying to buy him off. You're here to try to buy him for me. This is the most mortifying thing that has ever happened to me in my entire life."

Sullivan stiffened. "What's mortifying about it? I thought you wanted Gabe."

"For heaven's sake, Granddad. It's like you're offering him a dowry to take me off your hands. If he marries me and gets a chunk of H.I., everyone will say he did it for the money."

"Which is why I turned down the deal," Gabe replied softly.

She swung around to face him. "You did?"

"Shoot and damn." Mitchell waved a hand. "Why did you go and do something dumb like that? You coulda had the lady and one-third of H.I. That's what we call a win-win situation."

"What choice did I have?" Gabe gestured toward the papers on the coffee table. "If I sign those Lillian would always wonder if I married her for her inheritance."

"No, I wouldn't," Lillian said quickly.

Gabe looked at her. "I appreciate your faith in me but I'm afraid I can't accept you and one-third of H.I., too. I just finished explaining that to Sullivan."

"What if I just give up my shares in H.I.?" she asked.

Sullivan glared at her. "I'm not about to let you walk away from your inheritance, young woman. Wouldn't be right. I worked my tail off to build that company. I did it for you and Hannah and Nick."

Her refusing a third of H.I. would be a terrible blow to him, she realized.

"Evidently I'm fated to be doomed by my inheritance," she muttered.

"Depends," Gabe said.

She looked at him, hope rising. "On what?"

"There is a way around this. If you agree to marry me and if your family insists on endowing you, so to speak, you can put your share of your Harte inheritance into a trust for any children we might have. Okay with you, Sullivan?"

Sullivan looked thoughtful. "One way to handle it, I guess."

Joy flowed through Lillian, bringing a rainbow of colors.

"No problem," she whispered.

Gabe got to his feet. "You'll do it? You'll marry me?"

Neither Mitchell nor Sullivan so much as twitched. It was, Lillian thought, as if the whole world was holding its collective breath in anticipation of her answer.

"Well, sure," she said softly. "I mean, what else can I do after you turned down the chance to get your hands on a chunk of my family's company? It's such a truly Madison-style gesture. But I really don't want you to feel that you have to do this. It's not necessary, honest. I know you're not a fortune-hunter."

He gave her his slow smile, showing just a hint of teeth. "Honey, if I want Harte Investments, I'll buy the whole damn company when your dad puts it on the market in a year or two."

Everyone stared at him in dumbfounded silence.

Lillian met Sullivan's eyes. He grinned. She felt the laughter bubble up inside.

"Yes, of course," she gasped between giggles. "Why didn't I think of that. It's no secret that H.I. will be up for sale soon. You can buy it outright when Dad retires. No fuss, no bother, no need to get married."

"Trust me," Gabe said. "it would be a whole lot simpler that way."

Mitchell grunted. "Never thought of that."

"Probably because business is not your forte, Mitch," Sullivan growled. "It was obvious right from the start that Gabe didn't need to marry Lillian to get his hands on Harte. All he has to do is wait a few years and do a buy-out."

Gabe wrapped his fingers around Lillian's wrist. "Come on, let's go someplace where we can discuss our private affairs in private."

He opened the porch door and led her outside into the bright afternoon light. Together they went down the path toward the rocky beach.

Neither of them spoke until they reached the bottom.

"You're serious about this?" she said at last.

"Never been more serious in my life." He tightened his hand around hers. "Did you mean it when you said you'd marry me?"

"Yes. But you don't have to give up a share of Harte Investments for me. I mean, I appreciate the grand gesture but it's not necessary. Really."

"It's necessary."

"Why?"

He stopped and pulled her around to face him. "Because I'm a Madison. A Madison does things like turn down the offer of a third of a multimillion-dollar company for the woman he loves. It's in the genes."

The woman he loves.

"Oh, Gabe." The brilliant colors of happiness splashed through her, effervescent and glorious. She went into his arms. "I love you so much."

He kissed her.

Except for a few details such as the fact that they were on the beach, not on the bluffs, and she wasn't barefoot and there was no gossamer gown, the scene was just the way it had been in the romantic fantasy she had conjured up when she had set out to meet him on the path.

Perfect.

───────※───※───────

SULLIVAN surveyed the seating options in Mitchell's living room and chose the recliner that provided a view of the bay. He lowered himself into it with a long sigh and looked out at the water. The light was starting to go. He never liked this time of day.

"We came mighty close to screwing that up pretty bad, didn't we?" he said.

"What's with this *we* business?" Mitchell settled into the other well-worn recliner. "You're the one who damn near screwed things up. What the hell did you think you were doing trying to buy Gabe with a chunk of H.I.?"

"You're the one who told me I was supposed to fix things."

"You don't fix things between a Madison and a Harte with a business contract."

"Seemed like the logical thing to do. Pretty clear that Lillian wanted him and I just wanted to encourage him to see the benefits of marriage to her." Sullivan stretched out his legs, wincing when his joints protested. "How do you stand this damp, cold weather all year long?"

"I'm used to it. You've gotten soft living down there in Arizona."

"Not soft, smart. If you had any sense you'd move to the desert, too."

"I like it just fine here in Eclipse Bay." Mitchell rested his head against the back of the chair. "You figure to drive back to Portland tonight?"

"Had enough driving for one day. Knees stiffen up when I sit in a car for a long period of time."

"Yeah, I know what you mean." Mitchell absently rubbed one of his own knees. "Occurs to me that if you're gonna hang around town for a while, you might as well stay here with me."

"Why would I want to do that?"

"If you stay at the cottage you'll get in the way of Gabe's courting."

"Maybe I'll take you up on that offer. Don't want to interfere with the lovebirds." Sullivan chuckled.

Mitchell eyed him suspiciously. "What's so funny?"

"Just thinking about what the folks in town will say when they find out that I'm your houseguest."

"Huh." Sullivan grinned. "Probably figure we'll try to knock each other's teeth out."

"Probably."

"Now that's settled, maybe I should fill you in on some of the stuff that's been happening around here."

FIFTEEN minutes later Sullivan was ready to explode. "Why the hell wasn't I told about the break-ins? I didn't have a clue that Lillian was in danger."

"Take it easy. Like I just said, everything is under control. Gabe took care of Flint for you."

"I should have been informed."

"Gabe put the fire out before anyone realized just how big it was." Mitchell heaved himself up out of his chair. "Bryce will have dinner ready in a while. I generally have a glass or two of something beforehand. As I recall, you used to do the same."

"I haven't changed." Sullivan watched the darkness close in over the bay. "A little something at this time of day helps a man relax."

"That it does."

Mitchell went to a cabinet, hauled a bottle out of a cupboard and splashed whiskey into two glasses. He brought the two drinks back across the room and handed one to Sullivan without comment.

They drank their whiskeys and watched the darkness thicken outside the window.

After all these years, Sullivan thought, it was good to sit here and share the twilight with the one other person in the world who understood why this was such a bad time of day.

"They say the memories fade as you get older," Mitchell said after a while.

"They lie."

25

LILLIAN parked her car in the driveway behind Claire's red compact, got out and walked across the graveled drive toward the porch steps. All four doors and the lid of the compact's trunk were open wide. Two suitcases and a file box occupied the trunk.

The front door of the house banged open just as she reached out to knock. Claire lurched forward, head down, onto the porch, struggling with an oversized suitcase. She was dressed in sweats and running shoes. Her hair was anchored in a ponytail.

The loud, strident voice of a radio talk-show host holding forth on politics poured out of the doorway behind her.

"Need a hand?" Lillian asked above the hammering of the radio pundit.

Claire jolted to a stop, breathing hard. She looked up quickly, startled.

"Lil." She let go of the suitcase. "Sorry, didn't hear you drive up. What are you doing here?"

"You told me you were leaving town today. I came by to see if I could help with the packing."

"Thanks." Claire looked at the compact's trunk and then down at the suitcase that she had angled through the doorway. "I underestimated the job. Guess I hadn't realized how much stuff I had accumulated here in Eclipse Bay. I'm taking the essentials with me in the car. The moving-van people will be here at two o'clock for the rest."

"Point me in the right direction."

"I finished my office. I was just getting started on the bedroom and bath. If you want to take the kitchen. I would be forever grateful."

"No problem." Lillian moved through the doorway.

Claire followed her. She went to the table where the radio blared and turned off the political hot talk. The sudden silence left an uncomfortable vacuum.

"You're a good friend," Claire declared. "Unlike some others I could mention.

You will notice how none of the other members of the *team* bothered to show. Turns out they all had something unexpected come up at the last minute. Why am I not surprised?"

"Claire—"

"Getting fired from a political campaign staff endows you with instant invisibility. Did you know that? Like being in the wrong crowd in high school."

Lillian cleared her throat. "Where are the packing cartons?"

"In the laundry room off the kitchen. Help yourself."

Lillian went toward the kitchen.

"There's coffee on the counter," Claire called after her. "And some croissants from Incandescent Body. You know, that bakery is one of the few things I'm going to miss about this place."

"Understandable. It's very good."

Lillian went into the kitchen and opened the cupboard doors. She did a quick survey of the contents of the cabinets, getting a feel for the size of the job, and then went into the laundry room to look for boxes.

The small space was crowded with the usual jumble of odds and ends that tend to wind up in laundry rooms. A long shelf above the aging washer and dryer held a collection of soap, bleach, and dryer-sheet packages, together with squeeze bottles of glass cleaner and stain remover. A mop and a broom were propped in a bucket in the corner. The basket on the floor next to it was filled with rags.

A selection of empty cardboard cartons was stacked on top of the washer and dryer. She chose two and went back into the kitchen. Methodically she began emptying Claire's cupboards.

Impulse had brought her here today. She did not know what she was looking for. She only hoped that she would know it when she saw it.

Half an hour later, the two cartons filled, she went out into the living room and down the hall to the room Claire had used as a second office. The desk and file cabinet were still there but they had been cleaned out.

Claire appeared in the hall, a box filled with bathroom items in her arms.

"Finished with the kitchen already?"

"No. I need some strapping tape."

"On the table in the living room."

"Thanks."

"Don't know what I'd have done without you today." Claire went past her toward the front door. "Next time you're in Seattle, give me a call. I'll take you to dinner."

"I'll do that."

She waited until Claire disappeared outside and then ducked into the bedroom. The closet doors and the drawers in the chest beneath the window stood open, making a quick search easy. She examined an array of shoes first. Ignoring the high heels and pumps, she looked for a familiar pair of loafers.

They were nowhere in sight. Maybe they had already been packed. She opened one of the unsealed cartons.

Claire's footsteps sounded on the porch. Adrenaline surged through Lillian, making her hand tremble.

This was pointless. She was wasting her time. She dropped the lid of the carton and hurried out of the bedroom. She started back along the hall.

Too late. Claire was already in the living room, looking at the strapping-tape device that rested on the coffee table. She turned and saw Lillian. A frown crossed her face.

"Didn't you find the tape?" she asked.

"I stopped to use the bathroom." Lillian kept moving. She went to the coffee table and picked up the tape. Her pulse was pounding. "I'm almost finished with the kitchen."

"Terrific."

She took a deep breath and made herself walk briskly but not too briskly back into the kitchen. She knelt beside the cartons and went to work sealing them.

Claire's footsteps receded back down the hall toward the bedroom.

Lillian wondered if her heart would ever stop pounding. Clearly she was not cut out for this kind of thing. But there would never be a better opportunity to satisfy her curiosity.

She finished taping the boxes, got to her feet and went back into the laundry room for more cartons. Her pulse had finally slowed. She moved two large boxes aside to get at the medium-sized one that looked right for the contents of the silverware drawer.

She noticed the crumpled piece of navy blue cloth on top of the rag basket when she put the boxes down beside it. The blue fabric was not faded or torn. It looked new.

It looked familiar. She had an artist's eye for colors. She remembered them.

Her pulse picked up speed again. Her heart was pounding now.

Don't get too excited. Probably nothing. Just a rag.

Cautiously she reached into the basket, picked up the wad of navy blue cloth and shook it out. It was the shirt Claire had worn the day she had stopped by the cottage to warn her that Marilyn still wanted Gabe.

There did not appear to be anything wrong with the garment. No rips or holes that would have explained how it had come to be relegated to the rag pile. Could have fallen out of the laundry hamper by accident, she thought.

She flipped the shirt around to examine the back.

The smear of dried red paint on the right cuff made her go cold.

"Oh, damn," she whispered.

She had come here this morning on the off chance that she might get some answers. *Be careful what you wish for.*

"How are you doing in here?" Claire came to stand in the doorway of the laundry room. "Need more boxes? I've got some—"

She broke off at the sight of the navy blue shirt dangling from Lillian's fingers. Her eyes went to the paint-stained cuff.

"It was you who trashed my studio." Lillian put the shirt down on the washer. "I knew there had to be some evidence somewhere. It's almost impossible to work with a lot of paint and not get some on your clothes."

The blood drained from Claire's face. She swallowed twice before she managed to speak.

"You can't prove anything," she stammered. "You can't prove a damn thing, do you hear me?"

"Probably not. Unless, of course, you kept the VPX 5000. But I'm sure you had enough sense to ditch it. Did you throw it into the bay? That's what I did with my client files."

Claire's eyes filled with tears. She seemed to collapse in on herself.

"There was no need to injure Arizona," Lillian said. "She had nothing to do with this. Do you realize what might have happened if you had hit her even a little bit harder? She's an elderly woman, Claire. You could have killed her."

"I didn't want to do it but I had no choice."

"No choice? What are you talking about. No one made you hit her and steal her camera."

"I had to get the camera." Claire's hands knotted into fists at her sides. "Don't you understand? She had pictures."

"Pictures of you breaking into my cottage?"

"I didn't see her until I left. I had parked my car in the woods nearby. But when I started to drive away, I saw her truck parked on the opposite side of the road. She wasn't in it so I knew she was probably nearby conducting her idiotic surveillance rounds. I was afraid she might have spotted me coming out of your cottage."

"For heaven's sake, Claire, you know as well as I do that it wouldn't have mattered if she had noticed you in the vicinity of the cottage. No one ever pays any attention to A.Z.'s claims and theories. Everyone knows she's a little weird."

"When she came out of the woods a short time later she was carrying that damn camera. I panicked. Of course, no one would have listened if she had claimed to see me near your cottage on the day a break-in was reported. Everyone knows she's paranoid about people who work at the institute. But they sure as hell would have paid attention if she had produced some time-and-date-stamped photos of me coming out the back door of your place with a tire iron in my hand."

"You followed her home, waiting for an opportunity to take the VPX 5000 from her, didn't you? She knew that she was being tailed."

"I watched her for a while but I realized that sooner or later she would go back to that fortress. I got there ahead of her, hid the car in the trees and waited on her back porch behind the woodshed."

"You planned to attack her."

"*No.*" Claire wiped away her tears with the back of her hand. "I didn't know exactly what I was going to do. I couldn't think straight. I guess I had some vague idea of catching her off guard when she went into the house. I just wanted to get that camera."

"But something made her walk around the porch to check the rear door. You saw your chance, grabbed the plant stand and hit her."

"I didn't mean to put her in the hospital." Claire's voice rose on an anguished wail. "You have to believe me. I just wanted to knock her down. Make her drop the camera."

"You gave her a concussion, Claire. You could have killed her."

"I told you, I never meant to hurt her." Claire sniffed. "What's more, you can't prove that I took the camera. Just your word against mine."

"Sure." Lillian leaned back against the dryer and gripped the white metal edge on either side. "And since it's just us girls talking here, I've got some questions. What gave you the idea of going after my client files in the first place? Did you come up with it all on your own or was it something Anderson said?"

Rage infused Claire's face. She turned a shade of red that rivaled the paint on the shirt.

"Flint. I heard that bastard tell Marilyn about your files the day he came to see her at the institute. He actually bragged about them to her. He used them to talk his way into *my job*. Promised her he could get them for her."

"I see."

"Got to give credit where it's due. Marilyn is no fool. She understood the value of those files immediately."

"Did Anderson tell her he planned to steal them?"

"Of course not. He just said he was working an angle to get them. Told her not to worry. He'd handle all the details."

"Where were you when they had that conversation?"

"I was packing up my desk in the adjoining office. Marilyn closed the door but I simply switched on the recording system." Claire smiled bitterly. "That was one of my jobs, you know. Recording Marilyn's meetings and conversations with important people. She plans to publish her memoirs someday."

"Later you decided to see if you could find my client files before Flint got to them, right?"

Claire shrugged. "He said they were on your computer. Sounded easy enough. I could have used them the same way Flint planned to use them."

"To buy your way into another job?"

"Yes. The data on your high-end clients would be worth a fortune to any candidate in the Northwest." Tears welled in Claire's eyes again. "But I couldn't find your computer when I broke into the cottage. And there was Arizona with her damned camera when I came out. Everything went wrong. All that risk for nothing. It's not fair."

"That day you stopped by the cottage to warn me to watch out for Marilyn, you overheard my conversation with Gabe when he was on his way back from Portland. You learned that we had concluded I might be the target of a stalker. That made you very nervous, didn't it? You realized that we were no longer dismissing the break-in as the action of a transient. So you came back to trash my studio to add some credibility to our theory."

"I got scared. Really scared. This is Eclipse Bay. I knew that if a Harte and a Madison were putting pressure on Sean Valentine, he might actually conduct a serious investigation. I didn't know where that would lead. I thought that I would be safe if everyone continued to blame the break-in on a stalker who could conveniently just disappear."

"Oh, Claire." Lillian shook her head. "What were you thinking?"

The bitterness tinged Claire's voice. "How did you figure it out?"

"I suppose you could say it was a process of elimination. Gabe and a private investigator cleared the only real potential stalker we had on our list. When we talked to Anderson, he denied the break-ins here in Eclipse Bay. Adamantly."

Claire widened in scorn. "And you actually believed that bag of sleaze?"

Lillian shrugged. "The forced entry didn't fit with what I knew about him. Anderson is the sort who tries to talk his way in and out of situations."

"What about Marilyn? She should have been on your list. She was the one who had the most to gain from those files."

"The thing about Marilyn is that she is very up-front about what she wants. She doesn't sneak around. You, on the other hand, have a history of sneaking around."

Claire flinched. "What do you mean?"

"She was right when she said that you had an affair with Trevor Thornley, wasn't she?"

"I told you, I never slept with Trevor."

"I don't believe you."

Claire watched her warily. "Why not?"

"Because I found out that you were sneaking around with Larry Fulton in the back of his father's van the summer that he and I were dating."

"Larry Fulton." Claire's mouth fell open. "But that was years ago. We were in *college*."

"I know. I was pretty sure that he was fooling around with someone else that summer. I just hadn't realized that the other woman was you. The Willis brothers set me straight a few days ago. They gave me a whole new perspective on you, Claire. Once I started asking the right questions, things fell into place."

Claire backed out of the laundry room, never taking her eyes off Lillian. "You can't prove anything."

"You keep saying that." Lillian came away from the washer. "I'm not arguing the point. I came here today for some answers, not to get you arrested."

"Get out."

"I'm on my way." Lillian crossed the living room, paused at the front door and looked back over her shoulder. "Just one more question."

"I said, get out of here."

"You told me that Trevor was into high heels and ladies' lingerie and that his tastes would be a real turnoff. Can I assume you lied about that, too?"

"I hated the dressing up part," Claire explained. "But the man was on track to be a U.S. senator. I figured I could overlook a few eccentricities if it meant I would be a senator's wife."

"Did he really tell you that he would divorce Marilyn and marry you after he was elected?"

"He promised." Claire looked down at the blue shirt crumpled in her hands. "Just like Larry Fulton promised we would get engaged after he broke up with you. Nothing ever works out the way it's supposed to. It not fair, you know? It's just not fair."

GABE prowled back and forth across the cottage kitchen. "You shouldn't have confronted her on your own."

"You've mentioned that several times already." Lillian propped her elbows on the kitchen table and rested her chin in her hands. "I've explained that I went there on impulse."

"What if she had turned violent?"

"She's not the type."

"You can't be certain."

"Gabe, she knows I can't prove anything."

"Unfortunately."

"I guess this is one of those situations where you have to let karma happen."

"Karma never happens to people like her. Karma is bullshit. The Claires of this world always skate."

Lillian looked out the window. "I wouldn't say that Claire has done a lot of skating in her life. She said that things have never worked out for her. None of her big plans ever jelled. Larry Fulton and I broke up but he didn't marry her. He married Sheila. Trevor Thornley crashed and burned, so she didn't get to marry him and become a senator's wife. She lost her job with Marilyn's campaign. All and all, Claire hasn't been what anyone would call a winner."

THEY drove into town for warm croissants and coffee the next morning. Gabe parked in the lot in front of Incandescent Body. He studied the warmly lit interior of the bakery through the windows. A handful of people were clustered inside. The array of vehicles standing in the rain outside included Mitchell's big SUV, Arizona's aging truck, and Sean Valentine's cruiser.

"Looks a little cozy in there," he said. "Want to go somewhere else?" he asked.

"There is nowhere else where we can get croissants like the ones they make here." Lillian pulled up the hood of her rain cloak and reached for the door handle. "Come on, we can deal with this."

"I don't know about that." Reluctantly he opened the driver's side door. "It's a little early for a Harte-Madison scene."

"Nonsense. Never too early for one of those."

He hunched deeper into his jacket and walked quickly beside her through the drizzle to the entrance.

He opened the glass door and immediately registered the serious tone of the atmosphere inside. The buzz of conversation was more intense than usual. His first thought was that the sight of Mitchell and Sullivan sharing coffee together had electrified the gossip circuit. But then he realized that no one was paying much attention to the pair, who were seated at a small table with Bryce and Sean.

Predictably, everyone looked toward the door when it opened. Lillian pushed back the hood of her cloak and bestowed a bright smile on the crowd. Gabe nodded brusquely and headed for the counter. He needed some coffee before he dealt with Mitchell and Sullivan.

"What's up?" he asked the Herald who took their orders for croissants and corn bread.

"Haven't you heard?"

Before she could explain, the curtain opened behind her. Arizona leaned out and beckoned urgently.

"Come on back here, you two," she hissed. "I'll brief you along with the others."

Gabe looked at Mitchell and Sullivan. They had resumed their conversation with Sean. He was in no great rush to join them, he thought. One of Arizona's briefings promised to be a lot more entertaining. He glanced at Lillian. She shrugged and turned to go behind the counter.

He picked up his corn bread and followed her.

A familiar group of Heralds, including Photon, was gathered at the large worktable. They nodded somberly when Lillian and Gabe joined them.

" 'Morning," Gabe said.

"What's going on?" Lillian asked.

Arizona rapped a rolling pin on the floured table. "A very interesting development has just occurred. 'Course, the mainstream media and the local authorities, including Sean Valentine, have bought into the cover story being handed out by the gang up at the institute. But that's only to be expected." She shook her head. "Poor dupes."

Gabe propped one shoulder against the wall and savored a bite of warm corn bread. "What's the story?"

"Official version is that Claire Jensen was injured in a single-car accident on her way out of town yesterday. She's in the Eclipse Bay hospital as we speak."

"Good heavens." Lillian stared at Arizona. "Is she all right?"

"Sean says she's pretty banged up but she'll be okay. He investigated the crash. Said she was driving like a bat outta hell in the rain. Took a curve way too fast. But we all know the truth."

Heads nodded around the table.

Lillian cleared her throat. "Uh, what is that?"

"It's obvious. She must have seen somethin' she wasn't supposed to see up there at the institute. Probably stumbled into the underground lab. *They* faked an accident to try to get rid of her. Lucky for her they botched the job."

Lillian looked at Gabe. "And you say you don't believe in karma."

"I stand corrected," Gabe said. "Learn something new everyday."

He took her arm and steered her back through the curtain into the main room. Several pairs of eyes followed them as they made their way to the small table where Mitchell and Sullivan sat with Bryce and Sean.

Lillian leaned down to give Sullivan a kiss on his cheek. " 'Morning, Grand-dad."

"Good morning, honey."

Gabe nodded at Mitchell and Sullivan. "Glad to see that the two of you didn't knock each other's teeth out last night."

"When you get to be this age," Sullivan said, "you have to think twice about risking your teeth. Not that many good ones left."

She greeted the others and sat down beside Sullivan.

"Arizona give you her version of the accident?" Mitchell asked Gabe.

Gabe set his coffee and partially eaten corn bread down on the table and took one of the chairs. "All part of the big conspiracy up at the institute, according to A.Z."

Sullivan chuckled.

"Got to admit that her take on local news is always a lot more interesting than mine," Sean allowed.

"So it was an accident?" Lillian asked.

"Definitely." Sean took a bite out of a large, jelly-filled pastry. "She must have been in a real hurry to get out of town. Had to be doing seventy when she took that curve out by the Erickson place."

Bryce shook his head in solemn disapproval. "Everyone knows that's a real bad curve."

"The medics who pulled her out of the car said she was spittin' mad when they got to her." Sean swallowed the bite of pastry and reached for his coffee. "Kept saying something about how unfair it all was."

26

ON the night of the reception at the Eclipse Bay branch of the Bright Visions Gallery, Sullivan stood with Mitchell, a glass of champagne in his hand, and watched the large crowd ebb and flow around Lillian and her paintings. Warm pride flowed through him.

"Not like it was in Portland last week," Mitchell observed. "Only press here is from the *Journal*. But, what the heck, Eclipse Bay isn't exactly the art capital of the western world."

"Portland was all about publicity and media coverage," Sullivan reminded him. "It worked just like Octavia Brightwell said it would. It introduced Lillian to important collectors and the museum and gallery crowd. But this event is special for Eclipse Bay."

"And they're lovin' it." Mitchell grinned. "Look at 'em, all dressed up and swilling champagne. I doubt if a lot of these folks know much about art, but they're sure having a good time."

The throng that filled the gallery was composed largely of local townsfolk. Everyone from the Willis brothers to the strangely dressed group from Incandescent Body had turned out. Sullivan had a hunch that it wasn't a keen interest in art that had brought so many of the residents of Eclipse Bay out on a wet night. The driving motivation for this crowd was its lively curiosity about Hartes and Madisons. Everyone knew that both families would be in town for the event and they were all well aware that Gabe and Lillian were engaged.

The free drinks and hors d'oeuvres were just icing on the cake as far as most folks were concerned tonight.

"Who would have thought that a Harte would turn out to be an artist?" Mitchell said.

"Who would have believed that anyone in your family could create a profitable business like Madison Commercial?"

"Gotta say that Octavia sure knows how to give a party." Mitchell helped himself to a cheese canapé. "First-class all the way, too. Lot of people here tonight wouldn't have noticed or cared if she had served cheap champagne and second-rate food. But she pulled out all the stops, same as she did for the Portland crowd."

"Showing respect for the locals." Sullivan nodded. "Very smart. Good public relations."

"She's a smart young woman. But she's real, too, if you know what I mean. She didn't put on this bash just for publicity purposes. She did it because she really wanted to show folks that she appreciates them as much as she does the Portland crowd."

Sullivan took a sip of his champagne. "I'll buy that."

"Huh."

"What's that supposed to mean?"

"Can't help noticing that she and your grandson, Nick, are having themselves a mighty serious conversation over there."

Sullivan followed his gaze, searching for the pair over the heads of the crowd. He spotted Nick, dressed in formal black and white, standing with Octavia on the far side of the gallery.

The conversation looked more than serious, he thought. It had a close, intimate quality. Nick had one hand casually flattened on the wall behind Octavia's head. He leaned slightly in toward her, his broad shoulders angled in a way that subtly but effectively cut her off from the crowd around them. Sullivan recognized the body language and knew that every other man in the room understood it, too, if only on a subconscious level. It was a clear statement of possession, a this-woman-is-mine-tonight message.

"Oh, brother," he said softly. "Here we go again."

"I wouldn't worry about it, if I were you," Mitchell said cheerfully. "Like I said, Octavia's a nice young woman."

"Red hair."

"So what? You got a problem with red hair?"

"There's something familiar about her, Mitch."

"You've seen her before. She attended Hannah and Rafe's wedding. And you met her at the Portland reception last week."

"No, I mean something *really* familiar."

"Like what?"

"The red hair, the profile. The way she holds herself. Take a good look, man. She remind you of anyone?"

Mitchell studied Octavia for a long time.

"Well, shoot and damn," he said at last. "She's a dead ringer, isn't she? Funny, I never noticed before."

"Might explain why you took to her right off, though."

"Well, shoot and damn," Mitchell said again, this time sounding dazed. "What the hell is going on here?"

"Beats me," Sullivan said. "But I figure this isn't a coincidence."

"Nope." An expression of bemused wonder gleamed in Mitchell's eyes. "No coincidence. Tell you one thing, Nick better behave himself with her."

"What business is it of yours, how he behaves?"

"Octavia's alone in the world. No family to protect her."

"So you're going to take on the job, is that it?" Sullivan asked.

"Someone's gotta do it. That grandson of yours has a reputation for playing it fast and loose with the ladies."

"He just hasn't found the right woman to take Amelia's place."

"Way I hear it, he's not lookin' real hard for a wife," Mitchell observed. "Seems like he prefers a more casual arrangement with his lady friends, one that doesn't involve rings and a ceremony and a commitment. I hear tell they call him Hardhearted Harte in some circles."

"Damn it, my grandson's love life isn't any of your business."

"I won't let him take advantage of Octavia, got that?" Mitchell set his jaw. "She's not gonna be just another one of his short-term flings. You better set him real straight on that score or there'll be hell to pay."

Glumly, Sullivan studied the pair on the other side of the room.

"This could get complicated," he said.

"Sure could."

Sullivan didn't know precisely what Mitchell was thinking, but he was willing to bet his companion was recalling the same scene he himself remembered so well. It was a scene out of their shared past: an eerie, unsettling memory of the day a flame-haired woman in a short skirt and high heels opened the door of their little office on Bay Street and told them she would make them both very rich.

They both stared, fascinated at Octavia. No doubt about it, Sullivan thought, she bore an uncanny resemblance to Claudia Banner, the mysterious creature who had blazed through their lives all those years ago, singed them both badly and turned their world upside down before she disappeared with the assets of Harte-Madison.

"Who the hell is Octavia Brightwell and what is she up to here in Eclipse Bay?" he asked very quietly.

27

SHE listened to him climb the stairs and walk down the hall toward her studio. She continued to clean her brushes. His strides were easy, smooth, full of purpose and determination. A lot of the essence of Gabe Madison was distilled in the way he moved.

She put down the brushes and went to open the door. He came to a halt in front of her. He had left his jacket in the car and removed his cuff links. The collar of his charcoal-gray shirt was open, the silver-and-black striped tie loose around his neck. He was not smiling.

"You're late." She stood on tiptoe to kiss him.

"Ummm." He wrapped an arm around her when she made to pull back, holding her close for a long, slow, blood-warming kiss.

When he finally released her she was flushed and breathless. She saw the lazy, sexy gleam in his eyes and knew that she wasn't the only one who had been affected by the embrace.

"Thanks, I needed that," he said. "I had a hell of an afternoon."

"What happened?"

"Mitchell, Sullivan, and your father all arrived unannounced in my office two hours ago, just as I was thinking of leaving early for the day. It was nothing short of an ambush."

She wrinkled her nose. "Now what?"

He did not answer immediately. Instead he went to stand in front of her newest creation, an unfinished portrait of her mother and her grandmother and herself. The three figures were arranged around Eclipse Arch. They looked out at the viewer with steady gazes, each woman bringing the perspective of her particular phase of life to the scene, each silently acknowledging her links to the other two.

Gabe studied the picture.

"Damn, you're good," he said at last. "You really are good."

"Thanks, but you're avoiding the subject."

"I'm a CEO. I've got a natural aptitude for avoiding unpleasant subjects."

She did not like the sound of this. "What did they want, Gabe?"

"They presented a new business proposition."

"Uh-oh."

"Yeah, that was sort of my response, too."

"Gabe?"

"They want to do a merger."

She stared at him. It took her a few seconds to get her tongue untied. "A merger? You mean of Madison Commercial and Harte Investments?"

"Yeah."

"Oh, my."

"An equal exchange of stock between the companies. Family members only would be allowed to possess shares in the new corporation. The board of directors would consist of an equal number of Hartes and Madisons. I would be the CEO."

"Oh, my."

"In many ways, there is a lot to be said for the deal," Gabe continued, sounding as if he was reading from an investor's prospectus. "It would double the assets of the company overnight. It would allow us to extend the range and scope of our activities. It would give us the opportunity to provide extended management and consulting services to our clients."

"Oh, my." She felt the laughter bubble up inside and hastily clapped a hand over her mouth.

"It is also of course, my worst nightmare."

"I can understand that." She gave up the attempt to swallow her laughter. "The very thought of having to ride herd on a board of directors and a group of stockholders composed entirely of Hartes and Madisons would be enough to strike terror into the heart of any prudent, cautious, sensible CEO."

"You can say that again."

"But you're a Madison. I'll bet you didn't even swallow hard or blink. So, what are we going to call this new company?"

"The suggestion was made that the new firm should be known as Harte-Madison. Your father's idea, I believe. Some sentimental claptrap about recreating the original company founded by Mitch and Sullivan. I, however, took strong exception."

"So what is it going to be?"

He turned away from the portrait and came toward her, giving her the patented Madison grin, the really sexy one that showed his excellent teeth and made her pulse beat faster.

"Madison-Harte, of course," he said.

"Of course. I like it. It's got a ring to it."

"It does, doesn't it?"

He wrapped his arms around her and pulled her close. His mouth came down on hers in a kiss that demonstrated once again that nothing came between a Madison and his passion.

SUMMER IN ECLIPSE BAY

For Michele Bradshaw—
a lady who knows how to stay calm
even when we're all late for the wedding!

1

REJECTED again.

Sixth time in five weeks.

Not that he was counting.

Nick Harte put down the phone very deliberately, got to his feet, and went to stand at the living room window of the cottage.

Six rejections in a row.

A man could get a complex at this rate. Why was he doing this to himself anyway?

He looked out into the wall of gray mist that shrouded the landscape. Summer had arrived, just barely, in Eclipse Bay, and with it the familiar pattern of cool, damp, fog-bound mornings and long, sunny afternoons. He knew the season well. Growing up he had spent every summer as well as school vacations and long weekends here. His parents and grandparents maintained permanent homes elsewhere and he and his son lived in Portland most of the time, but that did not change the fact that for three generations the Hartes had been a part of Eclipse Bay. The threads of their lives were woven into the fabric of this community.

Summers in Eclipse Bay meant that on weekends the town swarmed with tourists who came to walk the breezy beach and browse the handful of shops and galleries. Summers meant the age-old ritual of teenagers cruising in their cars along Bayview Drive on Friday and Saturday nights.

Summers meant the summer people, outsiders who rented the weathered cottages along the bluffs for a few weeks or a month at a time. They shopped at Fulton's and bought gas at the Eclipse Bay Gas & Go. A few of them would even venture into the Total Eclipse to buy a beer or play some pool. Their offspring would flirt with some of the local kids on warm nights near the pier, maybe get invited to a few parties. But no matter how familiar they became, they would remain forever *summer people.* Outsiders. No one in town would ever consider them to be real members of the community with roots here. Eclipse Bay had its own private rules. Around here you knew who belonged and who did not.

The Hartes, like the Madisons, belonged.

But as much at home as he was here, Nick thought, he had long ago given up spending entire summers in Eclipse Bay. Probably because his wife, Amelia, had never really liked the town. After her death nearly four years ago, he had never gotten back into the habit of spending a lot of time in Eclipse Bay.

Until this summer. Things were different this year.

"Hey, Dad, I'm ready for you to look at my pictures now."

Nick turned to see his almost-six-going-on-thirty-year-old son standing in the doorway. With his lean build, dark hair, and serious dark-blue eyes, Carson was a miniature version of himself and all the other males in the Harte family.

But Nick was well aware that it wasn't just his physical appearance that marked him a true member of the clan. It was his precocious, frighteningly organized, agenda-driven nature. Carson's ability to focus on an objective with the unwavering precision and intensity of a battlefield commander told you he was a Harte to his toes.

At the moment he had two clearly defined goals. The first was to get a dog. The second was to exhibit a picture in the upcoming Children's Art Show scheduled to take place during the annual Eclipse Bay Summer Celebration festivities.

"I'm no art critic," Nick warned.

"All you gotta do is tell me which one you think Miss Brightwell would like best."

"Got news for you, kid. I'm rapidly coming to the conclusion that I'm the last person on earth who knows what Miss Brightwell likes."

Carson's small face tightened with sudden alarm. "Was that her on the phone just now?"

"Uh-huh."

"She turned you down again?"

"Afraid so."

"Geez, Dad, you gotta stop calling her up all the time and bothering her." Carson thrust out his hands, exasperated. "You're gonna ruin everything for me if you make her mad. She might not pick any of my pictures."

"I don't call her *all* the time." Damn. Now he was on the defensive with his own son. "I've only called her half a dozen times since Lillian's show."

He had been so sure that things had clicked between himself and Octavia that evening. The proprietor of Bright Visions, an art gallery business with two stores, one in Portland and one here in Eclipse Bay, Octavia had staged a gala reception to display his sister's work. The entire town had been invited and most of the locals had turned out for the show. The crowd had included everyone, from Virgil Nash, owner of Virgil's Adult Books & Video Arcade, to the professors and instructors of nearby Chamberlain College. Several members of the staff at the Eclipse Bay Policy Studies Institute had also deigned to appear.

They had all crowded into Bright Visions to drink good champagne, nibble on expensive hors d'oeuvres, and pretend to be art connoisseurs for a night. Nick had walked into the crowded room, taken one look at Octavia, and immediately forgotten that he was there to view Lillian's paintings.

The image he carried in his head of Octavia from that night was still crystal clear. She had worn a pale, fluttery dress that fell to her ankles and a pair of dainty, strappy little heels that had emphasized her elegantly arched feet. Her dark red hair had been brushed back behind her ears in a style that had framed her interesting, delicately molded features and mysterious sea-green eyes.

His first impression was that, although she was in this world, she was not completely anchored to it. There had been an ethereal, almost fey quality about her; perhaps she was a fairy queen visiting from some other, magical dimension where the rules were a little different.

He had stayed as close to her as possible that evening, aware of a visceral need to lure her to him and secure her by whatever means required. He did not want to allow her to float back to wherever it was she had come from.

The unfamiliar sense of possessiveness had made him want to bare his teeth and show some fang whenever another man had hovered too long in her vicinity. It was a completely over-the-top reaction, coming, as it did, after nearly four years of practicing what his sisters annoyingly described as commitment-free, serial monogamy. Okay, so he'd had a few discreet affairs. If anything that should have made him all the more immune.

The truth was, he had been stunned and bemused by his own reaction to Octavia. The only saving grace was that he had gotten the distinct impression that she was just as attracted to him as he was to her. Something in her big sea-colored eyes had registered her interest in him.

It had come as a shock at the end of the evening when she had politely turned down his invitation to dinner. He'd convinced himself that he'd heard regret in her voice, so he'd tried again a few days later when they were both back in Portland.

She had declined a second time with the explanation that she had to rush back to Eclipse Bay. It seemed the assistant she had left in charge of the gallery there, Noreen Perkins, had resigned without notice in order to run off with one of the artists whose work was exhibited in Bright Visions.

Octavia had returned to Portland on only one other occasion after that, and her stay had been extremely brief. He had asked her out for the third time, but she had told him that she was there to oversee a reception for one of the artists who showed in her gallery and had no time to socialize. The following morning she had flitted back to Eclipse Bay.

It had become obvious that she was not going to return to Portland any time soon. That had left him a limited number of options.

Two weeks ago he had made the decision to spend the summer in Eclipse Bay with Carson. But proximity was only making Octavia more inventive when it came to excuses for turning down dates.

The thing that should really concern him, he thought, was that he was working even harder to come up with reasons to call her one more time.

As far as he could tell, she did not have a complete aversion to men. She had been seen having dinner with Jeremy Seaton twice this past week.

Jeremy was the grandson of Edith Seaton, owner of an antiques shop located next door to Bright Visions Gallery. The Seatons had roots in the community that went back as far as those of the Hartes and the Madisons. Although Edith's husband, Phil, had died several years ago, she continued to take an active role in local affairs. Her son and daughter had moved away, but Jeremy had recently returned to take a position as an analyst at the Eclipse Bay Policy Studies Institute. The social and political think tank was one of Eclipse Bay's few claims to sophistication.

He knew Jeremy very well from the old days. They were the same age and they had been good friends at one time. But things had changed a couple of years ago. Women sometimes had that effect on a friendship.

He looked at Carson. "Miss Brightwell obviously doesn't think highly of me, but it's pretty clear that she likes you."

"I know she likes me," Carson said with exaggerated patience. "That's because I bring her coffee and a muffin every morning when we go into town to get the mail. But she might change her mind if you make her mad."

The sad fact was that Carson had made a lot more headway with Octavia than he had, Nick realized. His son adored the Fairy Queen of Eclipse Bay. For her part, she seemed to be very fond of Carson. The two of them had developed a relationship that somehow completely excluded him, Nick thought. It was frustrating.

"Don't worry," he said. "She's not the type to hold a grudge against you just because she doesn't want to go out with me."

He was pretty sure that was the truth. Octavia was a great mystery to him in many ways, but when it came to this aspect of her personality, he felt very sure of himself. She would never hold the sins of the father, whatever they might be, against the son.

Carson remained dubious. "Promise me you won't ask her out again until after she chooses one of my pictures."

"Okay, okay, I won't call her again until she makes her selection."

That was a safe promise. He figured it would be at least another three or four days before he could fortify himself to make a seventh phone call.

"Let's see your pictures," he said.

"They're in the bedroom." Carson whipped around and dashed off down the hall.

Nick followed him around the corner and into the downstairs room that his sister Lillian had turned into a temporary studio a few months earlier.

Three large squares of heavy drawing paper were arranged in a row on the hardwood floor. The pictures were all done in crayon, per the rules of the exhibition.

Nick went to stand looking down at the first picture. The scene showed a house with two stick figures standing very close together inside. The taller of the two figures had one arm extended protectively over the head of the smaller figure. A yellow sun shone brightly above the peaked roof. There was a green flower with several petals in the right-hand corner.

"That's you and me," Carson said proudly. He indicated the stick figures. "You're the big one."

Nick nodded. "Nice colors." He moved on to the next drawing and pondered it for a moment. At first all he could make out was a vague oval shape done in gray crayon. There were several jagged lines around the outside of the oval. He was baffled until he noticed the two pointy projections on top. Dog ears.

"This is Winston, I take it?" he said.

"Yeah. I had a little trouble with his nose. Dog noses are hard."

"Good job on the ears."

"Thanks."

Nick studied the third picture, a scene of five brown, elongated shapes thrusting out of a blue crayon circle. "The rocks in Dead Hand Cove?"

"Uh-huh." Carson frowned. "Aunt Lillian said it would make a good picture, but I dunno. Kind of boring. I like the other two better. Which one do you think I should give to Miss Brightwell?"

"That's a tough question. I like them all."

"I could ask Aunt Lillian. She's a real artist."

"She and Gabe are stuck in Portland for a while because Gabe is tied up with Dad and Sullivan while they hammer out the plans for the merger. You'll have to make the choice without her advice."

Carson studied the two pictures with a troubled expression. "Huh."

"I've got an idea," Nick said smoothly. "Why don't you take all three pictures with you tomorrow when we go into town? You can show them to Octavia when you take her the coffee and muffin. She can choose the one she likes best."

"Okay." Carson brightened immediately, clearly pleased by that suggestion. "I'll bet she goes for Winston. She likes him."

Not yet six and the kid was already displaying an intuitive understanding of the client, Nick thought. Carson was a natural for the business world. *Unlike himself.*

He had hated the corporate environment. His decision to leave Harte Investments, the company his grandfather Sullivan had founded and that his father, Hamilton, had taken over had not gone down well. Although his father had understood and supported him, his grandfather had been hurt and furious at the time. He had seen Nick's refusal to follow in his footsteps as a betrayal of everything he had worked so hard to achieve.

He and Sullivan had managed a rapprochement eventually, thanks to the intervention of everyone else in the family. They were back on speaking terms at any rate. But deep down, Nick was not certain that Sullivan would ever entirely forgive him.

He did not really blame his grandfather. Sullivan had poured his blood and sweat into building Harte Investments. He had envisioned the firm descending through generation after generation of Hartes. The company had been a personal triumph for him, a phoenix rising from the ashes after the destruction of Harte-Madison, the commercial real estate development business he had founded with his former partner, Mitchell Madison, here in Eclipse Bay.

The collapse of the company decades earlier had ignited a feud between Sullivan and Mitchell that had thrived until recently. The bad blood between the Hartes and the Madisons was legendary in these parts. It had provided fodder for the gossips of Eclipse Bay for three generations.

But the first crack in the wall that had separated the two very different families had come last fall when Rafe Madison, the bad boy of the Madison family, had married Nick's sister Hannah. Several more bricks had crumbled last month when his other sister, Lillian, had wed Gabe Madison.

But the earth-shattering news that Harte Investments and Gabe's company, Madison Commercial, were in the process of merging had been the final blazing straw as far as the good people of Eclipse Bay were concerned. The newly formed corporation, after all, effectively re-created the company that had been ripped apart at the start of the feud. Life had seemingly come full circle.

"You may be right about the Winston picture," Nick said. "But the house is pretty good, too. The green flower is a great touch."

"Yeah, but there will be lots of houses and flowers in the art show. All the kids I know like to draw houses and flowers. Probably won't be any other dogs, though. Hardly anyone can draw a dog, especially not one as good as Winston."

"Winston is unique. I'll give you that."

Carson looked up at him with a considering expression. "I've been thinking, Dad."

"What?"

"Maybe you shouldn't come with me when I take my pictures to Miss Brightwell tomorrow."

Nick raised his brows. "You want me to wait in the car?"

Carson smiled, clearly relieved. "Good idea. That way she won't even see you."

"You're really afraid I'm going to mess up your shot at getting a picture into the gallery show, aren't you?"

"I just don't want to take any chances."

"Sorry, pal. I've got my own agenda here and I'm not about to waste a perfectly good opportunity to move ahead with it just because you're worried she won't hang your picture."

So he didn't have a lot of interest in the family business. He was still a Harte, Nick thought. He was just as goal-oriented and capable of focusing on an objective as anyone else in the clan.

"If you wait in the car," Carson said ingratiatingly, "I promise I'll tell Miss Brightwell that it would be okay to go out with you."

One of the Harte family mottos in action, Nick thought, not without a degree of sincere admiration. *When you find yourself backed into a corner, negotiate your way out of it.*

"Let me get this straight." He hooked his thumbs in the waistband of his jeans and looked down at his son. "If I agree to stay out of the way tomorrow, you'll put in a good word for me?"

"She likes me, Dad. I think she'd agree to go out with you if I asked her."

"Thanks, but no thanks. I may not have followed in the family footsteps like Dad and Granddad, but that doesn't mean I don't know how to get what I want."

And he definitely wanted Octavia Brightwell.

That, he thought, was the real reason he and Carson were in Eclipse Bay for an extended stay. He had come here to lay siege to the castle of the Fairy Queen.

"Well, okay, but promise you won't wreck things for me."

"I'll do my best."

Resigned, Carson turned back to the dog picture. "I think Winston needs more fur."

He selected a crayon and went to work.

SHE was an out-and-out coward.

Octavia sat on the stool behind the gallery sales counter, the heels of her sandals hooked on the top rung, and propped her chin on her hands. She regarded the phone as if it were a serpent.

One date.

How could it hurt to go out with Nick Harte just once?

But she knew the answer to that. If she accepted one invitation, she would probably accept another. And then there would be a third. Maybe a fourth. Sooner or later she would end up in bed with him and that would be the biggest mistake of her life. Some thrill rides were just too risky.

They called him Hardhearted Harte back in Portland. Nick had a reputation for confining his relationships to discreet, short-term affairs that ended whenever his partner of the moment started pushing for a commitment.

According to the gossip she had heard, Nick never went to bed with a woman without first having delivered what was known as "The Talk."

The Talk was said to be a clear, concise position statement that made it plain that he was not interested in any long-term arrangements like marriage. Women who chose to sleep with Nick Harte went into the relationship with their eyes wide open.

They said that even if you lured him into your bed, he would be gone long before dawn. He never stayed the night, according to the stories that circulated about him.

Here in Eclipse Bay, where gossip about the Hartes and the Madisons had been raised to a fine art, folks were certain that they knew the real reason for The Talk. The local mythology held that Nick, being a true Harte, was unable to love again because he was still mourning the loss of his beloved Amelia. He was under a curse, some said, doomed never to find another true love until the right woman shattered the spell that bound him. His reputation for never staying the night with any of his lovers only fanned the flames of that particular legend.

Of course, that did not stop shoppers in the narrow aisles at Fulton's Supermarket from holding forth on the subject of the importance of Nick marrying again in order to provide his son with a mother. They said the same thing at the post office and in the hardware store.

But Carson didn't need a mother, Octavia thought. Nick was doing a fine job of raising him, as far as she could tell. The boy was the most self-assured, well-adjusted, precocious little kid she had ever met in her life. And there was no shortage of feminine influence available to him. Carson enjoyed the warmth of a close-knit, extended family that included a doting grandmother, a great-grandmother, and two aunts, Lillian and Hannah.

She unhooked her sandals, rose from the stool, and went to stand at the front window of Bright Visions. The morning fog was thinning, but it had not yet burned off. Across the street she could just make out the pier and the nearby marina. The lights were on in the Incandescent Body bakery down the street, and she could see the erratic snap and pulse of the broken neon sign that marked the Total Eclipse Bar & Grill. The tavern's logo, "Where the Sun Don't Shine," was just barely visible.

The rest of the world was lost in a sea of gray mist.

Just like her life.

A shiver went through her. Where had that thought come from? She wrapped her arms around herself. She would not go there, she vowed silently.

But the moody feeling was a warning, loud and clear. It was time to make some new plans; time to take control of her future. Her mission here in Eclipse Bay had been a failure.

Time to move on.

Her mission.

For months she had told herself that she had come here to right the wrongs of the past. In the beginning she had established a schedule that had allowed her to divide her time between this gallery and the main branch in Portland. But as the months went by she had found more and more reasons to extend her visits in Eclipse Bay.

Deep down she had actually been elated when her assistant here had run off with the artist. On impulse she had placed the Portland branch in the capable hands of a trusted manager, packed her suitcases, and moved her personal possessions into the little cottage on the bluff near Hidden Cove.

What had she been thinking? she wondered.

It was obvious that the Hartes and the Madisons did not need her help in healing the rift her great-aunt, Claudia Banner, had created so many years ago. The proud families were successfully putting the feud behind them without any assistance at all from her. There had been two weddings in the past few months that had united the clans, and now those old warriors, Sullivan Harte and Mitchell Madison, could be seen drinking coffee and eating donuts together at the bakery whenever Sullivan was in town.

No one in Eclipse Bay needed her. There was no reason for her to stay. It was time to go.

But that was easier said than done. She couldn't just close the door of the gallery and disappear in the middle of the night. Bright Visions was a small business, but it was thriving, and that meant it was worth a goodly sum. She would have to make arrangements to sell up and that might take a while. And then there was the matter of her obligations to the various artists whose work she exhibited and the commitment she had made to the Children's Art Show.

The art show had been her idea. She was the one who had come up with the concept and lobbied the members of the Eclipse Bay Summer Celebration committee to include it as one of the activities associated with this year's event. Enthusiasm for the project ran high. She knew that the children who planned to draw pictures for the event would be crushed if she cancelled it.

All in all, she concluded, what with getting Bright Visions ready to sell and fulfilling her business and civic commitments, she would probably not be able to escape Eclipse Bay until the end of the summer. But by fall she would be somewhere else. She had to find a place where she truly belonged.

2

THAT afternoon she closed the gallery at five-thirty and drove over to Mitchell Madison's house. She got out of the car and waved at Bryce as she went past the open kitchen door. He looked up from the pot he was stirring on the stove and inclined his head in a solemn greeting.

She smiled to herself. Bryce was the strong, silent type. He had worked for Mitchell for years. No one knew much about his past before he had arrived in town, and Bryce had never felt any impulse to enlighten anyone on that subject.

She understood where he was coming from, she thought.

She wandered into the garden and looked around, savoring the little slice of paradise that was Mitchell's creation. She had spent enough time in Eclipse Bay to know that, while everyone in the vicinity was quick to point out his legendary character flaws and remind you of his several failed marriages, no one disputed Mitchell's brilliance as a gardener. Gardening was his passion, and no one came between a Madison and his passion.

She came to a halt on the other side of a bed of gloriously blooming rose bushes.

"I've made a decision, Mitch."

He looked up at her from the padded kneeling bench he was using to work around the plants. He had the face of an aging, beat-up old gunslinger, she thought fondly, one who had only hardened with the years; a guy who could still hold his own against the young toughs if called upon to do so.

"What kind of decision?" Mitchell demanded.

The sharpness of his tone was a surprise. Mitchell never spoke sharply to her.

"I'll be leaving town at the end of the summer," she said.

"You mean you'll be spending more time back in Portland." He nodded, evidently satisfied, and went back to his weeding. "I can see where you might need to give more attention to your gallery there come fall. It's a much bigger operation."

"No," she said gently, "I mean that I will be leaving Eclipse Bay for good at the end of the summer season. I plan to sell both branches of Bright Visions."

He stiffened, eyes narrowing against the fading sun. "You're gonna sell up? Well, shoot and damn. Why the hell do you want to go and do a thing like that?"

"It's time." She smiled to cover the wistful feeling. "Past time, really. In fact, I probably shouldn't have come here in the first place."

"Not a lot of money in the art business here in Eclipse Bay, huh?" He shrugged. "No surprise there, I reckon. Eclipse Bay isn't exactly the art capital of the universe."

"Actually, the gallery here is doing fairly well. We drew clients from Chamberlain College and the institute this past winter, and now with summer here, we're picking up a lot of tourist business. Bright Visions is starting to get a reputation as an important art stop here on the coast."

His brows bunched together. "You're saying your business here is doing all right?"

"Yes, I expect to sell at a profit."

"Then why the hell are you talking about pulling out?"

"As I said, I think it's time for me to go."

He squinted at her. "You don't sound right. You feeling okay today, Octavia?"

"Yes."

"Not coming down sick, are you?"

"No."

"Shoot and damn. What's going on here?" He holstered the trowel he had been wielding, gripped the handholds on the low gardener's bench, and hauled himself to his feet. He seized his cane and turned around to confront her, scowling ferociously. "What's all this talk about leaving?"

"There's something that I want to tell you, Mitch. I don't plan to let a lot of other folks know because I don't want to upset people and cause talk. Lord knows, there's been enough gossip about the Hartes and the Madisons in this town. But you and I are friends. And I want my friends to know who I am."

"I know who you are." He thumped the cane once on the gravel walk. "You're Octavia Brightwell."

"Yes, but there's more to the story." She looked at him very steadily and braced herself to deliver the shocker. "Claudia Banner was my great-aunt."

To her astonishment he merely shrugged. "You think we didn't figure that out a while back?"

She stilled. *"We?"*

"Sullivan and me. He and I have slowed down some over the years, but we haven't come to a complete stop. Not yet, at any rate."

She didn't know what to say. "You *know*?"

"Sullivan spotted the likeness the night you hosted that show for Lillian's paintings down at your little gallery. Soon as he pointed it out, I finally realized why there had always been something sort of familiar about you." He smiled faintly. "You look a lot like Claudia did when she was your age. Same red hair. Something about your profile, too, I think. The way you hold yourself."

"But how did you—"

"Sullivan made some phone calls. Did some checking. Wasn't hard to find the connection."

"I see." She was feeling a little stunned, she realized. Maybe a little deflated, too. So much for her big bombshell.

"Not like you tried to hide it," Mitchell said.

"No, but I certainly didn't want to make a big deal about it here in Eclipse Bay, given what happened in the past and all."

Mitchell reached down and plucked a lush orange-gold bloom. "Funny thing about the past. The older you get, the less it matters."

She fell silent for a long moment, shifting gears as she adjusted to the turn of events. "If Sullivan made some calls, you probably know about Aunt Claudia." She took a deep breath. "That she's gone, I mean."

"Yeah." Mitchell looked up from the rose. His gaze was steady and a little sad. "Heard she passed on a year and a half ago. Heart problems, Sullivan said."

She felt the familiar tightening inside. Eighteen months but she still had to fight back the tears. "She never managed to give up the cigarettes. In the end, the doctor said it was amazing she made it as long as she did."

"I remember Claudia and her cigarettes. She was always reaching for the next one. Had herself a fancy little gold lighter. I can still see her taking it out of her purse to light another smoke."

"Mitchell, let me get something straight here. Are you telling me that you and Sullivan don't care that I'm related to Claudia Banner?"

"Of course we care. But it's not exactly what you'd call a problem for us."

"Oh." She was not sure how to respond to that.

"Can't say we weren't a bit curious at first, though," he added dryly.

"I can imagine. Why didn't you say something? Ask questions? Demand an explanation? I've stopped by here almost every morning or afternoon when I'm in town to say hello. I must have talked to you dozens of times since Lillian's show. But you never said a word. I've seen Sullivan on several occasions, too. He never gave any indication that he knew who I was."

"It was your personal business. Sullivan and I talked about it some. Figured we'd let you tell us in your own time."

"I see." She thought about that for a while. "Did you, uh, mention your little insight to anyone else?"

"Nope. Didn't figure it was anyone else's affair."

"Believe me, I understand." She wrinkled her nose. "If word got out that Claudia Banner's great-niece was in town and that she had become friends with the Madisons and the Hartes, there would be no end to the wild rumors and speculation. That's exactly why I kept a low profile."

"Yeah?"

"It wouldn't have been fair to you Madisons or to the Hartes. You've all suffered enough over the years because of what happened when you got involved with Aunt Claudia."

Mitchell snorted. "Madisons and Hartes are used to folks around here talking about us. Claudia may have been the spark that started the feud, but you can't blame her for the fact that Sullivan and I kept it going all those years. Hell, Madisons and Hartes have been inspiring conversation here in Eclipse Bay all by ourselves for decades. Got a real talent for it. Sometimes I think the good Lord put us on this earth just to keep this town entertained."

In other words, her concern for discretion and the privacy of the Madison and Harte families had been a complete waste of time and energy on her part. She sighed inwardly. Not only was she not needed here, Mitchell and Sullivan hadn't even cared enough about her presence in town to ask for explanations.

The day was getting more depressing by the minute.

"Well, that's that, then, isn't it?" She straightened her shoulders, preparing to leave. "I just wanted you to know, Mitch." She took a step back. "Guess I'll be going." She retreated another step. "Your roses look incredible, by the way."

Mitchell rapped his cane on the gravel again. "Hang on a minute. I'm the first to admit that you've got a right to keep your private business private, but now that you've mentioned Claudia and what happened in the past, I think maybe I've got a right to know why you've suddenly decided to pull up stakes."

"It's hard to explain."

His hawklike eyes gleamed with shrewd comprehension. "It's Nick Harte, isn't it?"

She was dumbfounded. "I, uh—"

"He's been pestering you, hasn't he? I knew it. I saw the way he moved in on you the night of Lillian's show. When he turned up in town a couple of weeks ago and settled into the Harte cottage for the summer. I got right on the phone to Sullivan."

"You *what?*"

"I warned him that he'd better keep Nick reined in good and tight. Told him I wouldn't stand by and let his grandson play any of his love 'em and leave 'em games with you. I don't care if Nick is still broken up about losing his wife. That's no excuse to fool around with you. Time he got over what happened and straightened himself out. Time he started acting like a real Harte again."

"A, uh, real Harte?" she repeated carefully.

"Damn right. Hartes don't mess around and have affairs. Hartes get married."

"I've heard that theory," she said dryly. "But there are exceptions to every rule. In any event, set your mind at rest, Mitch. This has got nothing to do with Nick Harte."

Even as the words left her lips, she realized she was lying through her teeth. Leaving Eclipse Bay had everything to do with Nick Harte. She just wasn't sure how to explain the connection, not even to herself, let alone to Mitchell.

"Bullshit." Mitchell glowered. "Pardon my language. But you've got to admit that the timing is more than a tad suspicious."

"Look, Mitch, we're getting a little off-topic here. I stopped by to tell you about my link to Claudia Banner. But since you already know about it, maybe I should tell you why I came here to Eclipse Bay in the first place."

There was a short silence. She could hear the distant clatter of pots in the kitchen. The light breeze off the bay shifted tree branches in the corner of the garden. Birds chattered overhead.

"Sullivan and me, we decided maybe you were just curious," Mitchell said after a while.

"It was more than mere curiosity," she said quietly. "I should probably start at the beginning."

"If that's what you want to do."

She hesitated, looking for the right place to begin. "I was with my aunt a lot during the last couple of years of her life. She needed someone to take care of her and there wasn't anyone else. Aunt Claudia was not the most popular member of the family."

"Hell, I didn't even realize she had a family. She never mentioned the subject."

"She was the renegade. The black sheep. The one who was always a source of acute embarrassment. But I had always liked her a lot. And she liked me. Maybe it was because I looked so much like her. Or maybe she just felt sorry for me."

"Why would she feel sorry for you?"

"I think she saw me as a loner, just as she was. My parents divorced when I was small. They both remarried and started new families. I spent most of my youth shuttling back and forth between them but I never felt at home in either house. Aunt Claudia sensed that, I think."

"Go on."

"Claudia was very special to me. I know she had her faults, and her business ethics left a lot to be desired. But I loved her and she cared about me in her own way. She worried that I was too inclined to play it safe. She said I spent too much time trying to smooth things over and calm the waters. She kept urging me to take a few chances."

"*She* sure knew how to take 'em." Mitchell chuckled reminiscently. "Maybe that was one of the reasons I couldn't take my eyes off her back in the old days."

"She never forgot you, Mitch. When she became seriously ill, I went to stay with her until the end. It took over a year for her to die. We had a lot of time to talk."

"And one of the things you two talked about was Eclipse Bay? Is that what you're saying?"

"Yes. She became increasingly obsessed with what had happened here. Said she didn't have a lot of regrets, but the destruction of Harte-Madison was one of them. She talked about how she wished that she could make amends."

"She should have known she couldn't go back and fix something that happened so long ago." Mitchell said.

"I know. But the subject became more and more important to her. Maybe because toward the end she became a serious student of New Age metaphysics. She talked a lot about karma and auras and such. At any rate, she asked me to come here after she was gone to find out how things stood. She wanted me to see if there was anything I could do to repair some of the damage she had done."

"Well, shoot and damn." Mitchell whistled softly. "So that's why you showed up here in town late last summer?"

"Yes. But shortly after I arrived, Rafe and Hannah returned and fell in love and made plans for Dreamscape. And then Gabe and Lillian started getting serious about each other. I turned around one day and you and Sullivan were having coffee together at the bakery." She smiled slightly. "It has become very clear that the feud is a relic of the past. The Hartes and the Madisons don't need my help mending the old rift."

"Huh," Mitchell said again. Thoughtful now.

She cleared her throat. "So, I feel that it's time for me to go."

"Just like that? You plan to slip out of town and disappear into the sunset?"

"It isn't that simple. As I said, I have to sell the gallery. And then there's the Children's Art Show."

"Loose ends."

"Yes."

"I don't like it," Mitchell said flatly.

"What don't you like?"

"Something doesn't sit right here." He whacked his cane absently against the trunk of a tree and eyed her with growing suspicion. "You sure Nick Harte hasn't been making a pest of himself?"

"No." Another quick dance step back. This was getting sticky. "Really."

"Has he been calling you up since he hit town a couple of weeks ago? Asked you out?"

"Well, yes."

"Hah. I knew it."

"I hardly think that constitutes pestering. Besides, I declined his invitations."

"Obviously."

"Obviously?"

Mitchell grunted. "If you'd had a date with Nick Harte, the news would have been all over town in an hour. Question is, why'd you turn him down?"

She began to feel a little desperate. The last thing she wanted to do was instigate more trouble between the Hartes and the Madisons.

"I've been busy," she said quickly.

"Bullshit. You're avoiding Nick Harte, aren't you?"

"Not exactly."

"Exactly." Mitchell looked fiercely pleased. "It's because you've got him figured out, isn't that right? You know Harte's got a reputation with the ladies. And you're too smart to fall for his tricks."

"Look, Mitch, I've got to be on my way. I would love to stay and chat, but I have some things to do this evening. Business related." She crossed her fingers mentally. She had gotten very good at inventing excuses lately. Aunt Claudia would have approved.

"Hold on here. I'll be damned if I'll let Nick Harte run you out of town." Mitchell aimed the cane at her. "You stay right where you are down there at the gallery. If he gives you any more trouble, let me know and I'll handle it."

"Sure. Right. Thanks, Mitch."

She whirled and fled toward the car.

DAMN it, Mitch was right, she thought halfway back to her cottage on the bluffs. In a way she was allowing Nick Harte to run her out of town. It was a humiliating admission to confront but it was the truth.

She was acting like a coward. Madisons didn't run from anything. Neither did Hartes. Aunt Claudia had never run from a risk in her entire life.

Maybe it was time she stopped running, Octavia thought. At least for the summer.

3

THE ancient mauve Cadillac glided into the small parking lot with the majesty of a massive cruise ship coming into port. Nick had just switched off the engine of his own BMW. He admired the mile-long fins that graced the rear of the vehicle. Chrome gleamed on every curve and angle.

"They don't make 'em like that anymore," he said to Carson.

From his position strapped into the backseat, Carson craned to see out the window. "That's Mrs. Seaton's car."

"So it is."

Edith Seaton's dome of severely permed gray curls was just barely visible. Nick wondered if she could actually see over the top of the wheel or if she had to steer looking through it. Then again, he reminded himself, she had lived in Eclipse Bay all her life. She probably knew her way around blindfolded.

He climbed out of the silver BMW, popped Carson out of the rear seat, and then went around the long, long fins of the Cadillac to open the door for Edith Seaton.

"Good morning, Nick, dear. My, you and Carson are here bright and early this morning." Edith emerged from the vastness of the big car and dimpled up at him. "Enjoying your stay out at your folks' place?"

"Yes, thanks," Nick said. "How's the antiques business?"

"As slow as ever." Edith reached back into the front seat to collect a white straw purse. "Which is probably a good thing, because I've been so busy lately with my Summer Celebration committee work." She reappeared, purse in hand. "One argument after another, you know. Right now the big issue is whether or not to put up a banner at the intersection where the Total Eclipse is located."

"I take it some folks don't approve?"

"I should say not. There's a strong feeling in some quarters that placing a banner so close to the bar would make it appear that the Total Eclipse is somehow an official participant in the event." Edith made a *tut-tut* sound. "And I absolutely agree. We really don't want the summer people and tourists thinking that dreadful place is considered a respectable business here in town."

Nick smiled. "Come on, now, Edith. The Eclipse has been operating here since my grandfather's day. Hard to pretend it doesn't exist. Fred pays his taxes, like everyone else."

"The Summer Celebration was never intended to promote that sort of tacky establishment and there will be no banner placed near it on my watch." She turned to Carson. "What's that you've got there, dear?"

"I brought my pictures for Miss Brightwell to see," Carson said proudly. He brandished the three rolled-up drawings he held. "She's going to choose one for the art show."

"Ah, yes, the Children's Art Show event. The Summer Celebration committee is delighted to be including such a wholesome, family-oriented activity as part of the festival this year. The project is a wonderful contribution. We're all so pleased that Octavia is willing to sponsor it."

"I did a picture of Winston," Carson informed her.

"That's lovely, dear." She winked at Nick as they walked toward the row of shops opposite the pier. "Do we have another budding artist in the Harte family?"

"You never know," Nick said.

"Art makes a very nice hobby," Edith said, laying a decided emphasis on the word "hobby." "Everyone should have a recreational activity of some sort. Jeremy enjoys painting, you know."

"He always did," Nick said, keeping his voice neutral.

"That's true. He doesn't have much time for it now, of course, what with his new position up at the institute." Pride glowed in Edith's face. "I'm surprised the two of you haven't had a chance to get together yet. You and Jeremy were such good friends in the old days."

Nick smiled very casually. "Like you said, he's probably very busy settling into his new job." And dating Octavia.

"I must say, your writing career appears to be going very well. I saw your latest book in the rack near the checkout counter at Fulton's the other day."

Nick wondered if that was a gentle hint. "I'd be happy to sign a copy for you, Mrs. Seaton."

"Thank you, but that won't be necessary," she said airily. "I don't read that sort of thing."

So much for knowing a hint when he heard one. "Right."

"Who would have thought you'd be so successful with your book writing?" Edith continued, shaking her head a few times.

"Not a lot of folks," he admitted. Amelia, for instance.

"And walking away from Harte Investments after your grandfather and your father had poured their hearts and souls into the business." Edith clicked her tongue again. "Really, it was quite a shock to everyone. When I think of what Sullivan went through after that dreadful woman destroyed Harte-Madison all those years ago. I mean, one would have thought that you would have felt some sense of responsibility to the family firm."

Nick realized he was clenching his back teeth a little too tightly together and forced himself to relax his jaw. It was Sullivan who had poured heart and soul into Harte. His father, Hamilton, on the other hand, had taken over the responsibility only because he had felt trapped by a sense of duty and filial obligation. Hamilton had known firsthand how much blood and sweat his father had expended to create Harte Investments. Early on in life he had accepted the fact that he could not reject the company without appearing to reject Sullivan and everything he had accomplished.

But Hamilton Harte had stood firm when it came to passing along the suffocating weight of obligation to his own offspring. He had refused to apply the kind of pressure that had been applied to him to coerce any of his three children into following in their father's and grandfather's footsteps. *Life is too short to spend it doing something you hate,* he'd told his wife, Elaine. *Let them find their own paths.*

The best thing about the merger of Harte Investments with Madison Commercial, Nick thought, was that it had finally freed his father and mother to pursue their own interests. Hamilton and Elaine planned to endow and oversee a charitable foundation. They could not wait to get rid of the responsibility of H.I. And Gabe Madison, fortunately for all concerned, was more than willing to take the helm. Running a business empire came naturally to him.

Nick searched for a way to change the subject. He picked the one he was least eager to pursue, but which he knew was guaranteed to distract Edith.

"How's Jeremy doing up at the institute?"

Edith switched gears instantly, delighted to turn to the topic of her grandson. "Very well, indeed. He says he likes being back in Eclipse Bay again after all those years away in Portland. The divorce was very hard on him, you know."

"I know."

"But he's dating again, I'm happy to say." She lowered her tone to a confidential level and winked broadly. "He's been seeing Octavia Brightwell."

"I heard." He had known this would not be his favorite topic, he reminded himself.

"Such a nice young woman. I think they make a lovely couple, don't you?"

He couldn't imagine a worse couple, Nick thought. Jeremy and Octavia were totally unsuited to each other. Any idiot could see that. But he didn't think Edith Seaton would appreciate being called an idiot, so he dug deep in search of logic and reason. He managed to pull up a vague memory of an article he'd come across in the course of researching his last book, *Fault Lines*. The plot had set his hero, John True, on the trail of a killer who had murdered his ex-wife.

"They say it takes a couple of years to recover from a divorce." He tried to put the ring of authority into his voice. "The trauma, you see. Takes a while to get past it, and experts advise people not to make serious relationship commitments during that time."

"Nonsense." Edith snorted. "What do the so-called experts know when it comes to love and marriage? Besides, it's been a year and a half now, and I'm sure Jeremy doesn't need another six months to recover. He just needs the right woman to help him forget. I think Octavia is doing him a world of good. She's pulling him out of his shell. He's been a little down since the divorce, you know. I was worried about him."

Under any other circumstances, Nick thought, he would have avoided the topic of Jeremy's divorce the same way he would have gone out of his way to sidestep a cobra in his path. But the fact that Edith thought that Octavia looked like a good candidate to take the place of Jeremy's ex was an irritating goad that he could not ignore.

"I'm surprised to hear you say that," he began coolly. "Personally I wouldn't have thought they'd have much—"

He was interrupted by the blare of a horn. He glanced toward the street and saw a familiar battered pickup truck rumbling past. There was no mistaking the driver. Arizona Snow was garbed in her customary camouflage-patterned fatigues. A military-style beret slanted across her gray hair in a jaunty fashion.

He raised a hand in greeting. Carson waved madly. Arizona waved back, but she did not pause. A woman on a mission.

That was the great thing about being a professional conspiracy theorist, he thought. You always had a mission.

The pickup continued down the block and pulled into the parking lot in front of the Incandescent Body bakery.

Edith sighed. "Expect you heard the news about old Tom Thurgarton's will?"

"Rafe said something about Thurgarton having left all his worldly possessions to Virgil Nash, Arizona, and the New Age crowd running the bakery."

"Yes." Edith shook her head. "Of all the ridiculous notions. Just like Thurgarton to do something so bizarre. He was such an odd man."

Nick nodded. "Yeah, he was always a little weird, wasn't he? A real recluse. He lived here in town all the time I was growing up but I doubt if I saw him more than half a dozen times a year."

"They say that Thurgarton's phobia about leaving his house got worse as time went on. Everyone was so accustomed to not seeing him that no one even knew he was dead until Jake down at the post office finally noticed that he hadn't picked up his mail in over two months. When Sean Valentine went out to see what was going on, he found Thurgarton's body in the kitchen. Heart attack, they say."

"Wonder if he left anything valuable to Virgil and A.Z. and the Heralds," Nick mused.

"I doubt it." Edith sniffed as they came to a halt in front of the door of Seaton's Antiques. "The way Chief Valentine tells it, that old cabin was crammed with over forty years' worth of junk. A real firetrap, he said. Old newspapers and magazines stacked to the ceiling. Boxes full of unopened mail. Cartons of things he'd ordered from catalogs that had never been unpacked."

"Going to be interesting to see what kind of conspiracy theory A.Z. will weave out of this," Nick said with a smile. "She's nothing if not inventive."

"I'm afraid A.Z. is one brick shy of a load, and hanging out with the crowd from the bakery isn't improving the situation." Edith turned the key in the lock and stepped into her shop. "Goodbye, you two. Good luck with your pictures, Carson."

"Bye, Mrs. Seaton." Carson was struggling to be polite, but he was already edging off toward the neighboring shop door.

"See you later," Nick said.

He and Carson continued on to the front door of Bright Visions. Instead of rushing inside, Carson paused.

"Maybe you could stay out here on the sidewalk while I show my pictures to Miss Brightwell," he suggested hopefully.

"Not a chance."

Carson heaved a sigh, resigned. "Okay, but promise me again that you won't say anything to make her mad."

"I already said that I'd do my best not to annoy her." Nick glanced through the window into the gallery showroom. The Open sign showed through the glass, but he could not see Octavia. She was probably in her cluttered back room, he decided.

He wrapped his hand around the knob and twisted. The now-familiar sense of anticipation sleeted through him.

The door swung inward, revealing a universe of intense color and light. The artwork that hung on the walls ran the gamut from landscapes to the abstract, but the pictures were grouped in some inexplicably magical fashion that somehow managed to make the whole greater than the sum of its parts. A sense of connection and coherence pervaded the scene. The viewer was drawn from one to another in a subtle progression that took him deeper into the little cosmos.

There was an art to displaying paintings to their best advantage, Nick thought. Octavia knew what she was doing. No wonder she prospered. It was hard *not* to buy a picture when you were in this gallery.

Carson hurried inside, clutching his drawings in both hands.

"Miss Brightwell?" he called. "Where are you? I've got my pictures."

Octavia came to stand in the open doorway behind the counter. The sweeping hemline of a long, full skirt in the palest possible shade of ice blue swirled around her shapely calves. She wore a matching silk blouse. A tiny blue belt studded with small chunks of clear crystal encircled her trim waist. Her fiery hair was held back off her face by a pale aqua scarf that had been folded to form a narrow headband.

People in the art world were supposed to wear black, Nick thought. Until he'd met Octavia, he had always assumed it was a rule.

As always, he felt his insides clench at the sight of her. He ought to be getting used to this sensation, he thought. But the appearance of the Fairy Queen never failed to steal his breath for a few seconds.

When she met his gaze across the showroom, Nick could almost see the familiar, concealing veil slip into place. But when she looked at Carson, she was all smiles.

"Good morning," she said, speaking more to the boy than the man.

"Hi, Miss Brightwell." Carson blossomed in the warmth of her smile. "I brought my pictures to show you."

"You may have noticed that we're here a little early," Nick said dryly. "And we came without coffee and muffins. Carson was in a hurry."

"We'll get you some coffee and a muffin right after you see my pictures," Carson assured her, looking a little worried because of the oversight.

"I can't wait to see your pictures," Octavia said warmly.

"I brought three." Carson tugged the rubber band off the roll of drawings. "Dad said I should let you pick. But I'm pretty sure you'll like the picture of Winston best. I added some extra fur."

"Let's spread them out and take a look."

Octavia led the way to a long white bench at the far side of the room. She and Carson unrolled the drawings and arranged them side by side.

Octavia studied each picture in turn with rapt attention, her expression absorbed and serious—for all the world, Nick thought, as if she were considering the pictures for a real, high-profile, career-making show such as she had given Lillian a while back in Portland.

"The house is very good," she said after a moment.

"That's me and Dad inside," Carson said. "Dad's the big one."

Octavia gave Nick a fleeting glance. He could have sworn she turned a rosy shade of pink before hastily returning her attention to the picture.

She cleared her throat. "Yes, I can see that."

"This is Dead Hand Cove," Carson said, pointing to the next picture. "Aunt Lillian said I should include it, but I think landscapes are boring. Just rocks and water. Take a look at Winston."

Obediently Octavia moved to examine the furry gray blob with the pointy ears.

"You've certainly captured the essence of his personality very well," she said.

Carson was pleased. "I told Dad you'd like this one best. I brought my crayon with me. I can add some more fur if you want."

"No, I think he has precisely the right amount of fur," Octavia said decisively. "I'll hang this one in the show."

Carson bounced a little with excitement. "Will you frame it?"

"Of course. I'm going to frame all of the pictures in the show." She looked at him. "You forgot to sign it."

"I'll do it now." Carson whipped out his crayon and went to work inscribing his first name in large block letters in the right-hand corner of the picture. "I almost forgot," he added, not looking up from the task, "I promised Dad that if you liked my picture, I'd tell you that it was okay to go out with him."

A stunned hush enveloped the gallery. Nick looked at Octavia. Her veiled expression never flickered, but he saw something that might have been speculation in her eyes. Or was that just his imagination?

Oblivious to the electricity he had just generated, Carson concentrated intently on printing the last letters of his name.

"Sorry about that," Nick muttered.

"No problem," Octavia murmured.

There was another short, extremely uncomfortable silence.

"So?" Octavia said.

He frowned. "So, what?"

"So, are you going to ask me out again?"

"Uh——" He hadn't been caught this far off guard since high school. He felt like an idiot. He could only hope that he was not turning red. Something had changed in the situation, but he was at a loss to know what had happened. Only one way to find out, he thought. "Dinner tonight?"

She hesitated; honest regret showed on her face. He'd seen that look before.

"You're busy, right?" he said without inflection. A cold feeling coalesced in his gut. He couldn't believe she'd set him up like that.

"Well, I did promise Virgil Nash that I'd drive out to the Thurgarton house after I close the gallery this afternoon. He and Arizona Snow want my opinion on some paintings that they discovered stashed in one of Thurgarton's closets. The thing is, I don't know how long it will take me."

He relaxed. Maybe she hadn't set him up, after all.

"Forever," he said.

"I beg your pardon?"

"It'll take you forever to even find the old Thurgarton place unless Virgil gave you really, really good directions. Thurgarton liked his privacy. There's no sign on the road leading to the turnoff, and the drive is hidden in the trees."

"Oh." Her fine, red-brown brows wrinkled delicately in a small frown. "Virgil gave me a little map."

"Forget it," he said easily. "I'll pick you up after you close the gallery this afternoon and drive you out there. Later we can go to dinner."

"I suppose that might work," she said.

She sounded so damn casual, he thought. As if the decision she had just made weren't staggering in its implications. As if it weren't going to alter destinies and change the fate of nations.

Okay, he could deal with the world shifting in its orbit. What really worried him was the question of why it had done so. After six turn-downs in a row, the Fairy Queen of Eclipse Bay had agreed to go out with him.

Lucky number seven.

Be careful what you wish for.

4

THE little girl with the glossy brown hair and the big, dark eyes was back.

Octavia was discussing the merits of a charming seascape with a middle-aged tourist couple when she caught sight of the youngster on the sidewalk outside. This was the second time this week that the girl had appeared. On the first occasion she had been accompanied by her mother, a pretty but quietly determined-looking woman who wore the unmistakable cloak of single parenthood. The pair had wandered into the gallery and looked at pictures for a long time. The child had been as absorbed in the works of art as her mother—an unusual event. Most kids found the paintings boring in the extreme.

The woman had greeted Octavia politely and made it plain that she was not there to buy, just to look around. She had clearly been braced for a cool reception, but Octavia had assured her that she was welcome to browse.

The woman and her daughter had moved from picture to picture, talking seriously in low tones about some of them, showing little interest in others. They had been standing in front of a brilliant abstract when the woman had glanced at her watch, frowned in alarm, and hurried out of the gallery with the little girl.

The woman had not returned, but her daughter was here again, standing on the other side of the glass staring at the colorful poster in the window that announced the Children's Art Show.

I'm not going to lose her this time, Octavia thought.

"Excuse me," she said to the couple contemplating the purchase of the seascape. "I'll be right back."

She hurried behind the sales counter, reached down, and selected a large box of crayons from a carton that was nearly empty. She took a pad of drawing paper from the dwindling pile.

Crayons and pad in hand, she straightened quickly and looked out the window. The little girl was still there.

Octavia crossed the gallery, opened the front door, and stepped out onto the sidewalk. The child turned, looking a bit startled.

"Hello," Octavia said. "Would you like to enter a picture in the art show?"

The child stared at her. She did not speak.

"Every entrant gets a box of crayons and a pad of drawing paper," Octavia explained. "The rule is that the picture has to be on a piece of paper the size of one of these." She flipped through the blank sheets of drawing paper. "When it's ready, bring it back here."

The girl's anxious gaze shifted from Octavia's face to the pad of drawing paper and the crayons. She put her hands behind her back, evidently afraid that she might lose control and reach out to grab the art supplies.

She shook her head very fiercely.

"Anne?"

The woman who had accompanied the girl into the gallery a few days ago rushed out of Seaton's Antiques. Her head swiveled rapidly as she searched the sidewalk in both directions with the slightly frantic look a mother gets when she turns around and realizes her offspring has disappeared.

"Anne, where are you?"

"I'm here, Mom," Anne whispered.

Her mother swung around. Relief flashed across her face. The expression was followed by stern exasperation.

"You must not disappear like that." She walked swiftly toward her daughter. "How many times have I told you not to run off without telling me where you're going? This may not be Seattle, but the same rules apply."

"I was just looking in the window," Anne said in a tiny, barely audible voice. She kept her small hands secured very tightly behind her back. "I didn't touch anything, honest."

Octavia studied the woman coming toward her. Anne's mother appeared to be in her late twenties but if you had only seen her eyes, you would have added twenty years to her age.

"Hello," Octavia said in her best professional tone. "I'm Octavia Brightwell. You were in my gallery the other day."

"I'm Gail Gillingham." Gail smiled hesitantly. "I'm sorry if Anne was bothering you."

"Not in the least," Octavia said cheerfully. "I noticed that she was looking at the poster featuring the Children's Art Show. I thought she might like to participate. I have room for more pictures."

Gail looked down at Anne. "Thank you, but I'm afraid Anne is very shy."

"Who cares?" Octavia looked at Anne. "Lots of artists are shy. I'll tell you what, why don't you take these crayons and the paper home with you? You can draw your picture in private where no one else can watch you at work. When it's ready, just ask your mother to drop it off here at the gallery."

Anne looked at the crayons and the paper as though they were made of some magical, insubstantial substance that might disintegrate if she were to touch them.

Octavia did not say anything more. She just smiled encouragingly and held out the crayons and the paper.

For a long moment, Anne did not move. Then, very slowly she untwisted her arms from behind her back, reached out, and took the supplies from Octavia. Clutching them tightly to her chest, she stepped back and looked at her mother.

Surprise and a fleeting delight lit Gail's face. An instant later her pleasure was marred by what seemed to be uncertainty. She hesitated and then seemed to brace herself.

"How much do I owe you for the crayons and the paper?" she asked.

"The Children's Art Show has been underwritten by the Bright Visions Gallery, which is sponsoring it," Octavia said. "All the entrants receive the same basic supplies."

"Oh, I see." Gail relaxed visibly. "Thank Miss Brightwell for the crayons and paper, Anne."

"Thank you," Anne repeated in the barest of whispers.

"You're welcome," Octavia said. "I'll look forward to seeing your picture."

Anne tightened her grip on the art supplies and said nothing. She still looked as if she expected the crayons and paper to vaporize in her arms.

At that moment, a familiar silver BMW pulled into the small parking lot at the end of the row of shops. Octavia's stomach fluttered. She glanced at her watch and saw that it was almost five-thirty. Nick was right on time.

Gail gave Octavia a grateful smile. "I don't know if Anne will actually do a picture for your art show, but she loves to draw and paint. She will definitely use the supplies."

"Excellent," Octavia said. She looked at Anne. "But I really hope you'll make a special drawing for the show. If you do, you can choose the color of the frame."

"You're gonna put it in a frame?" she asked in astonishment.

"Of course."

"So it will look like a real picture?" Anne pointed toward the framed paintings hanging inside the gallery. "Like one of those?"

"Yes," Octavia said. "It will look like a real picture because it will be a real picture. Just like one of those inside my gallery."

Anne was clearly dazzled by the prospect.

"Come along, Anne," Gail said. "We have to stop at the store and then we have to go home to help Grandma fix dinner."

"Okay."

Anne and Gail moved off toward the small parking lot. Nick was out of his car now, walking toward the gallery. He wore a long-sleeved, crew-neck tee shirt and a pair of jeans. The snug fit of the shirt emphasized the contours of his strong shoulders and flat belly.

He paused to greet Gail and Anne with a friendly nod and a few words. When the short conversation was finished, Gail and her daughter got into an aging Chevrolet.

Nick continued toward the gallery.

Edith came to stand on the sidewalk next to Octavia.

"Such a sad situation." Edith shook her head and made a *tut-tut* sound when Gail and Anne drove past them down the street.

Octavia waved at Anne, who gazed fixedly at her through the car window. Hesitantly the girl raised a small hand in response.

"I assume you're talking about Gail and Anne?" Octavia said, watching Nick.

"Yes. Gail is the daughter of Elmore and Betty Johnson, the folks who run Johnson's Nursery and Garden Supply. She was such a pretty girl back in high school. Bright, too. Went off to college in Seattle." She paused and smiled at Nick when he came to a halt in front of her.

"Afternoon, Mrs. Seaton. Nice day."

"It is, indeed. I was just telling Octavia how Gail went off to college in Seattle and ended up married to that investor fellow who left her a couple of years ago and ran off with the decorator who redid his office."

"I'm afraid I didn't keep up with the gossip at the time," Nick said in a repressive tone that was clearly meant to change the subject. "I had my hands full in Portland."

"Gail got almost nothing out of the divorce, they say," Edith continued, oblivious to the unsubtle hint. "Word is her husband stashed all his assets on one of those little islands in the Caribbean, declared bankruptcy, and left the state. Never sees his daughter, of course."

"Poor little Anne," Octavia said.

"Ready to go?" Nick said pointedly to Octavia.

She glanced over her shoulder and saw that her potential clients were still contemplating a purchase. "In a few minutes."

"Gail lost her job in Seattle a couple of months ago and now she's back here in Eclipse Bay. She's living with her folks while she looks for work. Money is tight."

"She's job hunting?" Octavia looked down the street. Gail's Chevy had disappeared around a corner. "Is that why she was in your shop?"

"Yes. Unfortunately, I had to tell her that I just don't do enough business to warrant hiring an assistant. I gather she's tried several other places with no luck."

"Hmm," Octavia said.

5

THE middle-aged couple left a short time later with their newly acquired seascape wrapped in brown paper.

Octavia set the security alarm, locked the door of the gallery, and dropped her keys into the spacious bag that hung from her right shoulder.

Nick gave her an enigmatic smile and put on his sunglasses.

She would have given a lot to be able to read his mind at that moment, she thought. Then again, maybe it was better not to know what he was thinking. The knowledge would only have made her more tense. She was still wondering if this burst of recklessness was going to prove to be a disaster.

They walked together toward the parking lot. When they reached the BMW, he opened the door on the passenger side and held it for her. She searched his face quickly looking for any concealed signs of triumph. She saw none. If anything, she thought, he seemed as wary as she felt.

Now that was an interesting development.

She collected the folds of her skirt in one hand and slipped into the front seat. "What did you do with Carson?"

"He's spending the evening with Rafe and Hannah out at Dreamscape," Nick said.

"Oh." She realized she had become accustomed to seeing Nick and Carson together during the past two weeks. "Will he be joining us for dinner later?"

He smiled. "This is my date, not Carson's."

He closed the car door very deliberately.

She watched him walk around the front of the vehicle. He moved with an easy, fluid grace that was at once relaxed and purposeful. Probably the way most top-of-the-food-chain predators moved when they were going out to grab a gazelle for dinner, she thought. Fascinating, exciting. More than a little dangerous.

The sense of deep, sensual appreciation that swept through her caught her by surprise. She was still slightly awed by her decision to go out with him. Until tonight, the only big risks she had ever taken in life had involved the buying and selling of art. She trusted her intuition when it came to taking chances on unknown painters. But she had always been cautious when it came to men.

Nick got behind the wheel and closed the door. The interior of the BMW suddenly felt overwhelmingly intimate. She realized she was holding her breath.

"Couple of things you should know," she said carefully when he made to slip the key into the ignition. "The first is that, in case your grandfather hasn't told you, Claudia Banner was my great-aunt."

Dead silence.

Nick did not fire up the engine. Instead, he twisted slightly in the seat and rested his right arm on the back. He watched her very steadily through his dark glasses.

"Want to run that past me again?" he said.

"I'm related to Claudia Banner. The woman who—"

"Trust me, I know who Claudia Banner is."

"Was. My aunt died a year and a half ago."

"I see." Nick waited a beat. "This is for real? Not a joke of some kind?"

"No, it's not a joke." She gripped her bag very tightly in her lap. "Does it change things? Do you want to call off the date?"

"My grandfather knows who you are?"

"Yes. Sullivan and Mitchell both know. They figured it out the night of Lillian's show." She cleared her throat. "Obviously they haven't told anyone else in either family yet."

"Yeah. Obviously." He tapped the key absently against the leather seat back. "Well, hell."

"Is this a problem for you?"

"I'm thinking," he said. "Give me a minute."

"Look, if you're that rattled, I can find my own way out to Thurgarton's place."

"It isn't a problem and I'm not rattled." He took off his dark glasses and examined her with cool, faintly narrowed eyes. "I just find this news a little unexpected, that's all. It raises a few questions."

"I know. I answered some of them for Mitchell and I can do the same for you." She glanced pointedly at her watch. "But not now. We need to get going. I promised Virgil I'd meet him and the others at six."

"Right." He turned back and twisted the key in the ignition. The powerful engine growled softly. "I'm still waiting for the other shoe to drop."

"The other shoe?"

"You said there were a couple of things I needed to know." He checked his mirrors and reversed out of the parking space.

"I'll be leaving town at the end of the summer."

He shot her a quick glance and she knew that the news had taken him by surprise.

"You're leaving Eclipse Bay?"

"Yes, I'm going to sell the gallery."

He seemed to relax slightly. He gave an understanding inclination of his head. "Not surprised the gallery here isn't working. Makes sense to concentrate on the Portland branch."

She watched the road through the windshield. "Both galleries are successful, as a matter of fact. But I'm going to sell both branches."

"Getting out of the art business altogether?"

"Not that easy." She smiled slightly. "It isn't just a business. More of a calling, I'm afraid. I can't imagine not being involved in art. A couple of months ago I was offered a position in a large gallery in San Diego. I don't have to give them my official decision until next month, but I'm leaning strongly toward accepting the offer."

"San Diego, huh?"

"It's not a certainty. There's also a possibility that I'm looking at in Denver."

"I see."

He drove in silence for a few minutes, piloting the BMW carefully through the small business district, past the pier, the town's single gas station, and the Incandescent Body bakery.

"Sounds like you're cutting a lot of ties all at once," Nick said eventually. "Is that wise?"

"I don't have any personal ties in the Northwest. I didn't even move to Portland or open the galleries until a couple of months after Aunt Claudia died."

"You've only been in the area a little more than a year?"

"That's right. Not long enough to put down roots. There's nothing holding me here." It was time to accept that truth, she thought. Time to get on with her life.

She looked out over the expanse of Eclipse Bay. The sun was low in the sky. It streaked the clouds gathering out on the horizon with ominous shades of orange and gold.

Nick drove without speaking for a while, concentrating on the road, although traffic was almost nonexistent on the outskirts of town.

"Why did you come to Eclipse Bay?" he asked finally. "Why go to all the trouble of starting up a business in a small town in addition to one in Portland? That was a major undertaking."

"It's not easy to explain. Aunt Claudia talked a lot about what happened here all those years ago. The memories bothered her a great deal toward the end. She felt guilty about her part in the feud. I promised her that I would come back to see if there was anything I could do to put things right."

"No offense, but just what the hell did you plan to do to mend a three-generation rift?" Nick asked dryly.

She winced. His obvious lack of faith in her feud-mending skills hurt for some obscure reason. The worst part was that he was right. She had been a fool to think she could do anything constructive.

"I don't know," she said honestly. "I just decided to give it a whirl."

"I gotta tell you, that sounds damn flaky."

"I suppose it does. The thing is, after Aunt Claudia died there wasn't any-thing holding me in San Francisco."

"That's where you were living?"

"Yes."

"What about your job?" He flexed his hand on the wheel. "A significant other?"

"I had a position in a small gallery, but it wasn't anything special. And there was no particular significant other."

"Hard to believe."

"I was seeing someone before Claudia got so sick. But it wasn't that serious and we drifted apart when I started spending more and more time with my aunt. He found someone else and I sort of went into hibernation. By the time I resurfaced after the funeral, I had no social life left to speak of."

"Family?"

"Not in the San Francisco area. My folks are separated. Dad lives in Houston. Mom's in Philadelphia. They've both got other families. Other lives. We're not what you'd call close."

"So you just up and moved to Oregon."

"Yes." She wrinkled her nose. "I suppose that sounds very flighty to a Harte."

"Hell, it sounds flighty for anyone, even a Madison."

That irritated her. Given his track record with women, he had a lot of nerve calling her flaky and flighty.

"I like to think of myself as a free spirit," she said. She rather liked the sound of that now that she thought about it. *Free spirit* definitely sounded better than *flighty* or *flaky*. More mysterious and exotic, maybe. She arched her brows. "Do you have a problem with that?"

"Don't know," he said. "I've never actually met a free spirit before."

HE was still pondering all the possible definitions of *free spirit* ten minutes later when he turned into the narrow, unpaved road.

"You know, I think you were right." Octavia leaned forward a little, peering through the window at the trees that loomed on either side of the rutted path. "I might have spent hours searching for this turnoff. Mr. Thurgarton certainly didn't believe in making his place easy to find, did he?"

He shrugged. "Thurgarton was one strange man. Just ask anyone."

She smiled fleetingly. "Sometimes I think that being a bit odd or eccentric is a requirement for renting or purchasing real estate in Eclipse Bay."

"I will admit that the people we're about to meet certainly exemplified the finest in that local tradition."

He eased the BMW deeper into the trees and brought it to a halt at the edge of a small clearing.

Arizona Snow's pickup truck was parked under a nearby tree. Virgil Nash's vintage sports car stood next to it.

A gray, weather-beaten cabin occupied the center of the open space. It was on the verge of crumbling into the ground. The front porch sagged and the windows were caked with grime. There was a worn-out quality to the old house, as if it were content to follow its owner into the grave.

"It doesn't look like Thurgarton took good care of his property," Octavia said.

The touch of feminine disapproval in her voice almost made him smile. He thought about her pristine gallery with its sparkling windows and carefully hung paintings. The interior of her little fairy cottage out on the bluffs probably looked just as neat and tidy.

"Thurgarton was not real big on home improvement projects," he said.

He switched off the engine and climbed out from behind the wheel. Octavia did not wait for him to show off his first-date manners. She got out of the front seat all on her own.

Free spirit.

Virgil Nash opened the front door of the cabin as Nick and Octavia started toward the porch steps.

"He certainly doesn't fit the stereotypical image of a porn-shop proprietor, does he?" Octavia murmured in a very low voice.

Nick grinned. "Virgil's definitely one of a kind, and you've got to admit that his business offers a unique service to the community. Sort of like a library."

"Well, that is one way of looking at it, I suppose. There is something scholarly about him, isn't there? Maybe it's the frayed sweater vest."

"Could be."

It was true, Nick thought. With his gaunt frame, silver goatee, and preference for slightly frayed sweaters and vests, Virgil would have been at home in an academic environment. There was an old-fashioned, almost courtly air about him. No one knew where he had come from or what he had done before he had arrived in Eclipse Bay. His past was as shrouded in mystery as Arizona Snow's.

For as long as anyone could remember, Nash had operated Virgil's Adult Books & Video Arcade. The establishment was discreetly located a couple of hundred yards beyond the city limits and, therefore, just out of reach of ambitious civic reformers and high-minded members of the town council.

Virgil believed in the old saying that location was everything in real estate.

"Nick, this is a surprise." Virgil walked across the porch. "Good to see you again. Heard you were in town for the summer."

"Needed a change." Nick went up the steps and shook Virgil's hand. "Thought Carson would enjoy the beach."

"Good thing you drove Octavia out here." Virgil smiled ruefully at her. "I got to thinking later that it might not be easy for you to find this place, what with being new to the community and all."

"You were right," she said. "Left to my own devices, I'd probably still be looking for the turnoff."

"Thank you so much for coming all the way out here to look at the paintings. We certainly appreciate it."

"Happy to be of service," Octavia said. "Where's A.Z.?"

"Right here," Arizona boomed through the screen door. "You met Photon, here?"

"Yes, of course." Octavia nodded at the tall man in the long, flowing robes who stood behind Arizona. "Good evening, Photon."

"May the light of the future brighten your night, Miss Brightwell." Photon inclined his gleaming, shaved head in Nick's direction. "Light and peace, Mr. Harte."

"Thanks," Nick said. "Same to you, Photon."

Another resident eccentric, Nick thought. Photon was the leader of the New Age crowd that operated the Incandescent Body bakery. The group styled itself the Heralds of Future History. Their philosophy was a little vague, but their baking skills were outstanding. The incredible muffins, pastries, and corn bread produced at the bakery had gone a long way toward quelling local concerns that Eclipse Bay had been invaded by a cult.

"Come on inside." Arizona thrust open the screen door. "Got the paintings lined up here in the living room."

"We had to clear out two pickup loads of junk to make space to display them," Virgil said dryly.

Nick grinned. "There goes the inheritance, huh?"

"Let's put it this way," Virgil said. "It was nice of Thurgarton to think of us, but it's starting to look like being the beneficiaries of his will is more trouble than it's worth. The furniture is in such bad shape it isn't even worth the effort of putting on a yard sale. Other than the paintings, everything else is just junk. Personally, I'm not holding my breath that the pictures are worth much, either."

Nick ushered Octavia ahead of him into the cramped, dark living room. She came to an abrupt halt.

"Oh, my," she said. "This is really quite amazing."

"That's one word for it." Nick stopped just behind her and whistled softly at the sight of the truly monumental clutter. "The term 'firetrap' also comes to mind."

Faded magazines and yellowed newspapers spilled from the tops of row upon row of cardboard boxes stacked to the ceiling. Old suitcases were heaped in a corner. One of them was open, revealing a tangle of old clothes. The surface of the desk near the window was buried beneath piles of file folders and three-ring binders stuffed with notebook paper.

In addition to the desk and its accompanying chair, the only other furnishings in the room were a recliner and a reading lamp.

Octavia gave Virgil, Arizona, and Photon a quick, laughing smile. "And to think that this is all yours now."

Virgil chuckled softly. "You know, this is the first time anyone was thoughtful enough to remember me in his will."

"The property is worth something," Nick said, trying to be optimistic.

"Something," Photon agreed, "but not a lot. No view of the water. The house, itself, is a tear-down. The plumbing is in bad shape and the wiring is decades out of code."

Nick was mildly surprised by Photon's assured assessment of the house and land value. For the first time he wondered what the man had done before he became the leader of the Heralds of Future History. Everyone had a past.

"Hold on, here," Arizona said. "There's more to this than meets the eye. Only one reason Thurgarton would have left us in his will, and that's because he knew we were the only ones he could trust. He must have been working on something mighty big there at the end!"

Nick exchanged a knowing glance with Octavia and Virgil. He was pretty sure they were both thinking the same thing he was thinking. *Here we go with the ever popular, never dull Snow conspiracy theories.*

Virgil cleared his throat. "A.Z. has concluded that Thurgarton stumbled onto a secret operation at the Eclipse Bay Policy Studies Institute." He motioned with one hand to indicate the piles of papers that surrounded them. "She believes that he collected all of this in an attempt to unravel the conspiracy."

"Most of this is just camouflage, of course," Arizona explained. "Thurgarton probably figured that if he piled enough out-of-date newspapers and magazines around the place, folks would write him off as a crackpot. They wouldn't realize that he had hidden the results of his investigation here."

"Camouflage?" Octavia picked up an ancient, tattered copy of *Playboy* and studied the bouncy-looking woman on the cover with grave interest. "That certainly explains some of these magazines. And it definitely beats the old line about just reading them for the articles."

"I resent that remark," Nick said. "In our younger days, my friends and I learned a lot from those magazines."

She gave him an arch look. "I don't think I'll ask you to tell me exactly what it was you learned."

"Examining all of these papers and magazines is gonna take some time, unfortunately," Arizona continued, ignoring the byplay. "Not like we aren't already plenty busy with Project Log Book, eh, Photon?"

"The light of future history will show us the way to accomplish all that must be done in due course," Photon said.

He was out of his real-estate assessor's role and back into his fathomless serenity mode, Nick noticed.

He looked at Arizona. "What's Project Log Book?"

"Photon and I talked it over and we decided that the only safe way to ensure that none of the data in my logs gets destroyed by the operatives up at the institute is to put it all online," Arizona said.

"I thought you didn't trust computers," Nick said.

"I don't like 'em and that's a fact. But we've got to move with the times. Got to take advantage of technology if we're going to stay ahead of the bad guys. The Heralds are building a Web site and they're inputting the contents of my logs and journals as we speak. This is all real hush-hush, naturally, but I trust you and Octavia here to keep your mouths closed. And of course Virgil will keep it to himself."

"I won't tell a soul," Virgil promised.

"Loose lips sink ships," Octavia said solemnly.

Arizona nodded. "That's for damn sure."

"You've been keeping those logs and journals for years, A.Z.," Nick said. "You must have hundreds of them."

"The Heralds are working around the clock in shifts on the computer that we set up in my War Room. Logistics haven't been easy, I can tell you. Got to keep things running as usual at the bakery while we put the data online so we don't arouse suspicion. Don't want anyone up at the institute to come nosing around before we're ready to go live with the Web site."

"We expect to have Project Log Book completed by the end of the summer," Photon said.

"And now you've got to sort through all of this junk in addition to putting together a Web site project and operating the bakery." Nick shook his head at the enormousness of the task. "Don't envy you this job."

"We'll get it done," Arizona assured him with her customary can-do attitude. "No choice. Future of the country depends on making sure that the facts in my logs are available to the concerned citizens of this nation. The Internet is the only way to go."

"Uh, where are the pictures you wanted me to examine?" Octavia asked politely.

"Behind that row of boxes," Virgil said.

He led the way, forging a path through the maze of cartons and papers to the far side of the living room. Nick and Octavia followed him.

Four paintings in old, wooden frames were propped against the wall. In the gloom, Nick could see that the first three were landscapes. The fourth looked as if it had been splashed with a lot of dark paint.

Virgil switched on the reading lamp behind the recliner and aimed the beam at the paintings. "I suspect they're all worthless, but I wanted an expert opinion before we dumped them into the yard sale pile."

Nick watched Octavia's face as she studied the paintings. She had the same expression of rapt attention that she'd had when she looked at Carson's pictures. She was taking this seriously, he thought. Given that two of the people who had asked for her opinion were conspiracy freaks and the third ran an adult bookstore, it was going above and beyond the call of duty to show such respect.

She walked slowly past all four paintings and stopped in front of the one that looked as if it had been painted with a brush that had been dipped in chaos. She looked at it for a long time.

Then she crouched in front of it, heedless of the fact that the change of position caused her long, pale skirts to sweep across the dusty floorboards. She gazed intently at what looked like a scribble in the right-hand corner.

"Hmm," she said.

Everyone went very still. Nick was amused. He could feel the sudden tension that had leaped to life in the room.

"Does anyone know where or how Thurgarton got this picture?" Octavia asked, never taking her attention away from the painting.

Virgil shook his head. "We found it with the others in a closet. No way to tell how he came by it. Why?"

"I hesitate to say anything at this point because I don't want anyone to get too excited."

"Too late," Nick said. "We're excited! Is this thing valuable?"

Arizona frowned. "Looks like the artist dumped the contents of several tubes of paint on the canvas and smeared them around."

Virgil smiled. "That's mid-twentieth-century art for you."

Photon contemplated the abstract painting with a considering air. "The longer one looks at it, the deeper it appears. It is clearly an exploration of the absence of light."

Nick looked at him. "You think?"

"Yes." Photon inclined his gleaming head. "It is a statement of man's craving for light and his simultaneous fear of its power."

Octavia rose slowly to her feet and turned around to face the others.

"I agree with you, Photon," she said quietly. "And if we're right, it may be the work of Thomas Upsall. The signature certainly fits. He always signed his work in a very distinctive manner. And his technique was also quite unique. A very time-consuming method that required layer upon layer of paint."

"Wow," Nick said. "A genuine Thomas Upsall. Who would have believed it? Wait until this news hits the art world."

She gave him a reproving frown. "Very funny. Obviously you don't recognize the artist."

"Nope, can't say that I do."

"Me, either." Arizona looked hopeful. "This Thomas Upsall, was he famous or anything?"

"He produced most of his paintings in the nineteen-fifties," Octavia said. "His pictures were not very popular at the time, but in the past few years they have become extremely collectible. There isn't a lot of his work around because he destroyed a great quantity of it during the last year of his life. He died in the mid-eighties, alone and forgotten."

"What do you think this thing's worth?" Arizona asked.

Octavia looked at the painting over her shoulder. "If, and I stress the word 'if,' it is a genuine Upsall, it could easily fetch a couple hundred thousand at auction. Maybe two hundred and fifty."

They all stared at her.

Virgil exhaled deeply. "A couple hundred thousand *dollars*?"

"Yes. The market for Upsall's work is hot at the moment and getting hotter." Octavia gave them all a warning look and held up one hand. "But to be on the safe side, I'd like to get a second opinion from a colleague of mine who specializes in mid-twentieth-century abstract art. She works in a museum in Seattle. Unfortunately, she's on vacation until next week."

"Think we can get her to take a look at the picture when she returns?" Arizona asked.

"Yes, for a fee," Octavia said. "She consults. She may even want to purchase it for her museum."

"That brings up the question of what to do with it until we can get your colleague here to examine it," Virgil said. "Now that we know it's worth two hundred grand or more, I don't like the idea of leaving it here."

"I could take it home with me," Arizona replied. "My security is top of the line. But the spies up at the institute keep a round-the-clock watch on me. If they see me take something from this place into my house, they might get curious. Don't want to draw any attention right now while we're at such a critical point in Project Log Book."

"I've got a security system for the paintings in my gallery," Octavia said slowly. "I suppose I could store the Upsall in my back room for a week."

"Good idea," Virgil agreed. "It should be fine in your back room. Not like Eclipse Bay is home to a lot of sophisticated art thieves."

Photon smiled benignly. "You illuminate us with the radiant light of your kindness."

6

THE row of shops that lined the street across from the pier was dark and silent at this hour. The last rays of the summer sun were veiled behind the thickening layer of clouds. Whitecaps danced on the slate-gray waters of the bay.

Nick parked in the small lot. When he climbed out from behind the wheel, a snapping breeze tugged at his windbreaker. Storm on the way, he thought. Summer squalls were not unusual for this time of year here on the coast.

Octavia was already out of the passenger seat. The bouncy wind whipped her hair into a froth and caused her long, full skirts to billow around her legs. She laughed a little as she grabbed a handful of her skirts to keep them from blowing up around her thighs. Her eyes were bright. He got the feeling that she was savoring the raw energy of the approaching storm. Maybe she tapped into it for her fairy magic or something. Seemed logical.

"We'd better hurry," she said. "The rain will hit any minute."

"Right."

With an effort he wrenched his attention away from her flying hair and skirts and opened the rear door of the BMW. He reached inside and hoisted the painting. Octavia had wrapped the picture in old newspapers before leaving Thurgarton's cabin.

Carrying the painting under one arm, he walked with her to the door of Bright Visions.

"You really think this thing is worth a quarter million?" he asked.

"Between you and me? Yes. But we'll all feel more secure once we've had a second opinion."

She continued to struggle with her skirts with one hand while she withdrew her keys from her shoulder bag. She opened the front door and stepped quickly into the darkened interior of the shop to punch in the code that deactivated the alarm system. Then she flipped some switches to turn on the lights.

"Who'd have believed that old Thurgarton would have possessed a valuable work of art?" He carried the painting into the shop. "He was no collector. You saw how he lived. How the heck do you suppose he got hold of it?"

"I haven't got a clue." She led the way across the showroom to the long counter. "As I told you, there isn't a lot of Upsall's work around. It's amazing to think that one of his pictures has been sitting out here on the coast all these years."

"Who says we're not a bunch of real sophisticated art lovers here in Eclipse Bay?"

"Certainly not me." She opened the back room and turned on more lights. "You can put it there with that stack of paintings leaning against the far wall."

He surveyed the crowded back room. Rows of paintings were stacked five and six deep against every wall. Empty frames of all shapes and sizes were propped in the corner. The workbench was littered with tools and matting materials.

"No offense," he said dryly, setting down the painting, "but this place looks almost as cluttered as Thurgarton's cabin."

"Gallery back rooms always look like this."

He straightened. "The finding of a previously unknown Upsall should make for an interesting story in some of the art magazines."

She smiled. "I can see the headline now. CONSPIRACY BUFF, NEW AGE CULT LEADER AND PORN-SHOP PROPRIETOR INHERIT LOST UPSALL."

"Be interesting to see what they do with the money." He walked back to where she stood in the doorway. "Well, so much for tonight's thrilling adventure in the world of art. Are you ready for dinner? I'd take you to Dreamscape, but Carson is there and we wouldn't be able to talk in peace. How about the Crab Trap? It's not as good as Rafe's place, but it's not bad."

"You do realize that if we dine in any of the local restaurants, there will be a lot of talk tomorrow?"

"So what? Hartes are used to being talked about in this town."

"I know."

Belatedly it occurred to him that she was not accustomed to being the subject of local gossip. "Look, if this is a problem, we can go back to my place. I've got plenty of food in the house. Comes with having a growing boy around. I'm not saying that it will be what anyone would call gourmet, but—"

She cleared her throat. "I bought fresh asparagus and some salmon fillets this afternoon."

Fresh asparagus and salmon were not generally purchased on a whim. He considered the possibilities.

"You planned to invite me back to your place?" he asked finally.

"To be honest, it struck me that it would be more comfortable to eat there rather than in front of an audience composed of a lot of the good and extremely curious people of Eclipse Bay."

He smiled slowly. "Fresh asparagus and salmon sound great."

THE atmosphere was making him very uneasy, but for the life of him, he could not figure out what was wrong. On the surface, everything was perfect.

Dinner had gone smoothly. He had taken charge of the salmon while Octavia had dealt with the asparagus and sliced some crusty bread. They had sipped from two glasses of Chardonnay while they worked together in her snug, cozy kitchen. They had talked easily, for all the world as comfortable as two people who had prepared a meal together countless times.

It was almost as if they had already become lovers, he thought. A deep sense of intimacy enveloped them and it was starting to worry him. This was a far different sensation than he had known with other women in the past. It was not the pleasant, superficial sexual awareness he had experienced on previous, similar occasions. He did not understand the prowling tension that was starting to leave claw marks on his insides.

Maybe this had not been one of his better ideas. Then again, looking back, he was pretty sure he'd never had much choice. If you went hunting fairy queens, you took a few risks.

He stood at the sink in her gleaming, white-tiled kitchen and washed the pan that had been used to steam the asparagus. Nearby, Octavia, a striped towel draped over her left shoulder, went up on her tiptoes to stack dishes in a cupboard. When she raised her arms overhead, her breasts moved beneath the thin fabric of her blouse.

Damn. He was staring. Annoyed, he concentrated on rinsing the pan.

She closed the cupboard door and reached for the coffeepot. "Black, right? No cream or sugar?"

"Right."

She poured coffee into two cups and led the way into the living room. He dried his hands, slung the damp towel over a rack, and followed her, unable to take his eyes off the mesmerizing sway of her hips.

What the hell was wrong with this picture? he wondered. This was exactly how it was supposed to look, precisely how he had hoped it would look at this point.

She curled up in a corner of the sofa, one leg tucked under the curve of her thigh, mug gracefully cupped in her hands. The fire he had built earlier crackled on the hearth.

She smiled at him and he immediately felt every nerve and muscle in his body shift from Yellow Alert status to Code Red. An almost irresistible urge swept over him to pick her up off the sofa, carry her into the shadowy room at the end of the hall, and put her down on a bed. He flexed one hand deliberately to regain control.

It had been like this all evening, as though he were walking the edge of a cliff in a violent storm. One false step and he would go over into very deep water. It didn't help that outside the rain and the wind had struck land with a vengeance some forty minutes ago.

He crossed the living room to the stone fireplace, picked up an iron poker, and prodded the fire. The blaze didn't need prodding, but it gave him something to do with his hands.

"I've enjoyed your books," she said. "I've got all four in the series."

"I noticed." He put aside the poker, straightened, and glanced at the book-shelf where his novels were arranged between two heavy green glass bookends. "We authors tend to pick up on little details like that."

The bookends looked expensive, he thought. Dolphins playing in the surf. One-of-a-kind pieces of art glass, not cheap, utilitarian bookends picked up at a rummage sale.

There were other quietly expensive touches in the cottage. An exotically patterned carpet done in shades of muted greens and gold covered most of the hardwood floor in front of the dark-green sofa. The coffee table was a heavy sheet of green glass that rippled and flowed like a wave of clear lava. A couple of framed abstract paintings hung on the walls.

Not the kind of furnishings you expected in a weekend or summer house, he thought. He had the feeling that she had deliberately set out to make a home here. And now she was planning to depart for good.

"Tell me," she said, "was it difficult to make the decision to leave Harte Investments when you decided to write full-time?"

"Making the decision was easy." He sat down on the sofa and reached for his coffee mug. "Getting out of the family business was a little more difficult."

"I'll bet it was. You were the firstborn and from all accounts you showed a talent for investments."

He shrugged. "I'm a Harte."

She gave him a fleeting smile. "There must have been a lot of pressure on you to take over the helm after your father retired."

"My parents were very understanding and supportive." He took a swallow of coffee and slowly lowered the mug. "But Sullivan went off like Mount Saint Helens."

"I believe it. Harte Investments was your grandfather's creation. Everyone around here knows what he went through to recover and build a new company after Aunt Claudia—" She broke off. "After Harte-Madison went under."

He wrapped both hands around the mug. "Dad tried to shield me from the worst of the blast but no one could have suppressed that explosion. Sullivan and I went a few rounds before he finally realized that I wasn't going to back down and change my mind."

"It must have been a difficult time."

"Yeah." He took another sip of coffee. "But we got through it."

"It's a tribute to the strength of your family bonds."

"Uh-huh." He did not want to talk any more about that time in his life. It was tied up too closely with Amelia's death. He glanced around the room. "Looks like you planned to stay here for a while."

She raised one shoulder in a tiny shrug. "Plans change."

He couldn't think of anything to say to that so he tried another topic. "Heard you've been seeing Jeremy Seaton."

"We've had dinner together a couple of times." She sipped her coffee.

He looked at her. "Mind if I ask if there's anything serious in that direction?"

She pursed her lips and tilted her head slightly. Thinking. "I would describe my relationship with Jeremy as friendly."

"Friendly." What the hell did *friendly* mean?

"Jeremy and I have a lot of interests in common."

He nodded once. "The art thing. Jeremy paints."

She gave him polite concern. "Is there a problem here?"

"You tell me." He put his mug down with great care. "Is Jeremy going to have a problem with you and me having dinner tonight?"

"I doubt it." She looked surprised by the question. "But if he says anything, I'll explain the situation to him."

"How, exactly, do you intend to explain it?"

"I'll tell him that we're just friends. He'll understand."

"Just friends," he repeated neutrally.

"What else?" She put down her own mug and looked pointedly at the clock. "Good heavens, it's getting late, isn't it? I have to go into the gallery early tomorrow to frame some of the children's pictures, and I'm sure you're anxious to pick up Carson."

"Kicking me out?"

"It's been a long day," she said by way of an apology and got to her feet.

"Sure." He rose slowly, taking his time.

She handed him his black windbreaker and opened the door for him. Smiling all the while. Friendly.

He went outside onto the front porch. The squall was dying fast, leaving behind crisp, still-damp air.

"Drive carefully," she said.

"I'll do that."

He pulled on his jacket but did not bother to fasten it. He stuffed his hands into his pockets and stood looking out into the night. He could hear the distant rumble of waves crashing against the bottom of the bluffs behind the cottage.

He turned slowly back to Octavia.

In the porch light, her hair glowed the color of the flames on the hearth inside. He could feel the magic that swirled around her.

He'd had enough. He knew now what was wrong with this picture.

"Something you should understand before we go any further here," he said.

"What's that?"

He took two steps back across the porch, closing the distance between them. He kept his hands in the pockets of his jacket, not trusting himself to touch her.

"Whatever else this turns out to be," he said evenly, "it isn't about being just friends."

She blinked. Her lips parted but no words emerged.

Just as well because he did not want to talk.

He kissed her, hands still in his pockets, leaning forward a little to claim her mouth. She did not flinch or step back but he felt the shiver that went through her.

He deepened the kiss deliberately.

Her mouth softened under his. He got the feeling that she was tasting him; testing him, maybe. Or was it herself she was testing?

She made a tiny, unbelievably sexy little sound and his blood ran hot in his veins. His breathing thickened.

He raised his head slowly. Breaking off the kiss required a serious act of willpower.

"Definitely not just friends," he said.

He turned away, went down the steps, and got into his car.

A short time later he drove into the newly paved, heavily landscaped parking lot at Dreamscape and slotted the BMW into the empty space next to Rafe's Porsche. He glanced at his watch as he got out. It was after eleven. The restaurant had been closed for over an hour. The vehicles that remained in the lot belonged to the overnight guests. There were a number of them.

Dreamscape had been an immediate success from the first day of operation. In addition to tourists, the inn drew a steady clientele from the institute and Chamberlain College.

He walked up the steps of the wide veranda that surrounded the lower floor of the inn. The front door opened just as he reached out to lean on the little bell.

"Heard the engine," Rafe said. "Figured it was you." He stood aside to allow Nick into the front hall. "Want some coffee?"

"No, thanks. Just had some." He nodded at the balding, middle-aged man who emerged from the office behind the front desk. " 'Evening, Eddie."

"Hello, Nick. Come to collect your boy?"

"Yes."

"How was the hot date with the charming Miss Brightwell?" Rafe asked.

"No comment."

Rafe gave him a commiserating look and closed the door. "That bad, huh? You know, I wondered if she was really your type."

"No comment means no comment. I thought you Madisons were real big on a no-kiss-and-tell policy."

"Hey, we're family now, remember?" Rafe grinned. "I'm just trying to show a little brotherly interest in your personal affairs, that's all."

"Brotherly interest, my ass, you're just—" He broke off at the sight of Hannah appearing in the opening that led to the central corridor and the solarium.

"About time you got here," she said.

"It's not that late," Nick said, feeling oddly defensive. "Just because you old married folks go to bed early doesn't mean the rest of us are obliged to keep the same boring hours."

"Good point." Rafe raised a brow. "It isn't even midnight, Cinderella. What *are* you doing here this early? I told you we'd be happy to let Carson stay the night if you got lucky."

Hannah turned on Rafe with a withering glare. "You told him that? You actually said something so extremely tacky?"

"He's a Madison," Nick reminded her. "He was born tacky. We can only pray that your classy Harte genes will overpower his unfortunate genetic inheritance when you two decide to start making babies."

Hannah gave him an odd look. Rafe's mouth curved but he refrained from comment. Nick got the feeling he was missing the joke.

"Well?" Hannah said in that tone of voice that meant she was deliberately changing the subject and everyone else had better go along. "How was the date with Octavia? Did you have a nice time? Where did you two have dinner?"

He studied his sister. There was something different about her lately. He hadn't been able to put his finger on it but it was almost as though she harbored a special secret. Marriage definitely agreed with her, he thought. But, then, with the glaring exception of himself, it agreed with Hartes, in general.

"Her place," he said neutrally.

"Oh, man," Rafe muttered. "You went back to her place and she kicked you out before eleven o'clock. Not good." He shook his head. "I'd be happy to give you a little brotherly advice on how to behave yourself on a first date with a nice lady, Harte. Least I could do, you being family and all."

"You can take your helpful dating advice down to the Total Eclipse Bar and Grill and stuff it where the sun don't shine."

"Touchy, are we? Okay, but it's your loss, pal."

He'd had enough, Nick decided. He looked at Hannah. "Got my son?"

"Sound asleep in the library." Her expression softened. "Winston is keeping an eye on him." She hesitated. "He seemed a little concerned about your relationship with Octavia."

"Winston is concerned about my personal life?"

"Not my dog. Your son. He mentioned several times this evening that he was afraid you might make her mad."

Rafe sighed. "Apparently even little Carson is aware of your lack of finesse with the ladies."

"My son is first and foremost a Harte," Nick said dryly. "His chief concern is making sure that nothing gets in the way of his current objective."

"And that objective would be?"

"Getting his picture of Winston exhibited in the Children's Art Show."

"A worthy ambition," Hannah murmured. "And I'm sure the portrait is stunning. Winston, after all, is an excellent subject. But what does your relationship with Octavia have to do with getting the picture exhibited?"

Nick grimaced. "Carson is afraid that if I annoy Octavia she might refuse to hang the portrait in the show."

"A reasonable cause for anxiety under the circumstances," Rafe said cheerfully.

Hannah looked startled. "Oh. I really don't think she'd take out her hostility on a little boy. She isn't the sort of person who would do that. Octavia is very nice."

"So," Rafe said a little too easily, "what, exactly, are you doing to annoy such a *nice* lady, Harte?"

"You know," Nick said, taking another look at his watch, "it really is getting late, isn't it?"

"Yes, it is," Hannah said. She swung around on her heel and disappeared down the long, central hall.

Nick and Rafe followed her. They all came to a halt at the entrance to a comfortable, book-lined room. The dark expanse of the bay filled the space behind the windows. The library lights had been turned down low. Music played softly. A number of the comfortable, overstuffed chairs were occupied by guests who were sipping after-dinner cordials and coffee and talking quietly.

In the corner two small figures sprawled across a mound of pillows. Several children's books were scattered on the rug beside them. Most of the stories featured dogs.

Nick crossed the room and looked down at Carson, who was dressed in jeans, running shoes, and a sweatshirt. The boy was sound asleep, one arm flung across Winston. The Schnauzer raised his head from his paws and regarded Nick with intelligent eyes.

"Thanks for looking after him, Winston. I'll take over now."

Nick scratched Winston behind the ears and then scooped up his son.

Relieved of his nanny duties for the evening, Winston got to his feet and stretched. He snuffled politely around Nick's shoes and then trotted briskly toward Hannah.

Carson stirred a little and settled comfortably against Nick. He did not open his eyes. "Dad?"

"Time to go home."

"You didn't make her mad, did you?"

"I worked very hard not to make her mad."

"Good." Carson went back to sleep.

They all trooped down the hall to the front door and out onto the wide veranda. Winston vanished discreetly into the bushes. Hannah arranged Carson's black windbreaker—a miniature version of the one Nick wore—around the boy's sleeping form.

"We've got some news," she said softly.

"What's that?" Nick asked.

"We're pregnant."

"Hey, that's great." He grinned and kissed her lightly on the forehead. "Congratulations to both of you."

"Thanks."

Rafe put his arm around Hannah and pulled her close against his side. His pride and happiness were apparent. "You're the first to know. We'll start phoning everyone else in both families tomorrow."

Nick smiled. "Nothing else like it, you know."

"Yeah, sorta figured that," Rafe said.

Nick looked down at Carson lying securely in his arms. "You just wish it was this easy to protect them forever."

They stood there for a moment. No one spoke.

After a while Nick hugged his son a little more tightly to him and went down the steps. At the bottom he paused briefly and looked back. "Almost forgot I've got a little news of my own."

Hannah smiled encouragingly. "What?"

"Octavia Brightwell is related to our own local legend, Claudia Banner. Turns out that Claudia was her great-aunt."

Hannah's jaw dropped. "You're kidding."

"Nope."

"What the hell is she doing here in Eclipse Bay?" Rafe asked.

"I don't think she knows the answer to that one, herself. She said something about coming here to see if there was anything that could be done to mend the damage her great-aunt did. But I've got a feeling it's more complicated."

"What do you mean?" Hannah replied.

"From what I can tell, she's been drifting since Claudia died a year and a half ago. No close family. No real roots anywhere. Coming here to repair the damage her aunt did gave her a goal. But she tells me that she plans to leave at the end of the summer because it's clear to her that the Hartes and the Madisons have ended the feud all by themselves."

"Yeah, the good times never last, do they?" Rafe said laconically. His expression turned serious. "Does my grandfather know who she is?"

"She said Sullivan and Mitchell have known since the night of Lillian's show. Obviously they chose to keep the information to themselves."

"Figures," Rafe said.

———※———※———

THEY waited together on the veranda while Winston finished his business in the damp shrubbery. Hannah watched the BMW disappear into the night.

"What do you think is going on here?" she said after a while.

"Damned if I know." Rafe wrapped his hands around the railing. "Maybe it's like Nick said. Maybe Octavia came to Eclipse Bay to carry out her aunt's dying wish and then discovered there was nothing to fix."

"Nick is getting serious about her. I can tell. Octavia is different from the other women he's been seeing in the past few years. He's acting odd, too. I wonder if he's given her The Talk yet?"

"Don't know about that, but one thing we can say for sure. The curse has not yet been lifted. Nick didn't stay the night at her place."

"That business about the curse is absolute nonsense. The reason Nick never spends the night with any of his lady friends is because of Carson. He doesn't like to leave him alone with a sitter all night."

"That excuse doesn't fly," Rafe said flatly. "It's true that Nick doesn't leave Carson with sitters all night, but you know as well as I do that the kid stays overnight with family at times. Trust me, Nick wouldn't have a serious problem arranging to remain in some woman's bed until breakfast if that's what he wanted to do. If you ask me, he's avoiding it."

"I suppose you're right. Waking up with someone in the morning is a little different. More intimate, somehow. He's probably afraid that if he spends the night, the lady in question might get the wrong idea in spite of The Talk. He's done his best to avoid getting entangled in a real relationship since Amelia died."

"It's one thing to have hot sex and leave while it's still dark," Rafe agreed. "It's another thing to face the lady across the breakfast table. Takes the relationship to a whole new level."

Hannah smiled and patted her tummy. "Certainly had that effect on our relationship. But then, you can cook. That made a huge difference."

Winston trotted up the steps and kept going toward the front door. Rafe turned his head to watch the dog disappear inside the hall.

"Uh-oh," he said.

"Something wrong?"

"Just realized that we left the door open."

"So?"

"So Eddie is still at the front desk. He must have overheard everything we said when we talked to Nick a few minutes ago. Got a feeling he now knows just who Octavia Brightwell really is. Probably can't wait to tell everyone down at the post office first thing tomorrow morning."

Hannah groaned. "You're right. Uh-oh."

"What the heck. It was all bound to come out sooner or later. Not like there's any way to keep a secret in Eclipse Bay, after all."

"True." Hannah nibbled on her lower lip for a moment. "All the same, I think I'll give Octavia a call first thing in the morning and warn her. She's an outsider. She won't be prepared for what she's going to walk into tomorrow."

Rafe smiled. He said nothing.

She raised her brows. "What?"

"Just struck me that Octavia isn't that much of an outsider."

"What do you mean?"

"She's related to Claudia Banner, remember?" He tightened his arm around Hannah and steered her back toward the open door. "Her family has been involved in this thing from the beginning. Just like us Madisons and Hartes."

ALL eyes turned toward her when she walked into the Incandescent Body bakery shortly before nine the next morning. And just as quickly shifted away again.

Even if Hannah had not been kind enough to give her a wake-up call and a warning, Octavia thought, she had been in Eclipse Bay long enough to know what this peculiar attention meant.

There was fresh gossip going around and she was the focus of it.

She had been well aware of what would happen if she accepted a date with Nick Harte, she reminded herself. And the fact that everyone now knew that she was related to the infamous Claudia Banner just added a whole lot of very hot spice to the stew that was now brewing in Eclipse Bay.

She paused just inside the doorway and drew a deep breath. Hartes and Madisons handled this kind of stuff routinely. Aunt Claudia wouldn't have so much as flinched. If they could do it, so could she.

She gave the small crowd a polite smile and moved forward, weaving a path through the gauntlet of tables. It seemed a very long way to the counter, but she made it eventually.

"Good morning," she said to the brightly robed Herald who waited to take her order. "Coffee with cream, please."

"May the light of the future be with you today." The Herald's ankhs and scarab jewelry clanked gently when she raised her palm in greeting. "Your coffee will be ready in a moment."

The door opened again just as Octavia handed her money to the Herald. She did not need to glance over her shoulder to see who had walked into the bakery. The fresh buzz of excitement said it all.

"Hi, Miss Brightwell," Carson called from the far end of the room. "Dad said he saw you in here."

She turned, cup in hand. A deep sense of wistful longing welled up inside her at the sight of Nick and his son together. In his matching black windbreaker, jeans, tee shirt, and running shoes, Carson was a sartorial miniature of his father. But the resemblance went so much deeper, she thought. You could already see in Carson the beginnings of the strength of will, the savvy intelligence, and the cool awareness that were Nick's hallmarks. There was something more there, too. Carson would grow up to be the kind of man whose word was his bond because integrity was bred in the bone in the Harte family.

Like father, like son.

She squelched the sudden rush of emotion with a ruthless act of willpower. Nick and Carson had everything they needed in the way of a family. And she would be leaving at the end of the summer.

"Good morning," she said to Carson. She looked at Nick and felt the heat in his gaze go straight to her nerve endings, setting off little explosions. "Hello."

" 'Morning," he said.

There was an unmistakable intimacy in the low greeting, a dark, heavy warmth that she was certain everyone in the bakery had picked up on. She knew, with a certainty that was so strong she wondered if she'd developed telepathic powers, that he was thinking about that good-night kiss on her front porch.

Not that she had any right to complain. She was thinking about it, too.

Actually, she'd spent far too much of the night recalling it, analyzing it, contemplating every nuance and cataloging her own responses. She had examined that kiss the way she would have examined a painting that had the power to capture her attention and force her to look beneath the surface.

Her reaction had been over the top and she knew it. In fact, the all-night obsession with the details of that encounter on the porch had made her very uneasy this morning. You'd have thought it was her first serious kiss. And that made no sense at all. This was what came of being relationship-free for nearly two years. A woman tended to overreact when the long drought finally ended. She needed to get some perspective here.

Nick and Carson arrived at the counter. There was more than just amusement in Nick's eyes. There was some sympathy, too.

He glanced around with mild interest. "Don't worry about this. The news is out that you're related to Claudia Banner and that we were seen together in my car last night."

"Yes, I know. Hannah called me first thing this morning to warn me."

"It'll all blow over in a couple of days."

She wasn't so sure about that, but she decided this was not the time or place to argue the point. "Sure."

"Give me a minute to grab some coffee for myself and some hot chocolate for Carson," he said. "Then we'll walk you over to the gallery."

Before she could object or agree, he started to give his order to the Herald.

Carson looked up at her while they waited for the coffee and chocolate. "Have you framed my picture yet?"

"I'm going to do it this morning." She smiled down at him. "Want to help?"

Excitement bubbled through him. "Yes."

Nick collected the cups and a paper sack from the Herald and gave the bakery one sweeping glance as he started toward the door.

"Okay, you two," he said out of the side of his mouth in the stone-cold accents of an Old West marshal. "Let's get the heck out of Dodge."

"Miss Brightwell's gonna frame Winston today," Carson announced. "I'm gonna help."

"Cool," Nick said.

Carson whirled and dashed ahead, completely oblivious to the thinly veiled curiosity that permeated the room.

"A Harte to his toes," Octavia murmured.

"Oh, yeah."

Outside, the remnants of the morning cloud cover were starting to dissipate. The day promised warmth and sunshine by noon.

The shops across from the pier had begun to open for the day. Octavia noticed that the lights were on inside Bay Souvenirs, House of Candy, and Seaton's Antiques.

"Looks like I'm running a little late this morning." She stopped in front of the door of Bright Visions and slid her key into the lock.

Carson and Nick followed her into the gallery and waited while she deactivated the alarm and switched on the lights.

"Where's my picture?" Carson asked.

"In the back room with the others," Octavia said. "But we have to finish our chocolate and coffee first before we start framing. Don't want to risk spilling anything on the pictures."

"Okay." Carson went to work on his chocolate. He seemed intent on downing the contents of his cup in record time.

"Easy," Nick said quietly.

There was no threatening edge to the tone of his voice, Octavia noted; no boring lecture on good manners. Just a simple instruction spoken with calm, masculine authority.

Octavia waited until all three cups were in the wastebasket before she opened the door of the back room.

"All right," she said, "let's see about getting Winston into a suitable frame."

Nick followed as far as the doorway of the back room. He glanced at his watch. "The mail should be in by now. I'll run down to the post office while you two work on the picture. See you in a few minutes, okay?"

"Okay." Carson did not look around. His attention was concentrated on the matting and framing materials that Octavia was arranging on the workbench. "Are you gonna use a gold frame for my picture, Miss Brightwell? I think Winston would look good in a gold frame."

"We'll try gold and black and see which looks best," she said.

"Obviously I'm not needed here," Nick said. "See you later."

The door of the gallery closed behind him a few seconds later. Octavia and Carson, absorbed in their task, barely noticed.

<hr />

MITCHELL Madison ambushed him when he walked into the post office.

"Heard you had a date with Octavia Brightwell last night," Mitchell commented, looming in Nick's path.

"Word gets around."

"You went out to the Thurgarton place together, picked up some old painting, and then you went to her cottage. That right?"

"Yes, sir. You are well informed."

"Now, see here." Mitchell put his face very close to Nick's. "I thought I made it damn clear to Sullivan that I wouldn't stand by while you fooled around with Octavia."

"Whatever arrangements you made with my grandfather are your business, naturally, but I should probably tell you that I don't generally consult with Sullivan before I ask a woman out. I don't think you can blame him for the fact that I had dinner with Octavia last night."

Mitchell squinted in a malevolent fashion. "Is that so?"

"Also, just to set the record straight, I don't call what Octavia and I did last night *fooling around*."

"What the devil do you call it?"

"A date. Mature adults not otherwise involved in a committed relationship get to do stuff like that."

"Sounds like fooling around to me." Mitchell's jaw tightened. "She tell you Claudia Banner was her great-aunt and that Claudia's passed on?"

"I think the whole town is aware of those facts by now."

"I don't give a damn about the town. I'm only interested in what's going on between you and Octavia."

Nick lounged against one of the old-fashioned counters, folded his arms, and studied Mitchell with morbid fascination. "Mind if I ask why you're so concerned with the subject of my social life?"

"Because you've got a reputation for lovin' 'em and leavin' 'em and givin' your girlfriends The Talk so they know up front that you're not serious. I'll be damned if I'll stand by and let you treat Claudia Banner's niece that way. That girl's got no family around to look after her, so I'm gonna do it. You treat her right or you'll answer to me. We clear on that?"

"Very clear. Can I pick up my mail now?"

Mitchell's brows bristled, but he reluctantly got out of the way. "You know something, Harte?"

"What?"

"If you had any sense, you'd get married again. Settle down and give that boy of yours a mother."

"The day I want advice on my personal life from a Madison, I'll be sure to ask."

⁂

IN the end they went with the gold metal frame. Octavia privately thought that the black did a better job of accenting Winston's gray fur, but Carson was entranced with the flashier look.

When they finished the project, she put the picture together with the others she had prepared for the show.

"Winston looks great," Carson said, satisfied. "I can't wait for the show. I was afraid maybe you wouldn't want to hang my picture because Dad kept bothering you."

"Are you kidding?" She ushered Carson out of the back room into the gallery and closed the door behind them. "I'd never let my personal feelings get in the way of hanging a beautiful picture like yours. Wouldn't be good business."

"Great-Granddad says all business is personal. People just don't like to admit it."

"Everyone knows that your great-grandfather is brilliant when it comes to business."

"Yeah." Carson looked proud. "He says I'm gonna be brilliant at business, too. He says that in a few years I'll be running my own company."

"Is that what you want to do?"

"Sure."

She hid a smile. There was not so much as a flicker of doubt in the words. "Nice to know where you're going so early in life."

"Uh-huh." Carson's small brow puckered slightly. "Thanks for going out with Dad last night."

"You're welcome."

"He's been acting a little weird lately."

"I'm sorry to hear that."

"It's not your fault." Carson's expression was intent and very serious now. "It's just that everyone keeps telling him that he oughta get a new wife so I can have a new mom."

"Pressure."

"Yeah. That's what Uncle Rafe and Uncle Gabe say. I heard Granddad tell Grandma not to put so much pressure on Dad, but she and Aunt Lillian and Aunt Hannah all say he needs some pressure."

"Hmm."

"They think Dad doesn't want to get married again because he's still sad about my mom being in heaven and all."

"Well, that may be true," she said gently.

"Maybe." Carson was clearly dubious. "I don't remember her, but Dad does. He says she was really pretty and she loved me a lot."

"I'm sure she did love you very much, Carson."

"Yeah, and everyone says Dad loved her. But I don't think that's the reason he doesn't want to get married again. He told me once that if you lose someone, it doesn't mean you won't fall in love with someone else someday."

This was dangerous territory, she thought. Time to change the subject.

"Carson, maybe it would be better if we talked about something else."

He ignored that, intent on making his point. "I think Dad's just hasn't found a lady he really, really likes, you know?"

"Quite possible." She went behind the counter and pulled out a sheet of paper. "Now, then, I'm trying to decide how to hang the children's pictures. I've made a little map of the gallery. Want to help me choose a good spot for Winston?"

"Okay." He scrambled up onto the stool. "What about you, Miss Brightwell?"

That gave her pause. "Me?"

"Have you ever found a man you really, really like and want to marry?"

"Not yet." She picked up a pencil.

"Think you will someday?"

"Maybe. I hope so. I'd love to have a son like you someday."

"Yeah?" Carson looked pleased. "You could have a kid of your own if you get married."

"Yes." Way past time to change the subject. She pulled the gallery floor plan closer so that they could both view it. "Now, then, the first thing we have to keep in mind is that the pictures all have to be hung at the right height so that people your age can see them properly."

He studied the floor plan. "Not too high."

"Right." She sketched some pictures on a display panel. "I was thinking of grouping them according to the age of the artists, but I'm wondering if it might be better to arrange them by subject, instead."

"You mean like put all the animal pictures together?"

"Exactly." She made some more notations on the piece of paper. "In addition to your picture of Winston, I received a lot of pictures of horses and one or two cow portraits."

"You didn't get any other dogs besides Winston, did you?" he asked quickly.

"Not yet."

"Good. That means mine will be the best."

"I sense a certain streak of competitiveness here."

"Huh?"

"Everyone knows that Hartes are very goal-oriented. They like to win."

"Great-Granddad says winning is a lot better than losing."

"I'm not surprised to hear that. I suspect it's a family motto. And there's certainly some truth to it. But that viewpoint overlooks the fact that not all situations have to be viewed in terms of win-lose."

"Huh?"

She smiled. "Never mind. I was just thinking out loud. The point is, the Children's Art Show is not a competition. There won't be any prize for the best picture."

"Oh." He shrugged and let it go. "Mind if I ask you a question?"

"What is it?"

Carson looked up from the floor plan. "Do you like my dad, Miss Brightwell?"

She was amazed when she did not miss a beat in her response. "Yes, I do."

"A lot?"

"I like him enough to go out with him," she said cautiously.

"He likes you, too. A lot. That's why he called you so many times. He didn't mean to make you mad or anything."

"Carson, I really don't think—"

"He never, ever asked a lady to go out so many times after she turned him down once or twice."

She wrinkled her nose, amused in spite of herself. "I suspect that I may have unwittingly aroused those Harte competitive instincts we were just talking about." "Aroused" might not have been quite the right word under the circumstances, she thought. "Make that 'triggered.' "

"Huh?"

"That attitude about winning that we discussed a moment ago. It's possible that your father decided that persuading me to go out with him was a sort of game. He wanted to win, so he kept calling me until I said yes."

"Oh." Carson gave that some thought and then shook his head. "Nah. I don't think that's how it is with him. Dad says he doesn't like people who play games."

"Neither do I." Resolutely she turned back to the floor plan. "I think that the house pictures would look good on the two panels in the center of the room. What do you think?"

The door of the gallery opened. She looked up quickly, expecting to see Nick returning from the mail run. But it was Jeremy Seaton who strolled into the showroom.

He was good-looking in an angular way. His light-brown hair was cut in a close, conservative style as befitted a member of the institute staff. His clothes were left over from his days in academia: khaki trousers, an open-throated, button-down shirt, and expensive-looking loafers.

"Good morning, Jeremy. Something tells me you've heard about the Upsall."

"Yep. Couldn't resist coming by to see it for myself." He gave her a quick, easy smile and then looked at Carson. "I know you. You're Nick Harte's son, right? You're looking more like your dad every day. I'll bet you don't remember me. We haven't seen much of each other in the last couple of years. I'm Jeremy Seaton."

Carson shook his head. "I don't remember."

"Figured you wouldn't. Well, it doesn't matter. Your dad and I used to hang out together a lot in the old days."

Carson looked intrigued. "You knew Dad when he was a kid?"

"Sure did. We played some baseball together. And when we got a little older we also played a little pool down at the Total Eclipse."

"What else did you do?" Carson asked eagerly.

Jeremy stroked his jaw, looking thoughtful. "As I recall, we spent an inordinate amount of time cruising up and down Bayview Drive on Friday and Saturday nights showing off our cars and trying to get girls to look at us. Wasn't a whole lot to do here in Eclipse Bay in those days."

"Still isn't, as far as I can tell," Nick said from the doorway. "Hello, Jeremy. Been a while."

Octavia could have sworn that the temperature in the gallery plummeted at least twenty or thirty degrees. There was a definite chill in the air.

Jeremy lowered his hand and turned around with a deliberate air and a politely bland expression. "Harte." His tone remained civil, but all the warmth had leached out of it. "Heard you were in town for the summer."

"Heard you've taken up full-time residence and got yourself a job at the institute," Nick said in a voice that was equally lacking in inflection. "Giving up the academic life for good?"

The gallery was flooded with toxic levels of testosterone. Nick and Jeremy might have been good friends in the past, Octavia thought, but something had gone very wrong somewhere along the line.

"Thought I'd try something a little different," Jeremy said. "Everyone needs a change once in a while. How's the writing going?"

"Swell."

"Rumor at the post office this morning is that you're planning to use Octavia here to help with some in-depth research for your next book," Jeremy said coolly.

"You've lived in Eclipse Bay long enough to know better than to listen to post-office gossip."

"I sure wouldn't want to think that there was any truth to the rumors I heard today."

"When you get right down to it, it doesn't much matter if there's any truth to them or not," Nick said. "Either way, it's none of your business."

Confusion and something that might have been the beginnings of unease appeared in Carson's small face. She knew exactly how he felt, Octavia thought. This uncomfortable little scene had gone far enough.

"I've got the Upsall in my back room, Jeremy," she said briskly. "Come around behind the counter and I'll show it to you. You know something about art. I'd be interested to get your opinion."

Neither of the two men looked at her. They watched each other with the air of two lions facing off over a downed zebra.

I definitely do not look good in stripes, Octavia thought.

She cleared her throat. "Gentlemen, if you wish to continue this conversation, you may do so outside. I would like to remind you that there is a minor present. I would suggest you find someplace private where you can make idiots of yourselves without an audience."

That got their attention. Both men turned toward her. The chill in their eyes would have frozen water in two seconds flat.

"Can't wait to see the Upsall," Jeremy said tonelessly.

"This way." She spun around and walked back into the room behind the counter.

Jeremy followed. Nick came to stand in the opening. He did not enter the room. Carson hovered at his side.

"What's an Upsall?" Carson asked.

Octavia unwrapped the painting with a small flourish. "This," she said, "is an Upsall. I think."

Carson studied the swirling storm of color on the canvas. "Cool. Looks like the painter dropped a big bucket of paint and it splashed all over the place."

Nick's mouth twitched. "Couldn't have said it better, myself."

Jeremy said nothing, intent on the canvas. After a few moments of frowning scrutiny, he crouched in front of the painting and examined the brushstrokes in the corner of the canvas.

"Well?" Octavia asked. "What do you think?"

"It's certainly his style. Upsall had a way of putting paint on canvas that was very distinctive."

"Yes. That's how he obtained such incredible depth of color. It could be a copy, of course, but it looks like there's several decades worth of dirt and grime on it."

"Which means that if it was a copy, it was made years ago."

"Upsall's work didn't become popular until recently," Octavia said. "There wouldn't have been any incentive for someone to take the time and trouble to forge one of his paintings several decades back."

"Could be the work of an admirer or a student," Jeremy said, sounding doubtful. "What are the odds that an original Upsall has been sitting in old man Thurgarton's house all these years?"

"I'm no expert," Nick said from the doorway. "But following your logic, Seaton, what are the chances that Thurgarton would have had an excellent copy of the work of an obscure artist?"

Jeremy did not look at him. "Like you said, you're no expert."

"But Nick does have a point," Octavia said firmly. "It would be just as difficult to explain a fine copy as it would an original. All things considered, I'm strongly inclined to stick with my first instincts. I think this is a genuine Upsall. I'm planning to get a second opinion next week, though, just to be sure."

Jeremy straightened and shoved his hands into the pockets of his trousers. He continued to regard the painting for another long moment. Then he nodded once, abruptly.

"I think you're right," he said. "It's an Upsall. Which means that Arizona Snow, Virgil Nash, and the Heralds are all about to get a very nice windfall."

"Looks like it." Octavia rewrapped the painting.

"Who'd have believed it?" Jeremy shook his head. "A genuine Upsall hidden away in Eclipse Bay."

Nick smiled with icy amusement. "Who says Eclipse Bay isn't the center of the art world?"

8

ANOTHER summer storm was headed toward Eclipse Bay. Not a yippy little terrier of a storm like the one that had scampered through town last night and left everything damp. This one promised to be a real monster. It prowled and paced, sucking up energy from the sea while it waited for the cover of darkness.

Octavia stopped at the far end of the short stretch of beach and stood looking out over the quietly seething water. The tide was out. The brooding sensation was back.

A couple of days ago she had convinced herself that leaving Eclipse Bay at the end of the season was the right thing to do. Now she was not so certain. The strange feeling that she could not depart until she had accomplished whatever it was that she had come here to do had descended on her again.

Was her imagination going into high gear? Or was she already coming up with excuses to delay the day she walked away from Eclipse Bay and Nick and Carson Harte?

A shiver went through her. This was not good. This was risky rationalization and she did not do risky stuff. According to Claudia, the tendency to play it safe and not take chances was a major failing. She could still hear her aunt's words ringing in her head.

You know what I want you to do after I'm gone? I want you to go out and raise a little hell. Live it up. Take some chances. Life is too damned short as it is. You want to get to my age and have nothing interesting to look back on?

Okay, so she'd taken a mini-chance last night and what did she have to show for it? She'd cooked dinner for Nick Harte. Big deal. She'd kicked him out of the cottage before she'd even discovered whether or not he was sufficiently interested in having mad, passionate sex with her to bother to give her The Talk.

Playing it safe.

She had set out to walk off the restlessness after getting home from the gallery, but the exercise wasn't working as therapy. It was tempting to blame her mood on the advancing storm, but she knew there were other factors at work. One of them was the memory of the tension she had witnessed between Nick and Jeremy earlier that day.

Why was she allowing the thinly veiled hostility that had shimmered between those two get to her? It wasn't her problem if they had issues. She had her own issues. She had a business to sell. That sort of enterprise required planning and care. And then there was the move away from Eclipse Bay to engineer. For starters, she had to make arrangements to ship all of the stuff she had brought here. What on earth had made her bring so many of her personal treasures to the cottage? She should have left them at her apartment in Portland.

But the apartment in the city had always had a temporary feel. She had not been tempted to try to settle in there. It was her cottage here in Eclipse Bay that she had tried to turn into a home.

Lots of issues.

Nick Harte.

Yes, indeed. Nick Harte was a big issue.

What was it about him that drew her? He was not her type. She had more in common with Jeremy Seaton, when you got right down to it.

This was getting her nowhere. Brooding was a waste of time and energy and it never, in her experience, resulted in good outcomes. The negative feelings simply fed on themselves and got heavier and more bleak.

It was time to get a grip. Take charge. Act responsibly.

She turned and started determinedly back along the beach.

She had almost reached the bottom of the cliff path when the overwhelming, primordial knowledge that she was not alone jangled her senses.

She looked up quickly and caught her breath when she saw Nick standing at the top of the bluff. The ominous early twilight generated by the oncoming storm etched him in mystery. His dark hair was ruffled by the growling wind. His black windbreaker was open, revealing the black pullover and jeans he wore underneath. Too bad there wasn't a photographer around, she thought. This shot would have been perfect for the back cover photo on one of his books.

For a timeless moment it was as if she'd been frozen by some powerful force, unable to move, barely able to breathe. But an acute awareness arced through her, raising the small hairs on the back of her arms. She ought to be getting used to the sensation, she thought. Nick Harte had this effect on her a lot.

With an effort, she forced herself to move through the oddly charged atmosphere and started up the cliff path. She climbed carefully, conscious of how the wind was whipping her long, white skirt around her legs.

"Looks like the weather people missed the call on this storm," Nick said when she reached the top. He glanced toward the looming chaos that threatened on the horizon. "Going to be a lot stronger than they predicted."

"Yes." She held her hair out of her face. "What are you doing here, Nick?"

"I brought dinner." His tone was casual to the point of careless, but his eyes were anything but casual. A dangerous energy crackled there in the blue depths. "Unless you've got other plans?"

She'd had some plans, she thought. But none of them sounded nearly as interesting as dinner with Nick. Or as reckless.

"You cooked dinner?" she asked, buying herself a little time to analyze the situation before she did something really, really risky like invite him into her cottage.

His mouth curved in a rakish grin that showed some teeth.

"Now, why would I sweat over a hot stove all afternoon when I've acquired a brother-in-law who owns and operates a restaurant?"

She found herself smiling in spite of the invisible lightning in the air. "Good question."

"I brought a picnic basket that is stuffed to the hilt with some of Rafe's finest delicacies. Interested?"

Live it up. Take some chances. Life is too damn short. . . .

She breathed deep, inhaling the intoxicating vapors of the oncoming storm. "Are you kidding? If Rafe did the cooking, I'm more than interested. I'm enthralled."

"You know, I always knew that guy would turn out to be useful someday, even if he is a Madison."

"Where's Carson?"

"At Dreamscape."

"Handy built-in baby-sitting setup you've got there."

"I figure I'm doing Rafe and Hannah a favor by giving them a little hands-on practice."

She tilted her head a little. "Do they need practice?"

"Yeah. They're expecting. But don't say anything, okay? They're still in the process of notifying everyone in the family."

"A baby." A sweet, vicarious joy rushed through her. "That's *wonderful*. How exciting. When?"

"Uh, you'll have to ask Hannah. I forgot to check the date."

"How could you forget to ask when the baby is due?"

"I forgot, okay? So sue me."

"Men."

"Hey, I brought dinner. I think that's pushing the envelope of the SG thing far enough, don't you?"

"SG thing?"

"Sensitive Guy."

SHE arranged the contents of the picnic basket on the glass-topped dining room table while Nick built a fire. Rafe had outdone himself, she thought. There was an array of appetizing dishes, including a beautiful vegetable pâté, curried potato salad studded with fresh green peas, cold asparagus spears dressed in hollandaise sauce, little savory pastries filled with shrimp, and cold soba noodles steeped in a ginger-flavored marinade. There were also homemade pickles, Greek olives, and crusty bread from the Incandescent Body. A bottle of pinot noir bearing the label of an exclusive Oregon vintner rounded out the menu. Dessert consisted of tiny raspberry tarts.

"Oh, my," she murmured appreciatively. "This is lovely. Absolutely spectacular. And to think that I was going to fix a plain green salad for dinner. Rafe is amazing."

"Enough about Rafe," Nick said. He struck a match and held it to the kindling. "Let's talk about me."

"What about you?"

"I want full credit for selecting the wine."

"Well, I suppose I can give you that." She glanced at the label. "It's a very nice wine."

"Thanks." He uncoiled to his feet, crossed the room, and took the bottle from her. "I'll have you know that I went through almost every bottle of red in Rafe's cellar looking for it."

"A dirty job, but someone had to do it, right?"

"Damn right."

He carried the pinot noir into the kitchen, found the corkscrew, and went to work with a few deft, economical movements.

A moment later he poured wine into two glasses. He handed one of the glasses to her and raised his own in a small salute.

"To Hannah and Rafe and the baby," he said.

She smiled and touched her glass to his. "And to the end of the Harte-Madison feud. May you all live long and happy lives."

He paused, the glass partway to his mouth, and slowly lowered it. "You sound like you're saying goodbye."

"I am, in a way." She took a sip of the wine. "I've been in a strange place for the past few months—"

"Yeah, Eclipse Bay is a little weird, isn't it?"

"—but I think I've treaded water long enough."

"You're entitled to tread water for a while after you lose someone you love, you know."

"I know. But Aunt Claudia would have been the first to tell me to get on with my life." She did not want to pursue that topic, she thought. She turned away and opened a cupboard to select some of the green glass dishes she stored inside. "Mind if I ask what that scene at the gallery was about today?"

"Any chance I can get away with asking, 'What scene?' "

"No." She looked at him over her shoulder as she took the plates out of the cupboard. "But I suppose you could tell me to mind my own business."

He leaned back against the tiled counter and contemplated the bloodred wine in his glass for a moment. She knew that whatever he was going to tell her, it was not going to be the whole truth and nothing but.

"Jeremy and I go back a ways. We alternated between being buddies and friendly rivals in the old days here in Eclipse Bay. Competed a little with our cars and—"

"Getting dates with fast women?" she finished lightly.

"Fast women, sad to say, were always pretty scarce around Eclipse Bay."

"Too bad. Go on, what happened with you and Jeremy?"

"We had some adventures. Got into some trouble. Raised a little hell. We stayed in touch in college and we both wound up working in Portland. He took a position as an instructor at a college there and I dutifully tried to fulfill my filial obligations at Harte Investments. And then—"

"Then, what?"

He shrugged and drank some more wine. "Then he got married. I got married, too. Things changed."

"You lost track of each other?"

"Life happens, you know?"

"Sounds to me like the two of you did more than just drift apart." She carried the plates past him into the living room. "Today I got the impression that there's some serious tension between you two. Did something happen to cause it?"

"Yesterday's news." He prowled after her and settled into a chair near the window. His expression made it clear that he was about to change the topic. "How are things going with the Children's Art Show project?"

Well, it wasn't as though she had any right to push him for answers to questions she'd had no business asking in the first place, she thought.

She gave him her brightest smile and sank down onto the arm of the sofa. The embroidered hem of her long white skirt drifted around her ankles. Swinging one foot lightly, she took a fortifying sip of wine.

"Very well," she said, lowering her glass. "I'm quite pleased. I think I'm going to have nearly a hundred entries. Not bad for a small town like this."

"No." He stole a glance at her gently swinging ankle. "Not bad."

THE casual thing worked right up until the full fury of the storm struck land. She was washing the last of the dishes when the lights flickered twice and went out.

The sudden onslaught of darkness paralyzed her briefly. Her hands stilled in the soapy water. "Oh, damn."

"Take it easy," Nick said from somewhere nearby. "We lose power all the time around here during big storms. Don't suppose you have an emergency generator?"

"No."

"Flashlight?"

She cleared her throat. "Well, yes, as it happens, I do have a flashlight. A nice, big red one with a special high-intensity bulb and an easy-grip handle that I bought last winter after a major storm. It is a model of cutting-edge, modern technology. So powerful that it can be used to signal for help if one happens to be lost at sea or on a mountain."

"I sense a 'but' coming."

"But I forgot to buy some batteries for it."

He laughed softly in the darkness and came to stand directly behind her. "Spoken like a real city girl. Don't worry about it, I've got a flashlight in the car."

"Somehow that doesn't surprise me."

He put out his hands and gripped the tiled counter edge on either side of her body. In the shadows she was intensely aware of the heat of his body so close to hers. There was suddenly so much electricity being generated both outside and inside the cottage that she was amazed the lights did not come back on. Probably ought to get her hands out of the dishwater, she thought. A woman could have a major household accident in a situation like this.

Nick put his lips very close to her ear. "I was a Boy Scout. You know what that means?"

"Something to do with being thrifty and neat?"

"Wrong." He grazed her earlobe with his teeth.

"Something to do with getting to wear a cute uniform?"

"Try again." He touched his mouth to her throat.

"Something to do with always keeping spare batteries on hand?"

"You're getting closer. Much closer." He kissed her throat. "Something to do with always being prepared."

"Oh, yeah." She yanked her hands out of the sudsy water and grabbed a dishtowel. "I've heard about the always being prepared thing."

He tightened the cage of his body around her so that her backside was nestled snugly into his thighs. She realized at once that he was aroused. Her senses registered that information and responded with a shot of adrenaline. Her pulse raced. There was a faint trembling in her fingertips. Not fear, she thought. Excitement.

"I take the motto seriously." He brushed his lips along the curve of her throat just below her earlobe. "And not just when it comes to things like flashlight batteries."

She was abruptly grateful for the inky shadows of the kitchen. At least he could not see the flush of heat that was surely setting fire to her cheeks.

"You taste good," he whispered. "Better than those little raspberry things we had for dessert."

There was a new, rougher edge in his voice and she was the cause. All that was female in her rejoiced. Outside, the wind howled. Here in the dark kitchen, power flowed.

He kissed her throat again, his mouth gliding up along the underside of her jaw. She reveled in the intense pleasure and the heady rush of anticipation.

This was why she had tried to keep her distance, she remembered. This was precisely the reason she had been so careful these past few weeks, why she had worked so hard to find so many excuses to decline his invitations. She had known it would be like this: dangerous and unpredictable and very high risk.

And also incredibly exhilarating and intoxicating.

He must have felt her body's response because he shifted again, pressing closer still until she could feel him, hard and muscled, along the full length of her own much softer frame. The contrast thrilled her senses. The mysteries of yin and yang in action.

There was no room to move now inside the cage he had made for her. He had enclosed her in a seductive snare she had no desire to escape.

An urgent, drawing sensation traveled up the insides of her legs and pooled in her lower body. She dropped the dishtowel and clutched at the counter edge for support. Her head tipped back against his shoulder. She savored the strength and power in him and told herself that she would not give in to the almost overwhelming urge to purr.

"I don't think we're going to need that flashlight for a while," he whispered. "We can do this in the dark."

He let go of the counter and put his hands on her at last. His fingers closed around her, spinning her toward him. He pulled her fiercely into his arms. His mouth closed over hers with the inevitability of the steel door of a bank vault slamming shut.

The wild chaos of the storm outside was suddenly swirling here in her tiny kitchen. One glorious rush after another swept through her, leaving her trembling with need and anticipation. She wanted him, she thought. She needed this night with Nick. She owed this to herself.

She almost laughed aloud. Was she good at rationalizing, or what?

"Going to let me in on the joke?" he asked into her hair.

"Trust me, this is no joke."

She put her arms around his neck and kissed him with all of the searing, pent-up hunger and desire that had been making her so restless these past few weeks.

He picked her up and carried her into the living room. The glowing embers of the fire cast an enchanted golden light on the scene. Her head spun a little and her feet left the earth. The next thing she knew, she was lying flat on her back on the rug in front of the hearth.

He followed her down onto the floor, sprawling across her, anchoring her beneath him with one heavy leg flung across hers, his weight pushing her into the thick wool. She pushed her hands up under his pullover until she touched bare skin.

He undid the long row of buttons that closed her white linen blouse and then he unfastened the next set, the ones that sealed her long, white skirt.

"This is like opening a birthday present," he said when he reached her waist. "I've got this nearly overpowering urge to just rip into it."

"I know just how you feel," she said, struggling to free him of his sweater.

He laughed a little and sat up briefly beside her. Crossing his arms at his waist, he grasped the hem of the garment and hauled it off over his head in a single fluid movement.

"Much better." She smiled appreciatively at the sight of his firelit shoulders. "Much, much better."

Deeply intrigued by the ripple of skin over muscle, she reached out one hand and threaded her fingers through the crisp hair that covered his chest. He sucked in his breath and groaned.

He went back to work, unfastening buttons one by one until he reached the hem of her skirt.

"Best present I've had in a long, long time." He put one hand on her bare skin just above the band of her white lace panties. He flexed his fingers gently. "Definitely worth the wait."

The touch of his big, warm palm on her midsection sent shock waves through her. She stirred, feeling sinuous and incredibly sexy beneath his touch.

He leaned over her to take her mouth again. His fingers moved, sliding up her rib cage to rest just beneath her breasts. By the time the kiss had ended she was no longer wearing her bra.

He moved his lips to one nipple and tugged. She gasped and sank her nails into the contoured muscles of his back.

Time became meaningless. The wild night flowed around them, closing them off from the outside world. She was vaguely aware of the winds raging outside the cottage, but here in this intimate, magical place there was another reality, a world where every move brought new wonders and new discoveries.

When Nick found the tight, throbbing nub that was the epicenter of the small storm taking place inside her, he stroked lightly with fingers he had dampened in her own dew. At the same time he slid two more fingers just inside and probed gently.

Without warning, the gathering energy that had created such a delicious tension exploded. She barely had time to cry out in surprise before she tumbled headlong into a bottomless pool.

When she eventually surfaced, she was breathless and joyous with the pure pleasure of it all.

Nick looked bemused by her reaction. His mouth curved slightly. "You okay?"

"Oh, yes. Yes, indeed, I am very okay." She drew her fingertips slowly down his chest and belly until she could cup his heavy erection. "Never better. Yourself?"

He grinned slowly, a sexy, anticipatory smile that sent little sparkling shards of excitement through her.

"Going to be okay real soon," he promised.

He settled heavily between her thighs. In the firelight his face was tight and hard with the effort he was exerting to maintain his control. He used one hand to guide himself carefully into her.

He was larger than she had anticipated. In spite of the unbearable sense of urgency and readiness, she was startled by the tight, full feeling.

"Nick."

He paused midway.

"Don't you dare stop now." She grabbed his head in both hands, spearing her fingers into his hair, and lifted herself against him.

He plunged the rest of the way, filling her completely. When they were locked together he levered himself up on his elbows and looked down at her. His expression was one of desire and passion and other forces too strange and wondrous for her to label with words. But she knew the power of those driving, elemental waves of raw energy. She knew them in her heart and soul because they were sweeping through her, too.

Nick began to move, gliding cautiously at first. But when she tightened her legs around his waist, he made a hoarse, husky sound and drove himself into her in a series of fierce, swift thrusts that seemed beyond his control.

She felt the intensity of his climax in every muscle of his body, heard it in his guttural shout of satisfaction.

When he collapsed on top of her she could barely breathe. She stroked his back from shoulder to hip. He was slick with perspiration. He was giving off so much heat you'd have thought that he was in the grip of a raging fever.

All in all, she thought, it was a wonderful way to go.

⁂

A cold draft woke her sometime later. She realized it was coming from the front door. Nick was leaving.

The shock of it brought her wide awake. She scrambled to her feet, clutching the chenille throw around herself.

"Nick?"

"Right here." He closed the door. "I just brought the flashlight in from the car. I'll leave it here on the hall table."

"Oh. Thanks." Maybe she'd been a bit hasty in assuming that he was running out on her already.

"No problem." He glanced at his watch. "It's after midnight. I'd better be going."

He *was* leaving. Couldn't wait to be on his way. Outrage and pain knifed through her. Well? What had she expected? This was Nick Harte, after all. He wasn't exactly famous for hanging around until breakfast. It wasn't as if she hadn't known exactly what she was getting into when she went into his arms earlier.

But it still hurt far more than it should. This was why she preferred to avoid risks, she thought. There were good, solid reasons for not opening yourself up to this kind of pain.

Nick crossed the small space that separated them and kissed her lightly.

"Carson and I will stop in at the gallery when we come into town to pick up the mail."

He turned without waiting for a response, slung his jacket over his shoulder, and went back toward the door.

"That would be nice," she mumbled.

He paused, one hand on the doorknob. "Is there a problem here?"

"Aren't you forgetting something?" she asked evenly.

"Such as?"

"The Talk."

A terrible stillness came over him.

"You know about The Talk?" he asked carefully.

She was beginning to wish that she had kept her mouth shut. Maybe she would have had the sense to do just that if she hadn't been jolted out of her very pleasant dreams to find him already dressed and headed for the door.

"Everyone knows about The Talk," she said crossly.

"Is that so?" He sounded irritated. "You shouldn't believe every bit of gossip you hear about me."

"You mean it's not true about The Talk?"

He opened the door, letting in another gust of wet air. "I've got no intention of discussing the details of my private life at this particular moment."

"Why not?" Her chin came up. "None of my business?"

"No," he said grimly. "It isn't. But just so we're clear on this subject, I'd like to point out that we've already had The Talk."

"Is that so?" she asked in icy accents. "I don't recall it."

"Then you've got a short-term memory problem, lady."

"Don't you dare try to wriggle out of this." She strode forward, clutching the chenille throw to her throat, and came to a halt directly in front of him. She jabbed a forefinger against his chest. "You did *not* give me The Talk. I wouldn't have forgotten something like that."

"No," he agreed coolly. "I didn't deliver it. You did."

That stopped her cold.

She stared at him. "I beg your pardon?"

"Don't you remember?" He moved out onto the shadowy porch. "You made it clear that you're a free spirit and that you'll be leaving at the end of the summer. Sounded to me like you weren't looking for anything other than a short-term affair."

"Hang on here, I never said anything of the kind. You're putting words in my mouth."

"Trust me." He flicked on a little penlight and started down the front steps. "I know The Talk when I hear it."

She was too dumbfounded to speak for a moment. By the time she had recovered, he was in the car, driving away into the night.

She abruptly realized that her bare feet were very cold.

9

"WHAT do you think is going on?" Lillian asked on the other end of the line.

"I think they've started an affair." Hannah glanced out into the hall to make sure no one was eavesdropping on her conversation with her sister.

Satisfied that she and Winston had the office to themselves, she closed the door and went back to the chair behind the desk. Winston, stretched out on his belly on the rug, watched her alertly.

It was obvious that he sensed her tension.

"You're sure they're involved?" Lillian asked.

"Yes. You should have seen him last night when he came back here to pick up Carson. Whatever is going on between those two, it's serious."

"Did he give her The Talk?"

"I don't think so. I asked him point-blank and instead of making a joke out of it, the way he usually does, he acted pissed off."

"He was mad?"

"Yes. More or less told me to mind my own business. Believe me, he was not in a good mood last night."

"Hmm."

"I know," Hannah said. "I had the same reaction."

They both fell silent for a while, thinking. Hannah looked out the window. The air was crisp and clear in the wake of the big storm. The bay was unnaturally smooth. From where she sat she could see Rafe and the two gardeners working to clear some branches that had been downed by the high winds.

"He hasn't let any woman get to him since Amelia died," Lillian said eventually.

"I know. Give me your professional opinion."

"I'm out of the matchmaking business, remember? I'm an artist now."

"You must still have some instincts. Your intuition when it came to figuring out couples was always amazing."

"My instincts aren't any good when it comes to those two," Lillian said honestly. "I tried to read the situation that night when I saw them together at my show there in Eclipse Bay. I got nothing. A complete blank."

"Does that mean it's a bad match?"

"No, it means I just couldn't tell one way or the other. It's hard to explain, but it was as if there was some sort of invisible glass shield between them and my intuition. I couldn't get past it. Whatever is going on with those two is as much a mystery to me as it is to you."

"Personally, I'm hoping she's the one for Nick. I really like Octavia, and Carson adores her."

That caught Lillian's attention. "Carson likes her?"

"Yes. I've never seen him like this with any of the other women Nick has dated. You'd think he was trying to do a little matchmaking himself."

"Interesting." Lillian pondered that briefly. "Of course, in all fairness, Carson has never had much opportunity to get to know any of Nick's other girlfriends."

"That's because Nick has always gone out of his way to keep that part of his life compartmentalized and separate from his life with Carson. This time it's different. That's my big point here. The very fact that Nick has allowed Carson to develop a personal relationship of his own with Octavia is a very strong indicator that this is not business as usual. Don't you agree?"

"Maybe. Depends."

"On what?"

"Well, it could be that Nick isn't deliberately allowing Carson to get to know Octavia. It may just be the circumstances. Eclipse Bay isn't a big city. There's no way Nick could have a clandestine affair here. It's impossible to keep one's private life private in this town."

"And nobody knows that better than Nick. Yet he made the decision to spend the summer here and it looks to me as if he has actively encouraged Carson to form an attachment to Octavia. I swear, they find an excuse to stop by her gallery every single day when they go into town to pick up the mail or shop for groceries."

"All right, I agree that isn't Nick's usual M.O. when it comes to women and his personal life," Lillian said thoughtfully. "Could be significant. You're sure he hasn't had The Talk with her?"

"Almost positive. It may mean that he's finally ready to move beyond the loss of Amelia."

"About time," Lillian said.

"Hey, he's a Harte. When Hartes fall in love, they fall hard."

"Mmm."

"What's this?" A flicker of alarm wafted through Hannah. She exchanged a concerned look with Winston, who promptly got to his feet and crossed the small space to put his head on her knee. "You don't believe that Nick has really become Hardhearted Harte, do you?"

"I think," Lillian said carefully, "that there may have been more problems in his relationship with Amelia than he ever let on."

"I know you were never fully satisfied that they were a great match. But there is no absolutely perfect match. And it doesn't mean that Nick didn't love Amelia deeply."

"No. It doesn't mean that," Lillian agreed. "But I've always wondered if it was Nick's decision to leave Harte Investments that exposed the underlying weaknesses in that marriage. If Amelia had lived, they might have worked things out. For Carson's sake, if nothing else. She loved him as much as Nick does."

"Yes. Amelia was a good mother." Hannah touched her still-flat stomach. She had not yet grown accustomed to the sense of wonder that accompanied the realization of the small miracle that was taking place inside her. "No one would ever say otherwise. Especially not in front of Nick."

"True. But if I'm right and there were some serious problems in that marriage, it might explain why Nick has been so careful to avoid a serious relationship in the years since Amelia's death."

"Protecting himself? You think he's afraid of making another mistake?"

"He's a Harte. We're not supposed to screw up when it comes to love and marriage, remember? We're supposed to get it right every time."

"If he didn't get it right last time, he might be doubly cautious this time."

"Yes, and with good reason. After all, it isn't just himself he has to protect this time around. He's got Carson to consider, too."

Hannah hesitated a moment. "Speaking of children . . ."

OKAY, so she'd over overreacted.

So sue me, Octavia thought.

She pulled into the parking lot at the end of the row of shops and switched off the engine. A woman had a right to be angry when she surfaced after a bout of mind-bending sex and discovered that the man with whom she had just shared said mind-bending sex was heading for the door.

The least he could have done was make a bigger show of regretting the unseemly haste of his departure. And how dare he accuse her of giving him The Talk? All right, she had mentioned leaving town at the end of the summer once or twice. That was different.

She got out of the car, dropped the keys into her purse, and slammed the door shut. She was feeling short of both temper and patience, and more than willing to blame everything on Nick this morning. Her emotions were so mixed up and so unstable today that she knew she could not begin to sort them out.

One thing was indisputable, however. She was well aware that she had no one to blame but herself for this untenable situation and that, of course, only made the mess all the more irritating. She had known what she was getting into when she made the decision to take some chances with Hardhearted Harte.

It occurred to her that, in addition to feeling pissed off, she also felt strong and decisive this morning. Energetic. Bold. Powerful. Gutsy.

She stopped in the middle of the sidewalk, struck by that realization.

Everything seemed sharper and clearer today. She was intensely aware of the bright sun and the glare of the light on the bay. She was eager to open the gallery and frame the rest of the children's pictures.

Yes, she was mad as hell at Nick Harte, but even the anger felt good—cleansing in some weird way that she could not explain.

She was almost at the door of the gallery when she belatedly remembered Nick's flashlight. She had left it in the backseat.

With a groan, she turned around and went back to the parking lot to retrieve it. This time she made herself close the car door very gently.

Doing the mature thing.

The power had not failed in the heart of Eclipse Bay, she noticed. The lights inside the gallery worked when she flipped the switch and the security system was still functional. She punched in the code to disarm it and went around the counter to open the door of the back room.

The instant she stepped inside she knew that something was wrong.

It took her a couple of seconds to focus on what it was that seemed different. Then it hit her.

The Upsall was gone.

HE could not figure out where things had gone wrong last night.

He was still brooding over the disastrous ending to what had been a great evening when he pulled into the slot next to Octavia's little white compact the next morning and turned off the engine.

"Hey, look," Carson said excitedly from the backseat. "A police car."

Nick turned his head and frowned when he saw the familiar logo of Eclipse Bay's tiny police department emblazoned on the door of an SUV parked at the curb. "That's Chief Valentine's vehicle. Probably had some problems with the security systems in the shops because of the storm."

"Here comes A.Z.," Carson added.

Nick got out of the BMW and watched Arizona park her pickup while Carson scrambled out of the rear seat. When she climbed from the truck and started toward them, he raised a hand in greeting.

" 'Morning, A.Z.," Nick said.

Carson waved. "Hi, A.Z."

" 'Morning, you two." Beneath the rakish tilt of her military beret, Arizona's expression was that of a battlefield commander readying herself for action. "Expect you already heard we got us some trouble here."

"Problems with the storm last night?" Nick asked.

"Reckon you could say that. Just got a call from Octavia. Looks like the gang up at the institute used the storm as cover to hit us last night."

"Come again?"

Arizona angled her head toward Sean's vehicle. "I see Valentine is on the job, but I doubt that he'll be able to accomplish much. The institute has him and every other official here in town completely bamboozled."

Another car pulled into the lot. Virgil Nash got out and started toward them.

"Good morning, Nick. Carson." Virgil looked at Arizona. "Is Photon here yet?"

"Told him to stay at the bakery and watch things there. The action here last night might be a calculated attempt to draw our attention away from Project Log Book so that they can get at the computer."

Out of long habit, Nick automatically sorted through Arizona's customary conspiracy spin on the situation to get to the single grain of truth at the center.

"What action?" he said abruptly. "Did something happen here last night?"

Arizona angled her chin. "The institute crowd broke into the gallery and snatched our Upsall."

Nick glanced at Virgil for clarification.

Virgil did not look particularly reassuring. "I got a call, too. That's why I'm here. Looks like the Upsall's gone."

"*Octavia.*" Nick grabbed Carson's hand and started toward the shop.

"What's wrong, Dad?"

"Don't worry," Virgil called after them. "Octavia's fine. The painting was gone when she arrived this morning."

Nick paid no attention. He kept going toward the shop, moving so swiftly that Carson had to run to keep up with him.

"Is Octavia okay, Dad?" Carson asked anxiously.

They reached the open door of Bright Visions at that moment. Nick halted at the sight of Octavia inside. The first thing he noticed was that she wasn't wearing one of her usual icy-pale fairy queen dresses today. Instead she was dressed in a short jumper in a bright shade of purple. The golden-yellow boatneck tee shirt she wore underneath the dress had sleeves that came to her elbows. There was a wide amber bracelet on her wrist and more amber at her ears and throat.

When she moved one hand in a small gesture, he noticed that she had painted her nails with a vivid crimson polish that sparkled in the morning light. He looked down and saw her bare toes peeking out from under the red leather tops of a pair of sexy, backless slides. She'd painted her toenails, too. Must have gotten up early, he thought. But then, he'd rolled out of bed at the crack of dawn himself, unable to sleep after a nearly sleepless night.

Octavia looked at him. There was fire in her eyes.

"Yeah," Nick said softly to Carson. "Octavia's okay."

Sean Valentine looked up from the notes he was making on a pad. He gave Nick a brief, friendly nod. " 'Morning, Harte." His somber face lightened when he caught sight of Carson. "Hey, there, Carson. How are you doing today?"

"Hey, there, Chief Valentine. I'm fine," Carson declared with delight.

Kids always responded to Sean, Nick reflected. He was not certain why. Valentine was no Officer Friendly. He carried a lot of wear and tear on his face.

It was true that Sean did project a calm, professional competence, but he always looked as if he expected bad news. Children seemed to look right past the grim stuff and see something else beneath the surface, something they liked and trusted.

Nick noticed that Octavia was also watching Sean greet Carson. There was a thoughtful, reflective look on her face as though she, too, saw something in Valentine that she liked and trusted.

When she switched her gaze to Nick, however, the approval disappeared instantly from her expression.

What he got was cool appraisal. She was looking at him the way she might examine a painting that did not quite measure up to her standards.

Oh, shit. Talk about worst-case scenarios. This was bad. Very, very bad.

"Hello, Nick," she said without inflection. But when she switched her attention to Carson, the warmth returned to her voice. "Good morning, Carson. I like that shirt."

Carson beamed. He glanced down at the dark-green dinosaur emblazoned on his sweatshirt. "Thanks. It's a velociraptor. Dad bought it for me."

"I see."

"A velociraptor can rip you to shreds in seconds," Carson said cheerfully.

Octavia nodded. "I'll bear that in mind."

Nick met Sean's eyes. "What's going on here?"

"Octavia says that the painting Old Man Thurgarton left to A.Z. and Nash and the Heralds has disappeared." Sean rubbed the back of his neck. "Kind of a mystery how it happened. Apparently it was locked up in the back room and the security alarm was set as usual."

Arizona loomed in the doorway. "Getting past a standard security system would be child's play for that gang up at the institute. No offense, Carson."

"Okay," Carson said, clearly not offended.

Sean heaved a deep sigh. "I don't think we can blame anyone at the institute, A.Z. I know you're convinced that those folks up there are bent on subverting the government and running the world from their secret headquarters here in Eclipse Bay, but there's just no good motive for them to steal a painting."

"You want motive?" Arizona stalked toward the counter. "I'll give you motive. They know me and the Heralds plan to use our share of the profits from the sale of that picture to help finance our investigations. The last thing that crowd wants is for us to be able to expand the scope of our operations. If that ain't motive, I don't know what is."

Virgil Nash came through the doorway and nodded politely at everyone. He turned to Octavia. "Was the Upsall the only painting that was stolen?"

"Yes," Octavia said. "It was far and away the single most valuable picture here. Whoever took it must have known what he was doing."

Nick studied the paintings hanging on the wall and then shook his head. "I don't think you can assume that."

They all stared at him.

"What do you mean?" Octavia demanded. "The average person would probably have been more attracted to some of the scenes of the bay. Or that one." She swept out a hand to indicate the painting hanging behind her. "The watercolor with the gulls. To the untrained eye the Upsall looks dark and rather depressing."

"Probably because it is dark and depressing," Nick said.

She gave him a superior smile. "Which only goes to show how much you know about art, but that is neither here nor there."

Sean raised his brows a little at her crisp tone, but he made no comment. Instead he looked at Nick with some curiosity. "What makes you say that whoever took the picture didn't have to be an art expert?"

"The rumor that Thurgarton had left a valuable painting behind and that Octavia was going to get a second opinion on it was all over town by yesterday afternoon," Nick said mildly. "It wouldn't have taken a genius to figure out that she had it stored in the back room, and it would have been easy to recognize. Everyone was talking about how ugly it was."

Octavia did not look pleased with that quick summary. She glared. "How do you explain the thief having a key and knowing the security code?"

Nick glanced at the door. "There are usually several duplicates of a key floating around. And when was the last time the code was changed?"

She drummed her crimson nails on the counter. "It hasn't been changed since I had the Willis brothers install the system when I first opened the gallery."

Virgil frowned. "You had an assistant working here for several months. She would have had the code and the key."

"Of course," Octavia said. "But I don't think we can pin this theft on Noreen. She left town with her artist boyfriend last month, remember?"

Sean looked thoughtful. "Does anyone know where Noreen and the boyfriend are now?"

Octavia shook her head. "She just phoned in her resignation and took off. But now that you mention it, there's, uh, something else."

They all looked at her.

She grimaced. "A few days ago I came across a piece of paper with the code written on it taped inside one of the counter drawers. Noreen had trouble remembering it."

"Which means a lot of people might have had access to that code," Sean said. "Including the artist boyfriend."

Arizona snorted. "Wastin' your time, Valentine. This has the fingerprints of that bunch up at the institute all over it, I tell you."

Sean flipped his notebook shut. "One thing's for certain, Eclipse Bay isn't exactly crawling with experienced, high-end art thieves, and we don't have what you'd call a big market for stolen art, either. Whoever snatched the painting has probably already taken off for Portland or Seattle to try to unload it."

"True." Octavia slouched against the counter, looking very unhappy. "It would be the logical thing to do."

"Our best hope is that the guy trips himself up when he goes to sell the

Upsall," Sean continued. "I'll call some people I know in the Seattle and Portland police departments and tell them to keep a lookout for our missing picture."

"That's an excellent idea." Octavia brightened. "I'll contact a few friends in the art world, too, and make them aware that there's a previously unknown Upsall floating around."

"Good thought," Sean said. He started toward the door. "I think that's about all for now. I'll check back later."

"All right," Octavia said. "Thanks, Sean."

"Sure. See you, folks."

A short chorus of goodbyes followed Sean out onto the sidewalk. So did Nick. They walked together toward Sean's vehicle.

"Something I can do for you, Harte?" Sean asked mildly.

"Just wanted to ask what you think really happened to that painting."

Sean opened the door on the driver's side and paused. "You want my best guess?"

"That would probably be the most helpful under the circumstances, yeah."

"Past experience tells me that whoever stole the painting was probably closely connected to the situation. He knew the picture was valuable, he knew where it was stored, and he knew how to disarm the security system."

"Which means he had access to the code and a key."

"As you just pointed out, how hard would that be? Might not have even needed the key and code. That system the Willis brothers installed for Octavia is good enough for Eclipse Bay, but it isn't exactly state-of-the-art." Sean looked at the window of Bright Visions. "Wouldn't take a rocket scientist to disarm it, especially in the middle of the night during a major storm when no one was around."

Nick followed his gaze and shook his head in a flat negative. "Not A.Z. or Virgil."

"No. Although I gotta tell you that in this situation, any out-of-town cop would be looking real hard at both of 'em. They both have motive. Why split the profits from the painting three ways when you can have the whole pie?"

Nick shrugged. "Guess I'd have to agree that to an outsider they'd both look a little mysterious."

"Try damned suspicious. No one knows anything about either of them before they arrived in Eclipse Bay. I got curious a couple of years ago and did some digging, myself."

Nick looked at him. "Learn anything?"

"Zilch. It's like neither one of them existed before they came to this town."

"For what it's worth, there are some old rumors about them," Nick said. "My grandfather told me once that he thinks Nash may have done some government intelligence work at one time, which could explain why his past has been wiped out of the records. And most folks assume that A.Z. assumed a new identity somewhere along the way because she's so deep into her conspiracy theories. But neither of them are thieves. Rock-solid, upstanding citizens in their own weird ways."

"I'm inclined to agree."

"That leaves Photon and his happy little crew of bakers."

"Yeah. And between you and me, that bunch is right at the top of my very short list." Sean got behind the wheel and closed the door. He squinted a little against the morning sun. "I'm going to run some background checks on some of those Heralds. But keep that to yourself. I want to handle it quietly. If word gets out that the group is under suspicion, some of the locals might turn on 'em real fast."

"I know. There are still a few folks around who think they're running some kind of cult out of that bakery."

"Think I'll also track down Noreen Perkins and her new boyfriend and ask them a few questions, too."

"Why? They aren't even in town any longer."

"Just being thorough."

"Right. Catch you later."

Sean put the SUV in gear and rolled off down the street.

Nick went back into Bright Visions. He stopped just inside. Octavia, Arizona, Virgil, and Carson were all looking at him with expectant expressions.

He surveyed the ring of interested faces. "Did I miss something?"

Carson could scarcely contain himself. "Wait'll you hear A.Z.'s really cool idea, Dad."

Nick managed, just barely, not to groan aloud. He caught Octavia's attention, expecting a little understanding, maybe even some sympathy in spite of the tension between them. After all, everyone knew that any really cool idea that had been concocted by Arizona Snow was an accident waiting to happen.

But Octavia's expression reflected zero commiseration. Whatever this really cool idea was, it was getting serious consideration from her.

In desperation, Nick turned to Virgil.

"Nothing to lose," Virgil said, stroking his goatee.

"Only chance we've got and that's a fact," Arizona stated with satisfaction.

Nick surveyed each of them in turn. "Why do I have a bad feeling about this?"

Octavia cleared her throat. "Virgil's right. It probably won't work, but it's not like we have anything to lose. I say we go for it."

"Yeah!" Carson cheered.

"What, exactly, are you all planning to go for?" Nick asked warily.

"What we need here is a professional private investigator," Arizona announced. "Got to be someone we can trust. The future of Project Log Book may be riding on this."

"You're going to hire a private investigator?" Nick chuckled. "Good luck. I don't think we've got any of those in Eclipse Bay."

Arizona looked crafty. "Got one."

"Is that right?" Nick raised his brows. "Who?"

"Quit teasing, Dad." Carson bounced a little. "A.Z. means you."

"Yep." Arizona rocked on her boot-shod heels. "Far as I can tell, you're the closest we've got to the real thing here in Eclipse Bay."

10

"ARE you all crazy?" Nick planted both hands on the counter and leaned across it. His tone was low, but his jaw was granite. "I write novels about a private eye. Such books are called fiction. Do you know what fiction means? It means it is *not real.*"

"Calm down, Nick," Octavia said soothingly.

She was very conscious of Carson, who was just outside the front door now talking to a man who had a dog in the back of his truck. She did not want the boy to overhear this argument.

When Arizona and Virgil had left the gallery a few minutes earlier, she had slipped behind the counter. She had deemed it prudent to put a bit of distance between them. Given Nick's simmering outrage, it was clear that he was not thrilled with the idea of having been drafted. But the counter did not seem nearly wide enough.

"Pay attention. I. Am. Not. A. Real. Private. Investigator." Nick spaced each word out very carefully and deliberately, as though talking to someone from another planet who might not have a good grasp of the language. "I do not have a license. I do not investigate for a living. I write *fiction* for a living. And you know that as well as I do. Why did you and Virgil agree to go along with A.Z.'s zany scheme?"

"Because we don't have a lot of choice," she said briskly. "As you pointed out, there aren't any real investigators here in Eclipse Bay, and I agree with A.Z. about Sean Valentine. He's a good man, and he is no doubt a very competent cop. But I'm pretty sure that he intends to waste a lot of time looking in all the wrong places."

"Don't tell me you agree with Arizona's conspiracy theory? You really think Valentine should look for the culprit up at the institute?" Nick spread his hands. "Give me a break. That's nuts and you know it."

"I doubt very much that the painting was stolen by someone at the institute," she said coolly. "But that still leaves a lot of rocks to turn over and I don't think Sean will do that. I've got a hunch he'll concentrate on the Heralds."

Nick was silent.

"I knew it," she muttered. "He *does* think it was someone from the Incandescent Body, doesn't he?"

"He intends to do some background checks on some of them," Nick admitted. "It's a logical place to start. The Heralds constitute the largest group of newcomers and unknowns in town who would have had knowledge of the painting and where it was stored."

"That's not true. There are more newcomers and unknowns up at the institute and Chamberlain College."

"Okay, maybe. Technically speaking. But it's unlikely that many of them would have heard about the painting so soon. With a few exceptions, they're considered outsiders here in Eclipse Bay. Not full-fledged members of the community. Most of them are not hardwired into the gossip circuit. The Heralds, on the other hand, knew everything about the Upsall almost immediately because Photon and A.Z. told them."

"Others could have known, too," she insisted. "You know how word spreads in this town."

"Come to think of it, you're right," he replied curtly. "There are a lot of suspects, aren't there?"

She did not like the way he said that. "Not a lot. Some."

"Jeremy Seaton, for instance. Heck, you showed him right where the painting was stashed. You even let him take a really close look at it. And he's into art. Probably knows some underhanded dealers back in Portland or Seattle who would be willing to take a stolen Upsall off his hands, no questions asked."

Shock reverberated through her. It took a moment to recover. Then she flattened her palms on the counter very close to his own big hands and leaned forward so that they were only inches apart.

"Don't you dare imply that Jeremy took the painting," she said softly. "That is beneath contempt."

"You want a private investigator on the case? You gotta expect some uncomfortable speculation."

"You brought up Jeremy's name only because you don't like him very much," she said through her teeth.

"Just trying to be logical. That's what we investigators are paid to do."

"You know something? When A.Z. came up with the idea to hire you, it struck Virgil and me that there was some merit to the plan. After all, who would know Eclipse Bay better than a Harte? And with your family history and clout here in town, you can talk to anyone. Get through any door. People will take you seriously and open up to you."

He took his hands off the counter. "Because I'm considered one of the locals?"

"Yes. You've got access in a way that Sean Valentine does not." She moved one hand slightly. "And that's why I went along with A.Z.'s scheme. But now I'm having second thoughts."

"Good."

"I agree with you," she went on smoothly. "I think that with your poor attitude, it is highly unlikely that you will be of any use to us."

"Yes, he will," Carson said very earnestly from the doorway. "I'll help him."

"That's very nice of you, Carson, but your father is not interested in working for me, so I'll just have to investigate without him."

"Do you know how to be an investigator?" Carson asked, intrigued.

"I've read all your father's books about John True. How hard can it be?"

Nick's eyes went very narrow. "What's this about investigating on your own?"

She raised one shoulder in a deliberately careless shrug. "I don't see that I have much option."

His mouth thinned. "You're serious, aren't you?"

"Oh, yeah."

"This is a really, really dumb idea, Octavia. Stay out of it. Let Sean Valentine do his job."

She watched him just as steadily as he watched her. Damned if she would let him intimidate her, she thought. She was Claudia Banner's great-niece. She could handle a Harte.

"That Upsall was in my custody," she said. "I feel responsible for the loss and I intend to do whatever I can to recover it."

"You're trying to force my hand and I don't like it."

"I have no idea what you're talking about."

"Sure you do. You can't do this without me and you know it, so you're doing your best to manipulate me into a position where I have no choice but to play private eye for you."

"I wouldn't dream of trying to manipulate you," she said austerely. "I'm sure it would be impossible."

He folded his arms across his chest. He did not try to conceal his irritation.

"Okay," he said at last. "You win. I'll ask your questions for you."

"Thanks, but I really don't want you to do me any favors."

"I'm not doing you a favor," he said. "I'm doing it for A.Z. and Virgil." He glanced at Carson. "Come on, son, let's go. We've got things to do."

"Are we going to be private eyes?" Carson asked eagerly.

"Yep. You can be my assistant, at least until you get bored with the job, which probably won't take long."

"I won't get bored."

"Sure you will," Nick said. "Heck, I already know that *I'm* going to get bored."

"Look, if you don't think that you can keep your attention focused on this problem—" Octavia began.

"I'm a Harte, I can focus. Even when I'm bored." Nick turned on his heel and headed for the door. "Let's go, kid. We'll start at Rumor Central."

"Where's that?" Octavia called after him.

Nick glanced back over his shoulder. "The post office, naturally."

"I heard the Upsall disappeared sometime late yesterday or last night." Jeremy lounged back in his desk chair, cocked one tasseled loafer-shod foot on his knee, and tapped the tip of a pen against the armrest. "True?"

"I'm afraid so," Octavia said.

She sank down into the only other chair in the small office and admired the view through the window. The town, with its marina and pier, was spread out before her in a picture-perfect landscape that would have looked good hanging in her gallery.

The tide was out again. Eclipse Arch, the massive stone monolith that dominated the long sweep of beach framed by the arc of Bayview Drive, was fully exposed. Sunlight sparkled on the water. The air had been scrubbed so clean by last night's storm that she could make out Hidden Cove and Sundown Point, the two rocky outcroppings that marked the southern and northern boundaries of the bay. She could even see the elegant old mansion that Rafe and Hannah had transformed into Dreamscape.

She had gotten into the habit of taking a sandwich in to work with her, but she had neglected to bring one today. Feeling badly in need of a short break, she did something she almost never did: she closed up for the noon hour. She drove up the hillside above town with some vague notion of getting a salad at Snow's Café. Instead she'd steered straight on past to the institute. Luckily Jeremy had been in his office and had invited her to eat with him in the cafeteria. Now they were back, drinking coffee together.

"I assume our noble chief of police is on the case?" Jeremy said.

"Yes. Sean is looking into matters." She decided not to mention that Nick was also investigating.

She was almost certain that Nick hadn't been serious when he had named Jeremy as a likely suspect, but there was so much bad blood between the two men that she did not want to risk pouring gasoline on the fire.

"Got any theories?" Jeremy asked.

"No." She frowned. "I think Sean feels it might be one of the Heralds."

"A real possibility. No one knows much about that crowd down at the bakery. My grandmother still thinks they're some kind of cult. Not that the theory keeps her from buying her favorite lemon squares there, of course."

"When it comes to good lemon squares, you have to do what you have to do."

"Speaking of doing what you have to do, I think I've worked my nerve up at last. Can I persuade you to come up and view my etchings some evening this week?"

"Any time."

"Are you free this evening?"

She thought about how she had hoped that she would not be free tonight. But things had changed.

"As it happens, I am, indeed, entirely free this evening," she said.

LATE that afternoon Nick balanced, feet slightly apart, on the gently bobbing dock and looked down at the short, wiry man standing in the back of a boat. Young Boone was dressed in a pair of stained and faded coveralls that appeared to be at least thirty years old. He wore a blue peaked cap emblazoned with the logo of a marine supply firm.

Even on his best days, Young Boone was not what anyone would call chatty. He had inherited the marina decades earlier from his father, Old Boone. Young Boone was somewhere in his seventies and his father had died twenty years ago, but he would probably go to his grave known as Young Boone. If either of the Boones had had first names, they had long since been forgotten in the misty past of Eclipse Bay history.

For two generations the Boones, Old and Young, had made their home in the seriously weathered two-story structure at the edge of the marina. The lower floor housed a bait, tackle, and boating supply shop. The upstairs served as the Boones' living quarters.

"Heard you had a little damage down here last night." Nick surveyed the marina through his sunglasses.

"Some." Young Boone did not look up from the rope he was coiling in the back of the boat. "Nothin' that can't be fixed."

"Glad to hear it. Storm woke you up, I'll bet."

"Couldn't hardly sleep through that racket. Came out here to check on the boats."

"That's what I figured." Nick studied the view of the shops across the street. The front of Bright Visions was clearly visible. "Happen to notice anyone hanging around the art gallery during the storm? Maybe see a car parked in the lot? Should have been empty at that time of night."

"Nope." Young Boone straightened and peered at Nick from beneath the peaked brim of his cap. "Only vehicle I saw was yours. Figured you was headin' back out to your family's place after spendin' time with Miss Brightwell."

Nick kept all expression from his face. This wasn't the first time today that he had been obliged to listen to observations about his late-night drive home.

"Uh-huh," he said. Noncommittal.

Young Boone screwed up his haggard features into a frown that may or may not have been genuine curiosity. "This have anything to do with that picture they say went missin' from the art gallery last night?"

"Yeah. I'd really like to find it for A.Z. and Virgil."

Young Boone nodded. "Wish I could help you but I didn't see a damn thing last night. 'Course, I was real busy here securing the boats and such like. Might have missed something goin' on across the street."

"You didn't miss my car when I drove past the marina," Nick reminded him dryly.

"No, I didn't and that's a fact. But I finished up down here right after that and went back to bed."

Which meant that there had been long stretches of time during the night when no one would have noticed a car in the parking lot across the street, Nick thought.

Young Boone gave him a knowing wink. "Miss Brightwell's nice, ain't she?"

"Yeah."

"A man like you could do a lot worse."

"A man like me?"

"Raising that boy of yours alone. No wife or mother around. Reckon it's time you settled down and got married again, don't you?"

"I don't think about it much," Nick said.

"Well, you damn well should be thinkin' about it, if you ask me."

"I didn't ask you, but I'll take your opinion under advisement."

"Under advisement?" Boone wiped his hands on a dirty rag. "That a fancy way of sayin' you ain't interested in my opinion?"

"No. Just meant I'll consider it." He watched a familiar, monster-sized SUV abruptly wheel into the marina parking lot. Mitchell Madison. Bryce was at the wheel.

Damn. He did not need another scene with Octavia's self-appointed guardian, Nick thought. Time to leave.

"You consider it real good," Young Boone said. "Time you found yourself a wife. You're a Harte. Hartes get married and stay married."

"Say, Boone, I've got to be on my way. You'll let me know if you hear anything about that painting, won't you?"

"Sure. But it's probably gone for good."

That gave Nick pause. He turned back. "Why do you say that?"

"Can't see anyone around here hangin' a stolen painting in his house. Sooner or later, someone would be bound to notice the damn thing."

"Okay, I'll give you that. And I'll also admit that this Upsall picture isn't the sort of fine art that you'd expect would appeal to the connoisseurs among us here in Eclipse Bay."

"Heard it looked like something a kindergartner might turn out," Young Boone said.

"Hey, I've got a kindergartner who can do better-looking art. Yeah, the Upsall is sort of ugly. Sure hard to envision someone like, say, Sandy down at the gas station, going to the trouble to steal it just so he could hang it on the wall of the rest room. And it would look like a little out of place in the Total Eclipse, too."

Boone thought for a moment. "Still leaves all those fancy types up at the institute and Chamberlain College. They might go for that kinda thing."

"Maybe. If that's the case, we'll have to let Valentine deal with it. I'm just checking out the possibility that someone local might have taken it as a prank or on a dare. I can see some guy who'd had a couple-three-too-many beers down at the Total Eclipse deciding to swipe the painting as a stunt."

"Huh. Hadn't thought of that."

"In which case," Nick said in the same casual tone he'd been using all day long, "if it just shows up again there will be no questions asked."

Young Boone squinted knowingly and snapped his oily rag.

"Gotcha. I'll spread the word."

"Thanks."

Mitchell was out of the SUV. He had his cane in one hand and he was making straight for the dock where Nick stood.

"I'd better get going," Nick said. "Places to go, people to see."

Boone glanced past him toward Mitchell, who was advancing rapidly. "Good luck. Gonna be hard to avoid Madison. He's got a bee in his bonnet about you and that Miss Brightwell gal."

"I know." Nick assessed his chances of escape. He had the advantage of being several decades younger than Mitchell, and he hadn't developed any arthritis yet. If he moved quickly, he might just make it to the car before Madison intercepted him. "See you around, Boone."

"See ya."

Nick went swiftly along the gently shifting dock. He made it through the gate and was halfway across the parking lot when he realized he wasn't going to be able to dodge his pursuer. He could outrun him, of course, but that would have been the coward's way. Hartes did not run from Madisons.

"Hold up right there, Harte." Mitchell thumped his cane on the hard-packed ground as he veered to the right to block Nick's path. His bushy brows bristled across the bridge of his aggressive nose. "I want to talk to you."

Nick halted. Not much choice, he figured.

"Afternoon, sir," he said politely. "Storm give you any trouble last night?"

"Storms don't give me trouble." Mitchell planted himself in front of Nick and glowered ferociously. "Hartes give me trouble. Just what the hell kind of game do you think you're playing with Octavia Brightwell?"

"I don't want to be rude, sir, but I'm in a hurry here. Maybe we should talk about this later."

"We'll talk right now." Mitchell banged the cane again for emphasis. "I heard you spent the night out at Octavia's place."

"That, sir, is a flat-out lie."

Mitchell was startled into momentary speechlessness.

"You tellin' me it was someone else? You weren't the man who was out there last night?"

"I had dinner with Octavia," Nick said evenly. "I went home afterward. I did not spend the night."

"The way I hear it, you were there until nearly one o'clock in the morning."

"You've got spies on your payroll?"

"Don't need any spies. Young Boone saw you drive past the marina late last night. He told everyone at the post office first thing this morning."

"You know, sir, I hate to break this to you, but nowadays it's not all that unusual for a couple of adults to spend an evening together that doesn't wind up until one in the morning."

"Not here in Eclipse Bay, they don't, not unless they're foolin' around. And you two aren't a couple of adults."

"We're not?"

"Nope."

"Mind if I ask just how you classify us, if not as adults?"

"You're a Harte and Octavia is Claudia's great-niece."

"So?"

"Shoot and damn, son." Mitchell raised the cane and waved it in a slashing arc. "I warned you. If you think I'm gonna just stand by and let you take advantage of that gal, you're——"

"Mitch, wait." Octavia's clear voice echoed across the parking lot. "I can explain everything."

Nick turned his head and saw Octavia coming toward them at top speed. She left the sidewalk in front of her shop and raced across Bay Street, hair flying behind her.

He was amazed that she could actually run in the sexy little slides. They did not look as if they'd provide adequate support or stability for this kind of exercise. But, then, what did he know about ladies' shoes?

A car horn blared. Brakes screeched. Octavia paid no attention. She reached the opposite side of the street and kept moving, heading straight for Mitchell and Nick.

"You don't understand, Mitch," she shouted. "It's okay, really it is."

Mitchell glared at her with concern when she skidded to a halt, breathless and flushed, in front of him.

"See here, you all right?" he asked. "Something wrong?"

"No, no, that's what I'm trying to tell you." Still breathing hard, she shot a quick, unreadable glance at Nick and then turned back to Mitchell. "I just wanted to assure you that you don't have to protect me from Nick."

"I already warned him once that I won't stand by and let him fool around with you."

"That's just it, we are *not* fooling around."

"Well, just what the heck do you call it?" Mitchell demanded.

Nick waited with genuine interest to hear her answer.

Octavia drew herself up with astonishing aplomb. "Nick is working for me."

Mitchell gaped. "What the devil?"

She bestowed an icy little smile on Nick and then looked at Mitchell with cool determination. "He has kindly agreed to investigate the missing Upsall. A.Z. and Virgil and I don't feel that Chief Valentine can handle the case on his own."

"Well, shoot and damn." Mitchell looked bemused for a couple of seconds, but in true Madison style, he recovered swiftly. "That doesn't explain why he was out at your place until all hours last night."

"Relax," Octavia said smoothly. "Last night was no big deal."

Nick felt his insides clench. No big deal?

"It's true we had dinner together, but so what?" Octavia went on in a breezy manner. "The only reason he left as late as he did was because of the storm. My fault, entirely. I didn't want him driving home until the wind had died down a little. I was afraid about stuff like downed power lines and trees falling across the road."

She did not have to sound quite so damned casual, Nick thought.

But her tactics were working. Mitchell was starting to appear somewhat mollified.

"Well, shoot and damn," Mitchell said again. "So you kept him there at your place on accounta the high winds?"

"Violent storms make me a little nervous."

"That one last night was a tad rough," Mitchell admitted. "Worst we've had in a while. You say he's gonna play private eye for you? Just like the guy in his books?"

"Precisely," Octavia said firmly. "From now on whenever you see Nick with me, you may assume that we are discussing the case. Nothing more."

"Huh." Mitchell looked thoughtful now. "If you're sure that's all there is to it—"

"Absolutely certain," Octavia said. "Like I said, last night was no big deal. Just a friendly dinner that lasted a little longer than we anticipated because of the storm."

"Huh." Mitchell looked hard at Nick. "You think you can find that painting?"

"Probably not." Nick shrugged. "But Virgil and A.Z. and Octavia want me to ask around a little so I said I would. If you hear anything useful, let me know."

"I'll do that."

Mitchell nodded to both of them and stalked back toward the waiting SUV.

They watched him climb into the front seat and slam the door. Bryce put the behemoth in gear and drove out of the parking lot.

There was a short silence. Nick folded his arms, leaned back against the BMW, and looked at Octavia.

"Let's get something straight here," he said. "I don't need you to protect me from Mitchell Madison."

Octavia reached into her shoulder bag, removed a pair of sunglasses, and slipped them onto her nose. Leveling the playing field, Nick thought. Now he could not read the expression in her eyes any better than she could read his.

"I think I'm the one who should make things clear," she said crisply. "I have a vested interest in making certain that you are not distracted by Mitchell and his misguided attempts to protect me. I want you to concentrate on finding that Upsall. Do we understand each other?"

"Yeah, sure. We understand each other." He paused a beat. "Last night was no big deal, huh?"

She pursed her lips and tilted her head slightly. Light glared on the lenses of her glasses. "I may not have phrased that correctly."

"I'm glad to hear that."

"After due consideration, I've decided that last night was actually quite therapeutic for me."

Her deliberate, reflective, analytical tone sent a cold chill through him.

"Therapeutic?" he repeated cautiously.

"Don't laugh, but this morning, when I woke up, I felt like the princess in the fairy tale, the one who'd been asleep for a hundred years. Awake at last. Okay, so maybe it was more like having been asleep for a couple of years, but you get the picture."

He relaxed a little but not much. "I'm a little confused here. Are you saying I'm Prince Charming?"

She chuckled. "Hardly."

His belly tightened. "I was afraid of that."

"What I'm trying to explain is that, in a way, I've been living in a different world for nearly two years. I put a lot of things on hold while Aunt Claudia was ill, and I never went back to them after she died. I've been just sort of floating through my life, as it were."

"A free spirit."

"That's how I described it, but it was more like being unanchored or untethered, if you see what I mean."

That fit with what he had figured out for himself, he thought. "Sounds like a form of depression or something."

"Maybe." She snapped her fingers. "But whatever the problem was, it's fixed."

"Because we had great sex last night?"

"The quality of the sex probably wasn't as much of a factor as the fact that I actually did the deed." She smiled coolly. "It has been a while, you see. My social life was one of the things I put on hold when Aunt Claudia got so ill. I never really got back to it."

"Glad I could serve in a useful capacity."

"You were *extremely* useful." She pushed her glasses up more firmly on her nose and cleared her throat. "Since we're having this conversation, I should probably take the opportunity to apologize for that unfortunate little scene last night as you were running out the door. Let's just chalk it up to two years' worth of celibacy, the storm, and the last remnants of my weird emotional condition."

"A nice tidy list of reasons." He shoved his fingers through his hair. "And for the record, I was not *running* out the door. It was late and I had to pick up Carson and get back to the cottage."

"Of course." She glanced at her watch. "I'm glad we've got that settled. You'll have to excuse me. I need to get back to the gallery."

"Now who's running?"

Her mouth tightened. "I've got a business to see to and you've got a missing painting to investigate."

"Sure." He wished he could see her eyes behind those damn sunglasses. "Would you like to come out to my place and have dinner with Carson and me tonight?"

She hesitated. "Thanks, but I'm afraid I'm busy this evening."

The chill returned to his gut. "Seaton?"

"Why, yes, as a matter of fact. How did you know?"

"Lucky guess," he said grimly.

"He wants me to look at some of his paintings." She turned away to start back toward the gallery. "He has never exhibited his work and he wants me to give him a professional opinion on whether it might have commercial possibilities."

"Bullshit. He wants to talk you into bed."

She stopped and looked back over her shoulder. "Would you like to tell me what it is between you two?"

"What the hell. I never told anyone else." He wrenched open the driver's side door of the BMW and got behind the wheel. "Might be *therapeutic* for me."

"Nick, wait—"

He slammed the door and looked at her through the lowered window while he started the engine. "Seaton hates my guts because he thinks that I had an affair with his ex-wife while they were still married."

Her mouth opened but no words emerged. Her speechless condition gave him some satisfaction, but not much.

"One more thing," he added, snapping the car into gear. "What happened last night between you and me wasn't therapy. It was great sex. There's a difference."

He drove out of the marina parking lot, leaving her standing there in her bright purple jumper and ridiculously sexy shoes.

11

"WHAT the hell do you expect me to do?" Sullivan snarled into the phone. "I'm trying to put together a merger here."

"Hate to break this to you," Mitchell growled on the other end, "but my grandson and your son don't need any help putting the finishing touches on the Madison-Harte merger. Both of 'em have been running their own companies for years. They know what they're doing. You're just gumming things up, hanging over their shoulders there in Portland. Leave 'em be and pay attention to the larger issues."

"Larger issues? Never heard you use a fancy phrase like that before, Mitch."

"Must have picked it up from one of you silver-tongued Hartes. Look, we've got a problem here in Eclipse Bay."

Sullivan cranked back in the chair and contemplated the view from the window of the temporary office his new grandson-in-law, Gabe Madison, had provided for him. The headquarters of Madison Commercial, soon to become Madison-Harte, were located on the top floors of a Portland office tower. From his perch he could see the boat traffic on the Willamette River.

The summer afternoon was sunny and warm. The weather reporters claimed that it was hot down there on the city streets, but he spent most of his time in Phoenix these days. He knew hot, and this was not hot.

"Seems to me that *you* have a problem, Mitch," he said, stalling for time while he considered the *larger issues.* "Not me. You're the one who decided to take on the job of looking out for Claudia Banner's great-niece."

"This problem we're discussing involves your grandson," Mitch shot back. "I told you I wouldn't stand by and let him—"

"Shut up." Sullivan got up out of the chair very suddenly.

Phone in hand, he went to stand at the window. "Don't say it again."

"Don't say what?" Mitchell asked innocently. "That I won't let Nick sucker Octavia into an affair and then dump her when he decides he wants to replace her with some other lady?"

"This is my grandson you're talking about." Sullivan's hand clamped fiercely around the phone, but he managed to keep his voice level. "He is not a philanderer, damn it."

"That so? Then why hasn't he found himself a good woman sometime during the past four years and settled down again? That's what you Hartes do, isn't it? Get married and stay married?"

"Yes, Mitch. Unlike the sterling example of family values you set for your grandsons with your three or four wives and God only knows how many affairs, we Hartes are real big on family values."

"You leave my grandsons out of this."

"Hard to do that, given that they're married to my granddaughters."

"There's not a damn thing wrong with Gabe's or Rafe's family values and you know it. Lillian is Gabe's passion and Hannah is Rafe's. Nothing comes between a Madison and his passion. Those two boys are married for life."

"So was Nick," Sullivan said quietly.

Silence hummed on the line.

"That's the real problem, you see," Sullivan continued. "Nick figured he had married for life. He hasn't adjusted to the loss of Amelia. He's not heartless, he's just trying to protect himself."

"Look, I know folks here in Eclipse Bay like to say that losing her broke Nick's heart." There was a note of gruff sympathy in Mitchell's voice. "Expect it's true, what with him being a Harte and all. But that ain't no excuse for him playin' fast and loose with a nice girl like Octavia. She's had a rough time of it, too, damn it. But unlike your grandson, I don't think she's tough enough to protect herself."

"So you've decided to do it for her?"

"Someone's gotta do it. Not like she's got any family around to take on the job."

Sullivan hesitated. "All right, you've made your point."

"Got another one to make while I'm at it," Mitchell said grimly. "Your grandson spent last night at her place."

That gave Sullivan pause. "The whole night?"

"Well, maybe not the *entire* night—"

Sullivan relaxed slightly. "Didn't think so."

"But it's pretty damn obvious those two are foolin' around."

"Obvious to you, maybe."

"Yeah, obvious to me. You should have seen the way Octavia jumped to Nick's defense this afternoon when I cornered him down at the marina."

"What the hell do you think you're doing, cornering my grandson?"

"I was just makin' sure he understands he can't have his way with Octavia."

"Damn it, Mitch—" Sullivan broke off abruptly and backtracked to the other part of Mitchell's comment. "What did you mean when you said Octavia jumped to his defense?"

"She claimed he's sort of working for her."

"Nick? Working for Octavia Brightwell? Doing what, for crying out loud?"

"Playing private detective, I hear. Like that fellow in his novels."

Sullivan struggled valiantly to hang onto the few remaining wisps of logic that still dangled from the conversation. "Why does Octavia need an investigator?"

"Long story. That painting Thurgarton left to A.Z. and Virgil and the Heralds got stolen from her shop last night."

"What was it doing in her gallery? Never mind. I assume she notified Valentine?"

"Sure. But he's got his eye on the Heralds and she doesn't think he's looking in the right place. Neither does A.Z. or Virgil."

"So she hired Nick." Sullivan sank down onto the corner of his desk and digested that information. "And he agreed to investigate?"

"Appears that way."

"This is bizarre."

"Like I said, we've got a situation here, Sullivan. I hate to admit it, but I think I'm gonna need some help straightening this one out."

"Now, just a minute—"

"I'll keep you posted."

Mitchell cut the connection.

Very slowly Sullivan reached across the desk and punched in another, very familiar number. He needed advice from the one person whose insight he had come to trust the most over the years.

His wife, Rachel, answered on the second ring.

"Something wrong?" she asked.

"Why do you say that?" he grumbled.

"Because it's the middle of the day and you're supposed to be deep into the intricacies of the merger of Harte Investments and Madison Commercial."

He could hear birds. Somewhere in the background, water splashed. He knew that she was out by the pool of their desert home with his daughter-in-law, Elaine. The two women were holed up together in Phoenix, keeping each other company, while their menfolk worked the merger details with Gabe Madison.

Sullivan summoned up a vision of Rachel in her swimsuit, her body sleek and wet.

She was still the only woman for him, he thought. There had never been another since he had met her all those years ago in the wake of the financial disaster of Harte-Madison. He had been a driven man in those days, completely obsessed with the task of rebuilding his business empire.

But he had learned the hard way that the great strength in the Harte genes was also a potentially devastating flaw. It was the nature of a Harte to be goal-oriented and so focused that other things, important things, sometimes got pushed aside. If Madisons were driven by their passions, Hartes were sometimes inclined to be cold-blooded and relentless in their pursuit of an objective.

Rachel had quietly acted to counter his single-minded obsession with Harte Investments. She had centered him, given him a sense of connection. During the long, hard years when he had thrown himself into the struggle to create H.I., Rachel had been there, sometimes going toe-to-toe with him to remind him that he had other priorities, too. It was Rachel who had taught him the meaning of family. It was Rachel who had saved him from going down a path that would have left him a hollow shell of a man.

"Gabe and Hamilton don't need my help," he said. "They've shunted me off to a corner office on the floor beneath the CEO's suite and made it clear they'll call me if they need me."

"I take it they don't call often?"

"Nope. I'm getting a little bored here, to tell you the truth. I'm thinking of going over to the coast for a couple of days."

"What's wrong in Eclipse Bay?" she asked instantly.

"Nothing's wrong."

"Nick and Carson are there."

"So? Thought I'd spend a little time with my great-grandson. Carson's got a lot of me in him. Going to run an empire one of these days. He needs my guidance during his early, formative years."

"You still haven't told me what's wrong."

The problem with being married to a woman like this for so many decades was that she could read a man's mind.

"Just had a call from Mitch," he said carefully. "Seems like Nick and Octavia Brightwell are involved. Sort of."

"Well, well."

"What, exactly, does that mean?"

"It means it's about time Nick finally got serious about a woman."

"That's the problem, according to Mitch," Sullivan said. "He doesn't think Nick is serious about Octavia."

"Surely Nick wouldn't have an affair with her?" Rachel sounded genuinely concerned now. "Not there in Eclipse Bay. Think of the gossip."

"It's the thought of Mitch trying to manage the situation on his own that worries me."

12

"HONEST opinion, Octavia." Jeremy looked at the five pictures propped against the walls of the bedroom he was using as a studio. "I can handle it. Really. I think."

She gazed into the depths of the painting in front of her. It was a portrait of Jeremy's grandmother. It showed Edith Seaton seated in her antiques shop, a small, purposeful figure surrounded by the clutter of the past. There was an almost surrealistic quality to the old dishes and small relics housed in the glass cabinets and displayed on the tables.

The painting showed a room crowded with a lifetime of memories. Edith's face was a rich tapestry of emotions and determination layered on each other with such a strong, clear vision that it was possible to see the personality of the woman in every stroke.

"It's really quite wonderful, Jeremy." She did not look up from the painting. "When you said that you wanted to show me some pictures, I had no idea they would be of this quality."

Jeremy visibly relaxed. He looked pleased. "I did that one of my grandmother from a photo I took last year. You know, she's lived her whole life in this town. Hardly ever traveled even as far as Portland. Eclipse Bay is her whole world."

"How long has she been alone?"

"Let's see, Granddad died eight, maybe nine years ago. That's him in the framed picture hanging behind the counter. They both grew up here. Got married the day after they graduated from high school. They were together for nearly sixty years."

She studied the picture-within-a-picture and was able to make out the features of a man with the thin shoulders that often accompanied age. There was a certain self-confident, almost rakish quality to the tilt of the man's head. The viewer got the impression that at one time the senior Seaton had been a good-looking man and knew it.

"Sixty years is quite a marriage," she said. "No one in my family ever managed to stay together that long."

"Mom told me once that Granddad ran around a bit in his younger days. But Grandmother pretended not to know about his little escapades."

"Your grandfather had his affairs right here in town?"

"I guess so. He lived here all of his life and didn't do any traveling to speak of."

She shuddered. "Must have been hard on your grandmother."

"I'm sure it was. She's got a lot of pride in the Seaton name."

"Marriages are always mysterious when viewed from the outside." She turned away from the painting. "I'd love to give you a show, Jeremy. But as I explained, to be important to your career, it would have to be held at the Portland gallery, not here in Eclipse Bay."

"I know. Eclipse Bay isn't exactly on the art world's radar screen."

"No, and I'm afraid that I'm booked solid in the city. I've got shows scheduled every month until the end of summer there and then I plan to sell both galleries."

"I understand," he said.

"But I can certainly hang a couple of your pictures in my gallery here in town and see if they sell. I have a hunch they will. You've got a real commercial talent. What do you say?"

"I'll go with your intuition. You've got the eye, at least when it comes to art."

"Meaning that I don't have it when it comes to other things?"

"Okay, okay, I admit that I have some strong reservations about you seeing Nick Harte."

"I thought so." She folded her arms and propped one hip on the edge of the table. "He told me that you think he had an affair with your ex-wife."

Jeremy looked stunned. Then his expression darkened and his face tightened with suppressed anger. "I can't believe that he actually talked to you about that."

"He didn't discuss it in detail. He just made the statement that you thought your ex-wife had had an affair with him while you were still married."

Jeremy's hand closed into a fist. "So, he admitted it," he said softly.

"No, he did not admit it. He just said that was what you believed."

"It's not a guess, you know." Jeremy looked hard at the painting of his grandmother. "Laura told me she'd been with him."

"Where is Laura now?"

"Getting ready to marry again, I hear. A lawyer in Seattle."

"When did she meet him?"

"How the hell should I know? I don't keep track of her private life these days."

"You and Laura," she said cautiously, "I assume the two of you were having trouble for a while before you split up?"

"Sure. We argued a lot toward the end. That's usually what happens before you get a divorce, isn't it?"

"That's certainly the way it went in my family." She watched him intently. "Were the quarrels bad?"

"Bad enough."

"The kind of arguments in which both people say things that are calculated to hurt the other person as much as possible?"

Jeremy glanced at her, frowning. "Sometimes. Look, I really don't want to rehash the events surrounding my divorce, okay? It's not my favorite topic of conversation."

"I understand. But I can't help wondering if maybe Laura told you that she'd had an affair with Nick because she knew it would hit you harder than if she said she'd fallen in love with a man you'd never met. Also, it could have been a way of protecting the man she really was seeing at the time."

"What is this? You think you have to defend Harte? Don't waste your time."

"What a terrible position to be in, trying to figure out whether to believe your lifelong friend or your spouse. No one should have to make that kind of decision."

"Look, I'm not after sympathy here," he muttered. "It's over. I've moved on, like they say, okay?"

"Tell me something, did you ever ask Nick directly if he'd slept with Laura?"

"I told him once that I knew about them, yeah," Jeremy growled.

"You accused him. You didn't ask him."

"What's the difference? He denied it."

"Did Nick ever lie to you in the past about anything else that was important?"

"What does the past have to do with this?"

"Did he?" she pressed gently.

"No. But, then, maybe he never had any reason to lie to me in the past."

"You've been acquainted with him since you both were children. Have you ever known him to cheat or steal or betray a friend?"

"Things are different when it comes to sex," Jeremy said with ominous certainty.

"Do you think so? I don't. Cheaters cheat and liars lie. It's what they do whenever things become inconvenient for them or when they can't get what they want in any other way. Most of the people I've known who can lie to your face have had some practice. Aunt Claudia always said that scamming people was an art form that required skill and precision."

Jeremy looked grim. "Your aunt would have known, from all accounts."

"Yes. The only thing I can say in her defense was that she came to regret a lot of the damage she caused. But we're not talking about her. Tell me about Laura. Looking back, can you recall occasions when she lied to you?"

Jeremy started to say something but he closed his mouth before uttering a word. He just stood there, gazing at one of the landscapes he had painted.

"How long did you know her?" she asked.

"We were married three months after we met. She thought she was—" He stopped.

"She thought she was pregnant?"

Jeremy nodded. "It was okay by me, although my family was a little put off by the rush, and Grandmother was mortified. She's a little old-fashioned, you know."

"Yes. I know."

Jeremy grimaced. "She became my biggest supporter, however, after she found out that Laura came from a socially prominent family in Seattle. But as far as I was concerned, I was excited about starting a family. It felt right, you know? Nick had little Carson and I . . . Well, it didn't happen for Laura and me. Turned out she wasn't pregnant, after all."

"She lied about it?"

He shoved his fingers through his hair, looking hunted. "To tell you the truth, I don't know. I've sometimes wondered. She said it was a mistake at the time. The test didn't work properly or something."

"How long were you married?"

"Eighteen months. Like I said, her family was old Seattle money. Lots of connections. Her parents were never particularly thrilled with me. They felt she could have done better. Once or twice I got the feeling that maybe she'd married me just to defy them and then . . ."

"Came to regret her decision."

"Things got worse in a hurry when I told her that I was thinking of moving to Eclipse Bay. I said it would be a good place to raise a family. She hated the idea so I put it off."

"You like it here. Don't you?" Octavia asked.

He regarded the painting of his grandmother for a while. "It's strange, but I do kind of like it here. Feels like home, you know?"

A wistful feeling drifted through her. "Yes. I know."

Sometimes feelings for places were wrong, she thought, but there was no need to go off on that tangent. Her intuition told her that Jeremy was, indeed, at home in Eclipse Bay. Like the Hartes and the Madisons, he had several generations of family history here.

She had made the mistake of believing that she belonged in Eclipse Bay, too, but that had been wishful thinking on her part. She knew that now. Her search for home was still ongoing.

"Just out of curiosity," she continued, "did Laura have a problem with you spending time on your painting?"

Jeremy jerked slightly, clearly startled by the question. His mouth was a thin, hard line. "She called it 'playing artist.' "

"One last question. Did you see much of Nick while you and Laura were married?"

Jeremy was quiet again for a while. Eventually he shook his head. "No. Things change when you get married, you know? Laura had her own set of friends. We hung around with them for the most part."

"Yet she still found time to have an affair with Nick?" Octavia spread her hands. "Get real, Jeremy."

"What the hell is this? You think you can just walk into this situation and analyze it without knowing all of the people involved?"

"I know something about Hartes. Lord knows, they've got their flaws, but I honestly can't see any of the Harte men fooling around with another man's wife." She straightened away from the desk. "And after looking at your paintings, I know a bit more about you, too. You can see a person's personality and character clearly enough to translate it onto a canvas. Try looking at Nick with your artist's eye. Ask yourself how you would paint him."

"Hell, you really have got it bad for him, don't you?"

"My feelings for Nick have nothing to do with this discussion." She dug her car keys out of her shoulder bag and went toward the door. "But I will tell you one thing, Jeremy. I won't let you use me to punish him for what you think he did with Laura."

13

"HEAR you're investigating that missing painting." Sandy Hickson drew the squeegee across the BMW's windshield with professional expertise and flipped the dirty liquid off with a flick of his wrist. "Just like that private eye guy in your books."

Nick leaned against the side of his car while he waited for Hickson to finish servicing it. He studied Sandy through the lenses of his sunglasses. It was felt in some quarters that Sandy had been born to work in a gas station. Legend held that as a teenager, he'd had a penchant for collecting phone numbers off rest room walls, the kind that were preceded by the inviting phrase *for a good time call* . . .

Whether Sandy had ever gotten a date using one of the numbers he had found on the grungy white tiles in the station's rest room was still an open question, but one thing was certain: The Eclipse Bay Gas & Go was a nexus point of local gossip.

"You read my books, Sandy?"

"Nah. Nothing personal. I don't read a lotta fiction, y'know? I prefer magazines."

"Yeah, I know the kind of magazines you favor. They've all got centerfolds featuring ladies whose bra sizes exist only in the realm of virtual reality. Talk about fiction."

Sandy did not take offense. He dipped his squeegee into a bucket of water and aimed another swipe at the windshield. "I read 'em mostly for the articles, y'know."

"Sure. Since you know what I'm after, you got anything for me?"

Sandy looked sly. "Been some talk going around about that painting."

"Anything you think I can use to help me find it?"

"Well, now, a few people are saying that you're getting warm." Sandy snickered, evidently enjoying some private joke. "Real hot, in fact."

The snicker became a guffaw.

Nick did not move. Sandy's sense of humor had not matured much since his high school years.

"What have you heard?" Nick asked.

"Heard you were getting it on with the chief suspect, that's what I heard. Whooee. You're hot, all right, my friend. Probably couldn't get much closer if you tried."

Sandy could no longer restrain himself. He laughed so hard he lost control of the squeegee. It dropped into the bucket, splashing dirty water on his shoes. He paid no attention.

Nick watched him for a moment, contemplating his options. The urge to wring Sandy's scrawny neck was almost overwhelming, but he exerted an effort and managed to resist the temptation.

"The chief suspect," Nick repeated. "That would be Octavia Brightwell?"

"You got it." Sandy went into another round of howls.

Nick made himself wait until Hickson's laughter had subsided to a few snorts.

"Who told you that Octavia was the chief suspect, Sandy?"

"Couple of folks mentioned it." Still chortling a little, Sandy retrieved his squeegee.

"Give me a name, Sandy."

"Well, Eugene, for one. B'lieve he mentioned it to me first."

"Eugene Woods?"

"Yeah."

"That would be the same Eugene Woods who is usually between jobs and spends most of his time at the Total Eclipse nursing a beer and associating with his old buddy Dickhead Dwayne and pretending to look for work?"

"That Eugene, yeah." Sandy scrunched up his face into an expression of keen interest. "Why? You wanna talk to him?"

"Yeah. I think I want to talk to him."

Alarm flickered in Sandy's eyes. "Hang on, Nick, I don't know as that's a real smart idea. Eugene ain't changed much since he was a kid. He didn't get that nickname of Mean Eugene for no reason, y'know."

"People change, Sandy. They mature."

"Not Mean Eugene. He's the same as he was back in third grade. Still hold you up for your lunch money if he can figure out a way to do it. And Dickhead's the same, too. Always goin' along with whatever Eugene wants him to do."

"I'll bear that in mind, Sandy."

Nick shoved himself away from the side of the car and walked across the street to the entrance of the Total Eclipse Bar & Grill.

"WHAT does that key open?" Gail asked.

Octavia glanced at the key hanging from the hook inside the storage closet. "I don't know to be honest. Nothing here in the gallery, that's for sure. I tried it on all the locks. Must have belonged to Noreen. One of these days I'll toss it out. But I hesitate to discard it until I know for certain that it doesn't go to anything important."

"I know what you mean. There's something about a key that makes you think twice before throwing it out, isn't there? Even when you don't know what it unlocks."

"Yes." Octavia shut the closet door and turned around with a smile. "Okay, I think that's it. Any other questions?"

"Not at the moment."

They walked back out into the gallery and went to stand at the window. Outside on the sidewalk several tourists meandered. The day was sunny and pleasantly warm.

Octavia had awakened feeling inexplicably good again today, even though there had been no wild and crazy sex last night and even though she still had the same set of problems she'd had before life had turned so adventurous here in Eclipse Bay.

Gail also looked better today. She seemed cheerful, even a bit enthusiastic.

She was dressed in a dark, lightweight suit with a little scarf at her throat. Her honey-colored hair was brushed sleekly back into a neat knot at the back of her neck. Very formal for Eclipse Bay, Octavia thought. But then, she had come here to apply for a job.

"It's strictly a temporary position, I'm afraid," Octavia said. "I'm planning to sell the gallery at the end of the summer and there's no way to know if whoever buys it will want an assistant."

Across the street at the end of the block she could see Nick leaning against the side of his car, talking to Sandy Hickson at the town's only gas station. Just the sight of him, even from this distance, did things to her pulse. There was something deliciously compelling about the way the man *lounged,* she thought; a sexy, subtle, masculine grace that made her think extremely erotic thoughts.

Evidently the conversation with Sandy was a riveting one. She wondered if Nick was actively pursuing his investigation or just passing the time of day while Sandy put gas in the tank and washed the windshield. It was impossible to tell from this distance.

"I understand that you can't promise anything beyond the summer," Gail said quickly. "But this will buy me some breathing space to look around and try to line up something permanent up at Chamberlain or the institute. I really appreciate this, Octavia."

"Not as much as I appreciate your agreeing to take the position," Octavia said.

"I'm sure a few more questions will come up, but I think I've got the basics down. As I told you, I've had some experience in retail and I've always loved art. In a way, this is a perfect job for me. I'm going to enjoy it."

"You might as well start this afternoon. If you're free, that is?"

"Yes. Mom is looking after Anne. I'll give her a call and tell her that I've started working. She'll be very relieved."

"Good. I've got a lot of things to do in the next few weeks. I'm planning to move, you know. And then there's the Children's Art Show. Also, I have to get started on making arrangements to sell both branches of Bright Visions." The list of objectives had become her mantra, she realized. She ran through it in her mind whenever she felt dispirited or depressed about her life at the end of the summer. It kept her focused.

Gail hesitated. "I know it's none of my business, but do you mind if I ask why you feel you have to sell your galleries and leave the state?"

"I've been sort of drifting for a while," Octavia said. "Trying to decide what

I want to do with my future. I don't have all the answers yet, but I've definitely come to the conclusion that I need to move on."

Gail nodded sympathetically. "Believe it or not, I know exactly what you mean. I felt that drifting sensation for a while after my divorce. It was hard to make decisions. But having Anne to support emotionally and financially did a lot to make me pull up my socks and move forward."

"I'll bet it did." She watched Nick across the street and thought that, whatever else you could say about him, there was no denying that he was an excellent father. "Nothing like being responsible for a child to help you put your priorities in order."

"True. Kids come first."

I wonder if I'll ever have one of my own, Octavia thought. A picture of Carson's laughing face danced through her mind. She pushed it aside.

"I've got a question for you," she said to Gail. "Why did you come back to Eclipse Bay?"

"Anne has reached the age where she's starting to ask why her daddy doesn't come see her," Gail said. "I thought it would be good for her to spend more time with my father. The positive-male-role-model thing, you know?"

"Yes," Octavia said softly. "I know."

Down at the station, Nick had straightened away from his car, preparing to leave. Anticipation crackled through her. She wondered if he was getting ready to drive here to the gallery to give her an update on his progress. Maybe she would suggest that they talk over lunch. Yes, that sounded good. A business lunch. She could leave her new assistant in charge of the gallery.

But Nick did not get behind the wheel of his car. As she watched, he started purposefully across the street, heading toward the entrance to the Total Eclipse.

"What on earth?" She stepped outside onto the sidewalk to get a better look. "Good grief, he's going into that dive."

"Who?" Gail came through the opening behind her. She glanced down the street with a puzzled expression. "Nick Harte?"

"Yes. It's almost lunchtime. Maybe he decided to pick up a sandwich there."

"At the Total Eclipse?" Gail wrinkled her nose. "Good way to get food poisoning, if you ask me."

"You're right." Intuition kicked in. "I'll bet he's following a lead."

Gail glanced at her with open curiosity. "It's true, then? Nick Harte is playing private eye for you and A.Z. and the others?"

"He's not *playing* private eye. He's making serious inquiries into the situation."

"Hmm. I don't know how many serious folks he's going to find inside the Total Eclipse, especially at this time of day."

"Good point." She'd been in town long enough to have learned something about the clientele of the Total Eclipse. "You know, I don't like the looks of this. Who do you suppose he's going to talk to inside that joint?"

"Well, there's Fred, the owner," Gail said.

"Of course." She relaxed a little. "He tends the bar. Bartenders always pick up useful tidbits of gossip. The hero in Nick's books often consults them."

"And if memory serves," Gail continued dryly, "you can usually count on finding Mean Eugene and his sidekick Dickhead Dwayne in there most days."

"I know who you mean. I've seen them on the street and in Fulton's occasionally. They're always together. I've heard the Mean Eugene name but I hadn't realized the skinny one was called Dickhead."

"Dwayne and Eugene have been buddies for as long as anyone can remember. They tend to reinforce each other's worst characteristics. Eugene calls the shots and Dwayne goes along. It is generally felt in these parts that anyone who would do whatever Eugene told him to do would have to be a dickhead. Hence the name."

"I can see the logic."

"Back in the big city, folks would probably say that Eugene and Dwayne are the products of dysfunctional families. But around here we just call them bums."

NICK pushed open the door and stepped into the perpetual gloom of the Total Eclipse. He removed his sunglasses and let the smell of stale cigarette smoke, spilled beer, and rancid grease envelop him. The combination brought back a lot of memories.

Some things were a given in Eclipse Bay. A guy bought his first condom from Virgil Nash, not because Grover's Pharmacy didn't stock them, but because it was too damn embarrassing to buy a box from Pete Grover. The pharmacist knew everyone's medical history from date of birth and did not hesitate to make his opinion of your sex life clear. And he always tried to get names. Even if you got up the nerve to risk his beady-eyed scrutiny, you faced the very real threat that he would notify your folks or, worse yet, the girl's folks that the purchase had been made.

Showing up here at the Total Eclipse on the day you were finally old enough to buy a legal beer was another rite of passage for young males in Eclipse Bay. By the same token, if you were still buying a lot of your beers here at age twenty-five or beyond, it was understood that you were never going to amount to much and that you were probably doomed to live out your life at the bottom of the town's social ladder.

Mean Eugene and Dickhead Dwayne were shining examples of the accuracy of that hypothesis. They were in their mid-thirties and still bought their beers here.

Nick gave his eyes a few seconds to adjust to the shadows. The only lights in the Total Eclipse were the narrow spots over the pool tables in the room at the back, the green glass lamp next to the cash register at the bar, and the weak candles in the little red glass holders on the tables. The candles were Fred's notion of ambience.

The place was nearly empty at this time of day. Being seen at the Total

Eclipse at any time invited unpleasant comments from the more high-minded members of the community. The comments were always a lot more scathing if you hung out here when there was daylight outside.

But the prospect of societal disapproval did not worry guys like Eugene and his buddy, Dwayne.

Eugene Woods had been born to bully. In high school his size and weight issues had ensured that he went on to become a local football legend and a known thug at Eclipse Bay High. Eugene's post-football years had not gone well, however. The layer of padding that had stood him in good stead on the field had increased in volume, and his brutish ways had earned him an extremely limited circle of friends. Sooner or later his poor work ethic screwed up any job he managed to land.

Dwayne was his constant companion. Dickhead was not really an accurate descriptor, at least not when applied to Dwayne's features. He reminded Nick more of an oversized insect.

Dwayne was thin and brittle with spidery legs and arms. He looked as if he'd crunch if you stepped on him. He twitched a lot, too, like a bug that had been hit with a dose of pesticide.

Bar stools were uncomfortable for a man of Eugene's proportions. Nick looked for his quarry in one of the booths.

Eugene was there, sitting at a grimy table with Dwayne. The big man faced the door, in true Old West gunslinger style. There was just enough light coming from the little candle in the red glass holder to reveal the meanness in his eyes and the ragged tears in the grimy tee shirt stretched over his belly.

Interviewing Mean Eugene was not going to be easy.

Nick went toward the booth. He nodded once at Fred when he went past the bar.

"Fred."

"How you doin', Nick?" Fred did not look up from the little television set he had positioned behind the bar. He was watching a long-running soap opera. Fred was addicted to the soaps.

"Doin' okay, thanks," Nick said.

Civilities completed, he moved on to the booth and stopped. He looked at Eugene and Dwayne.

"Can I buy you gentlemen a beer?" he asked.

Dwayne, who'd been concentrating on a dripping cheeseburger, started and looked up with a startled expression. Clearly the word "gentlemen" had confounded him. And with good reason, Nick thought.

But Eugene, always the faster of the two, chortled. "So we're gentlemen now, huh? Hell, yes, you can buy us a couple of beers. Never say no to a free beer. Besides, it ain't every day a Harte wanders in here and makes an offer like that, now, is it? Sit down."

"Thanks." Nick considered and discarded the prospect of sharing one of the torn, orange vinyl benches with either Eugene or Dwayne. When you dealt with guys like this you did not want to find yourself wedged into a tight place.

He glanced around, spotted a scarred wooden chair at a nearby table, and grabbed it. He reversed it and sat down astride, resting his folded arms on the back.

Eugene swiveled his head, an amazing feat considering that he lacked any sign of an actual neck.

"Hey, Fred," Eugene called loudly. "Harte, here, is gonna stand me and Dwayne to a coupla beers. Give us some of that good stuff you've got on draft."

Fred did not reply, but he reached for two glasses without turning away from the television screen, where someone was dying bravely in a hospital bed.

Eugene squinted malevolently. "You didn't come here to be friendly, Harte. Your type doesn't hang out with guys like us. Whatcha want?"

"Yeah," Dwayne said around a mouthful of burger. "Whatcha want?"

Nick kept his attention on Eugene. "Mind if I ask you a couple of questions, Eugene?"

"You can ask." Eugene polished off the last of the beer he had been drinking when Nick arrived. He wiped his mouth on the back of his shirtsleeve. "I'll decide if I feel like answering."

"I hear you've been speculating openly on the question of who might have taken that painting that's gone missing from the gallery up the street," Nick said casually.

"Hell, I *knew* it." Eugene uttered a satisfied little snort, savoring his own brilliance. "So you're playing detective, huh? Just like the guy in your books? What's his name? True?"

Nick raised his brows. "You read my books, Eugene?"

"Nah. I don't read much. I'm more into the sports channel, y'know? *XXXtreme Fringe Wrestling* is my favorite program."

"Mine, too," Dwayne volunteered. "That's the one where the women fight almost buck-nekked. They just wear those little leather thong things, y'know? You oughta see those tits flapping around in the ring."

"Hard for a book to compete with that kind of upscale entertainment," Nick said.

"Yeah," Eugene agreed. "But I seen your novels down at Fulton's when they come out in paperback. They got that little rack next to the checkout counter, y'know?"

"Amazing that Fulton's even bothers to stock my books, given that so few people around here are inclined to read them."

"Hey, you're our only local author and besides, you're a Harte." Eugene's voice hardened. "Everyone thinks that gives you special status in Eclipse Bay."

Nick was saved from having to respond directly to that tricky conversational gambit by a loud, jarring crash. Fred had just slammed two glasses of beer down onto the top of the bar.

"Come and get it, Eugene," Fred called, turning back to his soap. "No table service until four-thirty when Nellie shows up for the evening. You know that."

"Allow me." Nick got to his feet and went to the bar to collect the beers. He set them on the table and sat down again.

"Well, well, well." Eugene grabbed his beer and hauled it closer. "Never thought the day would come when I'd get served by a Harte." He gulped some beer and lowered the glass. "How about that, Dwayne? One of the honchos of Eclipse Bay just bought us a beer and served it, too. What d'ya think of that?"

"Weird," Dwayne said. He snickered and downed a hefty swallow from his own glass. "Damn weird."

You couldn't discuss things rationally with these two, Nick reminded himself. It would have been the equivalent of engaging in a conversation concerning the origins and meaning of the universe with a pair of particularly dim-witted bulls. The best you could hope to do was prod them in the direction you wanted them to take.

"Heard you've been doing a little detecting, yourself, Eugene," Nick said. "Sandy over at the station says you've got a theory about just who might have made off with that painting."

Eugene blinked a couple of times and then managed to make the intellectual leap required to grasp the meaning of the sentence.

"Yep, that's me, all right," Eugene said, sounding pleased. "Detective Eugene Woods." He grinned at Dwayne. "Got a ring to it, don't it?"

Dwayne snorted. "A real ring."

Eugene turned back to Nick. "I know who took that painting, but you ain't gonna like it." He put the glass down with a decisive clang and wiped his mouth on the back of his shirt. "Makes you look downright stupid, Harte."

"I've looked that way before," Nick said. "I'll get past it."

Eugene cackled so hard he choked. It took him a while to recover his wind. "Always enjoyed the sight of a stupid-looking Harte."

"I can't help feeling that this conversation is losing its focus," Nick said gently. "Could we return to the subject at hand?"

Eugene stopped grinning. His heavy features twisted into an expression of deep suspicion. Probably worried that he had just been insulted and not quite certain how to react, Nick thought.

Eugene, being Eugene and therefore extremely predictable in some ways, did what he always did in such circumstances. He went on the offensive.

"You wanna know what I think, Harte? I'll tell you. Only solid suspect far as I can see is your new girlfriend, the gallery lady. And you're screwing her. Ain't that a kick in the head? The big-time detective is screwing the prime suspect." He looked at Dwayne. "Ain't that a kick in the head, Dwayne?"

"Yeah," Dwayne said obediently. "A real kick in the head."

Eugene leaned across the table to make his point to Nick. "How do you like them apples, Mr. High-and-Mighty Harte? Looks like the lady has you by the short hairs. How's it feel to be led around by your balls?"

"Before we go into that, maybe you'd like to tell me where you heard this theory," Nick said.

"What makes you think I heard it somewheres else?"

Eugene's features transformed as if by magic, shifting from malicious glee to a twisted glare. "Maybe I came up with it all by myself. You think you're the only smart one around here?"

Nick throttled back his temper with an effort. He was here to gather information, not get into a brawl. "You got any proof that Octavia Brightwell stole the painting?"

"Proof? I don't have to show you no proof. You're the private eye. Find your own proof." Eugene leered. "Just keep digging away. Who knows what you might find?"

"Okay, you don't have any proof," Nick said evenly. "Would you, by any chance, have a motive?"

"Motive?" Eugene glanced at Dwayne.

"He means like a reason why she would steal it," Dwayne said, surprising Nick with his insight and comprehension.

"Oh, yeah." Eugene switched his attention back to Nick. "I can give you a reason, all right. That picture is real valuable and it ain't insured or nothing. Not even mentioned in Old Man Thurgarton's will. There's no record it even exists, get it? No, whatcha call it, prominence."

"Provenance," Nick corrected softly.

"Right. So the way I figure it, little Ms. Brightwell is pulling a fast one on all of you. Works like this, see, she hides the picture, pretends it got stolen and later, when the heat dies down, she leaves town, maybe goes to Seattle or some place like that and sells the damn thing. That way she gets to keep all the money. Now do you get it, Harte?"

"Interesting theory," Nick said.

"Yeah, it is, isn't it?" Eugene quaffed more beer and lowered the glass. Pleased with himself.

"And you say you came up with it all on your own?"

"Yep."

Dwayne opened his mouth, but he closed it again very rapidly when Eugene threw him a warning glare.

"In that case," Nick said, "can I ask you two gentlemen to refrain from spreading it any further until we find out exactly what is going on and maybe get some proof?"

Eugene looked intrigued. "Why should we keep quiet?"

"For one thing, there's a lady's reputation at stake."

"What reputation? Everyone in town knows she's screwing your brains out."

"I was speaking of her professional reputation."

"Who cares about that?" Eugene asked blankly.

"I do, for one," Nick said. "And I think maybe you and Dwayne, being gentlemen and all, should care about it, too."

They both looked at him as if he'd suggested that they should care about quantum physics.

Eugene recovered first. "Hell with her pro-fess-ion-al rep-u-ta-tion," he said, sounding each syllable out with sneering precision. "I don't give a shit about her reputation. You give a shit, Dwayne?"

"Nope," Dwayne said. "I figure the fact that she's screwing Harte's brains out is a lot more interesting than her professional reputation."

Nick rose slowly to his feet. They both watched him, taunting challenge in their faces.

"Let me put it to you this way, gentlemen," Nick said coolly. "If you two cannot manage to refrain from further public comment on either Ms. Brightwell's personal or professional reputation, I have two words of wisdom for you."

"What two words?" Eugene demanded, looking ready to pounce in victory.

"Lavender and *Leather."*

Eugene's face went slack as if he'd just gone completely numb. Maybe he had, Nick thought. With shock.

Dwayne gaped. He looked frozen with horror.

Satisfied that he had made his point, Nick turned and walked through the shadowy tavern. He pushed open the door and went out into the sparkling sunlight.

And immediately collided with Octavia, who had just put her hand on the door to open it.

"Excuse me, I—" She began, stepping hurriedly back out of the way. Then she recognized him. "Oh, it's you."

"Yeah, it's me."

The transition from night to day dazzled his vision. Or maybe it was the sight of Octavia in a dress that was roughly the color of a tequila sunrise and was splattered with impossibly oversized orchids. He took his sunglasses out of his pocket and put them on.

She glanced past him toward the door of the tavern. "What happened in there?"

"I confirmed something that I have long suspected."

"What?"

"No one in this town reads my books."

14

"I read them," she said.

"You don't count. You're leaving town in a few weeks, remember?" He took her arm and steered her away from the entrance. "What the hell are you doing here? I hope you weren't planning to eat lunch at the Total Eclipse. You weren't raised in Eclipse Bay, so you probably lack the necessary immunity to survive Fred's cooking."

"I wasn't planning to eat there. I saw you go inside and I knew you had probably gone in to talk to someone about the painting."

"Brilliant deduction." Across the street, Sandy Hickson was watching them with great interest, a dripping squeegee dangling absently from one hand. Nick took Octavia's arm again. "Come on, let's get you out of here. There's enough talk about you going around as it is."

She skipped a little to keep up with him. "Did you learn anything in the Total Eclipse?"

"Always something to be learned in the Total Eclipse," he said flatly. "It is never less than an enlightening experience."

She frowned. "What happened in there?"

"Long story."

"It's lunchtime. Why don't we go somewhere and you can tell me this long story."

He looked at her.

"You know," she said with a determinedly bright smile. "You can give me a report."

A report, he thought. First he was therapy and now he was business. This relationship was not improving. On the contrary, it seemed to be going sideways. But an invitation to lunch counted for something.

"Okay," he said. "But you're the client, so you're buying."

She flushed a little and did not seem amused. "Certainly. Where shall we go?"

"I assume you have to get back to the gallery right away. We can grab a bite at the Incandescent Body."

"Well, actually, no, I don't have to get back to the gallery right away," she said smoothly. "I just hired an assistant for the summer. Gail Gillingham. She said she could handle the place for the afternoon."

"Gail?" He thought about that. "Good choice."

"I think so. Unfortunately, I can't offer her anything permanent, but she said that the position will give her some breathing space in which to hunt for a better situation. You know what they say, the best time to look for a job is when you've already got one."

"Yeah, I've heard that." He kept his grip on her arm and angled her across Bay Street, steering toward the gas station, where his car was still parked at the pump.

"Gail has a very professional attitude and she's smart," Octavia said, trotting briskly along beside him. "I think that eventually she'll turn up something at the institute or at Chamberlain."

"Probably."

Octavia finally noticed that they were halfway across the street. She frowned. "Where are we going?"

"To get my car."

"Oh."

When they reached the BMW, Nick opened the door on the passenger side and stuffed Octavia into the seat. He closed the door and reached for his wallet.

"What do I owe you, Sandy?"

"Twenty-three bucks." Sandy peered through the windshield, looking at Octavia. "Everything go okay in the Total Eclipse?"

"Sure." Nick handed him the cash and started toward the driver's side of the car. "By the way, turns out Eugene and Dwayne were mistaken about that rumor they were spreading around."

Sandy blinked. "You mean the one about Miss—" He broke off abruptly when Nick gave him a hard look. He swallowed heavily. "Wrong, huh?"

"Yeah." Nick opened the door. "Completely false. Be a good idea if you didn't pass it along. Know what I mean?"

"Right," Sandy said quickly and nodded. "Big mistake."

Nick got behind the wheel. "You got it," he said through the open window. "Big mistake."

He drove out of the station, aware that Octavia was watching him intently.

"What was that all about?" she asked.

"Nothing important."

"Don't give me that. You deliberately intimidated Sandy Hickson. I want to know why."

He turned the corner and drove up the street that led away from the waterfront. "I didn't do a damn thing to Sandy."

"Yes, you did. I saw you. Something about the way you looked at him. I call that intimidation. Why did you do it?"

He contemplated that question for a while. Then he shrugged. "Okay, you should probably know what's going on, seeing as how you're the *client,* and all."

"Absolutely." She put on her own dark glasses, settled back into her seat, and folded her arms beneath her breasts. "Talk."

"There's a rumor going around town that you're the one who swiped the Upsall."

For a couple of seconds she did not move, just sat there gazing blankly through the windshield. Then she whipped around in the seat.

"Someone thinks I stole it?"

"I picked up the story from Sandy. He said he got it from a couple of colorful types who hang out at the Total Eclipse—"

"Mean Eugene and Dickhead Dwayne."

He was a little taken aback. Somehow it was hard to envision her calling anyone "dickhead." He had to keep reminding himself that the Fairy Queen was not all sweetness and light. Not anymore.

"Uh, yeah," he said.

"Those two are spreading the rumor that I'm responsible for the theft, hmm?"

"Yeah."

"Well, I hate to say it, but you must admit that there is some logic to their theory. I mean, I do have motive, opportunity, and a good working knowledge of the art world. How hard would it be for a slick operator like me to scam a bunch of locals like A.Z. and Virgil and the Heralds? All I'd have to do is make the picture disappear, tell everyone it got stolen, and then, a few months from now when I'm settled in some big city, make it mysteriously reappear. Presto, my name is suddenly legend in the world of modern art."

"Not hard," he agreed.

"And no one back here in Eclipse Bay would have a clue."

"No one but me," he corrected mildly.

"You wouldn't have any way of knowing what had happened, either. Not unless you made it a point to keep up with events in the art world."

He did not take his eyes off the road. "I'd do that, though."

"You would?"

"Let's just say I'd keep up with events concerning you."

"Oh." She mulled that over for a while and then, apparently not knowing what to do with it, let it go. She tightened her arms around her midsection. "Well, it's all moot because I did not steal the painting."

"I explained that to Eugene and Dwayne."

"You did?" Something in her expression lightened. "That was very nice of you."

"That's me. Mr. Nice Guy."

"I'm serious," she said. "That rumor about me taking the painting sounds quite logical when you think about it. I can see where reasonable people might start to wonder if I was the thief. After all, I am related to Claudia Banner and everyone knows what she did here."

He said nothing.

"I appreciate your support."

"Hey, you're the client. I lose you, I lose my fee."

"What fee?" she asked warily.

"Good question. Been wondering about that, myself. What fee?"

"You're not expecting a fee and you know it," she said crisply.

"That right? No fee, huh?"

They were in the woods now, climbing the hillside above the town. The cool, green canopy cut the bright sunlight. He watched for the familiar sign.

"Stop making a joke out of this," she said briskly. "We both know why you're looking for the painting. You want to help A.Z. and Virgil and the others."

"Not exactly," he said.

"What does that mean?"

"Means, not exactly."

The sign inscribed with the faded words SNOW'S CAFÉ came into view. The parking lot was crowded with vehicles ranging from bicycles to Volvos. Most of them, he knew, belonged to students and staff from nearby Chamberlain College. Arizona had catered to that particular clientele since she had opened the restaurant.

He turned off the road and parked next to a shiny, little, yellow Volkswagen.

"You know," Octavia said coolly, "the macho-cryptic private eye talk reads well in your books, but it doesn't go over so great in person."

"I hate when that happens."

He unfastened his seat belt and climbed out before she could pursue that line of inquiry. He was not in the mood to explain that the real reason he was playing private eye was because of her. Something Eugene had said came back to him. *How does it feel to be led around by your balls?* That was Eugene for you, a real relationship guru. Downright insightful.

He shut the door and started around the rear of the car. By the time he got to her side she was already out of the front seat, moving toward him with a determined stride. She gripped the handbag slung over one shoulder very tightly and there was a dangerous look in her eyes.

Damn. He was getting hard.

He opened the door of the café and ushered her into the pleasant gloom of the comfortably shabby interior. Tough-looking rock stars of another era, thin and angry and wearing a lot of leather, glared down at them from the ancient posters that decorated the walls. The music piped through the old speakers came from the same time warp as the posters, but the decibel level was kept reasonably low so that you could hold a conversation without shouting.

Arizona did not spend much time here these days. She relied on employees she recruited from the work-study offices of Chamberlain. She trained a new crew at the beginning of each academic year and she paid them handsomely. The result was a remarkably loyal staff that, in turn, freed her to concentrate on what she saw as her chief mission in life: keeping tabs on the goings-on at the institute.

"Getting back to the way you *explained* things to Eugene and Dwayne." Octavia tossed her bag into the booth and slid in beside it. "Maybe you'd better tell me precisely what you said."

"Hard to recall *precisely* what I said." He flipped open the plastic-coated menu.

Portions of Arizona's bill of fare were occasionally updated to reflect passing trends such as soy products and veggie patties, but mostly A.Z. stuck with the basic student food groups: burgers, fries, and pizza.

"Talk to me, Nick. I'm very serious here. What did you say to Eugene and Dwayne?"

"Why is that conversation of such great interest to you?" he asked, not looking up from the menu.

"Because the more I think about it, the more it worries me. I don't know those two well, but from what I've heard about them, it would surprise me if they took good advice willingly."

"I tried to provide an incentive."

She went very still on the other side of the table. "That's what I was afraid of."

"Look, don't worry about it, okay?"

"I'm worried." She reached out and plucked the menu from his fingers. "What magic words did you use to make them back off those rumors?"

What the hell, he thought. She would probably find out sooner or later, anyway. He lounged against the padded seatback and contemplated her for a moment.

"*Lavender and Leather,*" he said finally.

"I beg your pardon?"

"*Lavender and Leather* is the name of a gay bar located in the Capitol Hill neighborhood in Seattle," he explained. "About a year ago, Eugene and Dwayne went off to the big city, had a few beers, and decided it would be amusing to hang out in the vicinity of the establishment. They planned to entertain themselves hassling some of the patrons."

She was instantly incensed. "And here I've gone out of my way to be polite to them whenever I see them on the street. I actually felt sorry for those two."

"The interesting part is that, being Eugene and Dwayne, they managed to misjudge their intended victims. They picked on a couple of guys who had studied the martial arts. In short, Eugene and Dwayne got their asses kicked. Literally. It was not, I am told, a pretty sight."

"Oh, good." Octavia brightened. "I love stories that end like that. They confirm Aunt Claudia's theories about karma."

"Eugene and Dwayne apparently got a real jolt of karma that night." He picked up the menu she had taken from him and opened it again. "As you can imagine, however, it is not an incident they wish to have widely publicized here in Eclipse Bay."

"Ah, so that's it. Now I understand. No one here knows about their humiliating experience in Seattle?"

"Trust me, it is, perhaps, the best-kept secret in Eclipse Bay. If it ever got out that two gay men had used Eugene and Dwayne to mop out an alley, I doubt if the dynamic duo would ever be able to appear in public around here again."

She propped her elbow on the table and rested her chin on her hand. "In other words, you threatened Eugene and Dwayne."

"That's pretty much what it comes down to, yeah. Subtlety does not work well with those two."

"Hmm."

He looked up at that. "What?"

"If no one here in Eclipse Bay knows about Eugene and Dwayne's excellent adventure in Seattle, how did you learn the details?"

"Virgil Nash."

"Virgil? What does he have to do with Eugene and Dwayne?"

"As little as possible, like everyone else. It's another long story but I'll give you the short version. Several years ago, back in our wilder days, a bunch of us used to get together with some other guys out on a road near the bluffs to race our cars."

"I thought drag racing was illegal."

"Hey, we were nineteen-year-old guys with cars. What else could we do?"

"Right. Guys with cars. Go on."

"At the time, Eugene's pride and joy was a Ford that he boasted could beat anything else on the road. He was winning regularly but one night I beat him. He didn't take losing well, to put it mildly. After the race he followed me home. It was one o'clock in the morning."

"Go on."

"He had Dwayne with him, naturally. They probably egged each other on.

At any rate, Eugene started playing games on the road that runs along the low cliffs just south of town."

"I know it. There are a lot of tight curves. What kind of games?"

"Coming up fast from behind, nipping at the bumper of my car, pulling up alongside and swerving toward us just as we went into a curve."

"Us?"

He shrugged. "Jeremy was in the car with me that night."

"I see." She looked thoughtful.

"We didn't know if Eugene was really trying to force us off the road or merely attempting to scare us. He was more than just annoyed because he had lost to me that night. He was crazy mad."

"What happened?"

"I figured I had two choices; I could either try to outrun Eugene, which would have been dicey on those curves, or try to fake him out. I went for faking him out. Jeremy watched him while I concentrated on driving. When Eugene made one of his moves to pull up alongside, Jeremy gave me the word. His timing was right on the mark. I braked hard. Eugene kept going and lost control. His car went over a low bluff and down a short incline, and landed in some shallow water."

"Whew. Well, obviously he and Dwayne weren't killed."

"No. The only thing that saved them was the fact that the tide was still partially out. I stopped at the top of the bluff and Jeremy and I went down to see how bad things were. Eugene was slumped over the wheel. At first we thought that he was dead but then we realized he was just badly dazed. Dwayne was frozen with shock. There was no time to get help because the tide was coming in fast. Jeremy and I hauled them both out of the car and dragged them out of the water. We wrapped them in some blankets I kept in the back of the car."

"In other words, you and Jeremy saved Eugene and Dwayne."

"And neither of them ever forgave us for the humiliation," Nick concluded dryly.

"Where does Virgil Nash fit into this story?"

"Virgil lives out near where the accident happened. After we got Eugene and Dwayne out of the car, we went to Virgil's house to get help. He was there when Eugene made some threats to Jeremy and me."

"Threats?"

"Eugene was really pissed, like I said. Blamed us for wrecking his beloved car. But mostly he was just furious because he had screwed up and we'd had to rescue him. Anyhow, Virgil took us aside later and said that we should watch our backs for a while. We did, but Eugene never made any moves. The years went by and we figured everyone involved had forgotten about what happened that night."

"But Virgil didn't forget?"

"No. Virgil's been watching Eugene ever since, and that means watching Dwayne, too, since for the most part they're inseparable. When they got into trouble last year in Seattle, Virgil heard about it from a colleague who runs a sex toy shop there. He e-mailed both Jeremy and me and told us the story. Reminded us that guys like Eugene don't change and that someday it might pay to have some ammunition on hand, just in case."

"And today you used your ammunition."

"You could say that."

She watched him with an odd, unreadable expression. "For my sake."

"Yeah, well, I didn't want them spreading that story around."

"It's the kind of thing your hero, John True, would do."

He should have been flattered, he thought. But for some reason it irritated him that she was making a connection between him and the character in his books. He wasn't John True. He was Nick Harte. He closed the menu a second time and looked at her very steadily.

"Don't," he said grimly, "get me mixed up with John True. He's pure fiction. I'm real."

The interesting expression on her face disappeared immediately behind a cool veil. She took her chin off her hand and sat back. "Got it. Trust me, I won't make that mistake."

"Good." He was more annoyed than ever now. What the hell was wrong with him today?

A young waiter appeared, saving him from getting too deep into the intro-spective thing. Octavia ordered a salad. Nick realized that he was hungry. The confrontation at the Total Eclipse had given him an appetite. He chose the over-sized tuna sandwich and fries, knowing from past experience that it would do the job.

When the waiter had disappeared, Octavia looked at him.

"Don't get me wrong, I appreciate what you did today," she said. "But do you think it was wise to threaten Eugene and Dwayne?"

"I'm not worried about those two," he said.

"Okay, so what *are* you worried about? I can see that you've got something else on your mind."

"Eugene and Dwayne are not the sharpest knives in the drawer, if you know what I mean."

"I sort of got that impression. So?"

"So, while they are both the type to spread false and malicious rumors, neither of them has the brainpower to concoct the one going around about you."

She elevated her brows. "I believe I see where you're going here."

"When you stop and think about it, that story Eugene and Dwayne were spreading about you is a fairly sophisticated piece of gossip. They gave you motive and opportunity and they've added a few inside bits about how the art market works. Eugene even tried to use the word 'provenance.' "

"Not the sort of word you'd expect a guy like him to have in his vocabulary."

"No."

"From what I've heard about those two, they aren't likely to know much about the art market, either."

"Highly doubtful," he agreed.

"Which means that they are probably not the source of the rumors."

"Probably not."

She was quiet for a moment. Her expression turned somber. "What do you propose to do next?"

"I'm going to try to find out who started the gossip about you," he said. "I figure whoever is responsible for the rumors might have had a motive for implicating you."

"Like, maybe, to cover up his own involvement in the theft of the painting?"

"Yeah." He hesitated and then decided to give her the rest of it. "There's something else that bothers me about that elaborate story, too."

"What?"

"It would have been a lot simpler to point the finger of blame at the Heralds. They already seem a little suspicious to most folks. Instead, whoever concocted it chose you for the fall guy."

"You think this may be personal?"

"Yeah," he said. "I do. I've come to the conclusion that someone isn't just looking for any scapegoat. Whoever took the painting wants to make you, in particular, look guilty."

15

ANNE came into the gallery with Gail the following morning. She clutched a carefully rolled-up sheet of drawing paper in both hands.

"I brought you my picture," Anne said in her whispery little voice. She held it out to Octavia.

"Thank you." Delighted, Octavia came around from behind the counter to take the rolled artwork. "I'm so glad that you decided to enter a drawing in the show, Anne."

Before she could unroll the picture, Nick and Carson walked into the gallery. Nick carried a paper sack bearing the Incandescent Body logo. Carson had a cup of hot chocolate in one hand.

"Morning, Gail," Nick said. "Hi, Anne."

"Hi," Gail replied. "Say hello to Mr. Harte, Anne."

"Hello, Mr. Harte."

"This is Carson," Nick said.

"Hi," Carson said cheerfully. He looked at Anne and then at the rolled-up drawing in Octavia's hand. "Is that your picture?"

"Yes," she said.

"I did one, too. Miss Brightwell put mine in a gold frame." He looked at Octavia. "We brought you some coffee and a muffin."

"Thanks," Octavia said. "That sounds good."

"Let me see Anne's picture," Carson said.

"I was just about to look at it myself, and then Anne can select her frame."

Octavia carefully unrolled the drawing and put it down on a low table. She looked at the picture, ready with admiring words. Then she took a second look, awed by the remarkable talent displayed in crayon.

The form, color, shading, and expression were astounding, especially given the age of the artist. In some ways it was clearly a child's picture, but in others it vibrated with the raw power of a gifted and as yet untrained artist.

"Anne," she said very gently, "this is a beautiful picture. Incredible."

Anne looked thrilled. "Do you really like it?"

Octavia took her gaze off the picture with some reluctance and looked at her. "Yes." She caught Gail's attention. "It is quite remarkable, to be honest."

"I told you she was good," Gail said with quiet pride.

"Brilliant is more like it," Octavia murmured.

Carson was alarmed now. "Let me see." He hurried closer and examined the picture with an expression of mounting outrage. "It's a *dog*."

"It's Zeb," Anne told him. "He's my dog. Well, partly mine. He belongs to Grandpa, but Grandpa says I can share him."

Carson rounded on her. "You can't do a dog for the art show. I did Winston."

"Carson." Nick spoke quietly. "That's enough."

Carson turned to him. "But, Dad, she can't do a dog. I already did one."

Anne started to look uncertain. She glanced from her mother to Octavia for reassurance and then glowered at Carson. "Miss Brightwell said I could make any kind of picture I wanted."

"That's right," Octavia said calmly. "No two dog pictures are the same, so we can have any number of them in the art show, just like we can have any number of house pictures and flower pictures."

Carson was not appeased, but he obviously knew that he was fighting a losing battle. "It's not fair."

"Take it easy, Carson," Nick said. "You heard Miss Brightwell. No two dog pictures are the same, so there can be lots of them in the show."

"Each one is special," Octavia assured him. "Each one is unique. Your picture of Winston doesn't look anything like Anne's picture of Zeb."

Carson's face tightened but he did not argue further.

Octavia smiled at Anne. "Come with me and we'll pick out a frame for your picture of Zeb. You have a choice of black, red, or gold."

Anne brightened instantly. "I want a gold one, please."

Carson clenched his hands into small fists at his sides.

NICK took Carson out of the gallery. They went across the street and walked out onto the pier.

Nick stopped at the end and braced a foot on one of the wooden boards that formed the railing. He peeled the top off his cup of coffee.

"You want to tell me what's wrong?" he asked.

"Nothing's wrong." Carson took a desultory swipe at one of the railing posts with the toe of his right running shoe. "It's just not fair."

"Why isn't it fair?"

"It just isn't, that's all. My picture was the only dog picture until now. That's why Miss Brightwell liked it so much."

So that's what this is all about, Nick thought. He took a swallow of coffee while he considered how to handle the situation. He understood Carson's position better than his son realized. Every time he thought about Jeremy and his artistic talent and how much Jeremy had in common with Octavia, he was flooded with a wholly irrational jealousy, too.

"Miss Brightwell made it clear that she likes both dog pictures," Nick said.

"She likes Anne's better than mine," Carson muttered.

"How do you know that?"

"Anne's is better," Carson said.

It was a simple statement, uttered in the tone of voice of a guy who knows his hopes are doomed.

"Mind if I ask why you care so much what Miss Brightwell thinks about your picture of Winston?" Nick asked. "Is this just a simple manifestation of the Harte competitive instinct, or is there something else going on here?"

Carson frowned. "Huh?"

Sometimes he had to remind himself that Carson wasn't quite six yet. He was smart, but words like "manifestation" and "competitive instinct" could still throw him.

"Remember, the Children's Art Show isn't a competition. Miss Brightwell isn't going to choose a winning picture. All the drawings will be exhibited. There won't be any losers."

"Doesn't mean Miss Brightwell doesn't like Anne's picture best," Carson grumbled.

"Why do you care? I mean, let's face it, you've never shown a lot of interest in art until you decided to draw a picture for Miss Brightwell's show."

"I want Miss Brightwell to like my picture best."

"How come?"

Carson shrugged. "She likes artists. If she thought I was a good artist, maybe she'd like me better."

"Better than what? Better than she likes Anne?"

Carson kicked the post again. The blow was not so forceful this time. More of a gesture of frustration. "I dunno."

"She likes you a lot," Nick said. "Trust me."

Carson took another halfhearted shot at the post with the toe of his running shoe. Definitely losing steam now. A little boy struggling to deal with complex emotions that he doesn't comprehend, Nick thought.

They stood there in silence for a while, morosely watching the sunlight dance on the waters of the bay. Nick finished his coffee.

I want her to like me, too. I don't want her to think of me as therapy or business. I want her to want me, the way I want her.

He heard a crumpling sound and looked down, vaguely surprised to discover that he had crushed the empty coffee cup in his hand. Irritated, he tossed the remains into the nearest trash bin.

An adult male struggling to deal with complex emotions that he doesn't comprehend, he thought. Well, at least he wasn't going around kicking fence posts. A definite sign of maturity.

"So," he said, "what do you say we ask Miss Brightwell to have dinner at our house tonight?"

"Think she'd come?" Carson asked with sudden enthusiasm.

"I don't know," Nick said, determined to be honest. "But we're a couple of Hartes. That means we go after what we want, even if we lose in the end."

"I know," Carson said, "she likes salads. Tell her we're gonna have a really big salad."

"Good idea."

"SALAD, hmm?" Octavia said a few minutes later when they presented her with their proposition.

"With lots and lots of lettuce," Carson assured her. "As much as you want."

Nick leaned back against the counter and folded his arms. "Maybe a couple of radishes, too," he promised.

She gave him that mysterious smile that left him in limbo. "I could hardly pass up an offer like that," she said. "It's a date."

Nick turned to Carson. "Guess we'd better hit Fulton's before they run out of the best lettuce."

"Okay." Carson whirled and rushed toward the door.

Nick looked at Octavia. "Thanks. He's dealing with his first-ever case of professional jealousy. Anne's picture of Zeb hit him hard."

"I noticed."

Outside, Jeremy drove his Nissan into the little parking lot. Nick watched him climb out of the car and start toward the row of shops.

"Carson realized right away that Anne's picture was much better than his," he said to Octavia.

"The art show isn't a competition."

"Yeah, I reminded him of that." He crossed the showroom to the open door. "But he's a Harte. He had an agenda when he entered his picture of Winston in your show. He wanted you to think his drawing was the best. Now he's worried that he's been outclassed by a better artist."

She nodded. "I understand."

Outside on the sidewalk, Jeremy had paused at the entrance to Seaton's Antiques. He glanced at Nick, his face impassive. Then he opened the door and disappeared into his grandmother's shop.

"I'm really glad to hear that you understand," Nick said softly. "Because I'm having a similar problem."

She leaned her elbows on the counter. "You're worried that you've been out-classed by a better artist?"

"Professional jealousy is tough to deal with at any age."

He went outside to join Carson.

AT six that evening she stood on the top of the bluff with Carson and looked down at the five finger-shaped stones that thrust upward out of the swirling waters at the base of the short cliff.

"It's called Dead Hand Cove," Carson explained, cheerfully morbid. "Dad named it when he was a kid. On account of the way the rocks stick up. Like a dead hand. See?"

"Got it." The day had been pleasantly warm but there was a mild breeze off the water. Octavia stared down into the cove. "The stones really do look like fingers."

"And there's some caves down there, too. Dad and I went into them yesterday. We found some marks on the walls. Dad said he put them there when he was a kid so that Aunt Lillian and Aunt Hannah wouldn't get lost when they went inside."

"That's a Harte for you," she said. "Always planning ahead."

"Yeah, Dad says that's what Hartes do." Carson's mood darkened into a troubled frown. "He says sometimes all the planning doesn't work, though. He says sometimes stuff happens that you don't expect and things change."

"You mean stuff like Anne's picture of Zeb?" she asked gently.

He gazed up at her quickly and then looked away. "Yeah. It was better than my picture of Winston, wasn't it?"

She sat down on a nearby rock so that their faces were level. "Anne has a marvelous talent. If she decides to work hard at her drawing and if she has a passion for it, I think she could someday be a fine artist."

"Yeah." He kicked at a clump of grass.

"Different people have different kinds of talents," she said. "It's true that Anne has a gift for drawing. But the fact that you could see that her picture was so good means that you have another kind of talent."

He glanced at her, still scowling but intrigued now. "What kind?"

"It isn't everyone who can take one look at a picture and know that it is very good."

"Big deal."

"Yes, it is a big deal," she said matter-of-factly. "You have an eye for excellence, and that talent will be an enormous asset to you in the years ahead."

"How do you know?" he grumbled.

"Because it's the same talent I've got."

That stopped him for a few seconds. Then he looked appalled. "The same kind?"

"Yes."

"But I don't *wanna* run an art store. I wanna run a big company like Grand-dad Hamilton and Great-Granddad Sullivan. Dad says that's probably what I'll do on account of it's in my genes or something."

"The talent to recognize quality and beauty when you see it will be useful to you no matter what you do with your life," she said.

"You're sure?"

"Positive."

"Cause I don't wanna have to run a little art gallery like yours."

"Don't worry, I doubt if you'll end up doing that for a living. But you may decide to buy art to hang in your home or on the walls of your office someday, and with your talent you'll be able to buy really excellent art. You won't have to pay a consultant to tell you what's good and what's not so good. You'll be able to make your own decisions."

"Huh." But he was clearly somewhat mollified by the prospect of making decisions.

"Who knows?" she said. "Maybe someday you'll be in a position to buy one of Anne's paintings."

"I'm not gonna buy any pictures of her dumb dog, that's for sure."

DINNER went well, Nick thought later. He was unaccountably relieved, even pleased. It had, after all, been a new experience for him. Not that he couldn't do salad and boil a pot full of some of Rafe's ravioli stuffed with gorgonzola cheese, spinach, and walnuts. He had, after all, been cooking for himself and Carson for quite a while now.

But when he had resumed a social life a year or so after Amelia's death, he had consciously or unconsciously confined himself to women who, he was fairly certain, would not have been comfortable sitting at a kitchen table with a precocious kid.

Maybe the women of the Harte family had been right all along, he thought. Maybe he just hadn't wanted to see any of his dates in a domestic light. You looked at a woman differently after you'd seen her hanging out in your kitchen, carrying on an intelligent conversation about dogs and dinosaurs with your son.

Whatever the case, one thing was certain. When he looked across the old kitchen table this evening, a wooden table that had been scarred and scuffed with the marks of three generations of Harte family meals, it had hit him with shattering clarity that Octavia looked perfect sitting here with Carson and himself.

THEY played all of the ancient board games that had accumulated in the hall closet over the years until Carson reluctantly fell asleep on the sofa. Nick carried him upstairs to bed. When he returned to the living room, Octavia was in her coat, fishing her keys out of her pocket.

"It's getting late," she said, smiling a little too brightly. "I'd better be on my way. Thanks for dinner."

She was the one running away this time, he thought.

"I'll walk you out to your car."

He collected his jacket from the closet and put it on without buttoning it. When he opened the front door he smelled the sea and saw the trailing wisps of a light fog.

"Good thing I'm going now," Octavia said. She stepped out onto the porch and looked around. "This stuff looks like it's going to get heavier."

"Probably." He followed her outside, leaving the door ajar. "Thanks for what you said to Carson earlier. He's feeling a lot better now that he knows you're not going to judge him solely on his art."

"No problem."

"The kid's a Harte, what can I say? He wants you to like him and he'll do whatever he thinks will work."

"He doesn't have to worry. I like him. A lot. He's a pretty terrific kid."

He gripped the railing with both hands and looked out into the gathering mist. "What about me?"

"You?"

"I'd better warn you that this is a case of like son, like father."

She went still on the top step and gave him a politely quizzical look. "You want me to like you?"

"I want you to like me a lot."

She jangled her keys. "If this is about sleeping with me again—"

"It *is* about sleeping with you again," he said deliberately. "But it's also about explaining why I left in such a rush the other night."

"I know why you left in a rush. You panicked."

He released the railing and swung around abruptly to catch hold of her by the shoulders. "I did not panic."

"Sure you did. You're obviously dealing with a lot of unresolved issues connected to the loss of your wife, and when you get too close to a woman, you panic."

"Bullshit."

She gave him a gentle, sympathetic pat on the arm. "It's all right, I understand. I spent some time going through the grieving process after Aunt Claudia died. I can't even imagine how hard it would be to lose a beloved spouse."

He tightened his hands on her now. "It was hard, all right. But not for the reasons you think. I'm going to tell you something that no one else, not even anyone in my family, knows."

She stiffened. "I'm not sure I want to hear it."

"Too late, I'm going to tell you, whether you want to hear it or not. You probably know that the man at the controls of that small plane that crashed with Amelia on board was a family friend."

"Yes. Everyone knows that."

"Yeah, well hardly anyone else except his wife and me knows just what a very good friend he was of Amelia's."

"Nick, please stop."

"I found out after the funeral that they had been lovers at one time. They'd quarreled and each of them wound up marrying someone else. A couple of months before that plane crash, they had reconnected. It seems they'd both reached the earthshaking conclusion that they had married the wrong people."

She touched his cheek and said nothing.

"They were going off to spend the weekend together at a ski resort that day. His wife thought he was out of town on business. I thought Amelia had gone to visit her sister in Denver."

Octavia said nothing, just shook her head sadly.

"After the funeral his widow and I talked. We both decided that, for the sake of her son and mine, we would let the story stand about her husband having given my wife a lift to Colorado. Everyone bought it."

"I see." She lowered her fingers. "I'm sorry, Nick."

"I don't want you to feel sorry for me." He took his hands off her shoulders and cupped her face between his palms. "I just want you to understand why I've been a little reluctant to rush back into a serious relationship."

"You're scared."

He set his jaw. "I am not scared."

"Yes, you are. You made the kind of mistake that Hartes aren't supposed to make. You screwed up and married the wrong woman once, and you're absolutely terrified of screwing up again. So it's easier to play it safe."

"I made a mistake. I'll give you that much. And it's true that Hartes don't usually make those kinds of mistakes. But I'll never regret it."

She comprehended immediately. "Because of Carson."

"Amelia gave me my son. I will always be thankful to her memory for that."

"Of course you will, and that is as it should be. But that doesn't mean that deep down you're not afraid of trusting your emotions again."

"I am not afraid," he said evenly, "but I am damn careful these days. Amelia and I rushed into marriage because we both thought passion was enough. It wasn't. Next time around, I'm going to take my time and make certain that I know what I'm doing."

"Know what I think? I think you're being so careful that you get nervous when there's even a hint that a relationship might cross the line between casual and serious." She searched his face. "Is that what happened the other night? Did you panic because you thought our one-night stand might turn into something more than that?"

"For the last time, I did not panic. And for the record, I never intended it to be a one-night stand."

"I beg your pardon, did you freak out because you were worried that *our little summer fling* might get too heavy and too complicated?"

He refused to let her push him into losing his temper. He was trying to accomplish an objective here. Hartes never lost sight of their goals.

"Correct me if I'm wrong," he said, "but I was under the impression that you weren't looking for anything more than a short-term arrangement either, Miss Free Spirit."

She flushed. "I wasn't the one who ran for the door that night. I was doing just fine with the summer-fling thing."

"I did not run for the door. I left in a hurry, but I did not run."

"Details."

"Important details. And I'd like to remind you that I showed up at your gallery the next morning," he said. "It's not like I didn't call. And how the hell do you think I felt when you told me that the sex had been therapeutic? You made it sound like a good massage or a tonic, damn it."

She bit her lip. "Well, it was, in a way."

"Great. Well, do me a favor. The next time you want physical therapy, call a masseuse or a chiropractor. Or buy a vibrator."

Her eyes widened. She was starting to look a little unnerved, he thought. For some reason, that gave him an unholy amount of satisfaction.

"Don't push me," she warned.

"I haven't been pushing you." He hauled her close. "*This* is what I call pushing you."

He kissed her, using everything he had to seduce her into a response. He was not sure what he expected, but he knew what he wanted. He had his agenda. He was going to make her admit that the sex hadn't been merely a therapeutic tonic.

He was vaguely surprised and somewhat reassured when she made no move to free herself. After an instant's hesitation, her mouth softened under his. Her arms went around his neck and her fingers sank into his hair. Heat swirled through him, igniting his senses.

He had been right about this much, at least, he thought. She still wanted him. Nothing had changed on that front. He could feel the passion quickening within her.

When she shivered in his arms and tightened her hold on him, his triumph was tempered by the sheer enormousness of his sense of relief.

He dragged his mouth away from hers and nibbled on her earlobe. "It was good between us. Give me that much at least."

"I never said that it wasn't good." She tipped her head back, giving him access to her throat. "It was great."

"Then why not enjoy it?" The taste of her skin and the herbal fragrance of her hair combined into an intoxicating perfume. He knew that he would never forget her scent as long as he lived. "We have the rest of the summer."

She tensed in his arms. Her fingers stopped moving through his hair. Very slowly she pulled away and raised her lashes. "Maybe you're right."

He kissed the tip of her nose. "No *maybe* about it."

"It's possible that I overreacted the other night."

"Understandable," he assured her. "You were coming off a difficult year. A lot of emotional stuff going on in your life. You're making some major decisions about your business and your future. Lot of stress."

"Yes."

"Maybe you were right about one thing," he offered, feeling generous now. "Okay, it's not easy to think of myself as a sort of physical therapist, but I have to admit that there is a therapeutic side to really good sex."

"Probably releases a lot of endorphins, and then there's the exercise aspect."

"Right. Exercise." He was not sure this was going the direction he had intended, but it wasn't like he had a lot of alternatives.

"Rather like taking a brisk walk on the beach, I think," she mused.

He made himself count to ten and forced a smile. "No need to analyze it too much. Sex is perfectly natural and there's no reason that two healthy, responsible adults who happen to be single and uncommitted shouldn't enjoy it together."

She did step back then, slipping out from under his hands. "I'll think about it."

He did not move. "You'll *think* about it?"

"Yes." She turned and went down the steps. "I can't give you an answer tonight. I'm not thinking clearly right now, and I don't want to make another rash decision based on overheated emotions. I'm sure you can understand."

"Now who's panicking?" he asked softly.

"You think I'm afraid of having an affair with you?"

"Yeah. That's exactly what I think."

"Maybe you're right." She sounded regretful but accepting of that possibility. "As you said, I've been under a lot of stress lately. It's difficult to sort out logic and emotions."

He followed her down the steps, shadowing her to the car. When she stopped beside the vehicle he stopped, too, very close behind her. He reached around her, letting his fingers skim across the lush curve of her hip, and opened the door.

"I'll see you in the morning," he said. "Meanwhile, try to get some sleep."

She slipped into the front seat. "I'm sure I'll sleep just fine, thank you."

"Lucky you."

She started to put the key into the ignition and then paused. "One more thing I wanted to say."

He gripped the top of the car door. "What's that?"

"I think you should give Jeremy a call. Invite him out for a beer or whatever men do when they want to talk things over."

"Now, just why in hell would I want to do that?"

"Because you were once good friends and there's no reason why you can't be friends again. Deep down, he knows that you didn't have an affair with his wife."

She turned the key in the ignition, pulled the door shut, and drove away into the night.

16

NICK knew it was going to be a bad day when he drove into the parking lot of the Incandescent Body bakery the following morning shortly after ten and saw the black limo sitting near the front door. The driver was behind the wheel, sipping coffee and reading a newspaper.

"I don't need this," Nick said to himself while Carson scrambled out of the backseat. "I definitely do not need this."

Carson looked up at him. "What don't you need, Dad?"

"You'll find out in a minute." He closed the rear door and started toward the entrance to the bakery.

"I'm gonna have hot chocolate and an orange muffin this time," Carson announced with relish. "And we can get some coffee and a muffin for Miss Brightwell, too, okay?"

"I'm gonna have to think about that." He was still feeling pretty pissed off by her parting remarks last night, he thought. She'd had a lot of nerve suggesting that he take the lead in repairing his shattered friendship with Jeremy.

Carson looked startled. "How come? We always bring her some coffee and a muffin."

"The situation is getting complicated."

"But we gotta take her coffee and a muffin. We always take her that stuff. She 'spects it now. Dad, you promised you wouldn't do anything to make her mad."

"Okay, okay, we'll get her coffee and a muffin."

He opened the door of the bakery. Carson spotted the two men sitting at the small table immediately. Excitement galvanized him into motion. He raced forward at full speed.

"*Great-Granddad.*" Carson looked back over his shoulder. "Dad, it's *Great-Granddad.* He's here."

"I noticed," Nick said. He met Sullivan's eyes over the top of Carson's head. Then he flicked a glance at Mitchell, who was looking smug. "What a surprise."

He took his time following Carson to the table where the two men sat together over coffee. Two canes were propped against one of the chairs. Misleading, those canes, Nick thought. At first glance you might make the mistake of assuming that they indicated weakness. Nothing could be further from the truth.

He had seen photos of Mitch and Sullivan when they had been in the military together decades earlier. They had been young men in their prime at the time, strong and competent, ready to take on their futures. But the picture had been taken shortly after they had survived the hell of combat in a far-off jungle, and the experience had left an indelible imprint on them. If you looked closely, you could still see it in their eyes today. These were two very tough men, the kind you wanted at your back if you decided to walk down a dark alley.

They were also both stubborn as hell and downright bloody-minded when it came to getting their own way. But in fairness, Nick thought, those traits ran through every generation of both the Madison and the Harte families.

Sullivan grinned at Carson when the boy barreled to a halt at his chair. He gave Carson a hug and ruffled his hair affectionately.

"Hello there, sport, how are you doing?"

"Hi," Carson replied. "Did you come to see my picture in the art show? 'Cause if you did, you'll have to wait for a few days. The show isn't until next weekend. I did a picture of Winston."

"I won't miss the show," Sullivan assured him. He gave Carson a gentle push toward the front counter. "Go get yourself a muffin on me."

"Okay." Carson hurried away.

Nick looked at Mitchell. "This is your doing, I assume?"

"Just thought your grandfather oughta be made aware of what was going on here in Eclipse Bay," Mitchell said with malevolent good cheer.

"I hear you've been busy lately, Nick." Sullivan picked up his coffee. "Trying to find a painting that used to belong to Thurgarton and seeing Octavia Brightwell on the side."

"Not necessarily in that order, but, yeah, that pretty much sums up my summer vacation so far." Accepting the inevitable, Nick grabbed a chair and sat down. "But I've got hopes that the situation will improve."

<hr />

AFTER lunch at Dreamscape and some hurried conversation with Rafe and Hannah, who were busy with a crowd in the restaurant, Nick and Sullivan took Carson and Winston down to the beach below the old mansion.

Sullivan watched his great-grandson dart all over the landscape, following Winston from one tide pool to another.

"One of these days you're going to have to get that boy a dog of his own," he said.

"When he turns six," Nick agreed.

"That's next month."

"Yeah, I know. Carson reminds me just about every day."

"Six years old." Sullivan shook his head in wonder. "Where the hell did the years go? I remember when I used to walk on this same beach with you and Hamilton and a dog named Joe."

"If this is another one of those little grandfatherly chats on the subject of how the years are slipping away and how Carson needs a mother and how it's time I got married again," Nick said, "could we just skip to the end? I've heard it so many times that I've got it memorized."

"Take it easy. We're all worried about you and Carson. Harte men are family men, you know that."

"Carson and I have plenty of family. Every time I turn around, I'm running into family. Take this morning, for example. I walk into the local bakery to get a cup of coffee and what do I see? Family."

"Not like a Harte to be playing the field at your age."

"I do not play the field."

"What do you call it when you have relationships with several different women?"

"I call it a social life. And for the record, I did not have those relationships simultaneously. Hell, I've only dated maybe a half dozen different women in the past three years. I don't think that's excessive."

"Your mother and your grandmother and your sisters do."

"They're all obsessed with the idea of getting me married again."

"They think you've got some kind of psychological block. They've all decided that you've got a problem with getting serious about another woman because you're afraid of losing her the way you lost Amelia."

Nick watched Carson poke at a hole in the sand with a long stick while he tried to decide how to respond to that. "What do you think?" he said at last.

"Me?" Sullivan seemed surprised to be asked for his opinion. He halted beside a rock. "I think you just haven't found the right woman."

Nick realized he had been braced for a lecture. He allowed himself to relax slightly. "Yeah, that's sort of how I see it, too."

"But Octavia is different, isn't she?"

So much for letting down his guard. "Mitchell sent for you, didn't he? That's why you're here."

"Mitch feels protective toward Octavia Brightwell."

"Octavia can take care of herself."

"What about you?" Sullivan asked quietly.

It took Nick a beat or two to grasp that. "Don't tell me that you're afraid that I'm the one who might be in trouble here."

Sullivan's gaze rested on Carson and Winston, who had moved on to explore the entrance of a shallow cave. "Got one question for you."

"What?"

"Did you give Octavia The Talk?"

"Damn. I'm starting to think that everyone in the Northwest knows all the details of my social life. A guy could get paranoid."

"You didn't answer my question. Did you give Octavia your patented lecture on the subject of keeping things light?"

"You know what? I'm not going to answer that question."

Sullivan nodded. "Things went wrong this time around, didn't they? Mitch was right."

"I think we'd better change the subject, Granddad."

"Probably a good idea. Relationship counseling isn't exactly my forte. But for what it's worth, I came here to see what was going on, not to put pressure on you. I figure you can handle your own love life without my interference."

Nick raised his brows. "I'm stunned. Since when did anyone in our family ever hesitate to apply pressure whenever the opportunity arose?"

Sullivan exhaled heavily. "I put enough pressure on you when you were growing up. Always figured you'd take over Harte Investments, you know."

"I know."

"I didn't handle it well that day when you came to me and told me that you were leaving the company. Lost my temper. Said some things I shouldn't have said."

"We both did," Nick said quietly.

"Hamilton cornered me in my office that same afternoon. He was mad as hell. Angrier than I'd ever seen him. Told me to back off and leave you alone. Told me that you and Lillian and Hannah all had the right to make your own choices in life the same way I'd made mine and that he wasn't going to stand by and let me pressure any of you into doing what I wanted you to do. He really let me have it that day."

"Dad said all that?" Nick was surprised. He had known that he'd had his father's support when he made the decision to leave the company but he hadn't realized that Hamilton had gone toe-to-toe with Sullivan over the issue.

"Yes. Looking back, I can see that he was trying to protect you and your sisters from the kind of pressure I'd put him under when he was growing up. I didn't mean to force anyone into a mold, you know. It's just that I had always had this vision of H.I. descending down through the family. I couldn't believe that my grandson didn't want what I had spent so much of my life creating."

"The thing is," Nick said, groping for the words he needed, "Harte was your creation. I needed something that was all mine."

"And you found it in your writing. I understand that now." Sullivan's jaw tightened. "Something I've always wondered, though."

Nick glanced at him warily. "What?"

"Was it your leaving Harte after your first book was published that put the strain on your marriage?"

Nick sucked in a deep breath. "How did you know?"

"I didn't. It was your grandmother who guessed that things weren't going so well between you and Amelia there at the end. She had a hunch that the problems started when you decided to quit Harte. She always felt that, for Amelia, the company was part of the deal."

He did not know what to say, Nick thought. He had never realized that anyone had known about the fault line in his marriage.

"Grandmother is right," he said after a moment. "Amelia was having an affair with the man who was flying the plane that day. I think that, if she had lived, there would have been a divorce. She wanted out."

"And you wouldn't have been able to handle her cheating. You're a Harte."

"Yeah."

"Figured it was something like that." Sullivan kept his attention on Carson and Winston. "That's the real reason why you've been so cautious about getting serious with another woman. Got burned once and you're a mite nervous about sticking your finger back in the fire."

"Shit. Seems like everyone is trying to psychoanalyze me these days."

Sullivan's brows bristled into a sharp frown. "Who's everyone? Far as I know, only Rachel figured out the problems between you and Amelia. We never mentioned them to anyone else in the family or outside, for that matter."

"I told Octavia about how it was between Amelia and me. She leaped to the same conclusion that Grandma did."

"Huh. Women. Always trying to analyze what makes a man tick."

"Yeah."

"If only they knew how simple we really are."

"Better to keep 'em guessing," Nick said. "Probably makes us appear more interesting."

"True." Sullivan dug the tip of his cane into the coarse sand and started walking again. "Well, I think we've exhausted that subject. Tell me about this missing painting. You really trying to play private eye like that guy, John True, in your books?"

"I got into it because Virgil, A.Z., and Octavia asked me to look around a bit." Nick fell into step beside him. "They didn't think Valentine was looking in the right places, and they may have had a point. He suspects one of the Heralds probably took it and arranged to unload it in Seattle or Portland. He figures it's long gone."

"Mitch told me that much."

"I got a lot more serious about the situation after I heard the rumor that Octavia had been voted Most Likely Suspect."

"Octavia?" Sullivan scowled. "Now, that's interesting."

"I thought so." Never let it be said that the old man was losing it mentally, Nick thought. Sullivan had grasped the implications immediately. "Especially when you consider that she's well-liked here in town. It would have been a lot easier to cast suspicion on the Heralds, who are viewed as the local weirdos and outsiders."

"You figure it's personal, don't you? Someone is out to pin the blame on Octavia for some specific reason."

"That's how it looks to me."

"You sure she hasn't managed to piss off someone here in town? Maybe refused to market some artist who's decided to get even?"

"I don't think so." Nick shot him a searching glance. "I'm starting to wonder if this could be coming out of the past."

"Claudia Banner."

"Yes."

"But the only folks who got hurt when Claudia pulled off her scam all those years ago were Mitch and me. And we're both a little too old for revenge, even if we had a notion to go after it."

"I doubt if anyone gets too old for revenge if the motivation is strong enough, but I agree that you and Mitch are not the ones behind this. What I want to know is, do you think there's anyone else in Eclipse Bay who might harbor a grudge against Claudia Banner that would be big enough to make him go after Octavia?"

Sullivan contemplated that in silence for a while.

"If there's one thing I've learned about business in the past sixty years," he said finally, "it's that it's always personal. And when the deal involves as much cash as Claudia's scam did, there's usually a fair amount of collateral damage."

"Meaning maybe someone besides you and Mitchell Madison got hurt?"

"Could be. It's possible. I can't give you any names but I'll tell you what I'll do. I'll go over this with Mitch. You know, he and I never really talked about the details of what happened when Claudia put us into bankruptcy. We were too busy blaming each other and firing up the feud. But maybe we can discuss it calmly now. Put our heads together and reconstruct events, so to speak."

"Thanks. Let me know if you come up with anyone who might still be so pissed off at Claudia Banner that he would go after her niece."

"All right. It's a long shot, though. You do realize that?"

"Sure. But that's all I've got at the moment. Long shots."

"I can see that." Sullivan came to a halt and stabbed the cane into the sand a few times. He gave Nick a beatific smile. "Now that that's settled, how about I do you a favor and give you some time to yourself?"

"You offering to baby-sit?"

"Figured I'd take Carson back to Portland with me for a few days. Lillian and I can look after him while Gabe and Hamilton argue about the details of the merger. You'll have time to work on finding that missing painting."

"Sure. If he wants to go, you're welcome to take him with you, but don't pretend that you're trying to do me any favors. You just want another opportunity to mold him in your image. You think you can turn him into the next major empire builder in the family."

"You've got to admit, the boy's got a flair for business." Sullivan chuckled. "Remember how much money he made off that lemonade stand he set up in front of the house a few months ago when you brought him down to Phoenix? Talk about a natural aptitude."

Nick regarded his son playing with Winston and felt a rush of pride. "We'll see."

"We will, indeed. By the way, don't tell me that I'm not doing you any favors by removing young Carson from the vicinity for a while. I'd think you'd appreciate me giving you a little space in which to do your courting."

"*Courting.*" Nick stumbled over a rocky outcropping. He caught his balance and glowered at Sullivan. "What the hell are you talking about?"

"I figure I owe you that much," Sullivan continued smoothly, "after the way I tried to coerce you into taking over Harte Investments. And I've got to say, I think you've made a fine choice. I'm rather fond of Octavia."

"Damn it, who said anything about me courting Octavia Brightwell?"

"Gives me a good feeling to be helping you out like this. I do believe I'm getting downright sentimental in the twilight of my life."

"Twilight, my ass. You're not getting sentimental, you're still trying to run things, the way you always have."

"What can I say? It's in the blood."

———

THEY set out for Portland two hours later. Sullivan waited until they passed the You Are Now Leaving Eclipse Bay sign before he picked up the cell phone and punched out Mitchell's number.

"Well?" Mitchell demanded. "Did you get Nick straightened out?"

Sullivan glanced at Carson seated beside him. The boy was immersed in a book about dogs. "There's no need to worry about my grandson's, uh, association with Miss Brightwell."

Mitchell snorted loudly on the other end. "So you say."

"You'll have to take my word on that subject, Mitch. Meanwhile, something has come up in regard to that missing painting. Nick's got a hunch that there's a personal angle here. He thinks the thief might be someone who is still holding a grudge because of what happened when Claudia took Harte-Madison apart."

"But you and I were the ones who went bankrupt all those years ago. As far as I know we were the only people who got ripped off. Why the hell would anyone else still hold a grudge?"

"I don't know. I suggest we start with a list of everyone we knew at the time who might have had anything to do with Claudia and Harte-Madison."

"That's gonna take some thinking."

"I know. Tell you what. You put your list together and I'll make up mine. Then we can talk and compare notes. Maybe something will hit us."

"I'll see what I can do." Mitch paused. "You're sure Nick is gonna get his act together with Octavia?"

"Count on it."

Sullivan ended the call and looked at Carson. "Picked out the kind of dog you want?"

"I want one just like Winston."

"Can't go wrong with another Winston." Sullivan ruffled the boy's hair, then reached into his briefcase. "That reminds me, I brought a printout of your investment portfolio with me. Want to see how those lemonade profits are doing?"

Carson slammed the dog book closed. "How much money did I make?" he asked excitedly.

"You did very well with those ten shares in Fast Toy, Inc."

"I told you they made good toys."

"So you did." Sullivan put the brokerage statement on the seat between them. "Take a look at that bottom line. You made three hundred dollars."

"Oh, wow." Carson snatched up the statement and immediately started asking questions about the various entries.

Sullivan settled back against the seat and prepared to indulge himself in one of his favorite hobbies: teaching his eager great-grandson the finer points of investment strategies.

Life was good, he thought. He had Carson, and two hours ago Hannah had informed him that he was soon to become a great-grandfather for the second time. Judging by the intimacy and the joy he witnessed when he was with Gabe and Lillian, he was almost certain there would be more good news coming from that quarter one of these days.

All he had to do was get Nick and Octavia on the right track and life would be damn near perfect.

17

AN eerie green light emanated from Arizona's War Room. Octavia studied the glow seeping around the edge of the heavy steel door with great interest.

"Think maybe she's thawing some of those frozen space aliens she claimed the institute was trying to hide a few months ago?" she asked.

"When it comes to A.Z. and her conspiracy theories, nothing would surprise me." Nick pushed open the door and stood back to allow Octavia to enter the room.

In any normal house, the space would probably have been described by the architect as a study. But Arizona didn't live in a normal house. Her cabin was fortified with locking metal shutters on all the windows. The doors had been reinforced with steel bolts. Rumor had it that Arizona had six months' worth of supplies and food stored on the premises.

Octavia had lived in Eclipse Bay long enough to know that the reason no one in town got nervous about Arizona was because it was a fact that she had no interest in weapons of any kind. In her bizarre fantasy world, her mission was to collect and analyze intelligence data on the various conspiracies she was certain lay just below the surface at the Eclipse Bay Policy Studies Institute. The fact that the institute dismissed her as a quaint, local eccentric suited Arizona just fine. As she had explained to Octavia on one occasion, the disdain from the institute staff only made her job of spying on them simpler.

Octavia stepped into the War Room and saw that the mysterious green light radiated from a computer screen. Three people garbed in flowing robes and wearing a lot of the vaguely Egyptian-style jewelry favored by the Heralds sat hunched over the table. Two of them were going through heavy, leather-bound log books. The third was pounding away on the keyboard. They barely glanced up when Octavia and Nick entered.

There was a spartan, military-spare look to the furnishings. A large topographical map of Eclipse Bay was laminated to the surface of a massive desk. Rows of log books were arranged on the metal shelving that lined one wall.

Arizona, dressed in her customary camouflage-patterned fatigues, occupied the aging wooden chair behind the desk. A chubby, unlit cigar stuck out of the corner of her mouth. The narrow beam from the desk lamp was aimed low to illuminate the topo map. Most of Arizona's face was in shadow.

"About time you two got here." Arizona motioned toward the chairs that sat opposite her on the other side of the desk. "Have a seat. Coffee?"

Octavia glanced toward the machine in the corner. She could detect the unmistakable odor of burned coffee from where she stood. The glass pot had been sitting on the hot plate for a long, long time.

"No, thanks," she said politely. She took one of the chairs. "I've had enough today."

"I'll pass, too." Nick dropped into the chair beside her. He angled his chin toward the three Heralds. "How's Project Log Book going?"

"Right on schedule, and I intend to keep it that way." Arizona permitted herself a small moment of intense satisfaction. "Those bastards up at the institute aren't going to stop us. But we've got a problem."

"What's up?" Nick asked easily.

"The institute crowd has started a rumor. Heard it at Fulton's this morning," Arizona stated, clearly agitated.

Octavia sighed. "That would be the rumor that I'm the one who stole the painting and faked a break-in at my gallery to cover my tracks?"

"Bingo." Arizona snorted. "So, you've heard it, too, eh?"

"Yes," Nick said. "Seemed to be coming from Eugene and Dwayne. I took steps to keep them quiet, but I had a hunch that they weren't the original source."

"I reckon that the institute tried to use them to spread it for obvious reasons," Arizona said. "Not like those two blockheads would question the source of a story. They'd just happily blab to anyone who would listen. Whoever used them knew that was their nature."

Nick thought for a minute. "You said you heard the rumor at Fulton's?"

"Checkout counter," Arizona said. "Overheard Betty Stiles talking about it to Marjorie Dunne."

An unpleasant whisper of unease went through Octavia. Marjorie Dunne was the mother of little Katy Dunne, one of the children who had entered a picture in the Children's Art Show. Gordon Dunne served on the town council and had made it clear that he intended to run for mayor in the next election cycle. The family took its role as pillars of the community seriously.

"Betty and Marjorie, huh?" Nick leaned back in his chair and thrust his legs out toward the desk. He steepled his fingers. "What we need to do is trace this rumor back to the source."

"We know where it got started," Arizona snapped. "That crowd up at the institute concocted it. I'll bet they've got that painting stashed somewhere up there, too. Now, I've come up with a plan—"

"No." Nick unsteepled his fingers and held up one hand, palm out, to silence her. "Don't even think about it. You are not going to send Octavia and me into the institute to search for that painting."

"Got to go in," Arizona declared. "Don't see any other way to find the picture."

"Give me a few more days," Nick said. "I'm working on some angles."

Arizona looked skeptical. "What angles?"

"It's a little complicated and I'm not ready to talk about it yet. Let's just say that I think this thing has roots in the past. I've asked my grandfather to help. He and Mitch Madison are doing some deep background research. When I get the results I'll contact you."

"Deep background, huh?" Arizona chewed on her cigar while she pondered that. "When do you expect a report from 'em?"

"Soon," Nick promised. He got to his feet. "Any day now. Hold off on your plans to go into the institute until I get back to you, okay? If you move now, you may alert the folks who are behind this and they'll probably move that painting. Maybe ship it to California. We'll never find it if they take it out of town."

Arizona munched on her cigar a couple of times and then nodded decisively. "All right. I'll give you a few days to finish your deep background. But if you don't get anything useful out of Sullivan and Mitch, we're gonna have to go in. It's our only option."

"Right. I'll be in touch." Nick took Octavia's arm and hauled her up out of the chair. "Come on, we've got work to do, honey."

The *honey* bemused her a little. She got the feeling that he wasn't even conscious of having used the endearment. She thought about that while she allowed herself to be dragged from the War Room.

Outside, a light summer rain was falling. The woods surrounding the fortified cabin were cloaked in a gray mist. Nick hustled her into his car, and then went around the front and got in beside her.

She looked at him as he quickly reversed and drove back along the thin, rutted path that served as Arizona's driveway.

"Deep background?" she said dryly.

"I thought it sounded good. Had a nice military ring."

"It did seem to impress Arizona, but you only bought us a little time. What do you expect to accomplish?"

"Beats me. But I didn't have much choice. I had to come up with something fast. I definitely do not want to get tangled up in one of Arizona's little clandestine recon projects at the institute."

"From what Mitch told me, it's sort of a family tradition. Hannah and Rafe carried out a mission for Arizona and so did Lillian and Gabe."

"And it was just damn good luck that none of them got picked up for illegal trespass." Nick turned the wheel and drove out onto the main road. "I've got no intention of following in their illustrious and heroic footsteps, thank you very much. Especially when there's no reason in hell to think that the painting has been hidden up there at the institute."

Her small flash of amusement faded. "But you do believe that it's still somewhere in town, don't you?"

"Yes." He did not take his attention off the road. "I think whoever took it did it for personal reasons, not for profit. That means it's probably still somewhere in town. We need to find the source of those rumors."

A few minutes later Nick drove into town, turned onto Bay Street, and parked in the lot at the end of the row of shops. He got out and walked with Octavia to the door of the gallery.

The flicker of unease she had experienced a short time ago when Arizona had recounted the scene at Fulton's returned. Inside the gallery, Gail stood at the counter. She was engaged in an intense conversation with Marjorie Dunne.

"That's a ridiculous rumor, Mrs. Dunne," Gail said forcefully. "I can't imagine who started it, but it has absolutely no basis in fact."

Marjorie was clearly not about to be reassured or placated. Clad in tailored slacks and a fashionable cream silk blouse and wearing a lot of gold jewelry, she was, as usual, overdressed for Eclipse Bay. Her blond hair was cut in a short, sophisticated bob that Octavia was pretty sure had not come from Carla's Custom Cut & Curl. The local beauty shop specialized in two distinctive looks: Very Big Hair and the Senior Citizen Helmet.

"I'm sorry," Marjorie said, not looking particularly remorseful, just very determined, "but regardless of whether or not the rumors are true, I must insist that you give me my daughter's picture. I can't allow Katy to participate in the art show so long as there's a cloud hanging over Octavia Brightwell and this gallery. I have to think of my husband's position in the community."

Octavia felt Nick go very still beside her. Alarmed by the anger she sensed humming through him, she stepped forward quickly to defuse the situation.

"I assume this is about the gossip that is going around concerning me," she said calmly.

Gail and Marjorie both turned quickly. Gail's expression was every bit as resolute as Marjorie's.

Marjorie looked momentarily taken aback at the sight of Nick standing next to Octavia. She started to speak to him, but Gail overrode her.

"Katy will be crushed if her picture isn't in the show," Gail said to Octavia. She gave Marjorie a brief, pointed look. "I'm sure Mrs. Dunne wouldn't want her daughter to feel left out because of some stupid gossip. You know how sensitive children are."

Marjorie flushed a dull red, but she was resolved. "I'm sorry about this, Octavia. Katy may not understand why I'm doing this, but it's for her own good. I'm sure you can see my position here. Dunnes have been respected members of this community for three generations."

"You must do what you feel is best for your daughter," Octavia agreed. "It's unfortunate that you believe the rumor that I stole the Upsall, but that is your choice. I'll get the picture for you."

Marjorie's mouth tightened. "I didn't say I believed the gossip. I'm sure there's nothing to it. But it just wouldn't look good for Katy's picture to be in the show."

"That's ridiculous," Gail fumed. "The best way to help us squelch that gossip is to allow your daughter's picture to be exhibited with the others. If you pull it, you'll just add fuel to the fire and you know it."

Octavia was touched, but she was not about to let Gail fight this battle for her. "It's all right. I'll get the picture."

She circled the counter, opened the door of the back room, and went inside.

"I'm sorry about this," Marjorie said coldly, "but it really is not my problem, is it?"

"Depends how you look at it, Marjorie," Nick said.

In the back room, Octavia winced. Nick was in a dangerous mood.

Marjorie, however, apparently did not recognize the razor-sharp edge of the blade buried in the too-soft words.

"Nick." She was suddenly overflowing with warmth and cordiality. "I heard you were in town for the summer. Nice to have you back in Eclipse Bay for a while."

"Thanks," Nick said.

"I saw your latest book on the rack at Fulton's," Marjorie said. "A very intriguing cover."

"Think so?"

"Yes, indeed. I have an excellent sense of color and design, you know. I'm sure the story is very good, too. I understand you've become quite popular. Unfortunately I don't have much time to read these days."

"Why am I not surprised?" Nick murmured.

Octavia stifled a groan and hurriedly went to work sorting through the framed paintings to find Katy's picture. If she didn't get out there fast, there would be blood on the floor of the gallery.

"Gordon is getting ready to run for mayor, you know," Marjorie continued in a blithe, chatty fashion, evidently unaware of the ledge she was walking. "And what with all the campaign work and Katy's summer activities schedule. I haven't had a chance to read anything other than a newspaper for months."

"I know what you mean," Nick said. "I've been a little busy myself lately. I'm working on finding out who started those rumors that are circulating about Octavia."

"Oh, yes." Marjorie sounded nonplussed, as if she hadn't intended the conversation to go in this direction. "Yes, I did hear that you were asking around about the painting. Uh, any luck yet?"

"Yes, as a matter of fact. I'm getting close."

"That's wonderful," Marjorie said vaguely.

"I'm working on this theory, you see. I figure that when I find out who started the rumors, I'll have the thief."

Marjorie cleared her throat. "Is that so? I don't see why there would be any connection . . . ?" She let the remainder of the question dangle in thin air.

"There's a connection, all right," Nick assured her with the grave authority of an expert in his field. "It's obvious that someone is promoting the gossip in order to divert attention from himself." He gave it half a beat before adding very deliberately, "Or *herself,* as the case may be. It's an old tactic."

"It is?" Marjorie asked warily.

"Sure. Thieves and bad guys use it all the time. That's why the first thing law enforcement types do is check out the rumors surrounding a crime. They call it following leads."

"I see." Marjorie cleared her throat again. "I didn't know that."

"Probably because you've never read one of my books," Nick said very politely.

Octavia gritted her teeth. Things were getting nasty out there. She tried to sort more swiftly through the pictures. She was pretty sure Katy had done a drawing of a house. And she thought she recalled a big yellow flower, too.

"I'm making a list of everyone who repeats the gossip," Nick explained. "Checking out the sources. See who's trying to spread the rumors."

"That doesn't sound very helpful." Marjorie sounded a little desperate now.

"When I'm done, I'll give the list to Sean Valentine so that he can take a closer look at some of the people on it. I figure it's safe to say that someone on the list will prove to be the guilty party."

"I don't think you can make that assumption." Alarm registered in Marjorie's voice. "I mean, that's ridiculous. Everyone in town is spreading that gossip."

"Not quite everyone," Nick said. "For instance, I'll bet Gail, here, hasn't repeated the rumors."

"Nope, not me," Gail assured them with ferocious glee. "I wouldn't spread that kind of outrageous nonsense. I've got my position in the community to consider. After all, my family is third-generation here in Eclipse Bay. Same as yours, Marjorie."

"Well, I heard the story from Betty Stiles down at Fulton's," Marjorie said. Defensive now. "I have no idea where she got it."

"Thanks, I'll talk to Betty," Nick said smoothly.

"Why waste your time?" Marjorie asked. "It's Sean Valentine's job to find that painting."

"I'm doing this as a favor," Nick said. "Octavia is what you might call a close friend of the family."

There was another short pause.

"I see," Marjorie said cautiously.

Octavia spotted Katy's picture and snatched it out of the stack of framed drawings. She hurried toward the door.

"Here's your daughter's picture." She thrust it across the counter toward Marjorie. "It's a lovely drawing. Nice feel for color. Tell her she can keep the frame. Compliments of the gallery."

"Thank you. I truly do regret this. But I have to consider Gordon's position." Marjorie took the picture somewhat uncertainly and turned back to Nick. "Good luck with your little investigation."

"I'm sure we'll find out who took the painting," he said with astounding confidence. "My list is almost finished."

"Yes, well, I certainly hope you get the situation resolved soon." Marjorie summoned up a polished smile. "By the way, since you're in town for the summer, I'll be sure to send an invitation to Katy's birthday party to Carson. Katy's turning six in August, you know."

"I appreciate the thought," Nick said, "but it would probably be better not to bother with the invitation. I'm sure you can understand my situation here. I can't allow Carson to attend a birthday party given for a child whose mother's name is on my list. Got to consider Carson's position in the community, you see."

Marjorie's jaw dropped visibly. Shock and horror blended in her expression.

Octavia had a sudden urge to cover her face with both hands. Beside her, Gail did not make any attempt to conceal a satisfied grin.

Marjorie pulled herself together with commendable speed. "How dare you imply that I . . . that I'm on your list."

"Don't worry about it, Marjorie," Nick said. "When this is all over, I'm sure everyone will eventually forget who was on the list and who wasn't."

"Of all the—" Marjorie was overcome with outrage. Unable to speak, she simply stood there, glaring helplessly.

"You know," Nick went on as if nothing awkward had been said, "if you'd like to assist in the investigation, I'd be very grateful. In fact, everyone in my family would really appreciate the favor. Given your position in the community, you could be very helpful."

Marjorie's mouth worked once or twice before she managed to speak. "Well, of course, I'd love to help you but I honestly don't see how I could be of any more assistance. I told you, it was Betty Stiles who is spreading the story."

"I'll be talking to Betty next," Nick assured her. "But, since you've offered to help, there is one thing you could do that would go a long way toward narrowing my list."

"What's that?"

Nick glanced at the picture Marjorie clutched in her beringed hands. "Leave Katy's drawing here with the others. It will send a strong signal to the community that you don't think the rumors are true."

Marjorie was trapped and they all knew it. She shot a fulminating look at Octavia, and then she put the picture down on the counter and turned back to Nick with an earnest smile. "Well, if you really think it would help—"

"Oh, yeah," Nick said. "No question about it. Like I said, I really appreciate it."

"About your list," Marjorie added delicately.

"Obviously I won't have to add you to it," Nick said.

That seemed to cheer Marjorie slightly. She went quickly toward the door. "I hope it won't take you and Sean long to end this matter."

"It won't," Nick said.

They all watched in silence as Marjorie fled out the door and down the sidewalk toward the parking lot.

Octavia rested both elbows on the counter, propped her chin on her hands, and looked at Gail and Nick in turn. "Don't get me wrong. I am deeply touched. But I'm not sure that coercing Marjorie into leaving Katy's painting here was smart."

"Who cares about smart?" Gail said. "It felt good."

"That was Marjorie Dunne, for heaven's sake," Octavia reminded her dryly. "She's the wife of a member of the town council. Probably the wife of the next mayor of Eclipse Bay."

"So what?" Gail said with a chuckle. "This is Nick Harte. His family can buy and sell the entire town council and the mayor, too. In point of fact, if old legends are to be believed, they have done just that on a number of occasions."

"Be fair," Nick said to her. "It's not our fault that the council and the mayor have historically shown a certain willingness to accommodate us Hartes in exchange for contributions to their library building funds and pier renovation projects."

Octavia studied him with fresh appreciation. "My, my. I believe I have just witnessed an exhibition of what is commonly called throwing one's weight around."

"Relax, Marjorie deserved it," Gail said. "She has a history of behaving badly to lesser mortals. She was the same in high school. I don't suppose it escaped your notice that she didn't offer to send one of those birthday party invitations to my Anne."

"I did notice the oversight," Octavia admitted.

"If it's any consolation," Nick said, "Anne will get an invitation to Carson's party next month."

Gail smiled. "Thank you. She'll be thrilled. She hasn't had a chance to make any friends yet here in town."

"She'll have plenty of opportunity to meet other children her age at Carson's party," Nick said. "Every kid in town will get invited. Even Katy Dunne."

18

LATER that afternoon Octavia was in the back, framing the last of the entries in the Children's Art Show, when she heard Jeremy's voice in the other room.

"Gail?" Jeremy sounded surprised and somewhat incredulous. "Gail Johnson?"

"Gail Gillingham these days. Hello, Jeremy. It's been a long time."

"You can say that again. The last time I saw you, you were just a kid."

"Not quite. I was in college the last time our paths crossed. I'm surprised you even remember. You had finished grad school and were getting ready to accept a position at a college in Portland, as I recall."

"That's right. My grandmother mentioned that you were back in town. Said you were looking for a job."

"I found one, as you can see. It's temporary because Octavia plans to sell her business at the end of the summer, but it will give me some time to look around. I'm hoping something will open up at the institute or at Chamberlain."

"I'm working at the institute," Jeremy said. "I'll keep my ears open for you, if you like. There's bound to be some turnover before the fall."

"Thanks. I'd really appreciate it."

There was a short pause.

"I guess you probably heard about my divorce last year," Jeremy said.

"Your grandmother mentioned it," Gail said gently. "I can empathize. I went through one a couple of years ago. That's the main reason I came back to Eclipse Bay. I wanted my daughter to have more family around her."

"Sounds like a smart move. Kids need a sense of belonging. Maybe everyone does."

"Is that why you came back?" Gail asked. She sounded genuinely curious.

"Maybe. In a way, Eclipse Bay will always be home. When the institute offered me the position, it just felt like the right time to make a move."

Octavia went to the door. Jeremy and Gail stood on opposite sides of the counter. They were looking only at each other, she mused. Neither of them noticed her. She could have sworn she felt vibrations in the air.

She cleared her throat discreetly. Both of them jumped a little and turned toward her with expressions of surprise. She nearly laughed. You'd have thought she'd been hiding in a closet and leaped out unexpectedly.

"Hi, Jeremy," she said. "Did you bring in your paintings?"

"Are you kidding? Of course I did." He gestured toward a wooden crate leaning against the counter. "Got two of them right here."

Gail leaned over the counter. "Octavia said you painted. Let's have a look."

"I just brought the landscapes with me today." Jeremy went to work opening the crate. "Octavia thinks that's my most likely market here in Eclipse Bay."

He hauled one of the pictures out of the crate and propped it against the closest wall. Gail and Octavia came out from behind the counter to examine it.

Gail reacted immediately, her approval evident in her excited tone. "The Arch at sunset. I love it. What's more, I can sell it. It'll be gone by the end of the week."

Jeremy and Octavia exchanged amused glances.

"Tell you what," Jeremy said to Gail. "If you sell this sucker in a week, I'll buy you dinner at Dreamscape."

Gail did not take her eyes off the painting. "It's a deal."

HE ran Betty Stiles to ground outside Carla's Custom Cut & Curl. Betty emerged from the beauty shop with a stiff, cotton-candy cloud of pink hair. The hairdo had been frozen in place with so much lacquer that Nick was pretty sure it could have withstood a nuclear blast. She wore a jaunty denim skirt with a matching vest over a red blouse.

Betty was a widow in her late seventies. She had made a hobby of following every nuance of local gossip for as long as Nick could remember.

" 'Afternoon, Mrs. Stiles." He came away from the fender of his car and walked toward her. "How are you doing?"

"Why, Nick Harte. How nice to see you. I heard you were in town for the summer."

"Yes, ma'am."

"Saw your new book down at Fulton's the other day."

"Did you?" He would not ask if she had read it, he promised himself.

"I would have bought it because I read a lot of mystery and suspense. But when I read the back cover it didn't say anything about a serial killer."

"Probably because I didn't put one in the story."

"I only read books about serial killers."

"Figures," Nick said.

"Who would have thought you'd have made a successful career as a writer? You know, the day I heard you'd quit Harte Investments I told Edith Seaton that you were making a big mistake. 'Edith,' I said, 'that young man is going to ruin his life and break his grandfather's heart.' "

"We all survived, interestingly enough. Mrs. Stiles, I wondered if I could ask you a few questions."

"You're trying to find that missing painting, aren't you?" Betty sighed. "Of course you can ask me some questions, but if what I've heard is true, I'm afraid you're wasting your time."

"Why is that?"

She lowered her voice. "Well, dear, as everyone knows, the most likely suspect is Octavia Brightwell."

"Funny you should mention that, Mrs. Stiles. I've heard the same thing and I'm trying to find out who started that rumor. Thought maybe you could tell me."

"You want to know who *started* it?" Betty asked incredulously.

"That's right."

"But why does it matter, dear? I mean, it's perfectly obvious when you think about it that Miss Brightwell is the person most likely to be the thief."

"It's not obvious to me," Nick said.

"Oh." Betty seemed baffled by that news. Then she gave him a pitying look and patted his arm. "Well, I suppose it's understandable that you would want to think the best of her under the circumstances. But for what it's worth, my advice is to find another girlfriend."

Nick smiled coldly. The hard part about being a real private eye, he decided, was that sometimes it was extremely difficult to avoid losing your temper. But there was nothing to be gained by telling Betty Stiles that she was an interfering busybody.

"I don't plan to take your advice, Mrs. Stiles. So that leaves me with no choice except to find the real thief."

"But if Miss Brightwell took the picture—"

"Octavia didn't take it."

She made a *tut-tut* sound. "You seem very sure of that."

"I'm sure, Mrs. Stiles."

"Really, Nicholas, I wouldn't have thought that you were the type to be so easily taken in by a woman's wiles."

"And here I thought you were too smart to be conned by a thief."

Betty bridled. "I beg your pardon?"

"Isn't it obvious? Whoever started the rumor is the person who stole the painting."

"But that's ridiculous."

"Where did you hear it first, Mrs. Stiles?"

Betty drew herself up with great dignity. "I heard it right here at the beauty shop."

Nick looked past her through the window and saw two women sitting under the hair dryers. They had magazines on their laps but neither was reading. Both were focused intently on the scene taking place outside the shop. The owner of the salon, Carla Millbank, was watching him in the mirror as she wrapped a client's hair in little pieces of aluminum foil.

His conversation with Betty was going to be all over town by nightfall.

His new problem loomed large. The gender divides in Eclipse Bay were still firmly entrenched. There were some places a man could not go. Carla's Custom Cut & Curl was terra incognita for every male in the community.

FIFTEEN minutes later he walked into Bright Visions, still fine-tuning the details of his new scheme.

The place appeared to be empty except for Octavia, who was sitting on the high stool behind the counter. She looked up from some notes she was jotting down on a sheet of paper.

"There you are," she said. "I was getting worried. Did you find Betty Stiles?"

"For all the good it did me." He studied the two framed paintings leaning against the wall. "I don't remember those. Are they new?"

An odd expression crossed her face. "Yes, as a matter of fact."

"I'm no expert, but I like them."

"So do I."

"Nice view of the Arch. The scene of the pier at night is great, too. Sort of moody with the fog and the dark water and that little light on the boat. Who's the artist?"

There was a movement in the doorway behind the counter. Jeremy appeared from the back room. He looked at Nick with a veiled expression.

"That would be me," Jeremy said.

Gail came to stand beside him. "Isn't he terrific?" She was bubbling with enthusiasm. "I've already got a client in mind."

Of course it would be Jeremy, Nick thought. What the hell was the matter with him? How could he have forgotten Jeremy and his *considerable commercial talent.* If he'd been paying attention instead of concentrating on how to get someone inside the beauty shop, he would have put it all together instantly as soon as he saw the pictures. Now he was stuck with doing the polite, civilized thing in front of Octavia and Gail.

"Congratulations," he said to Jeremy, keeping his voice absolutely level. "Nice work."

"Be even nicer work if it pays," Jeremy said. His tone was just as level as Nick's. "But I'm not going to quit my day job anytime soon. I mean, what are the odds of actually being able to make a living by painting? A million to one, maybe?"

"I'm sure Nick knows exactly how you feel," Octavia commented. "He must have had the same doubts when he put his first manuscript in the mail. Isn't that right, Nick?"

She had him neatly cornered, he thought.

"Sure," he said. "And every time I've put a manuscript in the mail since that first one. It always feels a lot like jumping off a cliff."

Obviously it had been a mistake to tell her what lay beneath the surface of this little feud he and Jeremy had going. What was it with her, anyway? Why couldn't she let the two of them conduct their private war without outside interference?

Jeremy looked serious. "The jumping-off-the-cliff thing never goes away?"

Nick shrugged. "Not that I've noticed. My advice is to get used to it. It'll give you an edge." He switched his gaze to Gail. "How would you like to play undercover agent?"

"Do I get to wear a trench coat?" Gail asked.

"Not unless you want to get the collar wet in the shampoo bowl."

Octavia hopped off her stool. "Carla's Custom Cut & Curl? You want Gail to see what she can pick up in the way of gossip in the beauty shop?"

"Yeah. Betty Stiles says that's where she first heard the rumors."

"You're really serious about this detective thing, aren't you?" Jeremy asked Nick.

"No, I just needed something interesting to put down in my journal under the subject of what I did on my summer vacation," Nick retorted.

"Okay, okay, I get the point," Jeremy muttered. "You're serious." He glanced at Octavia. "Is there anything I can do to help?"

"You'll have to ask Nick," she said smoothly. "He's in charge of the investigation."

Jeremy did not look happy with that, but he dutifully turned back to Nick.

"Let me know. My roots in this town run as deep as your own. I might be able to save you some time."

"That's very kind of you, Jeremy," Octavia said. "What do you say, Nick?"

She was not going to let up, Nick thought. She wouldn't be satisfied until he bit the bullet and invited Jeremy out for a beer. Maybe the easiest way out of this mess was to make the offer in front of her. Jeremy would turn it down and then they would both be off the hook.

He glanced at his watch and then at Jeremy. "It's nearly five. I want to talk to Gail about what I need her to do at the beauty shop tomorrow. Then I'm going to have dinner with Octavia." Out of the corner of his eye he saw her raise her brows at that news. But she kept silent as he expected. She knew where he was going with this and she wasn't about to put up any roadblocks. "I figured I'd hit the Total Eclipse later this evening to pick up the latest gossip. You want to join me? I'll buy you a beer and we can play a little pool, keep our ears open, and see what we come up with."

Jeremy's jaw went rigid. But to Nick's astonishment he moved slightly. It was a single, robotic inclination of the head, but it was a definite nod of acceptance.

"Why not?" Jeremy said.

Damn. Now they were both trapped, Nick thought.

Octavia looked quietly pleased. She gave him a warm smile of approval.

An electrifying jolt of awareness shot through him. It was as if the floor of the gallery had opened up beneath his feet and he had plummeted into the abyss.

Oh, shit. He had been asking the wrong question all along, he thought. He had been wondering why Octavia insisted on meddling with his life. The really important question here was why was he allowing her to do so?

THEY ate at the Crab Trap, surrounded by tourists, summer people, and a sprinkling of locals.

"You won't regret this," Octavia said earnestly.

"Uh-huh." He cracked open a crab leg and went after the tender meat with a vengeance.

"Jeremy wouldn't have agreed to have a drink with you if he still believed that you'd had an affair with his wife."

"Uh-huh." He reached for another leg and assaulted it with grim enthusiasm. The sound of crunching shell was good.

"It's obvious that he wants to mend the rift."

"Uh-huh."

"He was just looking for an opportunity and now you've provided it."

"Uh-huh." He looked around for another crab leg to destroy.

"It was the right thing to do, Nick."

"I don't like being manipulated."

"I didn't manipulate you."

"Yes, you did."

"I just made a suggestion."

He looked at her, not speaking.

She swallowed. "Okay, it was a forceful suggestion."

"You nagged me into this meeting tonight."

She reddened. "I'm sorry if you feel that way."

"I do feel that way."

She sat back and folded her napkin very deliberately, her expression troubled now. "You're really mad, aren't you?"

"Yes. I'm really mad. But mostly at myself."

"Because you're allowing me to strongarm you into this meeting with Jeremy?"

"Uh-huh."

"I see." Her voice was steady but when she put down the napkin, her fingers shook slightly. "Well, if you feel that way about it, why don't you cancel the arrangement?"

He smiled humorlessly, staring into the abyss. "It's too late." *In more ways than you can possibly know,* he added silently.

"I don't understand."

"Yeah, I can see that."

⁊ ꙅ

ESTABLISHMENTS like the Total Eclipse had their place in the universe, Nick thought. It was, for instance, the one venue in Eclipse Bay where two guys involved in a private feud could meet on neutral territory.

The tavern was starting to fill up for the evening, but the buzz of conversation was muted in the back, where the pool tables were located. Only one other green-topped table was in use at the moment, and mercifully no one was smoking, so the air was still relatively clear. The gloom hung in thick curtains interrupted only by the narrow bright spot over the center of each table.

If the bar was the place for this conversation, Nick thought, pool was the game. Attitude was everything.

Nick adjusted his stance slightly, made a bridge with his fingers, and leaned into the shot. He stroked the cue gently. Going for a little spin. Concentrating on the follow-through, the way his grandfather and father had taught him. The way he would one day teach Carson. He stayed down until the ball dropped into the pocket.

"You do realize that we've both been set up," he said, straightening.

On the other side of the table, Jeremy watched him from the shadows. "I got that impression. But, hey, she's going to hang my paintings in her gallery. Shooting a little pool with you and letting you buy me a beer doesn't seem like such a high price to pay for my chance at money and immortal fame."

"Uh-huh." Nick chalked his cue. "I figured that was the real reason you agreed. Octavia's got this compulsion to make things right, you know. Has to do with what her great-aunt did to Harte-Madison all those years ago."

"I figured that much out. She says she's leaving town at the end of the summer."

"Yeah." He studied the position of the balls on the table, doing the strategy thing. "That's what she says."

Jeremy studied him across the green felt. "She also says that you didn't have an affair with my ex."

"She's right. I didn't."

Jeremy did not respond to that. But he didn't hurl any more accusations either.

They played for a while, not speaking. The only sounds were the click and snap of the balls striking each other and the gradually rising noise from the front of the tavern. Someone had turned on the music. A country-western rocker was wailing away about a good woman gone bad.

Nick dropped another ball into the pocket. "You know, you're not the only guy in the world whose wife had an affair." He wasn't sure why he said it. It just seemed the right time.

Jeremy went still on the other side of the table. "Amelia?"

"The man who was at the controls of that plane."

"Jesus. I didn't know."

"Not many people do. I'd like to keep it that way."

"Sure. Believe me when I say I understand your feelings on that particular subject." Jeremy paused a couple of beats. "Octavia said I should ask myself whether you or Laura had ever lied to me about other things."

"Come up with any answers?"

"Yeah. Laura lied to me about a couple of other matters. Important stuff. Guess we had a communication problem." Jeremy used the chalk on the tip of his cue. "Couldn't think of any times when you had lied to me, though."

Nick studied the table. "No offense, but I didn't even like Laura very much. Always had the feeling that she figured she'd married beneath herself when she married you."

"No offense, but I didn't care much for Amelia. Figured she was more in love with Harte Investments than she was with you."

"You may have been right." He took his shot and waited until the ball dropped. "But she was a good mother."

"That counts," Jeremy said quietly.

"Counts for a lot."

"At least you have Carson. I found out the hard way that Laura didn't want kids. At least she didn't want them with me."

"Carson made it all worthwhile," Nick agreed.

The sound of the growing crowd in the other room got louder. Someone cranked up the music system another notch. The hard-driving song playing now was about guys getting drunk on cheap whiskey and engaging in bar fights over good women gone bad.

"And to think that we both thought we knew what we were doing when it came to the female of the species." Jeremy drank some beer while he watched Nick take another shot. "Guess we had a lot to learn."

"Yeah."

The atmosphere around the table was more comfortable now. A lot of the tension was leaking out of it. Maybe it was the beer.

"So," Jeremy said, "who do you think took the Upsall?"

"Whoever is trying to pin the blame on Octavia. This is personal. I can feel it."

"Doesn't make sense. Octavia hasn't hurt anyone here in town."

"No, but her great-aunt did."

"According to the old stories, Claudia Banner's victims were Hartes and Madisons." Jeremy made a bridge and angled his cue stick. "You think maybe there were others?"

"My grandfather used the term 'collateral damage.' "

Jeremy banked a shot. "You know, my grandmother was a woman in her twenties when Harte-Madison fell apart. She grew up in this burg and knew everyone. Plays bridge every week with three other women who also have a lot of history in this town. They might remember something useful about the good old days. Want me to talk to her? See if she can get anything out of her bridge group? I'm sure she'd enjoy playing Mata Hari."

"I'd appreciate that," Nick said.

The music got louder and so did the crowd. Other players drifted into the back room and took over the remaining tables. Smoke from the cigarettes of neighboring players started to foul the air.

"Getting late," Nick said.

Jeremy shrugged. "One more game?"

"Why not?"

Nick had just racked the balls for another round when a familiar voice rumbled from the opening that divided the pool room from the bar area.

"Well, if it isn't the SOB who thinks he's the king of Eclipse Bay." Eugene slurred most of the *s*'s and there were a lot of them in the sentence, but his meaning was clear. "And will you look at that, Dwayne? He's shooting a little pool with his good buddy Jeremy. Isn't that sweet?"

The players at the other tables did not look toward the pair in the doorway. Everyone pretended to concentrate on their games. But Nick knew that the crowd was listening intently to every word. The tension was suddenly so thick he could have carved it into topiary shapes.

"You were right," Jeremy said quietly. He did not bother to glance at Eugene and Dwayne either. "Time to go."

"What are you doin' here, anyway, Harte?" Eugene bellowed. "Shouldn't you be with that little redheaded suspect of yours? Everyone knows she's been screwing your brains out so's you'll overlook the fact that she stole that painting."

Nick set the cue down very slowly. On the other side of the table, Jeremy did the same. This time they both looked at Mutt and Jeff.

The dark room fell silent. None of the other players moved so much as a finger. Everyone waited for the other shoe to drop.

Nick looked at Eugene. "You don't want to say anything more, Eugene."

But it was obvious that Eugene was too drunk to worry about consequences.

"You think you can threaten me?" Eugene stalked closer, hands clenched at his sides. "You really think I'm gonna put up with that kind of shit from a Harte?"

"He's right, Eugene," Jeremy said softly. "You don't want to do this."

"I'm not takin' any crap off you, either, Seaton. You think you can come back to town after all these years and start actin' like you're better than the rest of us again just because your mama married a Seaton and you hang with Nick Harte? Got news for you."

"Let's go," Nick said to Jeremy.

"Fine by me." Jeremy started around the table.

"Something me and Dwayne, here, been wondering about, Harte." Eugene came to a halt, blocking the path to the door. He leered. "Is she a *natural* redhead? She as red *down there* as she is up on top?"

Nick moved around the corner of the table.

"Take it easy," Jeremy said out of the side of his mouth. "The plan is to get out of here, remember?"

"The plan," Nick said, coming to a halt directly in front of the pool table, "is to tell everyone here a little story about Eugene and Dwayne's excellent adventure in Seattle a while back."

"Shut your mouth, Harte," Eugene roared. "Just shut your damned mouth. Say one more word and I'll rip your head off your shoulders and use it for a cue ball."

"Think so?"

"Hey, nobody cares if you're screwin' the redhead. Nobody gives a shit about your sex life, Harte."

"Except you, apparently, Eugene," one of the other players offered helpfully. "But maybe that's because Harte's sex life is a lot more interesting than yours."

Eugene turned purple, drew his head into his shoulders in the manner of a large turtle, and lumbered forward. He was surprisingly fast for a man of his size and bulk. The old football training, Nick figured.

"Hell," Jeremy muttered. "So much for a quick exit."

Nick did not move until the last instant. Then he side-stepped the ferocious charge. Eugene still had speed, but his maneuverability was shot. He blundered straight on, past the point where Nick had stood a second earlier, and crashed into the table. He folded over and went facedown on the green felt.

"Okay," Jeremy said. "Now we leave, right?"

Nick ignored him. He grabbed hold of one beefy shoulder. There was no need to try to haul Eugene erect. The big man came up off the table, one massive fist already arcing through the air.

Nick ducked the blow and slammed both clenched hands into Eugene's midsection. It was like hitting a very solid pillow. The impact felt good, but it didn't do much damage. Nick stepped back hurriedly, shaking his numbed hand.

Okay, maybe that had been a mistake.

Fortunately Eugene was off balance, thanks to too many beers and the collision with the table. When he charged a second time, flailing wildly, Nick stuck out a foot. Eugene obligingly tripped and went down with a crashing thud that shook the floor.

Dwayne squealed, grabbed the nearest pool cue, and launched himself at Nick. Jeremy snatched the stick out of his hands as he went past.

"You know," Jeremy said, "if you'd ever bothered to read one of Nick's books, you'd know he never gets into a fight without his trusty sidekick, Bonner."

Robbed of his ersatz rapier, Dwayne scrambled to a halt and turned to throw a short punch at Jeremy. He caught one of the other pool players on the shoulder, instead.

"Hey, watch it, you little creep." The player took a swipe at Dwayne and sent him tumbling into one of the men who had come from the bar area to see what all the excitement was about.

A man standing behind Nick chuckled. "Man, the little redhead must be one hot number, huh? So what's the deal? Is she, or isn't she a natural—"

Nick swung around and punched the commentator in the chest. The man fell back against a table. His cue stick went sailing and struck someone else.

The pool room exploded in a firestorm of shouts and flying fists.

Nick turned back, searching for Eugene amid the swarm of sweating, heaving bodies.

"Son of a bitch, Harte." Eugene had managed to get up off the floor. He threw himself at Nick.

Nick moved out of the way and came up against Sandy Hickson, who had wandered into the pool room. The two went down together and rolled under a table.

Jeremy bent over to look at the pair beneath the table. "Everyone okay down here?"

Someone hauled him up and swung at him. Jeremy took the blow on the side of his jaw and reeled back against a table.

Nick untangled himself from Sandy and came out from under the table in a low rush. He tackled the man who had just hit Jeremy and they both went down, rolling in a small river of spilled beer.

FRED picked up the phone. Sean Valentine and two other officers arrived ten minutes later.

19

SHORTLY before midnight Nick and Jeremy stood with Rafe in the parking lot that fronted the Eclipse Bay Police Department.

"I gotta say, this is a real red-letter occasion for me." Rafe tossed his keys into the air and caught them. "Never thought I'd see the day when a Madison had to bail one of you fine, upstanding, pillar-of-the-community Hartes out of jail. To say nothing of a Seaton."

"If you're looking for undying gratitude, try the Yellow Pages." Jeremy put a cautious hand to his jaw.

"One thing I really hate," Nick muttered, "is a guy who bails you out of jail and then gloats."

"You two are going to look very colorful tomorrow," Rafe said, amused.

"You know, neither of us is in the mood for this." Nick gave him a sour look. "The only thing we want from you right now is a lift back to the Total Eclipse so that we can pick up our cars. Think you can manage that without further comment?"

"No," Rafe said. "You want a ride, you've got to put up with the witty remarks."

Nick exchanged glances with Jeremy. "We could beat him up now or we could do it later."

"I vote for later," Jeremy said. "To tell you the truth, I'm not really up for any more physical activity tonight."

"Okay, later." Nick turned back to Rafe. "Drive."

"My pleasure." Rafe led the way across the parking lot to where he had left Hannah's car.

At that moment another vehicle swung into the lot, briefly dazzling Nick's eyes with its headlights. It came to an abrupt halt nearby. Octavia's fairy-tale coach.

"The perfect end to a delightful evening," Nick said to no one in particular. "It just doesn't get any better than this, does it?"

They all watched the door on the driver's side snap open. Octavia shot out of the front seat. Her red hair was a wild, fiery tangle in the yellow glow of the street lamp.

"No," Rafe said. "It sure doesn't. Oh man, am I ever glad I'm not in your shoes, Nick. All I can say is good luck."

Octavia rushed toward them around the hood of the white compact. She wore a gauzy, ankle-length, flower-patterned skirt and a snug-fitting tee shirt with a deeply scooped neckline. When Nick glanced down, he saw that she was wearing slippers. She had dressed in a hurry.

"I just had a phone call from Hannah. Something about a tavern brawl. Tell me there's been some terrible mistake."

"There's been a mistake, all right," Nick said. "You forgot to put on your shoes. You know, the importance of proper footwear is often overlooked."

"Are you both all right?" she asked.

"Sure," Nick said. "We're fine. Aren't we, Jeremy?"

"We're fine," Jeremy said obligingly.

"They're fine," Rafe assured her.

Nick saw some of her tension ease. The slight shift in the set of her shoulders caused her breasts to move beneath the tee shirt. The thin cotton fabric clung briefly to her nipples and he realized that she was not wearing a bra.

He was suddenly intensely aware of Rafe and Jeremy standing there with him. They were looking at her, just as he was. Probably also noticing that she wasn't wearing a bra.

Annoyed, he yanked off his windbreaker and held it out to her. "Here. Better put this on. It's chilly out here."

She frowned at the jacket, as if she'd never seen one before. He moved closer, putting himself between her and Jeremy and Rafe, and tugged the jacket forcibly around her shoulders. It was so large on her that it fell like a cape in front. He wasn't entirely satisfied, but at least her nipples were no longer visible.

She ignored the jacket to glower at him. "What happened? How did the fight start?"

"Eugene Woods started it," Nick said. He glanced at Jeremy. "Isn't that right?"

"Definitely," Jeremy said. "Eugene Woods was the cause."

Rafe nodded. "Eugene Woods."

"You weren't even there when it happened, Rafe. How do you know?"

"You got a situation involving Mean Eugene and Dickhead Dwayne and you know who started it," Rafe explained.

"Just the way things are in Eclipse Bay," Nick said.

Jeremy opened his mouth to give his two cents' worth. She hushed him with a raised palm and turned back to Nick.

"What was the fight about?"

Nick shrugged. "Bar fight. They happen. Jeremy and I were just in the wrong place at the wrong time."

Suspicion gleamed in her eyes. She turned to Jeremy.

"Tavern brawls are sort of like whirlwinds and tornadoes," Jeremy said seriously. "Forces of nature. They erupt out of nowhere for no known cause."

She moved on to Rafe. "Do I get an answer from you?"

He held up both hands, palms out. Innocent as a lamb. "I wasn't there, remember?"

She looked at Nick again.

"Hey, it was your idea that I buy Jeremy a drink," he reminded her.

She planted her hands on her hips. The movement parted the edges of the windbreaker and stretched the tee shirt across her unconfined breasts. "So this whole thing is my fault? Is that what you're trying to say? Don't you dare blame this on me, Nick Harte."

Nick moved forward again to block his companions' view. "You can take me back to where I left my car."

"Wait a minute, I'm not finished here," she said.

"Yes," he said. "You are."

He put his arms around her shoulders, turned her smartly around, and shoe-horned her into the front seat of her car before she could say another word.

HE followed her back to her cottage and got out of the car to see her to her front door.

"There was no need to follow me home." She shoved her key into the lock.

"It's after midnight and this cottage is pretty isolated out here on the bluff."

"This is Eclipse Bay." She turned the key. "Probably has the lowest crime rate on the entire West Coast."

"It's still late. I'd have worried." But mostly he would have gone crazy alone in bed tonight, thinking about her. Maybe it was some kind of testosterone hangover, a residual effect of the brawl. Or maybe he was in worse shape than he had realized.

She got the door open, stepped inside, and switched on a lamp. Turning, she studied him from the opening. With the light behind her, it was impossible to read her expression. Her red hair formed a fiery aura around her face. She was doing the enigmatic Fairy Queen thing again. He wanted to put her down on a bed and bury himself so deep inside her that she would never be able to forget that she was as human as he was.

"Thank you," she said, ever so polite. "As you can see, I'm home, safe and sound. You may leave now."

He wanted her so badly he'd probably go out into the woods and howl at the moon if she forced him to leave tonight.

He reached out and gripped the door frame. "Invite me inside."

"Why should I do that?"

"How about because I've had a hard night and it was, as you have already noted, your fault."

"I told you not to blame that tavern brawl on me." She tipped her head a little. "By the way, you never told me how things went between you and Jeremy this evening. Were you able to work through some of your issues before the brawl erupted?"

"Oh, yeah, we definitely rebonded."

Her expression softened. "I'm so pleased."

He saw his opening and put one foot over the threshold. "Now can I come inside?"

"Nick—"

He leaned forward and shushed her with a slow, deep kiss, careful not to touch her. If he put his hands on her, he thought, he might not be able to take them off again. Not before morning, at least.

She did not retreat. He felt a little shudder go through her. Progress, he told himself. When he lifted his mouth he saw that her lips were soft and parted.

"You know what?" he said. "I am not in the mood to talk about my issues with Jeremy tonight."

"I understand." The tip of her tongue appeared at the corner of her mouth. "Are you sure you're all right?"

"You already asked me that earlier."

"Yes, I know, but you sound a little weird."

"Possibly because I am feeling a little weird." Also a little wired, he thought. As if he were running on a high-voltage electrical current.

"Maybe you're having some sort of delayed reaction to the violence."

"Maybe."

She raised her hand. He thought she was going to touch his face, but at the last instant she hesitated, fingertips an inch from his jaw. "Did you take any blows to the head?"

"I can't remember." He caught the drifting fingertips in one hand and raised them to his lips. "Could be that I did and it gave me amnesia."

"Nick." Softer now. And there was a broken edge on his name.

He drew one of her fingertips into his mouth and bit gently. She drew in a sharp breath.

He took that as an invitation and glided over the threshold. She moved back to allow him inside. He closed the door behind himself and reached for her.

"Oh, Nick."

And then she was in his arms, clinging wildly, her lips against his throat.

"I was so worried when Hannah told me there had been a fight," she whispered urgently against his neck. "And then she said you were at the police station and that you'd called Rafe to come bail you out and I got mad. But I was still scared, too. It was awful."

"It's okay," he said into her mouth. "Everything is okay."

"Are you sure you're all right?"

"I will be soon."

He scooped her up and carried her toward the hall. There was enough light from the single lamp she had switched on a moment ago to guide him past the darkened bathroom into the shadow-drenched bedroom.

His first thought when he saw the bed was that it was surrounded with ghosts. Then he realized that he was looking at a lot of pale, gauzy draperies. The hangings spilled from a wrought-iron frame that arched overhead.

The hidden bower of the Fairy Queen, he thought.

He let Octavia slide slowly down the length of his body until she was on her feet once more and then he peeled off the tee shirt. He'd been right about the lack of a bra. Her elegantly curved breasts fit perfectly into the palms of his hands. He moved his thumbs lightly across her taut nipples. She closed her eyes.

Another little tremor went through her. He felt his own body shudder in response.

He lowered his hands slowly down her sides, savoring the feel of warm, soft skin until he found the elasticized waistband of the long, flowing skirt. Sliding his palms beneath the band, he pushed the garment down over her hips.

And discovered that a bra was not the only item of underwear that she had neglected that evening.

He let the skirt drop to her ankles. Then he threaded his fingers through the triangle of curling hair. Damned if he would ever tell Eugene or any other man that Octavia was, indeed, a natural redhead.

"You're not wearing any panties," he said against her bare shoulder.

"I was in a hurry when I left the cottage tonight."

"I may go crazy here."

A smile played at the edges of her mouth. She started to unfasten his shirt. "Because I forgot to put on a pair of panties?"

"Doesn't take much to drive me over the edge when I'm this close to you."

"I'm glad."

She separated the edges of his shirt and flattened her palms against his chest. "I'm not feeling wholly sane myself at the moment."

He eased her backward, kissing her with every step, until she came up against the high bed. The ghostly bed curtains drifted gently behind her, guarding the interior of the secret bower.

He did not take his mouth from hers when he reached behind her to pull the hazy fabric aside. Grasping the quilt, he pulled it straight down to the foot of the bed, exposing pristine white sheets.

He picked her up, put her down on the pale bedding, and stepped back to finish undressing himself. The wispy bed hangings drifted closed. On the other side of the veil Octavia watched him through the misty material. She lay on her side, knees slightly bent, hips curved in graceful, seductive lines.

He stood there for a few seconds, every muscle rigid with the effort it took to exert some control over the aching, raging need that was uncoiling rapidly throughout his body. It had never been like this with any other woman, he thought, baffled and bemused. He could not seem to wrap his mind around this sensation. It was not just physical. He was old enough and sufficiently experienced to take the physical effects in stride.

There was something else going on here. He knew that in the depths of his soul. He'd been trying to ignore it, work around it, deny it, but there was no possibility of avoiding the reality. Octavia was different.

He looked at her through the drifting veils that surrounded the bed, and for a moment he wondered if she really was a sorceress who had somehow managed to enchant him.

He had no time to wonder about his predicament. The heaviness of his erection made it impossible to think clearly. He fought his way out of the rest of his clothing.

When he pulled the bed hangings aside the second time, Octavia reached for him, drawing him down onto the snowy sheets. He put one hand on the sweet, round curve of her hip and she twisted urgently against him.

"Nick."

"Not so fast," he whispered.

But she was moving, sliding, slipping along the length of him. He felt her mouth on his chest and then her tongue touched his belly.

When her fingers curled around him and her lips moved lower, he thought he'd disintegrate.

He rolled her onto her back, pinning her with one leg thrown across her thighs. "I meant what I said. We're going to take this nice and slow."

"Are we?" Her voice was both mischievous and sensual. A woman who knows she's in control of the situation. She wriggled a little beneath his weight. "Do you really want to go slow?"

"Most definitely," he said. "I want to go slow tonight. And what's more, I'm going to make sure that we do."

She drew her fingertips down the length of his back. "Wanna bet?"

"Oh, yeah."

He bent his head and covered her mouth with his own. When she was absorbed in the kiss, giving herself completely over to it, working her sorcery, he reached out and snagged one of the trailing bed hangings.

He looped the fabric around her left wrist and tied a quick knot in it.

"Ummph?"

She wrenched her mouth away from his. Her eyes snapped open.

He grasped a wispy hanging on the opposite side of the bed and anchored her other wrist.

"Oh, my." She looked up at him, sexy laughter sparkling in her eyes. "This is interesting."

He leaned over her, bracing his weight on his elbows. "I thought so."

"All this just to slow me down?"

"I'm a desperate man."

She could pull the airy bed hangings down and free herself with a couple of quick tugs, but somehow he didn't think she would do that. He sensed that she was in a mood to walk on the wild side tonight. He could tell because he was inclined in the same direction. A shining example of synchronicity at work.

"What happens next?" she murmured.

"I don't know." He slid one hand between her legs and found the pearl in the oyster. He smiled when he felt her move beneath him, seeking more. "Shall we find out?"

"Oh, yes." She licked her lips and looked up at him through veiled lashes. "Let's do that."

He stroked her slowly, dampening his hand in her dew.

She lifted her hips against his fingers, tempting him with her body. She could have lured an angel into trouble. And he was no angel.

He moved down her body with his mouth, going lower until her scent enveloped him. He was so hard now he dared not brush his erection against her skin for fear of losing the fragile grip on his self-control. This was going to be a test of endurance and he was determined to make sure that he won tonight.

Eventually, when she was moaning and restless, he found the small, sensitive nubbin with his mouth. She caught her breath and tensed.

"Nick."

He used his tongue until she was gasping and writhing.

"Yes, please, *yes*. Now, damn it."

He slid a finger into her, searching for the spot; pressed upward. She gasped.

"*Yes*. Right there. Oh, yes. Oh, yes, oh, yes, oh, yes. *Nick*."

She came in shuddering little waves of raw, feminine energy that took his breath away. He barely made it back up her body in time to sink himself fully into her before his own climax ripped through him.

She jerked her arms abruptly and then her nails were in his back and her legs were wrapped snugly around his hips. The last thing he remembered was the feel of the bed hangings floating down like so many silken cobwebs, tangling him in a snare he did not think that he would ever be able to escape.

※ ※

HE came back to his senses a long time later. For a moment he did not open his eyes, preferring to savor the satisfaction that hummed through him. He was content to drift forever in the aftermath of the lovemaking.

Then he felt the soft touch of gauzy fabric twining around his right wrist. He opened one eye. Octavia's breasts brushed across his chest when she leaned over him to secure his other wrist to the bedpost. He opened his other eye.

"What's going on here?" he asked with lazy interest.

She straddled him and smiled slowly. "My turn."

"Oh, wow."

※ ※

SHE felt him leave the bed again shortly before dawn. Dismay and regret and a strange resentment whispered through her. She opened her eyes and stared at the wall, listening to him pad barefooted across the floor.

Of course he was leaving. What had she expected him to do? Stay until morning? What would be the point? This was a summer affair.

But she was not about to let him just slide out like this. He could say a proper goodbye when he left her bed, damn it.

She turned on her side, searching for him in the shadows, expecting to see him making for the bathroom with his clothes. But he wasn't creeping across the carpet.

He stood at the window, one hand braced against the sill, and looked out at the moonlit bay. The pale glow streaming through the glass etched his shoulders in steely silver and cast his profile into deep shadow.

"Nick?" She levered herself up on her elbows. "What are you doing?"

He turned his head to look toward the bed. "I was just thinking."

"About what?"

"About what happens at the end of the summer."

She did not move. She did not even breathe. "This isn't The Talk, is it? Because if you're trying to sneak it in now—"

"It's not The Talk," he said, his voice roughening abruptly.

She stared at him. "Are you angry?"

"Maybe. Yeah. I think so. I'm trying to have a rational discussion here and you're throwing that crap about The Talk in my face."

He was angry, all right. Fair enough. She was rapidly losing her temper, too.

"Okay, sorry," she said stiffly. "I just wanted to be sure you weren't going to try to deliver that stupid talk now. Because it's much too late."

He did not move for a few seconds. Then he came away from the window and walked back to the bed to stand looking down at her.

"Too late?" he repeated neutrally.

"Whether you like it or not, we are involved in a relationship. It may not work out for a variety of reasons, but I'll be damned if I'll let you put some arbitrary limit on it."

"There seems to be some confusion here," he said coldly. "You're accusing me of trying to specify the time and date when this thing between us ends, but I'm not the one who keeps talking about leaving Eclipse Bay in a few weeks."

She opened her mouth to argue and then closed it quickly.

Okay, he had a point.

She cleared her throat. "That's different."

"Like hell."

She glowered. "I have to be pragmatic. I've got a business to sell. That takes time and planning. And then there's the move. A person can't make those sorts of arrangements on a last-minute basis."

He put one knee on the tumbled bedding. "You're the one who's running scared here."

"That's not true."

"Hell, maybe we've both been running scared for a while." He came down on top of her, pushing her back onto the pillows. "But I think it's time we both stopped."

"You do?"

"If you want to sleep with me, lady, you're going to have to take a few chances."

"Is that so?"

"Yeah."

"What about you?" she managed. "Are you willing to take a few risks, too?"

His smile was slow and enigmatic in the shadows. His eyes had never been more dangerous. Or promised so much.

"I've been taking chances since the day I met you," he said. "Want to know why I didn't give you The Talk back at the beginning of this affair?"

"Yes."

"I forgot about it, that's why. Never even crossed my mind to give you The Talk." He brushed his mouth across hers. "You see? Taking chances."

"Oh."

He bent his head again and put his mouth to her throat. She felt the edge of his teeth against her skin and excitement stormed through her. She wrapped her arms around him and stopped thinking about the end of summer.

20

GAIL rushed through the door of the gallery shortly after ten-thirty the next morning. "You won't believe this."

"What's that?" Octavia came around the corner of one of the display panels and stopped, staring in amazement. "You're right. I don't believe it. Good grief, what happened? You've got Very Big Hair."

"What? Oh, yeah, my hair." Gail grimaced and put up a hand to touch the crisply starched mountain of hair on top of her head. "You owe me for this, boss. Big time."

Octavia shook her head slowly in disbelief. She could not get over her hair. "That's amazing."

"Carla wanted to color it, too, but I drew the line at that."

"Let me guess. Blonde?"

"Probably. I didn't get into a discussion of shades. I told her I needed to think about such a major move." Gail waved that aside. "But that's not important. What's important here is what I heard while I was trapped in the chair."

"Ah, yes." Octavia propped a scene of Hidden Cove at dawn against the panel. "Your undercover assignment. I almost forgot. Well?"

Gail drew herself up proudly. "Laugh if you will, but I found out something you really ought to know."

Octavia reached up to remove a picture of the marina from a panel. "Okay, Madam Spy. What did you find out at the beauty shop?"

Gail leaned against the counter and examined her nails. "Not much."

"I'm not surprised." She set the marina scene aside and hoisted the picture of Hidden Cove.

"Just two tiny little snippets of information that you might find interesting."

Octavia hung the Hidden Cove picture on the panel in the space that had been previously occupied by the painting of the marina. "And those two tiny little snippets would be?"

"Well, for starters, I found out what caused the big fight at the Total Eclipse last night."

"It was a bar brawl." Octavia stepped back to study the position of the picture she had just hung. "I have it on excellent authority that such events are random acts of nature. They don't need a cause."

"This one apparently had a very specific cause," Gail murmured dryly.

"Really?" Octavia made a tiny adjustment to the frame. "And what was it?"

"You."

Octavia's fingers stilled on the frame. "Someone said that I was the cause?"

"Actually, *everyone* is saying it this morning."

Octavia turned slowly. "That's very irritating."

"Irritating? Is that the best you can do? I expected a more forceful reaction."

"Well, it's also extremely annoying and a complete misrepresentation of the facts."

Gail slumped back against the counter. "I don't believe it. I am doomed to go through a Very Big Hair day and all you can say is that the information I brought back from my mission is irritating, annoying, and a misrepresentation of the facts?"

Jeremy came through the open door of the gallery. He had three cups of coffee cradled in the wedge formed by his hands.

"What's irritating, annoying, and a misrepresentation of the facts?" He stopped abruptly, staring at Gail. "Oh, jeez. I see what you mean. They really did a number on you down at the beauty shop, didn't they? I hope the information you got was worth the torture you had to go through to get it."

"Unfortunately the torture has only begun." Gail sighed in exasperation. "I have to live with this hair for the rest of the day. But for the record, the information I picked up is downright fascinating."

"I sure hope so. Any news on the Upsall?"

"Unfortunately, last night's excitement dominated the conversation. No one was talking about anything else this morning." She studied him as he came toward the counter. "Good heavens, you've got a shiner."

"I've already looked in a mirror today." Jeremy put the cups down beside her. "Tell me something I don't know."

"It's from the brawl last night, isn't it?" Gail stepped closer, concern darkening her expression. "I knew you were at the Total Eclipse with Nick, but I didn't realize you got hurt. Have you seen a doctor?"

"I don't need a doctor. I'm okay." He peeled the lids off the coffee cups. "Here you go, sugar and cream."

"Thanks." She took the cup from him without glancing at it, still studying his black eye with a troubled air. "Did you put ice on it?"

"For a while. Don't worry about it. Looks a lot worse than it is." Jeremy handed the second cup to Octavia. "Cream, right?"

"Yes. Thank you." She took the cup in both hands and stared at his bruised face. "Are you sure you're all right?"

"I'm sure." He chuckled. "You oughta see the other guy."

"What other guy?" she asked swiftly.

"Nick. I've got a hunch he looks a lot worse than I do this morning. He was in the middle of most of the action last night, as I recall. Just my bad luck to be standing around in the vicinity when it all went down. Yeah, I expect old Nick has a couple of beautiful shiners this morning."

Octavia concentrated on removing the lid from her cup. She became aware of an acute silence. When she looked up she saw that both Gail and Jeremy were watching her with rapt attention.

"Something wrong?" she asked politely.

"Uh, no." Jeremy raised his brows. "Just wondered why you weren't a little more concerned about Nick, that's all."

"He looked fine last night when I saw him outside the police station."

"I looked okay last night, too. Bruises take a while to color up. I figure he's probably a real mess today."

"He's not," she said shortly.

"You're sure?"

"I saw him earlier." Octavia dropped the lid into the trash bin.

"Earlier," Jeremy repeated. "That would be earlier this morning?"

"Yes." She took a tentative sip of the coffee. It was still a little too hot for comfort. She blew on the surface of the liquid a few times.

"Precisely how early this morning would that be?" Gail asked with great interest.

"I don't recall the exact time. Why? Is it important?"

"Could be." Gail exchanged glances with Jeremy. "Especially if it was, oh, say sometime around dawn or thereabouts."

"That would be critical," Jeremy agreed.

"And it would confirm the second tidbit of information I got this morning," Gail added smoothly.

Octavia peered at each of them in turn. "Am I missing something here?"

"You can tell us, honey," Gail answered. "We're your friends."

"Sure," Jeremy said. "You can tell us everything."

"Out with it," Gail said. "We're on pins and needles here. The suspense is killing us. Did Hardhearted Harte really spend the whole night with you last night? Was he actually there for breakfast? Did you or did you not break the curse?"

Too late Octavia recalled the second part of the Nick Harte legend. *He always leaves before dawn.* She felt herself turn red. "I really don't think that's any of your business."

"Oh, gosh," Gail said. "Both of the rumors I heard at the beauty shop are true. Nick got into that brawl because of you *and then he spent the night with you.* You've done it. You've broken the curse on Hardhearted Harte."

Octavia choked on a mouthful of coffee. She sputtered and dabbed madly at her lips. *"That's* what they're saying at the beauty shop?"

"Yep."

"I've never met anyone who broke a curse before," Jeremy said. "How does it feel? Do you get a little rush when it happens? Or do you have to wait for results?"

"Yes, tell us every little detail," Gail said.

"Hold it right there." Octavia slapped the coffee cup down on the counter. Drops of coffee shot over the rim and splattered the wood surface. "Let's get something straight. Apparently Nick is having fun telling people that he got into the brawl because I suggested he have a drink with you, Jeremy. Big joke. Ha ha."

"Well—"

"Okay, okay, maybe it *was* my idea for you two to have a beer together and talk things over. But it's quite a stretch to say that the bar fight was therefore my fault. I certainly never intended for Nick to take you to the Total Eclipse for that beer and chat."

"Where else could a couple of guys go to talk over old times in this burg?" Gail asked innocently.

"You misunderstand, Octavia," Jeremy said gently. "Nick's not spreading the story that he got into the fight because of you. It's all over town this morning because it's the flat-out truth and everyone who was in the Total Eclipse last night knows it. There are witnesses. Lots and lots of them. They're the ones who are doing the talking."

"But all I did was suggest that you two have a drink." Her voice was rising. That almost never happened. "It's not fair to blame me."

"There's a little more to it than that," Jeremy said.

"And what's with this nonsense about breaking the curse?" She no longer cared that she was getting loud. "Are there witnesses to that, too?"

Nick appeared in the doorway at that moment, three coffee cups in his hands. He studied the trio in the gallery through the lenses of his dark glasses and appeared to make an executive decision.

"Maybe I should come back later." He started to step back out onto the sidewalk.

Octavia rounded on him. "Don't you dare leave. Get back in here right now. Do you hear me, Nick Harte?"

"Oh, yeah." Nick went to the counter and set down the three cups. "I definitely hear you."

She crossed her arms and faced the three of them. "Let's try to get some clarity on this issue."

"Damn." Nick removed his dark glasses with obvious reluctance and dropped them into his pocket. "Do we have to do clarity? I hate the clarity thing." He looked at the cup Gail held and the one that sat on the counter. "You've already got coffee."

"I brought it," Jeremy explained.

Nick glanced at him. "You look like hell."

"Which is extremely unfair," Jeremy said, "given that I was just an innocent bystander."

"Innocent bystanders have a very high accident rate," Nick informed him with an air of authority. "Look it up."

"I'll remember that. But, you know, you might want to show a little gratitude here, Harte. I'm the one who took that cue stick away from Dickhead before he could ram it where the sun don't shine."

Nick nodded. "I am, indeed, grateful for that. By the way, that reminds me. You mentioned True's sidekick, Bonner, last night. Do you read my books?"

"What can I say? A divorced man has a lot of spare time on his hands."

"Is that how you got the black eye?" Gail asked Jeremy. "Did Dickhead hit you with the pool cue?"

"Actually, it was a little more complicated than that," Jeremy said.

"Excuse me," Octavia said very loudly.

They all looked at her with polite expectation.

"As I was about to say before I was so rudely interrupted," she went on, not even trying to lower her voice, "I want to know why everyone in town believes that I was the cause of that stupid bar fight last night."

"Probably because, as I just told you, it's true." Jeremy took a swallow of coffee.

"It is *not* true," she shot back.

"According to the ladies down at the beauty parlor, it is," Gail offered. "That's all anyone could talk about. That and the fact that Nick spent the night at your place, of course."

Nick paused in the act of taking a sip of coffee. "Folks are discussing that, too?"

"With relish and zest," Gail assured him.

"Huh." He shrugged and drank more coffee.

Octavia threw up her hands. "Okay, so I suggested that you two have a drink together. How was I to know you'd be dumb enough to have that drink at the Total Eclipse?"

"It wasn't the fact that Nick bought me a beer that started the fight," Jeremy said with grave precision. "The fight started when Mean Eugene announced to the entire bar that you had bestowed your favors upon Nick for certain agenda-driven reasons."

She stared at him. "I beg your pardon?"

"Eugene implied that you had commenced an affair with Nick, here, with the goal of causing him to become so bemused and befuddled that he would be unable to think clearly. The net result would be that our intrepid investigator would be unable to detect that you were the person most likely to have stolen the Upsall."

Octavia made it to the end of the counter and grabbed hold of it to steady herself. "Good lord."

"Of course, Eugene didn't put it in precisely those words." Jeremy glanced at Nick for confirmation. "Don't think he used the words 'bemused' and 'befuddled,' did he?"

"No," Nick said. "I believe what Eugene said was that Octavia was 'screwing me senseless.'"

Jeremy shook his head. "Don't think he said 'senseless,' either. Maybe it was 'screwing your brains out.'"

"Right." Nick raised a cup in a small salute. "That was it. He said that Octavia was 'screwing my brains out' in an effort to distract me from my investigation."

Jeremy turned to Octavia. "There was also some question about the naturalness of your red hair. Naturally, Nick could not let Eugene and Dickhead get away with talking about a lady in such crude terms. Hence the bar brawl."

Octavia clutched the counter, feeling dazed and disoriented. She looked at Nick, hoping he would tell her it was all just a big joke. "The brawl really did start because of me?"

"Don't worry about the gossip," Nick said, dismissing the entire event with another shrug. "It'll blow over in a few days."

"Are you kidding?" Jeremy asked. "Folks around here still talk about the big fight between your grandfather and Mitchell Madison that took place outside of Fulton's decades ago. What makes you think that forty or fifty years from now, they won't be telling the story of what happened last night at the Total Eclipse?"

"Jeremy's right," Gail said. "You're a Harte, Nick, and Octavia is related to the woman who sparked the original Harte-Madison feud. Trust me, the legend of the big brawl at the Total Eclipse will live on forever."

Jeremy nodded in agreement. "Mostly because there's so little to talk about in a small town like this."

"WELL, it's only to be expected, I suppose. You do know she is related to that Claudia Banner woman. The one who started the Harte-Madison feud all those years ago."

Octavia froze in the act of putting the six-pack of bottled spring water in the basket of the supermarket cart. The voice came from the next aisle over, the one labeled CANNED VEG & BEANS.

"My Hank said there hasn't been a brawl like that at the Total Eclipse in ages. Not since that biker club came through town three years back. Fred claims that there was a couple of thousand dollars worth of damage done in the pool room last night."

She recognized the voices now. Megan Grayson and Sandra Finley. Both women had come into Bright Visions to browse on occasion and both served on the Summer Celebration committee.

"If you ask me, Fred's just taking advantage of a golden opportunity," Megan said. "One of the Willis brothers told my husband that Fred has been thinking about repainting the Total Eclipse for years. He put it off because he was too cheap to pay for the job. But he knows he can get the money out of Nick Harte and Jeremy Seaton now, so why not go for it?"

"You have to wonder why Nick and Jeremy were playing pool together in the first place. Those two haven't had much to do with each other in a couple of years. Not since Jeremy's divorce, in fact. Everyone assumed they'd had a falling out of some kind."

"And then they both went and dated Octavia Brightwell here in Eclipse Bay." Sandra made a disapproving noise that sounded a lot like the clucking of a chicken. "That can't have helped the situation. In fact, you'd have thought that those two would have been at each other's throats by now. Nothing like a woman coming between two men to cause trouble."

"Well, from all accounts they were on the same side in that bar fight last night. Sounds like they must have settled their differences."

"Who would have thought a Harte and a Seaton would get into a barroom brawl? Oh, sure, you expect that sort of thing from a Madison, but I always thought the Hartes and the Seatons were a lot more refined."

"Don't you believe that for one moment," Megan said. "Remember, it was Sullivan Harte who got into that fistfight with Mitch Madison all those years ago and launched the feud. And from what I've heard, the Seatons aren't all saints, either. I can imagine how poor Edith must feel today. They say she's absolutely beside herself this morning because of what happened last night. Didn't even open her shop. Probably can't face the gossip."

"More likely she can't stand to be civil to Octavia Brightwell," Sandra said. "I mean, everyone knows that Octavia was the cause of the fight that involved Edith's precious grandson."

"Edith has always been so proud of Jeremy. I swear his divorce hit her harder than it did him. She was so thrilled that he'd married into such a *fine* family, remember? Not that the *fine* family ever gave her the time of day, as far as I could tell. Word had it that they encouraged the divorce."

"And now he's involved in a free-for-all at the Total Eclipse. No wonder she doesn't want to show her face in public today."

"By the way, you did hear that Nick Harte spent the night with Octavia Brightwell?"

"I certainly did. His car was seen leaving her place at eight o'clock this morning."

Megan giggled. "Word is, she may have broken the curse."

"I think it's a lot more likely that Nick Harte is having himself a little fun this summer. It'll end when he goes back to Portland."

"If you ask me, it's Octavia Brightwell who ought to go into hiding. She should be ashamed of herself. When you stop and think about it, she's the real problem here."

"A real troublemaker," Sandra agreed. "Back in high school we had a name for women like that."

That does it, I've had enough, Octavia thought. She wheeled her cart around the corner and started down Canned Veg & Beans.

"Good morning, Sandra. Megan." She gave both women a brilliant smile. "Lovely day, isn't it?"

Sandra and Megan hushed instantly. They gripped the handles of their shopping carts and stared at her as though she had materialized out of thin air.

"I couldn't help overhearing your conversation." Octavia jerked her own cart to a halt a short distance away and blocked the aisle with it. "And I am very curious to find out exactly what word you had for *women like me* back in high school, Sandra."

Sandra Finley turned an unpleasant shade of red. "I don't know what you're talking about. You must have misunderstood."

"She's right," Megan said quickly. "You didn't hear her correctly." She looked triumphant. "It never pays to eavesdrop, you know."

"Hard to avoid hearing you two, since you insist upon discussing me in the middle of a grocery store aisle."

"You'll have to excuse me." Megan glanced at her watch. "I've got a committee meeting at three."

"So do I," Sandra said. She tightened her grip on the cart handle.

Octavia did not shift her shopping cart out of their path. "You know, speaking of names that we used back in high school, I remember one that fits both of you perfectly. Rhymes with rich."

Sandra got her jaw back into place. "Did you just call me a bitch?"

"I really don't have time for this," Megan said.

Having concluded that she could not go forward, she swung her shopping cart into a tight U-turn. And promptly banged into Sandra's cart. The baskets jammed together. The wheels snagged, making it impossible for either woman to maneuver out of the aisle.

Octavia surveyed her captive audience. "Now, then, I have a suggestion. Since the two of you are obviously going to spend the rest of the day spreading gossip, what do you say we take a few minutes to get one particular fact straight?"

"I don't know what you're talking about," Sandra said stiffly.

Octavia ignored that. "For the record, Nick Harte did *not* leave my cottage at eight o'clock this morning. That is a flat-out lie."

Megan and Sandra looked at her, suddenly rapt. Neither said a word.

"He left at precisely seven-thirty-five," Octavia said coolly. "I remember, because we had just finished breakfast together and I turned on the radio to catch the morning news."

Megan and Sandra blinked.

Octavia smiled. "Hey, you know what? I'll bet that *women like you* are the sort who will appreciate a few of the more intimate details about my relationship with Nick. I'm sure there are probably all kinds of stories going around about us and the techniques I used to break the curse."

Megan and Sandra's jaws dropped.

Octavia leaned forward, bracing her arms on the handle of her cart, and assumed a confidential air. "I imagine you'd like to hear just how I did it, wouldn't you? Are you ready for this? I made poached eggs and toast for Nick's breakfast."

A thunderous hush fell on the adjoining aisles. It seemed to Octavia that the whole of Fulton's had suddenly gone silent.

"My secret is a little Dijon mustard on the toast under the eggs." She winked. "Trust me, it really adds some zip. You should have seen Nick's face when I put that plate down in front of him. Talk about a man who looks like he thinks he's died and gone to heaven."

Megan and Sandra were no longer watching her. Their gazes were riveted on a point just beyond her shoulder.

I'm getting an audience, Octavia thought. Terrific. Another little scene, the details of which would be all over town by sundown. The really interesting thing was that she did not give a damn. Not right now at any rate. Right now she was on a roll.

"If you think that the thing with the mustard is kinky, wait until I tell you how Nick got his coffee this morning," she said in a gossipy tone. "Talk about getting down to the good stuff. So, there we were, sitting at the breakfast table and I can tell that he's ready for a second cup, you know? I mean, he's *really, really* ready for it. Wow. This man is *hot* for another cup, if you get my drift."

"Might be a good idea to give everyone some time to cool off before you tell them about the coffee thing," Nick said behind her. He sounded amused, but there was the barest hint of a warning in his voice. "I'm not sure Eclipse Bay is ready for the details of my second cup of coffee."

She spun around. Reality came back with a jarring thud.

"I think it might be a good idea to check out now," he said.

She wondered just how big a fool she had made of herself. He was right. This was a very, very good time to check out.

"Okay." She whipped the cart around and headed for the checkout counter, leaving Sandra and Megan still tangled up in Canned Veg & Beans.

"I hope you don't mind me interrupting back there," Nick said, falling into step beside her. "It's just that some things are personal, you know? That stuff about the second cup of coffee? That's special to a sensitive guy like me."

"Oh, for heaven's sake, Nick, you didn't even have a second cup of coffee this morning and you know it."

"Are you sure?"

"Of course I'm sure. Can't you remember what you had for breakfast?"

"It's all a blur after the eggs and mustard."

21

AT four o'clock that afternoon he went back to the gallery to check on Octavia. She had looked good during the scene with Sandra and Megan at Fulton's, but underneath he thought he had detected some additional strain.

"She's not here," Gail said the instant he walked through the door. "She went home early."

"She never goes home early," Nick said.

"She did today."

He was getting more concerned by the minute. "Is she okay?"

"I don't think so." Gail exhaled deeply. "She's lived in town off and on for over a year and she's been hanging out a lot with Hartes and Madisons, but that doesn't mean she's completely acclimated to our quaint little traditions here in Eclipse Bay. In spite of the way she handled Sandra and Megan, I think she's a lot more upset about the gossip that is going around than she's letting on."

Nick frowned. "You really think it's bothering her? Seemed like she was dealing with it fairly well earlier."

Gail watched him very steadily. "The brawl last night was bad enough. But the fact that everyone is talking about how you spent the night at her place is a real problem, I think."

"Why? Everyone knows that we're seeing each other. It's no secret. She's aware of that."

"No offense, but I do believe that you're missing the point here," Gail said. "You were seen driving away from her cottage at eight o'clock this morning."

"Seven-thirty-five, and so somebody noticed my car coming from the direction of her cottage early this morning. So what? Not the first time."

"Yes, it is, as a matter of fact."

"You're right, I am missing something here. You want to run that by me again?"

Gail picked up a stack of brochures announcing the Children's Art Show and made a pretense of straightening them. "Eight o'clock or, to be precise, seven-thirty-five, is well after dawn at this time of year."

"What about it?"

"Pay attention, Nick." She slapped the brochures back down on the counter. "The word has gone out that Octavia has broken the curse."

"Yeah? So?"

"You do know about the curse, don't you?"

"That idiotic story about me that claims that I never spend the entire night with a woman?" He waved that aside. "I've heard about it, sure."

"Well?" she demanded.

"It probably got started because I've never left Carson with a sitter overnight. But it doesn't follow that I never have any nights to myself. Carson stays with family once in a while. He's with his grandfather and his great-grandfather and Lillian and Gabe at the moment. Leaving me free to do as I please at night."

"So, does that mean that you *do* sometimes spend the entire night with a woman with whom you're romantically involved?" Gail asked with disconcerting interest.

"Guys don't get *romantically* involved."

"What do they get?"

"Involved, period."

"Oh, sure, I knew that. So, do you sometimes spend the entire night with women with whom you're *involved, period?*"

"You know, I didn't come here to discuss my love life with a woman who has Very Big Hair."

"That was a low blow." Gail patted the rigid outer layer of her voluminous hairdo. "I was only carrying out my assignment."

"Yeah." Nick went toward the door. "Too bad you didn't learn anything useful about that damned painting."

Gail straightened her shoulders and held her chin high. "In the long run, I feel that I discovered something infinitely more important."

"Such as?"

"The name of the woman who broke the curse on Hardhearted Harte."

He went out onto the sidewalk and slammed the door closed.

TWENTY minutes later he stood on the bluff above the small, crescent-shaped beach, looking down. She was sitting on a rock, knees drawn up under a long, geranium-red skirt, her face hidden beneath the wide brim of a big straw hat. The now-familiar flicker of intense awareness crackled through him, tightening his belly and heating his blood.

It was a deeply sensual feeling, but he could not slap the label *great sex* on this and let it go at that. He had known that from the beginning.

He watched her there in the sunlight, her skirt fluttering a little in the breeze, her gracefully rounded arms wrapped around her knees, and he finally understood.

This strange, bone-deep sensation that he always experienced when he thought about her or when he was in her vicinity wasn't merely desire or anticipation. It was a sense of connection. In some manner that he knew he would probably never fully comprehend, he was linked to her now.

He had never known this particular kind of bond, he realized. Perhaps it would have developed eventually with Amelia if they had had more time and if he had not screwed things up by quitting Harte Investments and if she had not turned to an old lover when the chips were down.

No. It would never have been like this with Amelia. It could never be like this with anyone else.

Maybe the rumors were right. Maybe he had been under some kind of curse.

But what was the point of being freed if he lost the lady who had the magic touch?

She turned slightly, obviously aware that someone was on the bluff behind her. The straw brim of the hat tilted at an angle and he caught a glimpse of her face. She had on a pair of dark glasses. He could not read her expression but he got the distinct impression that she was not overly thrilled to see him. She was certainly not waving.

He found the path that led to the beach and went down it swiftly. Tiny pebbles scattered before him.

When he got to the bottom he walked toward Octavia feeling as if he were walking toward his destiny. She did not take off her sunglasses. It occurred to him that he was still wearing his, too. Neither of them could tell what the other was thinking, he realized.

"Are you all right?" he asked.

"Yes."

"Gail was worried about you. She said you'd left the shop in a hurry."

"There's nothing to be concerned about. I just wanted to get away for a while. I need to think."

He sat down beside her on the broad, sun-warmed rock. Close enough to be intensely conscious of her nearness; not quite touching. A curious kind of panic started to gnaw at his insides. She really was upset. He was not sure how to deal with it.

"I'm sorry the three of us gave you so much grief this morning," he said. "We were just teasing you."

"I know."

"I realize these past few days have been rough on you. You're not accustomed to being the subject of local gossip."

"It's not that."

"People were bound to talk after it got out that we were seeing each other," he said. "But the gossip will fade when folks get used to the idea."

"I don't particularly care what people think of our relationship."

That did not sound good, he thought. He turned his head to get a better look at her profile. She remained enigmatic behind the shields of her dark glasses.

"You don't care that everyone's discussing our relationship down at the beauty parlor and in the aisles at Fulton's?" he asked carefully.

She unclasped her knees and braced her arms behind her, flattening her palms on the rock. "Well, it feels a little strange to be the subject of so much local interest, but I've had plenty of opportunity to see how the Hartes and the Madisons handle that sort of situation. I thought I was dealing with it very well."

"You are," he agreed immediately. "You're handling it beautifully."

"And, as you just said, the talk will fade in time."

"Sure." He mentally crossed his fingers. "Eventually."

She said nothing else; just sat there, gazing thoughtfully out over the bay.

"So," he said when he could no longer stand the suspense. "If it's not the fact that everyone is chatting about how I spent the night at your place that's bothering you, what, exactly, is the problem here?"

"The bar fight last night."

He exhaled slowly. "I was afraid it might be that. Look, I'm sorry it happened, but it was just a case of a bunch of guys who'd been drinking some beer and got carried away. Not the first time it's happened at the Total Eclipse, and it sure as hell won't be the last."

"I realize that." She finally turned her head to look directly at him. "But it is the first time anyone has ever gotten into a fight on account of me."

Dread settled heavily in the pit of his stomach. "Okay, so you're accustomed to dating a classier sort of guy. The type who doesn't get into bar brawls. Would it help if I told you that I don't make a habit of that kind of thing?"

She just looked at him for a small eternity. Her mouth twitched a couple of times.

And then she was laughing so hard that tears started to run down her face beneath the rims of her dark glasses.

He watched her for a while, fascinated. "Did I say something funny?"

"Yes." She yanked off the dark glasses and dried her eyes on the sleeve of her gold shirt. "Yes, you said something very, very funny."

"You know you're losing it when you don't get your own jokes."

She pulled herself together with a visible effort. The laughter faded into giggles and then shrank into a wide smile. Her eyes were warm and clear and bright with the remnants of her amusement.

"You're not losing it," she said. "We're just not quite in synch here. What I was trying to tell you is that I have never considered myself the type of woman who is capable of launching a barroom brawl."

"You're not."

"You're wrong. Clearly I must be that type because I did ignite that fight last night. The facts are on the record from dozens of witnesses, apparently."

He winced. "This is one of those no-win situations, isn't it? Any way I respond, I screw up big-time."

She ignored that. "I like it."

"What? That I'm trapped in a lose-lose scenario?"

"No, that I'm the type of woman who has what it takes to spark a tavern brawl."

"Huh."

"I also like being the type of woman who inspires gossip in the beauty shop and creates great excitement in the supermarket aisles."

"Uh-huh."

"The type who ties men up in bed."

"And the type who lets herself be tied up in bed," he reminded her.

"That, too. Aunt Claudia would be so proud."

"Yeah?"

"Definitely. She was always telling me that I had to stop trying so hard to smooth things over and fix things. She said I should learn to raise a little hell. I'm starting to wonder if maybe that's the real reason she sent me here to Eclipse Bay. Not to repair the damage she did but to discover this other side of myself."

"Interesting theory."

"The thing is, how could she have guessed that I'd get into so much trouble if I got tangled up with you Hartes and those Madisons? You think maybe there really was something to all that stuff about auras and New Age metaphysics that she studied during the last years of her life?"

He folded his arms on his knees and savored the sense of relief that was washing through him. Octavia wasn't sunk in depression. She wasn't even pissed off. There was still hope.

"Wouldn't take a lot of metaphysical intuition and aura reading to figure out that sending you here to get involved with Hartes and Madisons would get you into trouble," he said. "A woman as smart as Claudia Banner would have been able to predict exactly what would happen."

THE following morning Nick scrawled his name on a check and pushed it across the bar. Beside him, Jeremy signed his check with an artistic flourish and put it on top of Nick's.

"Thank you, gentlemen." Fred snapped up both checks and put them into the cash register drawer. "Always a pleasure doing business with you. You're welcome back to the Total Eclipse any time. I like to encourage a high-class clientele."

"I don't think we'll be able to afford to come back often," Jeremy grumbled.

Fred contrived to look hurt. "This is the thanks I get for dropping all the charges?"

"You know damn well we didn't do two thousand dollars' worth of damage here the other night." Jeremy waved a hand to indicate the shabby surroundings. "Hell, the joint doesn't look any different than it did before things got exciting."

"You ruined my walls."

"Right, the walls." Nick lounged on a bar stool and folded his arms. He glanced toward the far end of the room, where the Willis brothers were busy with a tape measure and a clipboard.

The brothers were fixtures in town. For as long as Nick could remember, they had worked as general contractors, doing everything from plumbing to roof repairs. They were identical twins, but no one in town had any trouble telling them apart.

From his cleanly shaved skull to his crisply laundered overalls, Walter Willis was as precise and polished as one of the gleaming tools he wore on his belt. Torrance, on the other hand, wore his thin, straggling hair in a greasy ponytail. His work clothes were stained with everything from paint splatters to pizza sauce.

"What color are you going to paint the place?" Jeremy asked.

Fred pursed his lips. "I'm thinking taupe."

"Taupe?" Jeremy stared at him. "You're kidding, right? Taupe isn't the color you use for a bar."

"What color is taupe, anyway?" Nick asked.

"Who knows?" Fred said. "Walt over there suggested it."

"Forget taupe," Jeremy advised. "I'd go with dark green and maybe a warm brown on the baseboards and trim."

"Listen to him," Nick said. "The man's an artist."

"Green and brown, huh?" Fred pondered that for a while. "Walt said he'd give me a special on the taupe. Said he had some left over from a job he and Torrance did for one of the summer people."

"Don't suppose it much matters what color you use," Nick said. "No one will be able to see it in here, anyway, what with the low lighting and all."

Fred scowled. "Gotta keep the lights low."

"Why?" Jeremy asked. "So folks won't notice the size of the roaches?"

"Gives the place ambience," Fred said.

The door opened. For a few seconds the glare of daylight silhouetted the distinctive figures of Eugene and Dwayne. Then the door closed again.

"Don't think you need a lot of ambience to attract those two," Nick said. "Just spray a little stale beer around the place and sprinkle some aged French fries under the tables."

Eugene came to a halt halfway across the room and staggered a bit, feigning astonishment. "Well, as I live and breathe, Dwayne, if it ain't our good buddies, Harte and Seaton."

Dwayne, who had been tailgating his companion, collided with Eugene's backside and ricocheted off a couple of feet. He regained his balance and peered at Nick and Jeremy.

"Oh, yeah," Dwayne said. "It's them, all right."

"Dwayne and me was just over at the station talkin' to Sandy," Eugene explained. He lumbered into gear again, making his way through the maze of empty tables. "Saw you guys come in here. We want to buy you a drink."

Jeremy straightened warily. "Much as we'd love to stay and chat, Nick and I have appointments today. Isn't that right, Nick?"

Nick did not take his eyes off Eugene. "You want to buy us a drink?"

"Sure. After all that fun we had together, it only seems fair." Eugene reached the end of the bar and gestured expansively. "Beers all around, Fred."

Fred shrugged and set out four glasses.

"Gee, Eugene," Jeremy muttered. "We don't know what to say, do we, Nick?"

"Speechless," Nick agreed dryly. "What's this all about, Eugene?"

"Hell, me and Dwayne figure we owe you two something for covering the damages Fred, here, claims he's owed for the other night. Ain't that right, Dwayne?"

"Right." Dwayne perched on the stool next to Eugene. "Mighty generous of you."

Fred put a full glass down in front of everyone.

Eugene hoisted his glass. "Here's to good times."

"Good times." Nick picked up his glass and drank some beer.

Jeremy hesitated and then followed suit.

Eugene beamed. "Never thought I'd see you in a bar fight, Harte. Or you, either, for that matter, Seaton. Who'd have believed that you two would turn out to be just a couple of regular guys, after all? You ever believe that, Fred?"

"Wonders never cease." Fred walked out from behind the bar. "I'm gonna go talk to Walt and Torrance. I kinda like the idea of green and brown on the walls."

Eugene waited until he had moved off into the pool room where the Willis brothers were now working. Then he looked down the bar at Nick and Jeremy. He stopped smiling.

"You know, Dwayne and me, we never thanked you two for getting us out of the car that night we went into the water," he said.

"Forget it," Nick said. "That was a long time ago."

"Yeah." Eugene took a long pull on his beer. "A long time ago."

No one said anything for a while. Eugene and Dwayne worked steadily on their beers.

"After it happened," Eugene said eventually, "we figured you'd go straight to Chief Yates, you know? Maybe tell him about that little game of chicken we were all playing."

"You mean, tell him how you tried to run us off the road?" Jeremy asked neutrally.

"Maybe things got a little outta hand," Eugene said. "Me and Dwayne were really pissed after you showed us up at the races that night. If you'd gone to Yates and told him your version of events, he'd have believed you on accounta you and Harte, here, come from such fine, upstanding families and all."

"I don't want to belabor the issue," Jeremy said, "but our version of events would have been the truth."

"We were just foolin' around," Eugene insisted. "Like I said, things got outta hand. But that ain't the point. Point is, Yates and everybody else would have believed you guys. Nobody would have even listened to our side of the story on accounta everyone around here figures me and Dwayne for trash."

Nick glanced at Jeremy. Eugene was right and they both knew it. Nobody in Eclipse Bay would have taken Eugene's or Dwayne's word over the word of a Harte or a Seaton, regardless of the circumstances.

Eugene looked at Nick. "The other night, I'd had a few beers. I maybe said some things about your girlfriend that I shouldn't have said."

Nick inclined his head. "True."

"You know, that Miss Brightwell always says something nice when she sees us on the street," Eugene continued. "Ain't that right, Dwayne?"

"Yeah." Dwayne drank more beer. "Always says somethin' like, 'Good morning,' or 'How are you?' or 'Beautiful day, ain't it?' "

Nick looked at Dwayne. "She says, 'Beautiful day, ain't it?' "

"Nah, that ain't right." Dwayne's thin face twisted into a tight little knot with the effort of trying to think. "She says, 'Beautiful day, isn't it?' Yeah, that's it. 'Isn't it.' "

"Sure glad we got that straight," Jeremy said under his breath.

"Anyhow," Eugene went on with a doggedly determined air, "point is, she's a nice lady, even if she did swipe that painting. Me and Dwayne shouldn't have said that stuff about her deliberately screwing your brains out just so you wouldn't figure her for the thief. I mean, so what if that's the reason she's sleeping with you? It's a damn good reason, if you ask me. Goes to show she's smart."

"It takes a real man to apologize," Nick said. "Far as I can tell, you were among the first to hear the rumors at Fulton's. If you really want to settle things between us, you can tell me the name of the person who gave you the story."

Eugene and Dwayne exchanged nods. "It was that prissy old bitch, Mrs. Burke, wasn't it? Remember, Dwayne, she was talking to Carla from the beauty shop? I was in the ice cream section getting a couple of quarts of chocolate fudge swirl and they were right across from me in frozen orange juice. Acted like they never saw us."

"Sure," Dwayne said. "I remember. Old Lady Burke and Carla from the beauty parlor."

Nick saw Jeremy's eyes narrow a little at the names. He put down his unfinished beer and got to his feet.

"Thanks, Eugene," he said. "You, too, Dwayne. I appreciate the information. And the beer, too."

"Same here." Jeremy set his unfinished glass down on the bar next to Nick's.

"Ain'tcha gonna finish your beers?" Eugene asked, looking offended.

"The thing is," Nick said, "you've given us a hot new clue and we've got to get to work on it immediately."

"A clue, huh?" Eugene sounded pleased. "How about that, Dwayne? We gave 'em a clue. If they find that missing picture it'll be on accounta us."

"You'll have our undying gratitude," Nick said.

"I like the sound of that," Eugene said. "You sure you don't want the rest of your beer?"

"I wish I could hang around to finish it, but time is of the essence," Nick said. "Help yourself."

"Don't mind if I do." Eugene picked up Nick's unfinished beer and dumped it into his own nearly empty glass.

Dwayne did the same with the remaining beer in Jeremy's glass.

"That strike you as sanitary?" Jeremy asked as they went through the front door into the sunlight.

"The alcohol probably kills all the germs," Nick said.

"Sure. Eugene and Dwayne would have considered that."

The sunshine was blinding after the endless night of the Total Eclipse. Nick reached for his dark glasses. "What's with Mrs. Burke? You know her well?"

"No, but my grandmother does. Mrs. Burke is a member of her bridge group," Jeremy said. "They've been playing together every Wednesday and Saturday for nearly forty years."

"Which means your grandmother might be able to tell us where Mrs. Burke got the story."

Jeremy exhaled heavily. "There may be a little problem with me interrogating Grandma at the moment."

"She's still upset about you being hauled off to the police station after the big brawl?"

"Yeah. I stopped by to see her again this morning. I wanted to explain things and then ask her some questions about her recollections of what happened in the past. But I didn't get far. She was just sitting there at her kitchen table looking more depressed than she did after my divorce. Evidently I am proving to be just one major disappointment after another."

"Want me to talk to her? Tell her it was all my fault?"

"She's already decided whose fault it is," Jeremy said. "Like everyone else in town, she blames Octavia."

The door of the Total Eclipse opened again behind Nick. He glanced over his shoulder and saw Walter Willis emerge from the gloom. Something clicked.

"Hey, Walt, got a minute?"

"No problem." Walt changed direction and veered away from the van at the curb. He went toward Nick, sunlight gleaming on his meticulously shaved head. "I need to get some tools but I'm in no rush. What can I do for you?"

"You and Torrance installed the security alarm system in Octavia Brightwell's gallery, didn't you?"

"Sure did. She asked us to put it in when she opened for business. Why? Got a problem with it?"

"No. I just wondered if anyone besides Octavia and her former assistant might have access to the code."

"This is about the missing painting, isn't it?"

"Yes. Any ideas?"

"Well, Torrance or I could override the system if need be. But we've never had to do it. A real solid alarm system. Hasn't failed yet, not even during that big storm the other night." Walter's expression clouded. "See here, you thinking maybe one of us used the override code to sneak in and steal that painting?"

"Never crossed my mind," Nick said with absolute sincerity.

Walter snorted and relaxed. "Should hope not."

"But can you think of anyone else who might be able to override that system?"

Walter stroked his square chin, reflective and willing to be helpful now that he had been assured that he and his twin were not suspects. "Torrance and I never gave out the code to anyone except Miss Brightwell. I know she gave it to Noreen Perkins, but that's about all I know. You'd have to find Noreen to ask her if she gave it to anyone."

"Sean Valentine is working that angle," Nick said. "Don't think he's tracked her down yet, but he will eventually. Thanks, Walt. I just wanted to make certain I wasn't overlooking something obvious."

"You bet." Walter winked broadly. "I figure it's the least I can do for you after what you and Seaton, here, did for me and Torrance. Told Fred years ago the place needed a new coat of paint but he kept putting it off on account of he was too damn cheap. But now he says he wants a first-class job. Bottom line, on behalf of the Willis brothers, I'd like to say thanks."

"It was nothing," Nick said. "Just doing our part to improve Eclipse Bay. Hartes and Seatons have got a deep sense of civic responsibility, you know."

22

"Way I figure it," Mitchell said into the cell phone, "getting into a bar fight over a lady like Octavia is as good as a marriage proposal. You'd damn sure better speak to that grandson of yours or I'm gonna have to do it for you."

"Stay out of it, Mitch," Sullivan said. "Things will get sorted out a whole lot easier if you don't interfere."

"Shoot and damn." Mitchell stabbed at some weeds with his trowel. He could hear the muted background noises of a vehicle in motion. Sullivan was calling from the backseat of the limo. "The whole blamed town is talking about her."

"Presumably the whole town is also talking about Nick."

"Well, sure, but that's different. He's a Harte. Around here everyone talks about you Hartes and us Madisons."

"If she's going to marry Nick, she'd better get used to being a subject of conversation there in Eclipse Bay."

Progress at last, Mitchell thought. The tough old bastard had at least used the word "marry" and Nick's name in the same sentence. He stopped assaulting weeds and tapped the trowel absently against a stake. "Just so long as he doesn't cut and run."

"You ever known a Harte to cut and run?"

"Nah. You're all too damn stubborn."

"Sort of like you Madisons, eh?"

"I reckon."

There was a short silence on the other end.

"Just got to hang on until dawn, Mitch," Sullivan said quietly.

The trowel went still in Mitchell's hands. The words echoed in his mind, bringing back the old memories. *Just got to hang on until dawn.*

He pocketed the trowel and pushed himself up off the low gardener's bench. Grabbing his cane, he made his way along the graveled path that wound between the richly planted flowerbeds, heading toward the greenhouse.

But it wasn't the glorious blooms of his roses that he saw in his mind now. Instead he was suddenly hit with visions of the ominous, eerie green of a jungle plunging inevitably into darkness. It would be a night in which death stalked at every hand. There would be no hope of rescue until dawn.

Survival that night had depended on silence and not giving in to the panic. Most of all, it had depended on being able to trust the man who guarded his back and whose back he, in turn, had guarded.

Just got to hang on until dawn were the last words that he and Sullivan had spoken to each other before they had settled in to keep watch in silence for the duration of that night.

The words had become a private code, a vow made between two young men who had gone through hell together. Neither he nor Sullivan would have made it until dawn if it hadn't been for the other and they both knew it. *Just got to hang on until dawn* meant *You can count on me. I'm with you here. We'll get through this together. You can trust me, buddy.*

He shoved the old images back into the furthest corners of his mind and concentrated on the present. He opened the door of his greenhouse and stepped inside.

"You got your list finished?" he asked.

"Yes, but it's damn short. You?"

"Same here. Most of the folks who were involved in Harte-Madison at the time have either moved away or died. There was our secretary, Angie, remember her?"

"Sure," Sullivan said. "But she died ten or twelve years ago. We both went to the funeral."

"Her son still lives here in town. Took over the hardware store."

"I can't see any connection. He wasn't even born when Claudia was with us. Besides, Claudia didn't do his mother any harm other than indirectly put her out of a job when the company went under. Angie wasn't all that upset about losing her position, as I recall. She went to work for George Adams and later married him. Who else have you got on your list?"

Mitchell fished the little notebook out of his pocket and flipped it open. He rattled off the names of the handful of other people who had been directly or indirectly connected with Harte-Madison in the old days. He paused when he came to the last person on his list.

"There is one more," he said slowly. He read the name aloud. "Remember him?"

"Hell, yes. He's on my list, too."

"You know, for a while I thought maybe he was the one who had screwed us."

"That's because you were so dazzled by Claudia that you couldn't see straight. You were willing to blame anyone else except her."

"Yeah, well, later when I got to thinking straight again."

"Think she cut him in on some of the action? Made him an offer he couldn't refuse so he'd cover up for her?"

"Something like that," Mitchell said.

They talked for a while longer, comparing notes, going over different scenarios, and eliminating other possibilities. At last they were both satisfied that they had a possible answer.

Neither of them was very happy about it.

"I'm not gonna take this to Nick and Octavia on my own," Mitchell said. "What if we're wrong?"

"I don't think we're wrong, but either way this is going to be very unpleasant for everyone concerned. Sit tight. Carson and I will arrive sometime around noon. What do you say we keep this to ourselves until after the Children's Art Show tonight? I don't want to go upsetting everyone and spoil the big event. No reason this can't wait until tomorrow morning."

"Yeah," Mitchell said. "No reason to ruin the fun tonight."

NICK sat in the old wooden porch rocker, heels stacked on the railing, and watched the gleaming black limo coast slowly toward him down the long drive.

He did not like the conclusions he had reached after his conversation with Mrs. Burke that afternoon, but he had to admit that when he put the pieces together, everything fit. The only problem now was how and when to confront the suspect.

It was going to be an extremely delicate operation, he thought. The reputation of an upstanding member of the community was at stake. And much as he would like to do so, he couldn't see any way to hush things up, not if Octavia was to be completely vindicated. And she was his top priority in this affair.

The truth would have to come out, he thought, watching the limo pick its way along the unpaved drive. He sure as hell was not going to let the cloud of rumor and suspicion hang over Octavia indefinitely. Someone had to take the fall and it wasn't going to be her. Which meant that there was no way around the unpleasantness that lay ahead.

The limo drifted to a halt in front of the cottage. The rear doors snapped open before the driver could extricate himself from behind the wheel.

"Dad." Carson pelted toward him at a hundred miles an hour. "Dad, we're back."

Sullivan levered himself out of the other side of the vehicle, cane in hand, and started around the rear of the car.

Nick looked at Carson running toward him. *My son.*

And then Carson was in his arms and he was swinging his boy around in the familiar greeting ritual.

When he set Carson back on his feet, he caught Sullivan watching them. There was fierce love and pride in the old man's face. He did not speak, but there was no need for words. Nick knew exactly what he was thinking. *I didn't do everything right along the way but by God, one thing you can count on, I'd go to hell and back for you two, no questions asked.*

Nick met Sullivan's eyes. I'd do the same for you, he thought. No questions asked.

Sullivan smiled slightly and Nick knew that he understood.

The limo driver put two suitcases down on the porch and looked at Sullivan. "Anything else, sir?"

"No, thanks, Ben. We're all set for a few days. I'll give you a call when I need you. Take it easy on the way back to Portland."

Ben nodded. "Will do."

"Bye, Ben," Carson said.

"So long, pal. I'll look forward to meeting your dog when you finally get him."

"Okay," Carson said.

Ben nodded to all of them and went back down the steps. He got behind the wheel of the big car, put it in gear, and drove off toward the main road.

Nick ruffled Carson's hair. "How was the trip?"

"We stopped along the way and I got ice cream and Great-Granddad and Ben got coffee and then we looked at some caves. Really big caves. Bigger than the ones we have in Dead Hand Cove," Carson reported with excitement.

"We stopped to stretch our legs," Sullivan said, coming up the steps, "but we made good time." He raised his brows. "Didn't want to risk being late for the art show."

Carson looked at Nick. "Has Miss Brightwell hung my picture yet?"

"When I stopped by the gallery a couple of hours ago it was closed to the public, so I didn't go inside," Nick said. "Octavia and Gail were very busy getting things ready for this evening. They're probably hanging your drawing of Winston as we speak."

"Oh, boy." Carson whirled around and raced into the house.

Sullivan stopped beside Nick. They watched the screen door swing shut behind Carson.

"Had a long talk with Mitch today when we set out from Portland," Sullivan said. "We came up with a name for you. But we think we ought to go with you when you confront the person. If we're right, this goes all the way back to the days of Harte-Madison. Mitch and I feel some responsibility for the situation."

"That collateral damage you mentioned?"

"Afraid so."

"What's the name of your suspect?" Nick asked.

Sullivan told him.

"That pretty well cinches it," Nick said. He picked up one of the suitcases. "I came up with the same name."

Sullivan hoisted the other suitcase. "No reason this can't wait until tomorrow, is there? When word gets out no one's going to be able to talk about anything else. Gonna be rough."

"If Octavia agrees, it can wait until tomorrow," Nick said. "But no longer. I'm sorry about what's going to come down when this becomes public knowledge, but I've got Octavia to think about."

Sullivan nodded. "And she comes first now, is that it?"

"That's it."

AT six o'clock that evening every parking lot was full. A large crowd of locals, Heralds, tourists, and summer people thronged the street and sidewalk.

Colorful balloons bobbed from the open doors of the shops and gallery. The temperature had been above average during the day, a balmy eighty-two, and the late summer sun was fending off the evening chill. The Annual Eclipse Bay Summer Celebration was in full swing.

Octavia breathed a sigh of relief when several kids, dragging their parents, surged into Bright Visions the minute the door was opened.

"It looks like the show isn't going to be a disaster after all," she said in a low voice to Gail, who was supervising the punch-and-cookies table.

Gail chuckled. "Told you not to worry. Did you really think anyone would stay away? Every kid with a picture in the show will be here tonight, and everyone else in town will come just to get a look at you and Nick together. After all, you're the lady who shattered the curse."

"And then, of course, there is the fact that I am a noted local art thief," Octavia said dryly.

"Hey, a little notoriety never hurts when it comes to publicity."

"Just goes to prove the old publicity axiom, I guess. 'I don't care what you call me so long as you spell my name right.' "

Gail's amusement faded. "It's true that people are very curious about your relationship with Nick. And I won't say that the rumors about the missing Upsall haven't piqued everyone's interest. But the bottom line is that a lot of people really like you, Octavia. You're a nice person."

Octavia made a face. "You mean, for an art thief?"

"Gail is right." Hannah appeared out of the crowd and helped herself to a chocolate chip cookie. "You and the Bright Visions Gallery are part of this town. Folks wouldn't be talking about you if you weren't considered a legitimate member of the community. Local folks never talk about outsiders. They're not interested in the summer people or the casual visitors."

"Like it or not, you belong here," Gail said.

Hannah glanced toward the door. "And here come a couple of your biggest admirers."

Octavia followed the direction of her gaze and saw Eugene and Dwayne enter the gallery. They looked different. It took her a few seconds to realize that both men had shaved and put on clean shirts and pants for the occasion. Eugene's hair was slicked down with some sort of shiny pomade, and Dwayne had tied his in a ponytail.

The pair came to a halt just inside the entrance, blocking traffic. Although they had walked into the gallery with a certain air of bravado, they now appeared uncomfortable. She got the feeling neither of them knew what to do next.

"Will you look at that," Gail murmured. "They've actually buttoned their shirts."

"Sort of ruins the image when you can't see Eugene's hairy belly through the holes in his undershirt, doesn't it?" Hannah mused.

Gail frowned. "I hope they're not here to start trouble."

"Don't worry," Hannah said. "Sean Valentine is just outside talking to Nick and A.Z. and Virgil. Eugene and Dwayne won't create any problems with the chief nearby."

"I agree, there's no cause for alarm." Octavia picked up two paper cups filled with punch. "They wouldn't have gone to all the effort to get cleaned up if they'd planned to start another brawl."

She made her way through the crowd to where Eugene and Dwayne hovered uncertainly.

"Hello," she said brightly, handing a cup to each man. "I'm glad you could make it tonight. Please come in and have a look around."

"Thanks." Eugene seemed to relax. He took one of the cups of punch. "Dwayne and me figured it was about time we educated ourselves about art, y'know?"

"Of course." She gestured toward the buffet table. "Help yourselves to cookies."

"Look, Dwayne, they've got free food."

He started toward the table.

"Excellent." Dwayne downed the contents of his punch cup and set off in Eugene's wide wake.

Nick sauntered through the door at that moment. His gaze tracked Eugene and Dwayne's progress. "Everything okay in here?"

"Yes, indeed," she said. "I was just welcoming a couple of other legitimate members of the community."

He raised his eyebrows. "Do I detect a trace of irony here?"

"Probably." She glanced at Carson, who stood with Anne in front of the picture of Zeb. The two children appeared to be deep in conversation. A couple of miniature art connoisseurs, she thought. "Tell me the truth, Nick. Would you say that I'm a real member of this community?"

"Are you kidding? You've got everyone from Mean Eugene and Dickhead Dwayne to the wife of the future mayor here tonight. You've also got representatives of both the Harte and Madison clans. Trust me, in Eclipse Bay, it doesn't get any more legitimate."

"You're teasing me, aren't you?"

"I'm dealing the truth here. And there's another thing that guarantees you a place of honor in our fair town."

"What's that?"

"You broke the curse."

She made a face. "If you mention that stupid curse one more time, I swear, I'll—"

"I'd appreciate it if you would not refer to the condition of my former sex life as stupid," he said with grave dignity.

"At least you had a previous sex life. When I look back, I've got to wonder if I was the one under a spell. Two years is a long time to go between dates."

He gave her a smile that curled her toes.

"But it was worth the wait, right?" he said.

"I am not going to respond to such a leading question. Not in public, at any rate. Now, you'll have to excuse me, I'm trying to host a show here." She made to move off.

"By the way," he added, lowering his voice, "there is one more thing I wanted to tell you."

She paused and looked at him inquiringly. "Yes?"

He glanced around, apparently checking to see if there was anyone within earshot. Then he grasped her arm and urged her into a quiet corner of the room. "Mitch and Sullivan and I think we've got a lead on the Upsall."

Stunned, she just stared at him for a couple of seconds. He was standing very close, one hand braced against the wall behind her. There was something utterly, dangerously masculine in the way he leaned into her slightly, cutting off her view of the room with his broad shoulders. His body language spoke of possession and a silent claim that she knew every other man in the room could probably read.

A sense of déjà vu swept through her. This was the way he had stood with her at Lillian's gallery show, she thought. He had put himself between her and the crowd that evening, too, cutting her out of the herd, making her intensely aware of him and then asking her out on a date. She had known in her heart where a date with Nick would lead and her nerve had failed her that night.

Oh, sure, later she had come up with lots of really good reasons for avoiding the risk of getting involved with him, but the stark truth was that her courage had failed at crunch time that first night. She had run from him that evening and several more times after that.

But tonight was different. Tonight, because she had finally taken the risk, she knew him far more intimately and deeply and she could see what lay beneath the surface. In addition to the intensely sensual threat he posed, there was strength and honor and integrity. *Dear God, I'm in love.*

Automatically she lowered her own voice to a whisper. "Who? What? Where? Tell me what's going on here, Nick."

He looked at her very steadily. "No one's got more of a right to answers than you do. But this afternoon Sullivan and Mitchell asked me to ask you to give them until noon tomorrow to confirm our hunch."

"Why the delay?"

"We need to be sure. We're talking about someone with deep ties throughout the community. People are going to be hurt. We can't afford to be wrong."

She searched his face. He was genuinely concerned about what might happen when it all came undone.

"And if you're right?" she asked gently.

"There will be a lot of fallout. And it won't all come down on the person who took the painting. There is someone else who will probably get dumped on, too. An innocent bystander."

"Collateral damage."

"Yes."

She shivered. "I hate those words. Translated, they mean that real people will get burned."

"Yes," he said again. But this time his eyes went cold. "I told Sullivan and Mitch that, although I'm willing to give them some time, I'm not going to let this thing get hushed up or swept under a rug. One way or the other, by tomorrow afternoon, your name will be cleared, no matter who gets hurt. I'm not going to let you take the rap."

He meant every word, she thought. He was making it blazingly clear that she was his first priority. The realization gave her an odd feeling. No one had ever fought any battles for her and now, in the space of less than a week, Nick had gotten involved in a barroom brawl and was about to expose an upstanding member of the community as a thief. All in her name.

"All right," she said. "Tell Mitch and Sullivan I'll wait until tomorrow."

"Thanks. They'll be grateful."

"I owe them that much," she said. "For Aunt Claudia's sake, if nothing else." She peeked around his shoulder. "I'd better go. This crowd is getting bigger and it looks like the cookies have disappeared."

She made to slide around the broad shield of his shoulders.

"One more thing I wanted to tell you before you run off," he said quietly.

She looked back at him, her mind on the cookie supply issue. "Yes?"

"Something I should have said that first night at Lillian's show. Something I knew at the time. Something I've known all along. Just didn't quite recognize it until recently. Probably because I'm a little out of practice."

"What's that?"

"I love you."

She stared at him, open-mouthed Bereft of speech.

He gave her a sexy, knowing smile. "Better go check on the cookies."

He pushed himself away from the wall and strolled off into the crowd.

⸎

"WHEN are you gonna get your dog?" Anne asked.

"Right after my birthday," Carson said. "That's when the puppies will be old enough to be 'dopted. Dad says we'll drive to Portland so I can pick out one. It's the same place where Winston was born."

"What are you going to name him?"

"I don't know yet. I'm still thinking."

"When you bring him back here to Eclipse Bay can I see him?"

"Sure," Carson said, feeling magnanimous. "You can come to my birthday party, too."

"Okay. Do you want to come to mine?"

"Yeah," Carson said. "When is it?"

"August fourteenth."

"I'll bring my dog with me," Carson promised. He looked across the room to where Jeremy stood talking to Hannah and Anne's grandparents. "Is he gonna be your new dad?"

"Maybe." Anne took a bite of her cookie. "Mom likes him a lot, I think. Grandma and Grandpa like him, too. Mom says they have good taste in men and this time she's going to listen to 'em."

"I like him, too. Do you?"

"Uh-huh." Anne nodded enthusiastically. "He came to our house for dinner last night and everybody laughed and we played games and stuff. He liked my pictures. It was fun." She looked at Octavia, who was moving across the room toward the cookie table. "Is Miss Brightwell gonna be your new mommy?"

"I think so," Carson said. Then he frowned, still a little troubled about some aspects of the situation. "Unless Dad screws up again."

OCTAVIA spied the Willis brothers shortly before the end of the event.

She was about to bid them a pleasant good evening and thank them for attending the show when she suddenly remembered the mysterious key she had found in the back room closet.

"Torrance? Walter? Have you got time for a quick question?"

"Thinking of doing a little remodeling in here?" Walter surveyed the gallery with a speculative expression. "A new paint job wouldn't hurt. We can give you a good price on a few cans of taupe."

"I'm not planning on doing any painting for a while. This is more of a hardware issue. I found a key in the closet. It doesn't fit either of the doors. You two did the security and locks here and I thought I'd see if you recognized it. If not, I'll toss it."

They followed her into the back room and looked around with interest while she took the key off the closet hook.

"Sure is cluttered in here," Torrance said. "We could build you some shelving or maybe some racks for stacking all these paintings."

"That's not a bad idea," she said. "I'll think about it." She held out the key.

Walter took it from her and gave it a quick, cursory glance. "No problem. Reckon we know what this goes to don't we, Torrance?"

"Sure do," Torrance said. "Leastways, it's the same brand we used for that job. I remember we ordered it in special after the problems with that little rash of break-ins we had a couple years back." He looked at Octavia. "Turned out to be some kids fooling around. Summer people, you know. Sean Valentine took care of the situation, but a few folks around here got nervous and asked us to upgrade their locks and such."

"Won't be hard to check and see if this key fits where we think it does," Walter said.

23

OCTAVIA parked in the drive in front of the old, two-story house, turned off the ignition, and got out of the car. It was six-thirty in the morning, but fog veiled the early light and cast a damp pall on the entire town.

Or maybe it was just her mood, she thought as she went up the steps and crossed the front porch. She had not slept much last night.

She banged the brass knocker on the front door. When there was no response, she banged it a second time.

Eventually the door opened a crack.

"What on earth are you doing here at this hour of the morning?" Edith Seaton demanded.

"I think you know why I'm here," Octavia said gently "I came to get the Upsall."

Edith stared at her through the narrow opening for a long moment. Without warning her face suddenly crumpled. In the space of five or six seconds she seemed to age at least a decade.

"Yes." She stood back and held the door open. "Yes, I suppose you'd better take it."

Octavia stepped into the shadowy foyer.

Edith turned, not speaking, and led the way toward the living room. She wore a long, faded dressing gown and slippers.

Octavia took a quick look around as she followed Edith. The house was decorated with what appeared to be leftovers from Edith's shop. There was a display of carnival glass in a case that stood against one wall. Small porcelain figures were arranged on the end tables. The furniture was heavy and old-fashioned.

Edith sat down very stiffly in a rose-patterned rocking chair. Octavia went to stand at the window that overlooked the garden.

"How did you figure it out?" Edith asked in a resigned voice.

"I came across a key in my back room. Last night I asked the Willis brothers if they recognized it. They said they had installed a special lock in the door of your shop. We checked. The key fit. Last night I got a phone call from Noreen Perkins. Sean Valentine had tracked her down to ask her about a missing painting and she was worried that I might think she'd had something to do with the theft."

"And you asked her about the key, I suppose," Edith said dully. "She no doubt told you that several months ago we exchanged keys and that she also gave me the security code to the gallery."

"Yes. She said that both of you had occasionally gotten accidentally locked out. She had trouble remembering the security code for the alarm system so she made sure you had it in case she ever needed it."

"We thought it would be a convenience for both of us," Edith said. "But after she left, I forgot all about having the code and a key in my desk. Just never gave it another thought."

"Until the day you and everyone else in town discovered that Claudia Banner was my great-aunt."

"I couldn't believe it." Color rushed back into Edith's face. Her gnarled, spotted hands knotted into fists. "It was as if her ghost had come back to haunt me. Worse yet, it was happening all over again, just like it happened all those years ago. But this time it was my grandson she, I mean *you*, seduced."

"I did not seduce Jeremy."

"All that talk about putting his pictures on display in your gallery. Encouraging him to do more paintings for you. It was seduction, all right, and well you know it."

"It was business, not seduction."

"You went out to dinner with him several times, too."

"We are friends, Mrs. Seaton. But not lovers."

"Only because something better came along," Edith shot back hoarsely. "You dropped my Jeremy like a hot potato when Nick Harte started to date you. Don't deny it."

"I do deny it. Every single word. You're putting your own spin on this, Edith, but I think deep down you know that it isn't the truth."

"You caused trouble between Jeremy and Nick the same way Claudia Banner did with Mitchell Madison and Sullivan Harte."

"So you took the painting the night of the storm and tried to destroy my good name in a noble attempt to defend Jeremy from my wiles?" Octavia shook her head. "I'm not buying that, Edith."

Edith sat in rigid, stubborn silence.

"Do you know what I think?" Octavia sat down in the chair across from the older woman. "I think you used Jeremy as an excuse to take revenge for something that Claudia Banner did to you all those years ago. She is beyond your reach and maybe you told yourself you had put it all behind you. But when you realized that I was her niece, the old anger came rushing back, didn't it?"

Edith flinched. "She got away with it. But then, Claudia Banner got away with everything. She never paid for the trouble and pain she caused."

"Tell me what my great-aunt did to you, Edith."

"She seduced my husband." Edith surged up out of her chair. "And then she used him."

Octavia was on her feet now. "How did she use him?"

"Phil was the accountant for Harte-Sullivan. She got him to doctor the company books while she carried out her scam. That was the reason Mitchell and Sullivan never saw the bankruptcy coming until it was too late."

Octavia drew a deep breath and let it out slowly. "I see."

"It was as if she was some sort of sorceress," Edith whispered. "She put my Phil under a spell for a time. The poor fool never realized how she'd manipulated him until he woke up one morning and discovered that she had vanished. He actually thought that she would contact him after the heat died down. He really believed that she loved him and wanted him to run off with her. It was months before he finally understood that he'd been used."

"Was that when you discovered his role in the bankruptcy?"

"Yes. I'd suspected he was having an affair with her, but I never dreamed that she had seduced him into helping her drive Harte-Madison into bankruptcy. I was stunned. He was a Seaton, after all. How could he do something like that?"

"But you kept the secret."

"I had no choice. I had to think of the family name. I had the children to consider. Just imagine what they would have had to face here in Eclipse Bay if it had come out that their father had had a hand in the destruction of Harte-Madison."

"It would have been rough on them."

"And then there was the financial situation. If the truth had surfaced, my husband's career as an accountant would have been destroyed. At the very least the shame and humiliation would have forced us to leave town. Where would we have gone? This was our home."

"So you buried the past as best you could. Your husband never told Mitchell and Sullivan what he'd done."

"Of course not. I pointed out to him that there was nothing to be gained by confessing his part in their disaster and everything to lose."

"You succeeded in protecting your husband and the Seaton name, but you never forgave him or Aunt Claudia."

"I swear she was some sort of witch. She never paid for her wicked works. Probably never even gave her victims a second thought."

"You're wrong there, Edith. Aunt Claudia thought about the past a lot toward the end. In a way, she was obsessed with it."

There was no need to get into the specifics, Octavia thought. No point bringing up the fact that Claudia had never even mentioned the name Seaton during those times when she had talked about her adventures in Eclipse Bay. The only people who had concerned her at the end had been the Hartes and the Madisons.

"I have no right to ask you to forgive me for what I did," Edith said. "My only excuse is that, for a while after I discovered who you were, I went a little mad. It was as if a curtain had opened and I was looking at the past again. It all came crashing back and the only thing I could think about was punishing that dreadful woman."

"It's called visiting the sins of the father on the son, or in this case, visiting the sins of the great-aunt on the niece."

"I told myself I was doing it to show Jeremy and Nick the truth about you, but you're right, of course. I did it to avenge myself."

"So you took the Upsall and started the rumors that I was the thief."

"When I finally came to my senses, it was too late. It will all come out now, won't it? What Phil did in the past and what I tried to do to you. This time I won't be able to keep the stain off the family name. Jeremy will be embarrassed. The rest of the family and most of the people in town will think I've gone senile. And as for my friends—" Edith trailed off, bowing her head.

So much for nearly four decades of Wednesday and Saturday bridge games and civic committee meetings, Octavia thought. Even if the community and her friends were willing to forget the affair, Edith would never be able to hold her head up high in Eclipse Bay again.

She put a hand on one of Edith's thin shoulders. "You know, it was Aunt Claudia who urged me on her deathbed to come to Eclipse Bay. She said she wanted me to see if perhaps I could repair some of the damage she had done here. I assumed that she was referring to the Harte-Madison feud, and I have to tell you that I was feeling pretty useless because the Hartes and the Madisons took care of that issue all by themselves."

Edith took a hankie out of the pocket of her old robe and dabbed at her eyes. "Yes. Those two stubborn men seem to have become friends again."

"They didn't need me," Octavia said. "But maybe I was looking in the wrong place. Maybe this was the damage I was supposed to repair."

"I don't understand," Edith said.

"I know. I'll explain it to you while you get dressed. Hurry, we don't have a lot of time."

"It's very kind of you to want to help me after what I did to you, but it's too late, my dear. The truth will be all over town by nightfall. It's only right after all this time."

"You're going to have to trust me on this, Edith. For Jeremy's sake and the Seaton family name."

"But—"

"Aunt Claudia owes you this much," Octavia said.

SHE unlocked the gallery an hour earlier than usual and went straight to work reorganizing and tidying up the shop.

She took down drooping balloons and swept the cookie crumbs off the floor. It required three trips to the Dumpster to get rid of all the used paper cups, plates, and napkins.

When the trash had been dealt with, she concentrated on the display panels. One by one she took down the framed drawings that had been done by the children and replaced them with the usual pictures. She stacked the kids' pictures in one corner in the back room, ready to be collected by the proud artists.

She was coming through the door that separated the back room from the showroom, a large seascape in her hands, when she caught a glimpse of Nick's car. He was just pulling into the parking lot. Directly behind him was Mitchell's big monster of an SUV.

Nick, Carson, and Sullivan, accompanied by Mitchell came through the front door two minutes later. They all looked at her, concerned and serious and a little baffled.

"Okay, we're here," Nick said. "What's this all about?"

"Hang on," she said. "I'll be right back."

She darted into the other room to scoop up the painting that she had left propped against the leg of the worktable.

She walked back out into the main room holding the picture aloft for all to see. "Look what I found when I started cleaning up after the art show this morning."

They all dutifully stared at the painting. None of the men said a word.

"Hey," Carson said gleefully, "I remember that picture. It's the one that belongs to A.Z. and Mr. Nash and the Heralds. The one everyone said had been stolen."

"It is, indeed," Octavia agreed. "You really do have a good eye for art, Carson."

He beamed.

She put the Upsall very carefully on the counter. "Evidently it got pushed behind a stack of pictures that was leaning against the wall. Heaven only knows how long it would have stayed back there if it wasn't for all the rearranging I had to do in here this morning."

"Well, shoot and damn," Mitchell said. The somber look evaporated from his eyes. A knowing expression took its place. "It was in your back room all along. How about that."

"Thank the good Lord we didn't rush off to confront our suspect last night," Sullivan said dryly. He grinned at Octavia. "Could have been more than a little awkward."

"Naturally, I feel like a complete idiot," Octavia said. "But at least this fiasco is finished and Nick no longer has to play detective."

Nick smiled slowly. He did not take his eyes off Octavia. "I was just starting to get the hang of it."

THAT evening Nick drove her back to the cottage after dinner with Carson and Sullivan at Dreamscape. There was obviously a conspiracy at work to give them some time together, Octavia thought, amused. No one had even been particularly subtle about sending them off by themselves this evening.

She made coffee and put two large, leftover chocolate chip cookies on a plate. When she carried the tray out into the living room, she found Nick slouched deep into her sofa. Looking comfortable, she thought. At home. Like he had every right to be there.

Something I should have said that first night at Lillian's show. Something I knew at the time. Something I've known all along. Just didn't quite recognize it until recently. Probably because I'm a little out of practice . . . I love you.

A deep sense of joy welled up inside her and shimmered through her senses.

Nick watched her set the tray down on the coffee table.

"Alone at last," he said.

"Mmm." She put one of the cookies on a napkin and handed it to him.

He took a healthy bite. "Okay, let's have the real story," he said around a mouthful of cookie.

"You refer to the case of the missing Upsall, I presume?"

"What else? It's the only thing this town is talking about at the moment." He stretched out his legs and sank deeper into the sofa. "With the exception of you and me, of course."

"Mmm."

He sounded so matter-of-fact about the *you and me* part.

"You can skip the version in which you miraculously discover the Upsall when you tidied up your back room, by the way. I'm not buying it for a second."

She curled one foot under her leg and took a tiny sip of coffee. "The other version is a little complicated."

"Let's start with the fact that Sullivan, Mitchell, and I all know that Edith Seaton took the picture."

"She had her reasons."

"Sullivan and Mitchell figured that out. Phil Seaton was their accountant in the old days. Can one assume that your great-aunt seduced him into covering her tracks for her?"

"I'm afraid so. And afterward Edith was so horrified at the thought of being caught up in the scandal that she covered up for Phil."

"But never forgave your aunt, I take it?"

"She blamed Claudia for everything, not without considerable justification, I might add. When word got out that I was related to her old nemesis, Edith freaked. After all, I was having dinner with Jeremy, encouraging him to paint, and then I started sleeping with you. Clearly history was about to repeat itself. It was just too much for her to handle."

"So she stole the picture and spread the rumors. Pisspoor sort of revenge, if you ask me."

"It was the only kind that was left to her," Octavia said simply. "And she could justify it to herself for a time because she truly believed that I was turning out to be a bad influence on Jeremy."

"Because you encouraged him in his painting?"

"Yes."

"Huh." Nick ate the last of the cookie. "She didn't have any qualms about taking the easy way out, did she? Obviously she went along with your scheme to make the Upsall magically materialize in your back room."

"To be fair, she was reluctant at first. But when I told her that we were doing it for Jeremy's sake and for the sake of the Seaton name, she went for it. I also told her that I was sure that was the way Aunt Claudia would have wanted it."

Nick raised his brows and reached for his coffee. "Think it's true?"

"To be honest, I'm not sure Claudia even remembered Phil Seaton, let alone worried much about the damage she did to his family. But even if that was the case, one thing is certain—she definitely owed the Seatons. And now the debt has been paid in some small measure."

"Thanks to you."

She put her empty cup down on the coffee table. "It was the least I could do, given that I never got the chance to fulfill my mission of repairing the Harte-Madison feud."

"I thought you had concluded that the real reason Claudia sent you here was so that you could get wild and crazy."

"Yes, well, if that's true, all I can say is, mission accomplished."

"Not quite." His mouth quirked in sexy promise. He reached for her and started to pull her close. "But you know what they say, practice makes perfect."

She spread her hands against his chest, holding him off for a moment longer. "Before we get to the wild and crazy stuff, there's something I want to tell you."

"And that would be?"

"It may have been Aunt Claudia who sent me here to Eclipse Bay but you're the reason I decided to stay on even after it became apparent that the feud was ending."

"Is that right?"

"I love you."

He smiled slowly. The look in his eyes was so dazzling she could hardly catch her breath.

"I was hoping you'd say that," Nick whispered against her mouth. "Now can we get to the wild and crazy stuff?"

"Of course," she said demurely. "I'm sure Aunt Claudia would have wanted it this way."

"Do me a favor." He pushed her gently down onto the sofa. "Don't mention your aunt again for a while, okay?"

"Okay."

She put her arms around his neck and kissed him with all the love and passion that she had discovered within herself here in Eclipse Bay.

Wherever you are, Aunt Claudia, she thought, thank you.

24

ON a sunny afternoon in the fall, Mitchell stood with Sullivan at the end of the long veranda that wrapped around Dreamscape. Each of them held a glass of champagne in one hand. Their canes hung, side by side, over the railing. From their vantage point they had a clear view of the newlyweds, who were dutifully working their way through a seemingly endless reception line.

The entire town, from the current mayor and his likely successor and his wife to Mean Eugene and Dickhead Dwayne, had turned out for Nick and Octavia's wedding.

"Knew all along Octavia belonged here with us," Mitchell said.

"You won't get any argument from me." Sullivan smiled to himself at the sight of Nick standing so close to Octavia, one arm wrapped protectively and possessively around her waist, the other outstretched to shake hands with the next well-wisher in line. "She and Nick and Carson are a family already."

Mitchell glanced at Rafe and the now obviously pregnant Hannah. The pair was busy supervising the buffet tables.

"And there's more family on the way," he said proudly. "I'm gonna have me a great-grandkid, real soon now."

"Probably more than one," Sullivan said dryly. He motioned toward Gabe and Lillian, who stood with Jeremy and Gail. "I think I recognize that rosy glow on Lillian's face."

"Yeah?" Mitchell followed his gaze and grinned. "Think so?"

"I do, indeed."

Mitchell swallowed some more champagne and grimaced at the taste. "I think Rafe said he stashed some beer in the solarium. Want to go see if we can find it?"

"Good idea. This stuff tastes like fizzy water, which is a real shame, given what I happen to know it cost."

They gripped their canes and made their way around the corner of the veranda to a side entrance. A bright red ball shot past in front of them. A small bundle of silver and gray exploded out of the open door. The young Schnauzer seized the ball in his jaws and kept going, heading for the open lawn at full speed.

Carson and Anne burst threw the door, chasing after the dog.

"Come back, Tycoon," Carson shouted. "You're supposed to get the ball and bring it to me when I throw it for you. You're not supposed to run off with it."

"Zeb always brings back whatever I throw," Anne said with cheerful superiority. "He's a really smart dog."

"Tycoon is smart," Carson informed her as he dashed down the steps in pursuit of his dog. "He's still learning how to do stuff, that's all. Winston's teaching him."

Winston trotted sedately out of the doorway, following in the wake of Tycoon, Carson, and Anne with an air of patient authority and attentive vigilance.

Sullivan watched the pack of dogs and children race across the lawn in pursuit of the renegade Tycoon. "I'd swear that dog of Hannah's must have been a butler or a nanny in his past life, the way he keeps an eye on those kids."

"That's a fact."

They went into the lobby of Dreamscape and made their way to the solarium. The beer was there, as promised, resting comfortably in a chest filled with ice.

Mitchell handed a bottle to Sullivan and opened one for himself.

They each took a long pull.

"Sure beats the hell out of champagne," Mitchell said.

"It does."

They went to the window and looked out at the happy scene.

"You know something," Mitchell said, "it wasn't always easy, but in the end, we did okay, you and me."

"We did just fine," Sullivan agreed. "We hung on until dawn."